INTRODUCTION TO
business

Laura Portolese Dias
Shoreline Community College

Amit J. Shah
Frostburg State University

McGraw-Hill
Higher Education

Boston   Burr Ridge, IL   Dubuque, IA   New York   San Francisco   St. Louis
Bangkok   Bogotá   Caracas   Kuala Lumpur   Lisbon   London   Madrid   Mexico City
Milan   Montreal   New Delhi   Santiago   Seoul   Singapore   Sydney   Taipei   Toronto

The McGraw·Hill Companies

McGraw-Hill
Higher Education

INTRODUCTION TO BUSINESS

Published by McGraw-Hill, a business unit of The McGraw-Hill Companies, Inc., 1221 Avenue of the Americas, New York, NY, 10020. Copyright © 2009 by The McGraw-Hill Companies, Inc. All rights reserved. No part of this publication may be reproduced or distributed in any form or by any means, or stored in a database or retrieval system, without the prior written consent of The McGraw-Hill Companies, Inc., including, but not limited to, in any network or other electronic storage or transmission, or broadcast for distance learning.

Some ancillaries, including electronic and print components, may not be available to customers outside the United States.

This book is printed on acid-free paper.

1 2 3 4 5 6 7 8 9 0 WCK/WCK 0 9 8 7

ISBN   978-0-07-337699-8
MHID   0-07-337699-X

Vice president/Editor in chief: *Elizabeth Haefele*
Vice president/Director of marketing: *John E. Biernat*
Sponsoring editor: *Natalie Ruffatto*
Developmental editor: *Tammy Higham and Kristin Bradley*
Marketing manager: *Keari Bedford*
Lead media producer: *Damian Moshak*
Media producer: *Ben Curless*
Director, Editing/Design/Production: *Jess Ann Kosic*
Project manager: *Jean R. Starr*
Production supervisor: *Janean Utley*
Designer: *Marianna Kinigakis*
Photo research coordinator: *Jeremy Cheshareck*
Photo researcher: *Keri Johnson*
Media project manager: *Mark Dierker*
Typeface: *10.5/13 New Astor*
Compositor: *Aptara*
Printer: *Quebecor World/Versailles*
Cover credit: *The Pleiades, satellite view. © Digital Vision/ PunchStock*
Credits: The credits section for this book begins on page 508 and is considered an extension of the copyright page.

Library of Congress Cataloging-in-Publication Data
Introduction to business / Laura Portolese Dias ... [et al.].
    p. cm.
  Includes index.
  ISBN-13: 978-0-07-337699-8 (alk. paper)
  ISBN-10: 0-07-337699-X (alk. paper)
  1. Business. 2. Industrial management. 3. Small business--Management.
  I. Dias, Laura Portolese.
  HF1008.I58 2009
  658--dc22

                                    2007051767

The Internet addresses listed in the text were accurate at the time of publication. The inclusion of a Web site does not indicate an endorsement by the authors or McGraw-Hill, and McGraw-Hill does not guarantee the accuracy of the information presented at these sites.

www.mhhe.com

dedication

To my late Uncle Don, whose leadership advice as I kid I didn't understand, as a teenager I didn't listen to, but as an adult I live by.

—Laura Portolese Dias

To my family, whose love inspires me and whose tuition bills keeps me working.

—Amit J. Shah

BRIEF
contents

contents

Chapter Four

Chapter Five

Chapter Six

Chapter Seven

208 Leadership and Motivation

Chapter Eight

240 Human Resource Management

Chapter Nine

282 Marketing: Product and Price

Chapter Ten

316 Marketing: Place and Promotion

Chapter Eleven

356 Information Technology in Business

Chapter Twelve

384 Understanding Financial Information and Accounting

Chapter Thirteen

Chapter Fourteen

ABOUT THE
authors

Laura Portolese Dias teaches at Shoreline Community College in Washington State. After earning her bachelor's degree from the University of Montana, Dr. Portolese Dias worked in corporate training and retail. She later accepted a position teaching at the Art Institute of Seattle. There, she taught business and marketing classes and then moved into program administration. Missing teaching, she joined Shoreline Community College's faculty and was awarded tenure in March 2006. At Shoreline, Dr. Portolese Dias teaches introduction to business, human relations, international business, and supervision. She is a co-advisor for the business club on campus, Delta Epsilon Chi (DEC), a college division of DECA, Inc. Her involvement in DEC began in 1999 at the Art Institute of Seattle and continues at both the school level and the national level where she serves on the Post Secondary Council.

Through the Shoreline Community College faculty exchange, Dr. Portolese Dias recently visited Denmark to teach at Business Academy West, where she taught finance, marketing, and banking to Danish as well as to international students.

Dr. Portolese Dias is also chairperson of the Student Success Committee. She is also involved in curriculum development, specifically for the AAAS business degrees.

Dr. Portolese Dias lives in Seattle with her husband, Alain, and two humane society rescue dogs. When not in hiding from the rain, she enjoys mountain biking, hiking, traveling, and golfing.

Amit Shah is a full professor of management and director of the Center for Community Partnerships at Frostburg State University (FSU) in Maryland. He has over 20 years of experience in industry and academia. Dr. Shah has taught a variety of business courses including management, strategic management, and international business. He has published over 60 refereed articles in various journals and published proceedings and has conducted training for various organizations in the area of business and strategy. In his capacity as a Center director, he works with various small-to-medium-size organizations—for profit, nonprofit, and government agencies—in organizing management development workshops and training. He has received several awards such as Frostburg State University's Outstanding Faculty Service Award, the FSU College of Business's Outstanding Faculty Research Award, and Outstanding SAM Student Chapter Advisor Award. He has also served as president of the Southeastern Chapters of the Decision Sciences Institute and president of the Institute for Operations Research and Management Sciences. When he is not in his classroom or engaged in community service, Dr. Shah enjoys being an entrepreneur serving coffee at Mountain City Coffeehouse and Creamery, which he owns with his wife.

People say that teaching is a noble profession. We often wonder if they say this because they know that while teaching you always have to be "on," standing in front of expectant faces and teaching about the topic at hand, while also teaching how to think critically and provoking thoughtful discussion.

Some say teaching is noble because they see our passion for the job and find that admirable. People may also find teaching noble because we educate tomorrow's career force and potential leaders. This burden is ours to bear, and we try to do the best every day to make sure this preparation occurs in the right way.

We find that teaching is noble for all of these reasons, but the most important one is the simplest. It is a noble profession because teachers wouldn't do it well if we didn't care about each and every student's success. As instructors, professors, full-time, part-time, and associate faculty, we are guiding lives in new directions and possibly into new phases, a powerful responsibility, and one that comes with a lot of opportunities! Our goal with this textbook is to ensure that students succeed and that instructors can easily prepare for the courses they teach so they can focus on what they do best: mentor tomorrow's leaders through caring, helping, and guiding.

Introduction to Business is concise and manageable for one quarter or one semester. The examples are current and focus on small, mid-size, and large businesses. Every chapter includes career information and advice for students relevant to their possible or ongoing careers. Every chapter also has an opening profile of a business relevant to that chapter's content as well as an applications feature that specifically shows how the information in that chapter can be used in our day-to-day lives and work lives. We strive to illustrate to students why the concepts and examples presented in this text are relevant to them now as well as after they graduate.

Please feel free to e-mail us—Laura (lporto@shoreline.edu) or Amit (ashah@frostburg.edu)—with any comments on this book. We would love to hear from you!

A SPECIAL NOTE TO STUDENTS

Sometimes it might be hard to remember that successful people around you were once students and had their own struggles. Perhaps they didn't "get" math, had to work to pay for college so they didn't have as much time as they would have liked to study, or maybe went to school while raising a family. In other cases, challenges might have been something as basic as having trouble managing time and learning the right way to study (thus the Study Skills feature found throughout the chapters of this text!). Whatever the challenges, anyone who has taken the time to earn a degree will say these challenges made them stronger and more ready for the workforce. Take every challenge as a learning experience, and also celebrate every triumph, even the small ones. At the end of every quarter or semester, take time to congratulate yourself on being 10, 15, or 20 credits closer to your dream career. Our advice as you continue on your educational journey is this: Always communicate with and stay in close contact with your instructors, learn lessons from any mistakes while not dwelling on them, and absolutely celebrate the wins! Remember that anything worth achieving will be difficult, and embrace this difficulty with enthusiasm, excitement, and positive attitude. We wish for you a successful quarter/semester, a successful year, and most of all, a successful career!

Warmest regards,
Laura Portolese Dias
and
Amit J. Shah

CHAPTERS THAT TAKE EXAMPLES BEYOND THE CLASSROOM . . .

Each of the 14 chapters follows a common structure with a range of assessment and progress measurement options for instructors to use.

Learning Objectives

Each chapter begins with a list of **Learning Objectives.** These objectives are tied directly to the chapter content and instructor's materials and help students better anticipate what they will be studying in each chapter and help instructors measure students' understanding.

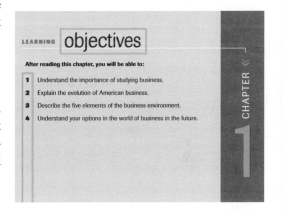

Key Terms

Developing a strong business vocabulary is one of the most important and useful goals of this course. To assist you, all key concepts in the book are highlighted in boldface type and are also defined in the margins. Page references to these **Key Terms** are listed at the end of each chapter. A full **Glossary** is found at the back of the book. You should rely heavily on these learning aids in adding to your vocabulary of business terminology.

Section Outlines

For the main sections in the chapters, **Section Outlines** are provided so students know exactly what topics will be covered in the coming pages.

> ### Section Outline
>
> **The Importance of Studying Business**
>
> **Defining Business**
>
> - Profit, Revenue, Loss, and Risk and Reward
> - Stakeholders and Shareholders

Self-Check Questions

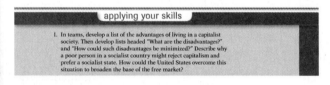

Self-Check Questions related to each section throughout the chapters allow frequent student assessment of comprehension. These questions work in conjunction with the Section Outlines and the Learning Objectives for the chapter.

Questions for Students

q: What big-ticket items do you own or desire based
» » on popularity? Which items seem more or less valuable because of the fluctuations in supply and demand?

The **Questions for Students** reinforce the chapters' key concepts by asking readers to think about the material in terms of their own experiences.

Applying Your Skills

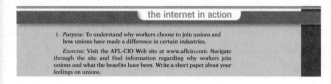

At the end of each chapter, **Applying Your Skills** review questions reinforce key learning outcomes. Team activities are also included in these exercises to promote collaboration in learning.

The Internet in Action

To encourage the development of Internet skills—specifically search skills—each chapter features **The Internet in Action** exercises that encourage students to locate and review useful Web sites for their ongoing development.

. . . AND INTO THE REAL WORLD!

Chapter Opening Profiles

At the beginning of each chapter students will find a **chapter opening profile** of someone working in the business world or of a company in the real world facing challenges relevant to the chapter content.

Real World Business Apps

Each chapter begins with a feature called **Real World Business Apps,** a hypothetical business situation in which a businessperson has questions about the area of business covered in the chapter. At the end of each chapter, the particular hypothetical situation is concluded, using concepts covered in the chapter.

Ethical Challenge

Even though many institutions now offer a separate business ethics course in their programs of study, we felt it was critical to emphasize the importance of ethical business practice in this text. As a result, the chapters feature a **Ethical Challenge** box in which the student is presented with an ethical dilemma. The ethical challenges are directly linked to the chapter material and the questions ask the student to relate the challenges back to their own experiences.

Thinking Critically

Each chapter includes a short business article relating to the learning objectives to get the students **Thinking Critically.** Articles come straight from the business news headlines, giving students a look into the real world of business. Students are asked to assess the material and answer critical thinking questions based on the content.

Study Skills

Student learning does not end when they leave the classroom. We know students often appreciate extra support. Each chapter provides helpful hints for students who aspire to learn and maintain good study habits. **Study Skills** boxes suggest proper study skills to help students thrive in their classes.

Study Skills

Subtitle if Needed

Management is the process of deciding the best way to use an organization's resources to produce goods or provide services. An organization's resources include its employees, equipment, and money.

Career Development

We also recognize the importance of supporting students as they transition from school to the professional world. Each chapter provides a **Career Development** box with ideas to aid students in their journey into their careers and unique insights and activities that will help students succeed.

STUDENT RESOURCES

Student Online Learning Center

Our online site for the text gives students supplementary materials to help them better understand and master chapter material. The student **Online Learning Center** has **narrated slides** (which are also available for students to download to their MP3 players), extra chapter quizzes, and other supplemental text materials. You can access the Online Learning Center by visiting **www.mhhe.com/diasbusiness**.

Student Study Guide

The **Student Study Guide** includes worksheets, practice tests, and supplemental learning materials including a business plan project so students can reinforce their learning of the chapter concepts. The Student Study Guide is organized by chapter and learning outcome to assist students in understanding each chapter's goals and objectives. This guide is available in both a print version or as part of the online enhanced cartridge.

Spanish Translations

Spanish-speaking students can take advantage of the **Spanish Translations** of the Glossary of key terms and online quizzes.

INSTRUCTOR RESOURCES

Online Learning Center—Instructor Content

The instructor's side of the **Online Learning Center (OLC)** serves as a resource for instructors and has several features that support instructors in the creation of lessons. Included on the OLC are the Instructor's

Manual (IM), which is organized by each chapter's learning objectives and includes page references, PowerPoint slides that include additional instructor teaching notes, and the Asset Map and other valuable materials. Visit the site at **www.mhhe.com/diasbusiness**.

Instructor's Manual

The **Instructor's Manual** outlines course materials, additional in-class activities, and support for classroom use of the text and has been organized by learning outcome to give instructors not only a basic outline of the chapter, but also assistance in all facets of instruction. For every question posed in the text, the IM provides a viable answer. The text page numbers provide easy reference for instructors. In addition, the Instructor's Manual guides instructors through the process of integrating supplementary materials into lessons and assignments. The Instructor's Manual also includes sample syllabi, video notes, and student success insights. Ultimately, this will be an instructor's greatest advantage in using all materials to reach all learners.

Test Bank

Every chapter provides a series of test questions, available in our Test Bank. Questions are organized by Learning Objective and Bloom's Taxonomy. A Test Table aligns questions with the content and makes it easy for you to determine the questions you want to include on tests and quizzes.

Instructor PowerPoint Slides

PowerPoint Slides created specifically for instructors include additional teaching notes, which include bonus examples, page referenced, and the Learning Objectives. Each slide also includes a text page reference for your convenience.

Videos

Our instructor DVD includes videos for every chapter of the text. Teaching notes for the videos can be located on the Instructor's Manual.

Asset Map

We know that instructors' time is valuable. To help you prepare, we have created an **Asset Map**. The Asset Map identifies by chapter, learning objective, and page number exactly which supplements are available for you to use. With the click of your mouse, find the PowerPoint slides, instructor note, or answer relating to every learning objective in the text. Visit our Web site to preview how the Asset Map can help, **www.mhhe.com/diasbusiness**.

ACKNOWLEDGMENTS

Every book is the product of a long list of people who contributed their time, energy, and effort, and ours is no exception. This text represents the culmination of the combined efforts of a large number of people.

Thank you to the amazingly talented team at McGraw-Hill, including Natalie Ruffatto and Tammy Higham, for providing the guiding light and vision for this text; and to Keari Bedford and Megan Gates, who are not only great marketers, but great people too! Also at McGraw-Hill, thanks to Jean Starr for keeping us on schedule, as well as to Benjamin Curless, Janean Utley, and Marianna Kinigakis for their efforts behind the scenes. We would like to thank the supplement writers, Gayle Ross, Barbara Barrett, Carol Johnson, Claudia Huiza, Theresa Mastrianni, and Jim Jump, for their outstanding dedication to this project.

LAURA'S ACKNOWLEDGMENTS

I give special thanks and appreciation to Amit Shah for his knowledge, expertise, and contributions to this book and the PowerPoint presentations for the supplements.

I would also like to thank the Starrs, the Loomises, and the McCloskeys who served as some of my favorite, inspiring people. I want to thank my DEC colleagues in Washington State and throughout the country whose devotion to student success inspires me. And I want to acknowledge my current and past students at Shoreline and the Art Institute of Seattle. Their growth and dedication to their career development invigorates me every quarter.

My mom and dad, JoAnn and Emanuele Portolese, deserve recognition for proofreading when they could have been golfing; for this and so many other reasons, I thank them. I honor my aunts and uncles, whom I am lucky to call my family. Family is the most important thing in life and I am thankful for mine: Rob, Lisa Victoria, and Veronica, Meme, Carlos, Rosemarie, Anne, Ken, and baby Wes. Last but not least, I thank my husband, Alain Dias, whose love, generosity, and support I appreciate every day (even if I don't always say it).

AMIT'S ACKNOWLEDGMENTS

First and foremost, I would like to thank my family—my parents for instilling the right values of hard work, ambition, positive attitude, respect for others, and drive to succeed; my kids, Raj and Riya, for giving up the family vacations and outings so I could meet my deadlines; my beautiful wife, Yashmi, for always being there without question and totally supporting my absolutely crazy and workaholic schedule in my quest for accomplishing different goals. I simply love you all!

I would be remiss if I did not thank my other family—my colleagues in my department who have always been there with total support and have put up with all my harassment; my dean, Danny Arnold, for creating an environment supportive of research and intellectual contribution; and my students, who have kept me young and always wanting to improve my teaching. Finally, I extend my thanks to Laura, who graciously welcomed me to this project.

REVIEWERS

We along with McGraw-Hill would also like to acknowledge all of the instructors whose valuable insights helped shape a text that we are all proud of:

Michele Adams, *Bryant & Stratton College*

Mark Alexander, *Axia College of University of Phoenix*

Vondra Armstrong, *Pulaski Technical College*

Lashun Aron, *Brown Mackie College*

Thomas J. Badley, *Baker College, Port Huron*

Larry Banks, *Eagle Gate College Group*

Ellen A. Benowitz, *Mercer County Community College*

Mary Jo Boehms, *Jackson State Community College*

Carl Bridges, *Lincoln Educational Services*

Dennis Brode, *Sinclair Community College*

Linda Bruff, *Strayer University*

Kay Conway, *Borough of Manhattan Community College, CUNY*

Pat DeBold, *Concord Career*

Joseph DeFilippe, *Suffolk County Community College*

Larry Dionne, *Robert Morris College*

Nick DiMartina, *Bryant & Stratton College*

Jon Doyle, *Corinthian Colleges, Inc.*

Lowell Frame, *Indiana School of Business*

Jan Friedheim, *Education Systems & Solutions*

Steve Friedheim, *Education Systems & Solutions*

Keeley Gadd, *National College*

Connie Golden, *Lakeland Community College*

Alfredo Gomez, *Broward Community College*

Katherine Groth, *Westwood College*

Beth Hall, *Tidewater Tech*

Karen Halpern, *South Puget Sound Community College*

Robin Hoggins-Blake, *American Continental University*

Juanita Johnson, *ITI Technical College*

Pat Kapper, *CCA Board Member*

John Keim, *Heald College*

John Lehnen, *Heald College*

Linda Morable, *Richland College*

Jaime Morely, *US Education*

John Olson, *ECPI*

Miguel A. Orta, *DeVry University*

Ken Pascal, *Art Institute of Houston*

Mary Ann Pelligrino, *IADT*

Robert Roehrich, *NAU*

Linda Rose, *Westwood College*

Kathleen Saxton, *Bryant & Stratton College*

David Schaitkin, *South Hills School of Business and Technology*

Angela Seidel, *Cambria-Rowe Business College*

Brenda Siragusa, *Corinthian Colleges, Inc.*

Rodo Sofranac, *Axia College of University of Phoenix*

Gerard Swain, *Virginia College at Autin*

Bob Trewartha, *Minnesota School of Business*

Pete West, *Colorado Technical University Online*

Charlie Zaruba, *Florida Metropolitan University*

INTRODUCTION TO
business

THE DYNAMIC BUSINESS ENVIRONMENT

Central Bark[1]

Central Bark is located in Seattle, Washington. The business offers doggie day care, grooming, self-service dog bathing, and boarding. Central Bark has an 8,000-square-foot facility and a private off-leash dog park. Curt Greenberg purchased the business in 2001 because of his love for animals. He started his career as a middle-school science teacher and worked in property management after his teaching career. After that, he decided he wanted to be his own boss, and he opened a kitchen store.

Curt Greenberg

Curt operated the kitchen store for 10 years and sold it in 2001. Then he purchased Central Bark. According to Curt, the biggest joy of his business is watching dogs grow into more social animals.

Curt knows he must be aware of all of the environments in which business operates. The business environments will be the focus of this chapter. First, in the economic environment, income and employment rates are extremely important. The more money people make, the more willing they will be to spend their money at Central Bark. In addition, if unemployment rates go up, people will have less need to use doggie day care during traditional work hours.

LEARNING objectives

After reading this chapter, you will be able to:

1   Understand the importance of studying business.

2   Explain the evolution of American business.

3   Describe the five elements of the business environment.

4   Understand your options in the world of business in the future.

In the legal environment, Curt has to be concerned about liability. For example, Curt has all new clients sign a form that says that they allow Central Bark to make decisions about the dog's health without prior consent from the owner. If a dog gets hurt while playing at Central Bark, Curt and his staff have the right to administer veterinary care. Curt's other legal concern is the well-being and safety of his employees. Dog bites, allergies, and accidents are all possibilities in Curt's business.

In the technological environment, Curt must manage his Web site because that is how many customers find his business. Technology advancements allow Curt to improve record keeping, such as client vaccination records and employee schedules.

The competitive environment is also extremely important to Central Bark. Since Curt purchased the business, five competitors have opened similar businesses nearby. In such a competitive environment, a business must provide something unique in order to differentiate its products and services. In this case, Curt believes the services provided to his human *and* canine customers must be outstanding.

Curt knows that several factors in the social environment affect his business. First, many people are waiting longer to have children in our current social environment. As a result, many choose to have a pet first, affecting Curt's business in a positive way.

Every business, from small to large, must have an awareness of the environmental factors that affect it. Understanding these factors allows a business to be more agile and to change based upon the needs of the customers, human and canine alike.

business

An individual or organization that seeks to provide goods and services to others while operating at a profit.

THE IMPORTANCE OF STUDYING BUSINESS

Business is an extremely exciting area to study, in part because business affects each of us in our daily lives. But what is business? **Business** can be defined as a person, partnership, or corporation that seeks to provide goods and services to others at a profit. By purchasing things we need, such as food and clothing, we participate in business. Many of you reading this text may become or already are business majors. The options are endless with a business degree. Even if you are not a business major, this textbook will give you insight into the process by which services and goods are provided to customers. This book explores many areas of business and demonstrates how business operates and affects our daily lives.

DEFINING BUSINESS

Businesses provide people with the opportunity to become wealthy. Sam Walton of Wal-Mart began by opening one store in Arkansas and, over time, became the richest person in America; his heirs are now worth billions of dollars. Bill Gates did even better. He started Microsoft and is now one of the richest people in the world. He is said to be worth about $56 billion[2] (however, take note that as the stock price of Microsoft changes, so does the worth of Bill Gates).

Wal-Mart started as one store and grew to a multi-billion dollar organization.

Rochelle Johnson owns a small 10-person marketing company. During a meeting, one of her employees, John, mentioned that they must keep stakeholders in mind when making business decisions. She asked him to define a "stakeholder." John said that a *stakeholder* is anyone who cares about the success of a business. For example, customers, suppliers, and people in the community are all stakeholders. Rochelle recognized why it mattered what customers thought, but she was puzzled as to why the rest of the stakeholders mattered. Her understanding was that business simply provided products or services, and if customers liked those products and services, they would buy them and her company would make a profit. Why did she care what other stakeholders thought?

John also mentioned learning during a business class about the five environments in which business operates. He said that an awareness of these five areas would help them make better business and marketing decisions for their clients. Rochelle knew she needed to be concerned about what the competitors were doing, but what other environments must she be concerned about?

Rochelle wanted answers to why the stakeholders are so important and what concerns she should have about the business environment. She did research immediately so she could find out. After all, what business owner doesn't want to make good decisions for her company?

At a more modest (and realistic) level, perhaps your goal is to support your family and provide for some luxuries or the education of your children. Owning a business if you are willing to be an **entrepreneur** or working for a business if you have managerial talents can help you meet this goal.

Profit, Revenue, Loss, and Risk and Reward

Profit is the amount of money a business earns above and beyond what it pays out for salaries and other expenses. For example, if you were to start a business selling hot dogs in the summer, you would have to pay for the cart rental, for the hot dogs and condiments, and for someone to run the cart while you were away. After you paid your employee and yourself, paid for the food and condiments you used, paid the rent on the cart, and paid your taxes, any money left over would be profit. Keep in mind that profit is over and above the money you pay yourself in salary. You could use any profit you make to rent or buy a second cart and hire other employees. After a few summers, you might have a dozen carts employing dozens of workers.

Revenue is the *total* amount of money a business takes in during a given period by selling goods and services. A **loss** occurs when a business's expenses are more than its revenues. If a business loses money over time, it will likely have to close. This is where risk comes in.

entrepreneur
A person who owns and operates his or her own business.

profit
The amount of money a business earns above and beyond what it pays out for salaries and other expenses.

revenue
The total amount of money a business takes in during a given period by selling goods and services.

loss
This occurs when a business's expenses are more than its revenues.

Starting small can lead to big things in entrepreneurship. One cart with good sales can turn into twelve carts and enough income to hire employees.

Starting a business always involves some risk. Steve Forbes of *Forbes* magazine says, "Risk-taking is the critical element for improving our standard of living."[3] **Standard of living** can be defined as the quality and quantity of products available to people and how these goods are distributed over the population. **Risk** is the chance an individual or organization takes of losing time and money on a business that may not prove profitable. Even among companies that do make a profit, not all make the same amount. Those companies that take the most risk may make the most profit. There is a lot of risk involved, for example, in making a movie. The much anticipated film *Gigli* fell far short of making money; with a budget of $54 million, the film grossed only $7.2 million (domestic and international).[4] On the other hand, some lower-budget movies can make a huge profit. *My Big Fat Greek Wedding,* for example, cost only $5 million to make and brought in over $368 million (domestic and international).[5]

As a potential business owner, you need to do research (for instance, talk to other businesspeople, read business publications, talk to customers, and many other activities to be discussed later in this book) to find the right balance between risk and profit for you. Different individuals have different tolerances for risk. In order to decide the best choice for you, you have to calculate the risks and the potential **rewards** of each decision. The more risks you take, the higher the rewards may be.

Stakeholders and Shareholders

Stakeholders are all the people who stand to gain or lose from the policies and activities of a business. Stakeholders (as we mentioned earlier in the Real World Business Apps box) include customers, employees, stockholders, suppliers, bankers who have made loans to a business, people in general in the surrounding community, and elected government leaders, among others (see Figure 1.1). All of these groups are affected by the products, policies, and practices of businesses, and their concerns need to be addressed.

All of us are stakeholders in many businesses. For example, if you shop at TJMaxx, you are a stakeholder of TJMaxx. Likewise, if you live in Framingham, Massachusetts, where the parent company of TJMaxx, TJX Companies, holds its corporate headquarters, you are also a stakeholder, because the success of TJMaxx will affect the community in which you live. As an example of the impact a company

standard of living

A grade or level of subsistence (basic needs) and comfort in everyday life enjoyed by a community, class, or individual.

risk

Exposure to the chance of a financial or time loss due to something that is not successful.

reward

The gratification as a result of some action.

stakeholders

All the people who stand to gain or lose from the policies and activities of a business.

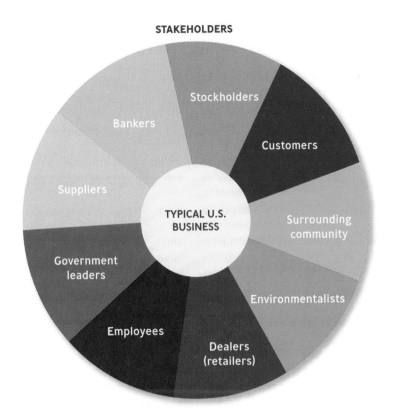

STAKEHOLDERS

figure 1.1

A BUSINESS AND ITS STAKEHOLDERS

Often the needs of a firm's various stakeholders will conflict. For example, paying employees more may cut into stockholders' profits. Balancing such demands is a major role of business managers.

has on a community, when Levi Strauss closed its last American factory in San Antonio, Texas, 800 jobs were lost.[6] At first, this might have appeared to affect only the laid-off workers. But in fact a ripple effect occurs when people in a community are laid off. Those workers in San Antonio might have cut down on dining out and other unnecessary expenses. As a result, the entire community of shops and restaurants could have lost money.

The challenge for organizations is to balance, as much as possible, the needs of all stakeholders. For example, the need for the business to make profits may be balanced against the needs of employees for sufficient income. The need to stay competitive may call for moving a business overseas, but that might do great harm to the community because many jobs would be lost.[7] It may be legal to move, but would moving be best for everyone? Business leaders must make decisions based on all factors, including the need to make a profit. As you can imagine, pleasing all stakeholders is not easy and calls for trade-offs that are not always pleasing to one or another stakeholder.

A **shareholder,** in contrast to a stakeholder, is a person who actually owns stock in a company. *Stock* is an intangible piece of ownership in a company. By owning stock, shareholders actually own a piece of the

shareholder
A person who actually owns stock in a company.

All Hail the Entrepreneur

"Big-and-old companies remain important. But in a global marketplace, start-ups are our best weapon."
—Carl J. Schramm, president and CEO of the Ewing Marion Kauffman Foundation, and author of *The Entrepreneurial Imperative*

Entrepreneurship is transforming America—not just for a few, but for all of us and for the better. Consider: Today roughly 45 million Americans, about 30 percent of the labor force, run their own businesses. Sometime during their careers, well over half of university graduates will start a business. Most Americans today work in firms that have entrepreneurial teams in charge. And most U.S. job growth and new technology comes from entrepreneurial companies. In short, ours is no longer an economy of big, old, stable corporations. Yes, we have many of those. But increasingly, we live in an economy of new, rapidly growing (and sometimes rapidly declining) entrepreneurial companies. America is unique in the world, a nation rebuilding itself on the principles of entrepreneurial capitalism. If all this comes as news to you, you are in good company. Until recently, even the most perceptive economists had missed this revolutionary development. One of the exceptions was Edmund Phelps, who won the Nobel Prize in Economics. He recently wrote of entrepreneurship as a source of dynamism, broader life satisfaction, and greater justice in society as a whole. Yet, as late as 1993, the founder of modern management and one of

the preeminent thinkers on economic matters in the 20th century, Peter Drucker, opined that we would never again see the likes of such entrepreneurs as John D. Rockefeller (founder of Standard Oil and the modern petroleum industry) and Henry Ford (founder of Ford Motor Company and the modern auto industry). But even as Drucker was writing, Bill Gates's Microsoft and Sam Walton's Wal-Mart were poised to surpass in market value the creations of Rockefeller and Ford.

One reason our new era of entrepreneurial capitalism has surprised so many is that it is so different from what came before it. From the mid-1940s through the mid-70s, America had an economy of the big—big business, big labor, big government—what some have called bureaucratic capitalism. Books such as William H. Whyte's 1956 classic *The Organization Man* and Sloan Wilson's *The Man in the Gray Flannel Suit* (1955) were assumed to describe a new and permanent change in our economic life. We all worked and would continue to work in gigantic organizations insulated from risk, and structured for efficiency—or so it was thought.

Then came the oil shocks and stagflation (defined in Chapter 2) of the late 70s, massive and sudden changes that gave an advantage to those who could adjust quickly, that is, to entrepreneurs. In the 1980s and early 1990s, the personal computer and the Internet delivered to men and women building new companies tools that allowed

company, however small the piece might be. Shareholders want to see return on their investments, and as a result, businesspeople are constantly under pressure to satisfy the needs of the stakeholders, including its shareholders.

SELF-CHECK QUESTIONS

1. Define business and explain why the study of business is important. Define *risk.* Are you willing to take risks in order to own your own business? Why or why not?

2. How are revenue and profit different? Are they related to each other also? How?

3. How are stakeholders and shareholders different? The same?

them to compete on an equal footing. By 2005, only 25 companies from the 1980 Fortune 100 even existed in the same capacity.

Does this mean big companies are all dying? Not at all. They are adapting. The smartest of them are joining forces with America's new culture of entrepreneurial capitalism. Want to see a vivid example of this new kind of alliance? Click to an old film on the American Movie Channel or Turner Classic Movies (both entrepreneurial companies, by the way, with Turner's now owned by a merger of two of the giant flagships of old-line industry, Time-Warner). Read the credits and you'll invariably see just one producer: Warner Bros., MGM, Paramount, or another of a select few. Now buy a ticket at your local theater to the latest major release. It doesn't matter which one. In just about all, the list of producers and production companies runs almost as long as the list of actors and crew. Films today involve numerous entrepreneurs and entrepreneurial companies partnering with a big studio. One of the best examples is Pixar Animation and Disney, with the former now owned by the latter.

It is a story typical of industries from pharmaceuticals to software to retail. Behind the familiar names are hundreds of alliances with independent and relatively new firms. In a world in which knowledge and imagination have joined labor, capital, and materials as factors of production, entrepreneurial companies often provide the creativity and take on the early risk while big companies chip in financial and marketing muscle when it's finally time to go national or even global. Factors of production are basically those things required for business to happen, such as land and labor. Factors of production will be discussed at length in Chapter 2.

In today's international marketplace, entrepreneurship is America's unmatched advantage. It is an infinitely renewable resource, one that economist William Baumol has called the "indispensable component" of growth and prosperity. We must respect and teach it in our schools. We must make sure our tax and regulatory policies don't create barriers to it. Most of all, we must recognize it as essential to America's continued economic and political leadership in the world.

QUESTIONS

1. How have "global alliances" helped big and small businesses?

2. Can you provide examples of companies whose success illustrates how "imagination and knowledge" have joined together?

3. The article uses the term "entrepreneurial capitalism." What is meant by this, in your opinion?

Source: Based on Carl Schramm, "All Hail the Entrepreneur," *Newsweek*, November 13, 2006. Copyright *Newsweek*, 2006.

EVOLUTION OF AMERICAN BUSINESS

Businesses in the United States have become very productive. The increasing impact of technology and global competition affects future employment and income levels. Where will the jobs be when you graduate? In the following section, we will explore briefly the progress of business in the U.S. economy.

Progress in the Agricultural and Manufacturing Industries

The United States has seen strong economic development since the 1800s. The agricultural industry led the way, providing food for the United States and much of the world. Cyrus McCormick's harvester,

Some of the most successful businesspeople started in the United States with nothing. Entrepreneurship is available to everyone in the United States, and many new ventures are being started by minorities.

Eli Whitney's cotton gin, as well as modern improvements on such equipment have done much to make farming a successful industry. The modern farming industry has become so efficient through the use of technology that the number of farmers has dropped from about 33 percent of the population to less than 2 percent in the United States. The number of farms in the United States declined from some 6.4 million at the beginning of the 20th century to approximately 2 million today.[8] However, the average farm size is now about 446 acres versus 160 acres in the past. In other words, agriculture is still a major industry in the United States. What has changed is that the millions of small farms that existed previously have been replaced by some huge farms, some merely large farms, and some small but highly specialized farms. The loss of farm workers over the past century is not a negative sign for the economy overall, since it means that U.S. agricultural workers are the most productive in the world. However, for many individual farmers it has meant the necessity of having to find new types of work to do.

Many farmers who lost their jobs were retrained and went to work in factories. The manufacturing industry, like agriculture, has also used technology to become more productive. As with agriculture, in the manufacturing sector fewer people produce more with new tools and machines. The consequence has been the elimination of many jobs. Again, the loss to society is minimal if the wealth created by increased productivity and efficiency creates new jobs elsewhere—and that's exactly what has happened over the past 50 years. However, while there may be a large benefit to society, the loss to individuals is often devastating.

This issue concerns many people. In his book *When Corporations Rule the World,* David C. Korten (2001) suggests that greed and power rule and the rights of human beings to earn a living are being squashed by corporations. Individuals are not having their basic needs met, while corporations are reaping gigantic profits.[9] Managers in business must have an awareness of employees when making decisions. The challenge managers face is balancing of profit with the good of the employees and society, which is one aspect of business we will explore in Chapter 4.

Progress in Service Industries

services

Intangible products (i.e., products that can't be held in your hand) such as education, health care, insurance, recreation, and travel and tourism.

Many workers who could no longer find employment in manufacturing have been able to find jobs in the service industry. **Services** are *intangible* products (products that can't be held in your hand) such as education, health care, insurance, recreation, and travel and tourism. In the past, the dominant industries in the United States produced goods (steel, railroads, machine tools, etc.). Today, the leading firms are in services: legal, health, telecommunications, entertainment, and financial industries. Although recently service-sector growth has slowed, it remains the largest

Understanding Career Planning

Career planning is the process by which an individual develops objectives for the future and acquires the necessary resources and takes appropriate steps to achieve a desired career outcome. In assessing an opportunity, then, the individual works within the career plan to judge the opportunity and reject or pursue it.

The career planning spirit motivates millions of people to obtain the necessary assistance, credentials, and personal growth to become successful professionals in the working world.

The question is, when it is hard enough just to find an attractive job, why would you make the considerable extra effort to plan a pathway and set goals by which your career will develop and be achieved? The answer is that nothing of value is gained without some vision and foresight. Think about the possibilities of your becoming a high-level executive, a small business owner, or a manager of a company you would like to work for. For this to happen requires a career vision to discover the practical steps needed to reach these lofty goals. Your planning work now can mean a huge payoff in a career where you can find great success!

area of growth.[10] Chances are very high that you may work in such a job at some point in your career. Figure 1.2 lists many service-sector jobs; look it over to see where the careers of the future are likely to be. Retailers like The Gap are part of the service sector. Retail is just one of many examples where college graduates can find employment.

Another bit of good news is that there are more high-paying jobs in the service sector than in the goods-producing sector. Given the projections that some areas of the service sector will grow rapidly, while others may have much slower growth, a good strategy for college graduates is to remain flexible and find out where jobs are being created!

Retailers are included in the service industry, the largest area of growth for U.S. employment.

q: What types of service industry jobs do you
» » think will continue to grow rapidly? Visit the U.S. Department of Labor at www.dol.gov/ and research service jobs you think would interest you. Are the projections positive or negative?

There's much talk about the service sector, but few discussions actually list what it includes. Here's a representative list of services as classified by the government:

LODGING SERVICES

Hotels, rooming houses, and other lodging places
Sporting and recreation camps
Trailer parks and camp sites for transients

PERSONAL SERVICES

Laundries	Child care
Linen supply	Shoe repair
Diaper service	Funeral homes
Carpet cleaning	Tax preparation
Photographic studios	Beauty shops
Health clubs	

BUSINESS SERVICES

Accounting	Employment agencies
Ad agencies	Computer programming
Collection agencies	Research and
Commercial photography	development labs
Commercial art	Management services
Stenogaphic services	Public relations
Window cleaning	Detective agencies
Consulting	Interior design
Equipment rental	Web design
Exterminating	

AUTOMOTIVE REPAIR SERVICES AND GARAGES

Auto rental	Tire retreading
Truck rental	Exhaust system shops
Parking lots	Car washes
Paint shops	Transmission repair

MISCELLANEOUS REPAIR SERVICES

Radio and television	Welding
Watch	Sharpening
Reupholstery	Septic tank cleaning

MOTION PICTURE INDUSTRIES

Production	Theaters
Distribution	Drive-ins

AMUSEMENT AND RECREATION SERVICES

Dance halls	Racetracks
Symphony orchestras	Golf courses
Pool halls	Amusement parks
Bowling alleys	Carnivals
Fairs	Ice skating rinks
Botanical gardens	Circuses
Video rentals	Infotainment

HEALTH SERVICES

Medical Assistants	Nursery care
Nurses	Medical labs
Chiropractors	Dental labs

LEGAL SERVICES

EDUCATIONAL SERVICES

Libraries	Computer schools
Schools	

SOCIAL SERVICES

Child care	Family services
Job training	

NONCOMMERCIAL MUSEUMS, ART GALLERIES, AND BOTANICAL AND ZOOLOGICAL GARDENS

SELECTED MEMBERSHIP ORGANIZATIONS

Business associations	Civic associations

FINANCIAL SERVICES

Banking	Real estate agencies
Insurance	Investment firms (brokers)

MISCELLANEOUS SERVICES

Architectural	Surveying
Engineering	Utilities
Telecommunications	

figure 1.2

WHAT IS THE SERVICE SECTOR?

SELF-CHECK QUESTIONS

1. What do you think is the biggest change that has occurred in business discussed in this section?
2. In what area of the service industry would you be most interested in working? Why?

THE FIVE PARTS OF THE BUSINESS ENVIRONMENT

The business environment consists of the surrounding factors that either help or hinder the development of businesses. Figure 1.3 shows the five elements in the business environment. The five elements are:

1. The economic and legal environment.
2. The technological environment.
3. The competitive environment.
4. The social environment.
5. The global environment.

According to the National Federation of Independent Businesses, there are 25.8 million small businesses in the United States and all of these businesspeople are acutely aware of the environments in which they must operate.[11] Or they should be, if they want to succeed.

A business owner can keep abreast of changes in the environment by reading the newspaper and various business publications. That way, she is constantly up to date on changes and can adjust her business accordingly. Business owners who are not aware of the environment around them necessarily have less success than those who are aware. Finally, business owners need to be aware of stakeholders in each of the business environments.

The Economic and Legal Environment

Businesses do not operate in a vacuum but rather within a framework of laws and economic forces. See Figure 1.4. People are willing to start new businesses if they believe that the risk of losing their money is not too great. Part of entrepreneurs' risk involves the economic system and how government works with or against businesses. Government can do a lot to lessen the risk of starting businesses and thus increase

Section Outline

The Five Parts of the Business Environment

- The Economic and Legal Environment
- The Technological Environment
- The Competitive Environment
- The Social Environment
- The Global Environment

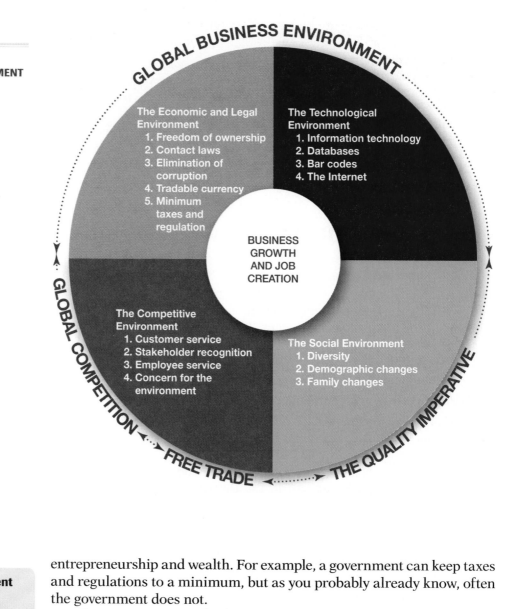

figure 1.3

**TODAY'S DYNAMIC
BUSINESS ENVIRONMENT**

GLOBAL BUSINESS ENVIRONMENT

The Economic and Legal
Environment
1. Freedom of ownership
2. Contact laws
3. Elimination of
corruption
4. Tradable currency
5. Minimum
taxes and
regulation

The Technological
Environment
1. Information technology
2. Databases
3. Bar codes
4. The Internet

BUSINESS
GROWTH
AND JOB
CREATION

The Competitive
Environment
1. Customer service
2. Stakeholder recognition
3. Employee service
4. Concern for the
environment

The Social Environment
1. Diversity
2. Demographic changes
3. Family changes

GLOBAL COMPETITION

FREE TRADE

THE QUALITY IMPERATIVE

**return on investment
(ROI)**

The money gained from
taking a business venture
risk. In addition to money,
investment of time is also
an important consideration
for businesspeople.

entrepreneurship and wealth. For example, a government can keep taxes and regulations to a minimum, but as you probably already know, often the government does not.

Entrepreneurs are looking for an acceptable **return on invest- ment (ROI).** Return on investment is the money gained from taking a business venture risk. In addition to money, investment of time is also an important consideration for businesspeople. If the government takes away much of what a business earns through high taxes, the ROI may no longer be worth the risk. This is true even in wealthy countries like the United States. States and cities in the United States that have high taxes and restrictive regulations tend to drive out entrepreneurs, while states and cities with low taxes and less restrictive regulations attract entrepreneurs. In 2006, the top three states with low tax rates for small businesses were South Dakota, Nevada, and Wyoming, mak- ing these states more appealing to entrepreneurs.[12] Laws that encourage entrepreneurship have been enacted all across the United States (and the world). Some of the tax laws that help small businesses include the provisions for deducting home office expenses, business travel and meals, and other business expenses.

Overall, a businessperson will benefit if he or she has an awareness of the laws affecting business and knowledge of the economic environment in which business operates. Economics will be discussed at greater length in Chapter 2.

figure 1.4

THE ECONOMIC AND LEGAL ENVIRONMENT

The Economic and Legal Environment
1. Freedom of ownership
2. Contact laws
3. Elimination of corruption
4. Tradable currency
5. Minimum taxes and regulation

What Can Government Do?

One way for government to actively promote entrepreneurship is to allow private ownership of businesses. In some countries, the government owns most businesses so there is little incentive for people to work hard or create profit. All around the world today, governments that previously owned most businesses are selling those businesses to private individuals to create more wealth. For example, China adopted a "gradualist" approach to privatization, whereas Russia started with the "big bang" approach of mass privatization.[13] One of the best things the governments of developing countries can do is to minimize the interference with the free exchange of goods and services.

Governments can lessen the risks of entrepreneurship by passing laws that enable businesspeople to write contracts that are enforceable in court. The **Uniform Commercial Code (UCC),** for example, covers things like contracts and warranties. In countries that do not yet have such codes, the risks of starting a business are much greater.

A government can also establish a currency that is tradable in world markets. That is, you can buy and sell goods and services anywhere in the world using that currency. The U.S. dollar, for example, is a **tradable currency.**

Governments can help minimize corruption in business and in their own ranks. However, some countries still face corporate and political corruption. For example, it is very difficult in such countries to get permission to build a factory or open a store without a government permit, which is obtained largely through bribery of public officials. According to Transparency International, a Berlin-based organization that conducts an annual corruption survey, Haiti, Myanmar, Iraq, and Guinea were the most corrupt countries in 2006. The least corrupt countries included Finland, Iceland, and New Zealand.[14]

Uniform Commercial Code (UCC)

A comprehensive set of commercial laws, adopted by every state in the United States, that covers sales laws and other commercial laws.

tradable currency

Money that is allowed to be exchanged for another country's money.

Among businesses themselves, corrupt leaders can threaten competitors to minimize competition.

There are many laws in the United States to minimize corruption, and businesses can flourish as a result. Nonetheless, corrupt and illegal activities at some U.S. companies negatively affect the business community and the economy as a whole.[15] Examples have included the Enron, Adelphia, WorldCom, Tyco, and ImClone scandals in the early part of the 2000s. The Enron scandal destroyed the company (and the pension funds of many who worked there), its accounting firm (Arthur Andersen), and other companies that had questionable accounting practices. Although when we think of corruption, we tend to think of large companies, but this is not always the case. Consider smaller companies where one of the employees is stealing money from the cash register or giving free food to friends. These examples are forms of corruption, and although we don't hear about them in the news as we do with major scandals like Enron, it is still important to recognize corruption as a concern for small businesses.

Bloomberg Personal Finance magazine reported that "one of the greatest threats to the U.S. economy . . . is the wholesale undermining of investor confidence in the stock market as a result of corporate deceptions like those of Enron."[16] In other words, when corporations behave unethically and illegally, investors may hesitate before investing in stocks. Lapses in the ethical environment have placed new emphasis on the need for laws restraining businesspeople from committing unethical and/or illegal acts, and such laws have recently been passed.

Recently, the Hewlett-Packard (HP) scandal rocked the headlines. This scandal involved Patricia Dunn, then the chair of the **board of directors** at HP who allegedly used unconventional methods to spy on board members to find out who was leaking information to the media. Because the board of directors is the entity that oversees the entire operations of a company, it is a serious ethical lapse to engage in this kind of behavior. The charges against Dunn, who resigned from HP in September 2006, were dismissed March 14, 2007.[17] Ethics will be discussed in more detail in Chapter 4.

The capitalist system relies heavily on honesty, integrity, and high ethical standards, and failure to adhere to those fundamental standards can weaken the whole system. The faltering economy of the early 2000s was due in part to such failure. The **capitalist system** is one in which the companies and businesses are owned by the citizens instead of the government. Given that a capitalist

board of directors

A group that oversees the activities of a corporation. Generally represents a mix—a small number of company executives and a greater number of outsiders.

capitalist system

Companies and businesses are owned by citizens instead of government.

Unethical behavior and corruption in business can impact more than just those involved.

Biz Majors Get an F for Honesty

Suddenly the business scandals of the past few years make a lot more sense. Research by the Center for Academic Integrity, a think tank affiliated with the Kenan Institute for Ethics at Duke University, shows that undergraduate business students do more cheating than just about anyone else, The survey of nearly 50,000 students at 69 schools found that 26% of business majors admitted to serious cheating on exams, and 54% admitted to cheating on written assignments, which includes plagiarism and poaching a friend's homework.

Bad as that is, business students didn't rank as the worst cheaters. That distinction belonged to journalism majors, 27% of whom said they cribbed answers. The most honest group? Those in the sciences, where 19% reported cheating on tests. The results come from surveys conducted over the past three years by Donald McCabe, a management professor at Rutgers Business School and founder of CAI.

McCabe says cheating has increased since he began doing surveys 15 years ago. He partly blames technology for making cheating easier. Papers can be downloaded off the Internet, and answers text-messaged to friends. But he adds that a "disturbing" number of students use recent corporate and political scandals to justify their behavior.

QUESTIONS

1. What do you think causes extensive cheating in school?

2. Do you think poor business practices of employers can be blamed for students who think cheating is okay?

Source: Based on Helena Oh, "Biz Majors Get an F for Honesty," *Business-Week* February 6, 2006.

---

system relies on high ethical standards, it is easy to see the damage caused to the system by the poor moral and ethical behavior of some businesspeople.

The Technological Environment

Since prehistoric times, humans have felt the need to create tools that make their jobs easier. Businesses always have been affected and even transformed by technological developments. See Figure 1.5. Various tools and machines developed throughout history have changed the business environment—sometimes dramatically, but few technological changes have had a more comprehensive and lasting impact on businesses than the recent emergence of information technology (IT): computers, modems, the Internet, cell phones, and so on. Chief among these developments is the Internet. Although many Internet firms failed in the early 2000s, the Internet has proven to be a major force in business today and in the future.[18] This section will discuss some of the concerns and awareness businesspeople should have involving technology.

By the time this book is printed, this phone my be a thing of the past.

q: What types of technology
» » exist today that did not exist
when you were in kindergarten?
In high school?

effectiveness

Producing the desired results.

efficiency

The ability to produce using the least amount of resources.

resource

Something used in the production of goods.

productivity

The amount of output you generate given the amount of input (e.g., hours worked).

Increased Productivity

When most of us think of technology, we often think of very fast computers or the newest and greatest cell phone. Technology, however, means everything from phones and computers, to medical imaging devices, personal digital assistants, and the various software programs that make business processes more *effective, efficient*, and *productive*. More will be discussed about technology in Chapter 11. **Effectiveness** means producing the desired results. **Efficiency** means producing goods using the least amount of **resources.** Technology clearly has resulted in greater efficiency.

Productivity is the amount of output you generate given the amount of input (for instance, hours worked). The more you can produce in any given period of time, the more money you are worth to companies. Tools and technology greatly improve productivity. Computer-aided design, computer-aided manufacturing, and artificial intelligence (AI) are used to automate tasks that would normally take people much longer to accomplish. For example, AI can be used to schedule work at a manufacturing plant or even be used to answer customer service questions submitted online.

Technology affects people in all industries, including farming. Don Glenn is a farmer in Decatur, Alabama. He uses his personal computer to compare data from last year's harvest with infrared satellite photos of his farm that show which crops are flourishing. He has a desktop terminal called a DTN that allows him to check the latest grain prices, and he uses AgTalk, a Web-based bulletin board, to converse with other farmers from all over the world. Glenn also bids for bulk fertilizer on XSAg.com, an online agricultural exchange. High-tech

The Technological
Environment
 1. Information technology
 2. Databases
 3. Bar codes
 4. The Internet

figure 1.5

**THE TECHNOLOGICAL
ENVIRONMENT**

equipment tells Glenn how and where to spread fertilizer and seed, tracks yields yard by yard, and allows him to maintain high profit margins.

One reason that workers make more money in the United States than in most other countries is that they have access to technology that allows them to be more productive (of course this is not true in all cases). Many countries may have less expensive labor, but that labor is not always as productive as it could be. Keep in mind, however, that increased productivity sometimes results in labor shifts or job losses. As previously mentioned, as machines are invented that improve processes, fewer human beings are needed to do the job. As these changes take place, businesses evolve to adapt to the new challenges.

Making Buying and Selling Easier

One of the most important recent environmental changes of interest to businesspeople is the growth of **e-commerce**— the buying and selling of goods over the Internet.[19] There are two major types of e-commerce transactions: **business-to-consumer (B2C)** and **business-to-business (B2B).** As important as the Internet has been in the consumer (B2C) market, it has become even more important in the B2B market, which consists of selling goods and services from one business to another, such as IBM selling consulting services to a local bank.[20] B2B e-commerce is already at least five

Farming is one of the largest and most important industries in the United States. Technology has led to increased productivity and has made farmers more efficient.

times as big as B2C e-commerce. While the potential of the B2C e-commerce market is measured in billions, B2B e-commerce is said to be measured in trillions of dollars.

The rise of Internet marketing came so fast and furious that it drew hundreds of competitors into the fray. Many of the new Internet companies failed. Companies such as Pets.com, CDnow, Internet Capital Group, eToys, and Kozmo.com have failed entirely or seen their stock prices drop dramatically. Many B2B stocks experienced similar failures. There is no question that some Internet businesses will grow and prosper, such as Amazon.com, but along the way there will continue to be lots of failures, just as there have been in traditional businesses.

e-commerce
Business conducted electronically over the Internet.

business-to-consumer (B2C)
A business that produces products to sell directly to the consumer.

q:
»»
How do you use the Internet to make purchasing decisions? Discuss it with classmates. Do you make similar purchases?

business-to-business (B2B)

A business that produces products to sell to another business.

Uniform Product Codes (UPC)

A series of lines and numbers that you see on most consumer packaged goods. The UPC identifies the type of product.

database

An electronic storage file where information is kept.

value

The relative worth, merit, or importance.

Success will come to those e-commerce businesses that offer quality products at good prices with great service. Many companies, such as JCPenney and General Electric, have combined their traditional brick-and-mortar operations with new Internet sites that make them more competitive.

Responsiveness to Customers

Businesses succeed or fail largely because of the way they treat their customers.[20] The businesses that are most responsive to customer wants and needs are more likely to succeed and those that do not respond to customers may not succeed.[21] One way traditional retailers can respond to the Internet revolution is to use technology to reach customers. For example, businesses mark goods with **Uniform Product Codes** or **UPCs** (bar codes)—the series of lines and numbers that you see on most consumer packaged goods. Bar codes can be used to tell retailers what product you bought, in what size and color, and at what price. A scanner at the checkout counter can read that information and put it into a database.

A **database** is an electronic storage file where information is kept. Consumer information can be saved in a database with cross-references to purchased product information. Grocery chains, movie rental stores, shoe stores, and other retailers offer "preferred customer" cards that can be scanned at checkout. Your contact information and purchase history then become part of the retailer's database. Because companies routinely trade database information, many retailers know what you buy and from whom you buy it. Using that information, companies can send you catalogs and other direct mail advertising that offers the kind of products you might want, as indicated by your past purchases. The use of databases enables stores to carry only the merchandise that the local population wants, and thus to maintain a smaller inventory, saving them money.

The Competitive Environment

Competition among businesses has always existed (see Figure 1.6), but it has never been greater than it is today. Some companies have found a competitive edge by focusing on quality. The goal for many companies is zero defects—no mistakes in making the product.[22] Some companies, such as Motorola in the United States and Toyota in Japan, have come close to meeting that standard. However, simply making a high-quality product isn't enough to allow a company to stay competitive in world markets. Companies now have to offer both high-quality products and outstanding service at competitive prices—this is what we mean by offering customers **value.**

The concept of *value* supports the idea that businesspeople must not only know what their competitors are doing, but also try to constantly improve their products and processes to meet customer expectations. The businessperson who is acutely aware of his competitors *and* his customers is more likely to be successful.

The Competitive Environment
1. Customer service
2. Stakeholder recognition
3. Employee service
4. Concern for the environment

figure 1.6

THE COMPETITIVE ENVIRONMENT

Customer-Driven Organizations

Customers require both high quality and high value, and for companies to stay competitive they must offer both. Figure 1.7 shows how competition has changed businesses from the traditional model to a new, world-class model.

Customer-driven organizations include Nordstrom department stores (they have a very generous return policy, for example) and Disney amusement parks (the parks are kept clean and appeal to all ages). The retail store Build-A-Bear Workshop provides great customer service through allowing customers to build their own stuffed animal.[23] Large and small businesses alike can succeed by providing outstanding customer service. Consider your doctor's office where the front staff knows your name or the paralegal who returns customers' phone calls the same day. These are examples of great customer service that keep customers coming back time and again. Big businesses and small businesses depend on their returning customers, and as a result, should go out of their way to make customers feel as if they are number one. Companies can successfully compete against Internet firms and

Traditional Businesses	World-Class Businesses
Customer satisfaction	Delighting the customer[1]
Customer orientation	Customer and stakeholder orientation[2]
Profit orientation	Profit and social orientation[3]
Reactive ethics	Proactive ethics[4]
Product orientation	Quality and service orientation
Managerial focus	Customer focus

figure 1.7

HOW COMPETITION HAS CHANGED BUSINESS

[1]*Delight* is a term from total quality management. *Bewitch* and *fascinate* are alternative terms.
[2]Stakeholders include employees, stockholders, suppliers, dealers (retailers), and the community; the goal is to please *all* stakeholders.
[3]A social orientation goes beyond profit to do what is right and good for others.
[4]*Proactive* means doing the right thing before anyone tells you to do it. *Reactive* means responding to criticism after it happens.

Study Skills

Study Skills Are a Learned Behavior!

What are your talents? What would you consider to be your greatest skills? Are you talented at singing, playing an instrument, playing sports, writing, painting, or renovating old cars?

Being good at studying is like anything you try. You might be better at some things than other things. Studying is a learned behavior like any activity, and you can improve your study habits and performance with more practice.

Two key areas will help you become better at studying: *study preparation* and *study execution*. Study preparation includes all the activities that help you get the most out of your reading and note taking. Study execution involves all the actions you take to stay on course to make sure you get the positive results you are seeking.

Companies such as FedEx offer high-speed delivery to keep up with the demands of customers worldwide.

empowerment
To give power or authority.

cross-functional teams
A group of people with different expertise working together to achieve a common goal.

other forms of competition if they continue to offer better and friendlier service. Successful organizations must now listen more closely to customers to determine their wants and needs, then adjust the firm's products, policies, and practices to meet those demands.

Have you noticed how everyone seems to be in more of a hurry today? The truth is that most people do live at a fast pace, and businesses need to respond or risk losing their business. For example, companies traditionally have had a six-week delivery time over the last several decades. Over time, many customers began to want things delivered in two days or less. That's why FedEx and other high-speed delivery firms are doing so well. Most of today's consumers want fast food, fast delivery, fast responses to Internet searches, and so on. Usually, the companies that provide speedy service are those that are staying ahead of the competition. Speed isn't everything, however. It has to be accompanied by things like good quality and reasonable prices. Some consumers may prefer less hurried but more helpful service, or slower pace with lower prices.

Employee Empowerment

To meet the needs of customers, firms must give their frontline workers (office clerks, front-desk people at hotels, salespeople, etc.) the responsibility, authority, freedom, training, and equipment they need to respond quickly to customer requests and to make other decisions essential to producing quality goods and providing good service, which is called **empowerment**—a concept that will be revisited throughout this book. To implement a policy of empowerment, managers must train frontline people to make decisions without the need to consult managers. The new role of supervisors, then, is to support frontline people with the training and technology to do their jobs well, including handling customer complaints quickly and satisfactorily. More will be discussed about empowerment and management in Chapter 6.

A key point to understand is that many businesses must reorganize to help their employees become more effective than they are now. Many firms have done so by forming **cross-functional teams**—teams made up of people from various departments—to work on a special project. These teams often work without close supervision; thus, they are sometimes called *self-managed* cross-functional teams.

One aspect of empowerment has been the elimination of managers and redistribution of workload. Companies that have implemented self-managed teams expect a lot more from their lower-level workers than they did in the past and can sometimes do without various levels of managers. Because they have less management supervision, workers need more education. Furthermore, empowered employees need to be treated as partners in the firm. Increasingly, a manager's job will be to train, support, coach, and motivate lower-level employees. As many companies have discovered, it sometimes takes years to restructure an organization so that managers are willing to give up some of their authority and employees are willing to assume more responsibility.

The Social Environment

The U.S. population is going through major changes, significantly affecting how people live, where they live, what they buy, and how they spend their time. Any businessperson needs to be aware of these massive shifts in society, in order to better meet the needs of the customer. See Figure 1.8.

The social environment is not only crucial for you as a businessperson to know about; it is a fun and interesting area to study. To learn more about the social changes and their impact on business, read as many publications as you can to find out about and keep track of these fast moving developments.

Diversity

The management of **diversity** is an important concern for businesspeople. An increasing percentage of the U.S. population in the future will be minorities—according to the U.S. Census Bureau, by the year 2050, non-Hispanic whites will be a slim majority. Over 24 percent will be Hispanic. In 2000, there were about 10.6 million citizens of Asian descent in the United States; in 2006 that number increased to about 12.9 million. The equivalent change from 2000 to 2006 for Caucasians is from about 197 million to 215 million, and for African Americans, from about 3 million to 9 million.[24] See Figure 1.9.

Businesses are concerned about having a diverse workforce for two main reasons. First, a business can better serve customers with a diverse workforce. Second, a diverse work environment brings about new, fresh ideas and perspectives. These new ideas might be implementation of a new system to make things easier and more efficient for workers, or even a new product. A diverse workforce is better overall for all companies. This affects each of us in the workforce because we will need to work with people of various ages, races, and backgrounds in order to be successful where we work. Having an understanding of diversity now will result in a greater ability to work with others later on.

Diversity has come to mean much more than recruiting and keeping minorities and women. In fact, many more groups are now included

diversity
Broad differences between people (ethnicity, gender, color, sexual orientation, body size, age).

figure 1.8

THE SOCIAL ENVIRONMENT

The Social Environment
1. Diversity
2. Demographic changes
3. Family changes

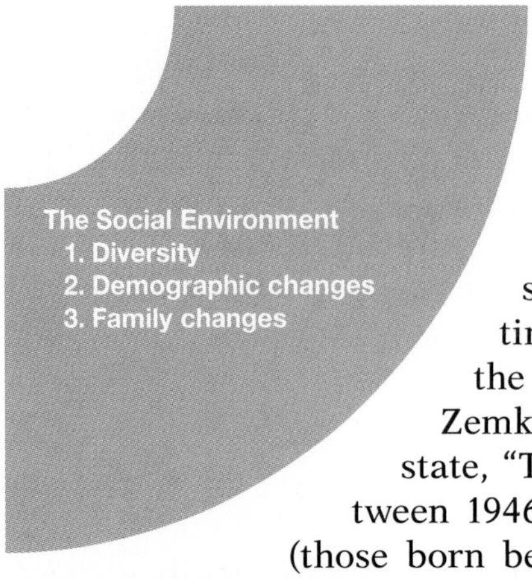

in diversity efforts. The list of 26 diversity groups identified by Federated Department Stores includes seniors, people with disabilities, gays and lesbians, atheists, extroverts, introverts, married people, singles, and devout individuals. Sometimes the issue is a difference in age. In the book *Generations at Work* (Raines, Zemke, and Filipczak, 2002), the authors state, "The Boomers (those people born between 1946 and 1964) say the Generation Xers (those born between 1965 and 1980) are slackers, whiners; they're rude, they lack social skills, and they always want to buck the system, and they don't want to spend time in the ranks. And the Xers say the Boomers are self-righteous: they're workaholics, they're more interested in politics than results, they talk a good talk but don't practice what they preach." You can imagine the conflicts that may develop between these two groups at work. Add another generation to that, Generation Y (those born after 1981), and it complicates matters even more! Generation Y (also known as the Millennial Generation) is known as the Echo Generation because its members are the children of Baby Boomers and they echo many of the work values of their parents. Generation Yers have many of the work–life balance requirements as Generation Xers, but view this balance differently. For example, Generation Yers prefer to keep work completely separate from personal life, whereas for Generation Xers

figure 1.9

SAMPLE CENSUS TABLE

Source: U.S. Census Bureau, 2006 American Community Survey, www.census.gov/.

	UNITED STATES	
	Estimate	**Margin of Error**
Total:	299,398,485	*****
White alone	226,537,259	+/−127,863
Black or African American alone	39,151,870	+/−34,212
American Indian and Alaska Native alone	2,035,551	+/−18,003
Asian alone	12,945,401	+/−28,537
Native Hawaiian and Other Pacific Islander alone	387,230	+/−8,034
Some other race alone	20,484,020	+/−115,113
Two or more races:	6,112,646	+/−62,937
Two races including Some other race	231,584	+/−10,146
Two races excluding Some other race, and three or more races	4,166,138	+/−45,582

the lines can be blurred. Perhaps the biggest difference at work, however, is that members of older generations view Generation Yers as too self-confident at work, which can grate on the nerves of both Generation Xers and Baby Boomers!

The management of diverse groups—whether they are different because of race, sex, age, sexual orientation, country of origin, religion, or some other classification—can be difficult. It becomes even more difficult as managers go overseas and must respond to all the cultural, political, and social issues that are specific to each country. As a future manager or business owner, you will discover that expertise in hiring and retaining a diverse workforce is key to a successful business.

One of the strengths of the United States is its ability to welcome people from all over the world. This photo shows a diversity seminar. These types of events allow people to learn about other cultures and practices.

Aging Consumers

Another social issue and concern is the fact that Baby Boomers are growing older; and as they retire, there will be more jobs than people qualified to fill those jobs. By 2030, the Baby Boomers will be senior citizens (many already are, in fact). People ages 45 to 64 are currently the richest group in U.S. society. They have a median income of $59,781.[25] They spend more than others on everything except health care and thus represent a lucrative market for restaurants, transportation, entertainment, and education.

According to the U.S. Census Bureau, there are now over 50 million citizens ages 60 and older.[26] By 2010 that number is expected to increase to about 56 million, and by 2020 there likely will be more than 74 million people over the age of 60. What do such demographics mean for you and for businesses in the future? Think of the products and services the middle-aged and elderly will need—travel, medicine, nursing homes, assisted-living facilities, adult day care, home health care, and recreation—and you'll see opportunities for successful businesses. Businesses that cater to the aging Baby Boomers will have the opportunity for exceptional growth in the near future. Baby Boomers are not aging the way previous generations did. Because of improvements in medical care and lifestyle choices, Boomers are more active than preceding generations. As a result, there is a growing market for adventure travel. Trips such as sailing

Understanding the differences in generations, in the workplace and in the consumer market, is important to continued business success.

through the Pacific islands or climbing Mt. Rainier are the sort of thing companies like Outer Quest provide and are a bit different than the traditional trips retirees once booked. All of this matters to managers because if they can better understand the wants and needs of consumers, they will be able to better provide products to meet those needs. Likewise, as students it applies to you because as Baby Boomers retire, it means more job openings for younger generations!

Dual Incomes

Dual-income families also play a role in the societal changes in the United States. A dual-income family is one in which both adult members of the household work. Several factors likely have led to a dramatic growth in two-income families in the United States. The high costs of housing and of maintaining a comfortable lifestyle, the high level of taxes, and the cultural emphasis on "having it all" have made it difficult if not impossible for many households to live on just one income. Furthermore, many parents today simply want a career outside the home.

One result of this trend is a host of programs that companies have implemented in response to the demands of busy two-income families. IBM and Procter & Gamble, for example, each offer employees pregnancy benefits, parental leave, flexible work schedules, and elder care programs. Some companies offer referral services that provide counseling to parents in search of child care or elder care. Such trends are creating many new opportunities for graduates in human resource management and related areas of study.

With more dual-income families in the workforce, many employers provide child care benefits of some type; some of these programs, such as the one at S. C. Johnson & Son, are on-site. Corporate day care centers are expensive to operate. Along with day care costs, individual employee needs and lifestyles have led companies to offer what are called cafeteria-style benefits packages, which enable families to choose from a menu of benefits. A couple may choose day care instead of a dental plan, for instance, and a single employee with no children may choose commuter reimbursement rather than child care.

Companies that offer varying benefits, including day care for parents and commuter reimbursement for public transit, report more motivated and productive employees.

Many companies are increasing the number of part-time workers, which enables mothers and fathers to stay home part of the day with children and still earn income. Some companies allow workers to telecommute, which means they work from home and keep in touch with the company through telecommunications (telephone, fax, e-mail). This lowers the company's cost for office space and also makes it possible for parents to meet the demands of both job and family.

Workplace changes due to the rise of two-income families create many job opportunities in day care, counseling, and other related fields.

Single Parents

The rapid growth of single-parent households has had a major effect on businesses as well. It is a tremendous task to work full-time and raise a family. Many individuals are working, raising a family, and going to school. This workload is hard to manage!

Many single parents struggle with the work–life balance, and they have encouraged businesses to implement programs such as family leave (where workers can take time off to care for a sick child) and flextime (where workers can come in or leave at selected times). These options have helped the plight of the single parent, but work/life balance remains a challenge.

Marriage

Society's views on marriage have changed. For example, in the past, individuals were married and had children at an early age. Now, people are getting married much later, if at all, and having children much later, if at all. As a result, unmarried people need products to meet the needs of a single lifestyle. In addition, many married couples have chosen not to have a child which, in turn, creates more wealth for these couples as well as the need for different products than would have been the case for couples of the same age in the past.

---

q: »» Find an article in a magazine or online news source that discusses a topic involving the social environment (aging workforce, dual-income families, single parents) and business. Compare your article with those found by your classmates. How do the trends influence you and your family? Your classmates?

The Global Environment

The global environment of business is so important, made clear as shown in Figure 1.3, as surrounding all other environmental influences (see also Figure 1.10). Global business will be discussed in much greater detail in Chapter 3. Two important environmental changes in recent years have been the growth

Sugar is being loaded for export at the port of Cebu in the Philippines. As countries continue to depend on one another for products, the global environment in business also becomes more important.

of international competition and the increase of free trade among nations. **Free trade** is the reduction of barriers to trade, such as elimination of tariffs (or taxes) on goods brought into another country.

Today, manufacturers in countries such as China, India, South Korea, and Mexico can produce high-quality goods at low prices. Better technology, machinery, tools, education, and training enable each worker to be more productive. U.S. companies such as Disney, FedEx, Intel, and Microsoft, as well as many smaller companies, are as good as or better than competing organizations anywhere in the world. But some businesses have gone beyond simply competing with organizations in other countries by learning to cooperate with international firms. Cooperation among businesses has the potential to create rapidly growing world markets that can generate prosperity beyond most people's expectations. For example, Hewlett-Packard has an alliance with Hitachi and Samsung, while Chevron has an alliance with Western Australia Energy Research Alliance.[27] The challenge is tremendous but so is the will to achieve.

It is extremely important to note that all sizes of businesses compete in the global marketplace. Often, when we think of global competitors, we think of the Microsofts and IBMs of the world. In fact, many medium-sized and small businesses sell their products overseas. Many entrepreneurs have found it is both profitable and challenging to sell products overseas. Technology has made this much easier through online selling and international shipping.

Few recent events have had a bigger effect on U.S. businesses than the terrorist attacks on the World Trade Center and the Pentagon on September 11, 2001. One of the obvious effects was on the travel industry; after 9/11 some people were afraid to fly, and this fear affected not only the airlines but also hotels, amusement parks, and restaurants. The impact was especially felt by companies like Boeing, which sells planes to the airline industry. Prior to 9/11, the stock market had already suffered a decline; the drop-off in business that followed the attacks only added to the woes.

The threat of terrorism on a worldwide level adds greatly to organizational costs, including the cost of security personnel, security equipment, and insurance. Firms are finding it difficult to get insurance against terrorist attacks; terrorism is usually excluded in insurance policies while acts of war can be included. Airlines have had to install stronger cockpit doors, buy more security equipment, and hire new security personnel. The U.S. government has also experienced huge cost increases because of homeland security issues.

free trade

The reduction of barriers to trade, such as elimination of tariffs (or taxes) on goods brought into another country.

With the increase in security needs in airports, the cost for personnel and high-tech equipment is growing.

The war in Iraq that began in March 2003 and ongoing threats of war in various parts of the world such as North Korea have had a major impact on businesses everywhere—global trade and travel have suffered. Some businesses like the defense industry (businesses that make bombs and other war materials) stand to gain profits as a result. As we have seen with the Iraq War, while some will gain, many companies as well as individuals will suffer losses in time of war.

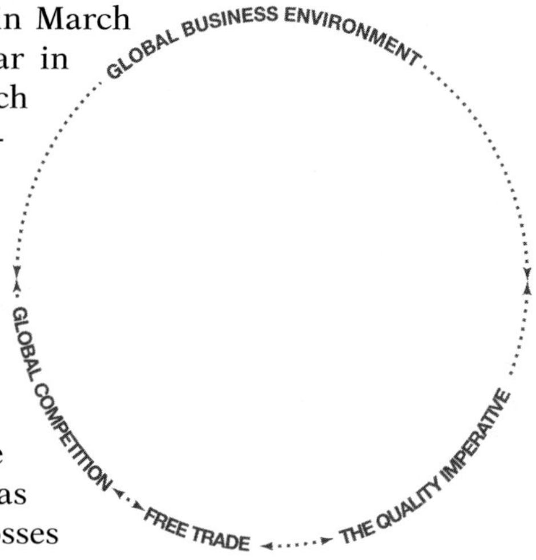

figure 1.10

THE GLOBAL ENVIRONMENT

GLOBAL BUSINESS ENVIRONMENT · GLOBAL COMPETITION · FREE TRADE · THE QUALITY IMPERATIVE

SELF-CHECK QUESTIONS

1. In what ways can the government make things easier for businesspeople? Do you think the government should do more? Why or why not?

2. Name two changes that have been brought about by technology? What kinds of long-term effects do you think these changes will have?

3. Why is social diversity an important concern for business?

4. What is free trade, and how does the issue of free trade impact businesses competing overseas?

YOUR FUTURE IN BUSINESS

We are in the midst of an information-based global revolution that will alter all sectors of the economy: agricultural, industrial, and service. It is exciting to think of the role you will play in that revolution. As you embark on your career in business, you have several choices. You can either start your own business or you can work for someone else. If you choose to work for someone else, it could be a large or small business, a nonprofit organization, or a government agency.

Entrepreneurship versus Working for Others

There are two ways to succeed in a business. One is to work for others, get experience and skills, and rise up through the ranks. Someone else is assuming the entrepreneurial risks in that case and paying your salary

Section Outline

Your Future in Business

- Entrepreneurship versus Working for Others

- Working for a Nonprofit Organization or a Government Agency

and benefits. Most people choose this option. It can lead to a happy and prosperous life.

The other riskier path is to start your own business (become an entrepreneur). One of the most famous rights in the United States Declaration of Independence is the right to "Life, Liberty, and the Pursuit of Happiness."[28] Does this right apply in business? Absolutely! If owning a business and being an entrepreneur gives you happiness, you have the liberty to live your life, to fulfill the dream of being your own boss.

Wanting to be his own boss, Curt Greenberg first started a kitchen store and then purchased Central Bark (see the chapter opening profile). This was his idea of fun, and it was his right! Obviously, as an entrepreneur, you are not getting paid vacations and sick leaves that you may receive when working for someone else. You have to provide these benefits for yourself. However, you reap the rewards for the risks you take. There are thousands of examples of successful entrepreneurs, and some famous ones such as Sam Walton of Wal-Mart, Bill Gates of Microsoft, Ray Kroc of McDonald's, and Steve Jobs of Apple. They all started small and grew their business and became very wealthy through hard work and the application of sound business principles—the same principles that you will be learning throughout this book.

Working for Other Businesses

As you graduate from college and choose a company, large or small, to work for, you may be happy to know that the earning power of a college graduate far outpaces that of less-educated individuals.[29] Most people follow the path of working for someone else. If you are looking for growth and advancement with potential to move higher, the choice of company to work for may be a medium-sized or large firm. However, if you are looking for job diversity, flexibility, and the chance to develop a broad set of skills, the choice may be to work for a small, entrepreneurial firm where the size of the firm may allow employees a lot of variety and latitude in decision making. Once you have the experience, either working for a large or small firm, you will have the ability and the opportunity, if that is your desire, to start your own business.

Entrepreneurial Challenge

Millions of people from all over the world have taken the entrepreneurial challenge and succeeded. For example, the number of Hispanic-owned businesses in the United States is growing at a pace three times the national average.[30] There is also rapid growth in businesses owned by Asian Americans, African Americans, Pacific Islanders, Native Americans, and Alaskan Natives. Some 37 percent of Koreans who immigrated to the United States now own their own business.[31] Women also have the same opportunity to engage in entrepreneurship as do men, and entrepreneurship is an attractive career path for an increasing number of women. The number of women business owners has dramatically increased in the last 20 years. In

1980, there were about 3 million women business owners; by 2005, there were over 10.4 million firms that were 50 percent or more woman-owned. Women now own over a third of all businesses in the United States.[32] Some famous names you may be familiar with include Oprah Winfrey, Donna Karan, Lillian Vernon, Martha Stewart—and many others.

Creation of Wealth

Have you ever wondered why some countries are relatively wealthy and others poor? Over time, economists have developed five factors that seem to contribute to wealth. They are called **factors of production** (see Figure 1.11):

1. Land
2. Labor
3. Capital
4. Entrepreneurship
5. Knowledge

> **factors of production**
> The resources used to create wealth: land, labor, capital, entrepreneurship, and knowledge.

If you were to analyze rich countries versus poor countries to see what causes the differences in the levels of wealth, you would have to look at these factors of production in each country. Russia and China, for example, both have vast areas of land with many resources but they are not rich countries (yet). In contrast, Japan and Hong Kong are relatively rich countries but are poor in land and other natural resources. Therefore, land is not the critical element for wealth creation. Similarly, most poor countries have many laborers. So it's not labor that is the primary source of wealth either. Finally, capital—machinery and tools—is now becoming available in world markets, and so mere access to capital is not the missing element.

What makes rich countries rich today is a combination of the last two factors—entrepreneurship and the effective use of knowledge. Entrepreneurship also makes some states and cities in the United States

Land: Land and other natural resources are used to make homes, cars, and other products.

Labor: People have always been an important resource in producing goods and services, but many people are now being replaced by technology.

Capital: Capital includes machines, tools, buildings, and other means of manufacturing.

Entrepreneurship: All the resources in the world have little value unless entrepreneurs are willing to take the risk of starting businesses to use those resources.

Knowledge: Information technology has revolutionized business, making it possible to quickly determine wants and needs and to respond with desired goods and services.

figure 1.11

THE FIVE FACTORS OF PRODUCTION

So, You Think You Want to Be . . . a Businessperson

A degree in business can apply to almost any career, and the possibilities are endless. First, a future businessperson should choose an industry that sounds interesting to her. Some of the possibilities in the service industry were listed in this chapter. For example, let's say someone is looking into the automotive industry, but she is not interested in actually working on cars. She could choose to go into the marketing area of business, helping publicize automotive dealerships. If she were more interested in the financial part of business, she could work in the accounting department of a dealership. Likewise, if she is interested in health care, she doesn't necessarily need to become a doctor.

She could work in the marketing department or financial department of a doctor's office.

Other areas of expertise might include management, information technology, economics, operations, international trade, or international business, to name a few. Every type of business in every type of industry has jobs in these areas.

Each chapter in this book will include a career focus. If the chapter was personally interesting to you, be sure to read the career spotlight to see the possible career options in that field. Of course, your instructors and advisors are also good people to connect with to discuss career choices.

rich while others remain relatively poor. The business environment either encourages or discourages entrepreneurship. The quality of a state's tax system plays a big role in creation of the entrepreneurial business environment. According to the Tax Foundation's 2007 State Business Tax Climate Index, top-rated states for best business tax climate include Wyoming, Alaska, Nevada, and Florida.[33] Should it be a surprise if these states were also the leaders in business start-ups?

Working for a Nonprofit Organization or a Government Agency

nonprofit organization

An organization whose goals do not include making a personal profit for its owners and organizers but rather the alleviation of some social problem.

Despite their efforts to satisfy all their stakeholders, businesses cannot do everything that is needed to make a community all it can be. Nonprofit organizations—such as public schools, civic associations, and charities—also make major contributions to the welfare of the society. A **nonprofit organization** is an organization whose goals do not include making a personal profit for its owners or organizers.[34] Nonprofit organizations often do strive for financial gains, but such gains are used to meet the stated social or educational goals of the organization rather than to amass personal profits.[35] *Social entrepreneurs* are people who use business principles to start and manage organizations that are not for profit and help alleviate social problems.[36]

A government agency is an organization accountable for overseeing explicit government functions.[37] You are no doubt familiar with various government agencies, from the federal Environmental Protection Agency to the Small Business Administration. Your interests may lead you to work for a nonprofit organization or a government agency. That does not mean, however, that you should not study business. On the contrary, if

After doing some research, Rochelle felt both relieved and more knowledgeable. Now she understands why stakeholders are important. First, stakeholders are your customers. Their needs must be met in order to sell products. Second, stakeholders can be anyone who "cares" about the decisions the company makes. For example, she realizes if her client does animal testing, there would be stakeholders, such as animal rights groups, that would be concerned with this policy. The more stakeholders you can satisfy, the more customers you will have. Of course, this results in revenue and profit!

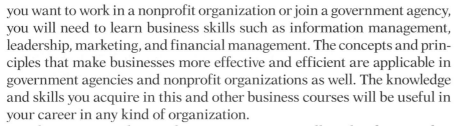

Rochelle also researched the types of environments that business operates: the economic and legal environments, the technological environment, the competitive environment, the social environment, and the global environment.

From her reading, Rochelle realizes that the social environment greatly affects the type of business she is currently operating—marketing. All of the changes that occur in society will change the types of products needed, and also change the way those products should be marketed. In addition, new technologies affect Rochelle's business because this could mean new ways of advertising to customers.

Although Rochelle had a subtle awareness of these environments before, she is now able to see how each of these areas might affect her business. Since she is an entrepreneur, she has realized she must read current events and business articles often to determine how these environments might be changing and how those changes could affect her business. Rochelle is determined to read at least three magazines and newspapers per week to stay up to date on changes in the business environment.

you want to work in a nonprofit organization or join a government agency, you will need to learn business skills such as information management, leadership, marketing, and financial management. The concepts and principles that make businesses more effective and efficient are applicable in government agencies and nonprofit organizations as well. The knowledge and skills you acquire in this and other business courses will be useful in your career in any kind of organization.

This is an introductory business text, so we will tend to focus on for-profit business. Nonetheless, we will remind you periodically that you can apply the concepts you are learning about in other areas, whichever career path you take that brings you happiness!

SELF-CHECK QUESTIONS

1. What are some of the advantages of working for others?
2. What do you gain and what do you lose by being an entrepreneur?
3. What are the five factors of production? Which factors are keys to wealth creation?
4. Who are social entrepreneurs? Can you apply the business principles in a nonprofit organization? Explain.

summary

This chapter provided an introduction to business, including defining business and explaining why the study of business is important. Profit, revenue, loss, risk, and reward were explained, and the difference between stakeholders and shareholders was discussed.

Changes in the business environment were discussed. One of the major changes over the last 200 years has been that the United States has moved away from manufacturing and agriculture and toward a service-driven economy. Much of this is due to new technology. Even long-established industries such as farming have used technology to make their work easier and more productive.

Entrepreneurship always has been a major part of business. Entrepreneurs face many challenges when starting a new business. They must be concerned with the five elements of the business environment. The economic and legal environment, for example, affects business as a result of regulations and taxes imposed on a business. The technological environment affects business through new technologies that can make jobs easier. The competitive environment must be on the minds of all businesspeople; having an awareness of what competitors are doing and what customers value is imperative to running a good business. The changes in the social environment result in constantly changing types of products customers demand, and managing diversity has become an important factor in business today. The global environment affects any size business. Free trade opens up markets that were previously difficult for small businesses to sell within. An awareness of new processes and technologies in business can come from simply reading publications and considering how such changes can affect business. The more understanding businesspeople have of the five environments, the more successful they will be.

Finally, the endless possibilities of your future in business were presented. The factors of production were introduced as they contribute to wealth. Options for using your study of business in a career include working for yourself, for a nonprofit organization, or even a government agency. Your future in business is open, and you are gaining learning tools to help you along the way.

key terms

business 4
profit 5
entrepreneur 5
revenue 5
loss 5

standard of living 6
risk 6
reward 6
stakeholders 6
shareholder 7

services 10
return on investment (ROI) 14
Uniform Commercial Code (UCC) 15

applying your skills

1. a. This chapter describes the growth trend in the numbers of businesses in the service sector. Look through your local Yellow Pages or go on the Internet to find and list five businesses that provide services in your area.

   b. The chapter also describes how certain demographic and social changes affect businesses. For each of the local service businesses on your list, describe how social trends might affect it. Include both negative effects and positive effects. Be prepared to explain your answers, either in small groups or using your online discussion board.

2. Form teams of four or five, either in class or using your online collaboration feature. Discuss the technological and e-commerce revolutions. If you are in an online class use your class Web site's collaboration feature to discuss in groups. How many students now shop for goods and services online? What have been their experiences? What other high-tech equipment do they use (e.g., cell phones, pagers, laptop computers, desktop computers, personal digital assistants, portable music players)?

3. This chapter defined and discussed the things that government can do to make things easier for entrepreneurs. Do you think the government makes things easier for entrepreneurs? Why or why not? Cite specific examples either in small groups or on your online discussion board.

4. What are the five parts of the business environment? Form teams, either in class or online (utilizing the class collaboration feature), and discuss which environment you think to be the most important to businesspeople.

5. What do you think are the advantages to working in a service-type business versus a goods or products type business? In groups or on your own, formulate a list of at least four things for each type.

6. In general, do you think businesses have a customer service focus? Why or why not? Do you think having this focus is more important in some businesses as opposed to others? Why or why not?

7. What generation do you consider yourself to be part of? Do you agree with the information provided in this chapter on generations? Why or why not?

8. Find articles using online sources on a successful minority entrepreneur. Develop a two- or three-page profile. What makes this person stand out? What lessons can be learned from her or his success? Share your findings with the class.

the internet in action

1. Read the latest issue of *Forbes, Fortune,* or *BusinessWeek.* What social changes are discussed that might affect business? What about technological and economic changes?

2. Select the Population Clock from the Census Bureau's homepage at www.census.gov. Record the time and population for the United States.

3. The U.S. Commerce Department (www.commerce.gov) conducts an economic census every five years (in years ending with 2 and 7). How do businesses use the information gathered in this census? To help answer this question, click on Economic Census, and then click on Slide Shows. There you'll find a slide show that reviews the scope and use of the economic census. (Hint: Be sure to scroll down to read the notes that explain each slide.) What are the three major ways businesses use the economic census data explained in the slide show?

4. Return to the U.S. Census Bureau's homepage. What is the population of the nation right now? Has the population changed since you started this exercise? If so, how? What does this tell you about the U.S. population? How could businesses use this information?

5. Find the latest statistics comparing women's pay to men's pay. Discuss some possible reasons for this difference and be sure to include the Web site where you found this information.

HOW ECONOMICS AFFECTS BUSINESS

WTRG Consulting[1]

Jim Williams owns WTRG Consulting, a business that provides macroeconomic and industry information to companies. Jim and his staff must follow economic trends very closely using various types of economic analysis to come up with information that helps his clients gain a competitive advantage. WTRG, located in London, Arkansas, is a small firm that Jim developed using what he had learned through his experience in larger companies. Jim has both an economics and a mathematics degree. After graduating, he taught at several local colleges. Then he landed a job at Thompson Greenspan consulting

Jim Williams of WTRG Consulting

(Alan Greenspan was a partner in the firm, before he became chair of the Federal Reserve Bank). His job involved developing models used to forecast changes in different industries, such as railroads and energy. These models helped build bridges between macroeconomics and clients' sales forecasts.

Later Jim moved to Texas, where he worked for Petra Chemical as a senior economist. There Jim scanned the marketplace for changes in the business and developed strategic plans and forecasts based on this information. Jim believes he was able to succeed in an industry he knew nothing about (chemicals)

After reading this chapter, you will be able to:

1 | Understand the basics of economics.

2 | Explain supply and demand.

3 | Describe free market capitalism and degrees of competition.

4 | Understand the differences between socialism and communism.

5 | Discuss the three major indicators of economic conditions.

simply because he talked with people. He believes that networking and asking questions of the experts in the field can be beneficial to anyone in business, but especially those just starting their careers. Jim left Petra to start his own consulting business, WTRG. Jim and WTRG consult for oil companies and help them better predict the price for oil. Jim also consults with stock traders and building owners. For example, a large skyscraper owner might want to know how much money it will take over a 10-year period to heat his building. Jim would develop a forecast to provide to his client based on past data and predictions of energy prices.

Jim says that economics applies to individuals as well as business owners on a daily basis. He points out that anyone who is a manager, in any field, needs to know a little about economics to be successful. For example, any manager would need to know what the job market looks like within the next couple of years in order to plan how many people might need to be hired. A manager would need to look at the prices of raw materials and competitors' products to determine what her business should charge for its products in the future.

From a personal perspective, economics applies to consumers on a day-to-day basis. For example, as consumers we know if a pest wipes out acres of orange crops in Florida, the price of oranges is likely to go up. This is a basic supply-and-demand concept we will talk about in this chapter. No matter what career path you take, understanding some basic economic concepts will help you better understand the world around you.

Section Outline

Understanding Economics

- Basics of Economics
- Microeconomics and Macroeconomics
- Economic Theorists
- Supply and Demand

UNDERSTANDING ECONOMICS

Every time we buy something, we are applying economics. When we go to work, economics is involved. If we choose not to purchase something because the price is too high, this decision is also based on economics. In this chapter, we will discuss the study of economics and its relationship to business. Economics impacts every business, small or large. As we discussed in Chapter 1, a business owner, no matter what size her business, must be aware of economics. This chapter will provide an overview of the study of economics using examples from small and medium-sized businesses.

Basics of Economics

Why is South Korea comparatively wealthy and North Korea suffering economically?[2] Why does China have an annual income of $1,740 per person[3] while Taiwan's is $9,775?[4] In this chapter, we explore the various economic systems of the world and how they either promote or hinder business growth, the creation of wealth, and a higher quality of life.

The economic contrast is remarkable. Business is booming in Seoul, South Korea (*left*), but North Korea (*right*), a communist country, is not doing well. This chapter will explore the differences in economies and why some do well while others do not.

Ashon was reading the newspaper online this morning, when he came across an article that said, "The U.S. economy is expected to weaken during the second half of the year, as unemployment and high energy prices take a toll on the housing market and consumer spending. In addition, GDP is expected to weaken to 2.7%. As a result, the Fed is considering lowering interest rates to stimulate growth."

Ashon skipped over this article, because he didn't understand what it meant to him and his newly formed Internet consulting business. However, Ashon thought about the meaning of the article throughout the day, nagged by the feeling that he should be reading and understanding all that economic talk. As a result, he read this chapter in the text to help him.

Economics is the study of how society chooses to employ resources to produce goods and services and distribute them for consumption among various competing groups and individuals. Remember from Chapter 1 that these resources (land, labor, capital, entrepreneurship, and knowledge) are called factors of production.

economics
The study of how society chooses to employ resources to produce goods and services and distribute them for consumption among various competing groups and individuals.

Microeconomics and Macroeconomics

There are two basic types of economic study, macro and micro. First, the term *macro* means something very big in scale. Therefore, **macroeconomics** looks at the operation of a nation's economy as a whole. **Microeconomics,** on the other hand, examines the behavior of people and organizations in particular markets. While macroeconomics looks at how many jobs exist in the whole economy, microeconomics examines how many people will be hired in a particular industry or a certain region of the country. Microeconomics, for example, might study the economics of San Francisco or the economics of your local nightclub.

macroeconomics
The study of the operation of a nation's economy as a whole.

microeconomics
The study of the behavior of people and organizations in particular markets.

Some economists define economics as the allocation of "scarce" resources. They believe that resources (such as food, water, land) are scarce and need to be carefully divided among people, usually by the government. They believe there is no way to maintain peace and prosperity in the world by merely dividing the resources we have today among the existing nations. There aren't enough known resources available to do that. **Resource development** is the study of how to increase resources and to create the conditions that will make better use of those resources. Outside of government, businesses may contribute to an economic system by inventing products that greatly increase available resources. For example, businesses may discover new energy sources, new ways of growing food, and new ways of creating needed goods and services.[5] Recently, one of the solutions to the challenge of scarce resources has been the development of genetically modified

resource development
The study of how to increase resources and to create the conditions that will make better use of those resources.

foods (GMF). GMF seeds are said to require less water and to produce larger crops on smaller pieces of land, which is one example of resource development.[6]

Economic Theorists

Imagine the world when kings and other landowners had most of the wealth and the majority of the people were peasants. The peasants had many children, and it may have seemed a natural conclusion that there would soon be too many people and not enough food and other resources to support them.

English economist Thomas Malthus made this argument in the late 1700s and early 1800s. In response to such views, Scottish writer and thinker Thomas Carlyle called economics "the dismal science." Followers of Malthus today (who are called neo-Malthusians) still believe that there are too many people in the world and that the solution to poverty is birth control, which includes such measures as limits on the number of children people can have (such as in China), forced abortions, and forced sterilization. The latest statistics, however, show that the world population is growing more slowly than was expected, and in some industrial countries (Japan, Germany, Italy, Russia) growth may be so slow so that there will be too many old people and too few young people to care for them.[7] In the developing world, on the other hand, population will continue to climb relatively quickly. Such studies about the effects of population growth on the economy are part of macroeconomics.

The challenge for macroeconomists is to determine what makes some countries relatively wealthy and other countries relatively poor, and then to implement policies and programs that lead to increased prosperity for everyone in all countries.[8] One way to begin understanding this challenge is to consider the theories of Adam Smith.

The Scottish economist Adam Smith was one of the first people to imagine a system for creating wealth and improving the lives of everyone. Rather than believing that fixed resources had to be divided among competing groups and individuals, Smith envisioned creating more resources so that everyone could become wealthier. The year was 1776. Adam Smith's book, *An Inquiry into the Nature and Causes of the Wealth of Nations,* often is called simply *The Wealth of Nations.*

He made the desire for improving one's own condition in life the basis of his general economic theory. According to Smith, as long as farmers, laborers, and businesspeople (entrepreneurs) can see economic rewards for their efforts (receiving enough money in the form of profits to support their families, for instance), they will work long and hard to achieve those rewards. As a result of their efforts, the economy

The Bill and Melinda Gates Foundation is just one of many foundations that provide needed funds for nonprofit organizations. This photo shows Moroccan students receiving a dose of Zithromax to prevent trachoma, a leading cause of blindness in developing nations.

as a whole will prosper—with plenty of food and all kinds of products available to everyone.

Under Adam Smith's theory, businesspeople don't necessarily deliberately set out to help others. They work primarily for their own prosperity and growth. Yet as people try to improve their own situation in life, Smith said, their efforts serve as a guiding "invisible hand" that helps the larger economy grow and prosper through the production of all kinds of needed goods, services, and ideas. Thus, the **invisible hand** turns self-directed gain into social and economic benefits for all. In other words, by individuals simply trying to benefit themselves, communities and other people end up benefiting as well.

However, some people end up with so much wealth, they would not be able to spend it all within a lifetime. As a result, many wealthy individuals help others. Bill Gates (the cofounder of Microsoft) and his wife, Melinda, set up the largest foundation in history, worth some $33 billion, according to the foundation's 2006 financial statements.[9] Their foundation will continue to increase, as Warren Buffet, the second richest individual in America and CEO of Berkshire Hathaway, has pledged to contribute money every year.[10]

Of course, business owners must meet the needs of customers when producing products or this wealth would not spread throughout the community. This is where the concepts of supply and demand come in.

invisible hand

A theory developed by Adam Smith that says that self-directed gain turns into social and economic benefits for all.

figure 2.1

THE SUPPLY CURVE AT VARIOUS PRICES

The supply curve rises from left to right. The higher the price of T-shirts (vertical-axis), the more sellers will be willing to supply.

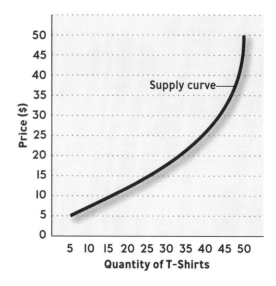

Supply and Demand

supply
The quantity of products that manufacturers or owners are willing to sell at different prices at a specific time.

Supply refers to the quantity of products that manufacturers or owners are willing to sell at different prices at a specific time. Generally speaking, the amount supplied will increase as the price increases because sellers can make more money with a higher price. For example, if T-shirts cost $5 each to a customer, manufacturers might be willing to supply only 5 T-shirts. On the other hand, if manufacturers could get $50 for a T-shirt, they might be willing to supply 100 T-shirts. Economists show this relationship between quantity supplied and price on a graph (see Figure 2.1). For our present discussion, understanding the definition of supply is what is most important.

demand
The quantity of goods that buyers will purchase at a particular price.

Demand refers to the quantity of products that people are willing and able to buy at different prices at a specific time. Generally speaking, the quantity demanded will increase as the price decreases. For example, if T-shirts were $5 each, most of us would be willing to buy one, and maybe more than one. However, if the price were $20, we would likely buy only one T-shirt, or none at all. In other words, as the price increases, the demand for the product decreases and vice versa (see Figure 2.2).

As you can see from the example, supply and demand are very much related to each other. If demand goes up, supply will go up—at least in an ideal world. If supply does not go up and the demand is still high, the price will then increase because there isn't enough of the product to meet the need of the

Various factors affect the supply and demand for T-shirts. The season and the price are major factors when consumers are deciding to buy. As consumer demand changes, the supply must change as well.

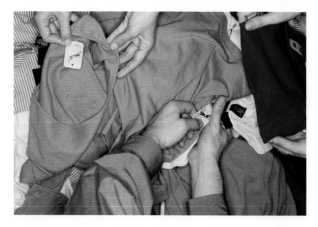

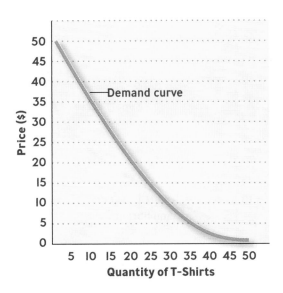

figure 2.2

THE DEMAND CURVE AT VARIOUS PRICES

The demand curve falls from left to right. The lower the price of T-shirts, the higher the quantity demanded.

→*SONY!!

customers. Consider the 2006 holiday season. The Playstation III was in very high demand, but Nintendo announced there was not enough supply to meet the demand of customers.[11] As a result, people were selling the consoles on eBay for several thousand dollars! However, as soon as there were enough Playstations on the market, the price returned to normal levels.

q: What big-ticket items do you own or desire based

》》 on popularity? Which items seem more or less valuable because of the fluctuations in supply and demand?

Another example of supply and demand is the oil industry. As more and more people purchase cars, there is a greater need for fuel. For example, according to the China Association of Automobile Manufacturers (CAAM) in 2007, demand for cars in China had increased nearly 26 percent.[12] As a result of many more people in the world buying cars, more fuel is required. Because demand has increased, and there is not enough supply to meet the demand, gas prices continue to rise. Finally, another example can be taken from your favorite clothing store. Most people do not want summer clothing in September, since the weather is changing and school will start again. As a result, most clothing stores will reduce the price of their clothing (supply) since the

figure 2.3

THE EQUILIBRIUM POINT

The place where quantity demanded and supplied meet is called equilibrium point. In the long-run, the market price will tend toward the equilibrium point.

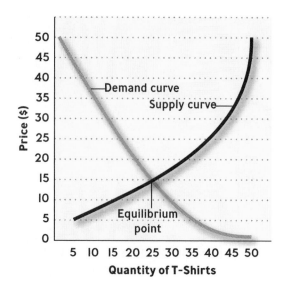

demand is not there for this type of clothing at this time of year. The ideal economic situation is when our economy is at an equilibrium point. The equilibrium point is the point where the amount of goods sought by buyers is equal to the amount of goods produced by suppliers, as you can see in Figure 2.3.

business cycle

The periodic rises and falls that occur in all economies over time.

Before we get further into economic theory, it is important here to say a quick word about what we mean by the **business cycle**. The *business cycle* denotes a common pattern where there is a period of rapid growth

figure 2.4

THE BUSINESS/ECONOMIC CYCLE

As you can see from this chart, through time the economy will experience contraction and expansion. During good economic times, we see the economy recover after a contraction and result in prosperous conditions.

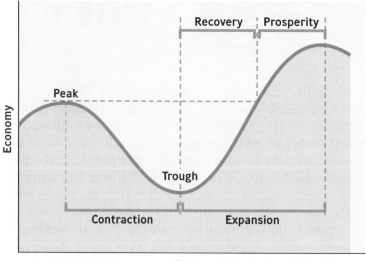

(recovery and prosperity) in the economy when supply and demand stimulate each other, alternating with a period of decline (contraction or recession) with diminishing demand and supply. The business cycle is also called the *economic cycle*. See Figure 2.4.

SELF-CHECK QUESTIONS

1. How are macroeconomics and microeconomics different?
2. What theory did Adam Smith develop? Describe it in your own words.
3. How are supply and demand interconnected?

FREE MARKET CAPITALISM

A **free market** is one in which decisions about what to produce and in what quantities are made by the market—that is, by buyers and sellers negotiating prices for goods and services. Consumers in the United States and in other free market countries send signals to tell producers what to make, how many, in what color, and so on. We do that by choosing to buy (or not to buy) certain products and services.

For example, if all of us decided we wanted T-shirts from the Indianapolis Colts, the clothing industry would respond in certain ways. First, manufacturers and retailers would increase the price of Indianapolis Colts T-shirts, because they know people are willing to pay more than before. Second, people in the clothing industry would also realize they could make more money by making more T-shirts. Thus, they would have incentive to pay workers to start work earlier and end later. Furthermore, the number of clothing companies making Colts T-shirts would increase. In short, how many T-shirts are made depends on how many we request or buy in the stores. The prices and quantities change as the number of T-shirts we buy changes. In other words, as consumers we have immense power in the market to determine the price of items and the availability of items.

Again, in a free market system, consumers ultimately decide what should be produced. The United States, of course, is a free market system. Those goods which are priced too high or not in demand will not sell, and as a result, we as consumers are telling the manufacturers what we want. In a free market system, competition is a major force. There are four types of competition, which we will discuss next.

Section Outline

Free Market Capitalism

- Competition in Free Markets

free market
A system in which decisions about what to produce and in what quantities are made by the market.

Competition in Free Markets

perfect competition

Exists when there are many sellers in a market, no seller is large enough to dictate the price of a product, and the products are similar.

monopolistic competition

Exists when a large number of sellers produce products that are very similar but are perceived by buyers as different.

oligopoly

A form of competition in which just a few sellers dominate a market.

There are four commonly recognized degrees of competition: (1) perfect competition, (2) monopolistic competition, (3) oligopoly, and (4) monopoly.

Perfect competition exists when there are many sellers in a market and no seller is large enough to dictate the price of a product. Under perfect competition, sellers produce products that appear to be identical. Agricultural products (apples, corn, potatoes) are often considered to be examples of such products. You should know, however, that there are no true examples of perfect competition. Today, government price supports and drastic reductions in the number of farms make it hard to argue that even farming is an example of perfect competition.

Monopolistic competition exists when a large number of sellers produce products that are very similar but are perceived by buyers as different (hot dogs, candy, personal computers, T-shirts). Actually, the competing products may even be interchangeable. Under *monopolistic competition* (not to be confused with monopoly, discussed in the following text), product differentiation (the attempt to make buyers think similar products are different in some way) is a key to success. Think about what that means for just a moment. Through tactics such as advertising, branding, and packaging, sellers try to signal to buyers that their products are different from those of competitors. (We will discuss more about these differentiation methods in Chapter 9.) Consider most fast-food burger companies. The fast-food industry, in which there are often pricing battles, offers a good example of monopolistic competition. Is a hamburger really that different if you go to McDonald's versus Wendy's or Burger King? The ingredients are virtually the same, with superficial variations and differences in presentation, making this a great example of monopolistic competition.

An **oligopoly** is a form of competition in which just a few sellers dominate a market. Oligopolies exist in industries that produce products such as breakfast cereal, tobacco, automobiles, soft drinks, aluminum, and aircraft. One reason some industries remain in the hands of just a few sellers is that the initial investment required to enter the business is tremendous.

In an oligopoly, prices for products from different companies tend to be close to the

Deregulation of the electric utilities industry in some states has given consumers a choice and allowed for more flexibility in some still regulated states. Are you willing to pay a little extra to go "green"?

Career Exploration and Professional Help

"Where are the jobs?" is perhaps the first question that graduating students ask. One of the challenges that students face is the career learning process. What companies would be a good fit to work for? Where are the high-paying careers? What is career aptitude testing? To help students learn more about career exploration, most colleges have a career center where such questions can be answered and tools are available that can help them along the job discovery process.

Visit your school's career center or one of your instructors and begin learning all the ways you can get your career headed in the right direction!

same. The reason for this is simple. Intense price competition would lower profits for all the competitors, since a price cut on the part of one producer would most likely be matched by the others. As in monopolistic competition, product differentiation, rather than price, is usually the major factor in market success under oligopoly. Note, for example, that most cereals are priced about the same, as are soft drinks. Thus, advertising is a major factor in determining which of the few available brands consumers buy because often it is advertising that calls attention to or even creates the perceived differences.

A **monopoly** occurs when there is only one seller that controls the total supply of a product and its price. In the United States, laws prohibit the creation of monopolies, which is one reason Microsoft got into trouble with the law: It appeared to have monopoly power in the market for computer operating systems.

The U.S. legal system has permitted monopolies in the markets for public utilities that sell natural gas, water, and electric power. These utility companies' prices and profits usually have been monitored and controlled by public service commissions (which are run by the government) that are supposed to protect the interest of buyers. New legislation has ended the monopoly status of utilities in some areas, thereby deregulating them. As a result, consumers in those areas are able to choose among utility providers. The intention of this deregulation is to increase competition among utility companies and, ultimately, lower prices for consumers.

Another example is the cable companies. Most communities have only one cable provider because of the high cost of installation. As a result, cable companies such as Comcast are carefully monitored to ensure prices are fair to consumers.

> **monopoly**
> Occurs when there is only one seller for a product or service.

q: What companies in your community operate

»» in perfect competition? Monopolistic competition? Which are parts of
an oligopoly or are a monopoly? Do you view the companies differently
because of the differences?

SELF-CHECK QUESTIONS

1. What is a free market system?
2. What are the four types of competition?
3. Do you think one type of competition would be better than another in developing countries? Why or why not?

---

socialism

An economic system based on the premise that some, if not most, basic businesses—such as steel mills, coal mines, and utilities—should be owned by the government so that profits can be evenly distributed among the people.

SOCIALISM AND COMMUNISM

Socialism

Socialism is an economic system based on the premise that some, if not most, basic businesses—such as steel mills, coal mines, and utilities—should be owned by the government so that profits can be evenly distributed among all the people. Such distribution of profits among everyone may come through health care benefits and retirement benefits. As you can imagine, private businesses and individuals are taxed relatively steeply to pay for such social programs. As we discussed in Chapter 1, however, high taxation can discourage entrepreneurship in a country. In many socialist countries, the top tax rate is very high. For instance, the individual top income tax rate in Denmark is 59 percent, in the Netherlands it is 52 percent, and in Belgium it is 50 percent.[13]

In addition to income tax, sales taxes may be high. While people in the United States pay sales taxes of about 5 percent (more in California, less—in fact, nothing—in Delaware),[14] socialist countries charge a value-added tax (which is something like a sales tax) of 15 to 20 percent on most goods purchased.[15]

Socialists acknowledge the major benefit of capitalism—wealth creation—but believe that wealth should be more evenly distributed than occurs in free market capitalism. They believe that the government should be the agency that carries out the distribution, which is why government owns many of the factors of production.

Socialism has become the guiding economic platform for many countries in Europe (Sweden, Finland, Belgium), Africa, India, and in much of the rest of the world. Socialist nations tend to rely heavily on the government to provide education, health care, retirement benefits, unemployment benefits, and other social services. Some countries, such as France, are moving slightly away from socialism, however, and leaning more to the center (between capitalism and socialism) to get their economies moving faster.

The Benefits of Socialism

The major benefit of socialism is supposed to be social equality. There is more equality of outcome in socialism than in capitalism because income is taken from the wealthier people, in the form of taxes, and redistributed to the poorer members of the population through various government programs. Free education (even through the college level), free health care, and free child care are some of the benefits socialist governments distribute to their people using the money from taxes. Workers in socialist countries usually get longer vacations than workers in capitalist countries. They also tend to work fewer hours per week and have more employee benefits, such as generous sick leave.

The Negative Consequences of Socialism

Socialism may create more equality than capitalism, but it takes away some of businesspeople's incentives and enthusiasm to start work early and leave work late. It can also take away the incentive to start new businesses or market new ideas. For example, tax rates in some socialist nations once reached 85 percent. Today, many professionals have very high tax rates (usually over 50 percent). As a consequence, many of them leave socialist countries for more capitalistic countries with lower taxes, such as the United States. This loss of the best and brightest people to other countries is called a **brain drain.** Of course, there are many other reasons for brain drain, socialism being only one of them.

brain drain
The loss of the best and brightest people to other countries.

Let's try to illustrate a socialist economy by imagining socialism in your own class: Say that after the first exam, those with grades of 90 and above have to give some of their points to those who make 70 and below so that everyone ends up with grades in the 80s. What would happen to the incentive of those who got As on the first exam? Would they study as hard for the second exam, knowing that they would have to give away any points above 90? What about those who got 70s? Would they work less hard if they knew that they would get extra points if they didn't do well? Can you see why workers may not work as hard or as well if they all get the same benefits regardless of how hard they work?

In some socialist countries, such as India, people suffer from lack of jobs and resources. While the system tries to distribute resources, sometimes there aren't enough resources to begin with. This photo was taken in a slum in New Delhi, India, a socialist country.

Capitalism results in freedom of opportunity, which is the freedom to keep whatever you earn. That creates incentives to work hard, but it also results in an unequal distribution of outcomes. In contrast, socialism strives for equality of outcomes. Socialist systems, therefore, tend to discourage the best from working as hard as they can. In the business world, socialism also results in fewer inventions and less innovation because those who come up with new ideas usually don't receive as much reward as they would in a capitalist system. As a result, people may not be motivated to try new ideas. Over the past decade, most socialist countries have simply not kept up with the United States in new inventions, job creation, or wealth creation. It is important, however, not to confuse socialism with communism.

Communism

The 19th-century German political philosopher Karl Marx saw the wealth created by capitalism, but he also noted the poor working and living conditions of laborers in his time. He decided that workers should take over ownership of businesses and share in the wealth. In 1848 he wrote *The Communist Manifesto*, outlining the takeover process. Marx thus became the founder of communism. **Communism** is an economic and political system in which the state (the government) makes almost all economic decisions and owns almost all the major factors of production, including housing for its people. It intrudes further into the lives of people than socialism does. For example, some communist countries do not allow their citizens to practice certain religions, change jobs, or move to the town of their choice.

communism

An economic and political system in which the state (the government) makes almost all economic decisions and owns almost all the major factors of production.

One problem with communism is that the government has no way of knowing what to produce because prices don't reflect supply and demand as they do in free markets. The government must guess what the economic needs of the people are. As a result, shortages of many items may develop, including shortages of food and basic clothing. Another problem with communism is that it doesn't inspire businesspeople to work hard because the government takes most of their earnings. Therefore, although communists once held power in many nations around the world, communism is slowly disappearing as an economic form.

Most communist countries today are suffering severe economic depression, and some people (for example, in North Korea) are starving. The people in Cuba are suffering from the lack of goods and services readily available in most other countries, and some people fear the government.[16] Some parts of the former Soviet Union remain governed under communist concepts, but the movement there is toward free markets. In fact, Russia now has a flat tax of 13 percent, much lower than the tax rate in the United States. When Russia introduced that low rate, tax revenues jumped by nearly 30 percent. With such low tax rates, people no longer did whatever they could to avoid paying them. The trend toward free markets is also appearing in Vietnam[17] and parts of China.[18] The regions in China that are most free have prospered greatly while the rest of the country has grown relatively slowly.

The Trend toward Mixed Economies

The nations of the world have largely divided historically between those that have followed the concepts of capitalism and those that adopted the concepts of communism or socialism.

1. **Free market economies** exist when the market largely determines what goods and services get produced, who gets them, and how the economy grows. *Capitalism* is the popular term used to describe this economic system.

2. **Command economies** exist when the government largely decides what goods and services get produced, who gets them, and how the economy grows. *Socialism* and *communism* are the popular terms used to describe variations of this economic system.

The experience of the world, however, has been that neither free market nor command economies have resulted in optimum economic conditions. Free market economies haven't been responsive enough to the needs of individuals who are poor, elderly, and disabled. It is thought that they do not take care of those people who may need it the most. Some people also believe that businesses in free market economies have not done enough to protect the environment. Over time, voters in free market countries, such as the United States, have therefore elected officials who have adopted many social and environmental programs such as Social Security, welfare, unemployment compensation, and various clean air and clean water laws.

On the other hand, socialism and communism, or command economies, haven't always created enough jobs or wealth to keep growing fast enough. As a consequence, communist governments are disappearing and socialist governments have been cutting back on social programs and lowering taxes on businesses and workers to compete better. The idea is to generate more business growth and thus generate more revenue.[19]

The economic picture we see in the real world today, thus, is more mixed. The trend has been for traditionally capitalist countries to move toward a more socialist system, that is, to provide programs to take care of poor or disadvantaged people and to safeguard the environment,

free market economies
The market largely determines what goods and services get produced, who gets them, and how the economy grows.

command economies
The government largely decides what goods and services get produced, who gets them, and how the economy grows.

while some of the socialist and communist countries have adopted elements of capitalism to a greater or lesser degree. As a result, there is a blend between capitalism and socialism in our world economy today. In a given society, this blend is called a *mixed economy*.

mixed economies

Economies where some allocation of resources is made by the market and some by the government.

Mixed economies exist where some allocation of resources is made by the market and some by the government. Most countries with mixed economies don't refer to themselves by such a name, however. If the dominant way of allocating resources is by free market mechanisms, then the leaders of the country still call their system capitalism. If the dominant way of allocating resources is by the government, then the leaders call their system socialism. Figure 2.5 compares the various economic systems.

Like most other nations of the world, the United States has a mixed economy. The optimal degree of government involvement in the economy today is a matter of debate, as it has been at various times in the past. The government has now become the largest employer in the United States, which means that the number of workers in the public sector is more than the number in the entire manufacturing sector. There's debate about the government's optimal role in health care, education, business regulation, and other parts of the economy. Many people believe the government should be more involved, many believe it should be less involved, while others believe the government should not be involved in these issues at all. Generally, the government's perceived ideal goal should be to grow the economy while maintaining some measure of social equality, but such a balance is very hard to attain. Few people on either side of the debate would disagree that the basic principles of freedom and opportunity should lead to economic growth that is sustainable.

Should we care about the types of economic systems other countries employ? Yes, because the trend we call *globalization,* discussed in the next chapter, causes us to depend on each other for products and services. What any one country does affects everyone else. As a result, it is in our best interest for other countries to prosper as well as ourselves.

SELF-CHECK QUESTIONS

1. What is the difference between socialism and communism? How are they the same? Which system, in your opinion, is the best and why?
2. Compare free market economies with socialism. What are the advantages and disadvantages of each?
3. What is a mixed economy?
4. Why is the trend going toward mixed economies? Do you think at some point the balance will likely change to one of the pure types? Why or why not?

	Capitalism	Socialism	Communism	Mixed Economy
Social and Economic Goals	Private ownership of land and business. Liberty and the pursuit of happiness. Free trade. Emphasis on freedom and the profit motive for economic growth.	Public ownership of major businesses. Some private ownership of smaller businesses and shops. Government control of education, health care, utilities, mining, transportation, and media. Very high taxation. Emphasis on equality.	Public ownership of all businesses. Government-run education and health care. Emphasis on equality. Many limitations on freedom, including freedom to own businesses, change jobs, buy and sell homes, and to assemble to protest government actions.	Private ownership of land and business with government regulation. Government control of some institutions (e.g., mail). High taxation for defense and the common welfare. Emphasis on a balance between freedom and equality.
Motivation of Workers	Much incentive to work efficiently and hard because profits are retained by owners. Workers are rewarded for high productivity.	Capitalist incentives exist in private businesses. Government control of wages in public institutions limits incentives.	Very little incentive to work hard or to produce quality goods or services.	Incentives are similar to capitalism except in government-owned enterprises, which may have fewer incentives.
Control over Markets	Complete freedom of trade within and among nations. No government control of markets.	Some markets are controlled by the government and some are free. Trade restrictions among nations vary and include some freetrade agreements.	Total government control over markets except for illegal transactions.	Some government control of trade within and among nations (trade protectionism).
Choices in the Market	A wide variety of goods and services is available. Almost no scarcity or oversupply exists for long because supply and demand control the market.	Variety in the marketplace varies considerably from country to country. Choice is directly related to government involvement in markets.	Very little choice among competing goods.	Similar to capitalism, but scarcity and over-supply may be caused by government involvement in the market (e.g., subsidies for farms).
Social Freedoms	Freedom of speech, press, assembly, religion, job choice, movement, and elections.	Similar to mixed economy. Governments may restrict job choice, movement among countries, and who may attend upper-level schools (i.e., college).	Very limited freedom to protest the government, practice religion, or change houses or jobs.	Some restrictions on freedoms of assembly and speech. Separation of church and state may limit religious practices in schools.

figure 2.5

COMPARISONS OF KEY ECONOMIC SYSTEMS

The Threat of Global Poverty

When Americans see televised images of bone-thin children with distended bellies, their humanitarian instincts take over. They don't typically look at UNICEF footage and perceive a threat that could destroy our way of life. Yet global poverty is not solely a humanitarian concern. In real ways, over the long term, it can threaten U.S. national security. Poverty erodes weak states' capacity to prevent the spread of disease and protect the world's forests and watersheds. It also creates conditions conducive to transnational criminal enterprises and terrorist activity, not only by making desperate individuals potentially more susceptible to recruitment, but also, and more significantly, by undermining the state's ability to prevent and counter those violent threats. Poverty can also give rise to the tensions that erupt in civil conflict, which further taxes the state and allows transnational predators greater freedom of action.

Americans can no longer realistically hope that we can erect the proverbial glass dome over our homeland and live safely isolated from the killers—natural or man-made—that plague other parts of the world. Al-Qaeda established training camps in conflict-ridden Sudan and Afghanistan, purchased diamonds from Sierra Leone and Liberia, and now targets American soldiers in Iraq. The potential toll of a global bird-flu pandemic is particularly alarming. A mutated virus causing human-to-human contagion could kill hundreds of thousands, if not millions, of Americans.

Today, more than half the world's population lives on less than $2 per day, and almost 1.1 billion people live in extreme poverty, defined as less than $1 per day. The costs of global poverty are multiple. Poverty prevents poor countries from devoting sufficient resources to detect and contain deadly disease. According to the World Health Organization (WHO), low- and middle-income countries suffer 90 percent of the world's disease burden but account for only 11 percent of its health care spending. Poverty also dramatically increases the risk of civil conflict. A recent study by the UK's Department for International Develop-

ment showed that a country at $250 GDP per capita has on average a 15 percent risk of internal conflict over five years, while a country at $5,000 per capita has a risk of less than 1 percent. War zones provide ideal operational environs for international outlaws.

If in the old days the consequences of extreme poverty could conveniently be confined to the far corners of the planet, this is no longer the case. The end of U.S.-Soviet competition, the civil and regional conflicts that ensued, and the rapid pace of globalization have brought to the fore a new generation of dangers. These are the complex nexus of transnational security threats: infectious disease, environmental degradation, international crime and drug syndicates, proliferation of small arms and weapons of mass destruction, and terrorism. Often these threats emerge from impoverished, relatively remote regions of the world. They thrive especially in conflict or lawless zones, in countries where corruption is endemic, and in poor, weak states with limited control over their territory or resources. The map of vulnerable zones is global—including parts of the Caribbean, Latin America, the Middle East, Africa, the Caucasus, and Central, South and East Asia. Fifty-three countries have an average per capita GDP of less than $2 per day. Each is a potential weak spot in a world in which effective action by states everywhere is necessary to reduce and combat transnational threats.

Questions

1. Do you think it is the responsibility of others to reduce poverty in developing nations? Why or why not?

2. Why do you think there is a link between internal conflict and GDP?

3. Do you think there might be a link between terrorist activities and GDP? Why or why not?

Source: Susan Rice, "The Threat of Global Poverty." *National Interest,* Spring 2006. Copyright © The National Interest, 2006. Used with permission.

ECONOMIC INDICATORS

So far we have discussed basic economic theory, such as the concepts of supply and demand, some theories of economics, and types of economies in the world. This section will discuss how a government determines how well the economy is doing.

The three major indicators of economic conditions are (1) the gross domestic product (GDP), (2) the unemployment rate, and (3) the price indexes. When you read business literature, you'll see these terms used again and again. Knowing and understanding these terms will greatly increase your ability to assess the nation's economy.

Gross Domestic Product

Gross domestic product (GDP) is the total value of final goods and services produced in a country in a given year within the United States. Either a domestic company or a foreign-owned company may produce the goods and services included in the GDP as long as the companies are located within the country's boundaries. For example, production values from Japanese automaker Honda's factory in Ohio would be included in the U.S. GDP because this production takes place within the country's borders. Likewise, revenue generated by the Ford car factory in Mexico would be included in Mexico's GDP, even though Ford is a U.S. company. Another way to measure GDP is per capita. The measurement takes the GDP number and divides it by the population. The United States had an estimated GDP per capita of $44,000 in 2006, according to the CIA's *The World Factbook*.[20]

Gross national product (GNP) is a similar term, but refers to the value of goods and services produced in the United States by Americans only.

If GDP growth slows or declines, there are often many negative effects on businesses. A major influence on the growth of GDP is how productive the workforce is, that is, how much output workers create with a given amount of input.

Almost every discussion about a nation's economy is based on GDP. The total U.S. GDP in 2006 was about $13.06 trillion.[21] The level of U.S. economic activity is actually larger than the GDP figures show because the figures don't take into account illegal activities (e.g., sales of illegal drugs). The high GDP in the United States is what enables Americans to enjoy such a high standard of living.[22]

Unemployment

Our second economic indicator is unemployment rate. The **unemployment rate** refers to the number of civilians at least 16 years old who are unemployed and who have tried to find a job within the prior four weeks. In 2000 the U.S. unemployment rate reached its lowest point in over 30 years, falling as low as 3.9 percent, but the rate rose rapidly to over 6 percent as a result of the economic slowdown of 2002–2003. The unemployment rate is finally stabilizing, at 4.5 percent in 2007.[23] Figure 2.6 describes the four types of unemployment: frictional, structural, cyclical, and seasonal. The United States tries to protect those who are unemployed because of recessions, industry shifts, and other cyclical factors.

Section Outline

Economic Indicators

- Gross Domestic Product
- Unemployment
- Price Indexes
- Fiscal and Monetary Policy

---

gross domestic product (GDP)

The total value of final goods and services produced in a country in a given year.

gross national product (GNP)

Similar to GDP, but only counts Americans producing products in the country, not other foreign nationals.

unemployment rate

The number of civilians at least 16 years old who are unemployed and who have tried to find a job within the prior four weeks.

figure 2.6

TYPES OF UNEMPLOYMENT AND U.S. UNEMPLOYMENT RATES FROM 1989 to 2007

The first type of unemployment is *cyclical unemployment*. Cyclical means there are not enough jobs for people who want to work and is usually a result of political or economic forces. The second type is *seasonal unemployment*. This type of unemployment might occur in some construction jobs, where workers are laid off during winter months. It can also include tourism jobs, where hotel workers might be laid off due to a low tourist season. *Frictional unemployment* is the third type of unemployment and occurs when people are "between" jobs. For example, if you quit your job and are planning on starting a new job as soon as you take two weeks' vacation, you would be considered frictionally unemployed. Finally, *structural unemployment* means that something within industries has changed that results in unemployment. For example, when the manufacturing of clothing in the United States started to move to China, this resulted in structural unemployment.

price indexes

Indexes of the changes in goods and prices of goods and services based on the prices of the same goods and services from a previous period.

inflation

A general rise in the prices of goods and services over time.

hyperinflation

When inflation increases beyond 50 percent in a given time period.

Nonetheless, for a variety of reasons, many of these individuals do not receive unemployment benefits.

Price Indexes

Our third economic indicator is **price indexes.** See Figure 2.7. The price indexes help to measure the health of the economy by measuring the levels of inflation, deflation, and stagflation. The consumer price index is one of the most popular indexes. The CPI measures the prices of products from month to month so economists can measure inflation. **Inflation** refers to a general rise in the prices of goods and services over time.[24] Some amount of inflation, about 2 percent, is perfectly normal. It means that goods are getting slightly more expensive to produce due to wages and other manufacturing costs increasing. **Hyperinflation,** on the other hand, is a phenomenon where the cost of goods is rising so quickly (second to second or minute to minute) that it renders the currency virtually worthless. One extreme example happened in December 1993 in Ukraine, where inflation

figure 2.7

ECONOMIC INDICATORS FOR THE U.S. ECONOMY

Note: Economists use economic indicators to measure the health of a country, economically speaking. Think of it as "taking the temperature" of the country. Most economists will look at not just one indicator to determine the health of the country, but rather will look at all indicators together to measure how well we are doing economically.

Sources: Federal Reserve Bank and White House Economic Statistics.

Gross domestic product and gross national product	Gross domestic product is the total value of final goods and services produced in a country in a given year within the United States. Gross national product is similar, but tracks only the value of goods and services produced in the United States by Americans.
Employment/Unemployment rates	The government tracks how many people have jobs as an indicator of our country's economic health. Obviously, the higher the unemployment, the higher the concern.
Price indexes	Price indexes track the price of goods over time. This allows us to see if we have inflation. Examples include the consumer price index (CPI) and the producer price index (PPI).
Household income	The government measures average household income to see how wage increases compare to increases the previous year.
Home sales	Home sales is the number of homes that sold during a given time period. Times of high home sales figures can mean economic prosperity.
Consumption	Retail sales and other statistics relating to how much we buy are tracked so the government can see how much we are spending.
U.S. trade	U.S. trade is tracked by a variety of measures to see how many goods we are trading when compared with different times in history.

peaked at 10,155 percent.[25] Although there is no set definition of where hyperinflation begins, many experts believe that inflation of over 50 percent is hyperinflation.

Stagflation occurs when both inflation and unemployment are high and occurring at the same time. According to many economists, the cause for stagflation is misguided fiscal and monetary policy (discussed in the next section). Obviously, stagflation is harmful to a country because it means that prices are rising while people are losing their jobs or do not have jobs.

Deflation means that prices are actually declining.[26] It occurs when countries produce so many goods that people cannot afford to buy them all (too few dollars are chasing too many goods, which is obviously a negative indicator, because it means that demand and supply are out of balance).

stagflation
When unemployment rates and inflation rates are high.

deflation
Prices are actually declining. It occurs when countries produce so many goods that people cannot afford to buy them all.

consumer price index (CPI)

Consists of monthly statistics that measure the pace of inflation or deflation. It tracks the price of 400 goods.

producer price index (PPI)

Similar to the consumer price index, but measures prices at the wholesale level.

fiscal policy

The federal government's efforts to keep the economy stable by increasing or decreasing taxes or government spending.

national debt

The sum of government deficits over time.

The **consumer price index (CPI)** consists of monthly statistics that measure the pace of inflation or deflation. Costs of about 200 categories of goods and services—including housing, food, apparel, and medical care—are computed to see if they are going up or down.[27] The CPI is an important figure because some wages and salaries, rents and leases, tax brackets, government benefits, and interest rates are based on it.

The **producer price index (PPI)** measures prices at the wholesale level. The PPI measures price change from the perspective of the seller whereas the CPI measures the price change from the purchaser's perspective.[28] Other indicators of the economy's condition include housing starts, retail sales, and changes in personal income. These are all statistics that are announced regularly and can provide some insight into the overall health of an economy. Remember, though, that not one of these measures alone will provide the full picture of the economy. They all must be studied in order to gain a more accurate picture.

Fiscal and Monetary Policy

Fiscal policy refers to the federal government's efforts to keep the economy stable by increasing or decreasing taxes or government spending.

The first half of fiscal policy involves taxation. Theoretically, high tax rates tend to slow the economy because they draw money away from the private sector and put it into the government. High tax rates may discourage small-business ownership because they decrease the profits businesses can earn and make the effort less rewarding. It follows, then, that—theoretically—low tax rates would tend to give the economy a boost.

Figure 2.8 illustrates where the government gets its money and where the money is spent. When you count all fees, sales taxes, and more, taxes on the highest-earning citizens could exceed 50 percent. As you can imagine, this causes concern for those who escaped high taxes in socialist countries.

The second half of fiscal policy involves government spending. The government spends money on highways, social programs, education, defense, and so on. The national deficit is the amount of money that the federal government spends over and above the amount it gathers in taxes for a specific period of time (namely a fiscal year). Over time, such deficits increase the national debt. The **national debt** is the sum of government deficits over time. As of October 2007, the national debt was a little over $9 trillion (see Figure 2.9). That's close to $30,000 for every man, woman, and child in the United States,[29] or over $112,000 for a family of four. (You can see what your current

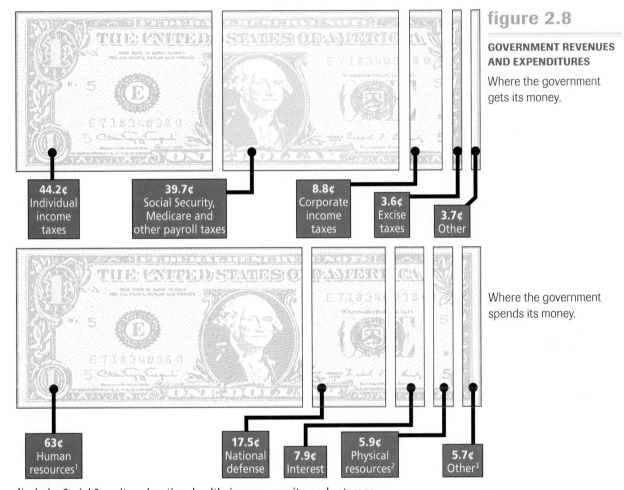

figure 2.8

GOVERNMENT REVENUES AND EXPENDITURES

Where the government gets its money.

44.2¢ Individual income taxes	
39.7¢ Social Security, Medicare and other payroll taxes	
8.8¢ Corporate income taxes	
3.6¢ Excise taxes	
3.7¢ Other	

Where the government spends its money.

63¢ Human resources[1]	
17.5¢ National defense	
7.9¢ Interest	
5.9¢ Physical resources[2]	
5.7¢ Other[3]	

[1]Includes Social Security, education, health, income security, and veterans.
[2]Includes commerce, housing, transportation, and environment.
[3]Includes international affairs, agriculture, science and space, and justice.

share of the national debt is by checking out the National Debt Clock at www.brillig.com/debt_clock.)

One way to lessen the annual deficits is to cut government spending. Many presidents have promised to make the government "smaller" by lowering government spending—but that doesn't happen very often. There seems to be a need for more social programs or more defense spending each year, and thus the deficits continue and add to the national debt. Some people believe that spending by the government helps the economy grow. Others believe that the money the government spends comes out of the pockets of consumers and businesspeople and thus slows growth.

In an economic boom, businesses do well. A **recession** occurs when two or more quarters show declines in the GDP, prices fall, people

recession
When the GDP falls for two consecutive quarters.

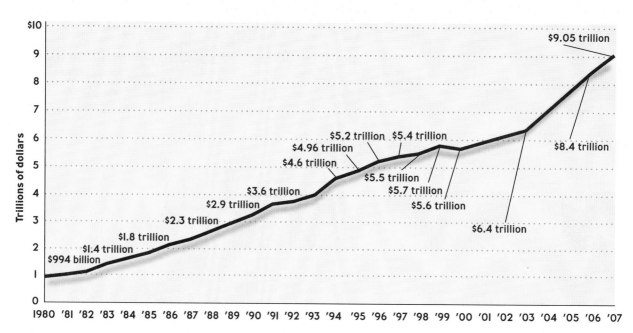

figure 2.9

THE NATIONAL DEBT

Every man, woman, and child in the United States' share of the national debt is close to $30,000.

depression

A severe recession, when the GDP falls for several quarters, and recovery is a long time off.

recovery

An improvement in the economy, marking the end of a recession or decline.

monetary policy

The management of the money supply and interest rates.

purchase fewer products, and businesses fail. **A depression** is a severe recession. A depression usually occurs during times of deflation and unemployment and is extremely serious. The Great Depression in the late 1920s and 1930s in the United States lasted almost an entire decade. **Recovery** occurs when the economy stabilizes and starts to grow again.

Monetary policy is ultimately what adds or subtracts money from the economy. Monetary policy is the management of the money supply and interest rates, and this is what helps control the growth or slowing of the economy.

Monetary policy is controlled by the Federal Reserve system. The Fed is a semiprivate organization that is not under the direct control of the government but does have members who are appointed by the president of the United States. Our current Federal Reserve chair is Dr. Ben Bernanke. He took over in 2006 after Alan Greenspan (the former Federal Reserve chairperson) retired.

The most obvious role of the Federal Reserve is the raising and lowering of interest rates. When the economy is booming, the Fed tends to raise interest rates, which makes money more expensive to borrow. Businesses thus borrow less, and the economy slows as businesspeople spend less money on everything they need to grow, including labor and machinery. The opposite is true when the Fed lowers interest rates. Businesses tend to borrow more, and the economy takes off. Raising and lowering interest rates should therefore help control the rapid ups and downs of the economy.

Focus on Ethics

RECON STILL CLEANING UP AFTER KATRINA

- 205,000 houses were severely damaged by the 2005 Gulf Coast hurricanes. As of May 2006, 60% remained unoccupied.
- Displaced families have moved an average of 3.5 times since the storms.
- In March 2006, *The New York Times* found that more than 1 in 10 New Orleans evacuees were homeless or had no permanent place to live.
- Fewer than 35% of New Orleans' 462,000 residents had returned to the city as of March. Only half are expected to return by September 2008.
- Eight months after Katrina, fewer than 1 in 10 New Orleans businesses had reopened.
- The Small Business Administration has rejected nearly 70% of the 2.4 million loan applications received from hurricane victims.
- 36 countries and international organizations donated $126 million to federal rebuilding efforts, half of which remained undistributed six months after Katrina.
- FEMA spent $431 million on 11,000 trailer homes that were never used, $3 million for 4,000 unused cots, and $10 million to fix up 240 rooms in Alabama that housed only six people.
- Carnival Cruise Lines got a six-month, $236 million contract to house evacuees on three of its ships, which sat half empty off the Gulf Coast for weeks.
- The GAO found that there was insufficient oversight on 13 reconstruction contracts, including $100 million to Bechtel.
- Experts predict there is a nearly 50% chance that a category 3 or greater hurricane will hit the Gulf Coast this season.
- On a scale of 1 to 10, FEMA director R. David Paulison gave the agency an 8 in terms of preparedness for this year's hurricane season.
- More than 100,000 families in Louisiana and Mississippi live in FEMA trailers that Paulison said "should not, or could not, ride out even a Category 1 storm."

Questions

1. What do you believe should be the role of the government after Katrina? Did the government fulfill their responsibilities? Explain.

2. From this article and other articles you have read, what other unethical practices took place in New Orleans after the hurricane?

Source: Excerpts from "Recon Still Cleaning Up After Katrina" *Mother Jones,* July/August 2006. Copyright © 2006. Foundation for National Progress. Used with permission.

The Federal Reserve also controls the money supply. A simple explanation is that the more money that the Fed makes available to businesspeople and others, the faster the economy grows. To slow the economy, the Fed lowers the money supply. Of course, the economic goal is to keep the economy growing so that more people can rise up the economic ladder and enjoy a satisfying quality of life. Many people wonder, why can't we just print more money if the government needs it? The main reason is fear of inflation. If the government printed more money, it would cost much more to buy the things we

Economics and You

Economics is an interesting field because it is truly a mix of business with a research component. It is unlikely that many of us will become economists, but we will definitely use economic concepts in our chosen career fields. As a small business owner or manager, it will be necessary to use all of the economic indicators to determine the direction we should take for our businesses. For example, the average household income can indicate to managers if wages have increased or decreased over last year. If salaries have increased, managers know that their customers likely have more money to spend in the current year. As a result, businesses may adjust prices. Increases in the average household income can also signify to managers that it might be time to give employees a raise!

GDP is another important indicator to the small business owner or manager. Knowing the overall health of the economy can help an entrepreneur determine if he or she should expand the business or hire more people. Following and understanding consumption figures is also crucial to being successful in business. Managers and business owners can determine where and how customers are spending money, allowing them to make better decisions about the types of products and services they offer.

Economic indicators are even important in your personal life. For example, if the home sales economic indicator is showing that home sales are slow, you know you may be able to get a better price on a house or even have a better selection of homes from which to choose. The unemployment rate is another indicator you may want to track personally. The higher the unemployment rate, the more difficult it could be to find a job. Likewise, the lower the unemployment rate, the better the choice of available jobs. You might be able to negotiate a higher salary, since there is a slimmer selection of potential employees. Sometimes we don't even know that we are using economic concepts. Think about buying gas for your car—do you complain about the price? The price goes up when supply is limited yet demand is still high. This is the basic supply and demand theory discussed in the chapter. Whether you use economic concepts in your workplace, personal life, or both, you will find this knowledge gets you one step ahead of your competition!

need, simply because there is more money available. This example relates to supply and demand, in that if there is more of something, in this case, money, the less it is worth. Some countries have printed more money with great regret, as their economies collapsed. Argentina faced the hyperinflation in 1990 when the inflation rate peaked at 20,266 percent.[30]

Printing more money is not always the answer. Inflation would increase the cost of necessities if a government printed more money.

SELF-CHECK QUESTIONS

1. Name and discuss the three economic indicators.
2. What are price indexes? What do they have to do with the economy?
3. What is the difference between monetary policy and fiscal policy?

When Ashon got home from work that day, he went back to the Web site he had read that morning and reread the article he couldn't understand earlier: "The U.S. economy is expected to weaken during the second half of the year, as unemployment and high energy prices take a toll on the housing market and consumer spending. In addition, GDP is expected to weaken to 2.7%. As a result, the Fed is considering lowering interest rates to stimulate growth."

He had learned a little about economics that day by reading this chapter of our text, and wanted to see if he could understand the article better now.

"Okay," he thought, "the economy will weaken because of more expensive housing and rising gas prices. Because of the weaker market, customers aren't spending as much as before. Whoever wrote this article must be looking at the price indexes to determine that consumer spending has gone down." After further reading, Ashon thought, "High energy prices mean that there is not enough supply to meet the demand of consumers. As a result, of course, prices will increase more. Prices will likely continue to increase until demand is less, or supply is more. GDP is also expected to weaken. This means that the entire growth of the economy will not be as fast as it has been in the past. This can be directly attributed to the fact that people are not buying as much. The good news, though, is that GDP is still expected to increase slightly by 2.7%. Finally, I think this article is saying that in order to stimulate more growth, the Fed may lower interest rates to make money cheaper to borrow."

Ashon was proud of himself. What had seemed like a foreign language before was much clearer to him. Most important, as a business owner, he now realized what the slowing growth of the economy might mean for his business. However, if interest rates were to go down, it might be a good time for him to borrow money, in order to expand his operations, because money would be cheaper to borrow. "Economics is not all theoretical," Ashon thought. "It really does apply to everyday life and business."

summary

Economics is the study of how society employs resources. This chapter introduced some basic economic concepts, such as the factors of production, supply and demand, and the business cycle. Supply is the availability of goods, while demand is the amount of goods consumers are willing to buy. If supply is higher than demand, the price of the good will normally decrease; if supply is lower than demand, a higher price can usually be charged.

Macroeconomics studies the economy on a broad or national scale, while microeconomics takes a narrower focus.

Malthus and his theory that the population would grow too fast to keep up with resources was contrasted with Adam Smith's theory that while trying to make a profit and help themselves, businesses are guided by an "invisible hand" to actually help others by creating jobs and wealth for others. Thus, in capitalism we see the phenomenon of resource development.

Capitalism, or free markets, is an economic system in which all or most of the means of production and distribution (land, factories, railroads, stores) are privately owned and operated for profit. In socialism and communism, on the other hand, most means of production and distribution are owned by the government, with the idea being to distribute wealth more evenly than in capitalism. In the world today there is a trend toward mixed economies, where the government owns some factors of production, while private businesses own others.

The chapter described the four levels of competition in a free market: perfect competition, monopolistic competition, oligopoly, and monopoly.

Economists use gross domestic product, unemployment rates, and price indexes as indicators of how well the economy is doing. Inflation means the normal rise of prices over time, while deflation means prices have gone down, normally due to an economic recession or depression.

Monetary policy refers to controlling interest rates and money supply, which helps stimulate or slow the economy when appropriate. Fiscal policy refers to rates of taxation and levels of government spending.

key terms

economics 41

macroeconomics 41

microeconomics 41

resource
  development 41

invisible hand 43

supply 44

demand 44

business cycle 46

free market 47

perfect competition 48

monopolistic
  competition 48

oligopoly 48

monopoly 49

socialism 50

brain drain 51

communism 52

free market
  economies 53

command
  economies 54

mixed economies 54

gross domestic product
  (GDP) 57

gross national product
  (GNP) 57

unemployment rate 57

price indexes 58

inflation 58

hyperinflation 58

stagflation 59

deflation 59

consumer price index
  (CPI) 60

producer price index
  (PPI) 60

fiscal policy 60

national debt 60

recession 61

depression 62

recovery 62

monetary policy 62

applying your skills

1. In teams, develop a list of the advantages of living in a capitalist society. Then develop lists headed "What are the disadvantages?" and "How could such disadvantages be minimized?" Describe why a poor person in a socialist country might reject capitalism and prefer a socialist state. How could the United States overcome this situation to broaden the base of the free market?

2. Do you think the United States should be concerned about brain drain, either in the sense of people immigrating to this country or people leaving this country for opportunities in other countries? Why or why not?

3. What do you think factors of production for a retail clothing store would be? What about the factors of production for an airplane manufacturer? List the factors of production either in groups or on your own.

4. Show your understanding of the principles of supply and demand by looking at the employment market today. Explain, for example, the high salaries that computer scientists are getting at Microsoft. Also explain why some PhDs aren't getting better pay than computer scientists who have only undergraduate degrees. Why do some librarians make less than some garbage collectors, even though the librarians may have a better education?

5. This exercise will help you understand socialism from different perspectives. Form three groups. Each group should adopt a different role in a socialist economy: One group will be the business owners, another group will be workers, and another government leaders. Think about your needs and desires in terms of the role you are playing. Within your group discuss and list the advantages and disadvantages to you of lowering taxes on businesses. That is, how will it improve things, and what problems might such a change in policy create in the context of a socialist society?

6. Draw a line and mark one end "free market capitalism" and the other end "central planning (command economy)." Mark where on the line the United States is now. Explain why you marked the spot you chose. Students from other countries may want to do this exercise for their own countries and explain the differences to the class.

7. Break into small groups, either in class or via the collaboration feature of your online classroom. In your group discuss how the following events or issues have affected people's purchasing behavior and their attitudes toward the United States and its economy: September 11, 2001; the war in Iraq; epidemics such as SARS (severe acute respiratory syndrome) and AIDS; the growth of the Internet; recent big business scandals such as Enron.

the internet in action

1. Do your parents or grandparents ever tire of telling you how much things cost back in their day? Sure, things were cheaper then, but the value of a dollar was different too. Think about something you bought today (shoes, soda, candy bar, haircut—whatever). How much did the good or service you bought today cost your parents when they were your age? Find out by using the handy tool on the Federal Reserve Bank of Minneapolis's Woodrow Web site (http://woodrow.mpls.frb.fed.us/research/data/us/calc). The calculator uses the consumer price index to compare the value of the dollar in different years. Enter the cost of the item you bought today, the year you would like to compare it with, and—presto—you'll find out how Mom and Pop could get along on such a small paycheck. (For an even bigger shock, compare the current dollar to the dollar in your grandparents' day!)

    a. How much would a $50 pair of jeans bought today have cost the year you were born?

    b. How much would a job paying $6 an hour today have paid in 1970?

    c. How much would a new car costing $18,000 today have cost the year your mother first got her driver's license?

2. Imagine your boss asked you to help her prepare the company's sales forecast for the next two years. In the past she felt that the trend in the nation's GDP and the employment trends in U.S. manufacturing and in manufacturing in Illinois were especially helpful in forecasting sales. She would like you to do the following:

    a. Go to the Bureau of Economic Analysis Web site (www.bea.doc.gov) and locate the gross domestic product data. Compute an annual figure for the last four years by averaging the quarterly data. Plot this on graph paper or a spreadsheet. Leave enough space for six years so that you can draw a projection line for the next two years.

    b. On the Bureau of Labor Statistics (BLS) Web site (www.bls.gov) go to the page with the information about the manufacturing industry. What is the employment trend in that industry over the last four years?

    c. On the BLS site, find the manufacturing employment for the state of Illinois. Using the data from July, plot the trend in manufacturing employment in Illinois over the last four years.

3. Look up current population. Look up current GDP. Calculate an estimated GDP per capita.

BUSINESS IN GLOBAL MARKETS

Brett Bats[1]

Brett Bats began selling baseball bats in the United States with a new, stronger wood technology. Soon, the company realized it was not cost effective to continue production of the bats in the United States. As a result, the owners of the company looked for factories in China to produce the bats. The venture required Joe Sample, one of the owners, to learn about Chinese culture and business practices. Joe found a production facility in China, and the two companies signed a contract making the factory the exclusive producer of Brett Bats. As Brett

Joe Sample from Brett Bats

Bats has grown, it has branched into other areas of baseball equipment. Joe Sample and his team now sell sunglasses, batting helmets, gloves, and catcher's equipment, all in China.

One of the challenges Joe has is communication with the factory in China. If he has a simple reorder of an existing product, it is a fairly easy process. However, when Brett Bats introduces a new product, it takes much more time and attention to detail to ensure the product is right.

LEARNING objectives

After reading this chapter, you will be able to:

1 Define global business.

2 Understand the importance of global trade.

3 Discuss the roles of comparative and absolute advantage in global trade.

4 Discuss the different strategies for reaching global markets.

5 Describe different types of trade protections and trade agreements.

6 Discuss the two indicators for measuring global trade.

7 Explain the forces affecting the global trade market.

For sunglasses, Joe sends specifications to the factory including colors and materials needed to produce the sunglasses. The factory then sends back a sample of the glasses. Joe suggests changes, such as smaller lenses or use of a different plastic for the frame. After the factory receives these changes, it adjusts the product and sends Joe another sample. Once a final prototype is approved, Joe places the order.

The Internet has made working with factories overseas much easier and more time efficient; however, cultural differences still exist when communicating with the factories in other parts of the world. This chapter will explore some of those communication differences as well as trade agreements and the forces that affect global markets.

Things may not have started off "pretty" for Ugly Dolls, but the two-person company has grown into a global business, selling its product in over 1,000 stores around the world. The dolls are a particular favorite in Japan.

UNDERSTANDING GLOBALIZATION

Global business is here to stay. It refers to any activity that seeks to provide goods and services to others across national borders while operating at a profit. Businesses large and small are finding many advantages to engaging in business globally. Businesses have entirely new markets in which to sell their products, and they can save on the costs of labor by producing overseas. Companies also face new cultural challenges when they engage in international business. Before we explore global business further, read the Real World Business Apps box in this chapter for an example of small company that has taken advantage of all global business has to offer.

global business

Any activity that seeks to provide goods and services to others across national borders while operating at a profit.

GLOBAL TRADE

Have you ever thought of traveling to exotic cities like Paris, Tokyo, Rio de Janeiro, or Cairo? While traveling to global destinations was far out of reach for most Americans for many decades, today the situation has changed. It is hard to find a major U.S. company that does not cite global expansion as a link to its future growth. A 2005 study noted that 91 percent of the companies doing business globally believe it is important to send employees on assignments in other countries, which can make for exciting career opportunities in global business.[2]

The United States is a market of over 300 million people, but there are over 6 billion potential customers in the 193 countries that make up the global market.[3] A market that large explains why the global market is attractive to large and small businesses alike! (See Figure 3.1 for a map of the world and important statistics about world population.) Even with this growing global market, 75 percent of the world's population lives in developing areas where technology, education, and per capita income still lag considerably behind those of developed (or industrialized) nations such as the United States. Over time, these nations will develop the resources to purchase goods from other countries, which is where business gets interesting for U.S. companies.[4]

Today Americans buy billions of dollars' worth of goods from countries such as India, Vietnam, and China. McDonald's is a popular restaurant in Germany, Saudi Arabia, and other global markets.[5] Major league baseball teams, the National Basketball Association, and the National Football League play games in Mexico, Italy, Japan, and elsewhere.

Angela Wilson owns a small but growing jewelry design business. She makes the jewelry by hand and sells her creations in small boutiques throughout the southwestern United States. One of her major clients just ordered 1,000 pieces and needs those pieces right away. Angela knows it would take her months to produce the jewelry herself and wants to find some way to produce it faster.

She considers outsourcing the production, but isn't sure how to start. Quite aside from the new rush order, Angela has been interested in finding out about selling her goods overseas, but isn't sure how to get started on that, either. She is hoping this chapter will give her a starting point to answer her questions and solve her problem.

Movie stars such as Harrison Ford and Angelina Jolie continuously draw crowds to movie theaters around the globe as American movies hold center stage in the global entertainment market. In his book *The World Is Flat,* Thomas Friedman discusses how the competitive field is leveling for all countries, including those which are still developing.[6] India, for example, is able to provide low-cost labor for the United States and other nations' companies for call center, customer service, and technology coding jobs, thereby increasing the quality of life for India's workers. Friedman discusses technology as being one of the main drivers of the phenomenon that he calls the "flattening of the world." It will be interesting to see over the next few years how the world continues to "flatten," especially in importing and exporting, which we will discuss in the next section.

The United States is the largest exporting and importing nation in the world. Not only large corporations, but also small businesses contribute to this statistic. **Exporting** is selling products to another country.

exporting
Selling products to another country.

Figure 3.1

WORLD POPULATION BY CONTINENT

Asia comprises over 60 percent of the world's population; however, the United States, only one part of North America, is the largest exporting and importing nation in the world.

Source: Central Intelligence Agency Factbook, www.maps. com, June 14, 2007.

North America 7.9%

Europe 12.5%

Asia 60.8%

Africa 12.7%

South America 5.6%

Australia 0.5%

importing

Buying products from another country.

free trade

The movement of goods and services among nations without political or economic trade barriers.

global trade

The exchange of goods and services across national borders.

comparative advantage theory

The theory that a country should sell to other countries those products that it produces most effectively and efficiently and buy from other countries those products it cannot produce as effectively or efficiently.

Importing is buying products from another country. Competition in exporting is very intense.[7] U.S. companies face aggressive competition from exporters in such countries as Germany, Japan, and China.[8] Today in the United States, small businesses account for only about 29 percent of exports while generating about half of the private-sector commerce, but they are becoming more involved in global markets as they see the potential for growth.[9]

Why Trade Globally?

In an economic sense, there are several reasons why countries trade with other countries. First, no nation, not even a technologically advanced one, can produce all of the products that its people want and need. Second, even if a country did become self-sufficient, other nations would seek to trade with that country in order to meet the needs of their own people. Third, some nations (for instance, China and Russia) have an abundance of natural resources and a lack of technological know-how, while others (Japan, Taiwan, Switzerland) have sophisticated technology but few natural resources. Trade relations enable each nation to produce what it is most capable of producing and to buy what it needs in a mutually beneficial exchange relationship. This happens through the process of free trade.[10]

Free trade is the movement of goods and services among nations without political or economic trade barriers. The degree to which trade should be free is often a hotly debated concept.[11] Some of the pros and cons of free trade are shown in Figure 3.2.

SELF-CHECK QUESTIONS

1. Why is the freedom of exporting and importing so important in global business?
2. Why do companies decide to engage in global business?

Section Outline

Comparative Advantage and Absolute Advantage

COMPARATIVE ADVANTAGE AND ABSOLUTE ADVANTAGE

Global trade is the exchange of goods and services across national borders. Exchanges between and among countries involve more than goods and services, however.[12] Countries also exchange art, sports, cultural events, medical advances, space exploration, and labor. **Comparative advantage theory** states that a country should sell to other countries those products that it produces most effectively and efficiently and buy from other countries those products it cannot produce as effectively or efficiently. Examples might be England selling wool

Figure 3.2

THE PROS AND CONS OF FREE TRADE

Free trade is often a hotly debated issue.

Pros

- The global market contains over 6 billion potential customers for goods and services.
- Productivity grows when countries produce goods and services in which they have a comparative advantage.
- Global competition and less-costly imports keep prices down so inflation does not curtail economic growth.
- Free trade inspires innovation for new products and keeps firms competitively challenged.
- Uninterrupted flow of capital gives countries access to foreign investments, which helps keep interest rates low.
- Free trade can create new jobs.

Cons

- Domestic workers (particularly in manufacturing) can lose their jobs as a consequence of increased imports or production shifts to low-wage global markets.
- Workers may be forced to accept pay cuts from employers, who can threaten to move their jobs to lower-cost global markets.
- Moving operations overseas because of intense competitive pressure often means the loss of service jobs and growing numbers of white-collar jobs.
- Copyright and intellectual property laws vary in every country. As a result, an entrepreneur may try to sell a product in a country that offers no protection on intellectual property.
- Domestic companies can lose any advantage they might have had when competitors build advanced production operations in low-wage countries.

and France selling wine. It is important to note here that every country has a comparative advantage in something. Comparative advantage theory, suggested in the early 19th century by English economist David Ricardo, has been the guiding principle supporting the idea of free economic exchange.[13]

A country has an **absolute advantage** if it has a monopoly on producing a specific product or is able to produce it more efficiently than all other countries. For instance, South Africa once had an absolute advantage in diamond production.[14] In addition, many Middle Eastern countries have an absolute advantage in the production of oil.[15] Most absolute advantage situations involve natural resources that one country has and others do not have. Absolute advantage can also be difficult to sustain if conditions change or resources are discovered elsewhere.

Because countries are interested in knowing how they compare in trading with other countries, there are several ways in which trade can be measured, which we discuss next.

absolute advantage

Occurs when a country has a monopoly on producing a specific product or is able to produce it more efficiently than all other countries.

Section Outline

Measuring Trade

- Balance of Payments and Trade Deficits
- Unfair Trade Practices

balance of trade

Ratio of a country's exports to imports.

trade surplus

When a country exports more than it imports.

trade deficit

Occurs when a country imports more than it exports.

MEASURING TRADE

Balance of Payments and Trade Deficits

In measuring the effectiveness of global trade, nations carefully follow two key indicators: balance of trade and balance of payments. The **balance of trade** is a nation's ratio of exports to imports. A *favorable* balance of trade, or **trade surplus,** occurs when the value of the country's exports exceeds that of its imports. An *unfavorable* balance of trade, or **trade deficit,** occurs when the value of the country's imports exceeds that of its exports. It is easy to understand why countries prefer to export more than they import. If I sell you $200 worth of goods and buy only $100 worth, I have an extra $100 available to buy other things. However, I'm in an unfavorable position if I buy $200 worth of goods from you and sell you only $100 worth.

The **balance of payments** is the difference between money coming into a country (from exports) and money leaving the country (for

Wisconsin-based Trek Bicycle Corporation started with small roots in 1976 and quickly moved to a broader market. In 1988, it made its first step into globalization with a research trip to Europe. It quickly became the largest bike manufacturer in the world, with locations in over 15 countries.

imports) plus or minus money flows coming into or leaving a country from other factors such as tourism, foreign aid, military expenditures, and foreign investment. The goal is always to have more money flowing into the country than flowing out of the country, in other words a *favorable* balance of payments. Conversely, an *unfavorable* balance of payments exists when more money is flowing out of a country than coming in.

For many years, the United States exported more goods and services to other countries than it imported. Every year since 1976, however, the United States has bought more goods from other nations than it has sold to other nations.[16] Remember, this is called a *trade deficit* or *unfavorable balance of trade*. For example, in 2006 the United States exported $55.2 billion worth of goods to China while it imported an astonishing $287.8 billion for a trade deficit of $232.6 billion.[17]

How then, you may ask, is the United States the world's largest exporting nation? Even though the United States exports the largest *volume* of goods globally, it exports a much lower *percentage* of its products than other countries do.[18] Figure 3.3 lists the major trading partners of the United States. In the early 1980s, for example, no more than 10 percent of American businesses exported products. However, slow economic growth in the United States and other economic factors lured more businesses to global markets beginning in the late 1980s.[19] Today, most large businesses are involved in global trade, and growing numbers of small and medium-size businesses are going global as well. Nevertheless, the percentage of total U.S. products that are exported is still low.

Unfair Trade Practices

In measuring trade, one of the concerns is unfair trade practices. Many countries enforce laws to prohibit these practices. One such

balance of payments
The difference between money coming into a country (from exports) and money leaving the country (for imports) plus money flows coming into or leaving a country from other factors such as tourism, foreign aid, military expenditures, and foreign investment.

Country	Total Value of Exports and Imports ($U.S. Billions, April 2007)
Canada	$46.22
China	29.07
Mexico	27.19
Japan	17.74
Federal Republic of Germany	11.88
United Kingdom	8.91
Korea, South	6.98
France	5.64
Taiwan	5.28
Netherlands	4.30

Figure 3.3

THE TOP TRADING PARTNERS OF THE UNITED STATES

Being neighbors, Canada and Mexico are among the top three trading partners of the United States. However, China has become a formidable trading partner of the U.S. as well.

Study Skills

Rate Your Study Skills

Consider the following areas:

- Study knowledge (understanding the many approaches to good study habits).
- Study preparation (utilizing all the tools to get the most out of studying).
- Study execution (transforming all the techniques and skills into maximizing your results, usually shown by consistently getting good grades).

Based on the above, how would you rate your skills in these areas? Give yourself a grade:

- Study knowledge _____
- Study preparation _____
- Study execution _____

How does your report card look? Stay tuned. Your grades might improve or decline as you work through each chapter's text boxes throughout this book. Be sure they improve!

dumping

The practice of selling products in a foreign country at lower prices than those charged in the producing country.

gray market

The flow of goods in a distribution channel other than those intended by the manufacturer.

unfair trade practice is called *dumping*.[20] **Dumping** is the practice of selling products in a foreign country at lower prices than those charged in the producing country. Dumping can also include selling products in a country below what it cost to produce the product. Japan and Russia, for example, have been accused of dumping steel in the United States, Canada of dumping softwood lumber.[21] U.S. laws against dumping are specific and require that foreign firms price their products to include 10 percent overhead costs plus an 8 percent profit margin.[22] It can take time to prove accusations of dumping, however. There is also evidence that some governments offer financial incentives to certain industries to sell goods in global markets for less than they sell them at home. Dumping promises to remain a difficult trade issue in the coming years because it can hinder a country from selling its own products domestically at a fair price. Dumping can impact and skew measurement trade data as well.

Another unfair trade practice occurs in the **gray market.** The gray market refers to the flow of goods in a distribution channel or channels other than those intended by the manufacturer. For example, suppose that a Chinese business owner is manufacturing Chanel suits in his factory. Chanel suits normally sell for several thousand dollars. If this business owner were to make "extra" of some of these suits and sell them on eBay, this would be selling on the "gray market." Another example might be a sales manager selling electronics products, such as cell phones, to unauthorized distributors. Of course, this would be highly unethical, but it is a gray-market practice that occurs frequently. (Ethics will be discussed in greater detail in Chapter 4.)

Now that we have discussed some basics of global business, in the next section we will explore how countries put policies into place to protect their local markets.

SELF-CHECK QUESTIONS

1. What are two indicators in measuring the effectiveness of global trade?
2. What role do unfair trade practices play in global trade?

TRADE PROTECTION AND AGREEMENTS

As we discussed in Chapter 1, economic and legal, technological, competitive, and social forces are all challenges to trading globally. What is often a much greater barrier to global trade, however, is the *political* atmosphere between nations. **Trade protectionism** is the use of government regulations to limit the import of goods and services. Advocates of trade protectionism believe it allows domestic producers to survive and grow, thus producing more jobs. Countries often use protectionist measures to guard against such practices as dumping; many countries are wary of foreign competition in general.[23]

One protectionist measure is a **tariff,** basically a tax on imports, thus making imported goods more expensive to buy. Generally, there are two different kinds of tariffs: protective and revenue. *Protective tariffs* (import taxes) are designed to raise the retail price of imported products so that domestic goods will be more competitively priced. These tariffs are meant to save jobs for domestic workers and to keep industries (especially new ones in the early stages of growth) from closing down entirely because of foreign competition. *Revenue tariffs* are designed to raise money for the government. Revenue tariffs are also commonly used by developing countries to help infant industries compete in global markets. Today there is still considerable debate about the degree of protectionism a government should practice. The United States publishes the **Harmonized Tariff Schedule,** which includes tariff costs for every product from every country.

An **import quota,** another type of protectionist policy, limits the number of products in certain categories that a nation can import. The United States has import quotas on a number of products, including beef and sugar. The goal of a quota is to prevent other countries from flooding the market with products, thereby driving down the price (according to the laws of supply and demand, which we discussed in the last chapter).

An **embargo** is a complete ban on the import or export of a certain product or the stopping of all trade with a particular country. Political disagreements have caused many countries to establish embargoes. The goal of an embargo generally is to get a country to change its policies. For example, the United States does not agree with many of Cuba's policies; therefore, we do not trade with Cuba at all.[24] In addition, the United States also prohibits the export of specific products globally. The Export Administration Act of 1979 prohibits the exporting of goods (e.g., high-tech weapons) that would endanger national security.

Nontariff barriers are not as specific or formal as tariffs, import quotas, and embargoes, but they can be quite detrimental to free trade. It is common for countries to set restrictive standards that detail exactly how a product must be sold in a country. For example, Denmark requires companies to sell butter in cubes, not tubs. This type of policy makes it difficult to trade a particular product with the country and is considered to be a kind of protectionist policy.

trade protectionism
The use of government regulations to limit the import of goods and services.

tariff
A tax on imported goods.

Harmonized Tariff Schedule
A publication by the U.S. government that lists the tariffs and quotas for every imported good.

import quota
Limits the number of products in certain categories that a nation can import.

embargo
Complete ban on goods to or from a country.

nontariff barriers
Restrictive standards that detail exactly how a product must be sold in a country.

Not all Americans see free trade as an economic benefit to our country. The members of the United Steelworkers Union believe the U.S. government should provide protection from global competition. On the other hand, others believe the United States is not capable of producing steel in an effective manner and that the government should not provide protection to this industry.

Another good example of nontariff barriers is Japan's keiretsu. Japan steadfastly argued that it had some of the lowest tariffs in the world and welcomed foreign exporters, yet for many years American businesses found it difficult to establish trade relationships with Japan. Observers insisted that a Japanese tradition, called *keiretsu* (pronounced "careyet-sue"), was the root of the problem. Under keiretsu, major companies (like Mitsui and Mitsubishi) built "corporate families" that forged semipermanent ties with suppliers, customers, and distributors with full support of the government. The Japanese believed such huge corporate alliances would provide economic payoffs by nurturing long-term strategic thinking and mutually beneficial cooperation.[25] As the Japanese economy has faltered, so has keiretsu. U.S. businesses are now finding Japan a friendlier place for their exports.

Despite these barriers to trade, there are many policies in place that are limiting, if not eliminating, barriers to trade.

The General Agreement on Tariffs and Trade and the WTO

In 1948, government leaders from 23 nations throughout the world formed the **General Agreement on Tariffs and Trade (GATT),** which established an international forum for negotiating mutual reductions in trade restrictions. In short, the countries agreed to negotiate to create monetary and trade agreements that might facilitate the exchange of goods, services, ideas, and cultural programs. In 1986, the Uruguay Round of the GATT was convened to specifically deal with the renegotiation of trade agreements. After eight years of meetings, 124 nations at the Uruguay Round voted to modify the GATT.[26] The U.S. House of Representatives and Senate approved the new agreement in 1994. Under the agreement, tariffs were lowered an average of 38 percent worldwide, and new trade rules were expanded to areas such as agriculture, services, and the protection of patents.

The Uruguay Round also established the **World Trade Organization (WTO),** which on January 1, 1995, assumed the primary task of mediating future trade disputes. The WTO, headquartered in Geneva, Switzerland, and comprising 151 member nations, acts as an indepen-

General Agreement on Tariffs and Trade (GATT)

An agreement signed by many countries to reduce the restrictions on trade with one another. It is overseen by the WTO.

Antiglobalization protests in Seattle, Prague, and Genoa (pictured here). The demonstrations vented their fear that globalization was being controlled by multinational corporations. They believe these entities have worked for their own benefit and addressed the needs of developing countries.

dent entity that oversees key cross-border trade issues and global business practices. It is the world's first attempt at establishing a global mediation center.[27] Trade issues are expected to be resolved within 12 to 15 months instead of languishing for years, as was the case in the past.

However, before you get the impression that all is well in global trade, it is important to note that the formation of the WTO did not totally eliminate the national laws that impede trade expansion. Therefore, in November 2001, a new round of talks (this time called the WTO Round) took place at Doha, Qatar, in the Persian Gulf.[28] Key topics discussed included dismantling protection of manufactured goods, eliminating subsidies on agricultural products, and overturning temporary protectionist measures that impede global trade. While the efforts of the WTO are admirable, many tough decisions lie ahead. The admission of China to the WTO in December 2001, along with the Chinese commitment to free trade, promises to stir differing emotions within the WTO.

Common Markets

One of the issues not resolved by the GATT rounds or at the WTO is whether common markets will create regional alliances at the expense of global expansion. A **common market** (also called a *trading bloc*) is a regional group of countries that have a common external tariff, no internal tariffs, and the coordination of laws to facilitate exchange among member countries. Two such common markets, the European Union (EU) and the South American Common Market (called Mercosur), are worth looking at briefly (see Figure 3.4). Common markets reflect nations' desire to be an economic union (using the same currency) as well as to have a means for focusing efforts on free trade.

World Trade Organization (WTO)

An organization that mediates trade disputes between countries and also sets policies in place to encourage trade.

common market

Regional group of countries that have a common external tariff, no internal tariffs, and the coordination of laws to facilitate exchange among member countries (also called a *trading bloc*).

figure 3.4

STEPS TO ECONOMIC
INTEGRATION OF THE
EUROPEAN UNION

This is an overview of the EU's major political, economic, and monetary achievements, from the signature of the Treaty of Rome in 1957 to the single currency of 13 Member States in 2007.

1950	May 9, Robert Schuman launches the idea of a European Community for steel and coal, created by the Treaty of Paris in 1951, which expired in 2002.
1957	The Treaties of Rome are signed, establishing the European Economic Community and the European Atomic Energy Community.
1958	The first European Commission takes office under Walter Hallstein.
1968	Customs Union is completed: all internal customs duties are removed and a common external tariff is applied.
1969	The Werner report sets out a path toward EMU (European Monetary Union).
1971	The Bretton Woods monetary system is partially abandoned; economic instability results.
1972	The European monetary "snake" is adopted to limit currency fluctuations between currencies.
1973	First enlargement: Denmark, the UK, and Ireland join.
1975	The European Regional Development Fund is set up to support the poorest regions; it later becomes one of the Structural Funds, spending a significant part of the EU budget.
1978	The European Monetary System is launched consisting of an Exchange Rate Mechanism based on the ECU, a basket of all the Community's currencies. It proves successful in promoting currency stability for the next decade.
1981	Second enlargement: Greece joins.
1984	The first EU Framework Program for Research and Development is launched.
1986	Third enlargement: Spain and Portugal join; the Single European Act sets a deadline for achieving the Single Market in 1992.
1989	The Delors report maps out the road to EMU in three stages; the Madrid Council agrees on a timetable to achieve EMU; the Berlin Wall comes down, ending the division of Europe.
1990	Launch of the first stage of EMU: economic policy coordination and the removal of obstacles to financial integration.

European Union (EU)

An agreement among European member countries to eventually reduce all barriers to trade and become unified both economically and politically.

The **European Union (EU)** began in the late 1950s as an alliance of six trading partners (then known as the Common Market and later the European Economic Community).[29] Today the EU is a group of 25 nations that united economically in the early 1990s. The objective was to make Europe—the world's second largest economy (behind the United States) with almost 20 percent of the world's GDP and representing some 360 million people—an even stronger competitor in global commerce. Europeans see economic integration as the major way to compete for global business, and particularly to compete with the United States. The EU may grow to 27 nations by 2008 because Bulgaria and Romania have been accepted.[30]

The path to European unification was not easy. A significant step was taken on January 1, 1999, when the EU officially launched its joint currency, the euro. The formal transition occurred three years later on

1991   The Maastricht economic convergence criteria are agreed on.

1992   Signature of the Maastricht Treaty.

1992-93 Foreign exchange speculation destabilizes the ERM and forces several currencies out: the fluctuation bands are widened.

1993   The Single Market is now in operation: goods, services, people and capital move freely throughout the EC (the "four freedoms").

1994   Start of the second stage of EMU: nominal convergence and creation of the European Monetary Institute (EMI), the forerunner of the ECB.

1995   Fourth enlargement: Austria, Finland, and Sweden join.

1997   The Stability and Growth Pact is agreed on at the Amsterdam European Council.

1998   The European Council and Parliament agree that 11 of the 15 Member States meet the criteria to adopt a single currency; the European Central Bank is created with a mandate to decide monetary policy for the euro area.

1999   The euro is launched as the single currency for 11 Member States. National banknotes and coins continue to circulate as subdivisions of the euro until 2002.

2000   European Union Charter of Fundamental Rights sets out the whole range of civil, political, economic, and social rights of European citizens and all persons resident in the EU.

2001   Greece joins the euro area.

2002   Euro banknotes and coins are introduced across the 12 euro-area Member States; the Erasmus program, started in 1987, celebrates its millionth student studying abroad.

2004   Fifth enlargement: the three Baltic States, Poland, Hungary, the Czech Republic, and Slovakia, Slovenia, Cyprus, and Malta join; constitutional treaty is signed, though rejection in French and Dutch referenda subsequently prevent its full ratification.

2007   Bulgaria and Romania join the Union, bringing membership to 27, and Slovenia joins the euro area.

Adapted from: The European Union Web site, http://ec.europa.eu/economy finance/een/006/article_5210_en.htm, April 2007.

January 1, 2002, when the separate currencies of 12 of the EU nations were transformed into a single monetary unit. EU members Great Britain, Sweden, and Denmark elected not to convert to the euro at that time. European businesses expected to save billions each year on currency conversions that had to be made prior to the introduction of the euro.

The EU clearly hopes that having a unified currency will bring its member nations more economic clout, as well as more buying power and greater economic and political stability. C. Fred Bergsten, director of the Washington-based Institute for International Economics, suggests that the euro will certainly be a worthy challenger to the U.S. dollar in global markets due to the economic strength and size of the EU. In late 2002 and early 2003, his words rang true as the dollar fell below the euro in value for the first time. The euro continues to climb as compared to the dollar.[31]

Mercosur is a common market made up of Brazil, Argentina, Paraguay, Uruguay, and associate members Chile and Bolivia. Mercosur was formed using an agreement called the Treaty of Asuncion, which was signed in 1990. Like the EU, Mercosur had ambitious economic goals that included a single currency. There was even talk of an agreement combining Mercosur and the Andean Pact (which includes Venezuela, Colombia, Peru, and Ecuador) that would pave the way for an economic free trade zone spanning South America. However, more than a decade after its formation, the Mercosur trade bloc seems to be on shaky ground. With currency problems in Brazil and a 2001 financial crisis in Argentina, Mercosur partners such as Chile are looking for better economic prospects elsewhere. The Mercosur nations have work to do if they want to attain their objectives.

Organization of the Petroleum Exporting Countries (OPEC)

OPEC

An organization, consisting of 12 oil-producing countries, to work collectively for oil interests.

OPEC is a major force today around the world. Because of the increased use of petroleum worldwide, OPEC is becoming ever more important to the world economy.

OPEC started in 1960 and today has 12 members: Algeria, Angola, Indonesia, Iran, Iraq, Kuwait, Libya, Nigeria, Qatar, Saudi Arabia, United Arab Emirates, and Venezuela. The mission of the organization includes the following:[32]

1. To coordinate and unify the petroleum policies of the member countries and to determine the best means for safeguarding their individual and collective interests.

2. To seek ways and means of ensuring the stabilization of prices in international oil markets, with a view to eliminating harmful and unnecessary fluctuations.

3. To provide an efficient economic and regular supply of petroleum to consuming nations and a fair return on capital to those investing in the petroleum industry.

The North American Free Trade Agreement (NAFTA)

North American Free Trade Agreement (NAFTA)

An agreement signed by the United States, Mexico, and Canada to reduce or eliminate tariffs on goods and to encourage trade between the countries.

A widely debated issue of the early 1990s was the ratification of the **North American Free Trade Agreement (NAFTA),** which created a free trade zone across the United States, Canada, and Mexico, the merits of which continue to be a political issue. It is important to note that NAFTA is quite different from an economic union and common market, such as the EU, which takes free trade to a much higher level than does NAFTA. The objectives of NAFTA were to (1) eliminate trade barriers and facilitate cross-border movement of goods and services among the three countries; (2) promote conditions of fair competition in this free trade area; (3) increase investment opportunities in the territories of the three nations; (4) provide effective protection and enforcement of intellectual property rights (patents, copyrights, etc.) in each nation's territory; and (5) establish a framework for further regional trade cooperation.[33]

Opponents of the ratification of NAFTA—led primarily by organized labor unions and business entrepreneur and former presidential candidate Ross Perot—warned of serious economic consequences if the U.S. Congress passed this agreement. Their primary concern focused on the loss of U.S. jobs and they predicted significant amounts of capital leaving the United States. In contrast, supporters predicted that NAFTA would open a vast new market for U.S. exports that would create jobs and market opportunities in the long term. In 1994, Congress approved NAFTA and President Bill Clinton signed it into law. Today, the three NAFTA countries have a combined population of 417 million people and a gross domestic product (GDP) of more than $11 trillion.[34] According to the agreement, the United States, Canada, and Mexico can lower trade barriers with one another while maintaining independent trade agreements with nonmember countries.

Since its approval, NAFTA has met with both success and difficulties. On the positive side, U.S. exports to NAFTA partners have increased approximately 85 percent, and Mexico has fared even better, experiencing a 225 percent increase in trade flows and replacing Japan as America's number two trading partner (behind Canada). On the downside, the devaluation of the Mexican peso in 1995 forced the United States to commit $30 billion in aid to Mexico. Also, it is estimated that the United States has lost almost 1 million jobs since the signing of NAFTA.[35]

Furthermore, annual per capita income in Mexico (about $7,300) still lags considerably behind that of the United States ($43,560) and Canada ($32,590)[36] causing illegal immigration to remain a major problem. Other concerns—such as a need for child labor laws and environmental protection, among many others—promise to keep NAFTA a much debated topic.

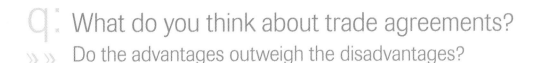

q: What do you think about trade agreements?

» » Do the advantages outweigh the disadvantages?

SELF-CHECK QUESTIONS

1. Why do countries engage in protectionist policies? Do you agree with using these policies in global business? Why or why not?

2. What are the advantages and disadvantages of countries agreeing to be part of a common market?

3. Do you think NAFTA should consider using a common currency?

STRATEGIES FOR REACHING GLOBAL MARKETS

licensing

Selling the right to manufacture a product or use a trademark to a foreign company (the licensee) for a fee (a royalty).

There are several strategies a business can use to enter the global market (see Figure 3.5). Note that a company can be involved in global business in varying degrees. Many smaller companies first "try out" the market by licensing or exporting. Then, as their success grows, they may consider getting more involved in global business.

Licensing

A firm (the licensor) may decide to compete in a global market by **licensing** the right to manufacture its product or use its trademark to a foreign company (the licensee) for a fee (a royalty). A company with an interest in licensing generally needs to send company representatives to the foreign producer to help set up the production process. The licensor may also assist or work with a licensee in such areas as distribution, promotion, and consulting. Simply put, a licensing agreement is simply one where a company allows another company to produce goods under their name. Of course, there can be benefits but many challenges to this as well.

A licensing agreement can be beneficial to a firm in several different ways. Through licensing, an organization can gain additional revenues from a product that it normally would not have generated in its home market. In addition, foreign licensees often must purchase start-up supplies, component materials, and consulting services from the licensing firm. Such agreements have been very profitable for companies like Disney, Coca-Cola, and PepsiCo. These firms often enter foreign markets through licensing agreements that typically extend into long-term service contracts. For example, Oriental Land Company and the Hong Kong government have licensing agreements with Walt Disney Company.[37] Oriental Land Company owns and operates Tokyo Disneyland and Tokyo Disney Sea Park under a licensing agreement. Licensing can also

figure 3.5

STRATEGIES FOR REACHING GLOBAL MARKETS

Licensing   Exporting   Franchising   Contract manufacturing   International joint ventures and strategic alliances   Foreign direct investment

LEAST   Amount of commitment, control, risk, and profit potential   MOST

Developing Skills for a Successful Career

Career planning and development are comprehensive skills that cannot be obtained by a single learning experience. To capture the necessary skills to become competent in building your career, you must perform many tasks, achieve some initial goals, and over time apply your growing body of knowledge pertaining to how to advance your career.

What skills will you need to become better at developing and executing your career goals? The list might look like this:

- Leadership skills
- Management skills
- Team-building skills
- Problem-solving skills
- Analytical skills
- Planning skills
- Marketing skills
- Empathetic listening skills
- Industry knowledge
- Technology skills

work well for small companies that have come up with a new product. A licensing agreement would allow a company to produce and sell the new product overseas.

However, companies that enter into licensing agreements may also experience some problems. One major problem is that often a firm must grant licensing rights to its product for an extended period, sometimes 20 years or longer. If a product experiences remarkable growth and success in the foreign market, the bulk of the revenues earned belong to the licensee. Perhaps even more threatening is that a licensing firm is actually selling its expertise in a product area. If a foreign licensee learns the company's technology or product secrets, it may break the agreement and begin to produce a similar product on its own. If legal remedies are not available, the licensing firm may lose its trade secrets, not to mention the agreed-upon royalties.

Exporting

As global competition has intensified, the U.S. government has created Export Assistance Centers (EACs) to provide hands-on exporting assistance and trade-finance support for small and medium-size businesses that choose to directly export goods and services. A nationwide network of EACs now exists in over 100 U.S. cities, with further expansion planned.[38] In 2002, over 50,000 small and medium-size businesses were helped by EACs.[39] This activity is critical because it is estimated that over 95 percent of the exporters in the United States are small and medium-size businesses.[40] EACs represent a strong source of future federal export promotion efforts.

A Pepsi sign hanging above a crowded New Delhi street. Pepsi and other American companies generate additional business from global markets, primarily through license agreements.

franchise agreement

An arrangement whereby someone with a good idea for a business sells the rights to use the business name and sell a product or a service to others in a given territory.

franchisor

A company that develops a product concept and sells others the rights to make and sell the product.

franchisee

A person who buys a franchise.

Still, even with the help of EACs available, many U.S. firms are reluctant to go through the trouble of establishing foreign trading relationships. In such cases specialists called export-trading companies (or export-management companies) are available to step in to negotiate and establish the trading relationships desired. An export-trading company not only matches buyers and sellers from different countries but also provides needed services (such as dealing with foreign customs offices, documentation requirements, even weights and measures) to ease the process of entering global markets. Export-trading companies also help exporters with a key risky element of doing business globally: getting paid.

Pizza Hut has locations around the world, and as a result, needs to appeal to different tastes. Franchises like Pizza Hut and McDonald's know the world is a big place and preferences in food can vary considerably.

Franchising

A **franchising agreement** is an arrangement whereby someone with a good idea for a business sells (the **franchisor**) to others (the **franchisees**) the rights to use the business name and sell the product or service (the franchise) in a given territory. Franchising is popular both domestically and internationally. Franchising is different from licensing in that where licensing might be for a single product, franchising allows the use of an entire *concept* including the label, how the good is manufactured or made, and the look and feel of the business. U.S. franchisors such

McDonaldizing the World

The United States changed the landscape of the global market with the tremendous expansion of franchising. Today small, midsize, and large franchises cover the globe, offering business opportunities in areas from exercise to donuts to education. Still, when the word *franchise* comes to mind, one name dominates all others: McDonald's. "McDonaldization" symbolizes the spread of franchising and the weaving of American pop culture into the world fabric. Whether in South Africa, Mexico, Germany, Brazil, or Hong Kong, no one adapts better and blends the franchise values into the local culture better than McDonald's.

For example, after setting up its first franchises in Hong Kong in 1975, McDonald's altered the breakfast menu after realizing that customers liked burgers for breakfast, then preferred chicken or fish for the rest of the day. The company also offers unique products such as curry potato pie and red bean sundaes for its Hong Kong customers. In Israel, all meat served in McDonald's restaurants is 100 percent kosher beef. The company also closes its restaurants on the Sabbath and on religious holidays. However, the company also operates nonkosher restaurants for Israelis who don't keep a strict kosher diet and desire to visit McDonald's on the Sabbath and religious holidays. To meet the unique challenge in India and respect the religious sentiments of the population, the company did not introduce beef or pork into the menu.

In Hong Kong, Israel, India, and all other markets in which McDonald's operates, the company continuously listens to customers and adapts to their culture and preferences. The company also must respond to problems and challenges that emerge at its more than 30,000 global restaurants—challenges such as the outbreak of mad cow disease in Europe and Asia. Profits fell by over 14 percent in Japan because of the outbreak of the disease. McDonald's is now funding research for a product that would let it test for the presence of *E. coli* or mad cow disease in its beef. Weak currencies in many countries (e.g., Brazil, Argentina) and government regulations also cause McDonald's global grief. In fact, in Beijing the company was told to remove 30 of its large landmark golden arches in the city because they didn't fit with the surrounding architecture. In 2003, the company closed 600 restaurants globally due to poor market conditions.

Yet, with all its problems and challenges, McDonald's is the leading restaurant in the world, serving over 47 million customers worldwide per day. By using adaptive strategies in global markets, the company has reaped a large payoff. Today, McDonald's derives more than half of its sales from abroad. Still, the challenge goes on. Some critics even ask whether the golden arches are doomed to fall. It seems the key question is: Can Ronald McDonald make meals all around the globe "happy meals"? Time will tell.

Questions

1. What has McDonald's done that has made it successful globally?

2. What do you think McDonald's needs to do in the future to stay successful?

3. Do you think McDonald's should investigate new global markets? Why or why not?

Sources: Carol Matlack and Pallavi Gogoi, "What's This? The French Love McDonald's?" *BusinessWeek,* January 13, 2003, p. 50; and "Big Mac Dips into Giant Loss," *The Mirror* (UK), January 24, 2003, p. 2.

as McDonald's, 7-Eleven, and Dunkin' Donuts have many global units operated by foreign franchisees. Global franchising is not limited to only the large franchisors. For example, Rocky Mountain Chocolate Factory, a Colorado-based producer of premium chocolate candies with 235 retail stores worldwide, entered into a franchising agreement with the Muhairy Group of the United Arab Emirates.[41] The Muhairy Group will open stores in Saudi Arabia, Oman, Kuwait, Bahrain, and Qatar, where chocolate is considered a gourmet luxury much like caviar is in the United States.[42]

Franchisors, however, have to be careful to adapt their product or service to the countries they serve. For example, KFC's first 11 Hong

Kong outlets failed within two years.[43] Apparently the chicken was too greasy, and eating with fingers was too messy for the fastidious people of Hong Kong. McDonald's made a similar mistake when entering the Netherlands market. It originally set up operations in the suburbs, as it does in the United States, but soon learned that the Dutch mostly live in the cities.[44] Pizza Hut originally approached the global market using a strategy of one-pie-fits-all. The company found out the hard way that Germans like small individual pizzas, not the large pies preferred in the United States. Preferences in pizza toppings also differ globally. Japanese customers, for example, enjoy squid and sweet mayonnaise pizza,[45] which is yet another example of why companies research before beginning their overseas ventures.

Contract Manufacturing

contract manufacturing

When one country produces goods with another country's company label on it.

Contract manufacturing involves a foreign company's production of private label goods to which a domestic company then attaches its own brand name or trademark. The practice is also known as *outsourcing*.[46] For example, Dell Computer contracts with Quanta Computer of Taiwan to make notebook PCs, on which it then puts the Dell brand name. Many other well-known U.S. firms, such as Levi-Strauss and Nike, practice contract manufacturing. Most of the clothing industry is involved in contract manufacturing, as is Cisco Systems, the world leader in Internet-routing gear, which depends heavily on contract manufacturers such as Solectron and Flextronics to manufacture its products.[47]

Contract manufacturing enables a company to experiment in a new market without incurring heavy start-up costs such as a manufacturing plant. If the brand name becomes a success, the company has penetrated a new market with relatively low risk. A firm can also use contract manufacturing temporarily to meet an unexpected increase in orders.

One of the major disadvantages is that intellectual property and copyright laws are different in every country. For example, let's say you get a really great idea for an innovative way to provide water to your dog while riding in the car. You spend lots of time and money building a model of this new product and decide to have it produced in China—where because of lax copyright laws, the manufacturer can copy your innovative design for a dog water dispenser and sell it itself. As global trade becomes more important, a worldwide standard for intellectual property laws will become more of a necessity.

International Joint Ventures and Strategic Alliances

joint venture

A partnership in which two or more companies (often from different countries) join to undertake a major project for a specified time period.

A **joint venture** is basically a partnership in which two or more companies (often from different countries) undertake a major project. According to Coopers & Lybrand, a New York–based international professional services firm, companies that engage in partnerships grow much faster than their counterpart companies that do not.[48] Joint ventures can even be mandated by governments as a condition of doing business in their country. It's often hard to gain entry into China, but agreeing to a joint venture with a Chinese firm can help a company gain such entry. For example, Volkswagen and General Motors entered into joint ventures with Shanghai Automotive Industrial Corporation, China's largest domestic car company, to build cars in China.[49]

Joint ventures are developed for other business reasons as well. Campbell Soup Company formed joint ventures with Japan's Nakano Vinegar Company and Malaysia's Cheong Chan Company to expand its rather low share of the soup market in both countries. Global Engine Alliance, a combination of DaimlerChrysler, Mitsubishi Motors, and Hyundai Motor Company, is a joint venture that will develop aluminum engines that will be used by both Asian manufacturers and DaimlerChrysler's U.S. Chrysler unit. Joint ventures can also bring together unique partners. For example, a few years ago, the University of Pittsburgh and the Italian government entered a joint venture to bring a new medical transplant center to Sicily.

The benefits of international joint ventures are clear:

1. Shared technology.
2. Shared marketing and management expertise.
3. Entry into markets where foreign companies are often not allowed unless their goods are produced locally.
4. Shared risk.

The drawbacks are not so obvious. An important one, however, is that one partner can learn the other's technology and practices, and then go off on its own and use what it has learned. Also, over time, a shared technology may become obsolete or the joint venture may become too large to be as flexible as needed.

An alternative to a joint venture is a Greenfield investment. A **Greenfield investment** means that a company will enter into a country and build factories and offices on its own. Of course, the disadvantage to this might be lack of knowledge of the country's ways of doing business. A Greenfield investment is a form of foreign direct investment that will be discussed later in this section.

Global market potential is also fueling the growth of strategic alliances. A **strategic alliance** is a long-term partnership between two or more companies established to help each company build competitive market advantages. Such alliances can provide access to markets, capital, and technical expertise. Unlike joint ventures, however, such alliances do not typically involve sharing costs, risks, management, or even profits. Many executives and management consultants predict that few companies in the 21st century will succeed in the global market by going it alone;[50] most will need strategic alliances. Strategic alliances can be flexible, and they can be effective between firms of vastly different size. Motorola, a large communications equipment manufacturer, once entered a strategic alliance with a small Canadian firm with only six employees. Oracle Corporation, a leader in computer software, has alliances with 19,500 different partners

Greenfield investment
When a company decides to enter a country and build offices and production facilities.

strategic alliance
An agreement between two or more companies to work together to achieve competitive market advantages.

Doing Bad by Trying to Do Good

The CEO of a major pharmaceutical manufacturer decided to set up what she considered to be a generous program to fight the growing AIDS epidemic in developing countries. She decided her company would give its expensive AIDS-related drug for free to government clinics in several of the poor countries. To her surprise, the decision was roundly booed by many humanitarian groups, which complained the company should instead lower the price of the drug so that everyone could afford it rather than give it away to only part of the affected population. The company currently charged regular customers approximately $8 for one pill. Critics claimed that the company could lower the price to 40 cents per pill (a few cents over cost) and really help fight the dreaded disease. Puzzled by the reaction, the CEO said, "We are doing more than anyone else and are still criticized. We should work together to fix this problem."

QUESTIONS

1. What are the CEO's alternatives? What are the consequences of each alternative?
2. What would you do?

that range from giant companies like Apple and Dell to emerging firms like Nantucket Nectars (a maker of juice-based beverages).[51] Many airlines also have strategic alliances, such as the one between Alaska Airlines and American Airlines. The airlines agree to offer frequent flyer mileage if a customer is flying on their "partner" airline.

Foreign Direct Investment

foreign direct investment (FDI)

The buying of permanent property and businesses in foreign nations.

Foreign direct investment (FDI) is the buying of permanent property and businesses in foreign nations. As the size of a foreign market expands, many firms increase foreign direct investment and establish a foreign subsidiary. A **foreign subsidiary** is a company that is owned in a foreign country by the home company (called the *parent company*). Such a subsidiary would operate much like a domestic firm in the foreign nation, with production, distribution, promotion, pricing, and other business functions under the control of the foreign subsidiary's management.

foreign subsidiary

A company that is owned in a foreign country by another company (called the *parent company*).

The legal requirements of both the country where the parent firm is located (called the *home country*) and the foreign country where the subsidiary is located (called the *host country*) have to be observed. The primary advantage of a foreign subsidiary is that the home company maintains complete control over any technology or expertise it may possess. The major shortcoming associated with creating a subsidiary is that the parent company is committing a large amount of funds and technology within foreign boundaries. Should relations with the host country falter, the firm's assets could be taken over by the foreign government. Such a takeover is called an **expropriation.** Obviously, creating a subsidiary might not be the best course of action for a smaller business; however, as a small company grows, this option for global business might be feasible.

expropriation

When a host government takes over a foreign subsidiary in a country.

Consumer products giant Nestlé is an example of a major firm with many foreign subsidiaries. The Swiss-based company spent billions of dollars acquiring foreign subsidiaries such as Ralston Purina, Chef America (maker of Hot Pockets), and Dreyer's Ice Cream in the United States as well as Perrier in France.[52] The company continues to look for opportunities around the globe. Nestlé is also an example of a multinational corporation. A **multinational corporation** is an organization that manufactures and markets products in many different countries; it has multinational stock ownership and multinational management. Multinational corporations are typically extremely large corporations, but not all large firms involved in global business are multinationals. For example, a business could literally be exporting everything it produces, thus deriving 100 percent of its sales and profits globally, and still not be considered a multinational corporation. Only firms that have *manufacturing capacity* or some other physical presence in different nations can truly be called multinational.

Becoming involved in global business requires selecting a strategy to enter a market that best fits the goals of the business. As you can see, the different strategies we have discussed reflect different levels of ownership, financial commitment, and risk that a company can assume. Whatever the operating strategy, it is important to be aware of key market forces that affect a business's ability to trade in global markets, the topic of the next section.

multinational corporation

An organization that manufactures and markets products in many different countries; it has multinational stock ownership and multinational management.

SELF-CHECK QUESTIONS

1. Why would a firm choose to export rather than become involved in a joint venture?

2. What do you think would be the best way to get involved in global business as a small soap manufacturer?

3. What are the advantages and disadvantages of creating a subsidiary?

FORCES AFFECTING TRADE IN GLOBAL MARKETS

Succeeding in any business takes work and effort, due to the many challenges that exist in all markets. Understandably, the hurdles are higher and more complex in global markets than in domestic ones. Global businesses must deal with differences in sociocultural forces, economic and financial forces, legal and regulatory forces, and physical and environmental forces. These forces affect any business, big or small, when entering foreign markets. Managers of even the smallest business must be aware of these forces when making strategic decisions.

Section Outline

Forces Affecting Trade in Global Markets

- Sociocultural Forces
- Economic and Financial Forces
- Legal and Regulatory Forces
- Physical and Environmental Forces

culture

The set of values, beliefs, rules, and institutions held to by a specific group of people.

ethnocentricity

Attitude that one's own culture is superior to all others.

Sociocultural Forces

The term **culture** refers to the set of values, beliefs, rules, and institutions held to by a specific group of people.[53] Primary components of a culture can include social structures, religion, manners and customs, values and attitudes, language, and personal communication. If you hope to get involved in global trade, it is critical to be aware of the cultural differences among nations. Geert Hofstede, a researcher on cross-cultural communications, suggests there are five main dimensions of cultures that critically affect communication among nations.[54] Awareness of these five dimensions has become the standard for businesspeople operating overseas, as they pertain to such areas such as gender roles and individualism. See Figure 3.6 for more on Hofstede's five dimensions of culture.

Different nations have very different ways of conducting business, and unfortunately American businesspeople are notoriously bad at adapting to those ways. In fact, American businesspeople have consistently been accused of **ethnocentricity,** which is an attitude that one's own culture is superior to all others. In contrast, foreign businesspeople are very good at adapting to U.S. culture. Think of how effectively German and Japanese carmakers have adapted to Americans' wants and needs in the auto industry. Japanese manufacturer Toyota attributed 70–80 percent of its sales revenues to the American market![55]

You should be aware of the differences in business practices around the world to compete successfully in the global market.

Religion

Religion is an important part of any society's culture and can have a significant impact on business operations. Consider the violent clashes between religious communities in India, Pakistan, Northern Ireland, and the Middle East—clashes that have wounded these areas' economies. Unfortunately, companies at times do not consider the religious implications of business decisions. Both McDonald's and Coca-Cola offended Muslims in Saudi Arabia by putting the Saudi Arabian flag on their packaging. The flag's design contains a passage from the Koran (Islam's sacred scripture), and Muslims feel their holy writ should never be wadded up and thrown away.[56] In another example, an American manager in

1. **Power distance** is the extent to which the less powerful members of organizations and institutions (like the family) accept and expect that power is distributed unequally. This represents inequality (more versus less), but defined from below, not from above. It suggests that a society's level of inequality is endorsed by the followers as much as by the leaders. Power and inequality are extremely fundamental facts of any society, and anybody with some international experience will be aware that all societies are unequal, but some are more unequal than others.

2. **Individualism versus collectivism** is the degree to which individuals are integrated into groups. On the individualist side we find societies in which the ties between individuals are loose: everyone is expected to look after him/herself and his/her immediate family. On the collectivist side, we find societies in which people from birth onward are integrated into strong, cohesive in-groups, often extended families (with uncles, aunts, and grandparents) which continue protecting them in exchange for unquestioning loyalty.

3. **Masculinity versus femininity** refers to the distribution of roles between the genders, which is another fundamental issue for any society to which a range of solutions are found. . . . Studies have revealed that (a) women's values differ less among societies than men's values; (b) men's values from one country to another contain a dimension from very assertive and competitive and different from women's values on the one side, to modest and caring and similar to women's values on the other. The assertive pole has been called "masculine" and the modest, caring pole "feminine." The women in feminine countries have the same modest, caring values as the men; in the masculine countries they are somewhat assertive and competitive, but not as much as the men, so that these countries show a gap between men's values and women's values.

4. **Uncertainty avoidance** deals with a society's tolerance for uncertainty and ambiguity. It indicates to what extent a culture programs its members to feel either uncomfortable or comfortable in unstructured situations. Uncertainty avoiding cultures try to minimize the possibility of such situations by strict laws and rules, safety and security measures, and on the philosophical and religious level by a belief in absolute truth. People in uncertainty avoiding countries are also more emotional, and motivated by inner nervous energy. The opposite type, uncertainty accepting cultures, are more tolerant of different opinions, and they try to have as few rules as possible. On the philosophical and religious level they are relativist and allow many currents to flow side by side. People within these cultures are more matter-of-fact and thoughtful and not expected by their environment to express emotions.

5. **Long-term orientation versus short-term orientation:** values associated with long-term orientation are thrift and determination values associated with short-term orientation are respect for tradition, fulfilling social obligations, and protecting one's "face."

Source: Five dimensions of culture from Geert Hofstede and Gert Jan Hofstede, *Cultures and Organization: Software of the Mind, Revised and Expanded 2nd Edition.* New York: McGraw-Hill USA, 2005. Copyright © 2005 Geert Hofstede. Used with permission.

figure 3.6

HOFSTEDE'S FIVE DIMENSIONS OF CULTURE

Islamic Pakistan toured a new plant under his control. While the plant was in full operation, he went to his office to make some preliminary forecasts of production. As he was working, suddenly all the machinery in the plant stopped. He rushed out, suspecting a power failure, only to find his production workers on their prayer rugs. Upon learning that Muslims are required to pray five times a day, the manager returned to his office and proceeded to lower his production estimates (it should be noted here that the manager should have done research before doing business in the country, making him more aware of how to do business in that culture).

Religion may very well be the most important of sociocultural forces.

Human Resource Management

Sociocultural differences can also affect important business decisions involving human resource management. In Latin American countries, workers believe that managers are placed in positions of authority to make decisions and be responsible for the well-being of the workers under their control. Consider what happened to one American manager in Peru who was unaware of this important cultural characteristic and believed workers should participate in managerial functions. This manager was convinced he could motivate his workers to higher levels of productivity by instituting a more democratic decision-making style than the style already in place. Soon workers began quitting their jobs in droves. When asked why, the Peruvian workers said the new production manager and supervisors did not know their jobs and were asking the workers what to do. All stated they wanted to find new jobs, since obviously this company was doomed because of incompetent managers.

Learning about sociocultural perspectives related to time factors, change, competition, natural resources, achievement, and even work itself can be of great assistance in global markets. Today, before managers and their families are sent on a global assignment, firms often give them training on how to adapt to different cultures. If the company does not provide training, it is up to the individuals to learn about the culture so they may better prepare to respect and deal with the culture when operating within it.

Communication

Sociocultural differences affect not only management behaviors but also global marketing strategies. Marketing, or the process of selling goods to consumers, will be discussed in greater detail in Chapter 8. **Global marketing** is the term used to describe selling the same product in essentially the same way everywhere in the world. Some companies have developed brand names—such as Intel, Nike, IBM, Sony, Ford, Dell, and Toyota—with widespread global appeal and recognition. However, even these successful global marketers often face difficulties. For example, translating an advertising theme into a different language can be disastrous if extreme care is not exercised regarding nuances and connotations of words. To get an idea of the problems companies have faced with translations, see Figure 3.7.

A sound philosophy to adopt in global markets is this: *Never assume that what works in one country will work in another.* Take for example Kids "R" Us, the clothing subsidiary of Toys "R" Us. Several years ago, the company missed its profit projections in Puerto Rico by banking heavily on back-to-school sales. Toys "R" Us planners failed to understand that Puerto Rican kids wear uniforms to school. They wrongly assumed that Puerto Rico's being a territory of the United States made the Puerto Rican market almost identical to the

global marketing

The term used to describe selling the same product in essentially the same way everywhere in the world.

- PepsiCo attempted a Chinese translation of "Come Alive, You're in the Pepsi Generation" that read to Chinese customers as "Pepsi Brings Your Ancestors Back from the Dead."
- Coors Brewing Company put its slogan "Turn It Loose" into Spanish and found it translated as "Suffer from Diarrhea."
- Perdue Chicken used the slogan "It Takes a Strong Man to Make a Chicken Tender," which was interpreted in Spanish as "It Takes an Aroused Man to Make a Chicken Affectionate."
- KFC's patented slogan "finger-lickin' good" was understood in Japanese as "Bite Your Fingers Off."
- On the other side of the translation glitch, Electrolux, a Scandinavian vacuum manufacturer, tried to sell its products in the U.S. market with the slogan "Nothing Sucks Like an Electrolux."

figure 3.7

OOPS, DID WE SAY THAT?

Translation problems can cause disasters for companies doing business in other cultures. Careful attention must be paid to the nuances and connotations of words.

U.S. market. Thousands of similar stories could be told. The truth is that many U.S. companies often fail to think globally. For many years U.S. auto producers didn't adapt automobiles to drive on the left side of the road, as is done in many countries, and they printed owner's manuals only in English. Also, the United States is one of only five nations in the world that still refuses to conform to the metric system.

Since global marketing works only in limited cases, it is critical that U.S. exporters thoroughly research their objectives before attempting to penetrate global markets. "Think global, act local" is a valuable motto to follow.

q: Why are cultural aspects of global business so
»» important for a businessperson to be concerned with?

Economic and Financial Forces

Economic differences can also muddy the water in global markets. Surely it is hard for us to imagine buying chewing gum by the stick instead of by the package. Yet this buying behavior is commonplace in economically depressed nations like Haiti because customers there have only enough money to buy small quantities. You might suspect that with over 1 billion people, India would be a dream market for companies like Coca-Cola and PepsiCo.[57] However, Indians annually consume an average of only three soft drinks per person, compared to the 50-plus *gallons* per person

The euro officially became the common currency of many EU member nations on January 1, 2002. Do you think the euro could replace the American dollar for leadership among the world's currencies?

exchange rate

The value of one nation's currency relative to the currencies of other countries.

Americans consume each year.[58] While it is true some of this uneven consumption may be due to cultural differences, it is also clearly related to the low per capita income level of Indian consumers. Thus, what might seem like the global opportunity of a lifetime maynot be a viable opportunity at all due to economic conditions.

Global financial markets unfortunately do not have a common worldwide currency. Mexicans shop with pesos, South Koreans with won, Japanese with yen, and Americans with dollars. Globally, the U.S. dollar is considered the world's dominant and most stable form of currency. This doesn't mean, however, that the dollar always retains the same market value. In fact, in recent years, the euro has been more valuable than the dollar. Since 2002, the euro has been the official currency of the European Union (EU). It replaced currencies such as the German deutschmark, the French franc, and the Italian lira.

In an international transaction today, one dollar may be exchanged for eight pesos; tomorrow, however, you may get only seven pesos for the same dollar. The **exchange rate** is the value of one nation's currency relative to the currencies of other countries. Changes in a nation's exchange rates can have important implications in global markets.[59] Such changes occur because people trade in currencies just as people trade in stocks. If the value of the dollar is high, the products of foreign producers are cheaper because it takes fewer dollars to buy them, but the cost of U.S.-produced goods become more expensive to foreign purchasers because of the dollar's high value. Conversely, a low value of the dollar means that a dollar is traded for less foreign currency.[60] Therefore, foreign goods become more expensive because it takes more dollars to buy them, but American goods become cheaper to foreign buyers because it takes less foreign currency to buy American goods. Obviously, all this is of huge concern to businesspeople. To earn the highest amount of profit, their hope is that the trading currency (such as the dollar) will remain high and stable.

Changes in currency values cause many problems globally. Consider a multinational corporation like Nestlé, which has over 500 factories and employs over 220,000 workers around the world. Labor costs can vary considerably as currency values shift.[61] Or consider a medium-size company like the H. B. Fuller Company headquartered in St. Paul, Minnesota. Fuller has direct operations in 36 countries in North America, Latin America, Europe, and Asia, making paints, adhesives, and coatings. Company president Al Stroucken believed that the most dramatic problem Fuller faced was dealing with currency fluctuations. The company learned to use currency fluctuations to its advantage by buying raw materials from sources whose currencies were lower in value.[62]

Currency valuation problems can be especially harsh on developing economies. Often, the only possibility of trade in many developing nations

(PRODUCT) RED

The world has become united because of business interests, but what about world health issues? Bono, the lead singer of U2, has a vision to get AIDS medication to Africa through world awareness of the problem. As a result, Bono and chair of DATA, Bobby Shiver, have teamed up and created a line of (PRODUCT) RED products where a portion of the profits from the sale of these products will go to support AIDS medication in stricken areas. They are working with companies such as The Gap and Motor-

THE (RED) MANIFESTO

ALL THINGS BEING EQUAL, THEY ARE NOT.

AS FIRST WORLD CONSUMERS, WE HAVE TREMENDOUS POWER. WHAT WE COLLECTIVELY CHOOSE TO BUY, OR NOT TO BUY, CAN CHANGE THE COURSE OF LIFE AND HISTORY ON THIS PLANET.

(RED) IS THAT SIMPLE AN IDEA. AND THAT POWERFUL. NOW, YOU HAVE A CHOICE. THERE ARE (RED) CREDIT CARDS, (RED) PHONES, (RED) SHOES, (RED) FASHION BRANDS. AND NO, THIS DOES NOT MEAN THEY ARE ALL RED IN COLOR, ALTHOUGH SOME ARE.

IF YOU BUY A (RED) PRODUCT OR SIGN UP FOR A (RED) SERVICE, AT NO COST TO YOU, A (RED) COMPANY WILL GIVE SOME OF ITS PROFITS TO BUY AND DISTRIBUTE ANTI-RETROVIRAL MEDICINE TO OUR BROTHERS AND SISTERS DYING OF AIDS IN AFRICA.

WE BELIEVE THAT WHEN CONSUMERS ARE OFFERED THIS CHOICE, AND THE PRODUCTS MEET THEIR NEEDS, THEY WILL CHOOSE (RED). AND WHEN THEY CHOOSE (RED) OVER NON-(RED), THEN MORE BRANDS WILL CHOOSE TO BECOME (RED) BECAUSE IT WILL MAKE GOOD BUSINESS SENSE TO DO SO. AND MORE LIVES WILL BE SAVED.

(RED) IS NOT A CHARITY. IT IS SIMPLY A BUSINESS MODEL. YOU BUY (RED) STUFF. WE GET THE MONEY. BUY THE PILLS AND DISTRIBUTE THEM. THEY TAKE THE PILLS, STAY ALIVE, AND CONTINUE TO TAKE CARE OF THEIR FAMILIES AND CONTRIBUTE SOCIALLY AND ECONOMICALLY IN THEIR COMMUNITIES.

IF THEY DON'T GET THE PILLS, THEY DIE. WE DON'T WANT THEM TO DIE. WE WANT TO GIVE THEM THE PILLS. AND WE CAN. AND YOU CAN. AND IT'S EASY.

ola to develop (PRODUCT) RED products and donate a portion of the profits to the Global Fund.

In addition to (RED), Bono has spoken with world leaders trying to utilize the power developed countries have to help poorer countries. Business and world health issues seem to be interconnected. It is true we are one world, and in business as in so many other ways we depend on each other. When the world is experiencing a health crisis such as AIDS, the economies of all nations suffer.

---

is through one of the oldest forms of trade: **bartering,** which is the exchange of merchandise for other merchandise or service for service with no money involved.[63] **Countertrading** is a complex form of bartering in which several countries may be involved, each trading goods for goods or services for services. It has been estimated that countertrading accounts for over 20 percent of all global exchanges, especially deals involving developing countries.[64] For example, let's say that a developing country such as Jamaica wants to buy vehicles from Ford Motor Company in exchange for Jamaican bauxite. Ford, however, does not have a need for Jamaican bauxite but does have a need for computer monitors. In a countertrade agreement, Ford may trade vehicles to Jamaica, which then trades bauxite to another country, say India, which then exchanges computer monitors with Ford. This countertrade is thus beneficial to all three parties. With many countries still in the developing stage, there is no question that countertrading will continue in global markets through much of the 21st century. Trading products for products helps businesses avoid some of the financial problems and currency constraints that exist in global markets.

Understanding economic conditions, currency fluctuations, and countertrade opportunities is vital to a company's success in the global market. In financing export operations in the United States, banks have traditionally been the best source of the capital needed for global

bartering

The exchange of merchandise for merchandise or service for service with no money involved.

countertrading

A complex form of bartering in which several countries may be involved, each trading goods for goods or services for services with the others.

1. Haiti
2. Bangladesh
3. Nigeria
4. Myanmar
5. Chad
6. Paraguay
7. Azerbaijan
8. Turkmenistan
9. Tajikistan
10. Indonesia

Source: Transparency International.

figure 3.8

COUNTRIES RATED HIGHEST ON CORRUPT BUSINESS PRACTICES

investment. However, when U.S. banks are not willing to provide export financing, exporters often turn to foreign banks and other sources for financing, which is especially true for small and medium-size businesses. These companies must be creative in scouring the globe for financing.

Legal and Regulatory Forces

In any economy, both the conduct and direction of business are firmly tied to the legal and regulatory environment. In the United States, for example, federal, state, and local laws and other government regulations heavily impact business practices. In global markets, no central system of law exists, so several groups of laws and regulations may apply. This makes the task of conducting global business extremely difficult as businesspeople find myriad laws and regulations in global markets that are often inconsistent. Important legal questions related to antitrust rules, labor relations, patents, copyrights, trade practices, taxes, product liability, child labor, prison labor, and other issues are written and interpreted differently country by country.[65]

American businesspeople are required to follow U.S. laws and regulations in conducting business globally. U.S. legislation, such as the Foreign Corrupt Practices Act of 1977, often creates competitive disadvantages for American businesspeople when competing with foreign competitors.[66] This law specifically prohibits "questionable" or "dubious" payments to foreign officials to secure business contracts. The problem is that this law runs contrary to beliefs and practices in many countries, where corporate or government bribery is not only acceptable but also perhaps the only way to secure a lucrative contract.[67]

For a partial list of countries where bribery or other unethical business practices are most common see Figure 3.8. Fortunately for U.S. companies, the Organization for Economic Cooperation and Development (OECD) is leading a global effort to fight corruption and bribery in foreign markets.

Physical and Environmental Forces

Certain physical and environmental forces can also have an important impact on a company's ability to conduct business in global markets. In fact, technological constraints may make it difficult or perhaps impossible to build a large global market. For example, some developing countries have such primitive transportation and storage systems that international distribution is ineffective, if not impossible, and this is especially true with regard to food, which is often spoiled by the time it reaches the market in certain countries. Compound this challenge with unclean water and the lack of effective sewer systems, and you can sense the intensity of the problem.

American exporters must also be aware that certain technological differences affect the nature of exportable products. For example, houses in most developing countries do not have electrical systems that match those of U.S. homes, in kind or capacity. An American appliance manufacturer obviously would have to take this into consideration, and this adds cost to the development of the product. Also, computer and Internet usage in many developing countries is minimal or nonexistent. You can see how this would make for a tough business environment in general and would make e-commerce difficult, if not impossible.

SELF-CHECK QUESTIONS

1. What are some forces that must be considered in global business? Give an example of a business consideration for each.

2. If you had to choose, which force affecting trade do you think would be the most important to consider for an Internet-based business? What about a business that manufactures paper products?

3. What is countertrade? Give an example not already provided in this chapter.

THE FUTURE OF GLOBAL TRADE

Global trade opportunities grow more interesting each day. New and expanding markets present great potential for trade and development. Changes in technology also have changed the landscape of global trade, as businesses find that many foreign markets are often no farther than a mouse click away. Let's look briefly at issues certain to influence global markets in the 21st century.

Advanced communication has made distant global markets instantly accessible. Also, the lure of over 6 billion customers is hard to pass up. Nowhere is the lure of global markets keener than in the developing countries in Asia, and particularly in the world's most populous country, the People's Republic of China. With more than 1.3 billion people, China is a fast-growing economy that's shifting its economic philosophy from central planning to free markets.[68]

Multinational companies such as General Motors, Caterpillar, and Levi-Strauss have invested heavily in China's future. Not long ago, such investments in China were considered too risky and not worth the effort. Today, however, U.S. companies are flocking to China and are eager to trade with the Chinese. Economists

Kazahkstan extracts over 63 million tons of oil each year. The oil field in the Caspian Sea is expected to be completed in 2008, raising the potential extraction to 3 million barrels of oil per day by 2015.

So, You Want to Be . . . Involved in Global Business

The concepts discussed in this chapter could help you launch a career in global business. There are many options in this field. In fact, just about any company you work for will likely have a global aspect to its operations. If you choose to work for yourself, you might decide to sell your products globally or have them manufactured globally. Either way, there are some general skills you should have.

First, an understanding of the country in which you are doing business is essential. As we discussed in this chapter, a familiarity with the sociocultural, economic, legal, and physical forces will serve you well. If possible, an understanding of the language as well as the customs of the country is extremely helpful.

In a career in global marketing, you develop global strategies for products that will be sold internationally. It is likely you might begin this career track (assuming little or no experience) in an administrative role. Once you have proven yourself in that role, you would likely be given small marketing projects and eventually become an international brand manager or marketer.

If the analytical side of business is more interesting to you, most large banks and financial institutions, such as American Express and Citibank, look for individuals who can analyze financial data from several countries, including currency valuation. This type of job might require you to live in a major metropolitan area, such as New York or London.

If you are an organized project–oriented individual, a job in global planning might be well suited for you. In global planning, it could be your responsibility to ensure parts for manufacturing from all over the world arrive at the specified time and location. Production can be entirely stopped if someone isn't ensuring the raw materials are available. This type of position might be called a sourcer or a planner, depending on the industry. In this type of job, you would do a lot of work on the phone and the Internet. It is also likely you might travel to some of your suppliers' factories to build good relationships.

Whatever track you choose in global business, at one point or another in your career, you will likely be working with individuals from a broad spectrum of countries. Today it is ever more true that it is a small world!

suggest that soon U.S. foreign direct investment could surpass exports as the primary means by which U.S. companies deliver goods to China. Concerns remain about China's one-party political system, its human rights policies, the growing trade imbalance with the United States, and difficulties in China's financial markets. Yet in 2000 the U.S. Congress granted China permanent normal trading rights, paving the way for China's acceptance into the World Trade Organization (WTO) in 2001. Still, many analysts warn that profits will take a long time to materialize for companies doing business with China.

Russia is also a prize coveted by global traders. Like China, Russia presents enormous opportunities. Philip Morris, Bristol-Myers Squibb, and Gillette are multinational firms with manufacturing facilities in Russia. PepsiCo has been doing business with Russia for many years. Chevron/Texaco and Exxon Mobil are hard at work in the Caspian Sea area looking to develop vast oil reserves. However, severe political and social problems still persist in Russia and in many of the former states of the Soviet Union. Even so, Russia's 150 million potential customers, craving American goods, represent an opportunity too good to pass up.

Angela is now a little clearer on where she needs to begin. For her immediate problem, Angela knows she must use contract manufacturing. Using the Internet, she will find a manufacturer who can produce the jewelry for her. Once she speaks with them, she plans to visit the factory and show them her needs before she signs the contract.

As for growing her business, Angela has determined it would be best to begin her foray into global business by simply exporting. She will first develop a Web site where her customers can view her product online and also order online. Then, she will develop the process for shipping goods to customers. She realizes, however, this is a short-term solution. She would obviously like to sell as much as possible, which will be difficult without using advertising to drive people to her Web site. Angela has decided she will export some of her jewelry to Europe. First, she will need to make contact with buyers there. Similar to the U.S. market, she will focus on small boutiques. After she has made contact and signed contracts with the overseas buyers, Angela will expand her production facility and ship directly to her customers in Europe. Angela knows that currency exchange rates will be a major factor to consider, depending on the strength of the dollar and the euro.

Angela now understands some of the forces affecting global business. For example, she knows religion can play a large role in a culture, and therefore she will make sure she does not inadvertently use offensive religious symbols in her designs. At first, she was going to sell her goods in Mexico, but realizes despite the attractiveness of NAFTA and Mexico's proximity to her location, it might not be the best market due to economic factors. Her jewelry is at the high end, and many of her potential customers in Mexico could not likely afford it. Finally, Angela looks into legal factors which could affect selling her jewelry in Europe. She sees there are some tariffs and quotas, which will be handled by the intermediary in Europe she has decided to hire. He will handle the receiving of the goods and also the distribution of goods once they enter Europe.

Finally, Angela would like to develop a global marketing strategy, so she will be sure her slogans and company name do not translate inappropriately into French, Spanish and Italian. After all of these efforts, Angela thinks she will double her revenues by the end of next year!

While China, Russia, and Japan attract most of the attention in Asia, U.S. businesses are not forgetting India (with over 1 billion people), Taiwan, Indonesia, Thailand, Singapore, the Philippines, Korea, and Malaysia. It's easy to see the great potential the Asian market holds for U.S. business.

As technology continues its unprecedented growth, markets not only in Asia but also in the rest of the world are instantly accessible. The growth of the Internet and advances in e-commerce enable companies worldwide to bypass normally required distribution channels to reach vast markets.

q: How do you see technology continuing

»» to change global business?

summary

Global business is any activity that seeks to provide goods and services to others across national borders while operating at a profit. There are many advantages of operating globally such as lower costs, newer markets, and enhanced revenues. The United States is the largest exporting and importing nation. Exporting is selling products to other nations and importing refers to buying products from other countries.

Global trade is the exchange of goods and services across national borders. The comparative advantage theory suggests that a country should sell to other countries those products that it produces most effectively and efficiently, and buy from other countries the products that it does not produce effectively and efficiently. Absolute advantage is having a monopoly on producing a product, which means a company can produce a product more efficiently than any other company.

The effectiveness of global trade is measured by two key indicators: balance of trade and balance of payments. The balance of trade refers to the ratio of exports to imports, whereas the balance of payment is the difference between exports and imports. The balance of payments also reflects the money received from tourism, foreign aid, military expenditures, and foreign investments.

Trade protectionism and trade agreements act as barriers to free trade. Trade protectionism such as tariffs and quotas limit the import of goods and services. Governments also use embargoes and nontariff barriers as tools to limit or restrict imports. The General Agreement on Tariffs and Trade (GATT), overseen by the World Trade Organization (WTO), was signed by many countries to reduce the trade restrictions with one another. Trading blocs such as the European Union (EU) and the North American Free Trade Agreement (NAFTA) create common markets for their members. Whether this free trade in common markets takes place at the expense of free global trade is the issue GATT needs to resolve.

There are several strategies a business can use to enter the global market ranging from licensing to foreign direct investment. Licensing refers to selling the right to manufacture a product or use a trademark to a foreign company for a fee. Exporting is the next level of commitment. Franchising is an arrangement whereby someone with a good idea for a business sells to others the right to use the business name and sell a product or a service to others in a given territory. Contract manufacturing, joint ventures, strategic alliances, and foreign subsidiaries are entry strategies with progressively increasing levels of commitment.

Finally, the chapter addresses the different forces that affect any business operating in a global arena. These forces are sociocultural, economic and financial, legal and regulatory, and physical and environmental forces. Managers of even the smallest business must be aware of these forces when making strategic decisions.

key terms

global business 72	**import quota** 79	**franchisee** 88
exporting 73	**embargo** 79	**contract manufacturing** 90
importing 74	**nontariff barriers** 79	**joint venture** 90
free trade 74	**General Agreement on Tariffs and Trade (GATT)** 80	**Greenfield investment** 91
global trade 74		**strategic alliance** 91
comparative advantage theory 74	**World Trade Organization (WTO)** 81	**foreign direct investment (FDI)** 92
absolute advantage 75	**common market** 81	**foreign subsidiary** 92
balance of trade 76	**European Union (EU)** 82	**expropriation** 92
trade surplus 76	**OPEC** 84	**multinational corporation** 93
trade deficit 76	**North American Free Trade Agreement (NAFTA)** 84	**culture** 94
balance of payments 76		**ethnocentricity** 94
dumping 78		**global marketing** 96
gray market 78	**licensing** 86	**exchange rate** 98
trade protectionism 79	**franchise agreement** 88	**bartering** 99
tariff 79	**franchisor** 88	**countertrading** 99
Harmonized Tariff Schedule 79		

applying your skills

1. Call or visit a business involved with importing foreign goods (such as a wine importer). Talk with the owner or manager about the problems and joys of being involved in global trade. Compile a list of advantages and disadvantages. Then get together with others in the class and compare notes.

2. Consider the cultural dimensions of Geert Hofstede mentioned in this chapter (see again Figure 3.6). Give some additional thought to them, and research them further if possible. If you had to choose one as most important when doing business overseas, which do you think it would be and why?

3. In a team or alone, prepare a short list of the advantages and disadvantages of trade protectionism. Share your ideas with others in the class and debate the following statement: The United States should increase trade protection to save American jobs and American companies.

4. Research the World Bank. Discuss three projects it has recently funded in developing countries.

5. Look up the Harmonized Tariff Schedule for the United States. Discuss five products that you can find in this schedule and discuss the tariffs charged for them.

6. Many U.S. firms have made embarrassing mistakes when trying to sell products overseas. Sometimes the product is not adapted to the needs of the country, sometimes the advertising makes no sense, sometimes the color or packaging is wrong, and so forth. Find an example of such a marketing mistake (one not provided in this chapter) and suggest how the company could have been more responsive to the needs of foreign markets. If possible, use a graphics program to illustrate a more appropriate advertisement or packaging option.

7. Jake Bower is a candidate for the U.S. House of Representatives from your district. He just delivered an excellent speech at your college. He spoke at great length on the topic of tariffs. His major arguments were that we need tariffs to

   a. Provide revenues.

   b. Protect our young industries.

   c. Encourage Americans to buy U.S.-made products because doing so is patriotic.

   d. Keep our military strong.

   e. Protect American workers and wages.

   f. Help us maintain a favorable balance of trade.

   g. Create a favorable balance of payments.

   Do you agree with Mr. Bower? Evaluate each of his major points by indicating whether you consider it valid or invalid. Justify your position.

8. Choose a good, service, or idea that you would like to market to a specific country. Identify the benefits of supplying the product to this market. Identify the sociocultural, economic and financial, legal and regulatory, and physical and environmental forces you might encounter. Provide alternatives you can use to address these forces.

the internet in action

Using research from human development reports (http://hdr.undp.org), financial data (www.worldbank.org), and population data (www.un.org/popin), answer the following questions. Be sure to properly cite your work.

1. Choose a product "your company" manufactures. Then decide which countries are most likely to buy your products.

2. Prepare a list of the 20 countries in the world with the largest populations.

3. Of the countries you listed in the previous question, which would be good countries to sell carbonated soft drinks in? Women's make-up? Electric shavers? Which might not be good places to sell these products?

4. Looking at the human development reports, which country do you think has the most potential to use technology regularly within the next 10 years? Which has the least potential?

DEMONSTRATING ETHICAL BEHAVIOR AND SOCIAL RESPONSIBILITY

WomenVenture

As the president of WomenVenture, Tené Wells is the essence of social responsibility. Tené Wells is one of those visionary people who see potential everywhere they look and by doing so, help others. Helping others is the core of being socially responsible. WomenVenture, the nonprofit organization she heads in the Twin Cities area (Minnesota), is a great example of a company that was founded on social responsibility and continues to thrive based on it. The goal of the organization is to teach women of all ages and levels of education and income how to thrive economically. The group's programs include business development to help women

Tené Wells

start small businesses, career planning for women, and financial literacy so women can become financially stable.

Tené first came to the agency she now leads to get some help for herself in crafting a winning résumé. In the mid-70s she was college-bound when she got pregnant. To support her twin daughters, she dropped out of school. After a series of odd jobs, she realized she needed a better life for her girls. "That's why I feel so strongly that our clients shouldn't have to settle, either. I needed a good job with growth potential and health benefits so I could make a life for us."

LEARNING objectives

After reading this chapter, you should be able to:

1. Define *ethics* and understand the approaches and the process of making an ethical decision.

2. Distinguish between compliance-based and integrity-based ethics codes, and list the five steps in setting up a corporate ethics code.

3. Describe the indicators of corporate social responsibility.

4. Examine corporate responsibility to various stakeholders.

5. Describe how social responsibility can be measured.

6. Discuss ethics and social responsibility on a global level.

In 1999, after a 20-year career at Honeywell and Medtronic, a medical technology company, she became president of the group that had helped launch her. At the time, WomenVenture's mission statement was to help women achieve economic self-sufficiency.

She sought new corporate and private funding and began offering popular market-driven courses. Today WomenVenture serves more than 5,000 women annually. One especially popular program teaches the skills for construction trades. For entrepreneurs in the Business Development program, the group offers micro-loans of up to $35,000. What makes her business socially responsible? It is the fact that it cares about others and that the organization's motive is to help others. It is businesswomen like Tené who not only inspire women around her, but also teach us what corporate social responsibly and good ethics are about.

Sources: Excerpt from "Women Who Inspire Us" Tené Wills, 11/1/06, "African American Women Step Up in the Business World," *USA Today,* August 24, 2006.

ETHICS IN BUSINESS

The American public was shocked when it learned in 2001 that Enron, the now bankrupt energy-trading company, created off-the-books partnerships to hide debts and losses. Enron's auditors were also found guilty of obstructing justice by shredding documents that related to the audit of Enron. This dishonesty caused deep concern among the American public about the honesty of businesspeople and corporations. Unfortunately, the Enron disgrace was soon followed by more scandals at major companies like Xerox, WorldCom, Tyco International, and ImClone.[1] Congress has stepped in to pass new legislation intended to make business more responsive to ethical concerns. Nevertheless, the truth is that there are plenty of honest businesspeople and companies out there who resolve to help others and who behave ethically. In this chapter we will discuss what it means to conduct business ethically.

ethics

The standards of moral behavior; that is, behavior that is accepted by society as right versus wrong.

Ethics Defined

We define **ethics** as our understanding of the standards of moral behavior—behavior toward others that is accepted by society as right versus wrong. Many Americans today have few moral absolutes. Many decide situationally whether it's okay to steal, lie, or drink and drive, for instance. They seem to think that what is right is whatever works best for the individual; that

Volunteers from PacifiCare Corporation came together from around Southern California to build one of two houses for families whose homes were destroyed during Hurricane Katrina. The houses will be constructed, then dissembled and shipped via semitruck to Texas, where they will then be rebuilt and completed on the site where the Katrina victim families are staying. PacifiCare paid $1,000,000 for the privilege of building a house for this project.

Marge Green, human resource assistant at a medium-size insurance company, was just told by her boss that she needs to develop an ethics standards program. Marge didn't take any courses that included ethics in college, so she did some research on the Internet to help her get started in writing the ethics standards program. But she was still unsure whether she understood every aspect of the program she was charged to

create. Although she understood intuitively what it means to be ethical, she also felt she should give more thought to the subject so she could be confident she would be personally satisfied with the program she would create. So she decided to read this chapter in the text to find out more on the subject.

each person has to work out for himself or herself the difference between right and wrong. That is the kind of thinking that has led to the recent scandals in government and business in America and in other countries. There is, in fact, a deep agreement in society as to matters of right and wrong and when individuals think otherwise they may be heading for disaster. In other words, as contributing members of society, businesses and individuals must meet the ethical standards of society or risk facing the consequences, as the recent scandals bear witness.

Religion and culture are generally our sources of ethics, which sometimes makes determining the "right" ethical course to take in a given situation a difficult task, since religion and culture vary among people. You can probably easily think of a number of recent and current issues in American public life about which people greatly disagree as to the "right" course to take in resolving them.

In a country like the United States, with so many diverse cultures, you might think it almost impossible to identify common standards of ethical behavior. However, among our various sources of ethics from many different times and places, we find astonishing similarity of values and standards for what is right and wrong. Think of such various sources as the Bible, Aristotle's *Ethics*, the Koran, and the *Analects* of Confucius, among many others, and you'll find in them the following basic moral guidelines: Integrity, respect for human life, self-control, honesty, courage, and self-sacrifice are right. Cheating, cowardice, and cruelty are wrong. Furthermore, all of the world's major religions support a version of the Golden Rule, even if it is stated only in the negative form: Do not do unto others as you would not have them do unto you. In other words, no matter where we live, ethics should, in a general sense, be the same. Of course, as a practical matter this isn't always the case, because even if they are operating from the same

Ethical Culture Crash

Communications and electronics giant Motorola describes itself as dedicated to "uncompromising integrity." Robert W. Galvin, Motorola's chair of the board, says that the company's ethical values and standards are an "indispensable foundation" for the company's work, relationships, and business success. But almost half of Motorola's employees are non-American, and more than half of its revenues come from non-American markets. Is it difficult for Motorola employees to adhere to the company's ethical values while at the same time respecting the values of the host countries in which Motorola manufactures and markets its products? Here's an example of how corporate ethics can clash with cultural ethics.

Joe, the oldest son of a poor South American cloth peddler, managed to move to the United States, earned an engineering degree, and got a job with Motorola. After five years, Joe seemed to have bought into the Motorola culture and was happy to have been granted a transfer back to his home country. Joe was told that the company expected him to live there in a safe and presentable home of his choice. To help him afford such a residence, Motorola agreed to reimburse him a maximum of $2,000 a month for the cost of his rent and servants. Each month Joe submitted rental receipts for exactly $2,000. The company later found out that Joe was living in what was, by Western standards, a shack in a dangerous slum area of town. Such a humble home could not have cost more than a couple hundred dollars a month. The company was concerned for Joe's safety as well as for the effect the employee's unseemly residence would have on Motorola's image. The human resource manager was ultimately concerned about Joe's lack of integrity, given that he had submitted false receipts for reimbursement. Joe was upset with what he considered the company's invasion of his

The giant accounting firm Arthur Andersen became famous for shredding Enron-related documents. While Andersen employees shown here thought it was funny to give document shredding lessons at an Arthur Andersen Night before an Oregon baseball game in 2002, no one is laughing now. Andersen's 28,000 employees lost their jobs when the company was found guilty of obstructing the government's investigation of Enron. The verdict was later overturned. Although the document shredding was eventually deemed to be legal, do you believe it was ethical?

basic values, people's cultures intervene to cloud particular issues. For example, consider a situation that happened with Motorola, a communications and electronics company, described in the Ethical Challenge box.

Keep in mind that ethics are not the same thing as the law. Generally, something that is **illegal** is also unethical, but the reverse is not always the case. *Illegal* means you could be fined or imprisoned by a court of law for engaging in a particular action. Something unethical doesn't always have to be illegal. For stealing company funds you could go to jail; such behavior is also obviously unethical. What about gossiping maliciously behind fellow employees' backs? It is not illegal to do so, but might be considered unethical. Remember, ethical standards are right versus wrong behavior according to society, down to the smallest actions in some cases. But as members of society we are also individuals with our own personal cultural backgrounds.

privacy. He argued that he should receive the full $2,000 monthly reimbursement that all of the other Motorola employees received. He explained his choice of housing by saying that he was making sacrifices so he could send the extra money to his family and put his younger siblings through school. This was especially important since his father had died and his family had no one else to depend on but Joe. "Look, my family is poor," Joe said, "so poor that most Westerners wouldn't believe our poverty even if they saw it. This money means the difference between hope and despair for all of us. For me to do anything less for my family would be to defile the honor of my late father. Can't you understand?"

Often it is difficult to understand what others perceive as being ethical. Different situations often turn the clear waters of "rightness" downright muddy. In Joe's case, one could see that Joe was trying to do the honorable thing for his family. One could also argue that Motorola's wish to have its higher-level people live in safe housing was not unreasonable, given the danger-

ous conditions of the city in which Joe lived. The policy of housing reimbursement supports Motorola's intent to make its employees' stay in the country reasonably comfortable and safe, not to increase their salaries. If Joe worked in the United States, where he would not receive a housing supplement, it would clearly be unethical for him to falsify expense reports in order to receive more money to send to his family. In South America, though, the issue is not so clear.

Questions

1. What do you think about the situation described here? Is there a genuine clash of ethical values, or is one side right and the other wrong?

2. What would you do if you were human resource manager at Motorola?

3. What would you do if you were Joe and the manager told you that your point of view was unacceptable?

Often this is what makes determining the right ethical course of action so difficult. It is what makes it difficult to understand what others perceive as being ethical or unethical.

PERSONAL ETHICS

Personal ethics are what guide us in making the right decisions. Many people use the idea "Will I be able to get away with it?" as a way of making ethical choices, which is not the best way to go about making ethical decisions! It takes some deeper consideration of an issue to find the right thing to do. We consult our consciences and we know that law, religion, and culture help define our ethics, but how can we ensure we are making correct ethical decisions?

There are five main approaches we can use when trying to make an ethical decision because we cannot always base ethics on law nor is it sufficient to consult our feelings in many cases. Rather, ethics must be based on some universally applied principles, such as the five shown in Figure 4.1.

Another framework we can use when making ethical decisions was developed by the Markkula Center for Applied Ethics at Santa Clara University. According to the framework, there are eight main

illegal

An action for which you could be fined or imprisoned.

Section Outline

Personal Ethics
- Five sources

figure 4.1

FIVE SOURCES OF ETHICAL STANDARDS

Source: Reprinted with permission of the Markkula Center for Applied Ethics at Santa Clara University.

1. THE UTILITARIAN APPROACH

Some ethicists emphasize that the ethical action is the one that provides the most good or does the least harm, or, to put it another way, produces the greatest balance of good over harm. The ethical corporate action, then, is the one that produces the greatest good and does the least harm for all who are affected—customers, employees, shareholders, the community, and the environment. Ethical warfare balances the good achieved in ending terrorism with the harm done to all parties through death, injuries, and destruction. The utilitarian approach deals with consequences; it tries both to increase the good done and to reduce the harm done.

2. THE RIGHTS APPROACH

Other philosophers and ethicists suggest that the ethical action is the one that best protects and respects the moral rights of those affected. This approach starts from the belief that humans have a dignity based on their human nature or on their ability to choose freely what they do with their lives. On the basis of such dignity, they have a right to be treated as ends and not merely as means to other ends. The list of moral rights, including the right to make one's own choices (such as about what kind of life to lead), to be told the truth, to not be injured by another, to have privacy, and so on, is widely debated; some now argue that nonhumans have rights, too. Also, it is often said that rights imply duties, in particular, the duty to respect others' rights.

3. THE FAIRNESS OR JUSTICE APPROACH

Aristotle and other Greek philosophers have contributed the idea that all equals should be treated equally. Today we use this idea to say that ethical actions treat all human beings equally, or if unequally, then fairly based on some standard that is defensible. We pay people more based on their harder work or the greater amount that they contribute to an organization, and say that is fair. But there is a debate over CEO salaries that are hundreds of times larger than the pay of others; many ask whether the huge disparity is based on a defensible standard or whether it is the result of an imbalance of power and hence is unfair.

4. THE COMMON GOOD APPROACH

The Greek philosophers have also contributed the notion that life in community is a good in itself and our actions should contribute to that life. This approach suggests that the interlocking relationships of society are the basis of ethical reasoning and that respect and compassion for all others—especially the vulnerable—are requirements of such reasoning. This approach also calls attention to the common conditions that are important to the welfare of everyone. This may be a system of laws, effective police and fire departments, health care, a public educational system, or even public recreational areas.

5. THE VIRTUE APPROACH

A very ancient approach to ethics is that ethical actions ought to be consistent with certain ideal virtues that provide for the full development of our humanity. These virtues are dispositions and habits that enable us to act according to the highest potential of our character and on behalf of values like truth and beauty. Honesty, courage, compassion, generosity, tolerance, love, fidelity, integrity, fairness, self-control, and prudence are all examples of virtues. Virtue ethics asks of any action, "What kind of person will I become if I do this?" or "Is this action consistent with my acting at my best?"

principles we should be concerned with in determining our own personal ethics:

- Concern for the well-being of others.
- Respect for the autonomy of others.
- Trustworthiness and honesty.
- Willing compliance with the law (with the exception of civil disobedience).
- Basic justice; being fair.
- Refusing to take unfair advantage.
- Benevolence; doing good.
- Preventing harm to others and the world around us.

On a day-to-day basis, we are all required to make ethical decisions. Should we download music to our computer that we didn't pay for? Should we run the stop sign, since no one is looking? Should we tell when we know one of our friends is cheating? We can use a five-step process to ethical decision making to help make ethical decisions in our personal lives:

1. *Recognize an ethical issue.* First, does the issue go beyond what the law requires? Can the conflict potentially have impact on individuals? If the answer is yes to these questions, you are probably dealing with an ethical issue.

2. *Get the facts.* What are the important aspects of this situation to be aware of? Whom does it impact? Are there some people who have a personal stake in how the ethical situation might turn out? Getting the facts in a situation allows us to see all sides of it.

3. *Evaluate alternative actions.* You may use the five sources of ethical standards (see Figure 4.1) to help you evaluate alternatives. Consider which option would do the most good and the least harm to the majority of individuals. Ask yourself if you would be okay with having your actions reported on the front page of a newspaper. If you had to explain your decision on television, would you be comfortable doing so?

4. *Act on your decision.* Put your ethical decision making into action as best you know how. In some cases it may be good to discuss things with a friend or mentor.

5. *Reflect on your decision.* Was it the right thing to do? Did you feel comfortable after the decision was made? Is there anything you would do differently?[2]

On a daily basis, we are all required to make ethical decisions. This type of framework allows us to better understand the ramifications of our decisions before we make them.

Just like individuals, corporations and those who run them must make ethical decisions on a daily basis as well. In the next section we will discuss ethics in a corporate environment.

CORPORATE ETHICS

Unlike the more informal way we make decisions based on our personal ethics, companies have found they must have a formal code of ethics by which employees must abide. Eighty-nine percent of the organizations surveyed recently by the Ethics Resource Center have written codes of ethics.[3] Whether or not a business has a written ethics code seems to be determined by the size of the company. Ninety percent of the organizations with more than 500 employees have written standards.[4] Keep in mind, however, that writing down ethical standards is much different than actually following them!

Although ethics codes vary greatly, they can be classified into two major categories: *compliance-based ethics* and *integrity-based ethics*.

Compliance-based ethics codes emphasize preventing unlawful behavior by increasing control and by penalizing wrongdoers. Whereas compliance-based ethics codes are based on avoiding legal punishment, **integrity-based ethics codes** define the organization's guiding values, create an environment that supports ethically sound behavior, and stress a shared accountability among employees. In both codes of ethics, the leadership of the company must set the pace for ethical standards. In other words, the leadership cannot act unethically and expect employees to act ethically.

The following five-step process can help improve America's business ethics:

1. Top management must adopt and unconditionally support an explicit corporate code of conduct.
2. Employees must understand that expectations for ethical behavior begin at the top and that senior management expects all employees to act accordingly.

compliance-based ethics codes

Prevent unlawful behavior by increasing control and penalizing violations.

integrity-based ethics codes

Define the organization's guiding values and create an environment that supports ethically sound behavior.

figure 4.2

STRATEGIES FOR ETHICS MANAGEMENT

FEATURES OF COMPLIANCE-BASED ETHICS CODES		FEATURES OF INTEGRITY-BASED ETHICS CODES	
Ideal:	Conform to outside standards (laws and regulations)	**Ideal:**	Conform to outside standards (laws and regulations) and chosen internal standards
Objective:	Avoid criminal misconduct	**Objective:**	Enable responsible employee conduct
Leaders:	Lawyers	**Leaders:**	Managers with aid of lawyers and others
Methods:	Education, reduced employee discretion, controls, penalties	**Methods:**	Education, leadership, accountability, decision processes, controls, and penalties

3. Managers and others must be trained to consider the ethical implications of all business decisions.

4. Outsiders such as suppliers, subcontractors, distributors, and customers must be told about the ethics program. Pressure to put aside ethical considerations often comes from the outside and it helps employees resist such pressure when everyone knows what the ethical standards are.

5. The ethics code must be enforced. It is important to back any ethics program with timely action if any rules are broken so all employees know that the code is serious. This last step is perhaps the most critical. No matter how well intended a company's ethics code is, it is worthless if it is not enforced. An ethics office must be set up. Phone lines to the office should also be established so that employees who don't necessarily want to be seen with an ethics officer can inquire about ethical matters anonymously.[5]

Sarbanes-Oxley

The **Sarbanes-Oxley Act,** also called the Corporate and Criminal Fraud Accountability Act, passed in 2002, has proved to be the most comprehensive act of its kind in regard to ethics. The bill passed into law with an overwhelming majority in Congress in response to the unethical behavior that occurred in the early part of the 2000s. Sarbanes-Oxley has been extremely important in requiring companies to act ethically.

The act has several components. First, **whistleblowers** (people who report illegal or unethical behavior) received greater protection from retaliation.[6] Second, the act set forth new penalties for boards of directors, accounting firms, and management if inaccurate or fraudulent financial reporting is found. In fact, CEOs (the chief executive officer is usually the person who runs and is responsible for an entire company) actually have to sign off on the financials, making them more accountable. Last, the act founded a new public agency that oversees, regulates, and inspects accounting firms.[7]

Although it would appear that the Sarbanes-Oxley Act affects only the leaders of a business, this is not true, as it can affect people from all areas of business.[8] For example, the act says that certain paperwork must be kept for a minimum time period. However, when an environmental group at a company gets together to recycle more paper the act can make the job of recycling more challenging since paper cannot be thrown away. The

> **Sarbanes-Oxley Act**
> Legislation passed in 2002 that set new standards for ethical codes of conduct within organizations.

> **whistleblowers**
> People who report illegal or unethical behavior.

As vice president for Corporate Development at Enron, Sherron Watkins sensed something was wrong with the financial reporting. She "blew the whistle" on her bosses at Enron. She is seen here testifying at the Enron Senate Hearings.

bill can affect just about every profession. Consider a situation where a medical assistant sees one of the doctors taking medication home for personal use and not paying for it. The bill protects the medical assistant, as a whistleblower, when she tells upper-level management of this behavior.

Some observers feel Sarbanes-Oxley is flawed. For example, the act only applies to companies that are publicly traded on the stock market, which means that private companies, no matter how large, are not held to the same practices and standards as those that are publicly traded.[9] Another flaw is the financial and time cost to business to implement the act's provisions, especially the cost to small business. In fact, there are many companies that now specialize in selling software to help companies make the transition to this new law.

As you can see, this law impacts both big and small business, investors and employees. It was passed in response to the recent major ethics scandals affecting corporations. It is one of the most far-reaching laws of its kind and time will tell if it is effective in making the changes it was supposed to make.

SELF-CHECK QUESTIONS

1. Define *ethics*.
2. What makes ethical decision making challenging?
3. What was the most recent ethical decision you had to make? After you reflected on your decision, did you feel it was the right one? Why or why not?
4. Do you think compliance-based ethics or integrity-based ethics are best used in a small company? Why?
5. What is a whistleblower?

Section Outline

Corporate Social Responsibility Defined

- Corporate Philanthropy
- Corporate Responsibility
- Corporate Policy

corporate social responsibility

The level of concern a business has for the welfare of society.

CORPORATE SOCIAL RESPONSIBILITY DEFINED

Corporate social responsibility is the concern businesses have for the welfare of society. It goes well beyond merely being ethical. Just as we all need to be good citizens, contributing what we can to society, corporations need to be good citizens as well. Of course, as can be said of many individuals, many corporations behave as good citizens only because they know it fares well for their business.

There are three determinants or categories by which we can judge social performance of a company. Those determinants are corporate philanthropy, corporate responsibility, and corporate policy.

Timberland is a company with a long-standing commitment to community service. The company's "Path of Service" program offers employees 40 hours of paid time off to serve in their communities. Here, at a sales meeting in Jacksonville, Florida, employees gather together for a day of community service. Do companies have responsibilities to the environment beyond obeying environmental laws? What other ways could companies contribute to their communities?

Corporate Philanthropy

Corporate philanthropy is one indicator of social responsibility. It includes charitable donations to nonprofit groups of all kinds. Corporate charitable donations amount to billions of dollars every year.[10] Strategic philanthropy involves companies making long-term commitments to one cause, such as McDonald's founding and support of Ronald McDonald Houses, which house families whose critically ill children require treatment away from home.[11] Philanthropy isn't limited to large corporations, as many small businesses also participate in corporate philanthropy.

corporate philanthropy
An indicator of social responsibility that includes charitable donations.

Corporate Responsibility

Corporate responsibility is all-encompassing because it includes everything from hiring minority workers, making safe products, minimizing pollution, using energy wisely, and providing a safe work environment—that is, everything that has to do with acting responsibly within society. Green Mountain Coffee Roasters is a perfect example of a company that behaves responsibly and has responsible methods. According to a 2006 survey in *Business Ethics* magazine, the company takes a dozen employees a year on tour throughout the coffee-growing regions of South America, hoping the employees will come away with a sense of the hard work and risk taking that go into growing coffee.[12]

corporate responsibility
An indicator of social responsibility that includes the actions the company takes that could affect others.

q : What companies in your area show corporate
»» responsibility?

corporate policy

The position a firm takes on social and political issues.

Corporate Policy

A company's **corporate policy** refers to the position a firm takes on social and political and sometimes internal business ethics issues. See Figure 4.3 for examples. So much news coverage has been devoted to the problems caused by corporations that people tend to get a negative view of the impact that companies have on society. If the news were more balanced, much more could be said about the positive contributions that businesses make. Few people know, for example, that Xerox has a program called Social Service Leave, which allows employees to

figure 4.3

EXAMPLES OF CORPORATE ETHICS POLICIES

Sources: ConMed Corporation, www.conmed.com/investor-ethics.php; The Food Company, 2007, www.thelocalfoodcompany.co.uk/ethical_policy.asp; and *The Olympian,* 2007, www.theolympian.com/ethics/; accessed November 6, 2007.

From ConMed, a company that sells medical products to hospitals:

A "conflict of interest" occurs when an individual's private interest is materially inconsistent with, in tension with, interferes with, or appears to be inconsistent with the interests of the Company. Conflicts of interest are prohibited as a matter of Company policy, unless they have been approved by the Company. In particular, an employee, officer, or director must never use or attempt to use his or her position at the Company to obtain any improper personal benefit for himself or herself, for his or her family, or for any other person.

Any employee, officer, or director who is aware of a conflict of interest or an improper personal benefit or is concerned that a conflict might develop is required to discuss the matter with the ConMed Legal Department promptly.

Ethical Trading Criteria for the Food Company, based in the UK:

1. All employment is freely chosen.
2. All staff are entitled to belong to trade unions and collective bargaining is respected, to the extent permitted by local law.

leave for up to a year and work for a nonprofit organization. While on Social Leave, the Xerox employee gets full salary and benefits, including job security.[13] IBM and Wells Fargo Bank have similar programs. In fact, many companies are jumping on the volunteerism bandwagon by allowing employees to give part-time help to social agencies of all kinds.[14] Hewlett-Packard, according to *Business Ethics* magazine's 2006 list of ethical companies, has a program called Digital Village where it sets up technology for developing communities and teaches them how to use the technology.[15]

Two-thirds of the MBA students surveyed by a group called Students for Responsible Business said they would take a lower salary to work for a socially responsible company. But when the same students were asked to define a socially responsible company, things got complicated. It appears that even those who want to be socially responsible can't agree on what it involves. One way to determine the "right" social responsibility is to look at it from the stakeholders' view: customers, investors, employees, and society in general.

3. Working conditions are safe and hygienic.
4. Child labor is not used.
5. Wages are fair and comparable to other retailers and wherever possible exceed the minimum wage.
6. Deductions from wages as a disciplinary measure shall not be permitted.
7. Working hours are not excessive.
8. No discrimination is practiced.
9. Regular employment is provided for those who are employed on a permanent contract.
10. No harsh, cruel or degrading treatment or practices are allowed.
11. No bribery, corruption, blackmailing or bullying is permitted.
12. Good environmental stewardship is practiced.
13. Suppliers and buyers are both free to sell and buy from any number of other businesses or outlets. No restrictions, as a way of guaranteeing business, are allowed.

RESPONSIBILITY TO STAKEHOLDERS

As we discussed in Chapter 1, a business has many stakeholders, and it has a responsibility toward each of these stakeholders. Here we will discuss a business's responsibility to the following key stakeholders: customers, investors, employees, and the society and the environment.

Customers

One responsibility of business is to satisfy customers by offering them goods and services of real value. A recurring theme of this book is the importance of pleasing customers. This responsibility is not as easy to meet as it seems. Keep in mind that three out of five new businesses fail—perhaps because their owners fail to please their customers. One of the surest ways of failing to please customers is by not being totally honest with them. For example, in 1988 a consumer magazine reported that the Suzuki Samurai was likely to roll over if a driver swerved violently in an emergency. When Suzuki executives denied there was a problem, sales plummeted.[16] In contrast, Daimler-Benz suffered a similar problem in 1997 during a test simulating a swerve around a wayward elk, when its new A-class Baby Benz rolled over. The company quickly admitted a problem, came up with a solution, and committed the money necessary to put that solution into action.[17] In addition, company representatives continued to answer questions in spite of aggressive press coverage. Daimler took out full-page ads that read: "We should like to thank our customers most warmly for their loyalty. You have given us the chance to remedy a mistake."[18] Since the test flip, only 2 percent of the orders for the vehicle were canceled. The solution cost the company $59 million in 1997 and $118 million each year thereafter. Analysts say those costs probably eliminate any profit on the vehicle. However, the quick resolution of the problem protected the company's reputation, thus allowing its other models to become such hits that Daimler's net earnings remained the same. Of course, by protecting its reputation, Daimler is also affecting future sales for its vehicles, benefiting the company in the long run.

The payoff for socially conscious behavior could result in new business as customers switch from rival companies simply because they admire the company's social efforts—a powerful competitive edge. Consumer behavior studies show that, all else being equal, a socially conscious company is likely to be viewed more favorably than less socially responsible companies. The important point to remember is that customers prefer to do business with companies they trust and, even more important, do not want to do business with companies they don't trust.

Investors

Milton Friedman, one of the most well-known American economists, who passed away in 2006, made the classic statement that corporatesocial responsibility means making money for stockholders. Ethical behavior is good for shareholder wealth. It doesn't subtract from the bottom line; it adds to it, which is similar to our last discussion about pleasing customers. Even if a mistake is made, a customer will continue to be loyal if the situation is remedied. In other words, the company will end up with more customers in the long run, which helps increase investor wealth.

Many people believe that it makes financial as well as moral sense to invest in companies that are planning ahead to create a better environment. By choosing to put their money into companies whose goods and services benefit the community and the environment, investors can improve their own financial health while improving society's health.

A few investors, known as inside traders, have chosen unethical means to improve their own financial health. **Insider trading** involves insiders using private company information to further their own fortunes or those of their family and friends. For example, let's suppose you own a publicly traded consulting firm. You know your firm is about to lose its biggest client and you know this will deeply affect your revenue. As a result, you decide to sell 20 percent of your stock in your firm. This is an example of insider trading. You had inside knowledge and information that others did not have, and as a result, you benefited from it.

You may remember the high-profile case of insider trading involving homemaking diva Martha Stewart. It was alleged that Stewart sold her 3,000 shares in ImClone, a pharmaceutical company, just before the government announced it would not approve a promising drug and the company's stock price fell dramatically. Stewart says it was just a coincidence and that she didn't know about the drug's rejection, but her phone records indicate that she made repeated calls that day to her broker. Stewart served jail time and paid fines for her involvement in this scandal. Although not convicted of insider trading, she was convicted of obstruction of justice.

Another form of social responsibility in terms of investors includes honest bookkeeping. WorldCom, for example, admitted that intentional accounting "irregularities" made the company appear $4 billion more profitable than it actually was.[19]

In other words, social responsibility to investors means doing the right thing to make money for stockholders and avoiding potential legal issues by trading stocks fairly and keeping accurate financial records.

Martha Stewart (*left*) leaves federal court in New York on June 4, 2003. Stewart and her former stockbroker both pleaded not guilty to all charges against them in a case built from Stewart's suspiciously timed sale of ImClone Systems, Inc., stock.

insider trading

Insiders of a company (such as employees) using private company information to further their own financial situation.

development

Knowledge Is the Key to Performance

Review the following information about how companies are structured and what that means to new hires, how and where to find potential jobs, and areas you can improve upon to increase your odds of getting hired!

LOOKING INSIDE COMPANIES

The communication of information, such as job opportunities, can be a by-product of the size of the company. Larger companies have many communication outlets such as company newsletters, job posting bulletin boards, and the intranet system (company information posted on the companies' internal Web pages) in which employees can be updated on job openings. Company sizes are defined by their basic structure, which is best described as slim and trim (typically small, family-owned companies), layered (very large, complex organizations), and home offices with satellites (midsize franchise-type companies). Job listings typically come from the human resources department (following legal hiring practices) from whom employees of the company can find out information such as job titles, job descriptions, and pay ranges. Employees often find new job opportunities within their own companies, and good companies do a better-than-average job of posting and communicating these opportunities for the benefit of their own employees.

HOW TO FIND A JOB

Jobs are found on job boards online, in local newspapers (print and online), through the development of your own personal contacts, or through the assistance of employment agencies. While these sources are helpful, the trend today for a comprehensive job search is to post a resume online, positioning yourself to companies that are looking for a larger pool of potential employees to hire. Individuals looking to maximize this job search format will be able to choose types of career titles they would like to pursue (such as education, sales, marketing, etc.) and locations they would have an interest in (major cities such as St. Louis, Chicago, Denver, etc.). These particular job Web sites can also help with creating a cover letter, resume writing, and identifying salary ranges that would also quantify the level of job acceptance you would realistically consider. The sites that are available and helpful to you in this online job search include Monster.com, Job-Hunt.org, JobPier.com, Simplyhired.com, and FedWorld (a Web site for listings of jobs with the federal government).

SKILLS TO AID YOU IN GETTING HIRED

Having the skills needed to perform a job is only one of the tools needed to actually get hired. Following are some important extra steps you can take to be seen as a leading candidate in a pool of job applicants:

- Assessing self-skills—determine what skills you can offer to a potential employer that others may not have.

- Learning career etiquette skills—study and practice proper business dining etiquette, polite phone skills, and professional greetings and introductions in a professional setting.

- Developing career goals—decide where you want to be in your career in one year, five years, and ten years, which will help you determine what you need to do to get there.

- Learning the skill of filling out a job application and submitting a resume—understand the importance of following written directions for applications and presenting yourself accurately in a resume.

- Learning about executing a job interview—practice interviewing skills with a school career counselor, instructor, or friend to evaluate what areas you can improve.

Employees

Businesses have several responsibilities to employees. First, they have a responsibility to create jobs if they want to grow. It has been said that the best social program in the world is a job. Once a company creates jobs, it has an obligation to see to it that hard work and talent are fairly rewarded. Employees need realistic hope of a better future, which comes only through a chance for upward mobility. People need to see that integrity, hard work, goodwill, ingenuity, and talent pay off. If a company treats employees with respect, they usually will respect the company in return.

Another stakeholder issue when it comes to employees is employee pensions. A **pension** is a promise of a steady income after retirement, assuming the employee has worked a minimum number of years with the company. Unfortunately, many companies are reneging on their promises to pay pensions to retirees. Struggling companies such as Ford and GM are having to make hard decisions about the millions of dollars they owe people through their pensions.

> **pension**
>
> A promise made by a company to pay a monthly dollar amount to employees who have worked a minimum number of years.

Given that replacing employees costs about 150 percent of their annual salaries, retaining workers is good for business as well as for morale.[20] When employees feel they have been treated unfairly, they often strike back. Getting even is one of the most powerful incentives for good people to do bad things. Not many disgruntled workers are desperate enough to resort to violence in the workplace, but a great number do relieve their frustrations in more subtle ways, such as blaming mistakes on others, not accepting responsibility for decision making, manipulating budgets and expenses, making commitments they intend to ignore, doing the minimum needed to get by, and making results look better than they are. The loss of employee commitment, confidence, and trust in the company and its management can be very costly—yet unnecessary.

In other words, social responsibility to employees means having a job that pays fairly, where promises are kept, and where people are treated with respect. Diversity is also part of a socially responsible company. According to the 2006 list of socially responsible companies that we mentioned previously, Hewlett-Packard ranked in the top 10 due to its diverse workforce, but also because it trains managers in other countries to look for diverse employees.

Society and the Environment

One of business's major responsibilities to society is to create new wealth. More than a third of working Americans receive their salaries from nonprofit organizations that actually, in turn, receive their money from businesses. Foundations, universities, and other nonprofit organizations own billions of shares in publicly held companies. As those stock prices increase, more funds are available to benefit

Study Skills

The Need to Succeed

We have a "need to succeed," and the objective of this exercise is to help identify the areas that you rate as needing the most attention to help improve your study preparation and study execution effectiveness. (Instructions: Put a number 1 next to the most important area you identify as needing improvement, a number 2 after the next most important in terms of needing your attention, then a number 3 . . . and so on until you reach the end of the list.)

Organization _____

Time management _____

Note taking _____

Listening _____

Writing _____

Reading _____

Prioritizing _____

Memorization _____

Test taking _____

Motivation _____

No more fabric spun by silk worms. Think recycled cola cans and fabric spun from corn. This picture shows Malden Mills, makers of Polartec Fabric made with recycled plastic bottles.

society. Businesses are also partially responsible for promoting social justice. Business is perhaps the most crucial institution of civil society. For its own well-being, business depends on its employees being active in politics, law, churches and temples, arts, charities, and so on. Rhino Entertainment, for example, is a vintage music and video distributor that has a simple mission: "To put out some great stuff, have some fun, make some money, learn from each other, and make a difference wherever we can." Individual staff members are assigned to oversee community and environmental activities. The company has bins for can and paper recycling as well as for clothing donations throughout its offices. Employees receive extra vacation days each year in exchange for 16 hours of community service.[21] They regularly participate in monthly activities at a local youth center. The company budgets a percentage of its revenues to go to charities that empower groups to help themselves. By promoting "doing the right thing" in its company, Rhino ensures that society benefits from its business as well as other social programs.

Businesses are also clearly taking responsibility for helping make their own environment a better place. Environmental efforts may increase a company's costs, but they also may allow the company to charge higher prices, to increase market share, or both. For example, Ciba Specialty Chemicals, a Swiss textile dye manufacturer, developed dyes that require less salt than traditional dyes.[22] Since used dye solutions must be treated before they are released into rivers or streams, having less salt and unfixed dye in the solution means having lower water-treatment costs. Patents protect Ciba's low-salt dyes, so the company can charge more for its dyes than other companies can charge for theirs. Ciba's experience illustrates that, just as a new machine enhances labor productivity, lowering environmental costs can add value to a business.

Not all environmental strategies prove to be as financially beneficial to the company as Ciba's, however. For instance, in the early 1990s StarKist responded to consumer concerns about dolphins dying in the process of tuna fishing because the nets meant to capture tuna also caught dolphins swimming over the yellowfin tuna schools in the eastern Pacific. The company announced that it would sell only tuna from the Western Pacific, where the skipjack tuna do not swim underneath dolphins.[23] Unfortunately, the company found that customers were unwilling to pay a premium for the dolphin-safe tuna and that they considered the taste of the skipjack inferior to that of yellowfin tuna. In addition, it turned out that there was no clear environmental gain: In exchange for every dolphin saved by not fishing in the eastern Pacific, thousands of

- Community-related activities such as participating in local fund-raising campaigns, donating executive time to various nonprofit organizations (including local government), and participating in urban planning and development.
- Employee-related activities such as establishing equal opportunity programs, offering flextime and other benefits, promoting job enrichment, ensuring job safety, and conducting employee development programs.
- Political activities such as taking a position on nuclear safety, gun control, pollution control, consumer protection, and other social issues; working more closely with local, state, and federal government officials.
- Support for higher education, the arts, and other nonprofit social agencies.
- Consumer activities such as ensuring product safety, creating truthful advertising, handling complaints promptly, setting fair prices, and conducting extensive consumer education programs.

figure 4.4

EXAMPLES OF SOCIALLY RESPONSIBLE BUSINESS ACTIVITIES

immature tuna and dozens of sharks, turtles, and other marine animals died in the western Pacific fishing process.

Environmental quality is a public good; that is, everyone gets to enjoy it regardless of who pays for it. The trick for companies is to find the right public good that will appeal to their target market. Many corporations are publishing reports that document their net social contribution. To do that, a company must measure its positive social contributions and subtract its negative social impacts. It is an interesting process that we will discuss next.

MEASURING SOCIAL RESPONSIBILITY

It is nice to talk about having organizations become more socially responsible. It is also encouraging to see some efforts made toward creating safer products, cleaning up the environment, designing more honest advertising, and treating minorities fairly. Keep in mind, however, that the majority of these efforts are made with the profit motive in mind. The companies know they will benefit by satisfying the demands of the customers. While talking about social responsibility is great, there is one measure of a company's social responsibility—a social audit. A **social audit** is a systematic evaluation of a company's progress toward implementing programs that are socially responsible. Normally the social audit is something initiated by the company but is handled by an outsider who specializes in this area.

The challenge is how to measure a company's performance in social audits. The idea is that positive actions (charitable donations, good hiring practices) will be subtracted from negative actions (layoffs, pollution) resulting in a net plus or minus. Another way to measure social responsibility would be to just record positive actions.

Section Outline

Measuring Social Responsibility

social audit
A systematic evaluation of a company's progress toward implementing programs that are socially responsible.

Sharing the Wealth

By giving in times of need, corporations can do good in the community—and for the bottom line.

It's not easy being a modern corporation. Not only is it expected to innovate the next big thing, manufacture it at the lowest possible cost, market it globally, and then blow the doors off the competition in terms of sales, but it is also expected to return significant results to shareholders each quarter, all the while having an elegant long-term strategic plan. On top of that, the modern corporation is expected to be a good citizen, too.

Corporate social responsibility (CSR) has never been more important than it is now, following scandals in highly visible global companies such as Enron, Parmalat, and WorldCom that dragged down the public perception of all corporations. In the public mind, perception equals reality. The result is that corporations today must act more aggressively—and publicly—to restore or maintain their reputations. Yet the world presents a seemingly infinite number of opportunities for them to demonstrate their goodwill: Relief efforts in the wake of the tsunami that devastated Southeast Asia in December 2004 and, more recently, in the United States, the response to Hurricane Katrina and the subsequent flooding

in New Orleans, and the response to the 2007 forest fires in California are the most high-profile examples.

In many ways, corporations behave like individuals. Indeed, many laws even treat corporations that way. W. M. Greenfield, in his article "In the Name of Corporate Social Responsibility" (*Business Horizons,* January–February 2004), writes that in the United States, for example, laws developed in the late 1800s defined a corporation as "an entity separate from the people who owned and operated it—a 'legal person.'" Just as some people seek anonymity in their good deeds while others are more public, many corporations act privately in the interests of the community, whereas others recognize significant advantages to creating a public perception of good citizenship. Increasingly, it is becoming a principle of business strategy to adhere to that old cliché about doing good and telling others about it. Ethicists may debate the differences between being good and acting good. But there's no doubt that regardless of motive, corporations realize significant impact against the bottom line with well-managed CSR programs. For example, according to a survey conducted by the PR firm Hill & Knowlton, 79 percent of Americans take corporate

In addition to the social audits conducted by the companies themselves, there are four types of groups that serve as watchdogs regarding how well companies enforce their ethical and social responsibility policies:

1. *Socially conscious investors* who insist that a company extend its own high standards to all its suppliers.
2. *Environmentalists* who apply pressure by naming names of companies that don't abide by the environmentalists' standards.
3. *Union officials* who hunt down labor law violations and force companies to comply to avoid negative publicity.
4. *Customers* who take their business elsewhere if a company demonstrates unethical or socially irresponsible practices.

What these groups look for constantly changes as the worldview changes. For example, until September 11, 2001, no group formally screened publicly traded companies to determine potential links to terrorism or the spread of weapons of mass destruction. Now some groups have begun to look at companies that may be even peripherally linked as the United States focuses on terrorism.

One important thing to remember is that it isn't enough for a company to be ethical and socially responsible; it must also convince the customers it is, too.

citizenship into account when making purchase decisions, and 71 percent consider it when making investment decisions. Likewise, the "Millennium Poll on Corporate Social Responsibility," for which the research firm Environics International interviewed 25,000 people around the world, revealed that impressions of individual companies are shaped more by corporate citizenship (56 percent) than by brand quality, reputation, or business fundamentals.

Corporate social responsibility, the fashionable management mandate to keep company goals in line with social issues, has gone beyond writing a check to charity or backing a corporate foundation for the tax benefit. Companies are beginning to realize that there is money to be made on social causes—tackling education, technology access, and housing—while applying business models to the problem. Result: Real progress, and money to the bottom line.

For the fourth year in a row, *Latin Trade* asked hundreds of companies in the region to explain their corporate social responsibility policies in detail. Three hundred and forty-three businesses replied, of all shapes and sizes. Of those, 40 percent reported annual sales of more than US $1 billion, while a third of them were small, posting revenues of less than $10 million. Interestingly, 56 percent of the respondents said corporate social responsibility is "integral to their business model."

Sapotek, a small Mexican technology firm, has invented an online desktop computer. For a small $60 fee or for free in many cases, users can draft documents, download their favorite songs, and even run their own personal Web sites. The company hopes to expand its revenue base by allowing distributors to sell its services to businesses and to launch an English version in the United States soon, says company founder Oscar Mondragon.

Questions

1. Do you think that companies engage in CSR programs only so they can "tell people about it" and gain from the publicity?

2. Do you think CSR programs are as important for small businesses as for large businesses? Why or why not?

Source: Excerpts from "Sharing the Wealth" by William Briggs and Archana Verma, *Communication World*, Jan/Feb 2006. Copyright © 2006 International Association of Business communications. Used with permission.

SELF-CHECK QUESTIONS

1. Name and discuss the three indicators of social responsibility.

2. Write down the stakeholders discussed in this chapter. Name at least two social responsibility concerns for each stakeholder.

3. Define *social audit*. Do you think it is a good way of getting companies to act socially responsibly? Why or why not?

ETHICS AND SOCIAL RESPONSIBILITY GLOBALLY

Section Outline

Ethics and Social Responsibility Globally

Ethical problems and issues of social responsibility are not unique to the United States. Top business and government leaders in Japan were caught in a major "influence-peddling" (read: bribery) scheme in Japan.[24] Similar charges have been brought against top officials in South Korea, the People's Republic of China, Italy, Brazil, Pakistan, and Zaire. What is new about the moral and ethical standards by which government leaders are being judged? They are much stricter than in previous years. Top leaders are now being held to a higher standard. Government leaders are not the only ones

So, You Want to Be . . . a CSR Specialist?

Corporate social responsibility is a relatively new career path. Many colleges now offer degrees in ethics and social responsibility. Whatever your educational background, you might qualify as a CSR (corporate social responsibility) specialist if you have demonstrated talents in this area, and a CSR specialist has many career options, both in the private and public sector.

Many of these opportunities exist in CSR departments. For example, Levi-Strauss might hire a CSR specialist to review factories' performance in this area and to write policies relating to human rights.

Another aspect of the CSR department may be public relations. In this job, a specialist would notify the public of the "good" things the company is doing, while this person may be the mouthpiece if something goes wrong and the company must manage a crisis.

Rather than have their own CSR departments, some companies are hiring outside CSR firms to evaluate social responsibility issues. In this case, the individual would be a consultant in CSR.

Many available jobs in this area are not billed as CSR jobs as such, but key phrases to look for would be "human rights programs," "reputation management," and "environmental risk."

Many American companies make a public stand against unethical practices in other countries. However, with the growth of multinational organizations, the lines are blurring when it comes to social and ethical responsibility in global business.

being held to higher standards. Many American businesses are demanding socially responsible behavior from their international suppliers by making sure their suppliers do not violate U.S. human rights and environmental standards.

For example, Sears will not import products made by Chinese prison labor. The clothing manufacturer Phillips–Van Heusen said it would cancel orders from suppliers that violate its ethical, environmental, and human rights code. Dow Chemical expects its suppliers to conform to tough American pollution and safety laws rather than just to local laws of their respective countries. McDonald's denied rumors that one of its suppliers grazes cattle on cleared rain forest land but wrote a ban on the practice anyway.[25] As we have discussed in the last section, it is in the best interest of companies to be socially responsible, as it creates more loyal customers, shareholders, and employees and it benefits society.

The justness of requiring international suppliers to adhere to American ethical standards is not as clear-cut as you might think. Is it always ethical for companies to demand compliance with the standards of their own countries? What about countries where child labor is an accepted part of the society and families depend on the children's salaries for survival? What about foreign companies doing business in the United States? Should they expect American companies to comply with their ethical standards? What about multinational corporations? Since they span different societies, do

Marge Green eagerly started on her ethics program development. First, she interviewed each of the top managers in the company and asked them what their values and the values for the company should be. Since many of the values are also listed in the company's mission statement, she was also able to draw values from that document. After compiling the data, Marge began to develop an integrity-based ethics program, which she had read about in this chapter of the text. For each company value, Marge was able to develop the ideology behind it and the objective, pinpoint who would be responsible for it, and describe the methods used to ensure the code was met. For instance, her first value was diversity:

Ideal: Hire a diverse workforce.

Objective: Allow us to serve customers better.

Leaders: Top managers. Human resources and hiring supervisors.

Methods: Education, application processes, rewrite of hiring manual.

After completing the ethics program document, Marge gave it to her supervisor to look over. Her supervisor was very pleased with her work. The supervisor then told Marge that in order for the program to work, they must get support from upper management, then the new ethics standards must be communicated to all employees, and finally the ethics code needed to be enforced. She asked Marge to write a plan to accomplish all of that, and Marge, with her newfound knowledge, was happy to oblige.

q: Do you think it is right for American companies

»» to have to apply the same ethical standards used domestically when conducting business globally?

they not have to conform to any one society's standards? Why is Sears applauded for not importing goods made in Chinese prisons when there are many prison-based enterprises in the United States? None of these questions are easy to answer, but they give you some idea of the complexity of social responsibility issues in international markets.

In an effort to identify some form of common global ethic and to fight corruption in global markets, the partners in the Organization of American States signed the Inter-American Convention Against Corruption. A similar anticorruption convention was signed by 29 member states of the Organization for Economic Cooperation and Development (OECD) and five other states that are home to nearly all of the major multinational corporations. The OECD convention covers only those companies and governments that offer bribes and not the individuals who accept them.[26] However, such loopholes are expected to be eliminated in the years ahead. In many places "Fight corruption" remains just a slogan, but even a slogan is a start.

q: Offering and accepting bribes happens in corporations
»» globally. Who deserves more punishment—those offering the bribes or those accepting them? What types of loopholes to anticorruption policies including bribery could there be in the next several years?

SELF-CHECK QUESTIONS

1. What are two ethical challenges when doing business overseas?
2. What can we do as customers to ensure companies are acting socially responsibly, both at home and abroad?

---

summary

Our discussion in Chapter 4 started out by defining ethics. Ethics involve obeying moral standards accepted by society. One of the challenges in acting ethically is that ethical sensitivities can vary from person to person. We discussed various ways to make personal ethical decisions. In companies, to set standards for ethics, companies can use compliance-based ethics codes or integrity-based ethics codes. Compliance codes involve forcing behavior and punishing if codes are not followed. Integrity codes are codes that set out the company culture and the ethics expected. No matter which type of code a company uses, the need for ethics codes has heightened over the last few years due to the many scandals that have involved unethical (and illegal) behavior.

Corporate social responsibility is defined as the level of concern a company has for society. There are three types of corporate social responsibility: corporate philanthropy, corporate responsibility, and corporate policy. Corporate philanthropy involves donations to charitable organizations, while corporate responsibility refers to a company's ability to avoid harm and even help society and the environment. Finally, corporate policy is the position a firm takes on political issues.

One way to determine social responsibility is to see what the stakeholders' concerns might be. Customers, the first set of stakeholders, want products to be safe and free from misleading advertising. Investors want to be assured that the accounting and financial statements of the company are accurate. Employees want to be paid a fair wage and be treated with respect. Finally, companies should avoid harm to society and the environment in their policies.

Another way to measure social responsibility is to perform a social audit. A social audit is a review of the positive and negative contributions of a company. The challenge of a social audit is the actual measure that is used.

Last, we discussed ethical challenges when doing business abroad. Some companies require suppliers to follow U.S. rules and have strict rules about importing and exporting. The challenge is that ethics and social responsibility can vary from culture to culture, and the question arises as to whose point of view should prevail.

key terms

ethics 110
illegal 113
compliance-based ethics codes 116
integrity-based ethics codes 116

Sarbanes-Oxley Act 117
whistleblowers 117
corporate social responsibility 118
corporate philanthropy 118

corporate responsibility 119
corporate policy 120
insider trading 123
pension 125
social audit 127

applying your skills

1. What sources have helped shape your personal code of ethics? What influences, if any, have ever pressured you to compromise those standards? Think of an experience you had at work or school that tested your ethical standards. What did you decide to do to resolve your dilemma? Now that time has passed, are you comfortable with the decision you made? If not, what would you do differently?

2. Name the three things that define ethics. Do you think one has more power in determining ethics than the others? Why?

3. Write an ethics policy for any small business either in groups or on your own. Use resources from this chapter as well as additional research to complete this assignment.

4. You are manager of a coffeehouse called the Morning Cup.
   One of your best employees desires to be promoted to a managerial position; however, the owner is grooming his son for the promotion

your employee seeks. The owner's act of nepotism may hurt a valuable employee's chances for advancement, but complaining may hurt your own chances for promotion. What do you do?

5. In groups, use the Internet to review ethics codes of three companies. Determine if each code is compliance based or integrity based. From what you can see, does the corporation adhere to its code? Why or why not?

6. In groups, describe and write down three questionable ethical situations and come up with possible responses. Then, switch your situations with another team's situations and compare possible actions.

7. What are some ethical global human rights issues in our society today? How would you solve these global issues?

8. Do you agree or disagree with the following statement: Corporate responsibility often would not exist if it weren't for the profit motive.

9. Take the test in Figure 4.5. Do you rely on an ethic of justice or ethic of care? Can you think of examples that prove the test correct?

the internet in action

1. *Purpose:* To demonstrate the level of commitment one business has to social responsibility.

   Exercise: Visit the Web site www.gapinc.com. The Gap touts the fact it is a socially responsible company. Explore the section on social responsibility and answer the following questions:

   - What does The Gap focus on in the area of social responsibility?

   - What efforts is The Gap making in each of these areas of focus?

   - Do you think there are any other areas of focus The Gap should include? If so, identify them.

   - How does The Gap communicate its social responsibility actions to investors, employees, and the public? Do you think this is an effective way? Explain.

   - Are there any recent updates to The Gap's social responsibility campaigns? If so, what are they?

2. Newspapers and magazines are full of stories about individuals and businesses that are not socially responsible. What about those individuals and organizations that do take social responsibility seriously? We don't normally read or hear about them. Do a little investigative reporting of your own. Identify a public interest group in your community and identify its officers, objectives, sources and amount of financial support, and size and characteristics of membership. List some examples of its recent actions and/or accomplishments.

Please answer the following questions.

1. Which is worse?
   A. Hurting someone's feelings by telling the truth.
   B. Telling a lie and protecting someone's feelings.

2. Which is the worse mistake?
   A. To make exceptions too freely.
   B. To apply rules too rigidly.

3. Which is it worse to be?
   A. Unmerciful.
   B. Unfair.

4. Which is worse?
   A. Stealing something valuable from someone for no good reason.
   B. Breaking a promise to a friend for no good reason.

5. Which is it better to be?
   A. Just and fair.
   B. Sympathetic and feeling.

6. Which is worse?
   A. Not helping someone in trouble.
   B. Being unfair to someone by playing favorites.

7. In making a decision you rely more on
   A. Hard facts.
   B. Personal feelings and intuition.

8. Your boss orders you to do something that will hurt someone. If you carry out the order, have you actually done anything wrong?
   A. Yes.
   B. No.

9. Which is more important in determining whether an action is right or wrong?
   A. Whether anyone actually gets hurt.
   B. Whether a rule, law, commandment, or moral principle is broken.

To score: The answers fall in one of two categories, J or C. Count your number of J and C answers using this key:
1. A = C; B = J; 2. A = J; B = C; 3. A = C; B = J; 4. A = J; B = C; 5. A = J; B = C; 6. A = C; B = J; 7. A = J; B = C; 8. A = C; B = J; 9. A = C; B = J

What your score means: The higher your J score, the more you rely on an ethic of *justice*. The higher your C score, the more you prefer an ethic of *care*. Neither style is better than the other, but they are different. Because they appear so different they may seem opposed to one another, but they're actually complementary. In fact, your score probably shows you rely on each style to a greater or lesser degree. (Few people end up with a score of 9 to 0.) The more you can appreciate both approaches, the better you'll be able to resolve ethical dilemmas and to understand and communicate with people who prefer the other style.

An ethic of justice is based on principles like justice, fairness, equality, or authority. People who prefer this style see ethical dilemmas as conflicts of rights that can be solved by the impartial application of some general principle. The advantage of this approach is that it looks at a problem logically and impartially. People with this style try to be objective and fair, hoping to make a decision according to some standard that's higher than any specific individual's interests. The disadvantage of this approach is that people who rely on it might lose sight of the immediate interests of particular individuals. They may unintentionally ride roughshod over the people around them in favor of some abstract ideal or policy. This style is more common for men than women.

An ethic of care is based on a sense of responsibility to reduce actual harm or suffering. People who prefer this style see moral dilemmas as conflicts of duties or responsibilities. They believe that solutions must be tailored to the special details of individual circumstances. They tend to feel constrained by policies that are supposed to be enforced without exception. The advantage of this approach is that it is responsive to immediate suffering and harm. The disadvantage is that, when carried to an extreme, this style can produce decisions that seem not simply subjective, but arbitrary. This style is more common for women than men.

To learn more about these styles and how they might relate to gender, go to www.ethicsandbusiness.org/kgl.htm.

Source: Excerpt (quiz) from Thomas I. White, *Discovering Philosophy, Brief Edition,* Copyright © 1996.

Figure 4.5

ETHICAL ORIENTATION QUESTIONNAIRE

ENTREPRENEURSHIP AND STARTING A SMALL BUSINESS

Loomis Sales Corporation

Before Chuck Loomis started his business, Loomis Sales Corporation, he was working for a company that manufactured commercial fishing crab pots. After many years of working for others, Chuck decided that he wanted to work for himself. He found a business broker, who helped him find a business that he could purchase and which matched his interest and expertise.

With a partner, Chuck started his company and focused on plastic injection molding, which is required to make a finished plastic product. One of the challenges of his business is keeping labor costs down so

Chuck Loomis

a reasonable profit can be earned. For a number of years, his business had manufacturing facilities in the United States. But, Chuck and his partner found they could reduce labor costs by over 40 percent by producing their plastic products overseas. Now, the company has all of its production in China.

Once all of the manufacturing facilities moved, Chuck realized he could work out of his home office, rather than spending money on an outside office. He says there are several advantages and disadvantages to having a home office. The advantages are that Chuck is able to save money on office space and

LEARNING objectives

After reading this chapter, you should be able to:

1 Explain the traits a successful entrepreneur possesses.

2 Discuss the types of business ownership and the advantages and disadvantages of each.

3 Describe the alternatives to starting your business from scratch.

4 Understand how a business can grow through mergers, acquisitions, and buyouts.

5 Describe the five main areas of focus when starting a small business.

commute expenses. He also enjoys the flexibility of not having to "punch a clock." The main disadvantage, he says, is that running a home office requires a great deal of self-discipline. On the other hand, because he lives and works in the same place, he must be sure not to work around the clock.

Chuck loves being an entrepreneur because he can change directions quickly, which allows him to be more creative in his business. He says the challenges of running his company include being responsible, not only for the employees but also for the livelihood of their families. For example, if he makes a poor decision, it affects not only his business, but all of those who work for him.

Chuck says that in order to be successful, it is imperative to have a partner agreement if you are not working alone. Second, he emphasizes the need for a business plan, including a strong section on how the company will be marketed. Having a mentor can also be hugely beneficial. He also says knowing your strengths and weaknesses, allowing you to hire people who possess strengths in the areas where you may lack expertise is also a big plus. Knowing a bit about all areas of the business, such as accounting and finance, can also make for a successful entrepreneur.

Just like Chuck, you can be a successful entrepreneur with the drive and ambition to run your own company. The concepts discussed in this chapter will provide you an overview of what it takes to be a successful entrepreneur.

Wacky Grocer Jim Bonaminio may put on his wizard suit and roller skate through his Jungle Jim's International Market, but he's serious when it comes to his business. Instead of competing on price against megagiants like Wal-Mart, Jungle Jim's competes on product variety. A case holding 1,200 kinds of hot sauce rests beneath an antique fire engine. Why do you think customers might remain loyal to Jungle Jim's?

INTRODUCTION TO ENTREPRENEURSHIP

Anyone can start a business. Obviously, there are many people who are not interested in starting their own business; there are many rewarding jobs available for those who do not wish to engage in entrepreneurship. However, entrepreneurship is a great way to apply your business skills to making a business out of a hobby, a passion of yours, or some special skill you possess. If you have the commitment, you may be very successful; but the proper preparation for starting your own business is essential. In this chapter we will discuss the process to be carried out and the decisions that must be made before starting a business of your own.

WHAT DOES IT TAKE TO BE AN ENTREPRENEUR?

One of the major issues facing the United States today is the need to create more jobs. You can get some idea about the job-creating power of entrepreneurs when you look at some of the great American entrepreneurs from the past and the present. The history of the United States is the history of its entrepreneurs. Consider just a few of the many entrepreneurs who helped shape the American economy:

Section Outline

What Does It Take to Be an Entrepreneur?

- Du Pont, which manufactures thousands of products under such brand names as Teflon and Lycra, was started in 1802 by French immigrant Éleuthère Irénée du Pont de Nemours. Some 18 shareholders provided $36,000 in start-up money.[1]

- Avon was started in 1886 with the $500 David McConnell borrowed from a friend.[2]

- George Eastman launched Kodak in 1880 with a $3,000 investment.[3]

- Procter & Gamble was formed in 1837 by William Procter and James Gamble with a total of $7,000 in capital.[4]

- Ford Motor Company began with an investment of $28,000 by Henry Ford and 11 associates.[5]

- Amazon.com began with investments by founder Jeff Bezos's family and friends. Bezos's parents invested $300,000, a huge portion of their retirement account. Today all who initially invested are billionaires![6]

Sam Leung and Richard McDonald are best friends. They have known each other since they were kids. Both have business degrees, and they have decided to open a business selling handcrafted wooden signs. The signs will be custom-made for each customer. While they both have business degrees, Sam is better at woodworking than Richard, although they both have an interest in it. Richard, on the other hand, is very good at accounting and record keeping. Sam and Richard are hoping to start their business within the next six months and need some help getting started, so they have decided to read this chapter and compare notes about it.

- Larry Page and Sergey Brin, two college buddies, founded Google when they were graduate students in 1998. The company started with an initial investment of $100,000 (given to them by one of the founders of Sun Microsystems). The two are now said to be worth $12.8 billion each.[7]

There are many other examples of small businesses growing into large companies not covered by this list. Although these entrepreneurs may not be billionaires (or aim to be), they *are* financially successful and offer important contributions to the communities and the people who are employed by them.

Their stories are remarkably similar: One or more entrepreneurs had a good idea, borrowed, and started a business. Those businesses now employ thousands of people and help the country prosper. Whether it is your goal to become the next conglomerate or to keep your business small and personal, there are common characteristics that all successful entrepreneurs have in common:[8]

- *Self-directed.* You should be thoroughly comfortable with your business and thoroughly self-disciplined, since you are your own boss. You will be responsible for your own success or failure.
- *Self-nurturing.* You must believe in your idea, even when no one else does, and be able to replenish your own enthusiasm. When Walt Disney suggested the possibility of the full-length animated feature film *Snow White,* the industry laughed. His personal commitment and enthusiasm caused the Bank of America to back his venture. The rest is history.
- *Action-oriented.* Great business ideas are not enough. The most important thing is a burning desire to realize, actualize, and build your dream into reality.
- *Highly energetic.* It's your business, and you must be emotionally, mentally, and physically able to work long and hard. For example,

Netflix CEO Reed Hastings sits in a mail delivery case of thousands of DVDs at the distribution plant in San Jose, California. The online DVD rental company is one of the Internet's rising stars. Hastings launched the subscription service in 1999. It grew to one million subscribers in less than four years. With close to 6.8 million users in 2007, the company hopes to reach 20 million by 2010. What advantage does doing business online offer companies like Netflix?

Tabitha Mageto and Remi Pageon, co-owners of Artisan Bakery in Virginia, often spend 18 hours a day in their shop. During the Christmas season, each pulls a 48-hour shift. "But that is better than working 18-hour days for someone else," says Mageto.[9]

- *Tolerant of uncertainty.* Successful entrepreneurs take only calculated risks (if they can help it). Still, they must be able to take some big risks sometimes. Remember, entrepreneurship is not for the squeamish or those with a high need for security.

q: What skills do you think you have that would

»» enable you to engage in an entrepreneurial adventure?

It is important to know that most entrepreneurs don't get the ideas for their products and services from some flash of inspiration. Rather than a flash, the source of innovation is more like a *flashlight*. Imagine a search party, walking around in the dark, shining lights, looking around, asking questions, and looking some more. The late Sam Walton used such a flashlight approach. He visited his stores and those of competitors and took notes. He'd see a good idea on Monday, and by Tuesday every Wal-Mart manager in the country knew about it. He expected his managers to use flashlighting too. Every time they traveled on business, they were expected to come back with at least one idea worth more than the cost of their trip. Even small businesses can use this flashlight approach to continue improving upon their business.

q: How do you think the flashlight approach to

》 》 life and business can help you as a student today?

We know from our discussion so far that starting a business can be risky. Despite this, many people decide to take the risk of becoming an entrepreneur for the following reasons:[10]

- *Opportunity*. The opportunity to share in the American dream is a tremendous lure. Many people, including those new to this country, may not have the skills necessary for working in today's complex organizations. However, they may have the initiative and drive to work the long hours demanded by entrepreneurship. The same is true of many corporate managers who left the security of the corporate life (either by choice or as a result of corporate downsizing) to run businesses of their own. Other people, including an increasing number of people with disabilities, find that starting their own businesses offers them more opportunities than working for others.

- *Profit*. Profit is another important reason to become an entrepreneur. At one time the richest person in America was Sam Walton, the entrepreneur who started Wal-Mart. Now the richest person in America is Bill Gates, the entrepreneur who founded Microsoft Corporation.

- *Independence*. Many entrepreneurs simply do not enjoy working for someone else. Many lawyers, for example, do not like the stress and demands of big law firms. Some have found enjoyment and self-satisfaction in starting their own businesses where they are independent.

- *Challenge*. Some people believe that entrepreneurs are excitement junkies who flourish on taking risks. Nancy Flexman and Thomas

African American Women Step Up in the Business World

More women of color today are taking the lead on the path to entrepreneurship.

Camille Young worked at big businesses for years, until she discovered an idea for her own company during a South Pacific vacation.

Back in New Jersey, she started looking for the food she ate in Fiji, frequenting fresh-juice bars in Manhattan because she couldn't find any near home. "Someone really needs to open a juice bar here," Young recalls thinking.

She quit her bank job last year to open the first of two juice bars in her BaGua Juice chain in Jersey City. She hopes the company will grow to as many as 50 locations.

Young, 34, is one of thousands of African American women starting businesses, research shows, in a trend that's tipping the balance of economic power in the African American community.

As women take entrepreneurship's lead, marketers from banks to tech companies are tapping African American women as a new source of revenue. "It's a huge opportunity," says Angela Burt-Murray, editor in chief of *Essence,* a leading lifestyle magazine for African American women.

African American women are launching companies for many of the same reasons spurring other women. They've gained corporate experience, but a glass ceiling keeps them from rising to the CEO's office. They're better educated. Self-employment offers more flexibility to care for children and aging parents.

Start-up costs have fallen as computers and other technologies grow cheaper. And the economy is shifting even more to retail and service businesses, which are well-suited to corporate refugees.

DRIVING START-UP GROWTH

The new research, published by the Small Business Administration, shows that women drive much of the growth in African American entrepreneurship.

African American women owned 547,341 companies in 2002, up 75% from five years before, when the Census Bureau last counted. The number owned by all men rose a smaller 29%, to 571,670, says the study by economist Ying Lowrey in the SBA's Office of Economic Research.

For the first time since the government began counting, African American women now likely own more companies than African American men, assuming growth rates stayed constant after 2002, says Gwen Martin, director of research at the Center for Women's Business Research.

African American women, like all female owners, still lag behind men by some key measures. The majority of their companies are part-time ventures, often run from home at night or on weekends to supplement daytime pay. Just 5% had employees, vs. 10% for African American men. Annual revenue averaged about $39,000, vs. $114,000 for African American men, Lowrey's research shows.

EXTRA PRESSURE

Still, many aim for bigger ventures, such as BaGua Juice, which employs six part-timers. Young worked for business consulting firms and the Bank of New York after getting degrees from Howard University and New York University's Stern School of Business. She says she was promoted quickly, but grew disenchanted with big-business bureaucracy. Some co-workers with less education but more seniority appeared, unfairly to Young, to get passed over for promotion. "Inequality is a very difficult thing to deal with."

Scanlan, however, in their book *Running Your Own Business,* contend that entrepreneurs take moderate, calculated risks; they are not just gambling.[11] In general, entrepreneurs seek achievement more than power.

Are you ready to be an entrepreneur? Start out by taking the entrepreneurship readiness test at the end of this chapter. Assuming you are ready and plan to start a business someday, the next section of this chapter will discuss how you can get started in your new business venture.

Also, as an African American woman, she felt extra performance pressure. "You must work harder just to be viewed as average," she says.

Young dipped into her 401(k) retirement account and savings for the $80,000 needed to open her first store on the ground floor of a Jersey City apartment building. She's opened a second in a Goldman Sachs cafeteria. Young, who is single, is living on savings until BaGua is profitable.

Lowrey says one of the most important factors fueling women's entrepreneurship is their "dramatically" rising academic credentials. Among African Americans, twice as many women as men earned bachelor's and master's degrees in 2004, the latest government figures show. The gap was narrower 20 years ago. African American women now get about 11% of all bachelor's and master's degrees.

"It just gives them many opportunities to do things on their own," says Martin, at the Center for Women's Business Research. The nonprofit center gets financial support from banks and other big companies seeking to do business with female entrepreneurs.

Mia Jackson, 38, leveraged her education to start a public relations and marketing business in North Bethesda, Maryland partly to solve her child-care quandary.

Jackson got a bachelor's in English from Stanford University. She worked in Charles Schwab's ad department before getting laid off in 2001, when the San Francisco–based discount broker trimmed operations amid a recession.

She moved to the Washington area, where she considered working for another company. But, the single mother no longer wanted to deal with the stressful "day-care dash," rushing out at 5:00 each afternoon to pick up her daughter. She started Doro Marketing Services five years ago, working alone from a home office. Clients include nonprofit groups, small companies, and government agencies. She spent about $15,000 from her 401(k) and from profits generated by the business itself for a computer and other essentials.

Jackson often works 50-hour weeks, including weekends. But as her own boss, she works around her daughter's schedule. "Every time I think about going back in the corporate setting, I can't do it."

CARING FOR AGING PARENTS

Tech-company founder Josie Cheri Lamkin launched Gypsy Lane Technologies to resolve another family challenge: elderly parents.

Lamkin, 34, started Gypsy last year after working for health care companies. It sells graphic design and computer training services. She spent about $30,000 to finish an office in her basement and purchase two desktop computers, a laptop, software, filing cabinets, and furniture.

She launched the business when her father and mother, now 82 and 72, got sick and she needed to spend time at a hospital. Lamkin is the only single adult among her five siblings; responsibility for her parents fell to her.

The time she needed to take off to go to the hospital was a big burden on her employer. Business ownership, she says, "allowed me a lot more flexibility."

Questions

1. Do you think the risks taken to be an entrepreneur are worth it? Why or why not?

2. Would you be willing to quit a high-paying job in order to start a business? Why or why not?

Source: Excerpt from "African American Women Step Up in Business World," Jim Hopkins, *USA Today*, 8/24/06. Copyright © 2007 USA Today. Used with permission.

SELF-CHECK QUESTIONS

1. What characteristics are required to be an entrepreneur? Are there any others not mentioned in the discussion that you think would be helpful?

2. Why do people start new businesses?

TYPES OF BUSINESS OWNERSHIP

In the United States every year 650,000 new businesses are created, triple the number created in 1960.[12] Two-thirds of these new businesses survive at least two years and about 56 percent will fail in the first four years,[13] which results in the entrepreneur being responsible for whatever debts were incurred by the business while it was still in operation. The purpose of this section is to ensure that you choose the correct form of ownership, which may help you incur fewer personal losses if your business does not succeed.

The first task any entrepreneur must do is decide the structure or legal form of the business. Each form has advantages and disadvantages. First we will describe the three main legal forms for a business, and then we will discuss some other important factors in making your new business a success.

Sole Proprietorships

sole proprietorship

A form of ownership that involves one individual.

A **sole proprietorship** is the easiest kind of business to start, and someone who starts a sole proprietorship is an entrepreneur. A sole proprietorship involves one person owning and running a business.[14] It might be a Web site development business run from home, a cabinet building business, or any other type of business in which the owner is an expert and wants to sell his or her skills. A sole proprietorship is a business operated by a **sole proprietor.** There are several advantages to a sole proprietorship, as opposed to the other forms of business.

sole proprietor

The name given to a person who owns a sole proprietorship.

First, all you have to do to start a sole proprietorship is to buy or lease the needed equipment (e.g., a saw, a word processor, a tractor, a lawn mower) and put up some announcements saying you are in business. Of course there are business names and licenses to consider as well. However, it is just as easy to get out of business; you simply stop. There is no one to consult or to disagree with about such decisions. You may have to get a permit or license from the local government, but this is usually very easy to do.

The second advantage is you get to be your own boss. You make all of the decisions and receive the benefits of those decisions. Entrepreneurs are proud of their work. Because many of them work alone; they get to take all of the credit (and risks) for providing goods and services to customers.

Besides the emotional satisfaction of owning a business, retaining all of the profit is a major advantage of a sole proprietorship. Along the same lines, profits from a sole proprietorship are taxed as the personal income of the owner, so there are no special federal taxes the business owner must worry about.

Study Skills

The Value of Time Management

Perhaps the most important personal skill that can enhance your overall effectiveness in reaching personal goals is the ability to manage your time and personal decision making. This skill is known as *time management.*

What time management can do: Provide the biggest payoff in the overall effectiveness of a person's performance.

What happens when time is misused: Life can become chaotic and frustrating when no importance is placed on setting priorities. Undesired outcomes are a result of this lack of development and maturity.

Learn to manage your time!

Despite these advantages, not everyone is equipped to own a business. It is often difficult to save enough money to start a business and keep it going. The cost of supplies, inventory costs (if it is a retail business), rent, and other expenses are sometimes too much to manage. Many would-be entrepreneurs have limited financial resources. It can be difficult for the owner to gather funds because there are limitations on how much an individual can borrow from others.

Many sole proprietors find they have skill gaps that affect their ability to manage a business. For example, someone may be very good at building Web sites, but may lack skill in keeping tax and accounting records. In other words, an entrepreneur must either be able to handle all aspects of the business, or find good people to manage those parts of the business where they lack strength.

The major disadvantage of operating as a sole proprietor, however, is that you, the owner, have **unlimited liability.**[15] This means that, from a financial perspective, there is no distinction between the business and the owner. For example, if the business were to fail, you the owner would be personally responsible for any of the debt you may have incurred in your business.

> **unlimited liability**
> The responsibility of business owners for all of the debts of the business.

Most sole proprietors start businesses because of their interest in the product or service they are selling. However, as you learned from the last section, entrepreneurs typically work many hours. Unlike a typical 8:00 a.m. to 5:00 p.m. job, where you get to leave at a specific time, an entrepreneur may find himself or herself working 8:00 a.m. to 8:00 p.m., or longer.

Another disadvantage is the lack of the fringe benefits that one often receives when working for someone else. Paying for your own sick leave, health insurance, and unpaid vacation time all cut into the profits of an entrepreneur.[16]

Finally, the fact that a sole proprietor has a limited lifespan is a disadvantage. If the entrepreneur dies or retires, the business no long exists (unless of course, it is sold or taken over by heirs).

Many entrepreneurs like their business the way it is, small and personal, and prefer it not to become too large to manage. They realize that trying to do too much for too many customers can make them less effective and may cause them to eventually lose valuable customers, and maybe even their entire business.

However, other sole proprietors may wish to expand their enterprise, but as sole proprietors they may have difficulty doing so and

Warren Brown's career is "rising." Brown left a promising law career to create Cakelove, a bustling bakery that specializes in making pastries from scratch using all-natural ingredients. Cakes, however, are his passion and the company's signature dish. Brown has appeared on the *Oprah* show and is regularly seen on the Food Network. Do you have a passion you would like to pursue as a business?

partnership

Legal form of business with two or more owners.

general partnership

A partnership in which all owners share in operating the business and in assuming liability for the business's debts.

limited partnership

A partnership with one or more general partners and one or more limited partners.

general partner

An owner (partner) who has unlimited liability and is active in managing the firm.

limited partner

An owner who invests money in the business but does not have any management responsibility or liability for losses beyond the investment.

limited liability

Means limited partners are not responsible for the debts of the business beyond the amount of their investment—their liability is *limited* to the amount they put into the company; their personal assets are not at risk.

master limited partnership (MLP)

Structured much like a corporation in that it acts like a corporation and is traded on the stock exchanges like a corporation, but taxed like a partnership and thus avoids the corporate income tax.

growing their business. There will be tips later in this chapter that entrepreneurs can use to obtain additional funding to grow their business.

If choosing to be a sole proprietor is not the right option for you, there are other options—partnership and corporations—that we will address next.

Partnerships

The second type of business ownership is a partnership. A **partnership** is defined as a legal form of business with two or more owners. There are several types of partnerships:[17] (1) general partnerships, (2) limited partnerships, and (3) master limited partnerships. A **general partnership** is a partnership in which all owners share business and financial obligations (debt, for example) of the business.

A **limited partnership** is a partnership with one or more general partners and one or more limited partners. A **general partner** is an owner (partner) who has unlimited liability and is active in managing the firm. Every partnership must have at least one general partner. A **limited partner** is an owner who invests money in the business, but does not have any management responsibility or liability for losses, beyond the investment. **Limited liability** means that limited partners are not responsible for the debts of the business, beyond the amount of their investment—their liability is *limited* to the amount they put into the company; their personal assets are not at risk.

A newer form of partnership, the **master limited partnership (MLP),** looks much like a corporation (which we discuss next) in that it acts like a corporation and is traded on the stock exchanges like a corporation, but it is taxed like a partnership, and thus avoids corporate income tax.

Another newer type of partnership was created to limit the disadvantage of unlimited liability. Many states are now allowing partners to form a **limited liability partnership (LLP).** LLPs limit partners' risk of losing their personal assets to only their own acts and omissions, and to the acts and omissions of people under their supervision.

When discussing partnerships, it is important to know that all states except Louisiana have adopted the Uniform Partnership Act (UPA) to replace other laws relating to partnerships.[18] The UPA was first developed in 1902 and revised several times, with the most recent revision being in 1997. Sometimes it is referred to as RUPA, the Revised Uniform Partnership Act. Ultimately, the UPA is a default agreement that guides the way partners must behave with one another in regard to ownership and shared profit and losses and also addresses the right to participate in managing the operations of the business. Although lawyers should still be consulted when writing a partnership agreement, the UPA can provide good guidelines for writing the agreement.

There are several advantages to a partnership, when compared to the other forms of business ownership. For example, there are more financial resources when two or more individuals can contribute to the business.

It's not hard to form a partnership, but it's wise for each prospective partner to get the counsel of a lawyer experienced with such agreements. Lawyers' services are usually expensive, so would-be partners should read all about partnerships and reach some basic agreements before calling a lawyer.

For your protection, be sure to put your partnership agreement in writing. The Model Business Corporation Act recommends including the following in a written partnership agreement:

1. The name of the business. Many states require the firm's name to be registered with state and/or county officials if the firm's name is different from the name of any of the partners.
2. The names and addresses of all partners.
3. The purpose and nature of the business, the location of the principal offices, and any other locations where business will be conducted.
4. The date the partnership will start and how long it will last. Will it exist for a specific length of time, or will it stop when one of the partners dies or when the partners agree to discontinue?
5. The contributions made by each partner. Will some partners contribute money, while others provide real estate, personal property, expertise, or labor? When are the contributions due?
6. The management responsibilities. Will all partners have equal voices in management, or will there be senior and junior partners?
7. The duties of each partner.
8. The salaries and drawing accounts of each partner.
9. Provision for sharing of profits or losses.
10. Provision for accounting procedures. Who'll keep the accounts? What bookkeeping and accounting methods will be used? Where will the books be kept?
11. The requirements for taking in new partners.
12. Any special restrictions, rights, or duties of any partner.
13. Provision for a retiring partner.
14. Provision for the purchase of a deceased or retiring partner's share of the business.
15. Provision for how grievances will be handled.
16. Provision for how to dissolve the partnership and distribute the assets to the partners.

figure 5.1

HOW TO FORM A PARTNERSHIP

Another advantage is pooled knowledge. One partner might be good at building Web sites, while another partner might be very good at marketing the business. They can use each other's abilities to make the business prosper.

One disadvantage is the division of profits. Unlike a sole proprietorship, where the owner keeps all of the profits, profits in a partnership must be divided among the partners.

Because of unlimited liability, each general partner is liable for the debts of the firm, no matter who was responsible for causing those debts. This is similar to a sole proprietor, in that general partners can lose their personal possessions if the company goes bankrupt.

Conflict among the partners is another disadvantage. How and where to spend money, and how the business should be managed, can create conflicts if the partners disagree. Because of these conflicts, a partnership agreement should be spelled out in writing, in order to protect all parties.[19]

limited liability partnership (LLP)

LLPs limit partners' risk of losing their personal assets to only their own acts and omissions and to the acts and omissions of people under their supervision.

When Mark Beckloff and Dan Dye's neighbors sniffed the all-natural treats Mark and Dan baked for their own dogs, they came begging for biscuits. It didn't take the two friends long to decide to form a partnership and open a bakery just for dogs. Today, their business is incorporated with more than 30 bakeries in the United States as well as stores in Canada, Japan, and South Korea. Can you think of innovative products that might fit into a specialized market?

Once a partnership has been established, it can be difficult to get out (other than by death). Even if all partners want to terminate the business, who gets what and how assets are divided can be a challenge.

Corporations

Although the word *corporation* makes people think of big businesses, such as General Motors, IBM, Ford, Exxon, General Electric, Microsoft, and Wal-Mart, it is not necessary to be big in order to incorporate. Many corporations are small and by their numbers contribute substantially to the U.S. economy. Before we discuss the types of corporations, it is important to mention the concept of **corporate governance,** which refers to the processes, customs, policies, laws, and institutions affecting the way in which a corporation is directed, administered, or controlled. When someone decides to form a corporation, she or he will put a set of corporate governance guidelines in place, that is, a written form of how the business will be run.

Part of corporate governance, especially in larger businesses, is a board of directors. The **board of directors** is the group ultimately responsible for the business. Many of them, however, do not actually work for the business; they are an outside source to provide guidance in the business.

C-Corporations

Incorporating may be beneficial for small businesses as well. A **conventional (C) corporation** is a state-chartered legal entity with the authority to act and have liability separate from its owners (the corporation's stockholders are its owners).[20]

What this means for the owners is that they are not liable for the debts or any other problems of the corporation, beyond the money they invested. Owners no longer have to worry about losing personal belongings, such as their house, car, or other property because of some business problem—a significant benefit. A corporation not only limits the liability of owners, but often enables many people to share in the ownership (and profits) of a business without working there or having other commitments to it. Corporations can choose whether to offer such ownership to outside investors or to remain privately held.

Besides the traditional C-corporation, two new forms of corporations have been developed over the years. First, it is important to point out that individuals can incorporate. It does not necessarily have to be a business with many employees and lots of assets. The advantage, of course, is that the owners have limited liability. In other words, the individuals cannot lose money, other than their original investments.

corporate governance

The processes, customs, policies, laws, and institutions affecting the way in which a corporation is directed, administered, or controlled.

board of directors

The group ultimately responsible for the decisions of a business.

conventional (C) corporation

A form of business ownership that provides limited liability.

S-Corporations

Another form of corporation is an **S-corporation.** The advantage to this type of incorporation is that it is created by the government and is taxed liked a sole proprietorship and partnership. There is still paperwork that must be filed, and there are also restrictions on which businesses qualify to be an S-corporation. Those restrictions are as follows:

1. Have no more than 100 shareholders.
2. Have shareholders who are individuals or estates and are citizens or permanent residents of the United States.
3. Have only one class of stock.
4. Have no more than 25 percent of income derived from passive sources (passive refers to things such as rent or interest).[21]

Limited Liability Companies (LLCs)

This form of corporation is similar to the S-corporation, but without the special restrictions. LLCs still enjoy limited liability, and can choose the form of taxation they want. In addition, the ownership rules are flexible, as is the distribution of profits and losses. LLCs also have more operating flexibility. For example, they do not have to hold annual meetings. Disadvantages are that they cannot sell stock and that there is more paperwork required to start an LLC, although not as much as with a traditional corporation.

One of the advantages of forming a corporation, as opposed to a sole proprietorship or partnership, is the ability to get more money for investment. Unlike the other two options, corporations are allowed to sell stock, which can boost the growth of the company. It is easy to change ownership, and can be easier to draw talented employees due to the ability to offer higher salaries and/or benefits. Another major advantage is that corporations have limited liability. One factor to remember about corporations and the way they are viewed by the government is that corporations are entities in and of themselves, separate from the owners.[22]

One disadvantage of incorporating is that there is a lot of paperwork that must be handled in order to form a corporation. Handling all of the paperwork by lawyers can be expensive. It is not unusual for it to cost several thousand dollars to create a corporation, but it is quite necessary. The Internet, however, has made incorporation much easier and less expensive. People are now able to incorporate online at a fraction of the cost it used to require, if they are Internet savvy.

Unlike a sole proprietorship where the owner and the business are taxed as one, a corporation has two tax returns (unless it is an S-corporation, which is taxed differently).

Filing of two tax returns can create **double taxation.**[23] First, since the corporation is viewed as a separate entity, it is taxed. Thus the people

S-corporation

A type of legal entity in which the biggest advantage is that it is taxed like a sole proprietorship.

double taxation

Occurs when the owners of the corporation are taxed twice—once when the corporation itself gets taxed and a second time when the dividends are taxed.

	Sole Proprietorship	PARTNERSHIPS		CORPORATIONS		
		General Partnership	Limited Partnership	Conventional Corporation	S-Corporation	Limited Liability Company
Documents Needed to Start Business	None; may need permit or license	Partnership agreement (oral or written)	Written agreement; must file certificate of limited partnership	Articles of incorporation, bylaws	Articles of incorporation, bylaws, must meet criteria	Articles of organization and operating agreement; no eligibility requirements
Ease of Termination	Easy to terminate: just pay debts and quit	May be hard to terminate, depending on the partnership agreement	Same as general partnership	Hard and expensive to terminate	Same as conventional corporation	May be difficult, depending upon operating agreement
Length of Life	Terminates on the death of owner	Terminates on the death or withdrawal of partner	Same as general partnership	Perpetual life	Same as conventional corporation	Varies according to dissolution dates in articles of organization
Transfer of Ownership	Business can be sold to qualified buyer	Must have other partner(s)' agreement	Same as general partnership	Easy to change owners; just sell stock	Can sell stock, but with restrictions	Can't sell stock
Financial Resources	Limited to owner's capital and loans	Limited to partners' capital and loans	Same as general partnership	More money to start and operate; may sell stocks and bonds	Same as conventional corporation	Same as partnership
Risk of Losses	Unlimited liability	Unlimited liability	Limited liability	Limited liability	Limited liability	Limited liability
Taxes	Taxed as personal income	Taxed as personal income	Same as general partnership	Corporate, double taxation	Taxed as personal income	Varies
Management Responsibilities	Owner manages *all* areas of the business	Partners share management	Can't participate in management	Separate management from ownership	Same as conventional corporation	Varies
Employee Benefits	Usually fewer benefits and lower wages	Often fewer benefits and lower wages; promising employee could become a partner	Same as general partnership	Usually better benefits and wages, advancement opportunities	Same as conventional corporation	Varies, but are not tax deductible

figure 5.2

COMPARISON OF BUSINESS OWNERSHIP FORMS

who own the corporation are taxed twice—once when the corporation itself gets taxed and a second time when the dividends are taxed. This of course can be a disadvantage. Finally, because corporations are required to have a board of directors, conflict often occurs between stockholders and board members.

figure 5.3

THE PROCESS OF
INCORPORATION

The process of forming a corporation varies somewhat from state to state. The articles of incorporation are usually filed with the secretary of state's office in the state in which the company incorporates. The articles contain:

- The corporation's name.
- The names of the people who incorporated it.
- Its purposes.
- Its duration (usually perpetual).
- The number of shares that can be issued, their voting rights, and any other rights the shareholders have.
- The corporation's minimum capital.
- The address of the corporation's office.
- The name and address of the person responsible for the corporation's legal service.
- The names and addresses of the first directors.
- Any other public information the incorporators wish to include.

Before a business can so much as open a bank account or hire employees, it needs a federal tax identification number. To apply for one, get an SS-4 form from the IRS.

In addition to the articles of incorporation listed, a corporation has bylaws. These describe how the firm is to be operated from both legal and managerial points of view. The bylaws include:

- How, when, and where shareholders' and directors' meetings are held, and how long directors are to serve.
- Directors' authority.
- Duties and responsibilities of officers, and the length of their service.
- How stock is issued.
- Other matters, including employment contracts.

SELF–CHECK QUESTIONS

1. What are the advantages of forming a partnership over a sole proprietorship?
2. Why would someone want to form a corporation rather than a partnership?
3. If you were to start a business, which form do you think you would use and why?

FRANCHISES AND COOPERATIVES

If starting your own business from scratch doesn't sound appealing, consider the following alternatives: starting a franchise, buying an existing business, or starting a cooperative.

Franchises

As we discussed in Chapter 3, franchising is an attractive entry form into global business. Domestically, franchising is a well sought out alternative as well to starting your business from scratch. Examples of

Section Outline

Franchises and Cooperatives

- Franchises
- Buying an Existing Business
- Cooperatives

franchises include 7-Eleven, Weight Watchers, Holiday Inn, Jiffy Lube, and McDonald's. A franchise is different from a chain store. A chain store is defined as a business that has central management (meaning all stores are run by the same people) and shares a brand name. Target and Wal-Mart are examples of chain stores. A franchise, on the other hand, shares a brand name but does not have central management. The owner of each franchise store is responsible for his or her own business. Sometimes, a chain owns some stores but franchises others, as McDonald's does. The stores a chain owns are called **company stores.**

company stores

A store owned by a chain that owns and franchises stores.

Keep in mind, a franchise is not a legal form of business, but rather a type of business. Someone who purchases a franchise will still have to determine his or own legal form of business, as we discussed previously.

Franchising has penetrated every aspect of American and global business life by offering products and services that are reliable, convenient, and competitively priced. Franchising clearly has some advantages. See Figure 5.4 for a list of the top 10 franchises.

q: Can you see yourself starting a franchise? What
» »   type of franchise business would you start and why?

1. Subway
2. Dunkin' Donuts
3. Jackson Hewitt Tax Service
4. 7-Eleven Inc.
5. UPS Store, The/ Mail Boxes Etc.
6. Domino's Pizza LLC
7. Jiffy Lube Int'l. Inc.
8. Sonic Drive-In Restaurants
9. McDonald's
10. Papa John's Int'l. Inc.

figure 5.4

TOP 10 FRANCHISES IN 2007

Source: Top 10 franchises in 2007 from *Franchise 500 for 2007*, www. entrepreneur.com/franchise500. Reprinted with permission from Entrepreneur's Magazine.

Perhaps one of the biggest advantages with franchising is marketing and management assistance.[24] Compared with someone who starts a business from scratch, a *franchisee* (the person who buys a franchise) has a much greater chance of succeeding because he or she has an established product (e.g., Wendy's hamburgers, Domino's pizza); help with choosing a location and promotion; and assistance in all phases of operation. It is like having your own store with full-time consultants available whenever you need them. *Franchisors* (the person or entity who owns the rights to the franchise) also provide intensive training. For example, McDonald's sends all new franchisees and managers to Hamburger University in Oak Brook, Illinois.[25] Some franchisors help their franchisees succeed by helping with local marketing efforts, rather than having them depend solely on national advertising. Many franchisors also offer financial assistance, such as loans, to their franchisees. Furthermore, franchisees have a whole network of fellow franchisees who are facing similar problems and can share their experiences. For example, The UPS Store provides its 3,600 franchisees with a software program that helps them build data banks of customer names and addresses. The company also provides one-on-one phone support and quick e-mail access through

Holiday Inn's Intercontinental Amstel hotel in Amsterdam has been celebrated as the Netherlands' most beautiful and luxurious hotel. Holiday Inn franchises try to complement the environment of the area they serve. This hotel is on the crossroads of Amsterdam's financial and exclusive shopping districts. What do you think would have been the reaction if Holiday Inn built the typical American-style hotel in this area?

its help desk. The help desk focuses on personalizing contact with the company's franchisees by immediately addressing their questions and concerns.

Another advantage of franchising is that you still enjoy the benefits of being a sole proprietor, if you so choose. A franchise operation remains your store, and you enjoy much of the incentives and profit of sole proprietors. You are still your own boss, although you must follow more rules, regulations, and procedures than you would with your own privately owned store.

A still further advantage is a lower failure rate, likely attributed to the support provided by the franchisor. Because the business has either a locally or nationally recognized name, there are already established customers who trust the product.

It almost sounds as though franchising is too good to be true. There are, however, some potential pitfalls. You must be sure to check out any such arrangement with present franchisees to get an idea of their experiences with the franchisor and possibly discuss the idea with an attorney and an accountant.

The biggest disadvantage to franchising is large start-up costs. For example, to open a Holiday Inn, it might cost upward of $5 million dollars!

Much like with a partnership, one of the disadvantages is that franchisees must share the profit. The franchisor often demands either a large share of the profits, in addition to the start-up fees, or a percentage commission based on sales, not profit.[26] The share demanded by the franchisor is generally referred to as a royalty. For example, if a franchisor demands a 10 percent royalty on a franchise's net sales, 10 cents of every dollar collected at the franchise (before taxes and other expenses) must be paid to the franchisor.

While we discussed management assistance as an advantage previously, it can also be a disadvantage. Because franchisors have an image to uphold, they have very tight restrictions on things such as signage, what can be sold, and even pricing, which allows little flexibility for the franchisee. Also, if the franchise experiences bad publicity, this can reflect negatively upon the individual franchisee. For example, an organization called the Center for Science in the Public Interest brought a lawsuit in early 2007 in hopes the KFC Corporation (KFC) would stop using trans-fat when cooking the chicken. Although KFC calls the lawsuit frivolous, this kind of bad publicity can affect the business. (KFC has stopped using trans-fat altogether as a result of this bad publicity.)[27]

Similar to the KFC example, other coattail effects can also be disadvantages. For example, if one fast-food restaurant causes food-borne illness, it is likely people will avoid all franchises with the same name.

In addition, there is the problem of cannibalization of existing businesses.[28] TCBY franchisees have complained that too many new stores have opened up, cannibalizing the business at existing locations. *Cannibalizing* means taking customers that might have gone to one TCBY but end up going to a different one because of location. To avoid this problem, many franchises, such as Cold Stone Creamery, severely limit the number of franchises that can be opened in a certain area.

Finally, if you decide to sell your franchise, there are likely restrictions on whom you can sell to. In order to control the quality of their franchisees, franchisors often insist on approving the new owner, who must meet the franchisor's standards.

See Figure 5.5 which shows the process of buying a franchise.

Buying an Existing Business

Another option to start a business is to purchase an existing business. There are many business brokers available who, just like real estate brokers, put buyers and sellers of businesses together. For example, consider someone who owns a craft store. If she decides to move she is unable to take the store with her, so she decides to sell the business. The advantage of purchasing this business is that there is already a customer base, inventory, and physical structure and location. The buyer can review important facts like sales numbers to determine if the business will be profitable enough. Often, the previous owner is willing to stay awhile and train new owners. Those who prefer not to use a business broker will find many businesses for sale through want ads on the Internet and newspapers. In either case, the most important thing is to determine the cost of the business versus the return (profit) you expect to make on the business.

Since buying a franchise is a major investment, be sure to check out a company's financial strength before you get involved. Watch out for scams, too. Scams called *bust-outs* usually involve people coming to town, renting nice offices, taking out ads, and persuading people to invest. Then they disappear with the investors' money.

A good source of information about evaluating a franchise deal is the handbook *Investigate before Investing,* available from International Franchise Association Publications.

CHECKLIST FOR EVALUATING A FRANCHISE

The Franchise

- Did your lawyer approve the franchise contract you're considering after he or she studied it paragraph by paragraph?
- Does the franchise give you an exclusive territory for the length of the franchise?
- Under what circumstances can you terminate the franchise contract and at what cost to you?
- If you sell your franchise, will you be compensated for your goodwill (the value of your business's reputation and other intangibles)?
- If the franchisor sells the company, will your investment be protected?

The Franchisor

- How many years has the firm offering you a franchise been in operation?
- Does it have a reputation for honesty and fair dealing among the local firms holding its franchise?
- Has the franchisor shown you any certified figures indicating exact net profits of one or more going firms that you personally checked yourself with the franchisee? Ask for the company's disclosure statement.
- Will the firm assist you with:
  A management training program?
  An employee training program?
  A public relations program?
  Capital?
  Credit?
  Merchandising ideas?

- Will the firm help you find a good location for your new business?
- Has the franchisor investigated you carefully enough to assure itself that you can successfully operate one of its franchises at a profit both to itself and to you?

You, the Franchisee

- How much equity capital will you need to purchase the franchise and operate it until your income equals your expenses?
- Does the franchisor offer financing for a portion of the franchising fees? On what terms?
- Are you prepared to give up some independence of action to secure the advantages offered by the franchise? Do you have your family's support?
- Does the industry appeal to you? Are you ready to spend much or all of the remainder of your business life with this franchisor, offering its product or service to the public?

Your Market

- Have you done a study to determine whether the product or service that you propose to sell under the franchise has a market in your territory at the prices you'll have to charge?
- Will the population in the territory given to you increase, remain static, or decrease over the next five years?
- Will demand for the product or service you're considering be greater, about the same, or less five years from now than it is today?
- What competition already exists in your territory for the product or service you contemplate selling?

Sources: U.S. Department of Commerce, *Franchise Opportunities Handbook;* and Rhonda Adams, "Franchising Is No Simple Endeavor," Gannett News Services, March 14, 2002.

figure 5.5

THE PROCESS OF BUYING A FRANCHISE

Developing Habits for a Successful Career

By now you are familiar with the expression, "Good habits lead to good outcomes." How you handle daily duties and activities, such as your job, school, eating and drinking choices, and so forth, creates opportunities to develop and maintain good habits. Here is a list of good habits that will help lead to personal and career success:

- Being on time
- Having an even temperament
- Doing your best
- Avoiding gossip
- Listening
- Being trustworthy
- Writing things down

- Showing consistent effort
- Exhibiting leadership
- Having a positive attitude
- Showing passion
- Completing all work
- Having character
- Volunteering

Cooperatives

cooperative

A business owned and controlled by the people who use it—producers, consumers, or workers with similar needs who pool their resources for mutual gain.

If buying a franchise or existing business doesn't sound interesting, another option would be to start a cooperative. Some people dislike the notion of having owners, managers, workers, and buyers as separate individuals with separate goals. These people have formed a different kind of organization to meet their needs for things such as electricity, child care, housing, health care, food, and financial services. Such an organization, called a **cooperative,** is owned and controlled by the people who use it—producers, consumers, or workers with similar needs, who pool their resources for mutual gain. In many rural parts of the country, for example, electrical power is sold through cooperatives. The government sells wholesale power to electric cooperatives at rates that are on average from 40 to 50 percent below the rates nonfederal utilities charge.[29] There are 47,000 cooperatives in the United States today.[30] Some co-ops ask members/customers to work at the cooperative for a number of hours per month as part of their duties. Members democratically control these businesses by electing a board of directors that hires professional management.

There is another kind of cooperative in the United States, set up for different reasons. These cooperatives are formed to give members more economic power as a group than they would have as individuals. The best example of such cooperatives is a farm cooperative. The idea at first was for farmers to join together to get better prices for their food products. Eventually, however, the organization expanded so that farm cooperatives now buy and sell fertilizer, farm equipment, seed, and other products needed on the farm, which has become a multibillion-dollar industry. The cooperatives now own many manufacturing facilities. Farm cooperatives do not pay the same kind of taxes that corporations do, and thus have an advantage in the marketplace. Credit unions are an example of a service co-op, while REI, a recreational equipment store, is an example of a retail co-op.

SELF-CHECK QUESTIONS

1. Why would someone want to open a franchise as opposed to starting from scratch?
2. What things would you tell someone to look for before buying a franchise?
3. What advantage would there be in buying an existing business?

CORPORATE EXPANSION

Yet another way to expand a business is to buy another business to help your business grow. This section will focus on types of buyouts. A **merger** is the result of two firms forming one company. An **acquisition** is one company's purchase of the property and obligations of another company. They are still joining as one, but in this case, one company is actually buying another rather than joining together as with a merger. Either way, companies are motivated to do this because it can add more customers to their business, create greater efficiencies in existing business, or break into new markets (such as global ones) in which the company has not yet been.

Mergers

There are three major types of corporate mergers: vertical, horizontal, and conglomerate. A **vertical merger** is the joining of two firms involved in different stages of related businesses. Think of a merger between a bicycle company and a company that produces bike wheels. Such a merger would ensure a constant supply of wheels needed by the bicycle manufacturer. It could also help ensure quality control of the bicycle company's products. A recent example of a vertical merger was Time Warner (cable operator) and Turner Corporation (produces CNN and other television programming).[31]

A **horizontal merger** joins two firms in the same industry and allows them to diversify or expand their products. An example is the merger of

Section Outline

Corporate Expansion
- Mergers
- Types of Buyouts

merger
The result of two firms forming one company.

acquisition
One company's purchase of the property and obligations of another company.

vertical merger
The joining of two firms involved in different stages of related businesses.

horizontal merger
Joins two firms in the same industry and allows them to diversify or expand their products.

figure 5.6

THREE TYPES OF MERGERS

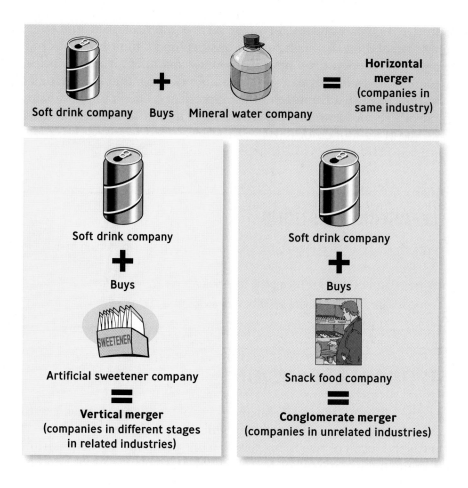

figure 5.6

THREE TYPES OF MERGERS

Soft drink company   **+**   Buys   Mineral water company   **=**   **Horizontal merger (companies in same industry)**

Soft drink company
+
Buys
Artificial sweetener company
=
Vertical merger (companies in different stages in related industries)

Soft drink company
+
Buys
Snack food company
=
Conglomerate merger (companies in unrelated industries)

conglomerate merger
Unites firms in completely unrelated industries.

hostile takeover
Attempts by the bidder to acquire a firm against the interest of the latter's management.

a bicycle company and a tricycle company. The business can now supply a variety of cycling products. A recent example would be AT&T Wireless merging with Cingular Wireless.[32] A **conglomerate merger** unites firms in completely unrelated industries. The primary purpose of a conglomerate merger is to diversify business operations and investments. The acquisition of a restaurant chain by a bicycle company would be an example of a conglomerate merger. Recent examples of conglomerate mergers are many. For example, Quaker sold the drink maker Snapple to Triarc in 1997. This merger was a conglomerate merger because Triarc is an investment firm that also owns some Arby's franchises.[33] See Figure 5.6 for a further description of mergers.

Rather than merge or sell to another company, some corporations decide to maintain control, or in some cases regain control of a firm internally. For example, Steve Stavro, the majority owner and head of a group that invested in the Maple Leaf Gardens Ltd. (owners of the Toronto Maple Leafs hockey team), decided to take the firm private (as opposed to taking a firm public). First, taking a firm public means to sell and trade shares of the company on the stock market. Once shares are sold on the stock market, it becomes a public company and must meet the needs of the shareholders. On the other hand, *taking a firm private* involves the efforts of a group of stockholders or management to obtain all of the firm's stock for themselves. In other words, they buy it back so it is no longer traded on the stock market. In the Maple Leaf Gardens situation, Stavro's investors group successfully gained total control of the company by buying back all of the company's stock.[34] For the first time in 65 years, investors in the open market could no longer purchase stock in the Maple Leafs.

When a bidder makes an offer for another company, it will usually discuss it with the board of directors first. If the board feels that the offer is a good one, it will likely make a recommendation that the shareholders accept the offer. If the board is presented with the offer and rejects it, however, but the bidder continues to pursue the offer, or if the bidder makes an offer without first approaching the board about it, this is an example of a **hostile takeover.**

Tony Lee took a job cleaning bathrooms in a factory until a job opened up for him on the production line. He worked so hard he eventually became supervisor. When the owners announced plans to close the factory, Lee knew he had to do something. With the help of a local law professor and an economic development group, Tony prepared a business plan. After attracting investors, selling his motorcycle, and taking a second mortgage on his home, Lee completed a leveraged buyout. Now he and the other investors own the $3 million company.

Types of Buyouts

Suppose the employees in an organization feel that there is a good possibility that they may lose their jobs, or suppose the managers believe that corporate performance could be enhanced if they owned the company. Do either of these groups have an opportunity to take ownership of the company? Yes—they might attempt a leveraged buyout. A **leveraged buyout (LBO)** is an attempt by employees, management, or a group of investors to purchase an organization primarily through borrowing. The funds borrowed are used to buy out the stockholders in the company. The employees, managers, or investors now become the owners of the firm. LBOs have ranged in size from $50 million to $6 billion and have involved everything from small family businesses to giant corporations such as R. J. Reynolds and Northwest Airlines.[35]

Another term for this is a **management buyout.** A management buyout occurs when employees of the company get together to purchase the business. Keep in mind, a management buyout may not always be a leveraged buyout, if the managers purchasing the company have cash to purchase the business. However, the majority of the time, a management buyout will also be a leveraged buyout, since *leveraged* means money is borrowed for the purchase, and often this is the case.

leveraged buyout (LBO)

An attempt by employees, management, or a group of investors to purchase an organization primarily through borrowing.

management buyout

When employees of the company get together to purchase the business.

GETTING STARTED IN YOUR OWN BUSINESS

There are five main areas of focus when starting a small business:

- Planning the business
- Financing the business
- Knowing your customers (marketing)
- Managing employees
- Keeping records (accounting)

This section will address each of these areas and provide insight into how you can begin your own business! As we mentioned at the beginning of the chapter, many new businesses *do* fail—but proper focus on each of the five areas will help ensure your business isn't one of them. Businesses usually fail due to one of the following reasons:[36]

- Lack of planning
- Lack of marketing
- Unrealistic financial expectations
- Wrong business partner
- Lack of business knowledge

This section will address how to avoid these pitfalls when starting your business.

Planning

business plan

Detailed written statement that describes the nature of the business, the target market, the advantages the business will have in relation to competition, and the resources and qualifications of the owner(s).

It is amazing how many people are eager to start a small business but have only a vague notion of what they want to do. Eventually, they come up with an idea for a business and begin discussing the idea with professors, friends, and other businesspeople. It is at this stage that the entrepreneur needs a business plan. A **business plan** is a detailed written statement that describes the nature of the business, the target market, the potential for customers, the advantages the business will have in relation to competition, and the resources and qualifications of the owner(s). It also includes market research. Market research can help

Focus on Ethics

IT'S ALL IN A NAME

An entrepreneur decided to start his own business. He looked at several franchises and settled on a fast-food restaurant franchise. However, once he found out how much it would cost in up-front costs and royalties, he decided to open his own restaurant. Although by law he could not use the same name as the franchise, he chose a similar name and sold exactly the same kind of food.

Questions

1. Is choosing a similar name for the franchise ethical? Why or why not?

2. Can you think of examples of companies that have similar names and similar products?

the business owner better develop products that meet the needs of the customer. (Market research will be further discussed in Chapter 9.)

A business plan forces potential owners of small businesses to be quite specific about the products or services they intend to offer, which helps them get their feet on the ground in a realistic way. They must analyze the competition, calculate how much money they need to start, and cover other details of operation. A business plan is also mandatory for talking with bankers or other investors. A good business plan takes a long time to write (usually about six months), but you must be able to convince your readers (bankers, investors) in five minutes that your plan is solid. Although there is no such thing as a perfect business plan, prospective entrepreneurs do think out the smallest details. Jerrold Carrington of Inroads Capital Partners advises that one of the most important parts of the business plan is the *executive summary* at the beginning of the plan. The executive summary has to catch the reader's interest, as it is usually an overview of the business in the first few pages of a business plan that may be all potential investors ever look at. Bankers receive many business plans every day. "You better grab me up front," says Carrington.

Sometimes one of the most difficult tasks in undertaking complex projects, such as writing a business plan, is knowing where to start. There are many computer software programs on the market now to help you get organized.

Getting the completed business plan into the right hands is almost as important as getting the right information into the plan. Finding funding requires research. In the next section, sources of money available to new business ventures will be covered. Finding money is of course one of the major factors when starting a business.

Before we discuss the funding part of entrepreneurship, it is important here to mention **intrapreneuring,** which may be described as a kind of internal or ongoing entrepreneurship once the business gets rolling, and

intrapreneuring

The process of continuing to innovate a small business.

When Sharon Lee and her brother Darryl wanted to start up a new seafood restaurant they turned to Bill Pelton for advice. Lee met Pelton, a retired sales and marketing executive, through the Service Corps of Retired Executives (SCORE). Pelton helped Lee complete her business plan and later sort through the stack of investment proposals from prospective backers that read about her business planning in a local newspaper article. How did Lee's business planning affect her chances of success?

how necessary it is once an entrepreneur starts to grow his or her business. If a business is successful, the entrepreneur must continue to innovate with new products, new processes, and new ideas. In other words, in *intrapreneuring,* an entrepreneur is constantly finding ways to improve and expand his or her business. How you plan to keep on intrapreneuring and innovating is one area that is great if addressed in the business plan.

Financing

An entrepreneur has several potential sources of capital: personal savings, relatives, former employers, banks, finance companies, **venture capitalists** (a person or investment company that loans money to businesses), and government agencies such as the Small Business Administration (SBA), the Farmers Home Administration, and the Economic Development Authority. There are also **angel investors.** Angel investors are individuals, usually wealthy, who invest their own money in a business for a share of the company. Angel investors are different from venture capitalists, in that venture capitalists usually invest other people's money, while angel investors invest their own funds. You may even want to consider borrowing from a potential supplier to your future business. Helping you get started may be in the supplier's interest if there is a chance you will be a big customer later. It's usually not a good idea to ask such an investor for money at the outset. Begin by asking for advice; if the supplier likes your plan, he or she may be willing to help you with funding.

The **Small Business Administration (SBA)** is a U.S. government agency that advises and assists small businesses by providing management training, financial advice, and loans. The SBA started a microloan demonstration program in 1991. The program provides very small loans (up to $35,000) and technical assistance to "prebankable" small-business owners. The program is administered through a nationwide network of 170 nonprofit organizations chosen by the SBA.[37] Rather than base the awarding of loans on collateral, credit history, or previous business success, these programs decide worthiness on the basis of belief in the borrowers' integrity and the soundness of their business idea.

The SBA microloan program helps people such as Karla Brown start their own businesses. Newly divorced and facing a mountain of debt, Brown needed to find a way to support her daughter. She bought two buckets of flowers and headed to the subway to sell them. Continuing the process, she made enough money to keep a steady inventory, but she needed help

venture capitalists

A company that has money to invest in small and large businesses, and in return for its investment will generally take a stake in the business.

angel investors

Individuals, usually wealthy, who invest their own money in a business for a share of the company.

Small Business Administration (SBA)

U.S. government agency that advises and assists small businesses by providing management training and financial advice and loans.

The SBA may provide the following types of financial assistance:

- *Guaranteed loans*—loans made by a financial institution that the government will repay if the borrower stops making payments. The maximum individual loan guarantee is capped at $1 million.
- *Microloans*—amounts ranging from $100 to $35,000 (average $10,500) to people such as single mothers and public housing tenants.
- *Export Express*—loans made to small businesses wishing to export. The maximum guaranteed loan amount is $250,000.
- *Community Adjustment and Investment Program (CAIP)*—loans to businesses to create new, sustainable jobs or to preserve existing jobs in eligible communities that have lost jobs due to changing trade patterns with Mexico and Canada following the adoption of NAFTA.
- *Pollution control loans*—loans to eligible small businesses for the financing of the planning, design, or installation of a pollution control facility. This facility must prevent, reduce, abate, or control any form of pollution, including recycling. The maximum guaranteed loan amount is $1 million.
- *504 certified development company (CDC) loans*—loans for purchasing major fixed assets, such as land and buildings for businesses in eligible communities, typically rural communities or urban areas needing revitalization. The program's goal is to expand business ownership by minorities, women, and veterans. The maximum guaranteed loan amount is $1.3 million.

Source: Small Business Administration, http://sba.gov, accessed on October 24, 2007.

figure 5.7

TYPES OF SBA FINANCIAL ASSISTANCE

from her friends to pay her bills. She thought she could make a living if she could take her flowers out of the subway and into a store. She obtained a $19,000 SBA microloan and rented a store in the heart of Boston. Soon after, Brown's flower shop brought in $100,000 in sales.[38] See Figure 5.7.

As we mentioned above, another way to get funding is through *venture capitalists*. A venture capitalist is a company that has money to invest in small and large businesses. A venture capitalist might loan money to a new business, fund an expansion of a business to new areas, or fund a company to help them market a new product. As a smaller business owner, it is important for you to consider venture capital and angel investor offers carefully. Normally, they provide funding in return for a stake in the business which can mean they will have a "say" into how your business is run.

Knowing Your Customer (Marketing)

One of the most important elements of small-business success is *knowing the market*. In business, a **market** consists of people with unsatisfied wants and needs who have both the resources and the willingness to buy. For example, most students have the *willingness* to take a Caribbean cruise during spring break. However, few of them have the resources necessary to satisfy this want. As a result, they probably would not be a good market to pursue for a travel agency.

market

Consists of people with unsatisfied wants and needs who have both the resources and the willingness to buy.

Katrina Markoff believes that chocolate can save the world. As founder of Vosges Haut-Chocolat, Markoff introduces her customers to different cultures by mixing her chocolate with exotic flavors from around the globe. It's easy to think of Japan when trying a wasabi truffle or of Italy when sampling a chocolate laced with taleggio cheese. After receiving an SBA loan, Markoff opened her first store in Chicago and then others in New York City, Las Vegas, and Japan.

Once the market and its needs have been identified, you must set out to fill those needs. The way to meet customers' needs is to offer top quality, at a fair price, with great service. Remember, it isn't enough to get customers—you have to keep them. As Victoria Jackson, founder of the $50 million Victoria Jackson Cosmetics Company, says of the stars who push her products on television infomercials, "All the glamorous faces in the world wouldn't mean a thing if my customers weren't happy with the product and didn't come back for more." Everything must be geared to bring customers the satisfaction they deserve.

One of the greatest advantages that small businesses have over larger ones is the ability to know their customers better, and to adapt quickly to their ever-changing needs. Now, let's consider the importance of effectively managing the employees who help you serve your market.

Managing Your Employees

As a business grows, it becomes impossible for an entrepreneur to oversee every detail, even if he or she is putting in 60 hours per week. This means that hiring, training, and motivating employees are critical activities. (More detail on the management of human resources will be presented in Chapter 7.) It is not easy to find good, qualified help when you offer less money, skimpier benefits, and less room for advancement than larger firms. That is one reason why employee relations are such an important part of small-business management.

Employees of small companies are often more satisfied with their jobs than are their counterparts in big business. Why? Quite often they find their jobs more challenging, their ideas more accepted, and their bosses more respectful. Entrepreneurs reluctantly face the reality that to keep growing, they must delegate authority to others. Nagging questions such as "Who should be delegated authority?" and "How much control should they have?" create perplexing problems. This challenge can be a particularly touchy issue in small businesses with long-term employees, and in family businesses.

As you might expect, entrepreneurs who have built their companies from scratch often feel compelled to promote employees who have

So, You Want to Be . . . an Entrepreneur

Are you an expert at something? Really good at something? Entrepreneurship is a way to utilize your skills and make money at it! As we discussed in this chapter, being an entrepreneur is more than having a good idea—it requires the personality traits we discussed plus careful planning to make sure the business works.

Many people take their hobby and decide to start a business, which is a great idea, as long as you don't mind the hobby becoming your main source of income! For example, individuals who love scrapbooking may decide to open a scrapbooking store. Fashion fanatics may decide to open a clothing store. The more technically savvy may choose to open a computer repair business. The types of businesses that can be opened are countless; it depends on what you enjoy doing—and what you can make money doing.

been with them from the start—even when those employees aren't qualified to serve as managers. Common sense probably tells you this sort of decision could be detrimental to the business. The same can be true of family-run businesses that are expanding. Attitudes such as "You can't fire family" or promoting certain workers because "they're family" can hinder growth. For example, Accent Administrative Staffing, located in Phoenix, is operated by a brother, sister, and mother team. When experiencing family problems, they went to counseling, and when that didn't work, the mother decided she would leave the business. Luckily, the family is still close, but according to *Entrepreneur* magazine, this is not always the case.[39] Sometimes the experience of operating family businesses can cause deep-rooted problems in families, which is why the relationship as a family member should be kept as separate as possible from the relationship as a business colleague.

Entrepreneurs can best serve themselves and the business if they gradually recruit and groom employees for management positions. By doing this, entrepreneurs can enhance trust and support of the manager among other employees and themselves. When Heida Thurlow of Chantal Cookware suffered an extended illness, she let her employees handle the work she once had insisted on doing herself. The experience transformed her company from an entrepreneurial company into a managerial one. She says, "Over the long run, that makes us stronger than we were."[40]

Record Keeping

Small-business owners often say the most important assistance they received in starting and managing their business involved accounting. A businessperson who sets up an effective accounting system early will save much grief later. It is highly recommended, however, that an

OUTLINE OF A COMPREHENSIVE BUSINESS PLAN

A good business plan is between 25 and 50 pages long and requires extensive research and detailed preparation.

Cover Letter

Only one thing is certain when you go hunting for money to start a business: You won't be the only hunter out there. You need to make potential funders want to read *your* business plan instead of the hundreds of others on their desks. Your cover letter should summarize the most attractive points of your project in as few words as possible. Be sure to address the letter to the potential investor by name. "To whom it may concern" or "Dear Sir" is not the best way to win an investor's support.

Section 1—Executive Summary

Begin with a two-page or three-page management summary of the proposed venture. Include a short description of the business, and discuss major goals and objectives.

Section 2—Company Background

Describe company operations to date (if any), potential legal considerations, and areas of risk and opportunity. Summarize the firm's financial condition, and include past and current balance sheets, income and cash-flow statements, and other relevant financial records (you will read about these financial statements in Chapter 17). It is also wise to include a description of insurance coverage. Investors want to be assured that death or other mishaps do not pose major threats to the company.

Section 3—Management Team

Include an organization chart, job descriptions of listed positions, and detailed resumes of the current and proposed executives. A mediocre idea with a proven management team is funded more often than a great idea with an inexperienced team. Managers should have expertise in all disciplines necessary to start and run a business. If not, mention outside consultants who will serve in these roles and describe their qualifications.

Section 4—Financial Plan

Provide five-year projections for income, expenses, and funding sources. Don't assume the business will grow in a straight line. Adjust your planning to allow for funding at various stages of the company's growth. Explain the rationale and assumptions used to determine the estimates. Assumptions should be reasonable and based on industry/historical trends. Make sure all totals add up and are consistent throughout the plan. If necessary, hire a professional accountant or financial analyst to prepare these statements.

figure 5.8

OUTLINE OF A COMPREHENSIVE BUSINESS PLAN

A full business plan is included in the student study guide. Keep in mind, business plans are usually approximately 25–50 pages in length and can take six months or more to write.

entrepreneur does not set up his or her own accounting system. When it comes to financials in a business, it is usually best to leave this to the experts.

Consider most new business owners who may be really good at their craft, say computer repair. Even though the business owner understands computers, she may not know a lot about accounting, so she may hire someone to set up the accounting system for her and keep records on a monthly basis. This solution allows the entrepreneur more time to focus on her occupation, rather than focusing on those things that may not be her strength.

Stay clear of excessively ambitious sales projections; rather, offer best-case, expected, and worst-case scenarios. These not only reveal how sensitive the bottom line is to sales fluctuations but also serve as good management guides.

Section 5—Capital Required

Indicate the amount of capital needed to commence or continue operations, and describe how these funds are to be used. Make sure the totals are the same as the ones on the cash-flow statement. This area will receive a great deal of review from potential investors, so it must be clear and concise.

Section 6—Marketing Plan

Don't underestimate the competition. Review industry size, trends, and the target market segment. Sources like *American Demographics* magazine and the *Rand McNally Commercial Atlas and Marketing Guide* can help you put a plan together. Discuss strengths and weaknesses of the product or service. The most important things investors want to know are what makes the product more desirable than what's already available and whether the product can be patented. Compare pricing to the competition's. Forecast sales in dollars and units. Outline sales, advertising, promotion, and public relations programs. Make sure the costs agree with those projected in the financial statements.

Section 7—Location Analysis

In retailing and certain other industries, the location of the business is one of the most important factors. Provide a comprehensive demographic analysis of consumers in the area of the proposed business as well as a traffic-pattern analysis and vehicular and pedestrian counts.

Section 8—Manufacturing Plan

Describe minimum plant size, machinery required, production capacity, inventory and inventory-control methods, quality control, plant personnel requirements, and so on. Estimates of product costs should be based on primary research.

Section 9—Appendix

Include all marketing research on the product or service (off-the-shelf reports, article reprints, etc.) and other information about the product concept or market size. Provide a bibliography of all the reference materials you consulted. This section should demonstrate that the proposed company won't be entering a declining industry or market segment.

If you would like to see sample business plans that successfully secured funding, go to the sample business plan resource center at www.bplans.com/samples. You can also learn more about writing business plans on the Small Business Administration Web site at www.sba.gov/starting.

However, even if an entrepreneur hires an accountant, she will still need to complete some record-keeping activities. (More on record keeping will be covered in Chapter 12.) Computers simplify record keeping and enable a small-business owner to follow the progress of the business (sales, expenses, profits) on a daily basis. An inexpensive computer system can also help owners with other record-keeping chores, such as inventory control, customer records, and payroll. A good accountant is invaluable in creating such systems and showing you how to keep them operating smoothly. Many business failures are caused by poor accounting practices. A good accountant can help make decisions

First, Sam and Richard must decide if they are right for entrepreneurship. They both decided their personal qualities make them a great match for entrepreneurship. They are both self-directed and not interested in working for anyone else. They are also willing to put in long hours to make the business succeed, so things look good.

Next, they must choose a type of business. They can choose either a partnership or a corporation, and they have reviewed the advantages and disadvantages of each. Because they don't have a lot of start-up money for legal fees, they have decided to form a partnership. Sam and Richard know that in a good partnership agreement, everything is spelled out. Although they trust each other completely, they both felt it necessary to sign a formal agreement. They decided that Sam would be the primary craftsman, unless they got too busy and needed Richard's help. They also decided that Richard would be responsible for keeping the books, and they would both do marketing for the business. They also decided how the assets would be divided, should one of them decide to quit the business.

Their next step was to develop a business plan. Using this business plan, their intention is to gain financing for materials and supplies. They plan to work out of Sam's garage at first, then move to a bigger location, once they are established. Sam and Richard will go to the microloan department of the SBA to see if the SBA can provide financing. If not, they plan to go to their bank with the business plan.

Their next step is to decide who their customers are. After doing some research and reading about marketing, Richard has tentatively decided they will market their signs on eBay as well as post flyers around town. They have identified their market as homeowners.

Sam and Richard will not hire employees just yet, but if they were planning on doing so, their next step would be to manage employees, figure out salaries, and so on.

Finally, because Richard is going to keep records for the business, they know they need to set up an accounting system set up in order to manage their finances. Richard has signed up for a short course on a bookkeeping computer program.

Sam and Richard feel confident they have done the proper planning to make their business a success!

such as whether to buy or lease equipment and whether to own or rent the building. Help may also be provided for tax planning, financial forecasting, choosing sources of financing, and writing requests for funds.[41] Other small-business owners may tell you where to find an accountant experienced in small business. It pays to shop around for advice.

SELF-CHECK QUESTIONS

1. Explain each of the five areas required to run a small business. Which one do you think you would enjoy the most? Which do you think would be most challenging for you personally?

2. What are the advantages of understanding some accounting, even if you don't do the accounting for your small business yourself?

summary

Chapter 5 covered the basics of entrepreneurship. Characteristics of successful entrepreneurs include people who are self-directed, self-nurturing, action-oriented, highly energetic, and are tolerant of uncertainty. Individuals take the risks of becoming an entrepreneur because of opportunity, profit, independence, and challenge.

The chapter presented the basic legal forms of ownership of a business. The sole proprietorship, which involves one individual owner, is the easiest kind of business to start. Partnerships involve two or more owners. There are various types of partnerships discussed: general partnership, limited partnership, master limited partnership, and limited liability partnership. Corporations can be large and small. The types of corporation include conventional (c) corporation, S-corporation, and limited liability companies. The advantages and disadvantages of sole proprietorships, partnerships, and corporations were explored as well.

The pros and cons of buying a franchise and buying an existing business were discussed as opposed to starting a new business from scratch. Opening a franchise can be a less risky way to become a business owner. Buying an existing business gives you access to an established customer base. Another alternative is to form a cooperative, which is owned and controlled by the people who use it. Once started, you can expand your business through mergers, acquisitions, and buyouts.

Finally, we discussed the areas of concern for an entrepreneur. First, he or she must have a written business plan. Second, the entrepreneur must obtain proper financing. This can be through friends and family, the Small Business Administration, or a venture capitalist. The entrepreneur should also be concerned with the business's market, or customers. Defining to whom a business is going to sell is extremely important. Next, if the entrepreneur plans on hiring employees, issues such as salary need to be determined, as well as the owner's willingness to delegate authority. Finally, the entrepreneur needs to keep accurate bookkeeping. It is highly recommended that a professional be hired to perform this task.

key terms

sole proprietorship 144
sole proprietor 144
unlimited liability 145
partnership 146
general partnership 146
limited partnership 146
general partner 146
limited partner 146

limited liability 146
master limited
   partnership (MLP) 146
limited liability
   partnership (LLP) 147
corporate
   governance 148
board of directors 148

conventional (C)
   corporation 148
s-corporation 149
double taxation 149
company stores 152
cooperative 156
merger 157
acquisition 157

applying your skills

1. Research businesses in your area and identify companies that use each of the following legal forms of ownership: sole proprietorship, partnership, corporation. Find some unusual businesses that are franchises.

2. Get into a team of 2 to 4 people. Discuss the following: Have you thought about starting your own business? What opportunities seem attractive? Think of people whom you might want for a partner or partners in the business.

3. Using your discussion from question 2, list all the financial resources and personal skills you will need to launch the business. Then make separate lists of the personal skills and the financial resources that you and your partner(s) might bring to your new venture. How much capital and what personal skills do you need that neither of you have? Develop an action plan to obtain them.

4. Let's assume you want to open one of the following new businesses. What form of business ownership would you choose for each business? Why?

   a. Video game rental store

   b. Wedding planning service

   c. Day care center

   d. Web-based jewelry business

5. Find issues of *Entrepreneur, Success,* and *Inc.* magazines in the library or on the Internet. Read about the entrepreneurs who are heading today's dynamic new businesses. Write a profile of one entrepreneur.

6. Select a type of small business that looks attractive as a career possibility for you. Talk to at least one person who owns such a business. Ask how he or she started the business. Ask about financing, personnel problems (hiring, firing, training, scheduling), accounting problems, and other managerial matters. Prepare a summary of your findings, including whether the job seems rewarding, interesting, and challenging—and why or why not.

7. Select a small business in your area that has gone out of business. List the factors you think led to its failure. Compile a list of actions the business owners might have taken to keep the company in business.

8. Choose a partner from among your classmates and put together a list of factors that might mean the difference between success and failure for a new company entering the business software industry. Can small start-ups realistically hope to compete with big companies, such as Microsoft and Intel? Discuss the list and your conclusions in class.

the internet in action

Purpose: To assess your potential to succeed as an entrepreneur and to evaluate a sample business plan.

Exercises:

1. Go to www.bizmove.com/other/quiz.htm and take the interactive entrepreneurial quiz to find out if you have the qualities to be a successful entrepreneur. Keep in mind that skills change over time. Even if you do not have a quality right now, chances are it can be developed if you work at it.

2. If you have entrepreneurial traits and decide you would like to start your own business, you will need to develop a business plan. Go to your study guide and review the sample business plan listed there. What would make you invest in this business? Are there any areas that might cause you concern if you were investing your own money?

Purpose: To find out more about the SBA.

Exercise:

1. Go to the SBA Web site and research the following:

   a. What is the SBA's advice on exit strategy?

   b. According to its Web site, what is an SDB?

   c. What kinds of things does the SBA do, besides lend money?

   d. If you were to start a business, in what ways would you use the SBA?

Purpose: To explore current franchising opportunities and to evaluate the strengths and weaknesses of a selected franchise.

Exercises:

Go to Be the Boss: The Virtual Franchise Expo (www.betheboss.com).

1. Take the self-test to see if franchising is a good personal choice for you. Find the test by clicking on Franchising, then on Franchising—An Interactive Self-Test under Franchising Basics.

2. Go back to the homepage and use the search tool to find a franchise that has the potential of fulfilling your entrepreneurial dreams. Navigate to the profile of the franchise you selected.

3. Discuss your choice.

entrepreneur readiness questionnaire

All kinds of people with all kinds of personalities have succeeded in starting small and large businesses. There are certain traits, however, that seem to separate those who will be successful as entrepreneurs from those who may not be. The following questionnaire will help you determine into which category you fit. Take a couple of minutes to answer the questions and then record your score at the end. Making a low score doesn't mean you won't succeed as an entrepreneur. It does indicate, however, that you may be happier working for someone else. Be as honest with yourself as possible to get the most out of the test. Each of the following items describes something that you may or may not feel represents your personality or other characteristics about you. Read each statement and then circle the response that most closely reflects the extent to which you agree or disagree with that statement. 1 means you agree entirely with the statement, 5 means the statement doesn't fit you.

1 ⟵——————————————————⟶ 5

Strongly Agree   **Strongly Disagree**

Looking at my overall philosophy of life and typical behavior, I would say that:

1. I am generally optimistic.   1 2 3 4 5
2. I enjoy competing and doing things better than someone else. 1 2 3 4 5
3. When solving a problem, I try to arrive at the best
   solution first without worrying about other possibilities.   1 2 3 4 5
4. I enjoy associating with co-workers after working hours.   1 2 3 4 5
5. If betting on a horse race I would prefer to take a chance
   on a high-payoff "long shot."   1 2 3 4 5
6. I like setting my own goals and working hard to achieve
   them.   1 2 3 4 5
7. I am generally casual and easy-going with others.   1 2 3 4 5
8. I like to know what is going on and take action to find out. 1 2 3 4 5

9. I work best when someone else is guiding me along the way. 1 2 3 4 5
10. When I am right I can convince others. 1 2 3 4 5
11. I find that other people frequently waste my valuable time. 1 2 3 4 5
12. I enjoy watching football, baseball, and similar sports events. 1 2 3 4 5
13. I tend to communicate about myself very openly with other people. 1 2 3 4 5
14. I don't mind following orders from superiors who have legitimate authority. 1 2 3 4 5
15. I enjoy planning things more than actually carrying out the plans. 1 2 3 4 5
16. I don't think it's much fun to bet on a "sure thing." 1 2 3 4 5
17. If faced with failure, I would shift quickly to something else rather than sticking to my guns. 1 2 3 4 5
18. Part of being successful in business is reserving adequate time for family. 1 2 3 4 5
19. Once I have earned something, I feel that keeping it secure is important. 1 2 3 4 5
20. Making a lot of money is largely a matter of getting the right breaks. 1 2 3 4 5
21. Problem solving is usually more effective when a number of alternatives are considered. 1 2 3 4 5
22. I enjoy impressing others with the things I can do. 1 2 3 4 5
23. I enjoy playing games like tennis and handball with someone who is slightly better than I am. 1 2 3 4 5
24. Sometimes moral ethics must be bent a little in business dealings. 1 2 3 4 5
25. I think good friends would make the best subordinates in an organization. 1 2 3 4 5

Scoring: Give yourself one point for each 1 or 2 response you circled for questions 1, 2, 6, 8, 10, 11, 16, 17, 21, 22, 23.

Give yourself one point for each 4 or 5 response you circled for questions 3, 4, 5, 7, 9, 12, 13, 14, 15, 18, 19, 20, 24, 25.

Add your points and see how you rate in the following categories:

21–25 Your entrepreneurial potential looks great, if you have a suitable opportunity to use it. What are you waiting for?

16–20 This is close to the high entrepreneurial range. You could be quite successful if your other talents and resources are right.

11–15 Your score is in the transitional range. With some serious work you can probably develop the outlook you need for running your own business.

6–10 Things look pretty doubtful for you as an entrepreneur. It would take considerable rearranging of your life philosophy and behavior to make it.

0–5 Let's face it. Entrepreneurship isn't really for you at this time.

Source: Entrepreneurship Readiness Test from Kenneth R. Van Voorhis, *Entrepreneurship and Small Business Management,* © 1980.

MANAGEMENT: FUNCTIONS AND STYLES

Ascentium Corporation

Ascentium Corporation is a business that has successfully used effective management principles to grow to over 300 employees and an annual revenue of $30 million in just six years. The company is based in Bellevue, Washington. It offers professional services, such as marketing and technology solutions, to clients. The founders, Jim Beebe and Curt Doolittle, exemplify the use of great management principles in a growing company. One of the major

Jim Beebe

prerequisites to having a great business is goal setting and planning to reach those goals. Managers in the business meet on a weekly basis for dinner to discuss the challenges and wins the company had that week. In addition, they use this time to plan strategy and goals for the company and create open communication among the leaders within the company. This planning has proven effective, as the company has grown rapidly.

objectives

After reading this chapter, you should be able to:

1 Define *management*.

2 Explain the four functions of management.

3 Understand the use of three tools: SMART, SWOT, and PEST analysis.

4 Understand the basics of organizational structure.

5 Describe various management styles and know when they are appropriate.

6 Explain the challenges for management in the new future.

The structure of the organization is also an important element in effective planning. The structure utilizes a partnership format. Although it is a corporation, it has 10 partners who oversee the business, along with the owners. The partners are managers in the company and receive quarterly dividends on profit, which motivates them to ensure that their area of the business runs smoothly and profitably. The business also has a very flat hierarchical structure (meaning there are not many layers of management). It is organized in this manner to better meet the market needs and demands of customers. Ascentium has found that this structure enables the company to adapt quickly and make decisions quickly to meet the needs of customers.

A core belief of Beebe and Doolittle is that decision making must occur in every level of the organization, which is especially true of those who work with clients every day. They make revenue, cost, and profit information available on the company intranet so that every employee can understand the implications of their decisions for the bottom line.

Beebe and Doolittle encourage their employees to be the best, and they expect a lot of them. Employees are expected to make the best decisions they can, while still being ethical in their decisions. As in all businesses, Beebe and Dolittle set the pace for Ascentium's ethics through showing by example, which truly is great management.

Source: www.ascentium.com/, accessed November 14, 2007.

management
The process of planning, organizing, leading, and controlling people and other available resources to accomplish organizational goals and objectives.

WHAT IS MANAGEMENT?

Effective management and leadership are the foundation of a flourishing business. Without good management, a company can offer the best product at a good price but still not be successful. It takes an excellent manager to plan, organize, control, and lead the business to not only sell, but to inspire others to want to do good for the company, too. Leadership, discussed further in Chapter 7, is different from management. Management is an appointed position with a title, while leadership tends to have a broader scope encompassing one's personal life too. To be effective, all managers must be leaders; however, all leaders do not necessarily have to be managers. In this chapter we will discuss the four functions of management, in which leadership is a key function. To be a good manager, you must perform all four of these functions well.

Management is the process of planning, organizing, leading, and controlling people and other available resources to accomplish organizational goals and objectives. Without management, organizations would be able to accomplish very little. Management is a position of power, a position that is granted to individuals because they are capable. Managers are expected to make decisions and make sure organizational tasks are accomplished. All managers are charged with four key functions.

FUNCTIONS OF MANAGEMENT

There are many tasks that managers must get done on a week-to-week basis. Conducting team meetings is one of those.

A manager's job is to ensure goals are met and tasks are completed. The four main functions of the job of management are planning, organizing, leading, and controlling.

Planning includes anticipating trends and determining the best strategies and tactics to achieve organizational goals and objectives. One objective is to please customers.[1] The trend today is to develop planning teams to help monitor the environment, find business opportunities, and watch for challenges. Planning is a key management function because the other functions depend heavily on having a good plan, no matter what the size of the business. For example, a restaurant owner needs to be constantly aware of the surrounding competition and base her goals and objectives on anticipated challenges.

Alice Nguyen is a sales associate at a trendy retail store at the mall near her home. Although Alice is in school full-time, her district manager has asked her if she wants to take a store manager position at a smaller store 10 miles away. Alice is excited about the promotion for several reasons. First, she would receive

a pay raise and second, it will allow her to use some of the skills she has gained in her business classes at school. Her current boss has a difficult management style, and Alice is determined to be a better manager than that. Alice googles "great management" to find some tips, and she decides to read this chapter of the text.

Organizing includes designing the structure of the organization and creating conditions and systems in which everyone and everything work together to achieve the organization's goals and objectives.[2] Many of today's organizations are designed around the customer. The idea is to design the firm so that everyone is working to satisfy the customer's needs, at a profit. Thus, organizations must remain flexible and adaptable because customer needs change, and organizations must either change along with them or risk losing business. For example, Dogwise, a small online bookseller specializing in books about dogs, decided to move its 5,000-square-foot office/warehouse to Wenatchee, Washington, in order to better meet its customers' needs.[3]

Leading means creating a vision for the organization and communicating, guiding, training, coaching, and motivating others to work effectively to achieve the organization's goals and objectives. The trend is to **empower** employees, giving them as much freedom as possible, so that they become self-directed and self-motivated. In other words, empowering employees means giving employees the authority (the right to make a decision without consulting the manager) and responsibility (the requirement to accept the consequences of one's actions) to respond quickly to customer requests. This function was once known as directing, that is, telling employees exactly what to do. In many smaller firms, that is still the role of managers. In most large modern firms, however, managers no longer tell people exactly what to do because knowledge workers and others often know how to do their jobs better than the manager does. Nonetheless, leadership is necessary to keep employees focused on the right priorities and timelines, while training employees, coaching them, motivating them, and performing the other leadership tasks.[4]

Controlling involves establishing clear standards to determine whether an organization is progressing toward its goals and objectives, rewarding people for doing a good job, and taking corrective action if

planning
Anticipating trends and determining the best strategies and tactics to achieve organizational goals and objectives.

organizing
Designing the structure of the organization and creating conditions and systems in which everyone and everything work together to achieve the organization's goals and objectives.

leading
Creating a vision for the organization and communicating, guiding, training, coaching, and motivating others to work effectively to achieve the organization's goals and objectives.

empower
Giving employees as much freedom as possible to become self-directed and self-motivated.

Our Mission and Vision: ABC Supply Co.

Since our founding in 1982, our mission has remained unchanged—make it easy for our customers. From the services we provide to the products we sell, we're committed to helping contractors succeed and grow their business.

We Fulfill That Mission By:

- Stocking the brands and products contractors want and need at a competitive price.
- Maintaining a state-of-the-art delivery system that ensures orders are delivered to the job site when and where they are needed.
- Actively listening to our customers to find out what they want and need, what we're doing well and how we can improve—and then implementing many of their suggestions.
- Providing ongoing training for every ABC Supply associate, ensuring they have the knowledge and expertise they need to provide world-class customer service.
- Training every ABC employee so they can provide contractors with the information and techniques they need to remain competitive.
- Challenging our associates to set goals for themselves and creating an environment that helps them realize those dreams.
- Judging our own success by the success of our customers. We know that we will only be successful when our customers are successful.

By staying true to this mission, we will realize our vision of being the supplier of choice for our contractor customers and being known as the greatest place to work in the United States.

Source: www.abcsupply.com/About.aspx?id=460, accessed September 4, 2007.

figure 6.1

MISSION AND VISION OF ABC SUPPLY CO.

controlling

Establishing clear standards to determine whether an organization is progressing toward its goals and objectives, rewarding people for doing a good job, and taking corrective action if they are not.

vision

A forward-looking statement that provides an encompassing explanation of why the organization exists and where it is headed in the future.

they are not. Basically, it means measuring whether what actually occurs meets the organization's goals.

The four functions just addressed—planning, organizing, leading, and controlling—are the heart of management. So let's explore these functions in more detail beginning with planning.

Planning

Planning, the first managerial function, involves setting the organizational vision, mission, goals, and objectives. Most successful companies employ several strategies to ensure planning is realistic. Part of planning involves creation of a **vision** and a **mission statement.** The *vision,* a forward-looking statement, provides an encompassing explanation of why the organization exists and where it is headed in the future. The *mission statement* is an outline of the organization's fundamental purposes. With the mission statement, an organization describes "what busines we are in."[5] Figure 6.1 shows the mission statement and the vision of ABC Supply Co.

Writing a Mission Statement

A meaningful mission statement should address the following components:

- Customer needs.
- Company philosophy and goals.
- The organization's self-concept.
- Long-term survival.
- The nature of the company's products or services.
- Social responsibility.
- Care for employees.

Mission statements can vary in length and content; however, an effective mission statement addresses the previously mentioned components. It should identify who your company is, what you stand for, what you do, and why you do it. An effective mission statement is best developed with input from all the members of an organization. Figure 6.2 shows sample mission statements of three different organizations. How well do they address all the components identified previously?

The mission statement becomes the foundation for setting specific goals. **Goals** are the broad, long-term accomplishments an organization wishes to attain. Goals need to be mutually agreed upon by workers and management. Thus, goal setting is often a team process. **Objectives** are specific, short-term statements detailing how to achieve the organization's goals. One of your goals for reading this chapter, for example, is to learn basic concepts of management. An objective you could

mission statement
An outline of the fundamental purposes of an organization.

goals
The broad, long-term accomplishments an organization wishes to attain.

objectives
Specific, short-term statements detailing how to achieve the organization's goals.

figure 6.2

OTHER SAMPLE MISSION STATEMENTS

- ***Mission statement for WCSU Daycare in Connecticut:*** The WCSU Childcare Center exists to provide a safe, developmentally appropriate environment for preschool and school age children. Our focus is to provide a stimulating early care and education experience which promotes each child's social/emotional, physical and cognitive development. Our goal is to support children's desire to be life-long learners.

- ***Mission statement for Zappos, an online shoe retailer:*** Our goal is to position Zappos as the online service leader. If we can get customers to associate the Zappos brand with the absolute best service, then we can expand into other product categories beyond shoes.

- ***Mission statement for Krusinski Construction Company in Illinois:*** Krusinski Construction Company is a leader in providing value-added construction services to our customers by creating a successful partnership with them throughout the construction process. Our pledge is to establish lasting relationships with our customers by exceeding their expectations and gaining their trust through exceptional performance by every member of the construction team.

figure 6.3

GUIDELINES FOR SETTING SMART OBJECTIVES

In this classic article, Doran explains the S.M.A.R.T. way to write goals and objectives. Over time, a few of the terms have been modified by other authors such as A = "agreed to" or R = "resource-based."

1. **Specific**—Make sure the objective is specific. Rather than saying "increase sales" say "increase sales by 10%."
2. **Measurable**—A company should be able to easily see if a goal is met. "Better customer service" is a hard goal to measure, but "increase customer service survey by 1 point in 6 months" is very measurable.
3. **Achievable**—Are the objectives achievable and attainable? Increasing company size by $1 million might not be achievable; however, increasing by $100k might be just difficult enough to be challenging, but not impossible.
4. **Realistic**—Can the company achieve the goal with the resources available? If a company does not have enough sales staff to increase sales, then increasing sales may not be the right goal. Hiring more people might be the better goal.
5. **Time**—What is the deadline for achieving goals? Is it 6 months, one year? Make sure it is realistic.

Source: SMART guidelines from George T. Doran, "There's a S.M.A.R.T. Way to Write Management Goals and Objectives," *Management Review,* November 1981, pp. 35–36. Copyright © 1981 American Management Association. Used with Permission.

use to achieve this goal is to answer correctly the chapter questions in the Student Study Guide that accompanies this text. To make goals and objectives most effective, you can use a framework called SMART objectives, illustrated in Figure 6.3.

SWOT and PEST

SWOT analysis

An analysis of the organization's **s**trengths, **w**eaknesses, **o**pportunities, and **t**hreats.

Another part of planning and setting goals might be to determine how well the company is doing at any given point in time. A **SWOT analysis** is useful for this. It is an analysis of the organization's **S**trengths, **W**eaknesses, **O**pportunities, and **T**hreats. The company begins such a process with an analysis of its business in general. Looking internally, what does the company do well? What does the company do poorly? Then, an external environmental analysis is performed. This analysis identifies external factors that could affect the business. For example, with advances in technology and a growing trend toward more people making online purchases,[6] an opportunity for a small retailer might include development of an e-commerce site, or selling products on eBay. Finally, threats include all existing external issues in a business's environment that would affect a business negatively. For example, if a national pizza chain were to open a store next to a family-owned pizza parlor, it certainly would have a negative impact on the family-owned pizza business. Also, with the oil prices up about 30 percent this year and expected to go even higher, they are impacting all businesses with increased gasoline and energy expenses.[7] Such events would be a threat for any small or large company in any industry. By performing a SWOT analysis, a company can better develop goals and objectives because managers can see the entire spectrum of their business both internally and externally. Figure 6.4 lists some of the potential issues companies consider when conducting a SWOT analysis.

Potential Internal STRENGTHS	Potential Internal WEAKNESSES
• Core competencies in key areas • An acknowledged market leader • Well-conceived functional area strategies • Proven management • Cost advantages • Better advertising campaigns	• No clear strategic direction • Obsolete facilities • Subpar profitability • Lack of managerial depth and talent • Weak market image • Too narrow a product line
Potential External OPPORTUNITIES	Potential External THREATS
• Ability to serve additional customer groups • Expansion of product lines • Ability to transfer skills/technology to new products • Falling trade barriers in attractive foreign markets • Complacency among rival firms • Ability to grow due to increases in market demand	• Entry of lower-cost foreign competitors • Rising sales of substitute products • Slower market growth • Costly regulatory requirements • Vulnerability to recession and business cycles • Changing buyer needs and tastes

figure 6.4

SWOT MATRIX

q: Develop a SWOT analysis for yourself. How can such
》 》 an analysis benefit your career?

The external environment of an organization can be divided into micro, or specific environment, and macro, or general environment. The micro or specific environment is comprised of factors such as the firm's customers, distributors, suppliers, and competitors. A company should pay close attention to these specific environmental factors because they have a direct impact on the firm's performance. Macro or general environments include factors that affect an organization indirectly. These factors are political, economic, sociocultural, and technological. A tool specifically useful in understanding and analyzing the macro environment is **PEST analysis.** PEST stands for **P**olitical, **E**conomic, **S**ocial, and **T**echnological. Similar to SWOT, a company would look at these four external areas to determine those things that may affect their business in the future. Political factors include political, legal, and regulatory issues and items, such as new laws being passed that could affect the businesses. In 2007, Congress passed the law to raise the federal minimum wage in three increments from $5.15 per hour to $7.25 per hour by 2009. The first of the increments took place on July 24, 2007, with minimum wage increasing to $5.85 per hour.[8] Although 30 states have a minimum wage higher than $5.85 per hour currently, the final wage rate of $7.25 per hour is bound to affect the small businesses. The manager would

PEST analysis

An analysis of outside factors that could affect a business: political, economic, social, and technological.

also look at economic factors such as interest rates, unemployment rates, availability of credit, inflation rates, and so on to determine how these might impact her business. For example, an unexpected drop in August 2007 payroll equaling higher unemployment rates has confirmed fears that the credit crisis has started to work its way to the broader economy beyond the housing market.[9] Higher unemployment rates result in lower disposable income which in turn results in lower consumer spending. If the trend continues with the unemployment rate, it could have significant negative impact on businesses. Sociocultural factors include items such as number of births, number of deaths, number of marriages, number of divorces, immigration and emigration rates, and so forth. For example, the U.S. life expectancy has grown from 47.3 years in the 1900s to a record 77.9 years in 2004.[10] What impact do you believe this has if you are a business owner? Finally, technology changes that can affect a business need to be considered. For example, the Internet has changed the way people communicate and do business. An effective Web site cannot only serve the purpose of information distribution but also can help create new revenue streams for a business. Using both SWOT and PEST, a business, big or small, can get a larger picture of those things that may require future planning.

Another way to view planning is to consider four forms of planning: strategic planning, tactical planning, operational planning, and contingency planning (see Figure 6.5).

strategic planning

Setting of long-term goals for the company.

Strategic planning is the setting of major, long-term goals for the company. Often, these goals have to do with the long-term growth of the company or new product offerings. It provides the foundation for the policies, procedures, and strategies for obtaining and using resources to achieve those goals. For example, a strategic plan for Mountain City Coffeehouse & Creamery in Frostburg, Maryland, includes long-term goals of

figure 6.5

PLANNING FUNCTIONS

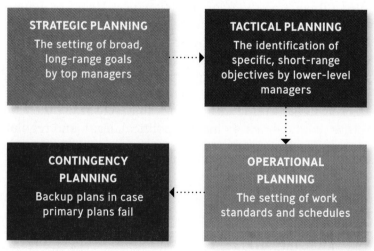

FORMS OF PLANNING

STRATEGIC PLANNING
The setting of broad, long-range goals by top managers

TACTICAL PLANNING
The identification of specific, short-range objectives by lower-level managers

CONTINGENCY PLANNING
Backup plans in case primary plans fail

OPERATIONAL PLANNING
The setting of work standards and schedules

Basics of Career Planning Objectives

For students to become more focused on their careers, they should ask themselves basic questions to help set themselves on the career track that will lead them to their highest aspirations.

To begin the process of planning career objectives, read the following questions and do your best to provide answers that will help you formulate your career aspirations:

- What is your ideal career?
- What companies would you consider to be a good fit to the career you are striving for?
- What skills do you have that might be a good fit to your ideal career?
- What desired salary and benefits do you expect from this career?
- Are you willing to relocate?
- What is keeping you from obtaining this career?

opening new locations and kiosks, establishing the coffeehouse as an art venue, and expanding catering menu selections.

Tactical planning is the process of developing detailed, short-term statements about what is to be done, who is to do it, and how it is to be done. These objectives are the short-term goals that must be achieved in order to meet the strategic plans and goals. Tactical plans for expanding catering menu selections for Mountain City Coffeehouse & Creamery include development of new specials separate from the in-store offerings by the chef and collecting local artists' information and organizing monthly art displays by the different artists.

Operational planning is the process of setting work standards and schedules necessary to implement the company's tactical objectives. The operational plan is the manager's tool for daily and weekly operations. For the coffeehouse, operational planning would include the weekly ordering of ingredients from different vendors (such as coffee roasters), scheduling of employees, and establishing and conforming to the daily opening and closing routines of the coffeehouse.

tactical planning
The development of several objectives for each goal. These are the short-term goals that must be achieved to attain long-term goals.

operational planning
Scheduling, budgeting, and any other necessary plans used to meet the tactical objectives.

q: Can you apply the different forms of planning to your
» » own career or your progress toward a degree? Explain.

contingency planning

Planning for "what if" scenarios and secondary plans in case the original ones do not work.

Contingency planning is the process of preparing alternative courses of action that may be used if the primary plans do not achieve the organization's objectives. For example, the contingency plans for meeting the sales goals for Mountain City Coffeehouse include advertising more to students on the campus of the local college, increasing the local radio advertising, and offering special discounts to regular customers tied to frequency and volume. *Crisis planning* is the part of contingency planning that involves reacting to sudden changes in the environment.

Organizing

organization chart

Visual diagram that shows relationships among people and divides the organization's work.

span of control

The optimal number of subordinates (employees) a manager supervises.

After managers have planned a course of action, they must organize the firm to accomplish their goals. Operationally, organizing means allocating resources (such as funds for various functions within departments), assigning tasks, and establishing procedures for accomplishing the organizational objectives. An **organization chart** is a visual diagram that shows relationships among people and divides the organization's work; it shows who is accountable for the completion of specific work, and who reports to whom. An organization chart includes top, middle, and first-line or supervisory managers (see Figure 6.6). In addition, it also shows the **span of control,** which is the number of subordinates a manager supervises. The optimum span of control depends greatly on the type of company and experience of employees.

q: Would you prefer to have a smaller or larger
»» span of control as a manager?

top management

It is the highest level of management and consists of the president and other key company executives.

Top management (the highest level of management) consists of the president and other key company executives who develop strategic plans. Terms you're likely to see often are Chief Executive Officer (CEO), Chief Operating Officer (COO), Chief Financial Officer (CFO), and Chief Information Officer (CIO), or (in some companies) Chief Knowledge Officer (CKO). The CEO is often the president of the firm and is responsible for all top-level decisions in the firm. CEOs are responsible for introducing change into an organization. The COO is responsible for putting those changes into effect. His or her tasks include structuring work, controlling operations, and rewarding people to ensure that everyone strives to carry out the leader's vision. The CFO is responsible for obtaining funds, planning budgets, collecting funds, and so on. The CIO or CKO is responsible for getting the right information to other managers so they can make accurate decisions.

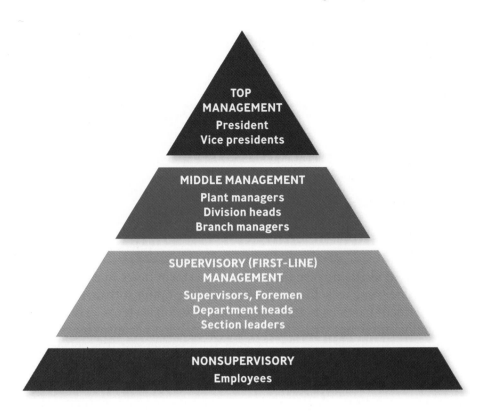

figure 6.6

LEVELS OF MANAGEMENT

This figure shows the three levels of management. In many firms there are several levels of middle management. Recently, however, some firms have eliminated middle-level managers because fewer are needed to manage self-managed teams.

Middle management includes general managers, division managers, district managers, and plant managers. These are the individuals who are responsible for tactical planning and controlling. Many firms have eliminated some middle managers through downsizing and have given the remaining managers more employees to supervise.

Supervisory management or **first-line management** are those who are directly responsible for operational planning, supervising workers, and evaluating their daily performance.

middle management

General managers, division managers, district managers, and plant managers or supervisors.

supervisory (first-line) management

Those who are directly responsible for supervising workers and evaluating their daily performance.

Tasks and Skills at Different Levels of Management

Few people are trained to be good managers. Usually a person learns a skill, such as providing excellent patient customer service in a medical office, and is selected to be a manager. The tendency is for such managers to become deeply involved in showing others how to do things, helping them, supervising them, and generally being very active in the operations-related tasks. The further up the managerial ladder a person moves, the less he may use his original job skills. Figure 6.7 shows that a manager must have three categories of skills:

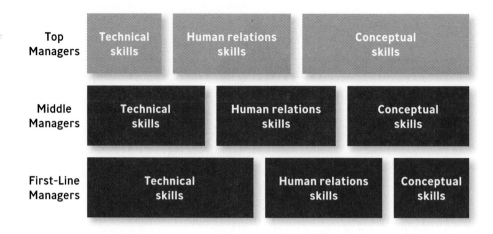

figure 6.7

SKILLS NEEDED AT VARIOUS LEVELS OF MANAGEMENT

All managers need human relations skills. At the top, managers need strong conceptual skills and rely less on technical skills. First-line managers need strong technical skills and rely less on conceptual skills. Middle managers need to have a balance between technical and conceptual skills.

technical skills
The skills required to do a specific job.

human relations skills
The ability to communicate and work with others.

conceptual skills
Ability to see the "big" picture.

1. **Technical skills** involve the ability to perform tasks in a specific discipline (such as selling a product or developing software) or department (such as marketing or information systems). This is especially important with supervisory managers, because they work closely, sometimes even side-by-side, with employees. Top-level managers may not need to use technical skills as much, as they are more focused on utilizing conceptual skills.

2. **Human relations skills** involve communication and motivation; they enable managers to work with and through people. Such skills also include those associated with leadership, coaching, morale building, delegating, training and development, and help and supportiveness. Human relations skills are critical in all three levels of management.

3. **Conceptual skills** involve the ability to picture the organization as a whole and the relationships among its various parts. Conceptual skills are needed in planning, organizing, controlling, systems development, problem analysis, decision making, coordinating, and delegating. Generally, this skill set is needed for top-level managers and may not be as necessary for first-line supervisors.

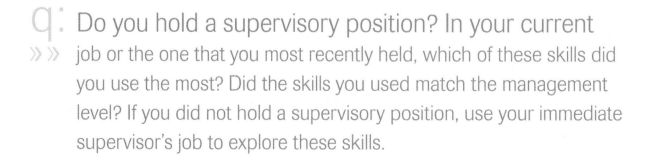

q: Do you hold a supervisory position? In your current job or the one that you most recently held, which of these skills did you use the most? Did the skills you used match the management level? If you did not hold a supervisory position, use your immediate supervisor's job to explore these skills.

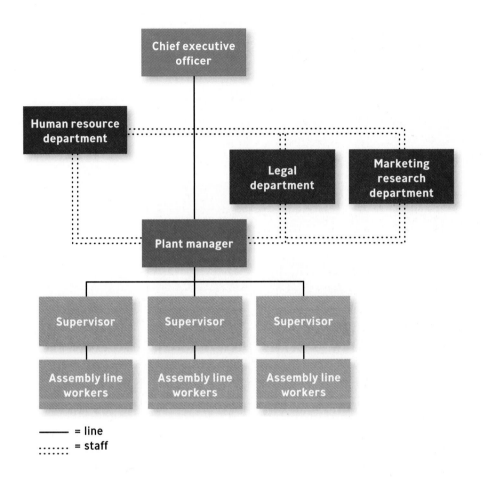

figure 6.8a

**LINE-AND-STAFF VERSUS
MATRIX ORGANIZATION**

Here are two sample
organizational structures.
The one on the bottom,
called a *line-and-staff
structure,* is most traditional.
It indicates a manager
overseeing employees.

Earlier we defined an organization chart. A major part of the organizing function is the parameter within which a manager must work. An *organizational structure* is the way a company is organized and where all employees fit into the bigger picture of the company. A manager must thoroughly understand what kind of structure her company has. There are several types of organizational structures a company can have, as noted by Figures 6.8a and 6.8b. A *line-and-staff* structure is one where the staff personnel advise and assist the line personnel in meeting the goals of the organization. Line personnel are part of the chain of command that are responsible for directly achieving organizational goals. A *matrix* organization, on the other hand, teams people from various departments to accomplish a common goal, such as getting a project done for a client. In a company that manufactures custom closets, for example, a salesperson, production person, and installer may all work together on designing a product for a customer.

An important element of organizational structure is the process of departmentalization. Departmentalization means to "group" related jobs or work processes into separate units. The traditional way to departmentalize organizations is by functions. Functional departmentalization is probably the most widely used grouping by small-to-medium-size

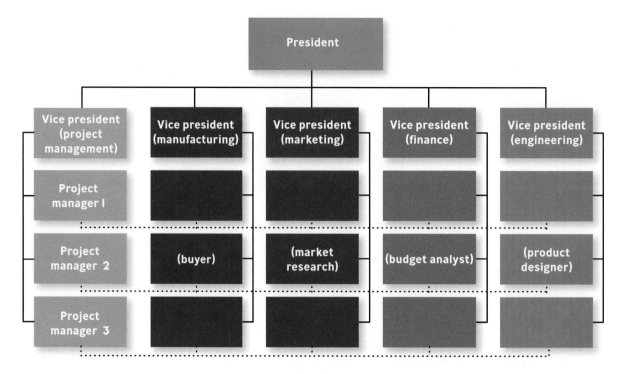

figure 6.8b

LINE-AND-STAFF VERSUS MATRIX ORGANIZATION

The second structure, called a *matrix organization,* utilizes a more nontraditional form with work teams made up of people from several departments. This kind of structure can be an advantage in many types of industries where several experts might be needed to complete one project.

organizations because of its simplicity. Functional structure is grouping of workers into departments based on similar tasks, expertise, or resources used. A company might have, for example, a production department, a transportation department, a finance department, and a human resource department. Figure 6.9 shows five ways a firm can departmentalize.

When a firm groups individuals and tasks around its major product lines, it is called product departmentalization. For example, a book publisher might have a textbook, a trade book, and a technical book department. In some organizations, it makes more sense to group activities around the major customers it serves. For example, a stock trading or brokerage firm may group its activities into small, individual clients, institutional clients, and a research department—in other words, types of customers it primarily caters to.

Many times organizations group the tasks and processes to meet the different needs of customers in different geographic regions. For example, a restaurant company may create units as northeast, southeast, northwest, southwest, and Midwest regions. A few firms find it most efficient to separate activities by process. For example, a small garment manufacturing firm might group activities as one department that sizes and cuts the garments, one that dyes the garments, one that stitches the material, and one that finishes the final product with accessories on them.

Many times firms use a combination of these departmentalization techniques—hybrid forms. For example, a firm could use function and

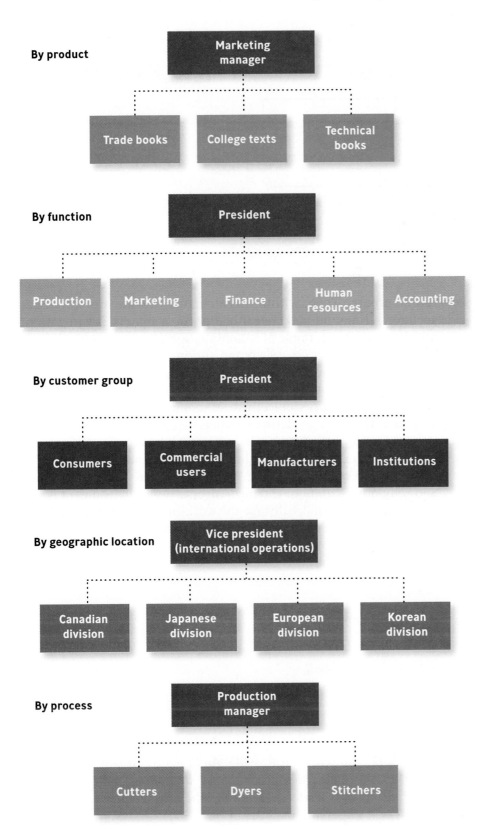

By product

Marketing manager

Trade books   College texts   Technical books

By function

President

Production   Marketing   Finance   Human resources   Accounting

By customer group

President

Consumers   Commercial users   Manufacturers   Institutions

By geographic location

Vice president (international operations)

Canadian division   Japanese division   European division   Korean division

By process

Production manager

Cutters   Dyers   Stitchers

figure 6.9

WAYS TO DEPARTMENTALIZE

A computer company may want to departmentalize by geographic location (countries), a manufacturer by function, a pharmaceutical company by customer group, a leather manufacturer by process, and a publisher by product. In each case, the structure must fit the firm's goal.

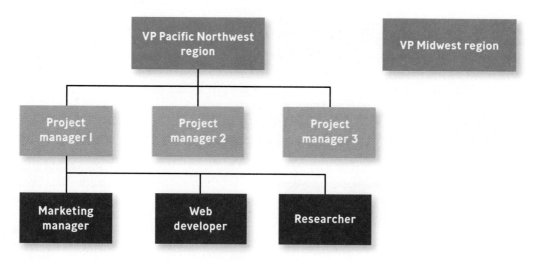

figure 6.10

GEOGRAPHIC DEPARTMENTALIZATION WITH MATRIX STYLE ORGANIZATION

An example of a software installation company departmentalizing by geographic locations and matrix style organization. As you can see, the regions are divided geographically (Pacific Northwest and Midwest), then the organization is further divided by projects.

geographic groups. Then, within this structure, a company would decide to have a line-and-staff organization or a matrix organization. Figure 6.10 shows an example of a combination of a geographic departmentalization with a matrix style organization.

Another aspect of organizations is **staffing.** Staffing involves recruiting, hiring, motivating, and retaining the best people available to accomplish the company's objectives. Managing diversity is also part of organizing. Diversity, as defined earlier, means to build systems and cultures that unite different people in a common pursuit, without undermining their individual strengths. Diversity includes, but also goes beyond, differences in race, gender, ethnicity, sexual orientation, abilities, and religious affiliation. Having a diverse work environment is key to success, because the more diverse the workforce, the more ideas from a variety of backgrounds can be generated. How to create a diverse workforce and manage it, as well as hiring the best people for the job, will be discussed further later in this chapter.

q: Consider your current workplace or a past workplace.
»» Do you think it is, or was, diverse?

staffing

Recruiting, hiring, motivating, and retaining the best people available to accomplish the company's objectives.

Leading

A leader is a person who can provide guidance to employees through establishment of values and ethics, but also can manage change through vision. We will discuss leadership more in the next chapter, but for now, the keys to good leadership include:

- *Communicate a vision and rally others around that vision.* In doing so, the leader should be openly sensitive to the concerns of followers, give them responsibility, and win their trust.[11]

- *Establish company values.* These values include a concern for employees, for customers, for the environment, and for the quality of the company's products. When companies set their business goals today, they're defining the values of the company as well.

- *Promote corporate ethics.* Ethics include an unfailing demand for honesty and an insistence that everyone in the company be treated fairly. Concern for social responsibility by leaders in a business can set the pace for ethics within the entire company. Many businesspeople are now making the news by giving away huge amounts to charity, thus setting a model of social concern for their employees and others.

- *Embrace change.* A leader's most important job may be to transform the way the company does business, so that the company becomes more effective (does things better) and efficient (uses fewer resources to accomplish the same objectives). One of the major challenges that managers may find is to help employees deal with change. Often employees do not understand the need for change or see change as affecting them negatively because they have to do things differently, which can make implementing the change difficult. If employees see a reason for a change, and have input into the change, they are much more likely to accept it. As we discussed earlier in this chapter, things often happen within the company (which require conceptual skills) that first-line supervisors or employees may not be aware of. Managers can help employees understand and accept a new change through open communication, participation, and feedback mechanisms.

Controlling

The control function involves measuring performance relative to the planned objectives and standards, rewarding people for work well done, and then taking corrective action when necessary. Thus, the control process (see Figure 6.11) is one key to a successful management system because it provides the feedback that enables managers and workers to adjust to any changes in plans or in the environment that have affected performance. Controlling consists of five steps:

1. *Establishing clear performance standards.* Employees should know exactly what is expected of them. Once the standards are clear to employees, and they know how they will be measured, the next step can take place.

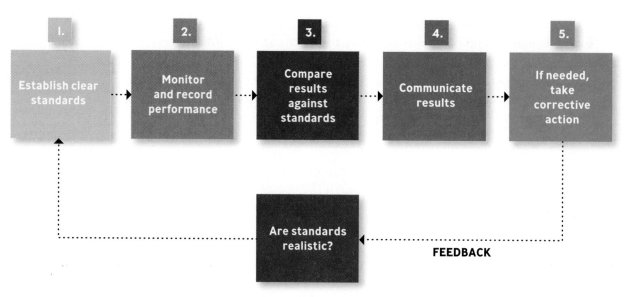

figure 6.11

THE CONTROL PROCESS

The whole control process is based on clear standards. Without such standards, the other steps are difficult, if not impossible. With clear standards, performance measurement is relatively easy and the proper action can be taken.

2. *Monitoring and recording actual performance.* A manager observes and records the performance of the employees against the standards that have been set.

3. *Comparing results against plans and standards.* After performance standards have been put into place and actual performance has been measured, the manager needs to compare the two.

4. *Communicating results and deviations to the employees involved.* If performance standards have not been met, or if they have been met or exceeded, the manager communicates it to employees.

5. *Taking corrective action when needed and providing positive feedback.* If the employees, for example, did not have proper training to run new machines, a corrective action would be to offer the needed training so that the employees involved can perform the tasks needed to meet the standard.

What Else Do Managers Do?

Obviously, the kinds of tasks managers do will vary greatly with the type of industry. Some managers may work directly with employees to get a task done, such as a supermarket manager who cashiers when the lines get too a long. But generally speaking, managers are also responsible for setting the tone of ethics, creating an environment for a good work–life balance, and also making sure high-quality products are being produced.

First, as we discussed in Chapter 4, managers establish the ethical framework. Employees tend to look up to managers for both guidance and example; therefore, if a manager acts unethically, there is a good chance employees will do the same. For example, if the manager takes longer than the hour allowed for lunch, the employees may start to do the same. If the manager arrives late to work, the employees may think it is not a big deal to be late or that it is acceptable to be late, and, as a result, might make on-time attendance a flexible issue.

Besides setting the tone for ethics, managers also need to do what they can to ensure a good work–life balance for employees. **Work–life balance** is a person's control over the interactions between his or her work life and family and personal life. A positive work-life balance can be achieved when persons feel satisfied about their personal life while still feeling satisfied and fulfilled by their work life. Managers can sometimes create work–life balance issues when their expectations exceed what a person can accomplish within a regular work week. At that point, the individual is working too much and generally does not have a good balance between work and life. Consider the manager who comes to your desk on Friday at 4 p.m. and expects a 30-page report to be completed by Monday morning at 9 a.m. Not only is this unrealistic, but it also creates stress for the employee. While the employee is working on the report, he or she probably does not have a good work–life balance, since to finish the report, almost every minute needs to be focused on work. There will always be circumstances where deadlines take precedence over a good work–life balance, but when these circumstances happen too often, it can result in an unhappy and burned-out employee.

Finally, the last (but hardly least) task of a manager is ensuring the good quality of products or services. This overall goal in a sense embodies and results from all other managerial functions. **Total quality management (TQM)** is a management strategy whereby quality goods are ensured at every phase of the production process, even in service organizations. In TQM, the manager must inspire employees to be concerned at every stage of production about providing excellent quality. The basis for TQM rests on attention to satisfying customer needs and continuous improvement in everything the organization does. For example, if a table manufacturer were to employ a TQM philosophy, all of the employees would be well trained in looking for defects in materials or flaws in procedure at every point in the manufacturing process. Everyone in the company would be responsible for ensuring the final high quality of the product from start to finish and thereby satisfying customer needs at the highest level possible.

Study Skills

Return on My Investment

If I spend more time on improving my study skills, what is my return on my investment?

By now, the basic concepts of study skills have been revealed, and your ability to understand these concepts and identify your strengths and weaknesses regarding them helps set realistic goals for your improvement.

What might be my return for this work? Perhaps some of the following:

- Improved grades
- Greater understanding of subjects
- More downtime from school
- Receiving an honor's degree
- More confidence toward graduation
- Improved time management skills
- More focus on expected career

---

work–life balance

The idea that an individual should have control over interactions between work and home.

---

total quality management (TQM)

A management strategy where quality is reviewed at every phase of the production process, even in service organizations.

SELF-CHECK QUESTIONS

1. What are the four functions of management? Which do you think is the most important? Why?
2. Perform a analysis and a PEST analysis on your school bookstore.
3. Why do you think TQM is so important in today's businesses?
4. Provide possible goals, objectives, and tactical plans for a company of your choice.

Section Outline

Management Styles

- Autocratic Leadership
- Participative Leadership
- Free-Rein Leadership
- Theory X
- Theory Y
- Theory Z

MANAGEMENT STYLES

Now that we have discussed what a manager does, it is important to know that there are several management or leadership styles by which to achieve goals. No one style is better than another, as it depends on the situation, and different styles work best in different situations.[12] Figure 6.12 shows the autocratic, participative, and free-rein styles.

Autocratic Leadership

Autocratic leadership involves making managerial decisions without consulting others.[13] For example, a manager might make a decision to change the bonus structure of the sales force. In this type of situation, it might not be best to consult employees, because it is unlikely they will have an unbiased view of salary. Tony Dungy, the coach of the Indianapolis Colts, led his

figure 6.12

LEADERSHIP STYLES

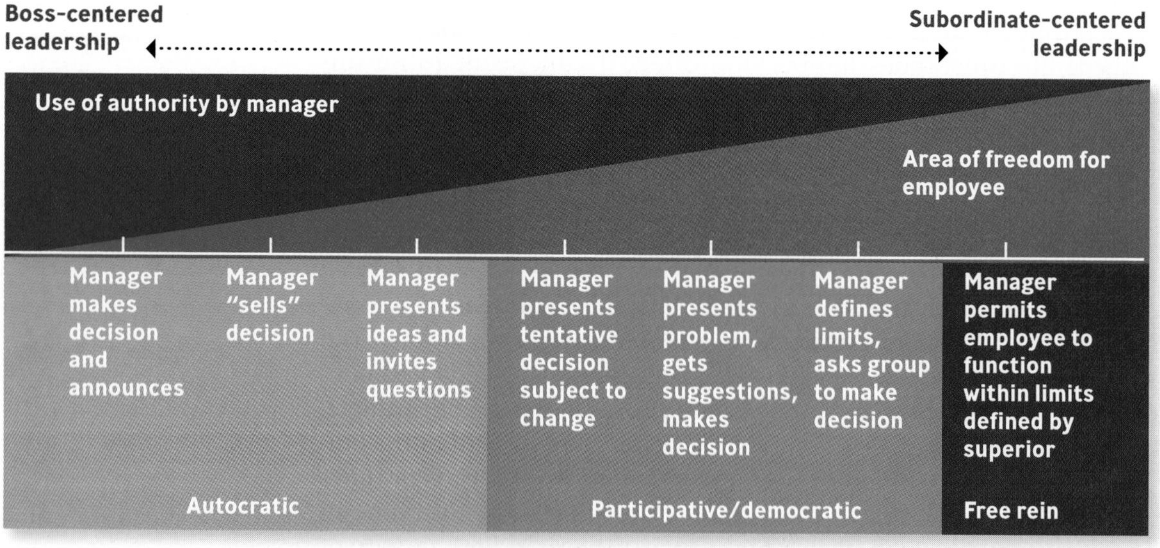
Boss-centered leadership
Subordinate-centered leadership
Use of authority by manager
Area of freedom for employee
Manager makes decision and announces
Manager "sells" decision
Manager presents ideas and invites questions
Manager presents tentative decision subject to change
Manager presents problem, gets suggestions, makes decision
Manager defines limits, asks group to make decision
Manager permits employee to function within limits defined by superior
Autocratic
Participative/democratic
Free rein

Source: Reprinted by permission of the *Harvard Business Review*. An exhibit from "How to Choose a Leadership Pattern" by Robert Tannenbaum and Warren Schmidt (May/June 1973). Copyright © 1973 by the Harvard Business School Publishing Corporation, all rights reserved.

team to a Super Bowl championship in 2007[14] by using an autocratic leadership approach. An autocratic approach is best when working with sports teams, because you want the coach to determine positioning and strategy, since he or she tends to see the bigger picture.

Coach Tony Dungy of the Indianapolis Colts during a game.

Participative Leadership

Participative (democratic) leadership consists of managers and employees working together to make decisions. Research has found that employee participation in decisions may not always increase effectiveness, but it usually increases job satisfaction. Many progressive organizations are highly successful at using a democratic style of leadership that values traits such as flexibility, good listening skills, and empathy.

Organizations that have successfully used this style include most small- to medium-size firms, such as Ascentium, described in the opening profile of this chapter. Even large firms, which often used an autocratic style, have effectively implemented this democratic style of management in their workplaces. For example, Cisco, IBM, and FedEx all recognize the importance of a more participative management style. Many small businesses have made this change as well and tend to find much better results. In such firms, employees discuss management issues and resolve those issues together in a democratic manner. That is, everyone has some opportunity to contribute to decisions.

Free-Rein Leadership

Free-rein leadership, also called **laissez-faire leadership,** involves managers setting objectives and then employees being relatively free to do whatever it takes to accomplish those objectives. In certain organizations, this can be the best management style. This style might be used when employees know the job very well and trust exists among management and employees. For example, an administrator of a hospital will likely use the free-rein method because doctors often know better than the administrator what is best for the patients. Likewise, managers in technical companies may not know how to develop new software; hence,

autocratic leadership

Making managerial decisions without consulting others.

participative (democratic) leadership

Managers and employees work together to make decisions.

free-rein (laissez-faire) leadership

Managers setting objectives and then employees being relatively free to do whatever it takes to accomplish those objectives.

Chess, Not Checkers

GREAT MANAGERS PLAY CHESS, NOT CHECKERS

Average managers play checkers, while great managers play chess. The difference? In checkers, all the pieces are uniform and move in the same way; they are interchangeable. You need to plan and coordinate their movements, certainly, but they all move at the same pace, on parallel paths. In chess, each type of piece moves in a different way, and you can't play if you don't know how each piece moves.

Great managers know and value the unique abilities and even the eccentricities of their employees, and they learn how best to integrate them into a coordinated plan of attack.

BEING A MANAGER IS DIFFERENT THAN BEING A LEADER

Great leaders discover what is universal and capitalize on it. Their job is to rally people toward a better future. Leaders can succeed in this only when they can cut through differences of race, sex, age, nationality, and personality and, using stories and celebrating heroes, tap into those very few needs we all share.

The job of a manager, meanwhile, is to turn one person's particular talent into performance. Managers will succeed only when they can identify and deploy the differences among people, challenging each employee to excel in his or her own way. This doesn't mean a leader can't be a manager or vice versa. But to excel at one or both, you must be aware of the very different skills each role requires.

GREAT MANAGERS CAPITALIZE ON PEOPLE'S UNIQUE ABILITIES

All that said, the reason great managers focus on uniqueness isn't just because it makes good business sense. They do it because they can't help it.

Like Shelley and Keats, the nineteenth-century Romantic poets, great managers are fascinated with individuality for its own sake. Fine shadings of personality, though

free rein is often the best style in that situation. The personal traits needed by managers in such organizations include warmth, friendliness, and understanding. More and more firms are adopting this style of leadership with at least some of their employees.

Theory X

Management theorist Douglas McGregor observed that managers' attitudes about their employees usually fall into one of two categories.[15] First, **Theory X** managers tend to believe:

- The average person dislikes work and will avoid it if possible.
- Because of this dislike, workers must be forced, controlled, directed, or threatened with punishment to make them put forth the effort necessary to achieve the company's goals.
- The average worker prefers to be directed, wishes to avoid responsibility, has relatively little ambition, and wants security.
- Primary motivators are fear and money.

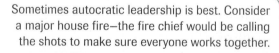

Sometimes autocratic leadership is best. Consider a major house fire—the fire chief would be calling the shots to make sure everyone works together.

they may be invisible to some and frustrating to others, are crystal clear to and highly valued by great managers. They could no more ignore these subtleties than ignore their own needs and desires. Figuring out what makes people tick is simply in their nature.

GREAT MANAGERS FIND WAYS TO AMPLIFY A PERSON'S STYLE

Great managers don't try to change a person's style. They never try to push a knight to move in the same way as a bishop.

They know that their employees will differ in how they think, how they build relationships, how altruistic they are, how patient they can be, how much of an expert they need to be, how prepared they need to feel, what drives them, what challenges them, and what their goals are. These differences of trait and talent are like blood types: They cut across the superficial variations of race, sex, and age and capture the essential uniqueness of each individual.

GREAT MANAGING IS ABOUT *RELEASING* NOT *TRANSFORMING*

To excel at managing others, you must bring that insight to your actions and interactions. Always remember that great managing is about release, not transformation. It's about constantly tweaking your environment so that the unique contribution, the unique needs, and the unique style of each employee can be given free rein. Your success as a manager will depend almost entirely on your ability to do this.

Questions

1. Have you ever had a manager who embodied these "musts" for managers? What was it like to work for that person?

2. What would you need to focus on to become this type of manager?

Source: Marcus Buckingham, *Harvard Business Review,* March 2005.

The natural consequence of such attitudes, beliefs, and assumptions is a manager who is very "involved" and who watches people closely, telling them what to do and how to do it. Motivation is more likely to take the form of punishment for bad work, rather than reward for good work. Theory X managers give workers little responsibility, authority, or flexibility. In other words, employees with a Theory X manager tend to be motivated by fear of "getting in trouble" rather than doing what is best for the company. This type of motivation may work in the short term, but it is unlikely this approach will work in the long term. Again, this type of approach does not take into account that everyone can be a leader.

Theory Y

The second theory of McGregor's is **Theory Y.** A Theory Y manager has very different beliefs and attitudes about employees:

- Most people like work; it is as natural as play or rest.
- Most people naturally work toward goals to which they are committed.
- The depth of a person's commitment to goals depends on the perceived rewards for achieving them.
- Under certain conditions, most people not only accept but also seek responsibility.

Theory X

Managers believe the average person dislikes work, has relatively little ambition, and wishes to avoid responsibility, so workers must be forcefully directed or threatened with punishment. Primary motivators are fear and money.

Theory Y

Managers believe most people like work and naturally work toward goals to which they are committed. People are capable of using imagination and creativity to solve problems. Each worker is stimulated by rewards unique to that worker.

- People are capable of using a relatively high degree of imagination, creativity, and cleverness to solve problems.
- In industry, the average person's intellectual potential is only partially realized.
- People are motivated by a variety of rewards. Each worker is stimulated by rewards unique to that worker (time off, money, recognition, and so on).

Rather than emphasize authority, direction, and close supervision, Theory Y emphasizes a relaxed managerial atmosphere in which workers are free to set objectives, be creative, be flexible, and go beyond the goals set by management. The trend in many U.S. businesses is toward Theory Y management. One reason for this trend is that many service industries, such as restaurants, are finding Theory Y helpful in motivating employees. Motivated employees usually mean happy customers, which of course results in higher profits!

Theory Z

Theory Z

Management theory that focuses on trust and intimacy within the work group.

Developed in the 1980s by William Ouchi, another theory is **Theory Z.** This style combines characteristics from Japanese and American management styles and includes a focus on trust and intimacy within the group (viewing employees as family). Theory Z blends a Japanese management style approach favoring consensus with appreciation of the value of individual rights and individual achievements, similar to American approaches. Managers implementing this style tend to believe in:

- Long-term employment in a company.
- Collective decision making. In other words, the entire group should assist in making decisions.
- Individual responsibility. All persons have an important role to play, and if they don't play that role, they are letting down their team.
- Slow evaluation and promotion. Employees are not promoted quickly, nor are their evaluations performed quickly. Ouchi believed this is the best way to nurture management skills.
- A specialized career path. All employees will be aware of the career path for their job.
- Holistic concern for employees and their families. Not only are the managers concerned about the employees' performance at work, they are also concerned about the home life of the employees.

Figure 6.13 shows a comparison of theories X, Y, and Z. Individual managers rarely fit neatly into just one of these categories. Researchers illustrate managing style as a continuum with varying amounts of

Theory X	Theory Y	Theory Z
1. Employees dislike work and will try to avoid it.	1. Employees view work as a natural part of life.	1. Employee involvement is the key to increased productivity.
2. Employees prefer to be controlled and directed.	2. Employees prefer limited control and direction.	2. Employee control is implied and informal.
3. Employees seek security, not responsibility.	3. Employees will seek responsibility under proper work conditions.	3. Employees prefer to share responsibility and decision making.
4. Employees must be intimidated by managers to perform.	4. Employees perform better in work environments that are nonintimidating.	4. Employees perform better in environments that foster trust and cooperation.
5. Employees are motivated by financial rewards.	5. Employees are motivated by many different needs.	5. Employees need guaranteed employment and will accept slow evaluations and promotions.

figure 6.13

A COMPARISON OF THEORIES X, Y, AND Z

employee participation, ranging from purely boss-centered leadership to subordinate-centered leadership.

Which management style is best? Research tells us that successful management depends largely on the goals and values of the firm, who's being led, and in what situations. For example, an autocratic leader might be best in a situation where things need to be done quickly, or when the employees are new and not yet familiar with the specifics of their job. A free-rein leader might be best if the employees are working on a long-term project. In other words, any management style, ranging from autocratic to free-rein, may be successful, depending on the people and the situation. In fact, a single manager should use a variety of leadership styles to match the people and the situations involved.

q: Which leadership style would you prefer to work with?

》 》 Which leadership style do you think you have?

SELF-CHECK QUESTIONS

1. Do you think you would work well under free-rein leadership? Why or why not?
2. Have you had a Theory X, Y, or Z manager? Describe your experience working for that person.

MANAGEMENT CHALLENGES

As you can see, human relations and conceptual skills are extremely important, perhaps more so than are technical skills, for dealing with a constantly changing workplace. The unique challenges managers face today include:

- Intense management scrutiny, caused by business scandals.
- Constant change in business.
- Global competition.
- Technological changes.
- Diversity in the workforce.
- Elimination of managerial and other jobs due to downsizing.
- The need to get things done by working with new generations of employees with different attitudes.

The business scandals of the early 2000s, such as those that occurred at Enron and WorldCom, have put business managers under intense scrutiny. Not only large but also small businesses have been part and parcel of the shady, unethical business dealings both in the United States and when doing business in foreign countries. Responding to public criticism adds new challenges to already pressure-filled jobs. New laws resulting from the scandals have complicated the lives of managers as well. However, the good news is that the Ethic Resource Center's (ERC) 2003 National Business Ethics Survey found that 90 percent of U.S. small-business respondents consider their top managers ethical, with only 18 percent admitting to having observed misconduct at work.[16]

Another current source of pressure on managers is the constant change occurring in today's business environment. For example, THQ Inc., an interactive entertainment publisher, is a fast-growing company in America. THQ used to stand for Toy Headquarters, reflecting the company's earlier days as a toy manufacturer. Today, THQ focuses exclusively on developing and publishing video games and employs approximately 2,000 people worldwide. It is one of the the largest video game makers, in the industry along with Nintendo, Sony PlayStation, and Electronic Arts. THQ has net revenues of over $1 billion.[17] The company went from employing a small informal group of workers, who knew each other well and communicated freely, to a larger corporation, in which knowledge sharing has become a challenge.

Such rapid change makes it more important than ever to have clear goals that enable a company to stay focused. The need to manage change has become increasingly important in light of today's emphasis on speed in the global marketplace. Global competition is just a click away, national borders mean less now than ever before, and competition

Focus on Ethics

WHAT WOULD YOU DO?

Suppose an employee of a retail store arrives at work and clocks in at 1:00 p.m., just in time for his scheduled shift. However, he still needs to use the restroom, eat his lunch, and check his voicemail. By the time he arrives on the floor, it is 1:15 and he has already been clocked in for 15 minutes. The manager doesn't say anything because they are friends.

Suppose a friend of yours is looking for a job, and you tell her about an opening where you work. You know that she is always late to work and doesn't pay attention to detail, but you recommend her for the job anyway. When the hiring manager comes to you as a reference, you still don't tell her the truth about your friend because you hope you can help your friend mend her ways.

QUESTIONS

1. Is the manager's behavior ethical? What would you do if you were one of the other employees?

2. What would you do if you were the friend and realized the situation? The hiring manager?

among companies has greatly increased. Outsourcing to India and other countries has caused major debates about the decrease in American jobs and global competition affecting U.S. labor markets negatively. Interestingly, new twists in globalization have created a sort of reverse outsourcing. Major global Indian firms are hiring Americans aggressively and even opening locations in the United States, thereby increasing the competition even more.[18]

The acceleration of technological change has resulted in a new breed of worker, one who is more educated and more skilled than workers in the past. Companies have a need for workers who are able to self-manage and also deal with change. At the same time, these new workers demand more freedom of operation and different managerial styles. Because of this new type of worker, managers need to use effective leadership skills in the workplace. Managers in most companies today tend to be friendly and generally treat employees as partners, rather than as unruly (Theory X) workers. Casual dress, parental leave, and flexible work hours are all new areas that managers must address with their employees.

The increasing diversity of the workforce is creating additional challenges. Currently, there are over four generations at work today, with different values and goals, working side-by-side. Each generation has a different expectation of management, which can create misunderstandings that must be dealt with by managers. Besides generational challenges, immigration and diverse national backgrounds in the workplace can also cause challenges for managers.

A diverse work environment includes not only people from a variety of races, but people from a variety of age groups.

downsizing (rightsizing)

Elimination of many management jobs, and other types of jobs, by using cost-cutting methods and technology, such as computers.

Communication, for example, can be a challenge when diverse languages are present.

Furthermore, because the workforce is becoming more educated and self-directed, much **downsizing,** or **rightsizing,** is occurring. *Downsizing* refers to shrinking of the organization by reducing the workforce. *Rightsizing* is often used synonymously with downsizing; however, rightsizing suggests matching resources to the need. So if the organization has excess human resources, some may be downsized or rightsized to match the need. Both reflect reduction in jobs. In addition, as layoffs and restructuring occur, managers may find themselves in the position of deciding who should be laid off and who will remain with the company, which can be emotionally draining.

Managers practice the art of getting things done through organizational resources that are available (e.g., workers, financial resources, information, and equipment). At one time, managers were commonly referred to as bosses, and their job consisted of telling people what to do, and then watching over them to be sure they did it. Bosses tended to be autocratic or lead by Theory X. Some managers still behave that way, but today, management is becoming more progressive. Many managers are being educated to guide, train, support, motivate, and coach employees, rather than simply telling them what to do. In other words, managers are as focused on leadership as much as they are on managing. For instance, managers at high-tech firms realize that workers often know more about technology than they do. Thus, most modern managers emphasize teamwork and cooperation rather than discipline and giving orders. Today's

So, You Think You Want to Be . . . a Manager

If management sounds like something you might be interested in for a future career, the possibilities are endless. Management jobs tie into every industry and career track. For example, as a nursing major, you may pursue a job at a hospital or a nursing home. Eventually, the hospital will need an administrator to oversee and manage the nursing staff. Likewise, if you aspire to a career in accounting, you may oversee and manage accounting clerks.

If you are an entrepreneur, the management skills will serve you well as you begin your own business. Effective management is really the key to a successful start-up, because you will depend a lot on others to make things happen for your business.

The best way to break into management is to first obtain your degree or certificate. Then, get established within a company, in a nonmanagement position. Make sure your supervisor knows you are interested in a management position someday. Take initiative; engage in extra projects, especially those that will put you in a leadership role. Your supervisor will take notice and your career in management will blossom!

managers face these challenges of global competition, downsized and diverse workforces, technological and other changes, and increased accountability and intense scrutiny. To be effective and efficient in accomplishing the organizational goals and objectives in today's challenging environment, managers must rely on appropriate leadership skills and motivational techniques. We will discuss these skills and techniques in the next chapter.

SELF-CHECK QUESTION

1. Why are managers facing intense scrutiny?
2. How is diversity affecting today's work environment?
3. Define *downsizing.* Is downsizing the same as rightsizing? Explain.

When Alice did the research, and after she read this chapter, she remembered the term *autocratic* and would use that to describe her current manager. Her manager is a nice person but only wants things done her way, which frustrated some of the employees to the point they actually quit. Alice decided it would be best in her situation to be a participative manager and allow employees to give feedback and input. She also realized that her company, even though there are only four stores, is a line-and-staff type of organization, which is departmentalized by function. She thinks the company made the right decision with this organization style, since it would be hard to be a matrix style as a clothing store. Finally, Alice found out she is more

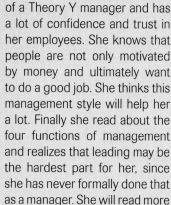

of a Theory Y manager and has a lot of confidence and trust in her employees. She knows that people are not only motivated by money and ultimately want to do a good job. She thinks this management style will help her a lot. Finally she read about the four functions of management and realizes that leading may be the hardest part for her, since she has never formally done that as a manager. She will read more about good leadership in the next chapter of this book in order to do a great job!

summary

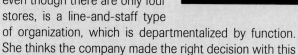

Management is based on the power or authority given to someone to make decisions that ultimately will meet the goals of a company. Management is the process by which such decisions are made. There are four main areas managers are responsible for: planning, organizing, leading, and controlling.

Goals are the long-term aims the company plans to accomplish, while objectives are the short-term operational tasks to meet those goals. Goals need to be specific, measurable, and realistic. SWOT analysis (strengths, weaknesses, opportunities, threats) can help a company understand its internal and external environment; PEST analysis helps understand the outside macro factors that will affect a company's prospects.

A company expresses its philosophy and describes its business in its mission statement. Its ultimate purpose for existing and where it wants to go in the future is reflected in its vision.

To execute her or his role most effectively a manager must understand what kind of organizational structure the company has because different structures call for different management styles. Top, middle, and first-line managers perform very different functions and require different kinds of expertise. Today companies are organizing more and more around self-managed teams.

As a leader, the manager is especially charged with setting the ethical tone for a company culture. The manager sets the example of proper and also efficient behavior in the workplace.

Managers employ different styles to guide employees to common goals. The autocratic style tells employees what to do; in the participative style managers and employees work together allowing employees to make more choices and provide input; the free-reign style sets goals and then employees are free to make things happen. Different styles are appropriate for different situations.

McGregor's Theory X states that workers need strong guidance; Theory Y suggests that employees will be most creative if given freedom and authority to direct themselves; and Theory Z emphasizes a management style in which workers and bosses arrive at decisions as a "family" or by consensus.

Finally, we discussed some of the recent challenges in management. From corporate scandals to ensuring diversity, the workplace has many new considerations which managers must be aware of. New generations of workers have expectations different from their older colleagues. Managers today face change in all areas, from composition of the workforce to technological change, faster than ever before.

key terms

management 176
planning 177
organizing 177
leading 177
empower 177
controlling 178
vision 178
mission statement 178
goals 179
objectives 179
SWOT analysis 180
PEST analysis 181
strategic planning 182
tactical planning 183

operational planning 183
contingency planning 184
organization chart 184
span of control 184
top management 184
middle management 185
supervisory (first-line) management 185
technical skills 186
human relations skills 186
conceptual skills 186
staffing 190

work–life balance 193
total quality management (TQM) 193
autocratic leadership 194
participative (democratic) leadership 195
free-rein (laissez-faire) leadership 195
Theory X 196
Theory Y 197
Theory Z 198
downsizing (rightsizing) 202

applying your skills

1. Discuss the best manager you ever had and the worst manager you ever had. What made them great or less than satisfactory? Discuss in small groups or write two paragraphs about it.

2. It has been said that planning is the most important function of management. Do you agree with the statement? Explain.

3. What is the difference between a goal and an objective? Give an example of each.

4. Perform a SWOT analysis on the company you intend to work for.

5. Perform a PEST analysis on a different company of your choice.

6. Identify a job of your choice. What skills would be appropriate for you to succeed in the job? What skills do you possess and where do you need to improve? Prepare a two-page assessment to discuss in small groups for feedback.

7. What are the main differences between Theory X and Theory Y managers? For whom would you rather work? Why?

8. Recently the behavior of a few managers has resulted in managers generally being held under suspicion for being greedy and dishonest. Discuss the fairness of such charges.

9. Do you see yourself being a manager someday? Explain why or why not.

the internet in action

1. Visit the following Web site: www.businessbureau-uk.co.uk/growing_business/employee_relations/motivation.htm. Take the management style test and report your results.

2. Research a company you might be interested in working for by going to www.google.com and typing the name of the company into the search box. Do you have a sense as to what the company culture and organization are like, and the management style the managers might practice? Explain why this makes the company more or less attractive to work for.

LEADERSHIP AND MOTIVATION

Nucor Corporation and Motivation[1]

What does having motivated employees mean to a business? It means a highly profitable, successful company. A case in point: it was about 2 p.m. on March 9, 2006, when three Nucor Corp. electricians from different plants got the call from their colleagues at the Hickman, Arkansas, plant telling them bad news. Hickman's electrical grid had failed. The electricians immediately dropped what they were doing and headed to the plant.

"It could have easily been a Hickman operator going to help the Crawfordsville, Indiana, mill," says executive vice president John J. Ferriola, who oversees the Hickman plant and seven others. No supervisor

Daniel DiMicco, president and CEO of U.S. Nucor Corporation

had asked them to make the trip, and no one had to. They went on their own.[2] The people of Nucor work hard because they are highly motivated to do so.

Nucor has nurtured one of the most dynamic and engaged workforces in existence. The 11,900 nonunion employees don't see themselves as worker bees waiting for instructions from above. Nucor's flattened hierarchy and emphasis on pushing power to the front line lead its employees to adopt the mindset of owner-operators.

At Nucor, the art of motivation is about an unblinking focus on the people on the front line of the

CHAPTER 7

LEARNING objectives

After reading this chapter, you should be able to:

1 Understand the difference between management and leadership.

2 Describe the qualities of a leader and the differing leadership styles.

3 Understand the importance of motivation.

4 Describe the key principles of employee improvement theories.

5 Explain how employees can be empowered in organizations.

business, which is clearly defined in the company's mission statement. It is about talking to the employees, listening to them, taking a risk on their ideas, and accepting the occasional failure.

Money can be a motivating factor for employees. However, at Nucor, the base salary is only part of the motivation. An experienced steelworker at another company can easily earn $16 to $21 per hour. At Nucor the guarantee is closer to $10 per hour, but a bonus tied to the production of defect-free steel by an employee's entire shift can triple the average steelworker's take-home pay. In addition, compared with other U.S. companies, pay disparities between workers and the CEO are modest at Nucor. In 2006, Nucor's chief executive collected a salary and bonus precisely 23 times that of his average steelworker, much less than the typical CEO who averages a salary 400 times that of a factory worker.

The company also has competition among facilities, and even among shifts. Since there is always room for improvement, plant managers regularly set up contests for shifts to try to outdo one another on a set goal, generally related to safety, efficiency, or output. Rick Ryan, the shipping department supervisor at the Auburn mill, says Nucor's Utah plant is the benchmark for such improvements. It is the most profitable plant, with the lowest costs per ton. "They've got everything down to a science," says Ryan, admiringly. "It gives you something to shoot for." Aiming for something more, being motivated, and being given the power to make decisions seems to be what makes Nucor tick.

Richard Tait and Whit Alexander, the creators of the game Cranium, make decisions as leaders based on the CHIFF criteria: clever, high quality, innovative, friendly, and fun.

INTRODUCTION TO LEADERSHIP AND MOTIVATION

Leadership and employee motivation are key factors in an organization's success. Nucor implements many of the leadership and motivation techniques we will discuss in this chapter: allowing employees decision-making ability, tying their pay to performance, and making it a fun, competitive place to work. We will also cover how leadership and motivation can make a business successful, the techniques used to become a leader, and how leaders can make a business a great place to work.

MANAGEMENT AND LEADERSHIP

What is the difference between management and leadership? As defined by *Webster's* dictionary, **leadership** is "the process of offering guidance or direction." **Management** is defined as "the act, manner, or practice of managing, handling, supervision, or control," as discussed in the last chapter. In other words, a leader provides guidance in the broadest sense, while a manager actively oversees and manages the specific activities that must be done to reach goals.

To offer guidance, a leader must be able to *motivate* others to want to do the things that he or she suggests need to be done. A leader may or may not have the responsibility and authority to make managerial decisions but is able to accomplish things anyway. There is a misunderstanding that one must have power in an organization in order to be a leader, but this is not always the case. Anyone can be a leader. For example, an employee can show a co-worker how to complete a project, or a parent can help a child with homework. Almost everyone has the ability to be a leader; she or he just has to be willing to provide guidance and be able to motivate others.

Consider a manager at a restaurant where you may have worked or may have dined. The manager handles daily scheduling, sets goals for the month and the year, and monitors the progress on a weekly and monthly basis. We know from Chapter 6 that planning, organizing, leading, and controlling are management functions. At the same restaurant, you observe someone who does not schedule anyone's work or set goals. This individual may not have any real power and authority, yet she motivates you because she is always upbeat, listens to her peers, and provides great customer service to restaurant guests. This

Sam Anderson is the owner of a sporting goods store in the suburbs of Atlanta called Casey's Sports. Sam is disappointed because his sales over the last six months have been declining. In fact, sales are down over 12 percent compared to last year's sales during the same period. As a small-business owner, Sam is highly concerned about the declining sales, which could affect the long-term survival of the business.

After speaking with several key employees and holding an all-staff meeting, Sam has determined that the declining sales are directly related to employee motivation. The employees do not seem to want to answer customers' questions, and they do not take the initiative to perform maintenance tasks around the store. Sam needs to figure out what he can do to motivate his employees. He believes that resolving the motivation issue will improve sales. This chapter discusses some of the long- and short-term techniques that Sam can use to increase sales by motivating employees.

person is a *leader*. While she may not have the authority or power to give you a pay raise, allow you to work more hours, or respond to a question a patron has about the bill at the end of the meal, she makes the whole operation run more smoothly and satisfactorily. If you are a fellow employee at the restaurant, the leadership that she exhibits in providing great customer service motivates you to do a better job too.

Consider the same scenario, but now your manager (who schedules and sets goals) is also very charismatic, caring, and enthusiastic. Your manager in this case is also a leader. Because of her leader characteristics you may want to work harder for her. You are more apt to stay at this job. She exhibits qualities of both a leader and a manager at the same time.

So, can you be a manager without being a leader and vice versa? Not every manager is a leader and similarly not every leader is a manager. However, it is hard to be an effective manager without also being a leader. It goes with the territory. On the other hand, there is no reason a leader must be a manager. Leaders are found in every walk of life and at every level.

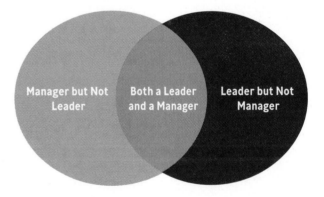

As we discussed in Chapter 6, to be an effective manager, an individual must be a good leader since leading is a key function of management. However, to be an effective leader, a person does not need to be a manager; leadership is a quality found among individuals at any level of the organization. Figure 7.1 shows the overlapping roles of management and leadership, and Figure 7.2 addresses typical characteristics associated with management and leadership.

figure 7.1

NOT EVERY MANAGER IS A LEADER—SEPARATE AND OVERLAPPING ROLES

You can be a manager and a leader when you possess the characteristics of both.

figure 7.2

TYPICAL CHARACTERISTICS ASSOCIATED WITH MANAGEMENT AND LEADERSHIP

Notice the complementary aspects of leadership and management.

Leaders	Managers
Innovate	Administer
Develop	Maintain
Inspire	Control
Hold a long-term view	Hold a short-term view
Ask what and why	Ask how and when
Originate	Initiate
Challenge the status quo	Accept the status quo
Do the right things	Do things right

Source: Distinctions were taken from W. G. Bennis, *On Becoming a Leader* (Reading, MA: Addison-Wesley, 1989).

q: How can you be a good leader without being » » a manager?

SELF-CHECK QUESTION

1. What are some differences between managers and leaders? Similarities?

Section Outline

Leadership Qualities

LEADERSHIP QUALITIES

Nothing has challenged researchers in the area of management more than the search for the "best" leadership traits, behaviors, or styles. Many studies have been performed to find characteristics that make leaders different from other people.[3] Intuitively, one would conclude the same thing that researchers have found: it is hard to pinpoint one set of distinct qualities that all leaders have or one set of leadership qualities that guarantees success as a leader. In fact, results from most studies on leadership have been neither statistically significant nor reliable. Some leaders are well groomed and tactful, while others are messy and abrasive, yet the latter may be just as effective as the former and vice versa. Even so, some tentative conclusions have been drawn about what may make for good leadership. We can look at a few of the leadership qualities that have been identified by researchers and authors in various fields as those characteristics which can help a leader lead. Following are the seven sets of qualities that tend to help leaders achieve effective results.[4]

Integrity, Ethics, and Self-Knowledge

Effective leaders tend to be, and are often perceived as being, highly ethical, trustworthy, and reliable. These individuals do the right things. Such leaders also know the importance of self-knowledge—what their strengths and limitations are, and what their principles, beliefs, and values are. Self-knowledge (sometimes called self-awareness) is critical in developing self-confidence. With the knowledge of his limitations, the leader is able to surround himself with people who bring complementary skills and fill the gaps or limitations of his own leadership. For example, Yvon Chouinard, founder and owner of outdoor gear company Patagonia, personifies these leader characteristics. Patagonia is a "green" business. Chouinard has defied all conventional wisdom and traditional corporate ideas of to do business. Environmental sustainability through less waste and recyclable material use, organic raw material such as cotton (even at 50 to 100 percent more cost), and advising customers to buy less or ship products via ground service (since air freight consumes a lot more energy) are a norm at Patagonia. Patagonia was one of the first companies to offer onsite daycare and both maternity and paternity leave to employees. Also, Chouinard supports his employees' outdoor interests with flextime—if the surf's up, employees take off. Chouinard has heard many times that he can grow his business like crazy and then take the company public to "make a killing." However, that is against everything that he believes in, and it would destroy what he stands for. Chouinard, with Patagonia's gross sales at $270 million, is setting the trend for industry giants like Wal-Mart, who are taking note of Patagonia's success and considering a potential move in the same direction. Matt Kistler, a senior vice president at Sam's Club, a division of Wal-Mart, says, "The one thing that impresses me is the power of the people who work at Patagonia. I was very impressed to see how involved in sustainability their employees are. They're tremendously knowledgeable and want to do the right thing."[5]

Having Vision, Understanding the Business, and Understanding the Tasks

Great leaders not only know the simple, basic tasks, but they also have a deep understanding of the business. More importantly, they have a forward-looking big picture of the organization. Successful leaders can

Yvon Chouinard, founder of Patagonia, resting on the Moose's Tooth in Alaska. Chouinard believes in employee flextime, allowing his employees to take time out for personal interests.

ABC Supply's founders Ken and Diane Hendricks believe in offering quality products for their customers and a great place to work for their employees.

visualize and articulate where they see the organization in 5 to 10 years. Leaders do not need to know every detail, but they should have a good grasp of the business. For example, Ken Hendricks, the founder and CEO of ABC Supply, spent the first few years on the job learning the business of roofing and siding while working with his father. That work resulted in Ken starting his own roofing company. In 1982, Ken and his wife Diane took a risk and acquired three supply centers, and ABC Supply was formed with a simple dream—to take better care of contractors for their exterior building needs than any other company. The company celebrated its 25th anniversary in 2007 with over 350 stores in 45 states, averaging a new store opening every one to two weeks. Having come from the trenches of learning the business hands-on, and with deep understanding of his business, Hendricks describes the vision of ABC Supply: "We will realize our vision of being the supplier of choice for our contractor customers and being known as the greatest place to work in the United States." Is Hendricks succeeding in his vision? In 2006, Ken received *Inc.* magazine's Entrepreneur of the Year Award, and in 2007, ABC Supply received the Gallup Great Workplace Award.[6]

Listening Willingly, Accepting Constructive Criticism, and Communicating

Great leaders are approachable, accessible, and always willing to listen. Often managers, and especially entrepreneurs, think that they have arrived at their position because of their talent, skills, and abilities. They believe they have the answers, more so than anyone else, which is a sure formula for disaster. The more a leader listens to others, is willing to accept constructive criticism and act on it, and keep the communication flow open, the more effective she or he will be in accomplishing the desirable vision and the goals of the firm. For example, Christine White, owner of Boudoir Baskets, a Web-based retailer of lingerie and other romantic accouterments in Santa Clara, California, always believed that she knew her business better than any sales representative of the company. So when a sales rep brought up a complaint about a new product, she ignored it, thinking that she had made the deal for the product, negotiated a good price, and stocked the warehouse with the product. Soon after, other reps started to bring in complaints, and then the customer complaints and the requests for refunds started. Yet, it took White a long time to pull the product off the shelf.[7] Could this damage have been avoided? Had White been willing to listen and act upon the first and second complaints, the problems with the customers and sales rep morale could have been avoided. Everyone makes mistakes. If you are willing to recognize, accept, admit, and act upon your mistakes, you not only earn the respect of your employees, but you also avoid potential business crises. White has now created an "open door" policy to invite constructive criticism and negative feedback.

Communication and Leadership

When asked to give a list of the qualities of a leader, most people will include "good communication skills." A sender is a person giving a message, and a receiver is a person receiving the message. It seems easy enough, but what are some things that can cause poor communication?

- Sender has poor knowledge of the subject or is inadequately prepared.
- Sender does not believe in the message or support the policy behind it.
- Receiver has poor knowledge of subject or is inadequately prepared.
- Receiver is not interested in the subject.
- Sender or receiver is temporarily preoccupied.
- People unintentionally fail to say what they mean.
- Sender and receiver have different vocabularies.
- Cultural differences exist between communicators.
- Professional differences exist between communicators.
- Communicators have different assumptions.
- Status differences (manager/employee) exist between communicators.
- One of the communicators has negative or hostile reactions to the other.
- One or both parties are unintentionally miscommunicating.
- Outside interference or distractions have occurred.
- Pressure of time does not allow effective communications to occur.

How many of these can you minimize in communication with others? What can you personally improve upon in your own communications?

Source: www.nsba.org.

Leadership and communication go hand-in-hand. Effective leaders are also great communicators. They must be able to articulate their vision and goals while communicating them in a simple yet inspiring way to their employees. Consider *BusinessWeek*'s list "The 50 Best Places to Launch a Career." In the 2007 list, the most desirable traits the top organizations look for in prospective hires are college degrees, leadership skills, and communication skills.[8] The "Communication and Leadership" box on this page identifies points that managers and leaders need to pay close attention to in order to keep their communication edge sharp.

Openness to Change

As the saying goes, "The only constant in life is change." Many managers do not like change; it represents added work in their busy work schedule. However, as management expert Peter Senge says, "Everything is in motion, continually changing, forever adapting." Leaders must be willing to stay open to change. It has been argued that when everything is going well, to keep the organization competitive and effective, great leaders figure out a way to change, innovate, and adapt. Leaders following this advice do not make drastic changes continually. They instead make continuous improvement in small increments and bigger changes when needed. For example, Julie Rodriguez, owner of Epic Divers & Marines, faced massive change during Hurricane Katrina. Her company repaired offshore pipelines and platforms and the business suffered severe damage due to the storm. Many employees were left homeless. Whether they worked or not during the two weeks following Katrina, Rodriguez kept everyone on the payroll. She was facing changes related to the pending jobs, physical location of the business, and employee issues. Rodriguez found that participative leadership was best under such circumstances. She had learned over time that managing a firm was more a matter of listening and responding to workers than telling them what to do. Change brings opportunities. Many firms were calling for Rodriguez's help, which meant more available work for her and her employees. But change also brings tremendous challenges. Rodriguez had to make employment decisions, building decisions, and other managerial decisions on the fly. She hopes that the tragedy will lead to more collaboration and camaraderie. She has empowered employees to do what they feel is best, and that is helping the company through the crisis.[9] It would be too easy for a business owner to cut back in face of such a disaster, but *embracing* change and working through it brings out the best in a company's leader and her employees.

Being Decisive and Committed

Decision making is very simply choosing among two or more alternatives. Even between only two alternatives there may be innumerable subtle factors to consider. Great leaders must seek opinions and feedback from others but, in the final analysis, must make the decision and be committed to it. Often, the downfall of a manager comes through an inability to make decisions or procrastination. Indecision causes confusion and loss of opportunities. Employees may not like the decision made, but they can respect it. When no decisions are made or the decisions are flip-flopped constantly, the employees lose confidence in the manager. For example, Amy Rees Lewis started her first business at the age of 24 as a reseller of medical software to doctors' offices from her home. Successfully running a variety of IT-related businesses for 10 years, she was offered an opportunity to come in as CEO of MediConnect, a struggling local company that retrieved, digitized, and organized medical records for insurance carriers. It was a big decision for Amy; she needed to be committed to the company because the turnaround and survival of the company would depend on her decisions and level of commitment.

Amy Rees Lewis is now CEO of MediConnect Global, Inc., and provides the leadership skills of decisiveness and commitment to continue her tradition of success in the company.

Amy accepted the challenge in 2004 and totally dedicated herself to her decision. She has not only managed to turn the company around, but she has also made it a thriving business with expanding reach as MediConnect Global with revenues over $26 million.[10]

Positive Attitude and Enthusiasm

Attitude is contagious. We as individuals make the choice whether we want to be positive or negative. If you give letters A to Z values of 1 to 26 and assign the appropriate numbers to the word "knowledge," it adds up to 96. The words "hard work" add up to 98. But, the word "ATTITUDE" adds up to 100.[11] The message here is that knowledge and hard work can get you close, but it is your attitude that gets you there. Effective leaders exude positive attitude and enthusiasm, which catches on professionally and personally.

Graham Weston uses creativity when taking care of his employees and inspiring them to perform better on the job.

Take Care of People and Inspire Them

Effective leaders always find ways to take care of their employees and inspire them to achieve uncommon goals. As a large company, Google has a lot of resources, but the company chooses to focus on taking care of its most important resource—its people. Google offers employees three free meals a day, a workout facility, a playroom, and the list goes on. It is hard to think of a perk that Google does not offer its employees. Google was named *Fortune*'s 2007 "Best Company to Work For" based on employee interviews and ratings.[12]

As a co-founder and CEO of Rackspace Managed Hosting in San Antonio, Texas, Graham Weston also finds creative ways to recognize his top performers, take care of his people, and inspire them to work hard and stay focused. As a perk, the top performer has the opportunity to choose between driving Weston's BMW M3 convertible or having access to Weston's vacation home for a week. He also offers flextime to workers going through personal problems. Employees feel that they do not have to ask for or fight for their fair share of rewards because Weston always takes care of them.[13]

From small to large companies, great leaders make great things happen through communicating their vision; possessing a willingness to listen and change; exuding ethical actions, a positive attitude, and enthusiasm; and committing to always take care of their people.

In order to be a good leader, it also helps to understand what *not* to do! Figure 7.3 shows the seven habits of unsuccessful executives.

q: Which of the qualities discussed can you identify

»» in your current or last manager? Which qualities would you have liked to see in your manager?

1. ***Dominance***—Leaders see themselves and their companies as dominating their environment. CEOs who fall prey to this belief suffer from the illusion of personal preeminence. They tend to see people as instruments to be used, as materials to be molded, or as audiences for their performances.

2. ***Totally identify with the company***—The CEOs identify so completely with the company that there is no clear boundary between their personal interests and the corporation's interest. The most slippery slope for these executives is their tendency to use corporate funds for personal reasons.

3. ***Know it all***—They think they have all the answers. Because of this need, they have no way to learn new answers.

4. ***Ruthless elimination***—They eliminate anyone who isn't 100% behind them. Doing this, CEOs cut themselves off from their best chance of seeing and correcting problems as they arise.

5. ***Obsessed with the company image***—They are consummate spokespersons, obsessed with the company image. Amid all the media frenzy and accolades, these leaders' management efforts become shallow and ineffective.

6. ***Underestimate obstacles***—CEOs become so enamored with their own vision of what they want to achieve that they overlook or underestimate the difficulty of actually getting there.

7. ***Tried-and-true methods***—They stubbornly rely on what worked for them in the past.

"Big-Time Failure CEOs" exhibiting at least 3 or more of these habits or qualities: William Smithburg, Quaker Oats; Dennis Kozlowski, Tyco; George Shaheen, Webvan; Jean-Marie Messier, Vivendi Universal; Jill Barad, Mattel; and Samuel Waksal, ImClone.

Source: Table from Sydney Finkelstein, "Seven Habits of Spectacularly Unsuccessful Executives," *Fast Company,* July 2003. Copyright © 2003 Fast Company. Used with permission.

figure 7.3

UNDESIRABLE LEADER QUALITIES

Seven qualities or habits of corporate CEOs that are admired by businesses but can do major damage to the organizations, if they are taken to extremes by CEOs.

SELF-CHECK QUESTIONS

1. What are the differing characteristics between managers and leaders?
2. What are seven qualities of a good leader? Which do you have and which do you plan to work on?

Section Outline

Leadership Styles

- Formal and Informal Leadership
- Transformational Leadership
- Transactional Leadership

formal leadership

Someone has been given authority to make decisions or lead a group.

LEADERSHIP STYLES

In Chapter 6 we discussed several styles of management. While management styles and leadership styles can cross over, remember that management is a position with authority, and official authority is not required in order to be a leader. Keeping this in mind, let us explore leadership styles as they relate to businesses.

Formal and Informal Leadership

In **formal leadership,** someone has been given authority to make decisions or lead a group; a manager or an appointed team leader would be a formal leader. On the other hand, **informal leadership** occurs when someone may not have official authority or position but chooses (or is chosen by others) to lead for a variety of reasons.

In a team or group in which nobody has been officially designated as a leader, the latter type of leadership may come to the forefront. According to Shannon Kalvar, a leadership researcher, two main types of leaders exist in groups: task leaders and social leaders. The **task leaders** plan activities and timelines and make sure the group stays on task. **Social leaders** make sure that everyone is comfortable with the decision being made and diffuse any potentially confrontational issues among group members. The same person might play both roles, or there may be some groups in which there are two leaders—one focusing on tasks and one on social aspects. Keep in mind, these leaders are likely to be *informal* leaders, so the roles can shift as the group shifts.

Task and social leaders in a group do not need to have a specific title such as manager; they simply need to have the willingness to step up and assume the roles. Consider the last time one of your instructors asked you to answer questions in teams. When people started talking about their weekend plans, there may have been one person who stepped up and said, "Let's get back to these questions so we can finish." Such a person would have been playing the role of an informal task leader. She was not granted authority by anyone but chose to take on the responsibility of getting everybody back on task.[14]

Transformational Leadership

A **transformational leader** has a clear vision of the direction in which he or she wants the company to go, has lots of energy, charisma, and enthusiasm that can be easily transferred to employees, and is able to inspire employees to sacrifice personal interests in order to achieve the organizational vision for collective good.[15]

When a transformational leader develops a vision, it takes several steps. The vision may come directly from the leader or may be collectively developed with other managers and employees the leader is enthusiastic about it. Second, the leader articulates the vision and gets collective buy-in. At this step, the leader's charisma, inspiration, and

informal leadership

Someone does not have "official" authority but is recognized as a leader by the group.

task leader

A leader who plans activities and helps keep the group on task.

social leader

A leader who ensures everyone in the group is getting along and agrees with the direction the group is going.

transformational leader

A leader who can transform the ideas of employees through inspiration, charisma, and a shared vision.

Study Skills

Being a Leader Now

Not managing others does not keep you from being a leader. To practice leadership skills while in school, here are some things you can do (or are already doing):

- Work part or full time. This gives you images of positive leadership (and not so positive) so you know how to behave when you are a manager and a leader.

- If your school offers on-campus clubs or professional student organizations, join them and take an active leadership role.

- When working on group projects in class, volunteer to take on more than you need to and help keep the group committed by praising and motivating them.

- Develop a positive attitude. Remember, positive ATTITUDE changes everything and helps you get there.

- Develop excellent listening skills. Focus on listening more than you talk.

- Respect your classmates and instructors. Remember the Golden Rule: treat others the same way you want to be treated.

Leadership Self-Test

Take the following test to determine what sort of a leader you are. Please circle true or false for each question.

1. TRUE or FALSE: I think more about immediate results than I do about mentoring others.

2. TRUE or FALSE: People will be motivated if you pay them enough.

3. TRUE or FALSE: It's nice to know about people's long-term goals, but it is not necessary to know this to get the job done.

4. TRUE or FALSE: If you have a consistent recognition system that rewards everyone in the same way, then that is enough.

5. TRUE or FALSE: The best way to build a team is to set a group goal that is highly challenging, maybe even "crazy."

6. TRUE or FALSE: The greatest pleasure in my job comes from making the work process more effective.

7. TRUE or FALSE: I spend more of my time and attention on my weaker performers than I do on my top performers, who basically take care of themselves.

8. TRUE or FALSE: It's better to know nothing about the personal lives and interests of the people who report to me.

9. TRUE or FALSE: Sometimes, it's as if I'm a "people collector" because I'm always recruiting and getting to know new people.

10. TRUE or FALSE: I like to surround myself with people who are better at what they do than I am.

11. TRUE or FALSE: I am a lifelong student of what makes other people tick.

12. TRUE or FALSE: People talk about "mission" too much — it's best just to let people do their work and not try to bring values into the conversation.

13. TRUE or FALSE: It's my job to know everything that goes on in my area.

14. TRUE or FALSE: I pay close attention to how and where I spend my time, because the priorities I put into action are the ones that other people will observe and follow.

15. TRUE or FALSE: I've worked hard to get along with and understand people who are very different from me.

Answers to this self-test can be found at the end of the chapter.

Questions

1. What do you think this test says about your method of leadership?

2. What things can you do to improve your leadership ability?

Source: Dr. A. J. Schuler, lecturer at the Wharton School of Business. Dr. Schuler is an expert in leadership and organizational change. To find out more about his programs and services, visit www.schulersolutions.com or call (703) 370-6545.

communication skills play a big role. Next, the transformational leader works with employees to come up with the strategies or the means to make the vision a reality. Finally, the leader "leads the charge" for executing the strategies to ensure that the vision comes to fruition. Yvon Chouinard of Patagonia is a classic example of a transformational leader who has created a new kind of company. He is a man of charisma and passion who cares about his employees, customers, and the environment. Using a variety of incentives and showing sympathy and flexibility in regard to his employees' needs, he has enabled his employees to transcend their self-interest to achieve the greater organizational and environmental good. He sets the example himself, sacrificing personal financial gains to help the environment through waste-reducing and other efforts. As a result, for every job Patagonia has to offer, it receives 900 applications, and the turnover rate at Patagonia is less than 4 percent.[16]

Transactional Leadership

Unlike the transformational leader, the **transactional leader** works by providing clear structure and guidelines to employees. As the term "transaction" suggests, this leadership style is based on the exchange process. Employees are given the performance standards and are rewarded or punished for the level at which the standards are met or missed. The majority of managers tend to follow the transactional leadership style. Few build upon the transaction and take the employees to the transformational level. Figure 7.4 shows the differences between transactional and transformational leaders.

> **transactional leader**
> A leader who gets people to do things by providing structure and guidelines based on the exchange process.

q: What leadership style do you prefer to work for?
» » What leadership style do you think you have?

Characteristics of Transactional and Transformational Leaders	
Transactional Leader	**Transformational Leader**
Contingent reward. Contracts exchange of rewards for effort, promises rewards for good performance, recognizes accomplishments	***Charisma.*** Provides vision and sense of mission, instills pride, gains respect and trust
Management by exception (active). Watches and searches for deviations from rules and standards, takes corrective action	***Inspiration.*** Communicates high expectations, uses symbols to focus efforts, expresses important purposes in simple ways
Management by exception (passive). Intervenes only if standards are not met	***Intellectual stimulation.*** Promotes intelligence, rationality, and careful problem solving
Laissez–faire. Abdicates responsibilities, avoids making decisions	***Individualized consideration.*** Gives personal attention, treats each employee individually, coaches, advises

figure 7.4

TRANSACTIONAL VERSUS TRANSFORMATIONAL LEADERS

A comparison of leadership styles.

Source: B. M. Bass et al., "Transactional to Transformational Leadership: Learning to Share the Vision," *Organizational Dynamics,* Winter, 1990, p. 22. Copyright © 1990 with permission of Elsevier, Inc.

SELF-CHECK QUESTIONS

1. What are the differences between formal and informal leaders?
2. What are the main differences between transformational and transactional leaders? Which aspects of these leadership characteristics do you plan to work on? Explain.

Section Outline

Importance of Motivation

- Taylor's Scientific Management
- Mayo's Hawthorne Studies
- Maslow's Hierarchy of Needs
- Herzberg's Two-Factor Theory

motivation

The drive to satisfy a need.

intrinsic reward

The personal satisfaction you feel when you perform well and achieve goals.

extrinsic reward

A reward given to an employee, such as a promotion or pay raise.

IMPORTANCE OF MOTIVATION

People are willing to work, and work hard, if they feel that their work makes a difference and is appreciated. People gain **motivation** in a variety of ways, such as recognition, accomplishments, personal goals, money, and status.[17] An **intrinsic reward** is the personal satisfaction you feel when you perform well and achieve goals. The belief that your work makes a significant contribution to the organization or society is a form of intrinsic reward. An **extrinsic reward** is something given to you by someone else as recognition for good work. Such things as pay raises, bonuses, promotions and public recognition are examples of extrinsic rewards. Figure 7.5 shows examples of extrinsic and intrinsic rewards. As we read in the opening profile, employees at Nucor are motivated by both extrinsic and intrinsic rewards. While ultimately motivation—the drive to satisfy a need—comes from within an individual, there are ways to stimulate people that bring out a natural desire to do a good job.

To help you understand the concepts, theories, and practices of motivation, we will discuss some of the traditional theories on motivation, as well as modern applications of motivation theories and the managerial procedures for implementing them.

figure 7.5

EXTRINSIC VERSUS INTRINSIC REWARDS

Intrinsic	Extrinsic
Personal satisfaction	Compensation
Being told you did a good job	Raise
Finishing something/accomplishment	Promotion
Interpersonal relations	Benefits

Taylor's Scientific Management

Many books have been written about how to effectively motivate people. It wasn't until the early 20th century that employee motivation was even discussed in the workplace. One of the most well-known books on employee motivation, *The Principles of Scientific Management*, was written by Fredrick Taylor and published in 1911. This book earned Taylor the title "father of scientific management." Taylor engaged in **time and motion studies**—studies of the tasks performed to complete a job and the time needed to do each task. The goal was to reduce the number of motions required to perform a task, thereby increasing efficiency and productivity.

By performing time and motion studies, Taylor found that an average person could shovel more dirt, coal, or any other substance (in fact, 25 to 35 tons more per day) using the most efficient motions and the proper shovel (the right training and the right tool). The findings led to time-motion studies of virtually every factory job. As researchers determined the most efficient ways of doing things, efficiency became the standard for setting goals.[18]

Figure 7.6 presents Taylor's four principles of **scientific management.** Scientific management had a profound impact on American industries and productivity. However, despite his noteworthy contributions, Taylor's philosophy and teachings had shortcomings—people were viewed largely as machines that needed to be properly programmed.[19] There was little concern for the psychological or the human aspect of the work. Taylor simply felt that workers would perform at a high level if they received high enough pay. There was no room for employee initiatives.

Taylor developed his principles early in the 20th century. Do they still apply today? Are organizations using any of them? Absolutely, they are. Some of Taylor's ideas are still being implemented. Car and computer manufacturing facilities, hospitals, and even many restaurants (such as McDonald's) function more efficiently due to the application of

Mr. Frank B. Gilbreth of Montclair, New Jersey, and his wife Lillian, having been appointed delegates to the scientific management congress to be held at the Masaryk Academy of Labor in Prague, Czechoslovakia, in 1925.

time and motion studies

Studies of the tasks performed to complete a job and the time needed to do each task.

scientific management

Studying workers to find the most efficient processes and then teaching people those techniques.

figure 7.6

TAYLOR'S SCIENTIFIC MANAGEMENT PRINCIPLES

1. Scientifically study each part of a task and develop the best method of performing the task.
2. Carefully select workers and train them to perform the task by using the scientifically developed method.
3. Cooperate fully with workers to ensure that they use the proper method.
4. Divide work and responsibility so that management is responsible for planning work methods using scientific principles and workers are responsible for executing the work accordingly.

Source: F. W. Taylor, *The Principles of Scientific Management* (New York: Harper, 1911).

UPS drivers are given specific instructions on how many packages they should deliver during one day, as well as other details on how their work is expected to be completed. What types of job-related details have you received from an employer?

scientific management principles.[20] For example, United Parcel Service (UPS) tells drivers how fast to walk (three feet per second), how many packages to pick up and deliver per day (an average of 400), and how to hold their keys (teeth up, third finger).[21] UPS's efficiency, productivity, technology improvement, and service delivery have earned the company sixteenth place in *Fortune* magazine's list of most admired companies in 2007.[22]

Others followed Taylor and researched employee efficiency. Frank and Lillian Gilbreth used Taylor's ideas in a three-year study of bricklaying. They developed the **principle of motion economy,** which showed that every job could be broken down into a series of elementary motions called a therblig. Then, each motion was analyzed to make it more effective.

Mayo's Hawthorne Studies

The research developed by Taylor also led to a six-year study from 1927 to 1933 at Western Electric Company's Hawthorne plant in Cicero, Illinois. The studies were conducted by Elton Mayo and his colleagues from Harvard University to determine the impact of physical conditions such as lighting, temperature, humidity, and so forth on worker productivity. For every change in environmental factors, such as either bright *or* dim lighting, productivity went up. In the series of 13 experimental periods, productivity went up *each time*. When everything was returned to normal conditions, with an expectation that the productivity should revert to the pre-experiment level, worker productivity increased yet again. When researchers interviewed the workers, they made astounding discoveries:[23]

Studies conducted at the Hawthorne plant gave birth to the theory of human-based motivation.

- The workers in the test room thought of themselves as a social group. The atmosphere was informal, due to the research study, and they felt they could speak freely with supervisors and each other, as well as to the researchers. They felt special and worked hard to remain in the group. This motivated them.

- The workers were involved in planning the experiments. For example, they rejected one kind of pay schedule and recommended another, which was eventually used. The workers felt that their ideas were respected and that they were involved in managerial decision making. This, too, motivated them.

- No matter what the physical conditions were, the workers enjoyed the atmosphere of their special room and the additional pay they got for more productivity. Job satisfaction increased dramatically.

To Share or Not to Share

First-line managers assist in the decisions made by their department heads. The department heads retain full responsibility for the decisions—if a plan succeeds, it is their success; if a plan fails, it is their failure. Now picture this: As a first-line manager at a construction management firm, you were sent new information on a report from corporate headquarters. The reason you were sent the report in the first place is that your department head is on her honeymoon in Europe, and she is not scheduled to return for two weeks. The findings in this report indicate that your department head's plans are sure to fail. If the plans fall short, as you suspect they will, the department head will probably be reprimanded or even demoted. You are the most likely candidate to fill the vacancy.

Questions

1. Will you give your department head the report?
2. What is your ethical responsibility?
3. What might be the consequences of your decision?

Researchers now use the term **Hawthorne effect** to refer to the tendency for people to behave differently when they know they are being studied.[24] Because of the findings from the Hawthorne studies, the emphasis of research shifted from Taylor's scientific management towards Mayo's human-based management. Out of many theories about the human side of motivation that emerged, one of the best known was Abraham Maslow's work on the hierarchy of needs.

Maslow's Hierarchy of Needs

Psychologist Abraham Maslow believed that in order to understand motivation at work, one must understand human motivation in general. It seemed to him that motivation arises from need. People are motivated to satisfy unmet needs; needs that have been satisfied will no longer provide motivation. He believed that needs could be placed on a hierarchy of importance. Figure 7.7 shows **Maslow's hierarchy of needs,** which is broken into the following levels:[25]

- *Physiological needs:* basic survival needs, such as the need for food, water, and shelter.
- *Safety needs:* the need to feel secure at work and at home.
- *Social needs:* the need to feel loved, accepted, and part of a group.
- *Esteem needs:* the need for recognition and acknowledgment from others, as well as self-respect and a sense of status or importance.
- *Self-actualization needs:* the need to develop to one's fullest potential.

principle of motion economy

Theory developed by Frank and Lillian Gilbreth that every job can be broken down into a series of elementary motions.

Hawthorne effect

The tendency for people to behave differently when they know they are being studied.

Maslow's hierarchy of needs

Theory of motivation based on unmet human needs from basic physiological needs to safety, social, esteem, and self-actualization needs.

figure 7.7

MASLOW'S HIERARCHY OF NEEDS

Source: Abraham H. Maslow, "A Theory of Human Motivation," *Psychological Review,* vol. 50, 1943, pp. 374–396.

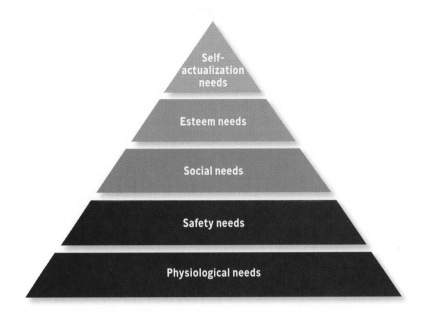

When one need is satisfied, another, higher-level need emerges and motivates the person to do something to satisfy it. The satisfied need is then no longer a motivator. For example, if you just ate a four-course dinner, hunger would no longer be a motivator (at least for several hours), and your attention could turn to your surroundings (safety needs) or family (social needs). Of course, lower-level needs (e.g., thirst) may emerge at any time, and if they are not met they tend to take attention away from higher-level needs, such as the need for recognition or status.

Most of the world's workers struggle all day to obtain basic physiological and safety needs. In developed countries, such as the United States, lower-level needs no longer dominate, and workers seek to satisfy growth needs (social, esteem, and self-actualization). This is important to management and leadership; if you can recognize at which level your employees are on the hierarchy, you can better develop programs to satisfy the needs they have. Reading the chapter's opening profile, at what level would you classify the Nucor employees on Maslow's hierarchy?

q: Where would you place yourself on Maslow's hierarchy?
»» You may be able to identify with something at each level, but which is your most dominating need at this moment?

Herzberg's Two-Factor Theory

So far, the exploration of motivation has been focused on extrinsic rewards or human needs. Fredrick Herzberg's theory explored what managers can do with the *job itself* to motivate employees. Of all the factors controllable by managers, which are most effective in generating an enthusiastic work effort?

A study conducted by Herzberg in the 1960s asked workers to rank various job-related factors in order of importance, relative to motivation.[26] The question was: what creates enthusiasm for workers and makes them work to full potential?

The results showed that the most important motivating factors were (in order of importance):

Pixar offers lunchtime classes at Pixar University in topics such as drawing and improvised comedy. Would this be a motivator for you? How can smaller businesses with smaller budgets implement these kinds of self-actualization motivators?

1. Sense of achievement
2. Earned recognition
3. Interest in the work itself
4. Opportunity for growth
5. Opportunity for advancement
6. Importance of responsibility
7. Peer and group relationships
8. Pay
9. Supervisor's fairness
10. Company policies and rule
11. Status
12. Job security
13. Supervisor's friendliness
14. Working conditions

Note that the factors receiving the most votes were all clustered around job content. Workers like to feel that they contribute to the company (sense of achievement was number 1). They want to earn recognition (number 2) and feel their jobs are important (number 6). They want responsibility, which is why continued training and learning is so important, and they want acknowledgment for that responsibility by having a chance for growth and advancement. Of course, workers also want the job to be interesting.

Herzberg noted further that factors centered on the job environment were not considered motivating to workers. Pay was one of those factors; note that pay is eighth on the list, which indicates that employee motivation is driven by more than salary. Workers felt that the absence of good pay, job security, friendly supervisors, and the like would cause

figure 7.8

**HERZBERG'S MOTIVATORS
AND HYGIENE FACTORS**

The factors in the left
column can be used to
motivate employees. The
factors in the right column
can cause dissatisfaction,
but changing them will
have little motivational
impact.

Motivators	Hygiene (Maintenance) Factors
Work itself	Company policy and administration
Achievement	Supervision
Recognition	Working conditions
Responsibility	Interpersonal relations (co-workers)
Growth and advancement	Salary, status, and job security

dissatisfaction, but the presence of those factors did not motivate them to work harder.

Herzberg concluded that certain factors, called **motivators,** did cause employees to be productive while giving them a great deal of satisfaction. The other elements of the job—**hygiene factors** (or maintenance factors)—could cause dissatisfaction if not present but would not necessarily motivate employees if enhanced. Figure 7.8 shows a list of both motivators and hygiene factors.

Considering Herzberg's motivating factors, we can reach the following conclusion: the best way to motivate employees is to make the job interesting, assist them in achieving their objectives, and recognize those achievements through advancement and added responsibility.

q: Do you see yourself being motivated by
» » Herzberg's motivators? Explain.

motivators

Job factors that cause
employees to be
productive and give
them satisfaction.

hygiene factors

Job factors that can cause
dissatisfaction if missing
but do not necessarily
motivate employees if
increased.

job rotation

A motivation technique that
involves moving employees
from one job to another.

As a leader and manager, you can implement these ideas in several ways. For example, managers must ensure employees have a path for promotion, are challenged by their jobs, and are recognized for good performance. Creating this type of environment is more important than merely offering a pay raise! Based on Herzberg's work, we know that the type of work an employee does is directly related to motivation. So what can managers do to *enrich* work? Make work different, more interesting, and more challenging? Managers can explore the concepts of job rotation, job enlargement, and job enrichment. **Job rotation** involves occasionally moving employees from one job to another to give them variety. **Job enlargement** combines a series of tasks into one challenging assignment. **Job enrichment** is a motivational strategy that involves making the job more interesting in order to motivate employees.

Researchers and managers who advocate all job enrichment techniques as listed suggest that there are five characteristics of work that are important in affecting individual motivation and performance:[27]

1. *Skill variety.* The extent to which a job demands different skills.
2. *Task identity.* The degree to which the job requires doing a task with a visible outcome, from beginning to end.
3. *Task significance.* The degree to which the job has a substantial impact on the lives or work of others in the company.
4. *Autonomy.* The degree of freedom, independence, and discretion in scheduling work and determining procedures.
5. *Feedback.* The amount of direct and clear information that is received about job performance.

Variety, identity, and significance contribute to the meaningfulness of the job. Autonomy gives people a feeling of responsibility, and feedback contributes to a feeling of achievement and recognition. Job enrichment is what makes work fun!

The word *fun* can be misleading, however. We are not talking about having parties all the time—although at Google, the number one ranked place to work on *Fortune*'s 2007 list, it seems like the employees are having fun all the time. Employees enjoy their jobs because they can be themselves. They are fully engaged in working toward accomplishing Google's mission (which the employees know well, making it a living statement), with all the amenities possible, such as free gourmet meals, on-premises gym for workout, pool tables, and swimming pools. Google employees come to work to get energized by their co-workers, and they do not feel like leaving work.[28] Would you want to leave work when the workplace is so much fun and you can be yourself?

job enlargement

A motivation technique that involves combining a series of tasks into one challenging assignment.

job enrichment

A motivational strategy that involves making the job more interesting in order to motivate employees.

q: Which strategy do you believe may better
» » motivate employees—job rotation, job enlargement, or job enrichment? Which would motivate you? Why?

SELF-CHECK QUESTIONS

1. Define *intrinsic* and *extrinsic rewards.* Provide examples of each.
2. How did scientific management set the stage for further research on employee motivation?
3. Describe how Maslow's hierarchy of needs theory can be used by managers in the workplace.

goal setting theory

The idea that setting ambitious but attainable goals can motivate workers and improve performance.

management by objectives (MBO)

A system of goal setting and implementation that involves a cycle of discussion, review, and evaluation of objectives among top and mid-level managers, supervisors, and employees.

EMPLOYEE IMPROVEMENT THEORIES

MBO and Goal Setting Theory

Goal setting theory is based on the idea that setting ambitious but attainable goals can motivate workers and improve performance. In order for the theory to work, the goals must be realistic, accepted, accompanied by feedback, and supported by organizational conditions. All members of an organization should have some basic agreement about the overall goals of the organization and the specific objectives to be met by each department and individual. If employees do not have a say in the goals, it is unlikely they will fully accept them. On the other hand, if employees help choose the company goals, they are more likely to be committed and motivated.

In the 1960s, Peter Drucker developed such a system to involve everyone in the organization in goal setting and implementation.[29] Called **management by objectives (MBO),** it is a system of goal setting and implementation that involves a cycle of discussion, review, and evaluation of objectives among top and mid-level managers, supervisors, and employees. Figure 7.9 describes the circular flow of MBO. The process begins when the managers and the employees establish a set of mutually agreed upon goals for a specific period of time. Then, the criteria for assessing work performance are determined. Once the criteria are established, the employees develop action plans to achieve their goals. Managers provide intermittent feedback to employees which serves both as a motivational tool and a control mechanism. At the end of the period, the employee performance is measured and

figure 7.9

THE CYCLE OF MANAGEMENT BY OBJECTIVES

Discussion, review, and evaluation of goals by all members of an organization creates the circular flow of MBO.

Source: K. Davis and J. Newstrom. *Human Behavior at Work: Organizational Behavior* (New York: McGraw-Hill, 1989), 209.

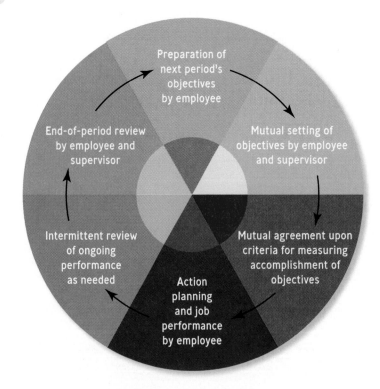

compared to the established goals. Appropriate rewards must be tied to the goal accomplishment, and the cycle continues.[30]

Problems can arise when upper-level management uses MBO as a strategy for forcing other managers and workers to commit to goals that are not mutually agreed upon. Employee involvement is the key to using MBO as a motivational tool. The more the employee is involved in the process, the better chance he or she will work harder to achieve the goals set.

Reinforcement and Equity Theory

Reinforcement theory is based on the idea that positive and negative reinforcement motivate a person to behave in certain ways. In this theory motivation is the result of the carrot-and-stick approach (reward and punishment). Individuals act to receive rewards and avoid punishment. Positive reinforcements are rewards, such as praise, recognition, or a pay raise. Negative reinforcement includes reprimands, reduced pay, and layoff or firing. A manager might also try to stop undesirable behavior by not responding to it, which is called *extinction*. Figure 7.10 illustrates how a manager can use reinforcement theory to motivate workers.

> **reinforcement theory**
> The idea that positive and negative reinforcement motivate a person to behave in certain ways.

> **equity theory**
> The idea that employees try to maintain equity between inputs and outputs compared to others in similar positions.

q: Can you think of examples of when you experienced
» » either positive or negative reinforcement? Explain.

Equity theory deals with questions like, "If I do a good job, will it be worth it?" and "What is fair?" The theory is based on perceptions of fairness and how those perceptions affect an employee's willingness to

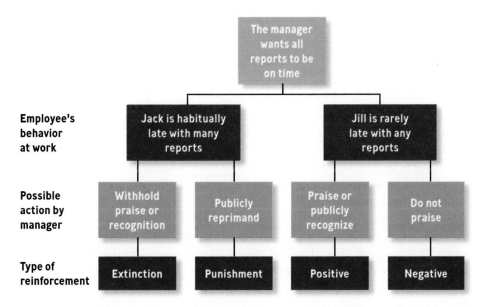

figure 7.10

REINFORCEMENT THEORY

Depending on an employee's performance, a manager can reward or punish with differing results.

perform. The basic principle is that employees try to maintain equity between inputs and outputs, compared to the inputs and outputs of others in similar positions. Equity comparisons are compiled from the information that is available through personal relationships, professional organizations, and other environments in an individual's life.[31]

When workers perceive *inequity*, they will try to reestablish equitable exchanges in a number of ways. For example, roughly putting in the same level of effort, if three co-workers received a 5 percent pay raise and one received only 2 percent, the latter employee would probably react in one of the following ways:

1. Reduce efforts in future work.
2. Ask the supervisor for a raise or an explanation.
3. Rationalize—"I was not working that hard anyway," or "The others must have put in more work than was evident."

Remember that equity judgments are based on perceptions and are therefore subject to errors in perception. It is the manager's job to minimize the misperceptions when and where possible through clear and frequent communication.

SELF-CHECK QUESTIONS

1. Define *goal setting theory* as it relates to employee performance.
2. Explain the steps in the cycle of management by objectives.
3. Compare and contrast reinforcement and equity theory.

---

empowerment

Allowing employees the ability and trust to make decisions.

EMPLOYEE EMPOWERMENT

Empowerment is a newer, recent concept and buzzword—if truly carried out, it is a great way to motivate employees. **Empowerment** of employees means trusting them to make the right decisions. In order to make this work, employees' decisions should not be second-guessed. If an employee makes a mistake, it should be accepted and corrected, but not punished. If employees are punished for making mistakes because they took a risk or made a judgment call, it sends the wrong message: do not take risks; be mediocre. Empowerment allows employees to feel a sense of ownership within the company.

Motivation does not have to be difficult. It begins with acknowledging a job well done. You can simply tell those who do a good job that you appreciate them, especially in front of others. Remember—praise in public and punish in private. It goes a long way with employees and their self-esteem.

So, You Want to Be . . . a Leader?

Everyone has the ability to be a leader in the various activities of everyday life and work life. To be a great leader, you must trust others, be positive, and maintain high levels of ethics and energy. Every company needs people with these characteristics; in fact, most businesses would prefer to hire people who exhibit leadership qualities rather than those who don't, even if they are otherwise qualified.

Consider practicing your leadership skills in every venue in which you are involved, such as professional or student organizations to which you belong or charitable or other organizations with which you can volunteer your time. Putting your innate leadership skills into action can help you develop the leadership talents you already possess.

q: Have you ever had a job in which you
»» felt empowered? How did it change your performance?

SELF-CHECK QUESTION

1. Define *empowerment*. Discuss a job you had in which you were not empowered, and a job you had in which you were empowered. Was your motivation level different at the two jobs?

Mini Maids must focus on teamwork and employee empowerment in order to stay on top of the cleaning business.

Sam Anderson's lack of motivated employees in his business, Casey's Sports, is an ongoing problem in most businesses. This is where leadership can help!

Sam now recognizes that he needs to work on his leadership style. He must make sure the goals of the store are clear to all employees and, more importantly, that the employees are involved in goal setting. Sam will have a monthly meeting to discuss goals, and he has implemented a special team of employees to conduct a goal analysis twice a year. He has not appointed one employee as team leader but expects the leader will be chosen informally as time goes on. The ideas generated through the analysis of the goals will be presented and discussed by the employees, not Sam. Beyond merely providing great information to Sam, participation in the analysis ensures employees will feel a sense of involvement and empowerment, which is part of Herzberg's theory on motivation. Sam expects to receive improved sales results because the employees will now feel trusted, respected, and empowered.

Sam understands that simply providing a paycheck to employees is not enough motivation. Job enrichment is another key to having motivated employees. Because of this, Sam will pay attention so every employee has a variety of interesting tasks to perform. He also will provide timely feedback and respectful performance reviews for every employee.

Sam has implemented several of the motivation theories discussed in this chapter. He has decided to offer employees a $5 bonus for selling tennis rackets, $10 for selling a set of golf clubs, $15 to the employee who has the most sales in a week, and a gift certificate for a local restaurant if an employee receives written, positive feedback from a customer. Extrinsic rewards such as those Sam is offering have proven motivating to employees.

Sam has also decided to implement Maslow's hierarchy in his employee motivation plans. Realizing that everyone has a need for self-actualization or self-fulfillment, he has started to offer product knowledge seminars to teach employees about new products.

Six months into Sam's management and motivation transformation, sales are up 8 percent! His employees seem happier and much more productive. He allows the employees to take responsibility for the day-to-day functioning of the store, which has made all the difference in sales, which is ultimately what employee motivation is about!

summary

In this chapter, we explored some differences between managing and leadership. We learned that management is a position of official authority, while leadership does not necessarily need to be a power position but is a quality exhibited at all levels in an organization. Leadership studies have not been very successful in explaining exactly what goes into developing leaders. Nevertheless, we can identify some of the characteristics of leaders, such as being inspiring, caring for others, having a vision and communicating it, and always being ethical.

In formal leadership, a person has been given authority to make decisions, whereas informal leadership occurs when someone may not have authority or position, but chooses or is chosen to lead. In groups and teams, two types of informal leadership that often develop from circumstances are social leadership and task leadership. Social leaders keep harmony in a group, while task leaders keep group members on target for goals.

A transformational leader has the ability to inspire others, has charisma, and is able to take employees beyond their self-interest for the greater organizational good. The transactional leader works in a more limited manner by providing clear structure and guidelines to employees.

The chapter discussed the various employee motivation theories applied to real work situations. The scientific management approach originally studied time and motion aspects of work and aimed to improve efficiency. Its limiting factor of not considering the human aspect came to light in Mayo's Hawthorne studies, which identified the importance of the social group. Maslow defined a hierarchy of needs to explain motivation, and Herzberg identified motivators that can be used to motivate and satisfy employees.

Management by objectives (MBO) emphasizes employee participation in a cycle of goal setting and implementation. Reinforcement theory offers the use of positive and negative reinforcement to motivate employee behavior. Equity theory explains the importance of perception and comparison (with others in similar positions) with regard to fairness of outcomes as this motivates or detracts from employees' willingness to perform at work.

Empowerment creates a sense of ownership in the company. Empowerment means really trusting employees and giving them the freedom to take risks and be creative and innovative at work.

key terms

leadership 210
management 210
formal leadership 218
informal leadership 219
task leader 219
social leader 219
transformational
  leader 219
transactional leader 221
motivation 222
intrinsic reward 222

extrinsic reward 222
time and motion
  studies 223
scientific
  management 223
principle of motion
  economy 224
Hawthorne effect 225
Maslow's hierarchy of
  needs 225
motivators 228

hygiene factors 228
job rotation 228
job enlargement 228
job enrichment 228
goal setting theory 230
management by
  objectives (MBO) 230
reinforcement
  theory 231
equity theory 231
empowerment 232

applying your skills

1. In groups, name and discuss at least five personal qualities you think are important for a person to be a good leader.

2. Write a personal improvement plan on the things you intend to do now to develop your leadership abilities.

3. Discuss three motivational theories. As a leader, how can you apply each of these theories to motivate your employees?

4. Describe the difference between management and leadership.

5. What are the levels of Maslow's hierarchy? Give an example of how you might motivate employees at each level of the hierarchy.

6. What are hygiene factors and what are motivators? Which specific ones are most motivating to you as an employee?

7. Discuss the importance of empowerment in employee motivation. Have you ever been empowered at a job? Explain.

the internet in action

1. Research a business leader who interests you. What characteristics make this person a leader? Share insight on this person in groups.

2. Understanding people's personalities can help managers and leaders better motivate them. Go to www.keirsey.com and answer the 36-item and 70-item questionnaires. Write a one-page report on the ways this test reflects your personality and the ways it doesn't. How might a manager use this test to better manage you as an employee?

self-test answers and discussion

1. **TRUE or FALSE:** *I think more about immediate results than I do about mentoring others.*
Managers focus more on the process and immediate efficiency than do leaders. Leaders think about how they invest their time to develop the strongest talent so that those people can grow and do more and more over time. Leaders figure that if they do that, those people will do a better job of watching and improving processes than they themselves will. "True" is more of

a manager's response, and "False" is more of a leader's response.

2. **TRUE or FALSE:** *People will be motivated if you pay them enough.*
Leaders understand that pay is a satisfier, not a true motivator. Once the satisfier is in place at an acceptable level, people are motivated by the nature of the work and challenges, opportunities to learn and grow, and whether or not they feel their bosses

support or care about them. "True" is more of a manager's answer, and "False" is more of a leader's answer.

3. **TRUE or FALSE:** *It's nice to know about people's long-term goals, but it is not necessary to know this to get the job done.*

   Someone once said that managers "get work done through people," but leaders "get people done through work." Because leaders need to know what makes individuals tick, they want to know about their long-term goals and aspirations. With this knowledge, they can craft ways to combine personal goals with the work at hand, or even the organization's goals. For a given project, it may be less important to know people's long-term goals, but for organizational success and growth, it is necessary. "True" is more of a manager's answer, and "False" is more of a leader's answer.

4. **TRUE or FALSE:** *If you have a consistent recognition system that rewards everyone in the same way, then that is enough.*

   Leaders recognize that everyone is motivated differently, and so consistency is not an absolute virtue in recognizing people. Some people may like public praise, and others may prefer the opportunity to have flexible family time, for example. Because managers emphasize systems more than they do people or personalities, "True" is more of a manager's response, and "False" is more of a leader's response.

5. **TRUE or FALSE:** *The best way to build a team is to set a group goal that is highly challenging, maybe even "crazy."*

   Managers tend to think more in terms of what has been done before, and then try to make incremental improvements. Leaders like to challenge people to bring out their best, in ways that they themselves may not have imagined possible. The best way to build team coherence is to take people through a shared, difficult challenge—something any military platoon leader can tell you. "True" is more of a leader's response, and "False" is more of a manager's response.

6. **TRUE or FALSE:** *The greatest pleasure in my job comes from making the work process more effective.*

   This is a classic manager's priority—deriving the most pleasure from process and efficiency. Leaders enjoy that a lot too, but what they tend to enjoy most is helping people and organizations grow. "True" is more of a manager's response, and "False" is more of a leader's response.

7. **TRUE or FALSE:** *I spend more of my time and attention on my weaker performers than I do on my top performers, who basically take care of themselves.*

   Leaders use their time as a reward, and seek to invest their attention where it can have the most upside impact. Generally speaking, people have the most opportunity to grow and become truly great where they already demonstrate strong performance. Therefore, managers often focus more of their attention on the people who are the best at what they do, since these people will bring the greatest process and performance improvements in the future. These same leaders tend to spend little time working with or overseeing weaker performers. Managers tend to focus more on problems to solve than they do on opportunities to boost people toward previously unachieved levels of excellence. "False" is more of a manager's response, and "True" is more of a leader's response.

8. **TRUE or FALSE:** *It's better to know little or nothing about the personal lives and interests of the people who report to me.*

   Leaders try to learn what makes each person tick, so that means getting to know them in a more personal way, without being invasive or inappropriate. Managers tend to be more cut-and-dried in their work relations. "True" is more of a manager's response, while "False" is more of a leader's response.

9. **TRUE or FALSE:** *Sometimes, it's as if I'm a "people collector" because I'm always recruiting and getting to know new people.*

   Some of the best managers are very good at studying best practices—ways to "build a better mousetrap" to improve performance and efficiency. Leaders tend to look more for the "Einsteins" and star performers of the world who are more likely to invent those better mousetraps in the first place. Leaders think about people and their talents as if they were investment opportunities, so "True" is more of a leader's response, and "False" is more of a manager's response.

10. **TRUE or FALSE:** *I like to surround myself with people who are better at what they do than I am.*

    This is a classic leadership statement, because leaders are all about finding and cultivating talent, and are not threatened by it. Managers may want to feel more in control of their surroundings—not least of all because highly talented people can be very independent and difficult to "manage"! Because leaders tend to have stronger social skills than do managers, and so are better prepared to deal with other strong egos,

"True" is more of a leader's response, and "False" is more of a manager's response.

11. **TRUE or FALSE:** *I am a lifelong student of what makes other people tick.*

    "True" is more of a leader's response, and "False" is more of a manager's response, for reasons already discussed.

12. **TRUE or FALSE:** *People talk about "mission" too much—it's best just to let people do their work and not try to bring values into the conversation.*

    Although it's true that "mission" and "vision" are concepts that have become watered down by careless misuse, leaders still understand that it is best to connect daily work and projects into a larger framework that gives work a sense of purpose and meaning. People who feel that their work has purpose and meaning do their work well and care about results. "True" is more of a manager's response, and "False" is more a leader's response.

13. **TRUE or FALSE:** *It's my job to know everything that goes on in my area.*

    Because leaders focus more on knowing the people who know what is going on, rather than on the details of everything that is going on, "True" is more of a manager's response, and "False" is more of a leader's response.

14. **TRUE or FALSE:** *I pay close attention to how and where I spend my time, because the priorities I put into*

action are the ones that other people will observe and follow.

Leaders realize that the little things they do ripple out in wider and wider ways, and that their priorities will be mimicked throughout an organization. As a result, they make their choices wisely, knowing that people, and other managers or supervisors, do imitate the "boss." "True" is more of a leader's response, and "False" is more of a manager's response.

15. **TRUE or FALSE:** *I've worked hard to get along with or understand people who are very different from me.*

    As headstrong as many leaders can be, they know from experience that being too headstrong can be a liability, and they have learned to work hard at listening to other points of view. Managers are more focused on what they believe is the "right way" to do some job or work process, and may be less open to widely divergent views. Leaders may not always enjoy hearing other views, but they understand the critical importance of the saying, "Let the best idea win!" Thus, "True" is more of a leader's response, and "False" is more of a manager's response.

Source: www.schulersolutions.com/leadership_self_test.html, reprinted with permission from A. J. Schuler, Ph.D. Dr. A. J. Schuler is an expert in leadership and organizational change. To find out more about his programs and services, visit www.SchulerSolutions.com or call (703) 370-6545.

HUMAN RESOURCE MANAGEMENT

Certes Financial Pros

Karen Oman has made the motto "we work to live, not live to work" the capstone of her business.[1] Oman, president and founder of Certes Financial Pros, believes that organizations should offer workers their choice of work arrangements. Job security is important to some workers, flexibility to others.

As their staff sizes rise and fall with the rhythms of the global marketplace, many companies say they require a flexible workforce made up of people who can come and go. At the same time, increasingly workers are demanding flexible schedules to help balance work

"We work to live, not live to work."

and life. Such schedules include nontraditional work arrangements, such as part-time and temporary jobs. That's where Oman comes in. Her company finds financial professionals to fit these flexible work environments. Certes employs the workers and sends them out to companies for temporary assignments. For example, financial officer Scott Eckes's wife is a teacher and his son is a 12-year-old with a full schedule of baseball games throughout the summer. Eckes takes the summer off from his Certes job to share the time with his family. Certes

After reading this chapter, you will be able to:

1 Understand how human resource managers recruit and select employees through the human resource process.

2 Illustrate the various types of employee training and development methods.

3 Describe different types of pay systems and how to evaluate employees.

4 Describe the most important laws affecting the workplace of which human resource managers need to be aware.

5 Describe the key human resource management challenges facing managers today.

will welcome him back in the fall, with no loss of his benefits. In fact, Certes employees can take up to six months off and still retain benefits.

Oman lives the motto of her company by treating her employees well—she not only gives them generous benefits and above-average wages, but also makes three vacation homes available to workers free of charge. Offering such generous benefits is not typical of temporary agencies, but doing so has helped Oman attract a loyal workforce. While the average turnover in temporary agencies is over 400 percent, Oman's turnover rate is around 25 percent. Certes Financial Pros' revenue increased from $100,000 when Oman started the company in 1994 to $7.4 million in 2001. Oman managed to increase revenues by 28 percent in 2001. Such dramatic growth, achieved while cultivating a balanced workplace environment,

earned Oman the Best Employer award from *Working Woman* magazine.

Temporary workers view their positions as opportunities to build their skills and gain experience. Employers say that hiring people for temporary work is an efficient way to "test-drive" employees before hiring them.

There is a caveat to this story: Labor leaders fear that such new employer–employee relationships will make it harder for employees to provide for their families. They fear the flexibility will actually cause workers to end up with less control of their lives, since part-time workers do not receive the same insurance and pension benefits as full-time employees. These issues face human resource managers today, as they strive to recruit, hire, train, evaluate, and compensate the best people to accomplish the goals of the organization.

INTRODUCTION TO HRM

People—human resources—are simply one of the most valuable assets that any company has. This chapter discusses some of the challenges of managing human resources—a company's people. Primary HRM challenges include determining how many people are needed and for how long, and executing the hiring and training process with employees. Once employees are hired, compensating them correctly is an important part of the process. Employees expect to be paid fairly for their work; therefore it is the human resource manager's job to motivate, compensate, and evaluate employees in an unbiased manner. Another responsibility held by human resource managers is to ensure employee schedules are appropriate to meet the organizational and employee needs. Above all else, human resource managers ensure employees are treated fairly and consistently, which are keys to running ethical businesses.

human resource management

The process of determining human resource needs and then recruiting, selecting, training and developing, compensating, appraising, and scheduling employees to achieve organizational goals.

THE HUMAN RESOURCE PROCESS

Human resource management is the process of determining human resource needs and then recruiting, selecting, training and developing, compensating, evaluating, and scheduling employees to achieve organizational goals (see Figure 8.1). Keep in mind that human resource management is not just a paper-pushing or record-keeping position;

Wegmans Food Markets is a grocery chain that has the feel of a family grocer. It achieves this by adding employee benefits such as profit sharing and fully funded medical coverage.

After being injured on his previous job, Tyrone Walker completed courses in the human resource management field. Eventually, he landed a new position as a staff member in the HRM department in the corporate offices of a retail store chain. Tyrone now has been at his new human resource job for just over six months, and the human resource vice president to whom he reports has asked him to do some research to help her prepare a report to determine human resource needs for the coming year in the region's stores. Tyrone knows that employees are discussing a computer program that will help track inventory easier, but he isn't sure how this program will affect their business. He has also spoken to a number of employees who are concerned they are not receiving enough on-the-job training. Tyrone has never completed a project like this one, and he wants to make a good impression on the vice president. He decides that in addition to conducting some research on the Internet, he will also consult some of the textbooks he has used in class. He particularly wants to reread this chapter in order to improve his understanding of human resource management.

rather, it is a job that is vital to the development and strategic planning (the overall plan of the company, discussed in Chapter 6) within the organization. Human resource departments have broad responsibilities. They are involved in the legal aspects of employment, such as monitoring for illegal immigrants, and are also responsible for motivating people (discussed in the previous chapter). All such HRM tasks require individuals who can think strategically and work closely with others. In addition, with the onslaught of outsourcing (see Chapter 3), human resource managers have to make difficult decisions about which, if any, jobs can be performed overseas and who may have to be laid off as a result.

Determining Human Resource Needs

All management, including human resource management, begins with planning. Five steps are involved in the human resource planning process:

1. *Prepare a human resource inventory of the organization's employees.* This inventory should include names, education, capabilities, training, specialized skills, and other information pertinent to the organization (e.g., languages spoken). Such information reveals whether or not the labor force is technically up-to-date, thoroughly trained, and so forth.

2. *Prepare a job analysis.* A **job analysis** is a study of what is done by employees who hold various job titles. Such analyses are necessary in order to recruit employees with the skills to do the job

job analysis
A study of what is done by employees who hold various job titles.

figure 8.1

THE HUMAN RESOURCE MANAGEMENT PROCESS

As this figure shows, human resource management is about more than just hiring and firing people. All activities in human resource management must coincide with the goals of the organization.

Determining human resource needs: Understand how many and what sorts of people you need and know the skills of the people you already have.

Recruitment: Determine if internal or external candidates are best, and choose the appropriate means to attract them.

Selecting: Choose the best person for the job through interviewing.

Training: Make sure employees are given the right amount of information and instruction to be able to do the job successfully.

Compensating: Determine a fair wage and benefits for the employees.

Appraising: Evaluate the performance of employees.

Scheduling: Decide what schedules work best for both the employees and the company.

job description

Specifies the objectives of the job, the type of work to be done, the responsibilities and duties, the working conditions, and the relationship of the job to other functions.

job specifications

A written summary of the minimum qualifications (education, skills, etc.) required of workers to do a particular job.

and to determine what supplemental training is needed. The result of job analysis is two written statements: job descriptions and job specifications. A **job description** specifies the objectives of the job, the type of work to be done, the responsibilities and duties, the working conditions, and the relationship of the job to other functions. **Job specifications** are a written summary of the minimum qualifications (education, skills, and so on) required of workers to do a particular job. In short, job descriptions are statements *about* the job, whereas job specifications are statements about the person *who does* the job. See Figure 8.2 for hypothetical examples of a job description and job specifications.

3. *Assess future human resource demand.* Because technology changes rapidly, training programs must be started long before the need is apparent. Human resource managers who are proactive—that is, who anticipate the organization's requirements identified in the forecast process—make sure that trained people are available when needed.

4. *Assess future supply.* The labor force is constantly shifting: people are getting older, becoming more technically oriented, being aware of diversity, and so forth. There are likely to be increased shortages of some workers in the future (e.g., computer and robotic repair workers) and an oversupply of others (e.g., assembly line workers).

5. *Establish a human resource strategic plan.* The plan must address recruiting, selecting, training and developing, appraising, compensating, and scheduling the labor force (note that this plan is different from the overall company strategic plan). As you can see, the previous four steps build into this last step, establishing the strategic plan.

JOB ANALYSIS	
Observe current sales representatives doing the job. Discuss job with sales managers. Have current sales reps keep a diary of their activities.	
JOB DESCRIPTION	**JOB SPECIFICATIONS**
Primary objective is to sell company's products to stores in Territory Z. Duties include servicing accounts and maintaining positive relationships with clients. Responsibilities include • Introducing the new products to store managers in the area. • Helping the store managers estimate the volume to order. • Negotiating prime shelf space. • Explaining sales promotion activities to store managers. • Stocking and maintaining shelves in stores that wish such service.	Characteristics of the person qualifying for this job include • Two years' sales experience. • Positive attitude. • Well-groomed appearance. • Good communication skills. • High school diploma and two years of college credit.

figure 8.2

JOB ANALYSIS

A job analysis helps a human resource manager develop the job description and job specifications.

Recruiting from a Diverse Population

Recruitment is the set of activities used to obtain a sufficient number of the right people at the right time; its purpose is to select those who best meet the needs of the organization. Recruiting may sound simple, but that is not always the case for the following reasons:

1. Some organizations have policies that demand promotions from within, operate under union regulations, or offer low wages, which make recruiting and keeping employees difficult or subject to outside influence and restrictions.
2. The emphasis on corporate culture, teamwork, and participative management makes it important to hire people who not only are skilled but who fit the culture and leadership style of the organization.[2]
3. Sometimes people with the necessary skills are not available; in this case, workers must be hired and then trained internally.
4. The geographic area or location of the business can make recruiting difficult. For example, if a business is located in a small town, it may be hard to find qualified people within the area to fill open positions.

recruitment

The set of activities used to obtain a sufficient number of the right people at the right time; its purpose is to select those who best meet the needs of the organization.

5. Globalization is adding a new challenge. As companies expand into overseas markets, recruiting becomes more complex because customs and cultures are different.

Because recruiting is a difficult task that involves finding, hiring, and training people who are an appropriate technical and social fit, human resource managers turn to many sources for assistance (see Figure 8.3). These sources are classified as either *internal* or *external*. Internal sources include employees who are already within the firm (and may be transferred or promoted); thus such prospects are called **internal candidates.** Another form of internal sources would be employees who can recommend others to hire. Using internal sources is less expensive than recruiting from outside the company. Maintaining employee morale is one of the great advantages of hiring from within.

It isn't always possible to find qualified workers within the company, so human resource managers must use external recruitment sources to hire **external candidates.** External candidates are people who are not currently working within the company. Some of the ways external candidates can be hired are through online or print advertisements, public and private employment agencies, college placement bureaus, management consultants, professional organizations, referrals, and walk-in applications.

Recruiting qualified workers may be particularly difficult for small businesses, because they do not always have enough staff members to serve as internal sources and may not be able to offer the sort of competitive compensation that attracts external candidates. Online tools for recruiting employees such as careerbuilder.com and monster.com can be very helpful in this case.

When Microsoft CEO Steve Ballmer offered the position of vice president of human resources to Lisa Brummel, she was hesitant because she did not have a background in HR. But Ballmer knew she was the right person to shake things up at Microsoft. After conducting "Listening Tours" with employees around the world, Brummel started implementing new office perks for the Microsoft employees, including an XBox lounge, desk side lunch delivery, flexible workspaces, and Mobile Medicine.

internal candidates
Employees who are already within the firm.

q : Do you think using an online resource is a good way for
» »   you to find a job? Do you think using an online resource is an
        effective way for companies to find employees?

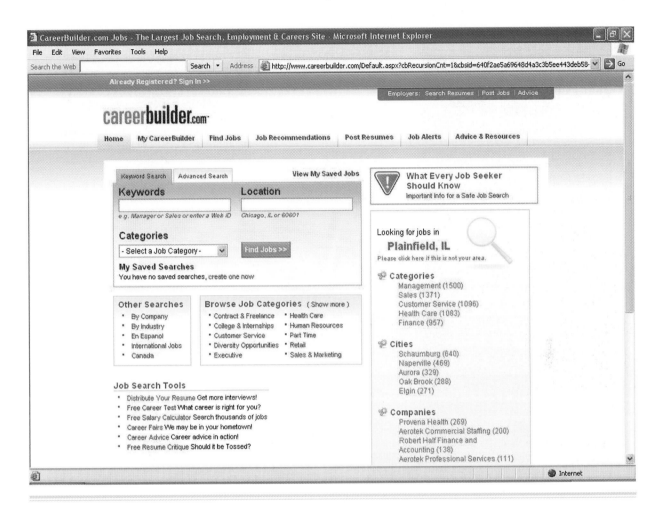

Selecting Employees

Selection is the process of gathering information and deciding who should be hired, under legal guidelines, for the best interests of the individual and the organization. Selecting and training employees, while extremely important to all business, have become very expensive processes in some firms. Think of what is involved: interview time, medical exams, training costs, unproductive time spent learning the job, moving expenses, and so on. It's easy to see how selection expenses can amount to over $130,000 for a top-level manager. It can even cost one and a half times the employee's annual salary to recruit, process, and train an entry-level worker.[3] A typical selection process involves six steps:

1. *Obtain complete application forms.* Today, legal guidelines limit the kinds of questions that may appear on an application form. Nonetheless, such forms help the employer discover the applicant's educational background, past work experience, career objectives, and other qualifications directly related to the requirements of the job. Large employers,

One Web site job seekers may find helpful is careerbuilder.com

external candidates

People who are not currently working within the company.

selection

The process of gathering information and deciding who should be hired, under legal guidelines, for the best interests of the individual and the organization.

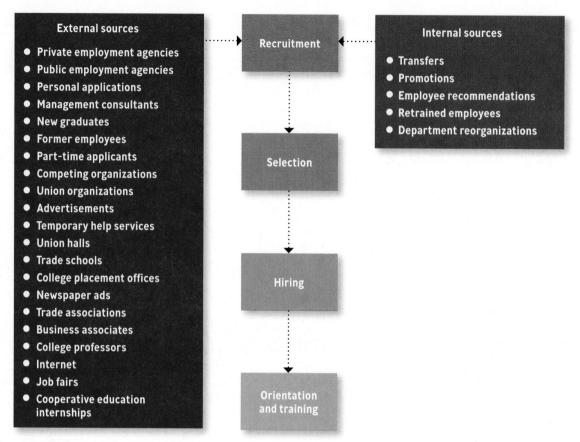

figure 8.3

EMPLOYEE SOURCES

Often, internal sources are given first consideration. However, there are many options when looking at external sources.

such as Target and Blockbuster, make the application process more effective and efficient by using an artificial intelligence program called Smart Assessment, developed by application-service provider Unicru (later acquired by Kronos). An applicant sits down at a computer and spends approximately one-half hour answering questions about job experience, time available to work, and personality. A report is e-mailed to a hiring manager. The report tells the manager whether to interview the applicant or not. If an interview is recommended, the report even suggests questions the manager can ask to find the best-fitting position for the applicant. Blockbuster says Unicru's system helped the company cut the hiring process from two weeks to three days and has reduced the employee turnover rate by 30 percent.[4]

2. *Conduct initial and follow-up interviews.* A staff member from the human resource department often screens applicants in a first interview. If the interviewer considers the applicant a potential employee, the manager who will supervise the new employee usually interviews the applicant as well. It is important that managers prepare adequately for the interview to avoid selection decisions they may regret.[5] Mistakes such as not asking the right questions or

being hasty about the interview questions to swiftly fill the position can become very costly. Other mistakes, such as asking an interviewee about his or her family, no matter how innocent the intention, could later be used as evidence if that applicant files discrimination charges.[6] Often, the initial interview is done over the phone to save the company time and money. Sometimes, if a department manager is interviewing a potential candidate, a human resource representative sits in on the interview to ensure nothing illegal is asked, which helps protect the company in case of any future lawsuits.

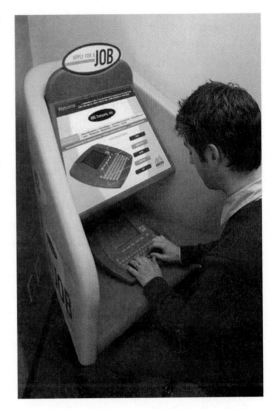

Providing a self-serve, electronic system for employment applications helps employers determine the best candidates before the interview process. Kiosks like the one pictured are available at retailers like Target and Blockbuster.

3. *Give employment tests.* Organizations sometimes use tests to measure basic competencies in specific job skills (e.g., welding, word processing) and to help evaluate applicants' personalities and interests.[7] By using employment tests, it is important the assessments be directly related to the job. Background checks can also help an employer identify which candidates are most likely to succeed in a given position. Web sites such as PeopleWise allow prospective employers not only to conduct speedy background checks of criminal records, driving records, and credit histories, but also to verify work experience and professional and educational credentials.

4. *Conduct background investigations.* Most organizations now investigate a candidate's work record, school record, credit history, and references more carefully than they have in the past.[8] Background checks help an employer identify which candidates are more likely to succeed in a given position.

5. *Obtain results from physical exams.* There are obvious benefits to hiring physically and mentally healthy people. However, medical tests cannot be given just to screen out individuals. In some states, physical exams can be given only after an offer of employment has been accepted. In states that allow pre-employment physical exams, the exams must be given to everyone applying for the same position. There has been some controversy about pre-employment testing to detect drug or alcohol abuse. It is beneficial to the company, from health, safety, and service perspective, to ensure employees do not abuse drugs and alcohol. For example, it would not be safe if an employee using drugs is responsible for operating heavy machinery. Can you imagine a physical therapist who abuses drugs trying to help a patient?

6. *Establish trial (probationary) periods.* Sometimes organizations hire employees conditionally, which allows the person to prove his or her worth on the job. After a specified probationary period (perhaps six months or a year), the firm may either permanently hire or discharge that employee on the basis of evaluations from supervisors. Although such systems make it easier to fire inefficient or problem employees, they do not eliminate the high cost of turnover.[9]

The selection process is often long and difficult, but selecting the correct employees for jobs is worth the effort in order to avoid the high cost of replacing workers. The process helps ensure that new employees meet the requirements in all relevant areas, including communication skills, education, technical skills, experience, and personality.

An option popular today is to hire contingent workers, rather than hire full-time employees. **Contingent workers** are defined as workers who do not have the expectation of regular, full-time employment. Such workers include part-time workers, temporary workers, independent contractors, and interns. Companies may hire contingent workers when demand is high, during maternity leaves, or when quick service is important to satisfy customers.

TRAINING AND DEVELOPMENT

Because employees need to learn how to work with equipment—such as computers and other job-related technology or equipment—companies often find that they must offer sophisticated training programs. Employers find spending money on training is usually money well spent. **Training and development** include all attempts to improve productivity by increasing an employee's ability to perform. Training focuses on short-term skills, whereas development focuses on long-term abilities. Training and development include three steps: (1) assessing the needs of the organization and the skills of the employees; (2) designing training activities to meet the identified needs; and (3) evaluating the effectiveness of the training.

Employee Training

Some common training and development activities are employee orientation, on-the-job training, apprenticeship, off-the-job training, online training, vestibule training, job simulation, and management training.

Employee Orientations

Employee orientations initiate new employees to the organization, to fellow employees, to their immediate supervisors, and to the policies, practices, and objectives of the firm. Orientation programs include everything from informal talks to more formal activities that last a day or more. They may involve such activities as visiting various departments and reading employee handbooks.[10]

On-the-Job Training

On-the-job training is often the most fundamental and valuable type of training. Employees being trained on the job immediately begin their tasks and learn by doing, or by watching and then imitating others. Salespeople, for example, are often trained by watching experienced salespeople perform. Naturally, this can be either quite effective or disastrous, depending on the skills and habits of the person being watched. On-the-job training is obviously the easiest kind of training to implement when the job is relatively simple (such as clerking in a store) or repetitive (such as collecting refuse, cleaning carpets, or mowing lawns). More demanding or intricate jobs require a more intense training effort. Intranets and other new forms of technology are leading to cost-effective, on-the-job training programs that are available 24 hours a day, all year long. Computer systems can monitor workers' input and give them instructions if they become confused about what to do next.

FedEx spends six times more than the average on employee training. It is finding it pays off with a low 4% turnover rate!

on-the-job training

This type of training immediately begins with the new employee learning by doing, or watching others for a while and then imitating them.

Apprentice Programs

Apprentice programs involve a period during which a learner works alongside an experienced employee in order to master the skills and procedures of a craft. Some apprenticeship programs also involve classroom training. Many skilled crafts, such as bricklaying and plumbing, require a new worker to serve as an apprentice for several years. Trade unions often require new workers to serve apprenticeships to ensure excellence among their members, as well as to limit entry to the union. Workers who successfully complete an apprenticeship earn the classification of *journeyman*. In the future, apprenticeship programs are likely to change due to changing industries. For example, the auto repair industry will require more intense training as computers in vehicles become more sophisticated.[11]

In the competitive and ever increasing global job market, take time to refine your writing skills!

apprentice programs

Involve a period during which a learner works alongside an experienced employee to master the skills and procedures of a craft.

Study Skills

Write Your Own Ticket!

Can you name a skill that will be critical to your career no matter what you are currently studying? Yes, it's *writing*.

What do great writing skills do for you? Beyond the obvious, consider that exceptional writing skills:

- Elevate your ability to communicate in all ways. If you write better you can speak better, too.

- Give you the ability to translate your knowledge or research into compelling and easily understood documents or proposals for practical use.

- Give you the ability to use language for critical multiple purposes, such as motivation, praise, and explanation.

Off-the-Job Training

Off-the-job training occurs away from the workplace and consists of internal or external programs to develop skills, or to foster personal development. Training is becoming more sophisticated as jobs become more sophisticated. Furthermore, training is expanding to include education (through higher level courses) and personal development—subjects may include time management, stress management, health and wellness, physical education, nutrition, and even art and languages. For example, 1800flowers.com started an internal school called Fresh University in an effort to retain their most talented employees. At Fresh University, employees improve their weak areas and develop their skills necessary to reach the next professional level.[12]

Online Training

Online training offers an example of how technology is improving the efficiency of many off-the-job training programs. You may have already enrolled in an online course. In such training, employees "attend" classes via the Internet. Another option is Web conferencing. This is a technology that allows for easy teleconferencing and online meetings. Many colleges and universities now offer a wide variety of Internet courses. Such programs are sometimes called *distance learning* because the students are separated by distance from the instructor or content source.[13]

Vestibule Training

Vestibule training (near-the-job training) is done in classrooms where employees are taught on equipment similar to that used on the job. Such classrooms enable employees to learn proper methods and safety procedures before assuming a specific job assignment in an organization. For example, x-ray technicians are responsible for not only prepping the patients but also adjusting, facilitating, and operating the equipment. They must be knowledgeable and comfortable with the equipment and the technology. These technicians are certified only after significant training on the equipment and they continue receiving the training with the advancement in technology.

Job Simulation

Job simulation is the use of equipment that duplicates job conditions and tasks so that trainees can learn skills before attempting them on the job. Job simulation differs from vestibule training in that the simulation attempts to duplicate the *exact* combination of conditions that occur on the job. This is the kind of training given to astronauts, airline pilots, army tank operators, ship captains, and others who must learn difficult procedures off the job.

Management Training

Managers need special training. To be good communicators, they especially need to learn listening skills and empathy. They also need time management, planning, and human relations skills. **Management development** is the process of training and educating employees to become good managers and then monitoring the progress of their managerial skills over time. Management development programs have sprung up everywhere, especially at colleges, universities, and private management development firms and corporations. For example, McDonald's, in addition to its Hamburger

---

off-the-job training

Occurs away from the workplace and consists of internal or external programs to develop any of a variety of skills or to foster personal development, such as health or stress management classes.

online training

Employees "attend" classes via the Internet to get the necessary training.

vestibule training

Also called near-the-job training, is done in classrooms where employees are taught on equipment similar to that used on the job.

job simulation

The use of equipment that duplicates job conditions and tasks so that trainees can learn skills before attempting them on the job.

management development

The process of training and educating employees to become good managers and then monitoring the progress of their managerial skills over time.

University, has started a new Leadership Institute for high-potential employees.[14] Managers participate in role-playing exercises, solve various management cases, and attend films and lectures. Management development is increasingly being used as a tool to accomplish business objectives.

COMPENSATING

Companies do not just compete for customers; they also compete for employees. One of the main purposes of compensation is to attract qualified employees. **Compensation** is the combination of salary, vacation time, paid health care, and other benefits. Often, compensation is the largest cost to a company. The long-term success of a firm—perhaps even its survival—may depend on how well it can control employee costs and optimize employee efficiency, which is one reason why human resources is such a strategic position. For example, service organizations such as hospitals, airlines, and banks have recently struggled to manage high employee costs, which is not unusual because these firms are considered **labor intensive.** That is, their primary cost of operations is the cost of labor.

compensation

The combination of salary, vacation time, paid health care, and other benefits.

labor intensive

A type of business where the primary cost of operations is the cost of labor.

A carefully managed compensation and benefit program can accomplish several objectives:

1. Attracting the kinds of people needed by the organization, and in sufficient numbers.

2. Providing employees with the incentive to work efficiently and productively.

3. Keeping valued employees from leaving and going to competitors or starting competing firms.

4. Maintaining a competitive position in the marketplace by keeping costs low through high productivity from a satisfied workforce.

5. Providing employees with some sense of financial security through insurance and retirement benefits.

Next, we will discuss some of the types of compensation systems that can be used to accomplish these objectives.

Many companies today are offering team-building cooking classes, where managers make a meal together and then devour it!

Pay Systems

Some of the different pay systems are as follows:

- *Salary:* fixed compensation computed on weekly, biweekly, or monthly pay periods (e.g., $1,600 per month or $400 per week). Salaried employees do not receive additional pay for any extra hours worked.

- *Hourly wage or day work:* wage based on number of hours or days worked, used for most retail, fast-food, and clerical workers.

- *Piecework system:* wage based on the number of items produced, rather than by the hour or day. This type of system creates powerful incentives to work efficiently and productively.

- *Commission plans:* often used to compensate salespeople, this type of compensation is pay based on employees earning some percentage of sales, called commission or **variable pay.**

- *Bonus plans:* extra pay for accomplishing or surpassing certain objectives. There are two types of bonuses: monetary and cashless. Money is always a welcome bonus. Cashless rewards include written thank-you notes, appreciation notes sent to the employee's family, movie tickets, flowers, time off, gift certificates, shopping sprees, and other types of recognition.[15]

- *Profit-sharing plans:* annual bonuses paid to employees based on the company profits. The amount paid to each employee is based on a predetermined percentage. Profit-sharing is one of the most common forms of performance-based pay.

- *Stock options:* being given the right to purchase stock in the company at a specific price over a specific period of time, which often gives employees the right to buy stock cheaply despite huge increases in the price of the stock in the marketplace. For example, Google has made many of its employees millionaires due to its stock options. If an employee receiving options in 2003 (exercise price of 30 cents to $35 per share) held on to all of his or her shares, they would now be worth $7.8 million based on the November 2, 2007, price of $711.25 per share.[16]

- *Fringe benefits:* include sick-leave pay, vacation pay, pension plans, and health plans that provide additional compensation to employees beyond base wages. Fringe benefits can include everything from paid vacations to health care programs, recreation facilities, company cars, country club memberships, and day care services.

- *Health benefits:* many organizations offer health care benefits to employees, spouses, domestic partners, and children. These benefits cover some or all of the cost of health insurance. For example, if it would cost $500 per month to cover an employee, the company may only charge the employee $100 (taken out of his or her

variable pay

Pay based on employees earning some percentage of sales.

paycheck) while covering the additional $400 of health care coverage.

- *401k plans:* many companies work with financial companies to set up investment funds so people can pay for retirement. In addition to setting these funds up for people, some companies will even contribute money, tax free, into the account on behalf of the employee. For example, suppose your employer matches 401k contributions. If you put in $100 per paycheck, the employer will also put in $100. More will be discussed on the advantages to contributing to a 401k in Chapter 14 on personal finance. Human resource departments generally administer these sorts of plans.

RSM McGladrey has over 120 offices across the country. The professional services firm understands the need to offer alternative benefits to its employees through a great work–life balance program. Flexible hours during busy seasons so employees can still spend time with their families is only one option for those working with RSM McGladrey.

Appraising Employees

Managers must be able to determine whether or not their workers are performing effectively and efficiently with a minimum of errors and disruptions. They do so by using performance appraisals. A **performance appraisal** is an evaluation in which the performance level of employees is measured against established standards to make decisions about promotions, compensation, additional training, or firing. Performance appraisals consist of these six steps:

> **performance appraisal**
>
> An evaluation in which the performance level of employees is measured against established standards to make decisions about promotions, compensation, additional training, or firing.

1. *Establish performance standards.* This is a crucial step. Standards must be understandable, subject to measurement, and reasonable. They must be accepted by both the manager and subordinates.

2. *Communicate those standards.* Managers often assume that employees know what is expected of them, but such assumptions are dangerous and not usually warranted. Employees must be told clearly and precisely what the standards and expectations are and how they are to be met. Besides communicating the standards, it is up to managers to work with employees to establish goals over the next performance appraisal period. By working together with their managers, employees have some say in their goals and will feel more comfortable meeting those goals.

3. *Evaluate performance.* If the first two steps are done correctly, performance evaluation is relatively easy. It is a matter of evaluating the employee's behavior to see if it matches the standards.

4. *Discuss results with employees.* Everyone fails or makes mistakes occasionally and it takes time to learn a new job and do it well.

Discussing an employee's successes and areas that need improvement can provide managers with an opportunity to be understanding and helpful, thus guiding the employee to perform better. Additionally, the discussion involved in a performance appraisal can be a good source of employee suggestions about how a particular task could be better performed.

5. *Take corrective action.* As an appropriate part of the performance appraisal, a manager can take corrective action or provide corrective feedback to help the employee improve his or her job performance. Remember, the key word is *performance.* One way to help employees improve is by working with them on a **performance improvement plan (PIP).** A PIP is a detailed document explaining what the employee needs to change and detailed steps on how to accomplish the change.

6. *Use the results to make decisions.* Decisions about promotions, compensation, additional training, and firing are all based on performance evaluations. An effective performance appraisal system is a way of satisfying certain legal conditions concerning such decisions.

Effective management helps employees achieve their goals and results in top performance, which is what performance appraisals are for—at all levels of the organization. Even top-level managers benefit from performance reviews made by their subordinates. One of the latest forms of performance appraisal, a 360-degree review, calls for feedback from all directions in the organization. Instead of basing an appraisal solely on the employee's and the supervisor's perceptions management gathers opinions from those under, above, and on the same level as the worker. The goal is to get an accurate, comprehensive idea of the worker's abilities.

Alternatives to Traditional Scheduling

By now, you are familiar with the trends occurring in the workforce that result in demands for more flexibility and responsiveness from companies. From these demands have emerged several new or renewed ideas such as flextime, in-home employment, and job sharing.

A **flextime plan** gives employees some freedom to choose when to work, as long as they work the required number of hours. The most popular plans allow employees to come to work between 7:00 and 9:00 a.m. and leave between 4:00 and 6:00 p.m. Usually, flextime plans incorporate core time. **Core time** refers to the period when all employees are expected to be at their job stations. For example, an organization may designate core time as between 9:30 and 11:00 a.m. and between 2:00 and 3:00 p.m. During these hours, all employees are required to be at work. Outside of core time, they can set their own hours. Flextime plans are

performance improvement plan (PIP)
A detailed document explaining what the employee needs to change and detailed steps on how to accomplish the change.

flextime plan
A type of scheduling that gives employees some freedom to choose when to work, as long as they work the required number of hours.

core time
Refers to the period when all employees are expected to be at their job stations, when referring to a flextime plan.

Assessing Your Strengths and Weaknesses

Understanding our own strengths and weaknesses is valuable. First, we are able to be true to ourselves in how we approach our lives and the job(s) we are willing and able to do. Second, the understanding of what we are good at and what we are not gives us confidence in the areas where confidence is justified and allows us to work on the areas in which we need improvement. Finally, the very idea that we are honest in accepting our shortcomings and willing to work through them guarantees further advancement in fruitful self-knowledge.

While it can be difficult to accept criticism at times, we learn and grow into better, more productive workers when we learn and understand our strengths and weaknesses.

What might be your own personal strengths? Your weaknesses? What can you do to improve your weaknesses and better use your strengths? Do a self-evaluation, and begin to find out how knowing strengths and weaknesses is knowing yourself!

designed to allow employees to adjust to the demands of the time; dual-career families find them especially helpful (see Figure 8.4).

There are some real disadvantages to flextime as well and it may not be a good fit for every organization. For example, flextime cannot be offered in assembly line processes where everyone must be at work at the same time. It also is not effective for shift work because in a shift, you may end up having more employees than the work planned for. Another disadvantage to flextime is that managers often have to work longer days in order to assist and supervise employees. Some organizations operate from 6:00 a.m. to 6:00 p.m. under flextime—a long day for supervisors. Flextime also makes communication more difficult; certain employees may not be there when others need to talk to them. Furthermore, if not carefully supervised, some employees could abuse the system, and that could cause resentment among others.

Another popular option used by approximately 33 percent of companies is a **compressed workweek.**[17] With compressed workweeks, employees

figure 8.4

FLEXTIME

In this flexible work schedule, employees can start work anytime between 6:30 and 9:30 a.m. They can take a half-hour lunch anytime between 11:00 a.m. and 1:30 p.m., and can leave between 3:00 and 6:30 p.m., as long as an 8-hour day has been worked.

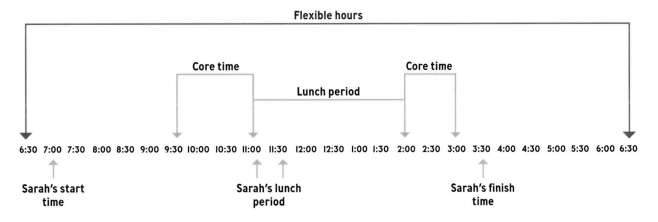

compressed workweek
When an employee works a full number of hours in less than the standard number of days.

telecommuting
Scheduling workers and work arrangements from home.

job sharing
An arrangement whereby two part-time employees share one full-time job.

work a full specified workweek in less than the standard number of days. For example, an employee may work four 10-hour days and then enjoy a long weekend instead of working five 8-hour days with a traditional weekend. There are the obvious advantages of working only four days and having three days off, but some employees get tired working such long hours, and productivity sometimes declines. Many employees are enthusiastic about this option and find such a system extremely beneficial.

Another popular option for scheduling workers and work arrangements is working from home, also called **telecommuting.** Nearly 10 million U.S. workers now work at least several days per month at home.[18] Home-based workers can choose their own hours, interrupt work for child care and other tasks, and take time out for various personal reasons. Working at home is not for everyone, however. To be successful, a home-based worker must have the self-discipline to stay focused on the work and not be easily distracted.

Telecommuting can be a cost saver for employers. For example, a small or medium-size business may save money on the number of desks it must buy and the amount of office space it must lease.

Job sharing is an arrangement whereby two part-time employees share one full-time job. Benefits to job sharing include:

- Employment opportunities for those who cannot, or prefer not to, work full time.
- A high level of enthusiasm and productivity.
- Reduced absenteeism and tardiness.
- Ability to schedule people into peak demand periods (e.g., banks on payday) when part-time people are available.
- Retention of experienced employees who might have left otherwise.

However, as you might suspect, the disadvantages of job sharing include having to hire, train, motivate, and supervise twice as many people and to prorate some fringe benefits. Nonetheless, most firms that were at first reluctant to try job sharing are finding that the benefits outweigh the disadvantages.[19] Because job sharing can create a great balance of work and life for employees, they are often motivated to give their best efforts to their companies.

SELF-CHECK QUESTIONS

1. List the seven areas of human resource management.
2. Discuss at least three types of pay systems. Which do you prefer and why?
3. Describe other types of compensation other than pay. Do you find any of the forms of nonmonetary compensation motivating? Why or why not?

LAWS AFFECTING HUMAN RESOURCE MANAGEMENT

The human resource department is responsible for knowing the laws related to the workplace and being sure they are followed in the seven areas of the HRM process we just discussed, as well as throughout the organization. This section will describe some major laws, as they apply to employment.

Laws and Government Programs Protecting Equal Opportunity

Legislation has made hiring, promoting, firing, and managing employee relations in general very complex and subject to many legal complications and challenges. Let's see how changes in the law have expanded the role and the challenge of human resource management.

The U.S. government had little to do with human resource decisions until the 1930s. Since then, though, legislation and legal decisions have greatly affected all areas of human resource management, from hiring to training and working conditions. These laws were passed because many businesses would not exercise fair labor practices voluntarily.

One of the most important pieces of social legislation ever passed by Congress was the Civil Rights Act of 1964. This act generated much debate and was actually amended 97 times before final passage. Title VII of that act brought the government directly into the operations of human resource management. **Title VII** prohibits discrimination in hiring, firing, compensation, apprenticeships, training, terms, conditions, or privileges of employment based on race, religion, creed, sex, or national origin. Age was later added to the conditions of the act. The Civil Rights Act of 1964 was expected to stamp out discrimination in the workplace. However, specific language in the act often made its enforcement quite difficult.[20] With this in mind, Congress took on the task of amending the law.

In 1972, the Equal Employment Opportunity Act (EEOA) was added as an amendment to Title VII. It strengthened the Equal Employment Opportunity Commission (EEOC), which was created by the Civil Rights Act of 1964. Congress gave rather broad powers to the EEOC. For example, it permitted the commission to issue guidelines for acceptable employer conduct in administering equal employment opportunity. The EEOC also set forth specific record-keeping procedures as mandatory. In addition, Congress vested the commission with the power of enforcement to ensure that these mandates were carried out. The EEOC became a formidable regulatory force in the administration of human resource management.

Probably the most controversial program encouraged by the EEOC has been **affirmative action** designed to "right past wrongs" by increasing opportunities for minorities and women. While this affirmative action is not a legal requirement, it is recommended and encouraged

Title VII

Prohibits discrimination in hiring, firing, compensation, apprenticeships, training, terms, conditions, or privileges of employment based on race, religion, creed, sex, or national origin.

affirmative action

Activities designed to "right past wrongs" by increasing opportunities for minorities and women.

HOW FMLA AFFECTS YOU:

The Family and Medical Leave Act (FMLA) allows "eligible" employees to take a leave of up to 12 workweeks in any 12-month period for the birth or adoption of a child, to care for a family member, or to care for themselves if they have a serious health condition.

- An "eligible" employee is an employee who has been employed by the employer for at least 12 months and worked at least 1,250 hours. The 12 months do not need to be consecutive. You are an "eligible" employee only if your employer employs 50 or more employees within 75 miles of the worksite.
- FMLA can be taken on an intermittent basis allowing the employee to work on a less than full-time schedule.
- The employees are entitled to have their benefits maintained, but they must continue to pay their portion during the leave. The employees also have the right to return to the same or equivalent position, pay, and benefits at the conclusion of their leave.
- The eligible employee must provide 30-day advance notice for foreseeable events. The employer is allowed to ask employees to obtain a certification from a medical provider testifying to the need for the employees to take the leave for themselves or for a family member. Upon completion of the leave the employer is allowed to require the employees to obtain a certification of fitness to return to work when the leave was due to the employees' own health concerns. The employer can delay the start of FMLA for 30 days if the employee does not provide advance notice, and/or until the employee can provide certification from a medical provider.
- If you and your spouse both work for the same employer, you cannot each take off 12 weeks for the birth of a child, when adopting a child, or to care for a parent with a serious health condition.

HOW FMLA AFFECTS YOUR COMPANY:

If your company is a public agency, you are subject to provide FMLA regardless of the number of employees employed. All schools, private or public, are considered public agencies.

An employer must give an employee requesting FMLA written notice, within two business days, if he or she is not eligible for FMLA. If the employer does not respond within two business days, the employee will be eligible to take the leave.

- The employer is not allowed to terminate FMLA if the employer falls below 50 employees for those employees currently on leave. Once the leave has been

that companies participate in affirmative action programs. Interpretation of the affirmative action law eventually led employers to actively recruit and give preference to qualified women and minority group members. Interpretation of the program has often been controversial. For example, consider the 2003 Supreme Court Ruling that race can be a factor in determining admissions.[21] The case began when two white women's applications to the University of Michigan were rejected due to the admissions policies that gave points based on race.

granted or the employee provides approval notice, the employer cannot alter the leave.

- The employee is required to provide 30 days' notice for foreseeable events that require FMLA. Foreseeable events would include scheduled surgery, adoption, or birth of a child. The employer is allowed to delay the onset of FMLA without a 30-day notice.

- The employer can ask the employee to provide a medical certification from a health care provider that substantiates the need to use FMLA. FMLA can be delayed until the certification has been received. In addition, the employer can ask for the employee to provide a fitness-for-duty certification prior to returning to work.

- The employee can ask to use FMLA to care for a family member, for his or her own physical/mental health care, and after the birth or adoption of a child. A spouse means a husband or wife as defined or recognized under your state's law. A parent is either the biological parent or the person who acted as the parent when the employee was a child. A son or daughter is either biological, adopted, under foster care, a stepchild, a legal ward, or any child for whom the employee is assuming parenting responsibility. The child must be under the age of 18 or can be over age 18 if a mental or physical handicap is present. The employer is allowed to ask for documentation (i.e., birth certificate, court documentation, or a medical provider's certification).

- An employer is allowed to periodically ask the employees on leave to report their status and intentions to return to work. If employees inform the employer that they do not intend to return to work, the employer may terminate the employment relationship and thus end the employee's FMLA. If an employee fraudulently obtains FMLA, he or she is no longer protected by FMLA in terms of job restoration and benefit maintenance.

- Ordinary illnesses do not qualify for FMLA, such as common cold, flu, earaches, upset stomach, headaches, and routine dental care. Substance abuse is covered when the employee is seeking treatment, and not just impaired by the usage. To be eligible for FMLA an employee must have a condition that makes him or her unable to perform the essential job function.

- Every employer covered by FMLA must post and keep posted a notice outlining the act's provisions. The posting must be in a conspicuous place whether or not the employer has any current eligible employees.

Source: U.S. Department of Labor, accessed on November 15, 2007.

Many people feel this kind of affirmative action is actually reverse discrimination.[22]

The **Family and Medical Leave Act** (**FMLA**) was passed in 1993 and stipulated that companies with more than 50 employees must provide up to 12 weeks of unpaid leave to an employee upon birth or adoption of a child.[23] It also stipulated that leave must be provided when an employee is taking care of an ill parent, spouse, or child. For a thorough description of the provisions of FMLA, see Figure 8.5.

Family and Medical Leave Act (FMLA)

Passed in 1993, stipulates that companies with more than 50 employees must provide up to 12 weeks of unpaid leave to an employee upon birth or adoption of a child or upon serious illness of a parent, spouse, or child.

Laws Protecting Disabled Employees

The courts have continued to address employment issues that human resource managers must be aware of. The Vocational Rehabilitation Act of 1973 extended the same protection against job discrimination on the basis of gender or race to people with disabilities. Today, businesses cannot discriminate against people on the basis of any physical or mental disability. The Americans with Disabilities Act of 1990 (ADA) requires employers to give applicants with disabilities the same consideration for employment as people without disabilities. It also requires that businesses make "reasonable accommodations" for people with disabilities. A **reasonable accommodation** would be an adjustment to the work environment that does not have high costs; for example, a company can provide an inexpensive headset that allows someone with cerebral palsy to talk on the phone or a TDD or a telecommunications device for the deaf. A TDD is a device that allows a deaf person to communicate over the phone by typing what he or she wants to say. Reasonable accommodation can also mean modifying equipment or widening doorways, for example.

reasonable accommodation

An adjustment to the work environment that does not have high costs.

Laws Protecting Aging Employees

Older employees are also guaranteed protection against discrimination in the workplace. Courts have ruled against firms in unlawful-discharge suits where age appeared to be the major factor in the dismissal. The Age Discrimination in Employment Act of 1967 (ADEA) protects individuals who are 40 years of age or older from employment discrimination based on age. The ADEA's protections apply to both employees and job applicants. Under the ADEA, it is unlawful to discriminate against a person because of age with respect to hiring, firing, promotion, layoff, compensation, benefits, job assignments, and training. The ADEA applies to employers with 20 or more employees. Additionally, the ADEA outlawed mandatory retirement in most organizations. It does allow age limits for certain professions, if evidence shows that the ability to perform a particular job significantly diminishes with age, or that a slowed response poses a danger to society. This applies to such professions as airline pilot

---

SELF-CHECK QUESTIONS

1. Explain the purpose of affirmative action. Do you agree or disagree with this program?
2. Explain how the Family Medical Leave Act (FMLA) affects you.
3. What does "reasonable accommodation" under the Americans with Disabilities Act mean?
4. What does the ADEA protect?

National Labor Relations Act of 1935. Established collective bargaining in labor–management relations and limited management interference in the right of employees to have a collective bargaining agent.

Fair Labor Standards Act of 1938. Established a minimum wage and overtime pay for employees working more than 40 hours a week.

Manpower Development and Training Act of 1962. Provided for the training and retraining of unemployed workers.

Equal Pay Act of 1963. Specified that men and women doing equal jobs must be paid the same wage.

Civil Rights Act of 1964. Outlawed discrimination in employment based on sex, race, color, religion, or national origin. Applies to employers with 15 or more employees.

Age Discrimination in Employment Act of 1967. Outlawed personnel practices that discriminate against people ages 40 and above. An amendment outlaws company policies that require employees to retire by a specific age.

Occupational Safety and Health Act of 1970. Regulated the degree to which employees can be exposed to hazardous substances and specified the safety equipment to be provided by the employer.

Equal Employment Opportunity Act of 1972. Strengthened the Equal Employment Opportunity Commission (EEOC) and authorized the EEOC to set guidelines for human resource management.

Source: www.eeoc.gov/welcome.html.

Comprehensive Employment and Training Act of 1973. Provided funds for training unemployed workers. (Was known as the *CETA program.*)

Employee Retirement Income Security Act of 1974. Regulated company retirement programs and provided a federal insurance program for bankrupt retirement plans. (Known as *ERISA.*)

Immigration Reform and Control Act of 1986. Required employers to verify the eligibility for employment of *all* their new hires (including U.S. citizens).

Supreme Court ruling against set-aside programs (affirmative action), 1989. Declared that setting aside 30 percent of contracting jobs for minority businesses was reverse discrimination and therefore unconstitutional.

Older Workers Benefit Protection Act, 1990. Protects older people from signing away their rights to things like pensions or to fight against illegal age discrimination.

Civil Rights Act of 1991. Applies to firms with over 15 employees. It extends the right to a jury trial and punitive damages to victims of intentional job discrimination.

Americans with Disabilities Act of 1990 (1992 implementation). Prohibits employers from discriminating against qualified individuals with disabilities in hiring, advancement, or compensation, and requires them to adapt the workplace if necessary.

Family and Medical Leave Act of 1993. Businesses with 50 or more employees must provide up to 12 weeks of unpaid leave per year upon birth or adoption of an employee's child or upon serious illness of a parent, spouse, or child.

and bus driver because research shows that the ability to perform these occupations decreases with age.

Other laws as they relate to human resources are shown in Figure 8.6.

figure 8.6

LAWS FOR HUMAN RESOURCE MANAGERS TO KNOW

CHALLENGES IN HUMAN RESOURCES

In most companies, the human resource department is responsible for maintaining good employee relations. Smaller companies may not have a human resource department, and if not, many of these challenges will naturally fall to the owner of the business. Challenges facing human

Would You Cross a Picket Line?

Assume you read over the weekend that Global Foods, a local grocery chain in your town, is seeking workers to replace members of the Commercial Food Workers Union who are currently on strike against the company. Some of the students at your college are employed at Global Foods and are supporting the strike, as are several people in your neighborhood. The strike has occurred because of Global Foods charging employees more for benefits, while not providing an adequate pay increase. Global Foods argues that its management has made a fair offer to the union and that the demands of the workers are clearly excessive and could ruin the company. Global Foods is offering an attractive wage rate and flexible schedules to workers willing to cross the picket line and come to work during the strike. You know of at least one other person who is thinking of crossing the picket line and taking a job. As a student, you could certainly use the job and the extra money for tuition and expenses.

Questions

1. Would you cross the picket line? Why or why not.
2. What are the possible consequences of your decision?

union

An employee organization that has the main goal of representing members in employee–management bargaining over job-related issues.

Knights of Labor

The first national labor union; formed in 1869.

resource personnel include issues as controversial as executive compensation and problems as serious as sexual harassment. Other challenges are embedded in the day-to-day workings of the organization.

Working with Unions

Like other managerial challenges, employee–management relations must be worked out through open discussion, goodwill, and compromise. It is important to know both sides of an issue in order to make reasoned decisions.

Any discussion of human resource challenges in the United States should begin with a discussion of labor unions. A **union** is an employee organization that has the main goal of representing members in employee–management bargaining over job-related issues.

Workers originally formed unions to protect themselves from intolerable work conditions and unfair treatment. Workers also united in unions to secure some say in the operations of their jobs. Some observers say that the downside to unions today is the cost and the lack of benefit union members feel they receive for their dues. Let's look at some labor union history before we discuss how unions and human resource managers work together.

The Industrial Revolution in the nineteenth century profoundly changed the economic structure of the United States. Enormous productivity increases gained through mass production and job specialization made the United States a true world economic power. This growth, however, brought problems for workers in terms of productivity expectations, hours of work, wages, and unemployment. Workers were faced with the reality that production was thought to be vital and they were but a factor of production. Anyone who failed to produce lost his or her job. People had to go to work even if they were ill or had family problems. Over time, the increased emphasis on production led firms to expand the hours of work. The length of the average workweek in 1900 was 60 hours, but an 80-hour week was not uncommon for some industries. Wages were low, and the use of child labor was widespread. Minimum-wage laws and unemployment benefits were nonexistent, which meant that periods of unemployment were hard on families which earned subsistence wages. As you can sense, these were not short-term issues that would easily go away. The workplace was ripe for the emergence of national labor organizations.[24]

The first truly national labor organization was the **Knights of Labor,** formed by Uriah Smith Stephens in 1869. By 1886, the Knights claimed a membership of 700,000. The organization offered membership to all working people, including employers, and promoted social causes as well as labor and economic issues.[25] The intention of the Knights was to gain significant *political* power and eventually restructure the entire U.S. economy. The organization fell from prominence after being blamed for a bomb that killed eight police officers during a labor rally at Haymarket square in Chicago in 1886.[26]

A rival group, the **American Federation of Labor (AFL),** was formed that same year. By 1890, the AFL, under the dynamic leadership of Samuel Gompers, stood at the forefront of the labor movement. The AFL was an organization of craft unions that championed fundamental labor issues. It intentionally limited membership of skilled workers (craftspeople), assuming they would have better bargaining power than unskilled workers in attaining concessions from employers. Note that the AFL was never one big union.[27] Rather, it functioned as a federation of many individual unions that could become members yet keep separate union status. Over time, an unauthorized AFL group, called the Committee of Industrial Organizations, began to organize workers in **industrial unions,** which consisted of unskilled and semiskilled workers in mass-production industries such as automobile manufacturing and mining. John L. Lewis, president of the United Mine Workers, led this committee.

Lewis's objective was to organize both craftspeople and unskilled workers.[28] When the AFL rejected his proposal in 1935, Lewis broke away to form the **Congress of Industrial Organizations (CIO).**[29] The CIO soon rivaled

American Federation of Labor (AFL)

An organization of craft unions that championed fundamental labor issues; founded in 1886.

industrial unions

Labor organizations of unskilled and semiskilled workers in mass-production industries such as automobiles and mining.

Starbucks is a popular place for students and professionals alike.

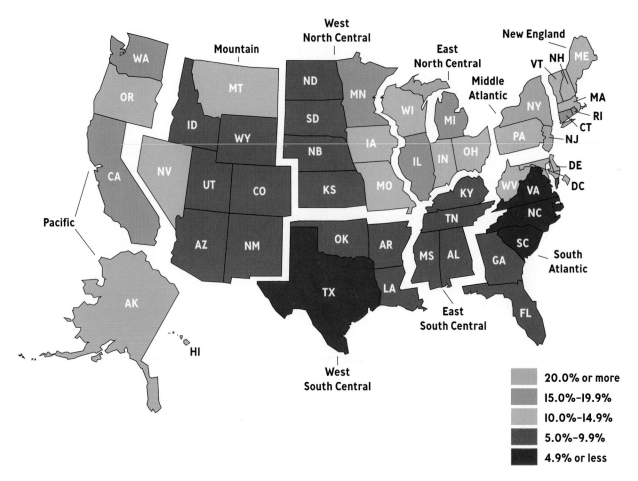

figure 8.7

UNION MEMBERSHIP BY STATE

Source: www.aflcio.org, 2007.

Congress of Industrial Organizations (CIO)

Union organization of unskilled workers; broke away from AFL in 1935 and rejoined it in 1955.

Legend:
- 20.0% or more
- 15.0%–19.9%
- 10.0%–14.9%
- 5.0%–9.9%
- 4.9% or less

the AFL in membership, partly because of the passage of the National Labor Relations Act (also called the Wagner Act) that same year. For 20 years, the two organizations struggled for power in the labor movements. It wasn't until passage of the Taft-Hartley Act in 1947 that the two organizations saw the benefits of a merger. In 1955, under the leadership of George Meany, 16 million labor members united to form the AFL-CIO. Recently, the AFL-CIO has begun to weaken. Seven unions, including the Service Employees International Union (SEIU), left the AFL-CIO in 2005 and formed a coalition called Change to Win. The SEIU was the AFL-CIO's largest union, with 1.8 million members.[30] Today, the AFL-CIO maintains affiliations with 53 national and international labor unions and has about 9 million members.[31] Figure 8.7 shows the union membership by state.

Historically, employees turned to unions for assistance in gaining specific workplace rights and benefits. Labor unions were largely responsible for the establishment of minimum-wage laws, overtime rules, workers' compensation, severance pay, child-labor laws, job safety regulations, and more worthwhile improvements in working conditions. As a consequence union membership soared in the early and middle part of the past century. Recently, however, union strength has waned.[32]

Starbucks and the Baristas Union

Working with unions can be a major management challenge, which is why many companies prefer that their employees not unionize. However, it is illegal to prevent unionization, and as a result, lawsuits can be filed against companies accused of attempting to prevent workers from unionizing.

Joe Agins, a Starbucks barista, was let go after becoming an outspoken member of the Industrial Workers of the World (IWW) union. The U.S. government accuses Starbucks of violating labor laws 32 times in order to prevent unionization at some of its stores. The resulting trial pits baristas against the mega-giant coffee corporation. It is now up to the government to prove that Agins was, in fact, fired for his role in the IWW union.

Besides dealing with unions, health care is another responsibility of human resource managers. Starbucks advertises that it provides health care to its full- and part-time workers. However, according to the union for Starbucks workers, IWW, only 42% of employees use the health care plan, even lower than the rate at Wal-Mart. Health care programs can be potentially too expensive for employees to participate in, making the benefit of health care less important when workers are choosing whether to work at a company such as Starbucks.

The union story at Starbucks hits on some interesting social responsibility issues, as well (see Chapter 4 of this text). Allowing the freedom to form a union is not only socially responsible, it is also a legal issue—this trial brings to question whether companies use the illusion of social responsibility to "look good" to customers.

The implications for human resource departments are clear. HR managers have to make sure the rights of their workers are truly respected, such as the right to unionize, and all the policies of the company are consistent with their social responsibility policies—or risk being judged not only a violator but a hypocrite as well.

Questions

1. What would some advantages to Starbucks supporting their baristas in forming a union?

2. If you were a barista at Starbucks, would you support the formation of a union? Why or why not?

Source: Based on Moria Herbst, "Starbucks: A Baristas Union?" *Business-Week*, August 17, 2007.

Throughout the 1990s and early 2000s, unions continued to lose the power they once had and membership continued to decline. Business observers suggest that global competition, shifts from manufacturing to service and high-tech industries, growth in part-time work, and changes in management philosophies are some of the reasons for labor's decline. Others contend that the membership decline is related to labor's success in seeing the issues it championed become law.[33]

Negotiation Tactics Used by Unions

Now that we have discussed some history, we can talk about some basic human resource issues in relation to unions. First, human resource departments are generally responsible for overseeing and carrying out the **negotiated labor–management agreement,** more informally referred to as the *labor contract.* This is the overarching contract that sets the tone and clarifies the terms and conditions under which the management and the union will function over a specific period. Negotiations for these contracts cover a wide range of topics and often take a long time to resolve. Figure 8.8 provides a list of topics commonly negotiated by

negotiated labor–management agreement

An agreement signed between unions and management for agreed-upon working conditions, benefits, and pay.

figure 8.8

ISSUES THAT MIGHT BE INCLUDED IN A NEGOTIATED LABOR–MANAGEMENT AGREEMENT

Labor and management often meet to discuss and clarify the terms that specify employees' functions within the company. The topics listed in this figure are typically discussed during these meetings.

1. **Management rights**
2. **Union recognition**
3. **Union security clause**
4. **Strikes and lockouts**
5. **Union activities and responsibilities**
   a. Dues checkoff
   b. Union bulletin boards
   c. Work slowdowns
6. **Wages**
   a. Wage structure
   b. Shift differentials
   c. Wage incentives
   d. Bonuses
   e. Piecework conditions
   f. Tiered wage structures
7. **Hours of work and time-off policies**
   a. Regular hours of work
   b. Holidays
   c. Vacation policies
   d. Overtime regulations
   e. Leaves of absence
   f. Break periods
   g. Flextime
   h. Mealtime allotments
8. **Job rights and seniority principles**
   a. Seniority regulations
   b. Transfer policies and bumping
   c. Promotions
   d. Layoffs and recall procedures
   e. Job bidding and posting
9. **Discharge and discipline**
   a. Suspension
   b. Conditions for discharge
10. **Grievance procedures**
    a. Arbitration agreement
    b. Mediation procedures
11. **Employee benefits, health, and welfare**

strike

A tactic by unions to negotiate a labor contract. It occurs when workers collectively refuse to go to work.

Union members from TWU local 100 picket outside the Jackie Gleason bus depot located in the Sunset section of Brooklyn during their strike. What impact does a union strike have on the public?

management and labor during contract talks. Usually, human resource departments are involved in the negotiations. When the negotiations do not go well, labor unions as well as management have some recourse.

The strike has historically been the most potent tactic unions use to achieve their objectives in labor disputes. In a **strike** workers collectively refuse to go to work. Strikes can attract public attention to a labor dispute and at times cause operations in a company to slow down or totally cease. For example, in November 2007, about 12,000 movie and television writers represented by Writer's Guild of America (WGA) went on strike against Hollywood producers. The WGA voted to strike for a greater share of the DVD sales and the digital streaming of the television shows.[34] The last strike by WGA in 1988 cost the industry an estimated $500 million.[35]

Unions also use boycotts as a means to obtain their objectives.[36] When a union mounts a **boycott,** it encourages both its members and the general public not to buy the products of a firm involved in a labor dispute. Strikes and boycotts are a last resort when there is a snag in negotiating contracts. Management and unions usually agree on a labor contract with no major problem resulting in such drastic action.

When unions and management have a difficult time negotiating the contract, mediation may help. **Mediation** introduces a third party into the negotiation; the mediator is a specialist who uses mediation procedures to encourage both sides in the dispute to come to an agreement.

Arbitration is a more extreme option than mediation to solve intractable labor disputes.[37] Under arbitration, both parties agree to allow an unbiased third party to make a decision about the disagreement. There are two types of arbitration, binding and nonbinding. In binding arbitration, an impartial third party hears the complaints of both sides and makes a decision that cannot be appealed. In nonbinding arbitration, parties present their case and the arbitrator offers an opinion, but the parties are not required to agree with or follow the opinion.

Negotiation Tactics Used by Management

Like labor, management also uses specific tactics to achieve its workplace goals. A **lockout** is an attempt by managers to put pressure on union workers by temporarily closing the business. If the workers are not working, they are not paid. Today, management rarely uses lockouts as a tactic to achieve its contract objectives. They do not use this tactic because generally it does not help solve the labor dispute; it only makes the situation worse with potential negative impact on employee morale, tarnished image of the company, and potential negative impact on the revenues.

An **injunction** is a court order directing someone to do, or to refrain from doing, certain acts. Management often seeks injunctions to order striking workers back to work, limit the number of pickets that can be used during a strike, or otherwise deal with actions that could be interpreted by a court as being detrimental to the public welfare. Strikebreakers, called "scabs" by unions, are workers who are hired to do the jobs of striking employees until the labor dispute is resolved. This tactic can help management by continuing production. However, the strikebreakers are generally not as well trained as people familiar with the job, and as a result, the quality can suffer.

Executive Compensation

The highest-paid CEO in 2007, according to *Forbes* magazine,[38] was Steven Jobs, the CEO of Apple, with over $646 million. Ray Irani, CEO of Occidental Petroleum, was second highest paid earning over $320 million in salary, benefits, and stock. In Chapter 2, we explained that the U.S. free market system is built on incentives, such as pay, that allow top executives to make such large amounts. For companies to have an excellent CEO, they often believe they must pay the "going rate" for that position in order

---

boycott
Occurs when organized labor encourages both its members and the general public not to buy the products of a firm involved in a labor dispute.

mediation
The use of a third party who encourages both sides in a dispute to come to an agreement.

arbitration
Occurs when both parties agree on an unbiased third party to make a decision about the disagreement.

lockout
An attempt by managers to put pressure on union workers by temporarily closing the business.

injunction
A court order directing someone to do, or to refrain from doing, certain acts.

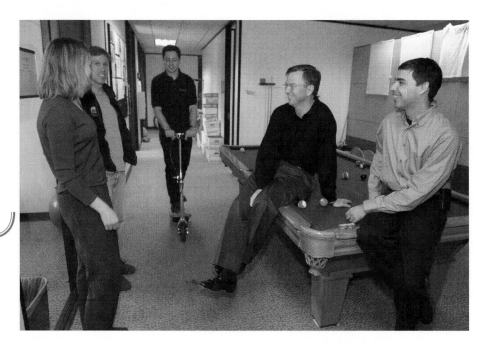

Dr. Eric E. Schmidt (second from right), Google's chair and CEO, holds an impromptu meeting with Larry Page (right), cofounder and president, Products, and Sergy Brin (on scooter), cofounder and president, Technology, at one of the recreation areas around the Google offices in Mountain View.

to attract the best person. On the other hand, CNN reported that the Google founders, Larry Page and Sergey Brin, took $1 in salary in 2005 and 2006.[39] According to *Forbes,* Steven Jobs also drew a nominal salary of $1 per year. In a moment, we will discuss how Jobs, Page, and Brin can happily accept this salary because of the stock options they receive. An average worker labors for a full year to earn what a highly paid CEO earns in one day. As you can imagine, this situation creates concern and large discrepancies of every sort between workers and high-level management. Let's look first at why salaries can be so high for CEOs.

In the past, executive compensation and bonuses were generally determined by the firm's profitability or an increase in its stock price.[40] The assumption in using such incentives was that the CEO will improve the performance of the company and raise the price of the firm's stock. For example, for the second year in a row, John Bucksbaum of the real estate trust fund of General Growth Properties earned his shareholders 39 percent in 2006, according to *Forbes,* while taking home a salary of $723,000.[41] Some may say this is a good return on investment. Note, though, that when calculating CEO compensation, the dollar figure is not just cash they receive. Today, most executives receive stock options (the ability to buy company stock at a set price at a later date) as part of their compensation. Ten years ago options accounted for only 27 percent of CEO compensation. Today they account for about 60 percent.[42] Company cars and use of company jets are also included in total compensation packages. The intent of incentives such as stock options is to encourage good performance from executives. As we mentioned earlier, the Google founders and Apple's Steve

Jobs can afford to take a salary of only $1 per year because they own significant amounts of company stock and receive additional stock options. Taking a smaller salary can signal shareholders and employees the commitment the CEO has to the organization, which in turn can help motivate employees. The problem with executive compensation is exacerbated and highlighted when highly rewarded CEOs may not be doing a good job running the company.

Many CEOs also have walked away with fat retainers, lucrative consulting contracts, and lavish perks when they retire,[43] regardless of whether or not they have helped their companies succeed. This is called a **golden parachute,** and aptly refers to the massive amount of bonuses received by upper-level executives upon leaving a company. Of course, leaving is not always the CEO's choice, so sometimes to get out of the contract the board of directors has to offer CEOs perks in order to entice them to leave quietly. For example, CEO Richard McGinn of Lucent Technologies was rewarded $12.5 million for getting fired.[44]

golden parachute
Aptly refers to the massive amount of bonuses received by upper-level executives upon leaving a company.

Despite the CEO compensation criticisms, many observers of the business environment believe the CEO of a company deserves and earns every penny. The stress of running a company, the personal toll it can take, the high commitment of personal time, the heavy responsibility, and the experience required all make the pay and stock options not only justifiable but reasonable as well. A person does not start out as CEO or jump into the position from nowhere. It takes years of hard work, excellent performances, and the drive for succeeding in the position. Yet, not everyone with these qualities can become a CEO.

Globalization

As companies continue to expand in new markets, globalization is becoming a growing concern to human resource managers. When companies expand into new markets, it is still up to human resources to perform the same functions they do in local offices. Because work and work life differ in various parts of the world, this can be a huge challenge. We learned in Chapter 3 that among other factors, sociocultural forces have a particular impact on the human resource management aspect of the business. HR managers must understand the cultural issues when dealing at the global level. Differences in religion, language, communication, and other cultural dimensions are critical for managers to understand and incorporate in their interactions as they can mean success or failure for the company.

Work–Life Balance

One of the recent concerns of human resource managers has become the need for a good work–life balance. Expectations are high in most

BEST MEDIUM COMPANIES	BEST SMALL COMPANIES
1. Holder Construction Company	1. Badger Mining Corporation
2. The Beryl Companies	2. InsureMe
3. Ultimate Software	3. Analytical Graphics, Inc.
4. Stark Investments	4. Heinfeld, Meech & Co., P.C., CPAs
5. ACUITY	5. Professional Placement Resources, LLC
6. Nevada Federal Credit Union	6. Triage Consulting Group
7. EILEEN FISHER	7. Root Learning, Inc.
8. The Integer Group	8. Insomniac Games, Inc.
9. Sage Products, Inc.	9. Dixon Schwabl Advertising
10. Orange County Teachers Federal Credit Union	10. McMurry, Inc.
11. MATRIX Resources, Inc.	11. Lincoln Industries
12. Hypertherm	12. Clark Nuber
13. The RightThing, Inc.	13. McWhinney Real Estate Services
14. AMX	14. Integrity Applications Incorporated
15. Park Industries	15. Northeast Delta Dental
16. Massachusetts Medical Society	16. Runzheimer International
17. CXtec	17. archer > malmo
18. Advanced Financial Services, Inc.	18. Bridge Worldwide
19. Hoar Construction, LLC	19. Bowen Engineering Corporation
20. Michigan State University Federal Credit Union	20. Kahler Slater
21. Urban Innovations, Ltd.	21. InPro Corporation
22. Digital Federal Credit Union	22. ENGEO Incorporated
23. SuccessFactors, Inc.	23. Schleuniger, Inc.
24. SJE-Rhombus Controls	24. Landrum Human Resource Companies, Inc.
25. Hand Held Products	25. Moody, Famiglietti & Andronico, LLP

Source: 2007 Best Small and Medium Companies to Work for in America, Accountingweb.com, www.accountingweb.com, accessed November 20, 2007.

Figure 8.9

2007 BEST COMPANIES TO WORK FOR IN AMERICA

How can your company make the list for the best companies to work for? Surprisingly, it is not about compensation as much as it is providing employee training programs, work–life flexibility, and low employee turnover.

companies, and many individuals feel they must work many hours in order to meet these expectations. Of course, long hours interrupt employees' personal lives, create more stress, and lower the quality of work. Human resource professionals are constantly trying to find ways to help employees balance their lives in terms of work requirements and home responsibilities and quality time with the family while still performing at high levels at work. In fact, it has been found that a good balance of work and personal life raises performance on the job. Having a good work–life balance is a win–win situation for both the company and the employees involved. Progressive companies, on a regular basis, are looking for opportunities to create or improve their work environment to move the company in the direction of improving the work–life balance of the employees (see Figure 8.9).

q: Is working for a company promoting work–life
»» balance important to you? What expectations do you have for a
good work–life balance?

Comparable Worth

A recent controversial human resource issue is that of pay equity, or
comparable worth, between women and men. **Comparable worth** is
the concept that people in jobs that require similar levels of education,
training, or skills should receive equal pay. This somewhat thorny issue has become more important as women have become a sizable and
permanent part of the labor force. In 1890, for example, women made
up only 15 percent of the labor force; in 2006, the rate was close to 46
percent.[45] Comparable worth goes beyond the concept of equal pay for
equal work. Federal and state equal-pay laws have been in effect for
many years. For example, the Equal Pay Act of 1963 requires companies to give equal pay to men and women who do the same job. Put
simply, it's against the law to pay a female nurse less than a male nurse,
unless factors such as seniority, merit pay, or performance incentives
are involved.

The issue of comparable worth, however, really centers on comparing the value of different jobs; for instance, bank tellers or librarians
(traditionally women's jobs) compared with truck drivers or plumbers
(traditionally men's jobs). Such a comparison shows that "women's" jobs
tend to pay less—sometimes much less. In the United States in 2006,
women earned approximately 81 percent of what men earned, though
the disparity varied considerably by profession, job experience and tenure, and level of education. In the past, the primary explanation for this
disparity was that women worked only 50 to 60 percent of their available
years once they left school (experience and tenure), whereas men, on the
whole, worked all of those years. This explanation doesn't hold much
substance today, because fewer women now leave the workforce for an
extended time. Other explanations suggest that many working women
devote more time to their families than do men, which causes them to
fall off the career track or voluntarily choose flexible jobs with low pay,
such as retailing, bookkeeping, nursing, or secretarial work. Feminist
thinkers suggest inherent discrimination is the cause. Whatever the
reason underlying the disparity, you can see the difference in pay in
Figure 8.10.

comparable worth
The concept that people
in jobs that require similar
levels of education,
training, or skills should
receive equal pay.

figure 8.10

COMPARABLE WORTH

Women have made important strides in all areas. However, when it comes to salary, women are still earning about 81% of what men earn.

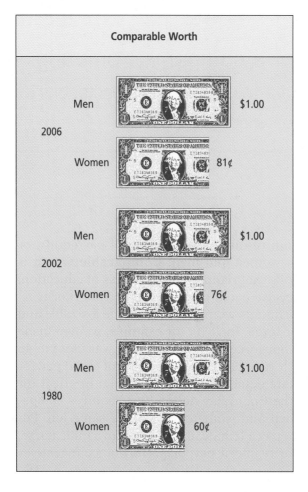

Comparable Worth

2006	Men	$1.00
	Women	81¢
2002	Men	$1.00
	Women	76¢
1980	Men	$1.00
	Women	60¢

sexual harassment

Unwelcome sexual advances, requests for sexual favors, and other conduct (verbal or physical) of a sexual nature.

hostile work environment

An environment created as a result of sexual harassment.

While this is hardly an easy issue to resolve, embedded as it is in society and the culture at large, human resource managers must be aware of the concept of comparable worth and the sensitivities around it when hiring and choosing compensation packages for employees, male or female.

Sexual Harassment

Sexual harassment refers to unwelcome sexual advances, requests for sexual favors, and other conduct (verbal or physical) of a sexual nature that creates a **hostile work environment.** It became a major issue in the workplace in the 1980s, but the furor over sexual harassment intensified in 1991 during the televised confirmation hearing of Supreme Court Justice Clarence Thomas. At the hearing before the Senate Judiciary Committee, attorney and college professor Anita Hill accused Thomas of sexual impropriety. Although the charge did not block Thomas's approval by the U.S. Senate and appointment to the Court, Hill's testimony on national television clearly heightened interest in this issue.

Legally, both men and women are covered under the Civil Rights Act of 1991, which governs sexual harassment. This fact was reinforced in 1997, when the Supreme Court agreed that same-sex harassment also falls within the purview of sexual harassment law. Women, however, still file the majority of sexual harassment cases. The number of sexual harassment complaints filed annually with the Equal Employment Opportunity Commission (EEOC) grew from 6,000 in 1990 to over 16,000 in 2000. The number of charges seems to be declining since 2000, dropping to about 12,000 charges in 2006.[46] It's also interesting to note that approximately 90 percent of sexual harassment suits are settled out of court. In evaluating sexual harassment, a person's conduct on the job can be considered illegal under specific conditions:

So, You Want to Be . . . a Human Resource Professional

Like many of the other careers we have talked about so far, human resources is far reaching, because every company needs a human resource department.

In smaller companies, the same human resource person might be responsible for recruiting, hiring, and administering benefits. In companies with more employees, the functions of human resource personnel might be divided into multiple departments. For example, there might be an HR subdivision that focuses on recruiting and another that focuses on benefits administration.

Another career possibility for you is a focus on compensation issues. Most people with little or no experience would likely begin their career in human resources as a coordinator or assistant. This position would be responsible for helping the human resource manager prepare reports and answer employee questions. If the assistant is able to handle the responsibility, he or she might be given more and more tasks and ultimately be promoted. Salary can vary greatly across HR departments, but can range into the six figures with several years of experience.

- The employee's submission to such conduct is made either explicitly or implicitly a term or condition of employment, or an employee's submission to or rejection of such conduct is used as the basis for employment decisions affecting the worker's status. A threat such as "Go out with me or you are fired" or "Go out with me or you will never be promoted here" would constitute **quid pro quo** sexual harassment.

- The conduct unreasonably interferes with a worker's job performance, or creates an intimidating, hostile, or offensive work environment.

This type of harassment is referred to as *hostile environment sexual harassment.*

In order to protect the company, many human resource managers hold mandatory sexual harassment seminars for employees to bring awareness about this workplace issue.

quid pro quo

An employee's submission to sexual harassment is made either explicitly or implicitly a term or condition of employment, or an employee's submission to or rejection of such conduct is used as the basis for employment decisions affecting the worker's status.

Securing and Retaining the Best Workers

One of the enduring major challenges for human resource management today is to ensure that the company hires the most qualified employees—and is then able to keep them. At the beginning of the chapter we discussed the selection process. Human resource departments are constantly working with department managers and supervisors to develop and implement new motivation plans in order to retain employees. Besides motivation plans, the human resource department generally administers benefits. In benefits administration, for example, human resources tries to find the best prices for health care and then provides information to employees on their health care plan options.

Tyrone knew this project would take several months, and he wanted to start on it right away. After delegating some of the work to his assistant, Tyrone sent an information sheet to all 150 employees. The inventory asked people to provide their names, education level, capabilities, training, military status, and any specialized skills. Upon receiving most of the forms, Tyrone noted that a majority of the employees had not recently had training in the latest software, nor did they have training in workplace issues, such as sexual harassment. Tyrone had one of his employees develop a database and put all of the entries into it, for easier record keeping.

Next, Tyrone prepared a job analysis. First, he took a survey of employees with various job titles to get specific information and spent some time observing employees on the job. After he had written a job analysis, he prepared a job description and a job specification. Although it was very time consuming, he knew that when there was an opening for a particular position, all of the information would be readily available to aid in recruitment. Tyrone also had one member of his team enter all of this information into a database on his computer.

After that, Tyrone needed to assess future human resource supply and demand. From his surveys, he saw that over 30 percent of the company would be at retirement age within two years, which caused some concern, because the company would have to hire new people. He also discovered that a brand-new computer program, specific to the retail business, would soon make tracking inventory much easier. The new program would be released in six months and would most likely cause a surge in business. As a result, Tyrone knew his company would need to hire some temporary workers in order to meet the anticipated business demand.

Finally, Tyrone was able to prepare the human resource strategic plan with help from members of his department. In his plan, he discussed the need for more recruiting in the next six months. He also addressed the issue of retirement, and the fact they would need to hire workers to replace those expected to retire. Tyrone noted that employees lacked training in some of the computer programs, and also lacked training in workforce issues, such as sexual harassment.

Having completed the report, Tyrone presented it to his boss, the VP of human resources, who was more than pleased with all of the work he had done on it.

It is extremely expensive to hire new employees. Therefore, the human resource manager wants to make sure employees are happy and as a consequence stay with the organization. One of the ways HR managers measure "happiness" with the company is through interviews and surveys of employee satisfaction. With the results in hand, the human resource personnel can coach the managers throughout the organization, pointing out areas for improvement.

SELF-CHECK QUESTIONS

1. What are unions for? Do you agree with the purpose of unions?

2. Discuss two of the other human resource challenges presented in this section. If you were an HR manager, which do you think would be most interesting to you? Why?

summary

In this chapter, we discussed the role of the human resource manager in an organization. There are seven areas for which human resource management is generally responsible: determining human resource needs, and then recruiting, selecting, training/developing, evaluating, compensating, and scheduling employees to achieve organizational goals. Determining human resource needs deals with understanding how many and what sorts of people an organization needs and knowing the skills of the people it already has. Recruitment addresses determining if internal or external candidates are best, and choosing the appropriate means to attract them. Selecting is choosing the best person for the job through interviewing. Training involves making sure employees are given the right amount of information and instruction to be able to do the job successfully. Appraising deals with evaluating the performance of employees. Compensating is determining a fair wage and benefits for the employees. Scheduling is deciding what schedules work best for both the employees and the company.

We also discussed some of the laws affecting human resources. Laws covering discrimination based on gender or race, disability, and age are all concerns for human resource managers who have to be sure their organizations stay within the law. The Civil Rights Act of 1964 prohibits discrimination in hiring, firing, compensation, apprenticeships, training, terms, conditions, or privileges of employment based on race, religion, creed, sex, age, or national origin. The Civil Rights Act created the Equal Employment Opportunity Commission (EEOC). Its affirmative action program was designed to "right past wrongs" by increasing opportunities for minorities and women. The Family Medical Leave Act (FMLA) stipulated that companies must provide up to 12 weeks of unpaid leave to an employee upon birth or adoption of a child as well as for taking care of an ill parent, spouse, or child. The Vocational Rehabilitation Act of 1973 extended the same protection against job discrimination on the basis of gender or race to people with disabilities. The Americans with Disabilities Act of 1990 (ADA) requires employers to give applicants with disabilities the same consideration for employment as people without disabilities and requires that businesses make "reasonable accommodations" for people with disabilities. Finally, the Age Discrimination in Employment Act of 1967 (ADEA) protects individuals who are 40 years of age or older from employment discrimination based on age.

The third section of this chapter discussed some of the challenges faced by human resource management, including dealing with labor union–management relations, executive compensation, work–life balance issues of employees, comparable worth, sexual harassment, and retention of employees. The negotiation tactics used by unions include strikes and boycott whereas the one by management include lockout and injunction. As a last resort, mediation and arbitration can be used. Executive compensation is taking a center stage with pay-for-performance. Work–life balance for employees is becoming important to keep employees healthy and stress-free. Pay equity or comparable worth argues for same pay for the same work regardless of gender. Unwelcome sexual advances, requests for sexual favors, and other conduct (verbal or physical) of a sexual nature refers to sexual harassment that HR managers need to mitigate in the workplace. Finally, hiring and retaining the best employees is an ongoing challenge facing HR managers.

key terms

human resource management 242
job analysis 243
job description 244
job specifications 244
recruitment 245
internal candidates 246
external candidates 247
selection 247
contingent workers 250
training and development 250
employee orientation 250
on-the-job training 251
apprentice programs 251
off-the-job training 252
online training 252
vestibule training 252
job simulation 252
management development 252

compensation 253
labor intensive 253
variable pay 254
performance appraisal 255
performance improvement plan (PIP) 256
flextime plan 256
core time 256
compressed workweek 258
telecommuting 258
job sharing 258
Title VII 259
affirmative action 259
Family Medical Leave Act (FMLA) 261
reasonable accommodation 262
union 264
Knights of Labor 264

American Federation of Labor (AFL) 265
industrial unions 265
Congress of Industrial Organization (CIO) 266
negotiated labor–management agreement 267
strike 268
boycott 269
mediation 269
arbitration 269
lockout 269
injunction 269
golden parachute 271
comparable worth 273
sexual harassment 274
hostile work environment 274
quid pro quo 275

applying your skills

1. Look in the classified ads in your local newspaper or on the Internet and find at least two positions that you might like to have when you graduate. List the qualifications specified in each of the ads.

Identify methods the companies might use to determine how well applicants meet each of those qualifications.

2. In groups, describe the best interview you have ever participated in and the worst. What made them great or terrible? Was the interviewer part of what made it best or worst? Explain.

3. Does your company offer health care benefits? What fringe benefits does it offer? What type of compensation did you/do you receive? Discuss in small groups. If you are not currently working, discuss how having health benefits would affect you as an employee.

4. In small groups, recall the various training programs you have experienced. Think of both on-the-job and off-the-job training sessions. What is your evaluation of such programs? Write a brief critique of each. How would you improve them? Share your ideas with the class.

5. Many health care professionals do not belong to a union. Nurses' pay has fallen behind compensation in industry, and doctors feel they are losing a good deal of control over their patients because of the strict rules enforced in many health maintenance organizations (HMOs). What are the pros and cons of doctors and nurses joining a union?

6. In small groups, either in class or online, discuss your personal experiences with a union.

7. What are other employee management issues you can think of? Compare your list with those of several classmates and see what issues you selected in common, and which ones are unique to each of you. Collectively select one or two workplace issues that you all agree will be important in the first decade of the new millennium, and then discuss their likely effects and outcomes.

8. Do businesses and government agencies have a duty to provide additional benefits to employees beyond fair pay and good working conditions? Discuss in groups and present your opinions.

the internet in action

1. *Purpose:* To understand why workers choose to join unions and how unions have made a difference in certain industries.

   Exercise: Visit the AFL-CIO Web site at www.aflcio.com. Navigate through the site and find information regarding why workers join unions and what the benefits have been. Write a short paper about your feelings on unions.

2. *Purpose:* The purpose of this exercise is twofold. From a manager's perspective, the purpose is to illustrate the types of questions man-

agers typically ask during interviews. From an applicant's perspective, the purpose is to practice answering such questions in a safe environment.

Exercise: Go to Monster Campus at http://campus.monster.com. Answer the sample interview questions in the Virtual Interview section. This interactive section gives you the opportunity to test your answers so that when you go on an actual interview you are less likely to fumble for answers.

MARKETING: PRODUCT AND PRICE

SSB Technologies

When Marco Sorani was 24, he broke his fifth cervical vertebra in a body-surfing accident. Sorani lost the use of his legs and the ability to move his fingers. That accident led Sorani in an entirely new direction, one that has benefited him and many others.

Sorani saw a new opportunity and took it. He noticed that many of the 54 million Americans with disabilities like himself were not able to access Web sites. That was a sizable market that really needed some help. Sorani became the chief executive at SSB Technologies, a San Francisco firm that helps companies make their

Marco Sorani

Web sites accessible to people who are disabled. SSB's software can read captions out loud so that people with visual impairments can hear what is on the screen. It can also caption Web audio, enlarge linking buttons, and enlarge the text.

When the U.S. government released guidelines for compliance with Section 508 of the Rehabilitation Act of 1998, it created an expanded opportunity for SBB. Guess what Section 508 calls for? It says that all information technology systems deployed by federal agencies must be accessible to people with disabilities. The

objectives

After reading this chapter, you should be able to:

1 Define *marketing* and its eight functions.

2 Understand market segmentation and name the types of segmentation.

3 Explain the process consumers go through when purchasing products and how consumer markets differ from business-to-business markets.

4 Describe the various aspects that go into the product element of marketing's 4Ps.

5 Describe the different types of pricing that should be considered in marketing products.

passage of this act meant that all government Web sites had to be adapted. SSB was ready to supply the government with the software to do the job. What Sorani did—noticing that people had needs that were not being met, finding a solution for those needs, and providing them with the needed goods and services—is called marketing.

This is an exciting time to be studying business and marketing. New technological innovations, such as voice-activated computers, cell phones that access e-mail, and software that enables individuals to send music, photos, and videos to others, make life easier and more exciting. Technology also provides an opportunity for students to find marketing careers in the high-tech firms that make such products. Such careers include marketing research to see what people want and need, product design and testing, selling, advertising, public relations, distribution, and follow-up services (such as training people how to use products and make repairs). Every day you are likely to see market opportunities as powerful as the ones Sorani saw. This chapter discusses some of the strategies that Sorani implemented: doing target marketing, understanding consumer behavior, and knowing about two of the "4Ps" of marketing—product and price.

INTRODUCTION TO MARKETING

marketing
The process of planning and executing the conception, pricing, promotion, and distribution of goods and services to facilitate exchanges that satisfy individual and organizational objectives.

Marketing is a fun business topic, because even if you don't intend to major in marketing, knowing a little about it can help you become a more informed and savvy consumer. It is important to understand that marketing goes beyond simply selling or advertising. **Marketing** is the process of planning and executing the conception, pricing, promotion, and distribution of goods and services to facilitate exchanges that satisfy individual and organizational objectives.

Section Outline

The Eight Functions of Marketing

THE EIGHT FUNCTIONS OF MARKETING

The eight functions of marketing are all about finding an unmet need in the market, and then providing that product or service to customers, but what does this really mean? As you have already learned, there is much more to marketing than advertising, which is commonly confused with marketing. The eight functions of marketing are (see Figure 9.1):[1]

Businessmen such as Lance Fried are constantly thinking of new products and services to market to consumers. Fried developed an MP3 player that could be used while doing water sports, such as surfing.

- **Exchange**
    1. **Buying:** Consists of inventing and developing or procuring products to fit the needs of the customer. These needs are determined through market research.
    2. **Selling:** When customers are informed of a product, selling is taking place, and it can be done through many methods; packaging and advertising to the consumers are two approaches.
- **Physical Distribution**
    3. **Transportation:** Obviously goods must be transported from the factory to the final place they will be sold via some mode of transportation. Transportation is much more complicated today because many companies are producing products overseas and bringing them to the United States to sell.
    4. **Storage:** Sometimes companies are not ready to bring products directly to the consumer. Consider a wine maker who must wait a year or more for the wine to age correctly and be ready to sell. Because of the long-term storage required for the product, a winery must plan for the cost of storage as well as the cost of insurance in case damage occurs while the wine is being stored.

Ariel Powell is a small-business owner who has just developed a brand-new product. The product is a device that allows dogs to walk more freely with their owners, while still restrained for safety. The device is something Ariel invented while still in college, and annoyed with the dog leash restraints currently on the market. She was able to  develop a prototype and find a manufacturer who can mass produce them for a reasonable price. Ariel has received opinions from friends, but isn't sure how to go about setting the price for her new leash or how to market and advertise it. So Ariel has decided to read this chapter in the text and find out.

- **Facilitating**
  5. **Quality and quantity:** Companies must understand the quality standards of the product they offer in order to meet or exceed customer expectations. A neighborhood grocer, for

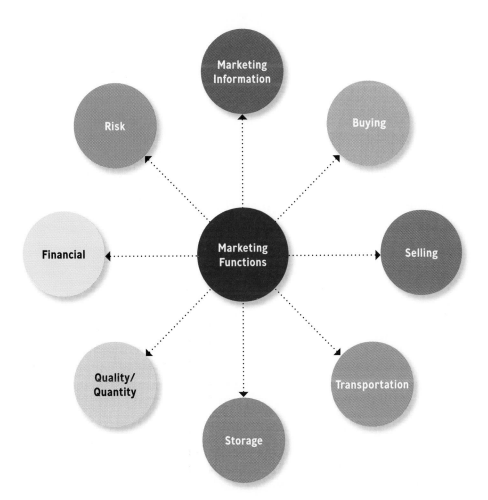

figure 9.1

THE EIGHT FUNCTIONS OF MARKETING

The functions of marketing are grouped into three broad categories: exchange, physical distribution, and facilitating. Think of the last purchase you made. Can you relate the eight functions in these three categories the marketer may have gone through to bring the product to you, the final consumer?

example, must constantly be concerned with the quality of produce it sells. If the produce is not of high quality, it is unlikely that customers will come back. Likewise, the grocer wants to ensure the quantity of an item needed to satisfy the consumer demand.

6. **Financial:** There needs to be methods and procedures for payment to those who provided the product, often the wholesalers and other suppliers. Also, the price that suppliers and wholesalers charge for the products to the company will in turn affect the company's pricing of its products to the consumers.

7. **Risk:** Buying, transporting, and selling products bear some risk to the marketer. Marketers must take possible risks into consideration, such as consumers not being willing to buy the goods or services at the prices offered or competitors offering products that are less expensive or of higher quality.

8. **Marketing information:** There are many tasks marketing professionals must complete in order to successfully sell products and services to consumers. Some of these tasks include setting prices, determining how sales of the product or service will help companies meet their financial objectives, reviewing market research, and analyzing competitors' marketing information. Based on the changing events in the business environment, a marketer must be prepared to change the message and the product or service accordingly.

The eight functions of marketing we just discussed will help you begin to understand marketing. Now that we have looked at the big picture, we will discuss how to start marketing. The first consideration is to determine who your customers are!

market segmentation
The process of dividing the total market into several groups whose members have similar characteristics.

MARKET SEGMENTATION

The total potential consumer market consists of over 6 billion people in global markets with a total of $10 trillion to spend by U.S. consumers alone, according to a 2007 study conducted by the Selig Center for Economic Growth in Athens, Georgia.[2] Because consumer groups differ greatly in age, education level, income, and taste, a business usually cannot fill the needs of every group. Therefore, it must first decide which groups to serve and then develop products and services specially tailored to their needs.

Take the Campbell Soup Company. You probably know Campbell for its traditional soups, such as chicken noodle and tomato. You may also have noticed that Campbell has expanded its product line to appeal to a number of different tastes. Campbell noticed the population growth in the American South and in the Latino community in cities across the nation, so it introduced a Creole soup for the southern market and a red bean soup for the Latino market. In Texas and California, where people like their food with a bit of kick, Campbell makes its nacho cheese soup spicier than in other parts of the country. Campbell is just one company that has had some success studying the consumer market, breaking it down into categories, and then developing products for separate groups of consumers.

The process of dividing the total market into several groups, whose members have similar characteristics, is called **market segmentation.**[3] Selecting which groups (market segments) an organization can serve profitably is called **target marketing.** For example, a shoe store may choose to sell only women's shoes, only children's shoes, or only athletic shoes. The issue is finding the right target market (the segment that would be most profitable to serve) for the new venture.

Campbell's traditional tomato soup is still popular, but the company has released several soup products to meet the needs of an expanding consumer base.

Segmenting the Consumer Market

There are several ways a firm can segment the consumer market (see Figure 9.2). For example, rather than trying to sell a product throughout the United States, you might focus on just one or two regions of the country. One option might be to focus on people in southern states, such as Florida and Georgia.

Dividing the market by geographic area (cities, counties, states, regions, and so on) is called **geographic segmentation.**

Another option for market segmentation would be to target persons of certain ages. For example, Hyundai targets consumers between ages 18 and 34 to compete with Honda and Toyota, according to *USA Today*. Hyundai's product line and pricing structure offers a better competitive advantage in this age group. Segmentation of a market by age, income, and education level or other such characteristics is **demographic segmentation.** Marketers might even segment according to religion, race, and profession. Demographics are the most used segmentation variable, but not necessarily the best.

You may want ads for your product to portray a target group's lifestyle. To do that, you could study the group's lifestyle, values, attitudes, and interests. This segmentation strategy is called **psychographic segmentation.** For example, if you decide to target Generation Y (late teens to early 20s), you could do an in-depth study of their values and interests. Such research reveals which TV shows they watch and which actors they like the best. That information could then be used to develop advertisements for those TV shows, using those stars. PepsiCo did such a segmentation study for its Mountain Dew brand. The resulting promotion dealt with Generation Y's "living life to the limit."

target marketing
Choosing the market segment for a marketer to focus its efforts on.

geographic segmentation
Dividing the market by geographic area (cities, counties, states, regions, etc.).

demographic segmentation
Segmentation by age, income, and education level, race, profession, or religion.

psychographic segmentation
Segmentation by lifestyle, values, attitudes, and interests.

MAIN DIMENSION	SAMPLE VARIABLES	TYPICAL SEGMENTS
Geographic segmentation	Region	Northeast, Midwest, South, West
	City or county size	Under 5,000; 5,000-10,999; 20,000-49,000; 50,000-99,999
	Density	Urban, suburban, rural
Demographic segmentation	Gender	Male, female
	Age	Under 5; 5-10; II-18; 19-34; 35-49; 50-64; 65 and over
	Education	Some high school or less, high school graduate, some college, college graduate, postgraduate
	Race	Caucasian, African American, Indian, Asian, Hispanic
	Nationality	American, Asian, Eastern European, Japanese
	Life stage	Infant, preschool, child, teenager, collegiate, adult, senior
	Income	Under $15,000; $15,000-$24,999; $25,000-$44,999; $45,000-$74,999; $75,000 and over
	Household size	1; 2; 3-4; 5 or more
	Occupation	Professional, technical, clerical, sales supervisors, farmers, students, home-based business owners, retired, unemployed
Psychographic segmentation	Personality	Gregarious, compulsive, extroverted, aggressive, ambitious
	Values	Actualizers, fulfillers, achievers, experiencers, believers, strivers, makers, strugglers
	Lifestyle	Upscale, moderate, budget conscious
Benefit segmentation	Comfort	Benefit segmentation divides an already established market into smaller, more homogeneous segments. Those people who desire economy in a car would be an example. The benefit desired varies by product.
	Convenience	
	Durability	
	Economy	
	Health	
	Luxury	
	Safety	
	Status	
Volume segmentation	Usage	Heavy users, light users, nonusers
	Loyalty status	None, medium, strong

figure 9.2

SOME METHODS MARKETERS USE TO SEGMENT THE MARKET

benefit segmentation
Determining which benefits are preferred and using those benefits to promote a product.

Mountain City Coffeehouse & Creamery in Frostburg, Maryland, offers a daily special of fresh and healthy ethnic vegetarian creation for its customers. Customers are becoming more health and nutrition conscious. They are looking for benefits such as different ethnic cuisines that are fresh and healthy, yet tasty. Determining which benefits are preferred and using those benefits to promote a product is called **benefit segmentation.** Separating the market by usage (volume of product use) is called **volume (usage) segmentation.** The coffeehouse also determines who are the big eaters of different ethnic vegetarian foods and targets them in their marketing for such items. Because the coffeehouse is near a university, at different times of the day, it attracts more faculty versus students and the promotion efforts are targeted for the different usage market.

The best segmentation strategy is to use all the variables possible to come up with a consumer profile (a target market) that is sizable, reachable, and profitable. On the one hand, that may mean not segmenting the market at all, and instead going after the total market (everyone). On the other hand, it may mean going after smaller and smaller segments. Targeting smaller but profitable market segments and designing or finding products and services for them is called **niche marketing.** For example, fridgedoor.com sells refrigerator magnets on the Internet, and offers about 1,500 different types. This product is reaching a very specific niche market, specifically targeted—people who find these items fun.

Market segmentation could include targeting people who are trying to find a lower-fat or lower-calorie alternative in fast-food menus. This photo shows John Martin, the Chief Executive Officer of Taco Bell, as he announces "Border Lights" new light menu items with 20% fewer calories.

As the world moves away from mass production and toward custom-made goods and services, marketers are focusing on **relationship marketing.** The goal is to keep individual customers over time by offering them new products that exactly meet their requirements. The latest in technology enables sellers to work with individual buyers to determine their wants and needs and to develop goods and services specifically designed for them (for example, hand-tailored shirts and unique vacations). The following are just a couple of examples of relationship marketing:

- Airlines, rental car companies, and hotels have frequent-user programs through which loyal customers can earn special services and awards. For example, a traveler can earn bonus miles good for free flights on an airline.
- The Hard Rock Café used customer relationship management software to launch a loyalty program, personalize its marketing campaign, and provide a contact center with more customer information. The result was that response times to customer inquiries were significantly improved and the company increased its sales.[4]

volume (usage) segmentation

Separating the market by usage (volume of product use) or how often a product is used.

niche marketing

The process of finding small but profitable market segments and designing or finding products for them.

relationship marketing

A marketing strategy with a goal to keep individual customers over time by offering them new products that exactly meet their requirements.

SELF-CHECK QUESTIONS

1. What are three ways in which marketers can segment markets?
2. Why do marketers choose to segment markets?

CONSUMER BEHAVIOR

The study of consumer behavior is important in marketing because before companies can sell effectively to someone, they must understand customer motivations and reasons for purchasing a product or service in the first place. Many people purchase new cars or particular brands of clothing, for instance, not because they absolutely need them (although we all need transportation and clothes), but because they perceive the purchase of these goods satisfies ego and can impress others or otherwise enhance their lives in intangible ways.

An important part of consumer behavior is the process we all go through when purchasing a product. Figure 9.3 shows the consumer decision-making process and some of the outside factors that influence it. The five steps in the process are problem recognition, information search, alternative evaluation, purchase decision, and postpurchase evaluation.

Problem recognition may occur, for example, when your washing machine breaks and you are unable to fix it yourself. This unfortunate situation leads to an information search—you may review the possibility of having your washing machine fixed or you may look for ads about new washing machines or read brochures about them. You may even check how specific machines perform, and then do other comparisons before making a decision.

Marketing researchers investigate consumer thought processes and behavior at each stage to determine the best way to facilitate marketing exchanges. Consumer behavior researchers also study the various influences that impact consumer behavior. Figure 9.3 shows several influences that affect consumer buying behavior: marketing mix variables (the 4Ps—see our discussion toward the end of the chapter); psychological influences, such as perceptions and attitudes; situational influences, such as the type of purchase and the physical surroundings; and sociocultural influences, such as reference groups and culture.

Other factors important in the consumer decision-making process, whose technical definitions may be unfamiliar to you, include the following:

- *Learning* involves changes in an individual's behavior resulting from previous experiences and information. For example, if you try a particular brand of shampoo and don't like it, you may never buy it again.

- A *reference group* is the group that an individual uses as a reference point in the formation of his or her beliefs, attitudes, values, or behavior. For example, a student who carries a briefcase instead of a backpack may see businesspeople as his or her reference group.

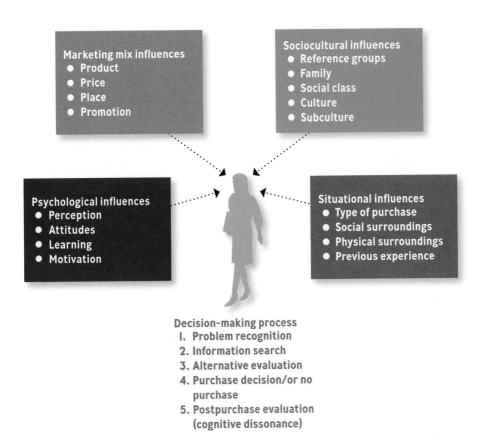

figure 9.3

OUTSIDE INFLUENCES
ON THE CONSUMER
DECISION-MAKING
PROCESS

- *Culture* is the set of values, attitudes, and way of doing things that is transmitted from one generation to another in a given society. The American culture, for example, emphasizes education, freedom, and diversity.

- *Subculture* is the set of values, attitudes, and ways of doing things that results from belonging to a certain ethnic group, religious group, racial group, or other group with which one closely identifies (e.g., teenagers). The subculture is one small part of the larger culture. Your subculture may prefer rap and hip-hop music, while your parents' subculture may prefer light jazz.

- *Cognitive dissonance* is a type of psychological conflict that can occur after a purchase, and is the same as buyer's *remorse*. Consumers who make a major purchase, such as a car, may have doubts about whether they got the best product at the best price. Marketers must, therefore, reassure such consumers after the sale that they made a good decision.

Study Skills

Importance of Good Communication Skills

What happens when you are faced with the challenge of speaking to a group of your peers? Or speaking one on one with your boss? Are you at ease or a bit nervous?

These situations are opportunities for displaying good communication skills. Improvement of your communication skills can give you a level of confidence and can move you ahead of others in the business world.

How far can you take your communications skills? College class work is a great learning and proving ground for working on your communication skills, and your instructor or professor can be a good critic.

An auto dealer, for example, may send positive press articles about the particular car a consumer purchased. The dealer may also offer product guarantees and provide certain free services to the customer.

q: Have you ever had buyer's remorse? How did it
»» impact future purchases?

The Business-to-Business Markets

It is important to remember that, although we have been discussing consumer markets, business-to-business (B2B) markets account for a significant number of sales, to say the least. The B2B marketers include manufacturers; intermediaries such as retailers; institutions (e.g., hospitals and schools); and the government.[5] The B2B market is larger than the consumer market because items are often sold and resold several times in the B2B process before they are sold to the final consumer. B2B markets buy items such as paper products, office machines (such as copiers), and other supplies. Manufacturing firms' B2B purchases will include office supplies, but also tools and component parts for the products they are manufacturing (such as door hinges or rubber mats in the auto industry). The marketing strategies often differ from consumer marketing because business buyers have their own decision-making process. Because B2B markets are so varied, it is important to look at the major differences (also see Figure 9.4):

Every customer goes through the five steps in the buying process when purchasing products.

1. The number of customers in the B2B market is *relatively* few. That is, compared to the 70 million or so households in the U.S. consumer market, there are relatively few construction firms, factories, or mining operations, among others.

2. The size of business customers is relatively large. That is, a few large organizations account for most of the employment and production of various goods and services. Nonetheless, there are many small- to medium-size firms in the United States that, together, make many attractive markets.

	BUSINESS-TO-BUSINESS MARKET	CONSUMER MARKET
Market Structure	Relatively few potential customers Larger purchases Geographically concentrated	Many potential customers Smaller purchases Geographically dispersed
Products	Require technical, complex products Frequently require customization Frequently require technical advice, delivery, and after-sale service	Require less technical products Sometimes require customization Sometimes require technical advice, delivery, and after-sale service
Buying Procedures	Buyers are trained Negotiate details of most purchases Follow objective standards Formal process involving specific employees Closer relationships between marketers and buyers Often buy from multiple sources	Accept standard terms for most purchases Use personal judgment Informal process involving household members Impersonal relationships between marketers and consumers Rarely buy from multiple sources

figure 9.4

COMPARING BUSINESS-TO-BUSINESS AND CONSUMER BUYING BEHAVIOR

3. B2B markets tend to be geographically concentrated. For example, oil fields tend to be concentrated in the Southwest and in Alaska. Consequently, marketing efforts may be concentrated on a particular geographic area. Distribution problems can be minimized by locating warehouses near industrial centers.

4. Business buyers are generally considered more rational (as opposed to emotional) than ultimate consumers (who may engage more in impulse buying) in their selection of goods and services; they use specifications and often more carefully weigh the total product offer, including quality, price, and service.

5. B2B sales tend to be direct. Manufacturers sell products, such as tires, directly to auto manufacturers, but tend to use intermediaries, such as wholesalers and retailers, to sell to ultimate consumers.

6. There is much more emphasis on personal selling in B2B markets than in consumer markets. Whereas consumer promotions are based more on advertising, B2B sales are based on direct selling because there are fewer customers who demand more personal service.

While Office Max offers business supplies to individual customers, the company also has a large corporate business base, offering direct order options for office supplies, document processing, and office equipment such as furniture and computer software. A dedicated corporate sales staff helps Office Max retain consumer and business-to-business customers.

7. Packaging tends to be more functional in B2B, rather than designed as a marketing tool, as with consumer markets.

SELF-CHECK QUESTIONS

1. What are the five steps in the consumer decision-making process?
2. Describe a recent purchase and how you went through this process.
3. What are some differences between the consumer market and the B2B market?

---

marketing management

The process of overseeing all of the aspects of marketing a particular product or service for the purpose of attracting and retaining customers.

4Ps

The ingredients that go into a marketing program: product, price, place, and promotion.

total product offer

Consists of everything that consumers evaluate when deciding whether to buy something.

THE 4PS OF MARKETING: PRODUCT

Marketing cannot occur without pleasing one's customers because no one would be in business without them! **Marketing management** refers to the process of overseeing all the aspects of marketing a particular product or service for the purpose of attracting and retaining customers. Much of what marketing people do has been conveniently divided into four factors, called the **4Ps** to make them easy to remember and implement.[6] The 4Ps are:

1. Product
2. Price
3. Place
4. Promotion

We will now take a closer look at product and price elements of the marketing mix or the 4Ps, while the next chapter will discuss place and promotion elements.

Total Product Offer

Reviewing the *total product offer* is the first, and perhaps most important, way to look at a product. A total product offer implies that a customer is not only buying a product or a service, but purchasing everything that goes along with it, such as service after the sale, or a brand name. In other words, **total product offer** consists of everything that consumers evaluate when deciding whether to purchase a good or service. Thus, the basic product or service may be a washing machine, an insurance policy, or a brand of soda, but the *total* product offer also may consist of the value enhancers that appear in Figure 9.5. Before consumers buy a product, they may evaluate and compare total product offers on all these dimensions.

Note that some of the attributes are tangible (the product itself and its package), whereas others are intangible (the reputation of the

The Importance of Positive Attitude

How would you respond to the question, "Are you a positive person?" What variables or experiences might affect your mental outlook? If you think about your attitude and disposition, how do they affect these areas of your life?

- Schoolwork and effort
- Your current relationships
- Your current job

- Your effort to get things done
- The perception of how others look at you
- Your potential to excel in your life

A positive attitude is the key to all the outcomes you encounter. A good attitude and a positive disposition have results that you can easily recognize if you think about it for a moment. They place you in a better light for all those with whom you come in contact!

producer and the image created by advertising). A successful marketer must begin to think like a consumer and evaluate the total product offer as a collection of impressions created by all the factors listed in Figure 9.5 and consider as a consumer what parts of the total product offer are important.

The total product offer consists of those things that are important to customers sometimes far beyond the product itself. As a businessperson, it is wise to talk with consumers in order to see which features and benefits are most important to them; that is, which value enhancers to include in the final offerings. Customers do not buy a product, they buy the total benefits of having or using the product.

But how can we know which benefits customers are looking for? This discovery process is where market research comes in.

Price	Brand name	Convenience	Package
Store surroundings	Service	Internet access	Buyer's past experience
Guarantee	Speed of delivery	Image created by advertising	Reputation of producer

figure 9.5

POTENTIAL COMPONENTS OF A TOTAL PRODUCT OFFER

q: What part of the total product offer is most important
» » to you?

Market Research

When a marketer knows what a customer wants, she and her team can develop the product and advertising to meet the exact needs of that customer, which is normally done through marketing research. **Marketing research** is the analysis of markets to determine opportunities and challenges, and to find the information needed to make good marketing decisions. Marketing research helps determine what customers have purchased in the past and what they might purchase in the future.[7] For example, marketers conduct research on business trends, the viability of new products, global trends, and more. Businesses need information in order to compete effectively, and marketing research is the activity that gathers that information.[8] Note, too, that in addition to listening to customers, marketing researchers should pay attention to what employees, shareholders, dealers, consumer advocates, media representatives, and other stakeholders believe.

Market research consists of four steps:

1. Defining the question (problem or opportunity) and determining the present situation.

2. Collecting research data.
3. Analyzing the research data.
4. Choosing and implementing the best solution.

CarMax is able to offer new and used cars to customers nationwide. With its Web site, potential consumers can locate the car they want, even in other parts of the country, and pick up at the location nearest them.

Market researchers must first determine what they need to know, in order to ask the appropriate questions. For example, they might want to know why a particular product is not selling well, or they might want to know how customers feel about a new advertising campaign. Once marketers have determined the information they need, they can start to collect the data.

Quantitative and Qualitative Research

Quantitative research involves the systematic scientific investigation of phenomena and their relationships. The data gathered are analyzed with statistical methods. Qualitative research, on the other hand, targets harder to measure attitudes and opinions. This type of research is usually used in marketing and the social sciences and involves focusing on a small group of people from which data are gathered for study. A focus group gathered to discuss what breakfast cereals the participants like and dislike would be an example of qualitative research, while a statistical study of 3,000 people and their purchase choices according to gender or income would be an example of quantitative research.

Data collection can occur in several ways. **Primary research** is research that a marketer creates; that is, the marketer implements the collection of the data firsthand. The goal of primary research might be to answer a question such as "Would consumers like a new flavor of our product?" Such research can be quite time-consuming and expensive. Primary research is usually conducted in the form of a survey or a focus group. A **focus group** is a small group of people who meet under the direction of a discussion leader who tries to understand their opinions about a product. (Focus groups are also used in political campaigns—where the product is a candidate.)

Companies conduct focus groups on their products to determine how the products can be improved to better meet the needs of the consumers.

Secondary research, on the other hand, seeks data already available to the marketer in government publications and journal articles and so forth. The disadvantage of secondary research is that it produces information that is not specifically developed for one marketer's purpose, so it may not meet the need. However, a powerful advantage of secondary research is that it is much more inexpensive to conduct and faster to gather information than using primary research. The savings in time and money make secondary research a popular research method.

Once the researcher gathers the data, all of the data are reviewed to form some sort of conclusion. The conclusion might be as simple as "customers want a quick, easy snack" or it might suggest a subtle shift in some aspect of a product to answer the original question or solve the problem.

It is important to note that most companies sell several products. A **product line** is a group of products that are physically similar, or intended for a similar market. Thus the costs of marketing research can often be spread over an entire product line, when the whole line is affected by the results of a research project.

focus group

A small group of people who meet under the direction of a discussion leader who tries to discover their opinions about a product.

secondary research

Data already available to the marketer, such as in government publications and journal articles.

product line

A group of products that are physically similar or intended for a similar market.

A company like Kashi may offer several types of cereals to meet the needs of more customers.

Product Differentiation

Product differentiation is the creation of real or perceived product differences. Actual product differences are sometimes quite small, so marketers must use a creative mix to make their product seem very special and different from the competition. Various bottled water companies, for example, have successfully attempted product differentiation. Although bottled water brands are quite similar, marketers have made the consumers think their bottled water is very different from the others. Coca-Cola and Pepsi are a well-known example of competition by product differentiation. Although for most people there is relatively little difference between the two, brand name, advertising, and other total product offer characteristics encourage the consumer to favor one soda over another. Consumers tend to develop strong loyalties over perceived differences in taste and other characteristics of such a product.

Several systems are used to classify consumer goods and services. See Figure 9.6. Once marketers know how goods are classified, they are better able to market to the consumers. One classification system, based on consumer purchasing behavior, has four general categories—convenience, shopping, specialty, and unsought.

product differentiation

The creation of real or perceived product differences.

1. *Convenience goods and services* (sometimes called *consumer products*) are products that the consumer wants to purchase frequently and with a minimum of effort, such as candy, gum, milk, snacks, gas, and banking services. One store that sells mostly convenience goods is 7-Eleven. We even use the generic term *convenience store*. Location, brand awareness, and image are important differentiators for marketers of convenience goods and services. The Internet has taken convenience to a whole new level, especially for banks and other service companies, such as real estate firms. Companies that do not offer such services are likely to lose market share to those who do, unless they offer outstanding service to customers who visit in person.

2. *Shopping goods and services* are products the consumer buys only after comparing value, quality, price, and style from a variety of sellers. Shopping goods and services are sold largely through shopping centers where consumers can make comparisons. Sears and Macy's are stores that sell mostly shopping goods. Because many consumers carefully compare such products, marketers can emphasize price differences, quality differences, or some combination of the two. Examples include clothes, shoes, appliances, and auto repair services.

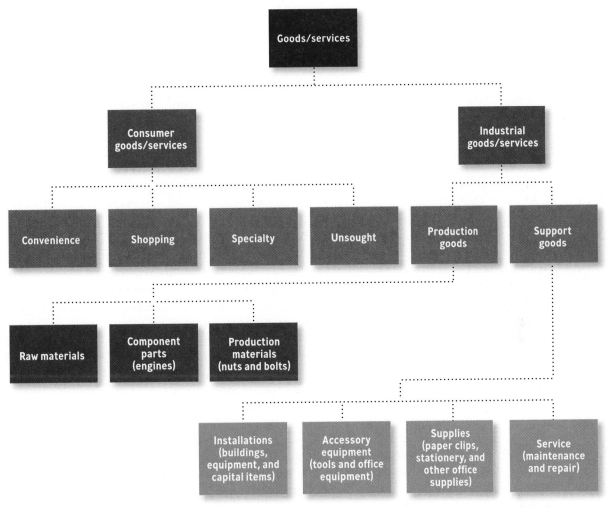

figure 9.6

VARIOUS CATEGORIES OF CONSUMER AND INDUSTRIAL GOODS AND SERVICES

3. *Specialty goods and services* are consumer products with unique characteristics and brand identity. Because these products are perceived as having no reasonable substitute, the consumer puts forth a special effort to purchase them. Examples include Rolex watches, expensive wine, fur coats, jewelry, Godiva chocolates, and expensive cigars, as well as services provided by medical specialists or business consultants. A Jaguar automobile dealer is an example of a specialty goods retailer. These products are often marketed through specialty magazines. For example, specialty skis may be sold through sports magazines and specialty foods through gourmet magazines. By establishing interactive Web sites where customers can place orders, companies that sell specialty goods and services can make buying their goods as easy as, or easier than, shopping at a local mall.

4. *Unsought goods and services* are products that consumers are unaware of, have not necessarily thought of buying, but suddenly find that they need to solve an unexpected problem. Some examples of unsought products are car towing services, burial services, and dental work. Marketing takes ingenuity for these products. The goal is to get the customer to seek out the product and services in a pinch, which requires a variety of promotional techniques. Consider the last time your plumbing was clogged at 10:00 p.m. As a consumer, you want the quickest fix possible; price isn't as much of a factor as with the other classifications of products we have discussed. You may look in the yellow pages and call the first plumber you see in a large, well-placed advertisement.

> **industrial good**
>
> A product that is used to produce or as a component of other products.

Another type of product is an **industrial good.** This product can be a good or service. Raw materials, major equipment, accessory equipment, components, process materials, maintenance items, and business services are industrial goods. For example, Boeing uses steel, rubber, glass, an array of bolts and fittings, and many other items, which are industrial products. Industrial products are generally not sold to individual consumers, but are sold in a business-to-business (B2B) market. The marketing of such products is a highly specialized field within the business area.

Packaging

Another important aspect of marketing is packaging. Because there are so many choices of products in a supermarket or a discount store, packaging is extremely important in order to get the customer's attention. The goals of packaging include the following:

Packaging can make a huge difference in the attractiveness of a product. Which packaging do you prefer for ketchup?

1. Protect the goods inside, stand up under handling and storage, be tamperproof, deter theft, and yet be easy to open and use.
2. Attract the buyer's attention.
3. Describe the contents and give information about the contents.
4. Explain the benefits of the product inside.
5. Provide information on warranties, warnings, and other consumer matters.
6. Give some indication of price, value, and uses.
7. Provide the dimensions and weight of the actual package.

A marketer who can design a package with all of these components will likely see an increase in sales.

Consider wine purchases. Many consumers do not know a good wine from a bad wine, so often the wine is chosen based on the packaging. The packaging of children's products is also very important because young children cannot read; the marketer must get the message to the child using visuals rather than writing. If you have gone grocery shopping with a child recently, you know the power of packaging!

Branding

Related to and in a sense summing up all the other aspects of the marketing process, the **brand** is the name and symbol that identify the product and position it over another similar product. **Brand equity** refers to the combination of factors that people associate with a given brand name. These factors include the reputation, image, and perceived quality of a product that are summed up in its brand. With proper brand equity, a marketer can achieve brand loyalty, which is the ultimate goal when developing products. **Brand loyalty** is the extent to which a customer will choose one product over another on a continual basis. For example, many individuals are brand loyal to a brand of toothpaste. It doesn't matter to brand loyal customers that a new brand of toothpaste is on the market because they tend to stick to the brand to which they are loyal. Aeropostale is an example of a store to which many people are loyal when purchasing clothing; these customers would rather not shop anywhere else.

brand
The name and symbol that identify the product of one seller over another.

brand equity
Refers to the combination of factors that people associate with a given brand name, such as image and perceived quality.

brand loyalty
The extent to which a customer will choose one product over another on a continual basis.

q: To what products are you brand loyal?
»» Why?

Product Development Process

The phases a company might go through in order to come up with a new product that meets the need of its customers is called the product development process. The process is outlined in Figure 9.7. First, companies must generate ideas for a new product. These new ideas can come from employees or even suppliers. Second, through product screening companies can look at the new ideas in terms of profit potential and marketability of the new product. After this phase, some products may not be developed any further. Product analysis involves number crunching to see the cost of making the product versus the sales forecasts of that product. If product numbers look good (i.e., the cost of making the product does not outweigh the revenue that a company could expect from making that product in the development and testing phase), the idea is

Celebrity Endorsements

Many producers use *brand association* to sell their products—often to young people. You are probably accustomed to seeing celebrities or sports stars, such as Queen Latifah or Tiger Woods, in print and television advertising to attract the attention of the audience.

Questions

1. Is it ethical for a celebrity to endorse a product or service that he or she does not use? Why or why not?

2. Is it ethical for a celebrity to endorse unhealthy products? Why or why not?

3. How responsible are you for your own buying behavior?

figure 9.7

THE NEW-PRODUCT DEVELOPMENT PROCESS

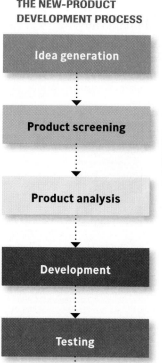

Idea generation

Product screening

Product analysis

Development

Testing

Commercialization

fully developed, and perhaps a prototype is made. Often, companies will use market research to ask customers their opinions on the new product. Once they receive these options, they may decide to make some changes to the product before the product is commercialized and made available to the general public.

SELF-CHECK QUESTIONS

1. What are the 4Ps?
2. What are four classifications of product?
3. Describe the difference between the two types of market research.

THE 4PS OF MARKETING: PRICE

As you can imagine, price setting is one of the most difficult parts of marketing. The price needs to reflect the quality, brand, and image of the product, and be high enough to make a profit while not being so high that people are unwilling to pay the price. A firm generally has several objectives in mind when setting a pricing strategy.

1. *Achieving a target return on investment or profit.* Ultimately, the goal of marketing is to make a profit by providing goods and services to others. Naturally, one long-run pricing objective of almost all firms is to optimize profit.[9]

2. *Building traffic.* Supermarkets often advertise certain products, such as diapers or paper towels, at or below cost to attract people

to the store. These products are called **loss leaders.** The long-run objective is to make profits by following the short-run objective of building a customer base. Yahoo! once provided an auction service for free in competition with eBay. Why give away such a service free? To increase advertising revenue on the Yahoo! site and attract more people to Yahoo!'s other services.

3. *Achieving greater market share.* The U.S. auto industry is in a fierce international battle to capture and hold market share. One way to capture a larger part of the market is to offer low finance rates (e.g., zero percent financing), low lease rates, or rebates. Many auto companies recently offered such discounts, but the result was a large loss in profits. Computer companies offered free digital cameras and printers, rebates, and daily sweepstakes to capture business from Dell. Dell responded by offering buyers the chance to win $50,000. Such counterattacks have enabled Dell to maintain, and even grow, its market share. Market share can be defined as the proportion of sales made by a company versus the total number of sales for that particular product. In 2006, for example, Coca-Cola lost market share of the soda market, dipping to just 42.9 percent of the soda market.[10]

4. *Creating an image.* Certain watches, perfumes, and other socially visible products are priced high to give them an image of exclusivity and status. Consider the cost of a $1,700 Prada jacket or a $12,000 Rolex watch. If the watch were to cost less, it might not have the same exclusivity and status.

5. *Furthering social objectives.* A firm may want to price a product low so that people with little money can afford it. The government often gets involved in pricing farm products so that everyone can get basic needs, such as milk and bread, at a low price.

Note that a firm may have short-run objectives that differ greatly from its long-run objectives. Both should be understood at the beginning of the marketing process and put into the strategic marketing plan. Pricing objectives should be influenced by other marketing decisions regarding product design, packaging, branding, distribution, and promotion. All of these marketing decisions are interrelated.

People believe intuitively that the price charged for a product must bear some relation to the cost of producing the product. (An understanding of this psychology goes into the marketer's pricing decision sometimes.) Generally this is so. Prices and cost aren't always related, however, as suggested previously.

Product Life Cycle

Besides meeting the pricing goals of the organization, price is based on the product life cycle. Most products go through this life cycle,

---

Section Outline

The 4Ps of Marketing: Price

- Product Life Cycle
- Cost-Based Pricing
- Demand-Based Pricing
- Competition-Based Pricing
- Break-Even Analysis
- Other Pricing Strategies

---

loss leader

When a store advertises certain products at or below cost to attract people to the store.

Avoiding the Black Hole of Business Start-ups

It is the Great American Dream to start your own business and become your own boss. It is not that complicated, either. Simply invest everything you own and as much as you can borrow, paint a rosy picture of how successful your product or service will be, grossly underestimate the cost in time and money, then sit back and watch the business fold in less than a year. Oh, and do not forget to ruin your credit rating, personal relationships, and health along the way.

You say no one deliberately sets out to fail in business? Perhaps not, but four out of every 10 start-ups will go under within the first year, six within the first five years. It seems that nothing succeeds like failure. Yet, many of the missteps and disasters that befall a new business are avoidable.

It is an idea that has been simmering in the mind of Carla, a pastry and dessert chef, who was told her cupcakes are second to none. At the urging of friends and co-workers, and with some credibility and success under her belt from working at reputable restaurants, she finally felt she had the resources to follow her dream. The idea was to open a small shop—a bakery boutique—that would feature her singular cupcakes. The real business, however, was to supply stores and retail outlets, and establish a name brand, a la "Famous Amos" chocolate chip cookies.

A viable idea, sound financial management, and hard work all are important, but first and foremost is the need for a well thought out strategic plan—the big picture of the business. It starts with the vision, mission, values, and operating principles. In addition to these basics, the plan will include financial data, market research, positioning information, competition review, and market description. This plan addresses the nuts-and-bolts issues of how to grow the business—it is a map for traversing the business jungle.

As part of this process, it is important to decide exactly what it is the company will be selling, whether it is a product or a service and, more importantly, to whom it will be sold. In other words: *identify the market.* A company can offer the finest, most affordable and efficient air-conditioning system known to man, but if the target market is north of Alaska, the company will not last the summer.

Define the market and the market will help to define the product or service. As such, it is critical to ask and answer these basic questions: Where are the prospective customers located? Who are they? What is their demographic? What are they looking for, and what is missing in the marketplace? What is the company's unique selling proposition?

The factors that will set a new company, product, or service apart from the competition not only will help determine the future marketing approach, but will act as a barrier to entry for future competition. Without this kind of thought process and planning, a new venture is vulnerable to being co-opted and imitated by the more established competition, thereby diluting its place in the market.

In Carla's case, an upswing in cupcake sales, indicating something of a trend, is what helped her decide this might be the right time to start her business. In her mind, the market already is defined. One of the challenges or opportunities was to build a brand that could not be imitated and takes on a certain cache in the marketplace. (Using the Famous Amos model, a cookie is a cookie, except when branded as "the" cookie.)

A common mistake start-ups make is setting prices according to the competition. It is better to start by calculating the profit margin needed to stay in business. What will the operating costs be? It is particularly important to shop for the best prices on equipment and materials and estimate labor costs by surveying what the competition pays, or by checking regional and industry averages.

Once costs have been determined, decide if pricing is where the new company will make its stand. Perhaps not. Quality of service or product may be the unique selling proposition that sets the company apart from the pack. If so, though costs may prevent the company from being the lowest priced offering, there still may be a niche that will attract the desired target market. In some cases, where prestige and status are the qualifying factors, a price that is too low may send the wrong message and actually lower market appeal.

Questions

1. Setting prices based on the competition is not always a good idea. Why?

2. What is a unique selling proposition?

3. What do you think is the most important part of owning a small business and marketing the product it sells?

Source: "Avoid the Black Hole of Business Start-Ups," Kenneth Sweet, *USA Today,* March 2006. Copyright © 2006 *USA Today.* Used with permission.

LIFE CYCLE STAGE	MARKETING MIX ELEMENTS			
	PRODUCT	**PRICE**	**PLACE**	**PROMOTION**
Introduction	Offer market-tested product; keep mix small	Go after innovators with high introductory price (skimming strategy) or use penetration pricing	Use wholesalers, selective distribution	Dealer promotion and heavy investment in primary demand advertising and sales promotion to get stores to carry the product and consumers to try it
Growth	Improve product; keep product mix limited	Adjust price to meet competition	Increase distribution	Heavy competitive advertising
Maturity	Differentiate product to satisfy different market segments	Further reduce price	Take over wholesaling function and intensify distribution	Emphasize brand name as well as product benefits and differences
Decline	Cut product mix; develop new-product ideas	Consider price increase	Consolidate distribution; drop some outlets	Reduce advertising to only loyal customers

figure 9.8

SAMPLE STRATEGIES FOLLOWED DURING THE PRODUCT LIFE CYCLE

product life cycle
A theoretical model of what happens to sales and profits for a product class over time.

consisting of four stages: introduction, growth, maturity, and decline (see Figure 9.8). The **product life cycle** is a theoretical model of what happens to sales and profits (the amount of money earned after expenses are paid) for a product class (e.g., all dishwasher soaps) over time. However, not all products follow the life cycle, and particular brands may act differently. For example, although frozen foods as a generic class may go through the entire cycle, one brand may never get beyond the introduction stage. Also, some products become classics and never experience much of a decline. Others may be withdrawn from the market altogether. Nonetheless, the product life cycle may provide some basis for anticipating future market developments and for planning marketing strategies. It can also help us, as consumers, see what products are about to be popular and what products are destined to die sooner rather than later! See Figure 9.8.

Some products, such as microwave ovens, stay in the introductory stage for years. Other products, such as fad clothing, may go through the entire cycle in a few months. Consider the purchase of a computer. By the time you purchase it and bring it home and use it for a time, there is already a much faster processor available! This results in a shorter life cycle for some products, especially high-tech products.

The life cycle affects pricing because the longer a product stays in the life cycle, more profit will be made. Remember, this success also

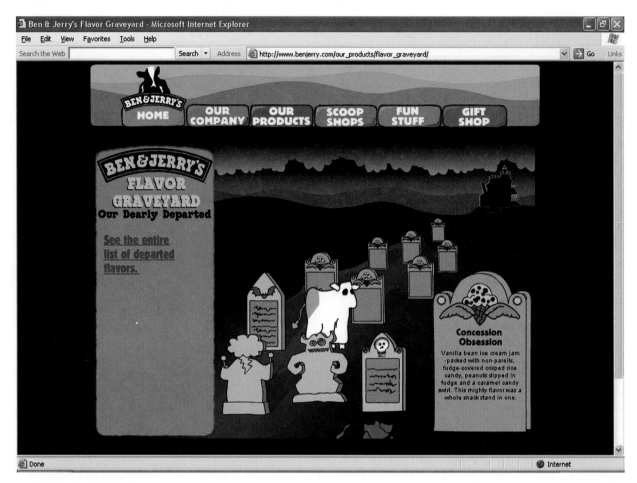

Sometimes a new flavor is not received as well by consumers as expected. Ben and Jerry's makes light of failed flavors in its "Flavor Graveyard" as shown on the Web site: www.benjerry.com/fun_stuff/#.

has to do with supply and demand for a product, as we discussed in Chapter 3. The higher the demand for a product, the higher the price that can be charged. Airlines, for example, charge more for airline tickets during peak times, such as the holidays. Likewise, a fad-type product, which goes through the life cycle quickly, must be priced to meet the expectations of customers and also be priced knowing that it will have a short sales cycle, resulting in fewer sales over time. See Figure 9.9.

Cost-Based Pricing

Producers often use cost as a primary basis for setting price. They develop elaborate cost accounting systems to measure production costs (including materials, labor, and overhead), add in some margin of profit, and determine the price. The question is whether the price will be satisfactory to the market as well. In the long run, the market—not the producer—determines what the price will be. Pricing should take

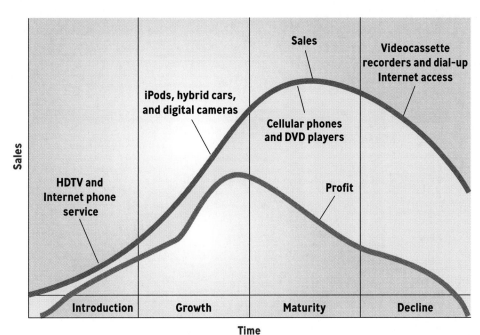

figure 9.9

SALES AND PROFITS DURING THE PRODUCT LIFE CYCLE

into account costs, but it should also include the expected costs of product updates, the objectives for each product, and competitor prices.

Demand-Based Pricing

An opposite strategy to cost-based pricing is target costing. **Target costing** is demand based, which means products must be designed to satisfy customers and meet the profit margins desired by the firm. Target costing makes the final price an input to the product development process, not an outcome of it. Companies estimate the selling price people would be willing to pay for a product and subtract the desired profit margin. The result is the target cost of production. Japanese companies, such as Isuzu Motors, Komatsu Limited, and Sony, have all used target costing.

target costing
Means to price based on demand. A product is designed so it satisfies needs and meets the profit margins desired by the company.

Competition-Based Pricing

Competition-based pricing is a strategy based on what all the other competitors are doing. The price can be at, above, or below competitors' prices. Pricing depends on customer loyalty, perceived differences, and the competitive climate. **Price leadership** is the procedure by which one or more dominant firms set the pricing practices that all competitors in an industry follow. You may have noticed that practice among oil, airline, and cigarette companies. For example, if one airline reduces the ticket prices, the competitors immediately follow.

price leadership
The procedure by which one or more dominant firms set the pricing practices that all competitors in an industry follow.

Shopping on the Internet has had a huge impact on the pricing strategies of marketers. Shopping.com, for example, allows consumers to view the same product at several different online stores and also allows them to compare prices.

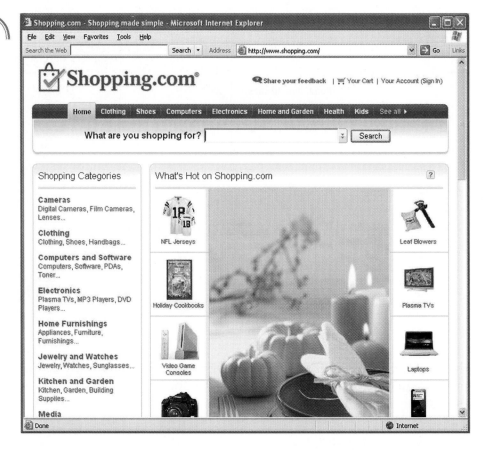

Break-Even Analysis

Yet another way to set price is to figure out how many of a product you would need to sell in order to make a profit. Perhaps you have decided to open a coffee shop on a busy corner. You would likely want to know how many lattes you would need to sell in order to make money. There is a simple calculation used to determine this:

$$\text{Break-even point (BEP)} = \frac{\text{Total fixed cost}}{\text{Price of 1 unit} - \text{Variable cost of 1 unit}}$$

For your coffee shop, let's say your fixed costs are your rent and electricity, totaling $600 per month. Your variable costs for one latte are $1 each. These include things like the milk and flavoring. So, let's say you decide to sell your lattes for $3 each. Here is what your calculation would look like:

$$\frac{\$600}{\$3 - \$1} = 300$$

This equation shows that you would have to sell 300 lattes to break even. Then, beyond 300 you would start to make a profit.

Other Pricing Strategies

One of the toughest parts of marketing is setting and keeping the right price, as you have probably already determined. One way a marketing professional can determine what price to charge is by using the pricing strategy matrix (see Figure 9.10). A marketer would look at the price of a product and then determine if the product has high, medium, or low value to the customer. Then, he or she would look at the price that is actually being charged. The place where the two meet would be the direction (higher or lower) the marketer should go on price. Keep in mind that this matrix is only one of many tools a manager can use to keep up-to-date on the right prices.

Let's look at pricing strategy for a specific product—high-definition television (HDTV) sets. A firm can decide pricing strategy by looking at the product life cycle. One strategy would be to price the TVs high to recover the costs of developing the sets and to take advantage of the fact that there are few competitors. A **skimming price strategy** is one in which a new product is priced high to make optimum profit while there's little competition. Of course, those large profits will attract competitors, which is what happened when high-priced HDTVs were introduced in the late 1990s. A second strategy would be to price the new HDTVs low, which would attract more buyers and discourage other companies from making sets, because the profit is so low. This strategy enables the firm to penetrate or capture a large share of the market quickly. A **penetration strategy,** therefore, is one in which a product is priced low to attract more customers and discourage competitors. For example, if Burger King wants to introduce a new

skimming price strategy
A pricing strategy in which a new product is priced high to make optimum profit while there's little competition.

penetration strategy
A pricing strategy in which a product is priced low to attract more customers and discourage competitors.

figure 9.10

THE PRICING STRATEGY MATRIX

	LOW PRICE	MEDIUM PRICE	HIGH PRICE
High value	Underpriced: value undercut by price. "What's wrong with this picture" pricing strategy.	Attractive pricing: ideal for market penetration. "More for your money" pricing strategy.	Premium pricing: prestige, prominence. "Connoisseur" pricing strategy.
Medium value	True bargain: may be a temporary special to raise revenue or to move discontinued items. "Inventory sale" strategy.	Price and value are in balance, exclusive of other factors. "Square deal" pricing strategy.	Overpriced: informed buyers will stay away; sales may be made to unsophisticated market. "Infomercial" pricing strategy.
Low value	Cheap stuff. Often sold with lots of "bonus" items or features. "Tourist trap" pricing strategy.	Turns sales into complaints. "Caveat emptor" pricing strategy ("Let the buyer beware").	Don't even think about it: the "Fleece 'em and run" pricing strategy.

CAREER spotlight

So, You Want to Be . . . in Marketing

Sales is a challenging area in which individuals can prove themselves, in order to possibly move up to sales manager or other positions of responsibility. Another option in the marketing arena is advertising. Advertising may appeal to those who are attracted to the tantalizing mix of psychology, communications, and art that advertisers blend to help market a product. Many companies hire graphic designers and copywriters to develop their advertising campaigns.

If you are interested in the numbers crunching part of marketing, market research might be an area to entertain as a possibility for your career. In this job, a researcher designs surveys and analyzes the data that the surveys provide.

Retailing offers a variety of opportunities, some more marketing oriented than others. In many companies, skill level is more important than having a four-year degree. Marketing skills can often be developed in two-year business programs and in real-world experi-

ence. Professional organizations, such as the American Marketing Association (AMA), give you the opportunity to network with others. There are many interesting publications on marketing for you to read, such as *Advertising Age* and *American Demographics,* that might be beneficial for you to start reading now, before you begin your career in marketing.

Some possible positions in marketing include:

- Market researcher
- Sales representative
- Purchasing agent (buyer)
- Advertising manager
- Public relations specialist
- Marketing manager

Visit the Bureau of Labor Statistics online (www.bls.gov/) for more information on salary, job duties, career paths, and prospects.

---

everyday low pricing (EDLP)

A pricing strategy where prices are set lower than other stores and do not have many special sales.

high–low pricing strategy

This strategy has regular prices that are higher than those at stores using EDLP, but they have many special sales in which the prices are lower.

sandwich, it may price the sandwich very low so people will be willing to try it. Small businesses can use this strategy as well. For example, neighborhood coffee shops can have a "drink of the day" where the drink is priced very low to attract and keep customers. A neighborhood Mexican restaurant might offer "1/2 off Fajitas on Tuesdays" to encourage customers to visit the restaurant on Tuesdays, but also on other days of the week.

There are several pricing strategies used by retailers. One is called **everyday low pricing (EDLP).** That's the pricing strategy used by Home Depot and Wal-Mart. Such stores set prices lower than competitors and usually do not have many special sales. The idea is to have consumers come to those stores whenever they want a bargain, rather than waiting until there is a sale, as they do for most department stores.

Department stores and other retailers most often use a **high–low pricing strategy.** The idea is to have regular prices that are higher than those at stores using EDLP, but also to have many special sales in which the prices are lower than those of competitors. The problem with such pricing is that it teaches consumers to wait for sales, thus cutting into profits. As the Internet grows in popularity, you may see fewer stores with a high–low strategy, because consumers will be able to find better prices on the Internet and will begin buying more and more from online retailers.

Some retailers use price as a major determinant of the goods they carry. For example, there are stores that promote goods that sell for only $1 or only $10. Outlet stores supposedly sell brand-name goods at discount prices. Other stores, sometimes called discount stores, sell "seconds," or damaged goods. Consumers must take care to carefully examine such goods to be sure the flaws are not too major.

Bundling occurs when two or more products are grouped together and priced as a unit, usually used to encourage people to purchase more, as they receive a discount for purchasing more. For example, a store might price washers and dryers as a unit. Jiffy Lube offers an oil change and lube, and then checks your car's fluid levels and air pressure and bundles these services into one price. Have you purchased socks recently? If you did, you know there are some socks that are around $3 for one pair, but if you buy the package with three, all three are only $8, saving you money for buying more.

Psychological pricing (odd pricing) means pricing goods and services at price points that make the product appear less expensive than it is. You are no doubt familiar with this strategy from seeing it in various circumstances. For example, a house might be priced at $199,500 with the idea that it sounds less than $200,000. Gas stations almost always use psychological pricing; $2.99 per gallon sounds less than $3.00.

As you can see from our discussion on pricing, many factors affect price: the cost of production, competitors' prices, the phase in the product life cycle, and product image, among many others. These factors, combined, can make it a challenge to set prices. However, if the correct mix of factors is brought to bear on the pricing decision, a marketer may find a correct price that will meet customers' expectations and make a profit.

bundling

Grouping two or more products together and pricing them as a unit.

psychological pricing (odd pricing)

Pricing goods and services at price points that make them appear less expensive than they are.

SELF-CHECK QUESTIONS

1. What are three objectives that might be used when setting pricing strategies?
2. Discuss three types of pricing strategies that might be used in marketing.

After reading this chapter in the text, Ariel has come to the conclusion that she needs to set her price high for her new dog leash to maximize profit, because it is a brand-new product and may induce imitators. She has decided to use a skimming pricing strategy, pricing the leashes at $22 retail. She plans to lower the price when sales reach the growth stage.

Ariel is also aware that she must brand her product. As a result, she had a graphic designer create a logo and a tag line, which will be on the tags and the leash.

She has now given some thought to packaging. She knows that the packaging must attract the buyer's attention. So, she had her graphic designer create a package that depicts a person straining to keep the dog under control while passing a cat. The drawings are cartoonish and create the exact image of the product Ariel wants—if you buy this, you won't have to worry about your dog being out of control while walking him.

Finally, Ariel has chosen a target market. She knows that it would be expensive to try to advertise or market to everyone, so she has decided to market based upon demographics. She has chosen men and women between the ages of 18 and 40. Another aspect of her segmentation will be by psychographics or lifestyle, however. She has decided to target the outdoor-loving person within her selected demographic. Now that she has her price, packaging, and target market figured out, she needs to know how to distribute the product and promote it. These topics will be discussed in the next chapter.

summary

Our discussion began with the eight functions of marketing and the concept of market segmentation. Marketers usually find it necessary to segment markets, or break them into smaller groups, so they can better develop products for and market products to targeted groups. For example, a marketer can segment potential markets based upon geographic parameters, demographic parameters, or psychographic parameters, among others. The best method is to come up with a mix that profiles the largest segment possible and target that. Niche marketing is marketing to a very special and narrow segment, but also a profitable, sustainable one.

Marketers must understand consumer buying behavior, which starts with consumers recognizing a need or a problem and progresses through information search and evaluation of alternative products to the final buying decision. Marketers must understand how to intervene in this process with the end in mind of influencing the customer to select their product. Marketers are helped in this endeavor by conducting marketing research, gathering either primary or secondary data about consumers. The information they acquire can help them develop a product in the first instance, change a product, or better market an existing product.

Marketers are helped by understanding the nature of their product to find the best means of selling it or advertising it. Products may be classified according to various systems. Types of products are convenience, shopping, specialty, and unsought.

The chapter introduced the first two of the 4Ps of marketing—product and price. Some of the concerns when developing products include proper research to meet the needs of consumers, packaging to appeal to customers, and understanding where in the product life cycle a particular product fits. Marketers seek to differentiate their product from the competition in order to develop a brand that inspires brand loyalty.

Pricing a product is a strategic decision of crucial importance in marketing. Pricing strategies we discussed were loss leader, target costing, price leadership, skimming price strategy, penetration strategy, everyday low pricing (EDLP), high–low pricing strategy, bundling, and psychological pricing (odd pricing). Costs involved in making a product are only one factor in the complex pricing decision.

key terms

marketing 284

market
  segmentation 286

target marketing 286

geographic
  segmentation 287

demographic
  segmentation 287

psychographic
  segmentation 287

benefit
  segmentation 289

volume (usage)
  segmentation 289

niche marketing 289

relationship
  marketing 289

marketing
  management 294

4Ps 294

total product offer 294

marketing
  research 296

primary research 296

focus group 297

secondary research 297

product line 297

product
  differentiation 298

industrial good 300

brand 301

brand equity 301

brand loyalty 301

loss leader 303

product life cycle 305

target costing 307

price leadership 307

skimming price
  strategy 309

penetration strategy 309

everyday low pricing
  (EDLP) 310

high–low pricing
  strategy 310

bundling 311

psychological pricing
  (odd pricing) 311

applying your skills

1. Working in teams of five, think of a product or service that your friends want but cannot get on or near campus. For example, maybe you would like a different food selection. What kind of

product would fill that need? Discuss your results in class and how you might go about marketing that new product.

2. Working in teams of four or five list as many brand names of pizza as you can, including brands from pizza shops, restaurants, supermarkets, and so on. Merge your list with the lists from other groups. Then try to identify the "target market" for each brand. Do they all seem to be after the same market, or are there different brands for different markets? How do they use product differentiation to make their product different from the competition?

3. Consider three different consumers and their purchases of shoes. What product qualities could they have been looking for when they chose those shoes? What was the importance of price, style, brand name, and color? Describe the product offerings you would feature in a new shoe store designed to appeal to a single working mother. What about a 19-year-old student?

4. A total product offer consists of everything that consumers evaluate when choosing among products, including price, packaging, service, image, and reputation. Working in teams, compose a list of factors in the total product offer that consumers might consider when evaluating the following products:

    a. vacation resort
    b. college
    c. new car
    d. new suit

5. How important is price to you when buying the following products: shoes, milk, computers, haircuts, and auto rentals? What nonprice factors are more important in making these choices? How much time or trouble does it take to evaluate factors other than price when making such purchases?

6. Where would you place the following items in the product life cycle and why?

    a. Alka-Seltzer
    b. Campbell's chicken soup
    c. iPod
    d. Starbucks lattes

7. Let's say you are determining how to price a cupcake and cookie fund-raiser you are having for your school. Your fixed costs are a table rental at $30 and your variable cost of ingredients per item will be 25 cents. Using the formula provided in this chapter, what is your break-even point? Do you think you could sell enough to make the fund-raising venture worth it?

the internet in action

1. *Purpose:* To demonstrate how the Internet can be used to enhance relationship marketing.

    Exercise: Nike wants to help its customers add soul to their soles and express their individuality by customizing their own shoes. See for yourself at www.nike.com. Click on NIKEiD, and then build a shoe that fits your style. What if you're in the middle of your shoe design and have questions about what to do next? Where can you go for help?

2. *Purpose:* To determine the appropriate pricing strategy for specific products.

    Exercise: Go to www.marketingteacher.com/Lessons/lesson_pricing.htm and review the various types of pricing strategies. Click on the Exercise button at the top of the page and place the products listed into the appropriate cells of the grid provided. Click on the Answer button at the top of the page to check your work. If you do not agree with the answers, scroll down the screen for an explanation.

MARKETING:
PLACE AND
PROMOTION

The Sunny Window

A good example of finding a niche and marketing to and meeting the needs of that niche is Nancy Engel. Nancy grew up in a welfare family and although she worked hard and got good grades, she could not afford to go to college. She did a variety of low-paying jobs, got married, and gave birth to a daughter. At that time in her life, she had to go on welfare. In 1981, in the middle

Nancy Engel

of a divorce and with the prospect of being a single mother, she ran across an article about selling spices from home. She took the last $30 of her welfare check and purchased assorted spices. She mixed them together, calling it her "Italian spice mix." The next day she took her mixes to a flea market and at the end of the day, she had no spices left, but $200 in her pocket!

objectives

After reading this chapter, you should be able to:

1 Explain place and how it pertains to marketing.

2 Describe logistics and different transportation modes.

3 Describe the types of retail competition and distribution.

4 Understand the five types of promotion.

5 Define *integrated marketing communication* and its role in promotion.

10

Engel kept reinvesting her profits, and eventually expanded her business to include soaps and potpourri with help from a loan from the SBA. Her business, now called The Sunny Window, is an excellent example of how, with nothing but the right product and ambition, $30 can become a $250,000 business! Engel says the thing she is most proud of is the fact she was able to send her daughter to college.

Source: Based on an article from Center for Women and Enterprise, "Success Stories," www.cweonline.org/content/view/102/49/ (accessed October 10, 2007), and *Business Fast Lane,* by Ron Ruiz, 2007.

place

The process of getting products to the places where they will be sold, or *distribution,* and to how the actual locations where the products are sold is determined.

Section Outline

The 4Ps of Marketing: Place

- Merchant Wholesalers
- Agents and Brokers
- Retail Intermediaries

marketing intermediaries

Organizations that assist in moving goods and services from producers to business and consumer users.

Advertising is one way that we, as consumers, learn about new products. This chapter discusses various promotional techniques, including advertising, which can be used to develop a great brand.

INTRODUCTION TO PLACE AND PROMOTION

In the last chapter, we discussed the first two of marketing's 4Ps, *product* and *price,* as well as market segmentation and consumer behavior. In this chapter we will focus on the final two Ps of the marketing mix—place and promotion.

Place refers to the process of getting products to the places where they will be sold, or *distribution,* and to how the actual locations where the products are sold are determined. We will discuss intermediaries that can be used to facilitate this process. Then, we will explore the logistics and the process of physically moving goods from production to retail. Finally, we will discuss retail outlets, usually the final destination for products.

In the second part of this chapter we will discuss *promotion,* our final "P." Promotion consists of five distinct areas—advertising, sales promotion, direct marketing, public relations, and personal selling.

THE 4PS OF MARKETING: PLACE

Consider the pair of shoes you most recently purchased. Now try to imagine the challenge of getting the raw materials together, making millions of pairs of shoes, as Nike does, and then distributing those shoes to stores throughout the world. That hurdle is what thousands of manufacturing firms—making everything from automobiles to toys—have to deal with every day. There are hundreds of thousands of marketing intermediaries whose jobs are to help move goods from the raw-material state to producers, and then on to consumers, which is what we mean by "place" or *distribution.* Place also refers to the marketing of services, in that the services must be accessible to the people who want them, according to researchers of the marketing mix, Boom and Bitner.[1] From a product perspective, there are several players in "place":

- **Marketing intermediaries** are organizations that assist in moving goods and services from producers to their business and consumer users. They are called intermediaries because they are in the middle of a whole series of organizations that join together to help distribute goods. A wholesaler is a marketing intermediary.

- A **channel of distribution** consists of the whole set of marketing intermediaries, such as agents, brokers, wholesalers, and retailers, that join together to transport and store goods in their path (or channel) from producers to consumers. B2B products, as discussed in the last chapter, have much shorter channels of distribution as compared to consumer products.

Wei Zhang is the owner of a small retail store that sells ethnic foods, such as spices and packaged foods. Wei has lived in the United States for only three years, but he knows there is a market for his products because he did extensive research and customer surveys. However, once he opened his store, he found that on a good day he might have 15 customers, which did not always equate to 15 *paying*

customers. Wei has begun to realize that he must take steps to bring more paying customers into the store and he wants to expand his business through successful marketing activities, but he doesn't have a lot of money. He needs some direction as to how to get started. He hopes that this chapter of the text will provide some answers.

- **Agents/brokers** are marketing intermediaries who bring buyers and sellers together and assist in negotiating an exchange, but do not take title to the goods, which means that they do not own or buy the goods at any point in the process.
- A **wholesaler** is a marketing intermediary that sells to other organizations, such as retailers, manufacturers, and hospitals. They are part of the B2B system. The final consumers usually cannot shop at the wholesalers.
- A **retailer** is an organization that sells to consumers (like you), that is, the final consumers. Old Navy and Hollister are examples of retail organizations.

Channels of distribution keep communication, the exchange of currency, and title of the goods flowing openly among the parties. These channels also help ensure that the right quantity and assortment of goods will be available when and where they are needed.[2] Figure 10.1 depicts selected channels of distribution for both consumer and industrial (or B2B) goods. After this introduction to the complicated process of distribution, we will discuss specific intermediaries that assist in marketing distribution: merchant wholesalers, agents and brokers, and retail intermediaries.

Merchant Wholesalers

Merchant wholesalers are independently owned firms that take title to the goods they handle (in other words, they buy the goods they handle). About 80 percent of wholesalers fall into this category. There are two types of merchant wholesalers: full-service wholesalers and limited-function wholesalers. *Full-service wholesalers* perform all of the distribution functions (see Figure 10.2). *Limited-function wholesalers* perform only selected functions, but try to do them especially well. Three common types of limited-function wholesalers are rack jobbers, cash-and-carry wholesalers, and drop shippers.

---

channel of distribution
The whole set of marketing intermediaries, such as agents, brokers, wholesalers, and retailers, that join together to transport and store goods in their path (or channel) from producers to consumers.

agents/brokers
Marketing intermediaries who bring buyers and sellers together and assist in negotiating an exchange, but don't take title to the goods (don't own the goods at any point in the process).

wholesaler
Marketing intermediary that sells to other organizations.

retailer
Organization that sells ultimately to consumers.

merchant wholesalers
Independently owned firms that take title to the goods they handle.

Channels for consumer goods

Channels for industrial goods

This channel is used by craftspeople and small farmers.

This channel is used for cars, furniture, and clothing.

This channel is the most common channel for consumer goods such as groceries, drugs, and cosmetics.

This is a common channel for food items such as produce.

This is a common channel for consumer services such as real estate, stocks and bonds, insurance, and nonprofit theater groups.

This is a common channel for nonprofit organizations that want to raise funds. Included are museums, government services, and zoos.

This is the common channel for industrial products such as glass, tires, and paint for automobiles.

This is the way that lower-cost items such as supplies are distributed. The wholesaler is called an industrial distributor.

Manufacturer

Manufacturer

Manufacturer

Farmer

Service organization

Nonprofit organization

Manufacturer

Manufacturer

Wholesaler

Broker

Broker

Store

Wholesaler

Retailer

Wholesaler

Retailer   **Retailer**

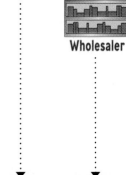

Consumers

Industrial users

figure 10.1

EXAMPLES OF DISTRIBUTION CHANNELS FOR CONSUMER AND INDUSTRIAL GOODS

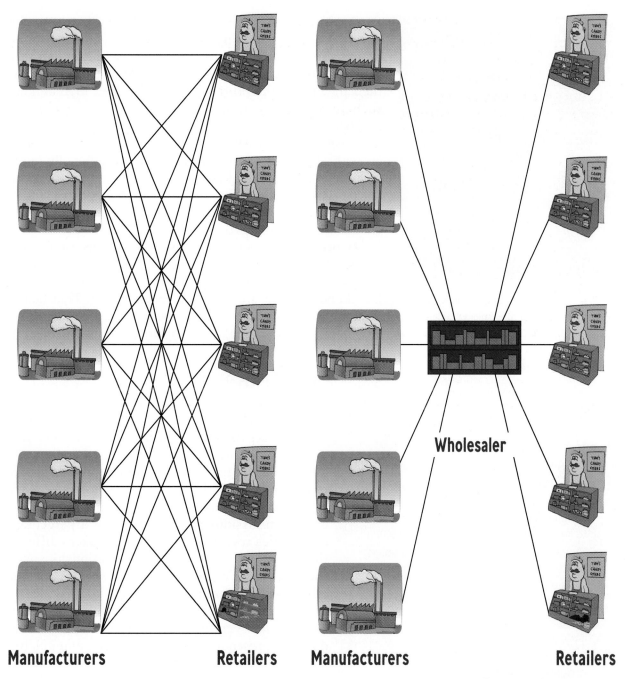

Manufacturers   **Retailers**   **Manufacturers**   **Retailers**

figure 10.2

INTERMEDIARIES CREATE EXCHANGE EFFICIENCY

Adding a wholesaler to the channel of distribution cuts the number of contacts from 25 to 10.

Whole Foods is a marketing intermediary that sells to consumers.

Rack jobbers furnish racks or shelves full of merchandise to retailers, including display products, and sell, for all practical purposes, on *consignment*, which means that they keep title to the goods until they are sold to customers, and then they share the profits with the retailer. Merchandise such as music, toys, hosiery (L'eggs panty hose), and health and beauty aids are sold by rack jobbers.

Cash-and-carry wholesalers serve mostly smaller retailers with a limited assortment of products. Traditionally, retailers went to such wholesalers, paid cash, and carried the goods back to their stores—thus the term *cash-and-carry*. Today, stores such as Office Depot and Staples allow retailers and others to also use credit cards for wholesale purchases.

Drop shippers solicit orders from retailers and other wholesalers and have the merchandise shipped directly from a producer to a buyer. They own the merchandise but do not handle, stock, or deliver anything. That task is done by the producer. Drop shippers tend to handle bulky products, such as coal, lumber, and chemicals.

Study Skills

Importance of Study Partners

What has been your experience using a study partner? Consider the advantages:

- Study partners help you schedule and participate in study time.
- They also keep you focused on the right amount of study time and frequency required to keep on top of the course requirements.
- Study partners are a great sounding board to the learning process, helping you fill in the gaps of what might be complicated subject materials.

However, there are some potential disadvantages to look out for:

- Study partners sometimes have other obligations that crowd study time, making scheduling complicated and nonproductive.
- Study partners sometimes have issues with an instructor or other students and allow these distractions to become a higher priority than the subject matter.

Sharing information with others is a great way to study—choose your study partners wisely!

Agents and Brokers

Agents and brokers bring buyers and sellers together and assist in negotiating an exchange. However, unlike merchant wholesalers, agents and brokers never own the products they distribute. As a rule, they do not carry inventory, provide credit, or assume risks. While merchant wholesalers earn a profit from the sale of goods, agents and brokers earn commissions or fees based on a percentage of the sales revenues. Agents and brokers differ in that *agents* maintain long-term relationships with the people they represent, whereas *brokers* are usually hired on a temporary basis.

Agents who represent producers are known as *manufacturer's agents* or *sales agents*. As long as they do not represent competing products, manufacturer's agents may represent multiple manufacturers in a specific territory. Manufacturer's agents are often used in the automotive supply, footwear, and fabricated steel industries.

Sales agents represent a single producer in a typically larger territory. Sales agents are used by small producers in the textile and home furnishing industries.

Brokers have no continuous relationship with the buyer or seller. Once they negotiate a contract between a buyer and seller, their relationship ends. Brokers are used by the producers of seasonal products (e.g., fruits and vegetables) and in the real estate industry.

Retail Intermediaries

Perhaps the most useful marketing intermediaries, as far as we as final consumers are concerned, are *retailers*. They are the ones who bring goods and services to our neighborhoods and make them available to us. Next time you go to the supermarket to buy groceries, stop for a minute and look at the tremendous variety of products in the store. Think of how many marketing exchanges were involved to bring you the 18,000 or more items that you see.[3] Some products, such as spices, may have been imported from halfway around the world. Other products have been processed and frozen so that you can eat them out of season (e.g., corn and green beans). We will discuss retailers further later in the chapter.

> **rack jobbers**
> Furnish racks or shelves full of merchandise to retailers, display products, and sell on consignment.

> **cash-and-carry wholesalers**
> Serve mostly smaller retailers with a limited assortment of products. Office Depot would be an example.

> **drop shippers**
> Solicit orders from retailers and other wholesalers and have the merchandise shipped directly from a producer to a buyer.

SELF-CHECK QUESTIONS

1. What are marketing intermediaries? Why are they useful?
2. What is the difference between a merchant wholesaler and an agent/broker?

LOGISTICS AND TRANSPORTATION

Clearly a major issue in marketing continues to be how to ship goods from city to city or from one country to another. The efficiency and effectiveness of such shipments offer the companies a competitive advantage in the marketplace through lower costs, faster deliveries, and increased customer satisfaction. In turn, identifying or developing such a system of shipments results in higher profits for the company.

Supply chain management is the process of moving goods and materials from one place to another. The way goods are physically moved from one place to another is a major part of marketing's third P, place.

The supply chain consists of the sequence of linked activities that must be performed by various organizations to move goods and services from the source of raw materials to the ultimate consumers. The supply chain is different from a channel of distribution because a supply chain encompasses every activity needed in the process. For example, supply chain management for apples might involve the farmer who grows the apples, the truck that picks up the apples from the farm, the warehouse where the apples are stored, the packaging and processing done to the apples at the warehouse, the truck or train used to transport the apples or apple products to a distribution center,

> **Section Outline**
>
> **Logistics and Transportation**

> **supply chain management**
> The process of moving goods and materials from one place to another.

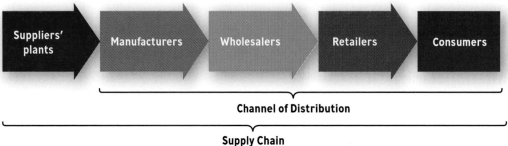

Channel of Distribution

Supply Chain

figure 10.3

THE SUPPLY CHAIN AND CHANNEL OF DISTRIBUTION

> **logistics**
>
> Planning, implementing, and controlling the physical flow of materials, goods, and related information from points of origin to points of consumption.

and the transportation used to get the goods from a Whole Foods distribution center to each individual Whole Foods store. As you can see, it is a lengthy process, and must go smoothly, especially for perishable products such as meats and produce.

Logistics involves planning, implementing, and controlling the physical flow of materials, goods, and related information from points of origin to points of consumption. In other words, logistics manages the supply chain and all of the processes that go along with it.

One of the major jobs of a logistics manager is to decide which mode of transportation will be used to get the goods from point A to point B. See Figure 10.4. Due to the growth of global business, this process has become much more complicated, as raw materials and goods can flow from one side of the world to the other.[4]

The amount of time a product spends in transit, as well as the associated costs, are two factors businesses must consider when choosing transportation. For example, bringing goods by water is inexpensive, but very slow. Trucks are good for small shipments and can be used for remote locations, while trains are great for large shipments, but not practical transport to remote locations. Air transportation is very speedy, but also very expensive. In recent years, the majority of logistics managers have used intermodal shipping. *Intermodal shipping is the use of multiple forms of transportation to complete a single*

figure 10.4

COMPARISON OF TRANSPORTATION MODES

MODE	COST	PERCENTAGE OF DOMESTIC VOLUME	SPEED	ON-TIME DEPENDABILITY	FLEXIBILITY HANDLING PRODUCTS	FREQUENCY OF SHIPMENTS	REACH
Railroad	Medium	38%	Slow	Medium	High	Low	High
Truck	High	25	Fast	High	Medium	High	Highest
Pipeline	Low	21	Medium	Highest	Lowest	Highest	Lowest
Ship (water)	Lowest	15	Slowest	Lowest	Highest	Lowest	Low
Airplane	Highest	1	Fastest	Low	Low	Medium	Medium

Intermodal shipping often involves the use of truck trailers.

shipment of freight. For example, imagine an automobile made in Japan for sale in the United States. It would be shipped by truck in Japan to a loading dock where it would be moved by ship to a port in the United States. Next, it would likely be placed on another truck, and then taken to a railroad station for loading onto a train that would take it across country. Once the vehicle arrived at the destination train station, it would be loaded onto another truck and moved to the local car dealer.

SELF-CHECK QUESTIONS

1. Define *logistics* and *supply chain management*. How do they differ?
2. What are the advantages of train transportation versus truck transportation?

RETAILING

A supermarket is a retail store. A retailer, remember, is a marketing intermediary that sells to ultimate consumers. The United States boasts approximately 2.3 million retail stores, which does not include the retail Web sites. The U.S. retail industry generates $3.8 trillion in retail sales annually not including the food service sales. Retail organizations employed more than 15.3 million people in 2005.[5] Retailers

Section Outline

Retailing

- Method of Competition in Retailing
- Retail Distribution
- Other Types of Retailing

TYPE	DESCRIPTION	EXAMPLE
Department store	Sells a wide variety of products (clothes, furniture, housewares) in separate departments	Sears, JCPenney, Nordstrom
Discount store	Sells many different products at prices generally below those of department stores	Wal-Mart, Target
Supermarket	Sells mostly food with other nonfood products such as detergent and paper products	Safeway, Kroger, Albertson's
Warehouse club	Sells food and general merchandise in facilities that are usually larger than supermarkets and offer discount prices; membership may be required	Costco, Sam's Club
Convenience store	Sells food and other often-needed items at convenient locations; may stay open all night	7-Eleven
Category killer	Sells a huge variety of one type of product to dominate that category of goods	Toys "R" Us, Bass Pro Shops, Office Depot
Outlet store	Sells general merchandise directly from the manufacturer at a discount; items may be discontinued or have flaws ("seconds")	Nordstrom Rack, Liz Claiborne, Nike, T Maxx
Specialty store	Sells a wide selection of goods in one category	Jewelry stores, shoe stores, bicycle shops

figure 10.5

TYPES OF RETAIL STORES

compete on different aspects of business. Some compete on price whereas others choose product variety or location as a competing and differentiation tool.

Method of Competition in Retailing

There are five major ways in which retailers compete for the consumer's dollar: price, service, location, selection, and entertainment, which makes retail not only a form of distribution, but also a form of competition. Consumers are constantly comparing retailers on price, service, and variety. Therefore, it is important for retailers to use benchmarking to compare themselves against the best in the field to make sure that their practices and procedures are the most advanced. Let's discuss the five major ways now.

q: Which is the most important to you when choosing a

»» retail store:price, service, location, selection, or entertainment?

Price Competition

Discount stores such as Wal-Mart, Target, Kmart, and TJMaxx, not to mention all the various Internet discount sites, succeed by offering low prices. It is hard to compete with these price discounters over time, especially when they offer good service as well. Service organizations also compete on price. One classic example of a business who is renowned for both an excellent service and competitive pricing is Southwest Airlines. The same is true of H&R Block in income tax preparation services and Motel 6 and Red Roof Inns for room rentals. Price competition is getting fiercer as Internet firms, such as mySimon.com and Shopping.com, help consumers find the best prices on a wide range of items. As you learned in the last chapter, prices are easy to match, so most retailers have to turn to other strategies—like service—to win and keep customers.

Service Competition

A second competitive strategy for retailers is service. Retail service involves putting customers first, which requires all frontline people to be courteous and accommodating. Retail service also means follow-up service, such as on-time delivery, guarantees, and fast installation. Consumers are frequently willing to pay a little more for goods and services if the retailer offers outstanding service. Some of the benchmark companies in this regard include Home Depot, The Men's Wearhouse, Southwest Airlines, and Nordstrom. Even lesser known companies, such as your neighborhood grocer or pet store, often compete based on excellent service. These retailers show that if businesses hire good people, train them well, and pay them fairly, they will be able to provide world-class service.

Many travelers will go with a particular airline because of price competition. What other ways do airlines attract customers? When you travel, do you pick the airline because of price, service, or location?

Location Competition

Many services, especially convenience services like banks and dry cleaners, compete effectively by having good locations, which is why you find automated teller machines in convenient places, such as supermarkets and train stations. Many fast-food restaurants, such as Burger King and Pizza Hut, now have locations on college campuses so that students can reach them quickly. Some dry cleaners pick up and deliver laundry at your home or business. Often, nothing is more convenient than shopping online. Many online retailers, such as Amazon.com and Zappos.com, have gotten the hang of speedy delivery and easy returns, since this is an important part of meeting convenience expectations of customers. As online retailers get better and better at meeting customer needs, competition between online stores and brick and mortar stores will continue to intensify.

Selection Competition

category killer

Stores that offer a wide selection of goods in a specific category (such as Toys "R" Us), at competitive prices.

A fourth competitive strategy for retailers is selection. Selection is the offering of a wide variety of items in the same product category. **Category killer** stores offer wide selection at competitive prices. They are called category killers because they are so competitive in their category that they usually overpower smaller competitors that don't offer comparable selection or price, and drive them out of business. Toys "R" Us stores carry around 8,000 to 10,000 distinct toys and other items, and the company has over 1,500 stores around the world.[6] Many small, independent toy stores closed their doors because they simply couldn't compete with the low prices and wide selection found at Toys "R" Us. Borders Books carries approximately 200,000 different books.[7] PetCo Animal Supplies and other pet superstores have around 10,000 items each.[8] Despite their initial success, many category killer stores are in turn being killed by discount stores like Wal-Mart. Wal-Mart has become a huge competition challenge to Toys "R" Us.[9] Consumers are finding it more convenient to shop for multiple items at stores like Costco rather than go out of their way to find stores selling only sports equipment or only pet supplies.

Costco is an example of a selection competitor—consumers can find almost everything at the warehouse store, including groceries, clothing and furniture.

Entertainment Competition

Last, many retailers utilize a competitive strategy called entertainment competition. In following this strategy, retailers attempt to offer a value-added aspect in the shopping experience of their customers. When you approach a Jordan's furniture store in New England, for example, you notice that the design team has recreated French Quarter facades like those in New Orleans. As you walk in, you see a Louis Armstrong look-alike playing in a room that resembles Bourbon Street (in New Orleans). There is even a replica of a riverboat that features live music every weekend.[10] You can eat a free fresh-baked cookie and, if it's raining, you can get an umbrella. One mall calls it "shoppertainment." It's all about making it fun to shop at stores and malls. At Bass Pro Shops, you are treated to giant aquariums, waterfalls, trout ponds, rifle ranges, and classes in everything from ice fishing to conservation.[11] In San Francisco, Sony's Metreon is a Sony Entertainment Center with a restaurant, an IMAX theater, and lots of exciting video games to play.[12] You get to see and experience all the latest high-tech equipment and have fun at the same time. Vans, Inc., a sporting goods retailer, opened a 60,000-square-foot skate park and off-road bicycle track at Ontario Mills Mall near Los Angeles.[13] If the experience was "fun" for the customers, it has the potential for building the loyalty and repeat business.

Many retailers compete in several of the areas we just discussed. For example, REI, a sporting goods retailer, offers a large selection of outdoor gear, from hiking and mountain climbing to skiing. REI is able to compete on selection because it offers all items one would need to go on a skiing trip or climb a mountain.[14] REI stores are also strategically located. They offer service competition as well because the salespeople are trained on the products they sell and can provide consumers with information about each product. They offer entertainment competition as well. Their store in Seattle, Washington, has a climbing wall, waterfalls to test waterproof gear, and various terrains to test hiking boots. The brick and mortar retailers of the future will likely have to meet expectations in several of the areas we have discussed in order to succeed.

Customers wander past barbecues, fishing boats, and rows of beverage coolers in the Bass Pro Shop's Outdoor World in Springfield, Missouri.

intensive distribution

Distribution that puts products into as many retail outlets as possible.

Retail Distribution

A major decision that marketers must face is selecting the right retailers to sell their products. Different products call for different retail distribution strategies. There are three categories of retail distribution: intensive distribution, selective distribution, and exclusive distribution. **Intensive distribution** puts products into as many retail outlets as possible, including vending machines. Products that need intensive distribution include convenience goods (discussed in Chapter 9), such as candy, gum, and popular magazines. Coca-Cola, for example, uses intensive distribution. It wants its products to be in as many retailers as possible.

Selective distribution is the use of only a preferred group of the available retailers in an area. Such selection helps assure producers of quality, sales, and service. Manufacturers of appliances, furniture, and clothing usually use selective distribution. Examples of companies that use selective distribution include Godiva Chocolatier, and Ralph Lauren clothing. H and M, a popular juniors clothing store, only has a few stores in major series, which makes their distribution strategy selective; in other words, consumers cannot find the products just anywhere as with products that have intensive distribution.

Exclusive distribution is the use of only one retail outlet in a given geographic area. The retailer has exclusive rights to sell the product and is therefore likely to carry a large inventory,

Godiva Chocolatier is another example of a company that uses selective distribution, having stores in select areas of the world, such as this store in Brussels.

ETHICAL challenge

Salespeople's Time and Trouble

After talking with some of your friends, you have discovered a practice that is quite common among them. It goes like this: They go to a local department or furniture store to shop. They talk to the salespeople and get all kinds of help with the choice of fabrics and other matters. They copy all the information from the product tag onto a piece of paper, including the name of the manufacturer, the model number of the piece they are looking at, and the price. Next, they call the manufacturer and order the item directly, thus saving the retail markup. Or, they simply go online and do the same. You need a new sofa for your apartment. The retail price at your local furniture store is $1,200. The price di-

rectly from the manufacturer is closer to $1,000, including shipping. You have spent lots of time with the salesperson at the store and she was very helpful. She courteously helped you pick out colors and fabrics. You wonder about the ethical issue of buying the sofa somewhere else.

Questions

1. Is purchasing online unethical in this scenario? Why or why not?

2. Have you been in a situation like this one? Would you repeat your actions? Why or why not?

give exceptional service, and pay more attention to this brand than to others. Luxury auto manufacturers usually use exclusive distribution; Tiffany's (the jewelry store) also uses exclusive distribution. With this kind of distribution, it is always a concern that products will end up in outlets other than those that were intended. For example, Tiffany's does not want its products to be sold on eBay because this lessens the exclusivity of the product. However, exclusive distribution does not always mean high-end products. Martha Stewart Everyday, for example, is a brand sold only at Kmart, but the Martha Stewart collection is a brand sold only at Macy's.

selective distribution
Distribution that sends products to only a preferred group of retailers in an area.

exclusive distribution
Distribution that sends products to only one retail outlet in a given geographic area.

Other Types of Retailing

Electronic retailing is selling goods and services to ultimate consumers over the Internet. Even though sales are transacted online, it is still retailing, with the same challenges. Getting customers to visit the Web site where products are sold is only half the battle. The other half is delivering the goods, providing helpful service, and keeping your customers. When electronic retailers fail to have sufficient inventory or fail to deliver goods on time (especially at holiday times and other busy periods), customers may give up and go back to brick and mortar stores. Most Internet retailers now offer e-mail confirmations for customer orders. But electronic retailers are not always good at handling complaints, accepting returns of goods that do not meet customer expectations, and providing personal help. Some Web sites are trying to improve customer service by adding help buttons that lead customers to almost instant assistance from a real person. Rightstart.com,

There are many examples of brick and mortar stores that also have Internet services for their customers' added convenience. Some people shop on the Internet and go to the store to buy the merchandise. Others both shop and buy on the Internet. What leads you to shop from a store rather than on the Internet? What are the advantages and disadvantages of shopping and buying on the Internet?

for example, is a seller of children's toys and products. It has added a live chat function to provide better service to its online customers. When customers have problems or questions, they can click the Live Help link and a customer-service representative will assist them. IKEA.com also offers a live chat feature to answer questions about products.

Telemarketing is the sale of goods and services by telephone. Some 80,000 companies use telemarketing today to supplement or replace in-store selling and to complement online selling. Many send a catalog to consumers and let them order by calling a toll-free number. There are two types of telemarketing: *outbound* and *inbound call centers*. With inbound call centers, the customer calls a toll-free number and inquires about the product. In an outbound call center, an employee calls people from a list and tries to sell a product.

q:
»» Many call centers are being outsourced overseas.

Consider your personal experiences. What are the advantages or disadvantages to outsourcing for telemarketing or customer service purposes?

The challenges facing companies that use outbound telemarketing are the National Do Not Call Registry (www.donotcall.gov), caller identification services, and other methods customers can use to screen out potential telemarketing calls. In the online world, many retailers use *spam*, e-mails that encourage potential customers to visit a Web site or purchase a product, to solicit business. The goal of spammers is to send out as many e-mails as possible in the hopes a few will decide to purchase the product or visit the Web site. Many people consider both outbound telemarketing and spam as nuisances—both, however, are successful means to attract customers.

Vending is another form of retailing you are no doubt quite familiar with. A vending machine dispenses convenience goods when consumers deposit sufficient money into the machine. Vending machines carry the benefit of location—they're found in airports, office buildings, schools, service stations, and other places that are extremely convenient for the customer. Now customers can even purchase iPods and cell phone charges at truck stops and airports because of more sophisticated vending machines!

Direct selling involves selling to consumers in their homes or where they work. Major direct sellers include cosmetics producers (Mary Kay Cosmetics) and vacuum cleaner manufacturers (Electrolux). Trying to emulate the success of those companies, other businesses are now venturing into direct selling. Lingerie, artwork, jewelry, candles, and cookware are just a few of the goods now sold at "house parties" sponsored by sellers.[15] Because many women work outside the home and are not available during the day, companies that use direct selling are sponsoring parties at workplaces or in the evenings and on weekends. Some companies, such as those in encyclopedia sales, have dropped most of their direct selling efforts door to door in favor of Internet selling.

Direct selling is a great way to reach consumers who are often too busy to go shopping themselves. The salesperson provides immediate attention and help, and the customer saves time. Have you ever bought goods in this way? What did you notice about the atmosphere of the sales situation that differed from in-store buying?

telemarketing
The sale of goods and services by telephone.

direct selling
Selling to consumers in their homes or where they work.

SELF-CHECK QUESTIONS

1. What are the three types of retail distribution? What type of distribution would convenience products use? Specialty products?

2. Name three forms of retailing that take place outside of brick and mortar stores.

promotion mix

The combination of tools a marketer uses: advertising, personal selling, public relations, and sales promotion.

integrated marketing communication (IMC)

Combines all the promotional tools into one comprehensive and unified promotional strategy.

THE 4PS OF MARKETING: PROMOTION

The final "P" in the 4Ps of marketing is *promotion,* which is an effort by marketers to inform and remind people in the target market about products and to persuade them to purchase particular products. The challenge of promotion is the communication process. The marketer must define the target audience, select methods to reach that audience, design the right message for the audience, and make sure they get the message. These tasks are all so challenging that many companies choose to hire advertising or promotion agencies. The advertising agency will develop the target market, create advertisements and promotional plans, and implement those plans. Many companies find that hiring such firms is a time-saver because they can leave promotion to experts in the field. But whether companies hire an agency to do this work for them or promote their products themselves, marketers use many different tools to promote products and services. Traditionally, as shown in Figure 10.6, those tools include advertising, personal selling, public relations, and sales promotion. The combination of promotional tools an organization uses is called its **promotion mix.**

Before we discuss all of these promotional tools, refer to Figure 10.7 for the steps that should be taken in development of a promotional campaign.

Integrated marketing communication (IMC) is a way of thinking about promotion that combines all the promotional tools and more into one comprehensive and unified promotional strategy. The idea is to use all the promotional tools and company resources to create a positive brand image and to meet the strategic marketing and promotional goals of the firm.[16] For example, IMC includes the promotion mix, but also the logo, music in commercials, packaging, and branding of the product. The concept goes well beyond traditional promotion, unifying all aspects of the product and its marketing and also the broader company goals in a concerted effort. Good IMC should provide the customer with the same compelling message about a product, regardless of the media mix or the way the product comes to consumers' attention in one situation or another. We will further our discussion of IMC later in the chapter.

Advertising

Advertising is paid, nonpersonal communication through various media by organizations and individuals who are in some way identified in the advertising message. Figure 10.8 lists various categories of advertising. Take a minute to review this information carefully because there is much more to advertising than television commercials.

The importance of advertising in the United States is easy to document. According to the *Television Bureau of Advertising Online,* the

figure 10.6

THE PROMOTION MIX

total ad volume for all media including television, radio, newspaper, and so forth in 2006 exceeded $281.6 billion.[17] No doubt, television is the number one medium. Figure 10.9 lists the expenditures on all types of media.

The public benefits greatly from advertising expenditures. Advertising allows us to learn about products, including prices, features, benefits, and so on, but also often provides us with free entertainment. Additionally, the money advertisers spend for commercial time, for

figure 10.7

STEPS IN A PROMOTION CAMPAIGN

1. Identify a target market. (Refer back to Chapter 9 for a discussion of segmentation and target marketing.)

2. Define the objectives for each element of the promotion mix. Goals should be clear and measurable.

3. Determine a promotional budget. The budgeting process will clarify how much can be spent on advertising, personal selling, and other promotional efforts.

4. Develop a unifying message. The goal of an integrated promotional program is to have one clear message communicated by advertising, public relations, sales, and every other promotional effort.

5. Implement the plan. Advertisements must be scheduled to complement efforts being made by public relations and sales promotion. Salespeople should have access to all materials to optimize the total effort.

6. Evaluate effectiveness. Measuring results depends greatly on clear objectives. Each element of the promotional mix should be evaluated separately, and an overall measure should be taken as well. It is important to learn what is working and what is not.

MEDIUM	ADVANTAGES	DISADVANTAGES
Newspapers	Good coverage of local markets; ads can be placed quickly; high consumer acceptance; ads can be clipped and saved.	Ads compete with other features in paper; poor color; ads get thrown away with paper (short life span).
Television	Uses sight, sound, and motion; reaches all audiences; high attention with no competition from other material.	High cost; short exposure time; takes time to prepare ads. Digital video recorders skip over ads.
Radio	Low cost; can target specific audiences; very flexible; good for local marketing.	People may not listen to ads; depends on one sense (hearing); short exposure time; audience can't keep ads.
Magazines	Can target specific audiences; good use of color; long life of ads; ads can be clipped and saved.	Inflexible; ads often must be placed weeks before publication; cost is relatively high.
Outdoor	High visibility and repeat exposures; low cost; local market focus.	Limited message; low selectivity of audience.
Direct mail	Best for targeting specific markets; very flexible; ads can be saved.	High cost; consumers may reject ads as junk mail; must conform to post office regulations.
Yellow pages–type advertising	Great coverage of local markets; widely used by consumers; available at point of purchase.	Competition with other ads; cost may be too high for very small businesses.
Internet	Inexpensive global coverage; available at any time; interactive.	Relatively low readership in the short term (but growing rapidly).

figure 10.8

ADVANTAGES AND DISADVANTAGES OF VARIOUS FORMS OF MEDIA

example, pays for the production costs of the television or radio programs we enjoy. Advertising also covers the major costs of producing newspapers and magazines. Consider a cable subscription for Home Box Office (HBO). Because HBO does not advertise products on its channels, customers must pay for the programming on a subscription basis. Advertising allows customers to watch network television and read newspapers and magazines for a reasonable price. Without advertising, consumers would no doubt pay more for the luxuries we currently enjoy. Figure 10.8 discusses the advantages and disadvantages of various advertising media to the advertiser, and shows the average cost for each. As you can see in Figure 10.9, television advertising, including cable and broadcast television, is very expensive, compared with other types of advertising.

Newspapers, radio, and the yellow pages are especially attractive to local advertisers. Television offers many advantages to national advertisers, but it is expensive. For example, 30 seconds of advertising during the Super Bowl cost $2.6 million in 2007.[18] How many cases of soda or bags of dog food must a company sell to pay for such commercials

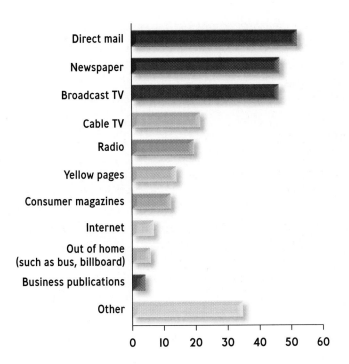

figure 10.9

EXPENDITURES IN 2006 FOR VARIOUS TYPES OF MEDIA

(remember break-even analysis in the last chapter)? The answer may seem to be "a lot," but few other media besides television have ever allowed advertisers to reach so many people with such impact. About 43 percent of U.S. households are reached by the Super Bowl.[19] That compares with the 26 percent reached by the Academy Awards.[20] The amount charged for 30 seconds of air time is directly related to the size of the potential audience.

Television advertising is not limited to traditional commercials that interrupt our favorite programs; sometimes the products *themselves* appear in the programs. Advertisers often pay to have their products appear on television where they will be seen by the viewing audience. This concept is called **product placement.** Have you noticed products that have been featured in movies and TV shows, such as the cars in James Bond movies or the General Motors vehicles prominently displayed in the 2007 blockbuster *Transformers*? Car manufacturers pay money or give the cars to the producers for free, just so they can be seen in the movie. Have you ever noticed when watching *American Idol* that the judges each have a glass of Coca-Cola in front of them? This is another example of product placement.

product placement
Paying to put products into TV shows and movies where they will be seen.

Personal Selling

Personal selling is the face-to-face presentation and promotion of goods and services. Personal selling can occur on a B2B level or on a consumer level. Either way, the steps are the same. Effective selling

personal selling
Face-to-face presentation and promotion of goods and services.

Product placement is often very subtle. It could be the watch an actor is wearing, or the shoes, or the clothes. It could be the beverage he is drinking—or the car he drives. In any case, advertisers are trying to influence you to purchase the product yourself. The next time you watch television, pay attention to the brand-name products that appear on your favorite shows—advertisers are trying to reach you!

is not simply a matter of persuading others to buy. In fact, it is more accurately described as helping others satisfy their wants and needs. Given that perspective, you can see why salespeople are using the Internet, portable computers, PDAs, Blackberries, and other technology. These salespeople can use this technology to help customers search the Internet, design custom-made products, review prices, and generally do everything necessary to complete the order. The benefit of personal selling is having a person help you complete a transaction. The salesperson should listen to your needs, help you reach a solution, and then make accomplishing that solution smoother and easier.

You are familiar with all kinds of men and women who do personal selling. They work in local department stores and sell all kinds of goods and services, like automobiles, insurance, and real estate. What could they do to be more helpful to you, the customer? Could you be a successful salesperson? What would you like to sell?

It is costly to provide customers with personal attention, especially since some companies are replacing salespeople with Internet services and information. Therefore, those companies that retain salespeople must train them to be especially effective, efficient, and helpful. Let's take a closer look at the process of selling.

Steps in the Selling Process

The best way to understand personal selling is to go through the selling process and see what tasks are involved. In both business-to-business and consumer selling, it is critical for the salesperson to know the product well and to know how it compares to competing products. Such product knowledge is needed before the salesperson begins the selling process. The selling process then consists of seven steps:

1. *Prospect and qualify:* The first step in the selling process is prospecting. **Prospecting** involves researching potential buyers and choosing those most likely to buy. This selection process is called *qualifying*. To qualify people means to make sure that they have a need for the product, the authority to buy, and the willingness to listen to a sales message. A person who meets these criteria is called a *prospect*. B2B sellers often meet prospects at trade shows, where they visit booths sponsored by manufacturers and have the opportunity to ask questions. Other prospects may visit a company's Web site seeking information. The best prospects, however, are often people at companies who were recommended to people by others who use the products or who know about them. How many times have you visited a store simply because one of your friends raved about it? In B2B situations, salespeople often e-mail potential clients with proposals to see if there is any interest, before making a formal visit. If you are in a retail store setting, a prospect is a person who visits the store, seeking a particular product.

2. *Preapproach:* Before making a sales call, salespeople must research to find out as much as possible about potential customers and their particular wants and needs. Salespeople must find out which people in the company are most likely to buy or use the product they are selling. In a retail store setting, this research can be done by asking questions to find out what the customer needs and wants.

3. *Approach:* An old saying goes, "You don't have a second chance to make a good first impression." That's why the approach is so important. When salespeople call on a customer for the first time, their opening comments are important. Salespeople must project friendly professionalism, create rapport, and build their credibility with customers in order to begin a relationship.

4. *Make presentation:* In the actual presentation of products, salespeople need to match the benefits of their value package to their clients' needs. Salespeople who have done thorough research to understand their customers' expectations can tailor their presentations to fit their clients. During the presentation is a great time to use testimonials (letters or statements from users praising the product) to show potential buyers that they are joining leaders in other firms in trying a new product.

prospecting
Researching potential buyers and choosing those most likely to buy.

5. *Answer objections:* Salespeople should anticipate any objections the prospect may raise and determine proper responses. These questions should be considered opportunities for creating better relationships, not as challenges. Customers may have legitimate doubts, and salespeople are there to resolve those doubts. Relationships are based on trust, and trust comes from successfully and honestly working with others. Often, salespeople can introduce customers to others in the firm who can answer their questions and provide them with anything they need. Today, many businesses can set up virtual meetings in which customers can chat with various members of a business in order to foster better relationships.

6. *Close sale:* Salespeople have limited time and cannot spend extended time with one potential customer answering questions and objections. A *trial close* consists of a question or statement that moves the selling process toward the actual close. Questions you might ask in a trial close include, "Would you like the blue one or the red one?" or, "Do you want to pay for that with your credit card?" The final step is to ask for the order and help the customer complete that order.

7. *Follow up:* The selling process is not over until the order is approved and the customer is happy. The sales relationship may continue for years as businesses respond to new requests for information. Selling is often described as a process of establishing relationships, not just a matter of selling goods or services. The follow-up step includes handling customer complaints, making sure that the customer's questions are answered, and quickly supplying what the customer wants. Often, customer service is as important to the sale as is the product itself. Most manufacturers have, therefore, established Web sites where information may be obtained and discussions may take place.

The selling process varies somewhat among different goods and services, but the general idea is the same. Salespeople share the goal of helping the prospect make a purchase and to make sure that customers are satisfied after the sale.

q: Have you ever used the steps of selling? Have

»» the steps been used on you?

Public Relations

Public relations (PR) is a management function that evaluates public attitudes, changes policies and procedures accordingly, and executes a program of action and information to earn public understanding and acceptance. A good public relations program has three steps:

public relations (PR)

The management function that evaluates public attitudes, changes policies and procedures accordingly, and executes a program of action and information to earn public understanding and acceptance.

1. *Listen to the public.* Public relations starts with good marketing research (discovering and evaluating public attitudes). The best way to learn what the public wants is to listen to people often, and in different forums, including on the Internet.

2. *Change policies and procedures.* Businesses do not earn understanding by bombarding the public with propaganda; they earn understanding by having programs and practices in the public interest. The best way to learn what the public wants is to listen to people often—in different forums, including on the Internet.

3. *Inform people that you are being responsive to their needs.* It is not enough to simply have programs in the public interest. Businesses must tell the public about those programs so that customers know you are being responsive.

Public relations demands a dialogue with customers so that information can be exchanged over time and trust can be developed through responsiveness.

Customers today often complain that they find it nearly impossible to speak with a human being when they have a question or complaint. They may spend literally hours on the phone going through automated choices, waiting, and still not being satisfied. In desperation, they often call someone else in a long and futile chase for someone to handle the problem. Today, however, PR is taking a much more active role in listening to consumers and working with them to handle problems. That means that PR must establish good relationships with production and service people so they can find answers to customer questions quickly.

The U.S. Bureau of Labor Statistics reports that public relations has become one of the three fastest-growing industries in the country.[21] One firm that has had huge success because of good public relations practices is Yahoo! It began its PR campaign when the World Wide Web was just starting to interest the general public (not just academics) in the early 1990s. Yahoo!'s idea was to get stories into the media about the growing importance of the Internet. The second phase of its public relations campaign came before Yahoo! sold any stock. It decided to use the media to promote the head of the company, Tom Koogle, and his professionalism. If investors had not been assured that Yahoo! had a good business model, the company would not have been able to sell much stock to first-time buyers. Once the company got started, the goal of Yahoo!'s public relations team was to show Yahoo! as a major Internet company, the equivalent to America Online, which was the major competitor at that time. The company also wanted to demonstrate that Yahoo! was as important to Internet commerce as it was in Internet communications. Much of the success of Yahoo!, then, is directly attributable to its long-term public relations strategy.

It is the responsibility of the PR department to maintain close ties with the media, community leaders, government officials, and other corporate stakeholders. The point is to establish and maintain a dialogue with all stakeholders so that the company can respond to inquiries, complaints, and suggestions quickly.

Publicity is the talking arm of public relations. It is one of the major functions of almost all organizations. Here's how publicity works: Suppose a bakery want consumers to know about a new location that is about to open, but the business owners have very little money for promotions. The bakery would need to get some initial sales to generate funds. One effective way to reach the public is through publicity. **Publicity** is any information about an individual, product, or organization that is distributed to the public through the media and that's not paid for, or controlled by, the seller. The bakery might prepare a publicity release, describing the new location and the grand opening events, and send the information to various media outlets such as local radio stations or newspapers. Much skill is involved in writing such releases so that the media will want to publish or broadcast them.[22] You may need to write different stories for different media. If the stories about the bakery opening are published, the message will reach many potential consumers (and investors, distributors, and dealers), and the business may be on its way to becoming a wealthy marketer.

Publicity works only if the media find the material interesting or newsworthy. Publicity has several other advantages over other promotional tools, such as advertising. For example, publicity may reach people who do not normally read a print advertisement. The information may instead appear on the front page of a newspaper or in some other prominent position, or the announcement could be given air time on a television news show. Perhaps the greatest advantage of publicity is its believability. When a newspaper or magazine publishes a story as news, the reader treats that story as news—and news is more believable than advertising. That's why Gardenburger and other companies that sell soybean products have been so intent on sending out press releases about the health benefits of their products.

There are several disadvantages to publicity as well. For example, marketers have no control over how, when, or if the media will use the story. The media are not obligated to use a publicity release, and most are thrown away. Furthermore, the story may be altered so that it is not so positive. There is good publicity (iPod sales are taking off) and bad publicity (Firestone tires cause accidents). Also, once a story has run,

publicity

Any information about an individual, product, or organization that's distributed to the public through the media and that's not paid for or controlled by the seller.

iPhone Premieres This Friday Night at Apple Retail Stores

Free Workshops, Genius Bar Support and One to One Personal Training

CUPERTINO, California—June 28, 2007—Apple's revolutionary iPhone™ will go on sale this Friday, June 28 at 6:00 p.m. local time at Apple® retail stores nationwide. All 164 Apple retail stores in the US will stay open until midnight, and customers can purchase up to two iPhones on a first come, first served basis. Beginning Saturday morning, iPhone customers can learn how to get the most out of the iPhone with free, in-depth workshops offered throughout the day at all Apple retail stores. Every Apple retail store will offer support for iPhone at the Genius Bar and personal training through Apple's new One to One program.

"Apple retail stores were created for this moment—to let customers touch and experience a revolutionary new product," said Ron Johnson, Apple's senior vice president of Retail. "With our legendary Genius Bar support, free workshops and our One to One personal training, we're here to help customers get the most from their new iPhone."

iPhone introduces an entirely new user interface based on a revolutionary multi-touch display and pioneering new software that allows users to control iPhone with just a tap, flick or pinch of their fingers. iPhone combines three products into one small and lightweight handheld device—a revolutionary mobile phone, a widescreen iPod®, and the Internet in your pocket with best-ever applications on a mobile phone for email, web browsing and maps. iPhone ushers in an era of software power and sophistication never before seen in a mobile device, which completely redefines what users can do on their mobile phones.

Pricing and Availability

iPhone goes on sale in the US on June 29, 2007 at 6:00 p.m. local time through Apple's retail stores and AT&T's select retail stores, Apple's online store will be taking orders for iPhone beginning at 6:00 p.m. PDT. iPhone will be available in a 4GB model for $499 (US) and an 8GB model for $599 (US), and will work with either a PC or Mac®. Beginning June 30 and continuing through the summer, Apple stores in the US will open early at 9:00 a.m. for iPhone sales. Customers can check iPhone availability at their local Apple retail store starting at 9:00 p.m. the night before at www.apple.com/retail.

Apple ignited the personal computer revolution in the 1970s with the Apple II and reinvented the personal computer in the 1980s with Macintosh. Today, Apple continues to lead the industry in innovation with its award-winning computers, OS X operating system and iLife and professional applications. Apple is also spearheading the digital media revolution with its iPod portable music and video players and iTunes online store, and will enter the mobile phone market this year with its revolutionary iPhone.

figure 10.10

A PRESS RELEASE ANNOUNCED APPLE'S INTRODUCTION OF THE iPHONE

it is not likely to be repeated. Advertising, in contrast, can be repeated as often as needed. One way companies can help ensure that publicity is handled well by the media is to establish a friendly relationship with media representatives through being open with them when they seek information. Then, when businesses want their support, the media will be more likely to cooperate.

Sales Promotions

sales promotion

Promotional tool that stimulates consumer purchasing and dealer interest by means of short-term activities.

Sales promotion is the promotional tool that stimulates consumer purchasing and dealer interest by means of short-term activities. These activities include such things as displays, trade shows and exhibitions, event sponsorships, and contests. Figure 10.11 lists some sales promotion techniques.

For consumer sales promotion activities, think of those free samples of products you get in the mail, the coupons you clip from newspapers, the contests that various retail stores sponsor, and the prizes in Cracker Jack boxes. Sales promotion programs are designed to supplement personal selling, advertising, and public relations efforts by creating enthusiasm for the overall promotional program.

There was a big increase in such promotions as the 21st century began, especially online. Sales promotion can take place both internally (within the company) and externally (outside the company). Often, it's just as important to generate employee enthusiasm about a product as it is to attract potential customers. The most important internal sales promotion efforts are directed at salespeople and other customer-contact people, such as complaint handlers and clerks. Internal sales promotion efforts include (1) sales training; (2) the development of sales aids, such as flip charts, portable audiovisual

figure 10.11

EXAMPLES OF BUSINESS-TO-BUSINESS SALES PROMOTION TECHNIQUES AND CONSUMER SALES PROMOTION TECHNIQUES

B2B	Consumer
Trade shows	Coupons
Portfolios for salespeople	Cents-off promotions
Deals (price reductions)	Sampling
Catalogs	Premiums
Conventions	Sweepstakes
	Contests
	Bonuses (buy one, get one free)
	Catalogs
	Demonstrations
	Special events
	Lotteries
	In-store displays

This international Manufacturing Trade Show in Chicago featured 4,000 booths, giving buyers for other businesses thousands of new products to explore and purchase. Can you see why trade shows in many industries are an efficient and necessary way to stay abreast of the latest developments, your competitors, and consumer reactions and needs?

displays, and videos; and (3) participation in trade shows, where salespeople can get leads. Other employees who deal with the public may also be given special training to improve their awareness of the company's offerings and to make them an integral part of the total promotional effort.

After generating enthusiasm internally, it is important to get distributors and dealers involved, so that they, too, are eager to help promote the product. Trade shows are an important sales promotion tool because they allow marketing intermediaries to see products from many different sellers and to make comparisons among them. At many conferences, you may see trade show booths set up to sell a product, which creates a great opportunity for personal selling, as you learned earlier in this chapter, but which also provides a great chance to show products that may be complicated to use or understand. Today, virtual trade shows—trade shows on the Internet—enable buyers to see many products without leaving the office. Furthermore, the information is available 24 hours a day, seven days a week.

After the company's employees and intermediaries have been motivated with sales promotion efforts, the next step is to promote to final consumers through distributing samples, coupons, displays, store demonstrations, premiums, contests, rebates, and so on. Sales promotion is an ongoing effort to maintain customer enthusiasm, so different strategies must be used over time to keep the ideas fresh. One popular sales promotion tool is **sampling**—letting consumers have a small sample of the product for no charge. If you have ever visited a Baskin Robbins, you have probably had an opportunity to sample a variety of its many

sampling
Letting consumers have a small sample of the product for no charge.

flavors of ice cream. Because many consumers won't buy a new product unless they've had a chance to see it or try it, many grocery stores, for example, often have people standing in the aisles handing out small portions of food and beverage products. Sampling is a quick, effective way of demonstrating a product's superiority at the time when consumers are making a purchase decision. Pepsi introduced its FruitWorks product line with a combination of sampling, event marketing, and a new Web site.

Event marketing occurs when companies sponsor events such as concerts or sporting events to promote their products, which is another effective method of sales promotion. Companies will also help with charitable organizations in order to give back to their communities while still marketing the positive image of their companies. An example of a company who has used event marketing to both promote its organization while being a good corporate citizen is New Balance, whose tennis shoes in 2007 were named the Susan G. Koman 3 Day Walk's official shoes. New Balance's presence as a corporate sponsor benefits both the Koman Foundation as well the company itself.[23]

event marketing
Sponsoring events such as rock concerts or being at various events to promote your products.

Other Types of Promotion

You know how important it is to get people talking about something, or "creating a buzz." Two related concepts and means of promotion that try to do this are *viral marketing* and *word-of-mouth*. **Viral marketing** (so-called because the campaign "spreads like a virus") is the term now used to describe everything from paying people to say positive things on the Internet to setting up multilevel selling schemes whereby consumers get commissions for directing friends to specific Web sites. Here is how Barnes & Noble does it: You send your friends an e-mail that tells them how much you enjoyed reading a certain book and gives them a link to the Barnes & Noble Web site. If they follow the link and buy a book, you get a 5 percent commission. Another example is Dish Network. The company will offer the current customers a credit of $50 ($5 per month for 10 months) for recommending their friends and if the friend subscribes, the recommending customer's account is credited with the money.

viral marketing
The term now used to describe everything from paying people to say positive things on the Internet to setting up multilevel selling schemes whereby consumers get commissions for directing friends to specific Web sites.

Word-of-mouth promotion today is often one of the most effective promotional tools because Internet word-of-mouth can reach so many people so easily.[24] In **word-of-mouth promotion,** people tell other people about products that they've purchased. The success of movies such as *Little Miss Sunshine,* made on a small budget, depends on word-of-mouth promotion. Anything that encourages people to talk favorably about an event, product, or organization may be effective word-of-mouth promotion. Clever commercials can also do the same. Have you ever heard someone say that a

word-of-mouth promotion
A promotional tool that involves people telling other people about products that they've purchased.

Make an Impression That Counts!

From the very beginning of our careers, we learn how important a first impression is when we interview, begin a new job, join a sports team, and attend the first day of classes.

In starting one's career, first impressions really count. Your positive attitude can let others know you are mentally prepared and ready to make healthy contributions to the work environment. Getting off to a good start can open doors and position you as a leader.

How do you make a best first impression? Try being prepared, positive, and mentally and physically ready. As the saying goes, "You get only one chance to make a first impression."

commercial on a show was better than the show? No doubt you have heard people talking about the new commercials seen during the Super Bowl.

The whole idea, of course, is the same behind every sort of promotion—to get more and more people talking about the products and brand names so that customers remember them when they want to purchase a product or service. One especially effective strategy for spreading positive word-of-mouth is to send testimonials to *current*

Viral marketing is used in the entertainment industry to create interest for a movie, video game, or event weeks or months before it is actually released. Viral marketing for the role-playing game *Alpha Omega* started with a series of puzzles and cryptic videos on a Web site called *ethanhaaswasright.com* over a month before the release of the game's details.

Small-Screen Dream: Launch a Cable Ad Campaign

For years, TV advertising was the bastion of big-business marketers. We learned not to "squeeze the Charmin" and "things go better with Coca-Cola" from ad campaigns on the three big TV networks that reached us without cable hookups or satellite dishes.

But all that has changed since cable networks have lured audiences away with specialized programming. Let Anheuser-Busch and Ford spend close to $2.5 million to reach the masses by running a single Super Bowl ad. Savvy entrepreneurs are pinpointing their target audiences and reaching them locally, regionally or even nationally for a tiny fraction of the cost. Now, local commercials are the mainstay of cable systems—in some regions accounting for as much as 70 percent of their ads—and major cable companies even provide low-cost ways to produce commercials.

You can reach a wide yet qualified audience by creating your own cable TV ad campaign; just follow these five steps:

1. *Define your audience.* There is cable programming to reach every target audience and suit any interest imaginable—from home and garden shows, to 24-hour news, to baseball, to comedy. To make an effective buy, you'll need to create a simple one- or two-sentence target audience profile starting with basic demographics (gender, age, household income, and any other important characteristics). If the product or service you're marketing is tied to a hobby or special interest, such as home improvement, be sure to include it in the profile. Next, consider geography. You can target prospects within a small radius, or on a citywide, regional, or national basis.

   Here is an example of a target audience profile: women; ages 25–54; with household incomes of $35,000-plus; who are homeowners; enjoy gardening; and reside in XYZ areas.

2. *Contact the cable systems.* Even if you plan to advertise in multiple markets, start by contacting the cable system provider in your market area; many cable companies have extensive coverage areas. Comcast, for instance, works with small-business owners in markets from Los Angeles to Miami through its advertising sales division, Comcast Spotlight. In south Florida alone, there are 19 different Comcast zones, and you can choose to advertise in as many as you wish.

3. *Identify the right programming.* A chief advantage of advertising on cable TV is that specialized programming successfully hooks audiences. Whether they're watching a hockey game or a fashion makeover, engaged viewers are more likely to see your spot and less likely to pay attention to other tasks. Once you provide your cable sales rep with your target audience profile, you can request a proposal based on research from Nielsen Media Research and Scarborough Research showing the best-targeted programming to reach your prospects, using between 40 and 60 different networks.

4. *Make your buy.* It's a good rule of thumb to budget a minimum of $1,500 per month for your spot buy. For best results, negotiate for a combination of fixed-position spots, which are guaranteed to air during specific programs, and run-of-station spots on the networks you choose. Run-of-station spots cost less but may air at any time, such as after midnight, when they'll reach the fewest number of viewers. So it's smart to specify the hours (or parts of the day) during which your spots may air.

5. *Produce your spot.* Cable companies seeking small-business advertisers have jumped into the production business. Comcast Spotlight, for example, produces local spots from just under $500 to about $1,200, depending on the market. This includes scripting, shooting, post-production and a professional voice-over. Even spots with actors and custom jingles can be created affordably. These spots have a more "local" look than big-budget ads from McDonald's and Nike, but you can count on them to successfully capture the attention of viewers for a whole lot less.

Questions

1. What are some other activities small businesses can do, with limited budgets, for advertising?

2. Which advertising may give a small restaurant owner in a rural area the most audience reach? Explain.

Source: Kim T. Gordon, "Small-Screen Dream: No Need to Spend Millions to Get on the Big Networks—Reach Your Best Customers with These 5 Simple Steps for Launching a Cable Ad Campaign," *Entrepreneur Magazine*, January 2006.

customers. Most companies use testimonials only in promoting to new customers, but testimonials are also effective in confirming customers' belief that they chose the right company. Positive word-of-mouth from other users further confirms their choice, so they will purchase again. A further extension is that some companies make it a habit to ask customers for referrals, or establish a reward for a referral.

In the final section of this chapter, we will talk about how to pull together all the promotional techniques we have discussed to have successful IMC (integrated marketing communication), a new concept that we introduced previously.

SELF-CHECK QUESTIONS

1. List each type of promotion we discussed.
2. Which method of promotion do you think is most effective in selling to you? Which is the least effective?

IMC: PUTTING PROMOTIONS TOGETHER

Section Outline

IMC: Putting Promotions Together

Ensuring that each target market has its own, separate promotion mix is very important. Because the customers are different in each market, the promotions should be different too. For example, for a small restaurant located in a downtown area, one target market might be busines people eating lunch at the restaurant, while another market

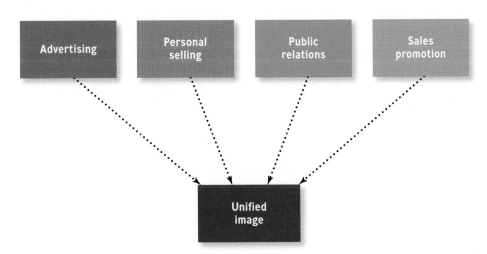

figure 10.12

INTEGRATED MARKETING COMMUNICATION

Integrated marketing communication means that all areas of promotion provide the same message to consumers. Companies should make sure their letterhead, logos, and signature colors as well as imagery on any advertisements are consistent and support the unified theme of the promotional mix.

So, You Want to Be . . . in Logistics

Logistics experts are needed in all businesses that sell products. Consider Old Navy, for example, a retailer with many stores. A logistics manager must ensure that clothing gets distributed to each store efficiently and just when it is needed. In industrial product companies such as Boeing, logistics managers keep track of components and raw materials that are ordered to make sure they arrive on time at the right stage of the process.

Freight companies hire logistics people to coordinate merchandise deliveries for their clients. Trucking companies have logistics experts to coordinate the arrival and delivery of goods across the nation.

Other logistics jobs within supply chain management include planners. A logistics planner forecasts the needs of the company, and ensures raw materials are shipped from suppliers in a timely manner. A supply chain manager might also be responsible for negotiating the price of raw materials ordered or reviewing the effective use of resources and developing plans to make the supply chain more efficient. These functions are all areas of *logistics*.

Most individuals starting in logistics or supply chain management will begin as an assistant to a director or a manager. At first, the job might be limited to data entry and other administrative duties. Once promoted, however, logistics managers' incomes can be large because of the expertise and analytical skills required.

could be people who bring their families to the restaurant for dinner. The promotions will be different for each group simply because each market has a different need and a different motivation for eating at the restaurant, *yet these various promotions are part of one concerted effort.*

As we mentioned earlier in the chapter, an *integrated marketing communication (IMC)* promotional approach is a formal method for uniting all the promotional efforts of an organization to make them more consistent with each other and more responsive to the organization's customers and other stakeholders. IMC includes all public relations and promotional efforts including everything from jingles in ads and packaging to the latest in Internet communications and interactive tools. The result is a unified image of the company in the public's mind.

In some cases, advertising is created by ad agencies, public relations is created by PR firms, and selling is done in-house. There is little coordination across promotional efforts. As a result, consumers often receive conflicting messages about a company and its products. For example, TV advertising may have emphasized quality, while the sales promotion people were pushing coupons and discounting. Such conflicting images

Wei Zhang did substantial research and found out that he did not necessarily need a lot of money to successfully market his retail store. He decided to apply a promotional mix in order to increase sales in his store.

First, Wei placed an advertisement in the yellow pages both in print and online because he did not have the budget for television or radio advertising. He has also decided to create a Web site, to provide information about his store and to enable customers to order select products online. Because Wei did not know much about Web site development, he hired someone to develop the site and update it for a minimal fee every month.

Wei has only two employees, but he realized they do not have as much product information as they should have; thus, they have had difficulty communicating with customers about the various products and spices. Wei decided that it is important for him to spend time after hours training the employees. Although it costs money to pay each of the employees during training, he recognizes the benefits—if employees know about the merchandise, selling that merchandise successfully is more likely.

Wei also decided to use public relations as part of his marketing plan. He wrote a press release about the new, unique store that he has opened, since there were none like it in his town. He was able to find many examples of press releases on the Internet to help him write his. He faxed the press release to each of the major newspapers and television stations in his town. Fortunately, one of the television stations was interested in the unique products in his store and came out to interview him. He even appeared on the 5:00 local news!

Finally, Wei has decided to use sales promotions as another promotional strategy. He implemented sampling in his store for each of the packaged goods he sells. He also sends out coupons to his regular customers, after getting their information from a signup sheet in the store. Wei also decided to offer a monthly Chinese cooking class using the food sold in his store.

After a couple of months of his promotional efforts, Wei is extremely pleased with the results. The cost has been very little compared to the return on his investment. Rather than 15 customers on a good day, Wei now has over 50!

are not as effective as a unified image created by multiple promotional means working in the same direction.

Small businesses that may not be able to use advertising agencies can nevertheless utilize IMC. Any signage, letterheads, and ads in the yellow pages should all carry the same message, right down to the same colors and logos. This way, the customer starts to identify the brand in a unified manner.

Today, more and more companies are trying to create an integrated approach to promotion. Ad agencies are buying direct marketing companies so that they can offer an integrated approach. Of course to implement an IMC system, companies must start with the basics: gathering data about customers and stakeholders and their information needs. Thus the unifying effort encompasses the entire marketing process starting with marketing research. Gathering data that gives the whole picture of the target audience, and making it available to everyone in the value chain, is a key to future integrated marketing success. All messages reaching customers, potential customers, and other stakeholders must be consistent and coordinated.

SELF-CHECK QUESTIONS

1. Explain why IMC is beneficial to businesses.
2. What are two items that are important to remember when developing a program of IMC?

summary

This chapter addressed the final of the 4Ps of marketing: place and promotion. Place means both the physical distribution of products and the strategy behind their distribution. First, we discussed the types of marketing intermediaries (merchant wholesalers, agents and brokers, and retailers) and the reasons they are used. There are two types of merchant wholesalers: full-service and limited-function wholesalers. Three common types of limited-function wholesalers are rack jobbers, cash-and-carry wholesalers, and drop shippers. Agents and brokers differ in their relationship with customers, long-term and temporary, respectively.

Supply chain management involves moving goods and materials from one place to another, whereas logistics manages the supply chain and all the processes that go along with it. The next section of the chapter addressed the five major ways in which retailers compete: price, service, location, selection, and entertainment. The three types of distribution strategies for retailers are intensive, selective, and exclusive. Other types of retailing involves electronic retailing, telemarketing, vending, and direct selling.

The second major section of the chapter discussed the four areas of promotion—advertising, personal selling, public relations, and sales promotions. Advertising is the paid, nonpersonal communication through various media. Television is the number one media for advertisements. Personal selling is the face-to-face presentation and promotion of goods and services. Steps in the personal process include prospect and qualify, preapproach, approach, make presentation, answer objections, close sale, and follow up. Public relations executes a program of action and information to earn public understanding and acceptance. Publicity is the talking arm of public relations. Sales promotion is the promotional tool that stimulates consumer purchasing and dealer interest by means of short-term activities. We also addressed other types of promotion such as viral marketing and word-of-mouth marketing.

The final part of the chapter addressed integrated marketing communications (IMC) which combines all the promotional tools into one comprehensive and unified promotional strategy.

key terms

place 318

marketing
  intermediaries 318

channel of
  distribution 318

agents/brokers 319

wholesaler 319

retailer 319

merchant
  wholesalers 319

rack jobbers 322

cash-and-carry
  wholesalers 322

drop shippers 322

supply chain
  management 323

logistics 324

category killer 328

intensive
  distribution 330

selective
  distribution 330

exclusive
  distribution 330

telemarketing 332

direct selling 333

promotion mix 324

integrated marketing
  communication
  (IMC) 334

product placement 337

personal selling 337

prospecting 339

public relations
  (PR) 341

publicity 342

sales promotion 344

sampling 345

event marketing 346

viral marketing 346

word-of-mouth
  promotion 346

applying your skills

1. Form small groups and diagram how Dole might get pineapples from a field in Thailand to a canning plant in California to a store near your college. Include the intermediaries and the forms of transportation each one might use.

2. Discuss the merits of buying and selling goods in stores versus over the Internet. What advantages do stores have? Has anyone in the class tried to sell anything on the Internet? What were the challenges of that?

3. Choose four ads from at least two different media—a newspaper, magazine, TV, or any other medium. Select two ads that you consider effective and two ads that you do not consider effective. Be prepared to explain your reasoning behind your choices.

4. Scan your local newspaper for examples of publicity (stories about new products) and sales promotion (coupons, contests, sweepstakes). Share your examples and discuss the effectiveness of such promotional efforts with the class.

5. In small groups, or individually, make a list of six products (goods and services) that most students own or use and then discuss which promotional techniques prompt you to buy these goods and services: advertising, personal selling, publicity, sales promotion, or

word-of-mouth, and other means. Which tool or tools seem to be most effective for your group? Explain why.

6. Do you think advertising is unethical in any way? If so, think of examples to support your opinion. Discuss in small groups or write a one-page opinion paper about it.

7. Research how a small restaurant with a promotion budget of $10,000 might be able to promote itself in your city. How might a retail store with the same budget spend the funds?

the internet in action

1. *Purpose:* To analyze how products move from online retailers to end customers.

   Exercise: Let's say that you are a consumer in the market for a particular product. You have done your research and have found the perfect product for your needs at the lowest price available and you have ordered it online. Now what? How does the online merchant get the product to you? One of the most commonly used delivery services is UPS. Go to *www.ups.com* and use what you find there to answer the following questions.

   - UPS delivers approximately 13 million packages a day. How did UPS grow from a Seattle-based messenger service started by 19-year-old Jim Casey with a borrowed $100 to a worldwide delivery service that invests $1 billion each year in information technology alone?

   - How does UPS work? That is, what happens from the moment a request is made to ship a product to the moment it arrives at the customer's doorstep?

   - In the mid-1980s, UPS shifted its emphasis from an operations focus to a customer needs focus. Today, UPS provides many tools that help its customers meet their shipping needs. What are some examples of such tools?

2. *Purpose:* To evaluate the promotional effectiveness of two Web sites.

   Exercise: A promotional Web site is more like a product than an advertisement; that is, it is more like a constantly changing magazine than a brochure. It should have an action-oriented design to pull consumers to the site and be geared to move the consumer closer to a sale. How well do the sites for Mountain Dew (www.mountain dew. com) and Rain Forest Café (www.rainforestcafe.com) use the Web to present their messages? Consider these criteria in evaluating the Web sites:

- Achieves marketing objectives (such as consumer awareness, image, trial, accelerating repurchase, attracting job candidates)
- Attracts target market
- Is useful to target market
- Is easy to navigate
- Is graphically pleasing
- Loads quickly

3. Choose one of the previously mentioned Web sites and write or discuss suggestions for improving the site.

INFORMATION TECHNOLOGY IN BUSINESS

Winchuck River Store

K aren Clark, a small-business owner, runs a thriving rustic lodge and cabin dé-cor eBay business and Internet store right from her home: *www.winchuckriverstore.com.* Her story is one of determination and success. Clark found herself in need of a job after a divorce, which was a difficult situation for her because she had been a stay-at-home mother for the previous 16 years.

Clark had previously dab-bled in selling antiques and had numerous volunteer experiences. She worked as an office assistant in the early 1980s, when

Karen Clark

technology was different than it is now. She worked for a company that rented time shares, and her job was to create files for new clients. Clark says that after she left that job, she didn't use a computer for a long time. After coming back to using one, she was pleased that they had become so user friendly.

When she was once asked if she had a fear of technology, she said she had no fear: "I look at technology as a 'dead' item. Nonliving things can-not hurt me. It isn't interested in hurting me, so people should just go in there and figure it out. It doesn't

LEARNING objectives

After reading this chapter, you should be able to:

1 Explain information technology's role in business.

2 Understand how information is managed.

3 Describe various types of software and hardware.

4 Discuss challenges in information technology.

recognize your failures, successes, or have an opinion about you. There is no judgment to using technology other than the one you give yourself."

Clark says that without technology her business would not even be possible. Technology helps her maintain her books, allows customers to virtually visit her shop, and allows her to market her products, which include everything from lighting to antiques to kayak building kits.

When asked what was most frustrating about technology, Clark replied without hesitation, "All technology can be frustrating. I try to keep in mind that technology just helps me get the job done. However, I know there

are limits to what I will learn and sometimes you need to find someone more knowledgeable in parts of the business. For example, I hired a professional Web designer. I knew I could have done it on my own, but it would have taken a lot of time. It is important to realize your strengths and weaknesses and spend time doing those things you know you are really good at."

The most rewarding part of technology, according to Clark, is what it does *for her!* She says that she appreciates the people who make the software useable for individuals and their businesses. The most rewarding part of running her own business, says Clark, is answering only to herself.

THE ROLE OF INFORMATION TECHNOLOGY IN BUSINESS

What is technology? How can it be used to help Karen Clark and the many other entrepreneurs around the world? First, always remember that business constantly changes. Business owners and managers who try to rely on outdated ways of operating will simply not be able to compete with those who have and know how to use the latest technology. To put this statement into perspective, think of the technology that exists now that did not exist when you were 10 years old. Now take a moment to imagine what the next 10 years will bring. Would you be confident in a job interview tomorrow if you only had an understanding of the technology that existed when you were a child? Probably not! The ability to adapt by embracing technology can result in better business results.

This chapter will discuss how technology helps manage information in businesses. This chapter will discuss how technology helps, software, and hardwere and challenges in information technology today.

Technology impacts our daily lives more than we realize.

As the owner of a banner and sign printing business, Jose Diaz is stressed out because he has seen a decrease in his company's profits over the past two years. He attributes this decrease to his competitors using technology to produce signage and handle other parts of their businesses, such as invoicing and customer service. His business, on the other hand, is *not* using technology for the signs, banners, or day-to-day business activities.

Jose and his team spend a great deal of time on every order. Each letter or logo has to be created either using vinyl or paint and every item is crafted by hand. Customers must sometimes wait for over two weeks for their orders, and he has been receiving more complaints than usual. His competi-

tors are using digital printing technology and are able to complete more orders in a much shorter time frame.

At the end of every business day and sometimes on the weekends, Jose must handle the accounting for his company. He is using a printed ledger to keep track of invoices and payments as well as employee paychecks, utility bills, and other expenses. The time it takes to handle this task is eating away at both his professional and personal satisfaction.

Despite the challenges he knows he is facing, Jose is reluctant to embrace technology as a solution because he fears it will have a negative impact on his creativity. He is also not sure where to start.

Brief History of Information Technology

To understand why technology matters today, one should have a basic understanding of the past. Business technology has often changed names and roles. In the 1970s, business technology was known as **data processing (DP).** Although many people use the words *data* and *information* interchangeably, they are different. **Data** are raw, unanalyzed, and unorganized facts and figures. **Information** is the processed and organized data that can be used for managerial decision making. Data processing was used to support an existing business; its primary purpose was to improve the flow of financial information.

In the 1980s, business technology became known as **information systems (IS).** While data processing was a behind the scenes activity, information systems soon moved into the center of the business. Its role changed from *supporting* the business to *doing* business. Customers began to interact with a wide array of technological tools, from automated teller machines (ATMs) to voice mail. As businesses increased the use of information systems, they became more dependent on them. Until the late 1980s, business technology was just an addition to the existing way of doing business. Keeping up-to-date was a matter of using new technology on a base of old methods (such as using a fax machine instead of the United Postal Service). But change

data processing (DP)
The name for business technology in the 1970s. Its primary purpose was to improve the flow of financial information.

data
Raw, unanalyzed, and unorganized facts and figures.

information
The processed and organized data that can be used for managerial decision making.

information systems (IS)
The name for business technology in the 1980s. Its role changed from supporting the business to doing business. Technology such as ATMs and voice mail are examples.

It may seem that technology moves slowly, but when we look at the world 20 years ago, we know it was very different in terms of technology:

- When you send an e-mail, there is a line that says "cc." This comes from the typewriter days — if you needed another copy, you used carbon paper between two sheets of paper to make a second copy! Although we obviously don't use carbon paper on e-mail, the term *carbon copy* stuck!
- Did you know that the word processor first came out in the early 1970s? No, it wasn't a computer program but an actual device, similar to a typewriter that had memory and could store data. According to IBM, the device could store a whopping 20 pages of text on a cassette tape!
- Want to store music like an iPod? The only way to store it was a "dual" cassette tape recorder where you could record one tape onto another, or even record onto a cassette tape!
- If you like video games today, consider what they used to look like back in the 1980s:

- Keeping in touch with friends, but how about using a "block phone"? The cost in 1983 was $3,995 and weighed two pounds!

- Finally, how about adding a new way of cooking food? Do you think you would need a class on it? In the 1980s, the introduction of the microwave brought about much confusion; so much, in fact, that courses were launched to teach people how to use them!

figure 11.1

HOW FAR HAVE WE COME?

began to accelerate as the 1990s approached. Businesses shifted to using new technology based on new methods. Business technology then
became known as **information technology (IT),** and its role became
to *change* business.

Time and Place with Information Technology

Time and place have always been at the center of business. Customers
had to pay attention to business hours to satisfy their needs. They went to
stores to buy clothes. They went to banks to arrange for loans. *Businesses*
decided when and where customers did business with them. Today, IT
allows businesses to deliver goods and services whenever and wherever
it is convenient for the customer. Thus, today you can order clothes from
the Home Shopping Network while sitting at home, arrange a home
mortgage loan by phone or computer, or buy a car on the Internet at any
time you choose.

Consider how IT has changed the entertainment industry. If you
wanted to see a movie 35 years ago, you had to go to a movie theater.
Thirty years ago, you could wait for it to be on television. Twenty years
ago, you could wait for it to be on cable television or go to a video store
and rent a VHS tape. Ten years ago, you could go to a video store and rent
or buy a DVD. Now, you can order video on demand by satellite or cable,
download it to your Xbox Live, order DVDs for rent online, or download
the movie over the Internet to your computer.

At work, Internet and intranet communication using shared documents and other methods allows contributors to work on a common
document without time-consuming meetings.

> **information technology
> (IT)**
> The name given to
> business technology in
> the 1990s. Its role became
> the way of doing business,
> rather than just using
> technology to help with
> business functions.

q: How do you use technology as a consumer?

Information Technology and Independence of Location

As IT breaks time and location barriers, it creates organizations and services that are independent of location. For example, the NASDAQ (USA)
and the Eurex (Europe) are electronic stock exchanges without trading
floors. Buyers and sellers make trades by computer. Being independent
of location brings work to people instead of bringing people to work.
Data and information can flow more than 8,000 miles in a second, allowing businesses to conduct work around the globe continuously, making

figure 11.2

HOW INFORMATION
TECHNOLOGY IS
CHANGING BUSINESS

Organization	Technology is breaking down corporate barriers, allowing functional departments or product groups (even factory workers) to share critical information instantly.
Operations	Technology shrinks cycle times, reduces defects, and cuts waste. Service companies use technology to streamline ordering and communication with suppliers and customers.
Staffing	Technology eliminates layers of management and cuts the number of employees. Companies use computers and telecommunication equipment to create "virtual offices" with employees in various locations.
New products	Information technology cuts development cycles by feeding customer and marketing comments to product development teams quickly so that they can revive products and target specific customers.
Customer relations	Customer service representatives can solve customers' problems instantly by using companywide databases to complete tasks from changing addresses to adjusting bills. Information gathered from customer service interactions can further strengthen customer relationships.
New markets	Since it is no longer necessary for customers to walk down the street to get to stores, online businesses can attract customers to whom they wouldn't otherwise have access.

virtualization

Accessibility through technology that allows business to be conducted independent of location.

instant messaging (IM)

Allows businesses to communicate in real time, for free, via computer.

physical location less important. Regardless of business size, effective use of technology frees companies from the constraints of a physical location. Rather, team members and clients can communicate in several ways, called *virtualization*.

Virtualization is accessibility through technology that allows business to be conducted anywhere at any time.[1] For example, you can carry a virtual office in your briefcase, pocket, or purse, using such tools as Blackberries or wireless-enabled laptop computers. Likewise, people who otherwise would not have met are forming virtual communities through computer networks.

The way people do business drastically changes when companies increase their technological capabilities. Electronic communications can provide substantial time savings, whether you work in an office, at home, or on the road. E-mail ends the tedious game of telephone tag and is far faster than paper-based correspondence. **Instant messaging (IM),** best known as the preferred way millions of people contact each other, is now a favorite business real-time communication tool. For example, the first thing many businesspeople do after they turn on their computers is to see who is logged onto IM. Many business professionals

Instant messaging has made its way into the workplace, sometimes increasing efficiency in teams as a communication tool. How do you use instant messaging? Do you use similar functions for an online course as for communicating with your instructors and fellow students?

can participate in multiple conversations at once. The advantage to IM in business is that IM is immediate, even more so than e-mail, and there is no additional incremental cost, which makes overseas communication easier and cheaper.

e-Business and e-Commerce

e-Business, or electronic business, refers to any electronic business data exchange using any electronic device, including selling products online,[2] which is called **e-commerce.** e-Business involves much more than just selling. It can be as simple as being able to log on to a Web site and see the availability of a particular product. It can mean being able to check bank statements with your bank online, or being able to visit a company Web site to view new products on the market. So, unlike e-commerce which results in a transaction or exchange, electronic business does not always have to be an exchange of money or goods; e-business is often simply information sharing. It is important to understand the difference between these terms, as many people use them interchangeably when they are actually quite different. In other words,

e-business
Any electronic business data exchange using any electronic device.

e-commerce
Selling products or services online through e-business.

e-commerce consists of selling a product or service online, while e-business pertains to doing any sort of business or data exchange using technology.

any business participating in e-commerce is engaging in e-business, while a business may engage in e-business without necessarily doing e-commerce.

For example, if someone decides to get a haircut at a new salon, he or she may be able to make an appointment online, so the salon is engaging in e-business. If the salon also sells products online to that person, the parties are also engaging in e-commerce.

Business has become easier in many ways with the help of technology, but sometimes there can be too much of a good thing. Perhaps we have all had the experience of going into a restaurant with a very long menu and feeling overwhelmed with the choices available. Today there is so much information out there that it can sometimes be mind-numbing. One of the challenges of both e-business and e-commerce is that both can cause *information overload* to the consumer, which we will address in the next section.

SELF-CHECK QUESTIONS

1. What is data processing? How has technology changed from data processing to information technology?

2. How has instant messaging changed the way we do business? How has this technology affected you directly?

---

infoglut
The phenomenon of information overload in business.

MANAGING INFORMATION

The new technologies we have today make a difference in our lives every day, but they can be useless or somewhat oppresive if we do not know how to use and manage the information we receive. With voice mail, e-mail, the Internet, iPods, text messaging, and IM, businesspeople can feel overwhelmed with information.[3] This information overload is called **infoglut.** However, there are some preventive measures we can take, as businesspeople, to ensure we are getting the right amount of information at the time we need it.

---

q: Have you ever experienced *infoglut?*

First, in managing information, we have to know what is useful and what is not useful. *Usefulness* is based on these four characteristics:

1. *Quality:* Quality means the information is accurate and reliable. For example, when a retail store enters a sale into the register, it will automatically be calculated into the day's total sales. If that information is wrong, it can have a domino effect on all other information such as revenue projections, and so on.

2. *Completeness:* There must be enough information to allow individuals to make a decision but not so much as to confuse the issue. Today, as we have noted, the problem is often too much information rather than too little.

3. *Timeliness:* Information must reach business owners and managers quickly. Sales information from two years ago must be available when needed to accurately compile a sales forecast. If locating that information takes several weeks to pull up that information, it may be virtually useless, because a decision may already have been made.

4. *Relevance:* Information systems often provide us with too much data. Managers need to learn to ask the right questions, in order to get the relevant data they need.

The importance of information management cannot be overemphasized. For most companies, the proper management of information is the core of their business. For example, Princess Cruises has a third party manage a database with all of the information on its passengers. Since each passenger must complete a "cruiser information form," the company gets excellent data about its customers. With this information, it can send special offers and last-minute deals. The data is so important, in fact, that it is transported via a Brink's truck with special locks.

People must get easy to use, organized data when they need it, which is where data storage comes in. A **data warehouse** stores data on a specific subject over a period of time. However, the warehouse is not very useful if the data are difficult to retrieve. **Data mining** looks for hidden patterns in the data in a data warehouse and discovers relationships

data warehouse

An electronic storage place for data on a specific subject (such as sales) over a period of time.

data mining

Looking for hidden patterns in the data in a data warehouse and discovering relationships among the data.

Small businesses can find many types of software that fit their needs and their budgets, such as Office Accounting by Microsoft, which can help eBay businesses list new items and send invoices.

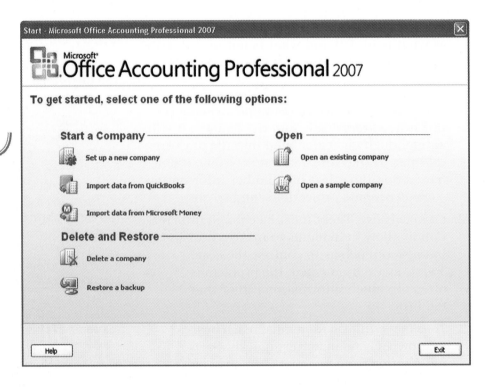

among the data. In Internet retail, data mining is called *shopping cart analysis*. Using shopping cart analysis, a manager can see what items people buy together, and as a result make recommendations on product placement. Thus, this kind of data can increase sales. Data mining can be useful to all businesses, big and small.

SELF–CHECK QUESTIONS

1. What are the four characteristics of useful data?
2. What is data mining?

Section Outline

The Backbone of Knowledge: Hardware and Software

- Hardware
- Software

THE BACKBONE OF KNOWLEDGE: HARDWARE AND SOFTWARE

Hardware

The advances in computer hardware come along so fast that what is powerful as of the writing of this textbook will not likely be so by the

It May Change Everything, But It Doesn't Cure All

The United States may be able to produce more missiles and microwaves than any other country, but our global domination in mass production didn't mean much on September 11, 2001. Armed with low-tech box cutters, terrorists were able to hijack high-tech airplanes and fly them into symbols of U.S. high-tech engineering—the World Trade Center and the Pentagon. Ironically, U.S. Special Forces had success in Afghanistan riding on the backs of borrowed horses and using air strikes by 50-year-old B-52 bombers.

Sure, both the United States and the terrorists have a long list of cutting-edge gadgetry and sophisticated weapons, but the critical element for the terrorists' "success" on 9/11 was something more intangible: it was information. The terrorists' box cutters weren't their deadliest weapon on 9/11; it was their understanding of U.S. air transportation. Information technology made manuals and flight schedules readily available to them. Online access to news articles gave them enough information to know that U.S. aircrews are trained to collaborate with, rather than confront, hijackers in an effort to save passengers' lives.

It was information that allowed U.S. planners to coordinate missions over Afghanistan by way of Central Asian airstrips, aircraft carriers, and U.S. bases. Digital communication devices on the ground transmitted precise coordinates to bombers overhead. Global positioning system satellites in space steered the bombs to those coordinates. Without the information systems, U.S. forces could have been blindly blasting at mountaintops. But it is not just information that makes the difference between a shot in the dark and a direct hit—it is getting the right information into the right hands at the right time.

Anyone who has done a Web search knows that quantity of information isn't the key to meeting your goals.

"Being submerged in data is not very productive," said Kenneth Watman, director of warfare analysis and research at the Naval War College in Newport, Rhode Island. "You've got to have some sort of intelligent scheme for putting things together." And that's where the government fell short before 9/11. There are countless local, state, and federal information networks, but they were not linked to share information before 9/11. For example, when Florida state police ticketed alleged terrorist ringleader Mohammed Atta for driving without a license in April 2001, they did not have access to federal intelligence information that would have told them he was on a CIA terrorist watch list. Since 9/11, government agencies have tried to find ways to connect their networks to ensure that another attack, and a lack of shared information, doesn't happen again.

Questions

1. How did technology make it easier for 9/11 to occur? Do you believe it can be prevented today? How can technology assist in such prevention?

2. Based on your knowledge of the changes so far implemented by the government, do you believe they are adequate?

Sources: Based on Freedbery, Sydney, "Governance in IT Changes Everything," *National Journal,* May 11, 2002; Krane, Jim, "Information Is US Military's Most Lethal Weapon," *AP Worldstream,* February 19, 2002; The 9/11 Commission Reports, accessed November 7, 2007, www.9-11commission.gov/report/911Report_Ch12.htm; Buchbinder, David, "In Afghanistan, a New Robosolider Goes to War," *The Christian Science Monitor,* July 31, 2002, accessed November 7. 2007, www.csmonitor.com/2002/0731/p01s03-usmi.html; and Rosen, Steven Peter, "The Future of War," *Harvard Magazine,* May-June 2002, accessed November 7. 2007, www.harvardmagazine.com/on-line/050218.html.

time you read this chapter. Hardware includes computers, pagers, cellular phones, printers, scanners, fax machines, personal digital assistants (PDAs), iPods, and much more. The mobile worker can find travel-size versions of computers, printers, and fax machines that are almost as powerful and feature-laden as their big brothers. An interesting development in office equipment is the merging of older

The iPhone was released to an eager market in June 2007. After only a few months, Apple dropped its 4GB model and decreased the price of the 8GB model, issuing a $100 coupon to customers who had purchased the item prior to the price change. Technology is always adapting, which makes new products outdated very quickly.

technologies with newer ones; for example, the ability to network computers to the copy machine saves companies money because they do not have to provide or pay for the upkeep of individual printers for everyone.

All-in-one devices that address the entire range of your communications needs are also available. For example, there are handheld units, such as Treos and iPhones, that include a wireless phone, MP3 player, fax and e-mail capabilities, Web browser, and personal information managers (PIMs) such as calendars.

Computer hardware is very useful—as long as it works. You may have experienced the frustration of getting paper stuck in a copier and having to figure out how to clear the jam without damaging the original copies. IBM is working on a solution to computer breakdowns with an approach called SMASH: simple, many, and self-healing.[4] The hope is to build computers made of many small components that have the ability to monitor their own performance and solve problems. IBM's inspiration was biology. A hangnail doesn't stop you from typing (although it might be a good excuse to stop typing!); a software or hardware problem should not stop your computer from working either. After all, we take such semi-intelligent automation for granted in other technology. With SMASH technology, for example, a telephone system, with its vast networks, switches, and services providers, would automatically send signals around a faulty circuit. In other words, it would be self-healing.

Wireless Information Appliances

wireless networking

Refers to the ability of a computer or device to transport signals through the air.

wireless fidelity (Wi-Fi)

The technology used to obtain an Internet connection without having to connect to a phone line or cable line.

Some experts think we have entered the post-PC era toward an array of Internet appliance options. They include equipment like PDAs (such as Blackberry), smart phones, and in-dash computers for the car. The standardization of **wireless networking** has set the common PC free from cords. No longer chained to their desks, laptop computer users find it liberating to have the mobility and flexibility to work on the Internet or company network anywhere they can tap into a wireless network. Wireless networks use a technology called **wireless fidelity (Wi-Fi).** Wireless local-area networks in hotels, airports, and even restaurants such as Panera Bread allow users with laptops outfitted with wireless modems to connect to the Web and download at 50 times the speed of typical dial-up connections.[5] The point is that people are taking the Internet with them, tapping in anytime and anywhere, to gather information and transact business.

Intranets, Extranets, Firewalls, and VPNs

An **intranet** is a companywide network closed to public access that uses Internet-type technology. To prevent unauthorized outsiders (particularly the competition) from accessing their sites, companies can construct a **firewall** between themselves and the outside world to protect corporate information from unauthorized users. A firewall can consist of hardware, software, or both. Company intranets, as well as individuals using home computers, use firewalls because they do not allow certain information from the intranet computer to be accessed by a computer from the outside. The firewall uses certain guidelines for what can be accessed, thereby protecting the computer from viruses or identity theft. Of course, firewalls are not foolproof, but using them is one way that individuals and companies can protect themselves.

Some companies use intranets only to publish information for employees, such as phone lists and employee policy manuals. The better return on investment for intranets, however, is time-saving applications—allowing forms to be filled out on the intranet (such as vacation requests), payroll information, and supply requisitions. These applications eliminate paper handling and enable more effective decision making. AmeriKing, the largest independent Burger King franchisee in the United States, estimates that it saves about a half a million dollars a year on printing and distribution costs for things such as physician directories, employee profiles, and employee contact information, by using its intranet.[6]

intranet

A companywide network, closed to public access, that uses Internet-type technology.

firewall

Can consist of hardware or software; prevents outsiders from accessing information the user does not want others to see.

You can now access Wi-Fi hot spots at coffee shops, restaurants, the airport, and many other locations. Does constant availability to access keep you more efficient?

q: Do you know if you have a firewall on your home
»» computer? What types of security systems do you encounter on
school computers?

Intranets are used in both the business and consumer markets. Here a shopping cart computer is connected to a store's intranet to indicate past purchases and supplies a store map.

extranet

A semiprivate network that uses Internet technology and allows more than one company to access the same information or allows people on different servers to collaborate.

figure 11.3

HOW HAS THE INTERNET CHANGED BUSINESS?

Extranets

Many businesses choose to open their intranets to other, selected companies through the use of *extranets*. An **extranet** is a *semiprivate* network that uses Internet technology and allows more than one company to access the same information, or allows people on different servers to collaborate. One of the most common uses of extranets is to extend an intranet to outside customers, such as suppliers. For example, a department store design department may want to use an extranet with its manufacturer located in China, in order to share new fashion designs and place orders.

Cisco Systems completes 90 percent of its purchasing and sales contracts electronically.[7] Cisco employee Brad Boston says that in the year after he joined the company, he signed only three pieces of paper: his employment contract, his tax return, and one contract with a Cisco supplier that insisted on having a hard copy.[8] Notice that we described an extranet as a semiprivate network, which means outsiders cannot access the network easily; but because an extranet does use public communication lines, knowledgeable **hackers** (people who break into computer systems for illegal purposes, such as transferring funds from someone's bank account to their own without authorization) can gain unauthorized access. Most companies want a network that is as private and secure as possible. One way to increase the probability of total privacy is to use dedicated lines (lines reserved solely for the network). There are two problems with this method:

	20 YEARS AGO	TODAY
Airlines	Reservations made in person or phone, wait times were often long	Reservations are made online, check in occurs online
Banking	Customers received monthly statements	Customers balance checkbook and pay bills online
Retail stores	Had to visit several stores to compare prices and see availability of products	Customers can check inventory online, shop online, and compare prices
Auto dealerships	Customers visited the dealership to see what cars were available and to view new models	Customers can build their own vehicle online, shop dealer inventory online
Manufacturing	Phone calls were required to place orders, purchase orders sent via mail	Businesses can order raw materials from suppliers online, send purchase orders electronically

(1) dedicated lines are expensive, and (2) dedicated lines limit use to computers directly linked to those lines. What if your company needed to link securely with another firm or individual for just a short time? Installing dedicated lines between companies in this case would be too expensive and time-consuming. Virtual private networks are a solution, and we will discuss them in the next section.

VPNs

A **virtual private network (VPN)** is a private data network that creates secure connections, or "tunnels," over regular Internet lines.[9] The idea of the VPN is to give the company the same capabilities at much lower cost by using shared public resources, rather than private ones, which means that companies no longer need their own leased lines for wide-area communication, but can instead use public lines securely. Just as phone companies provide secure shared resources for voice messages, VPNs provide the same secure sharing of public resources for data and allow for on-demand networking: an authorized user can join the network for any desired function, at any time, for any length of time, while keeping the corporate network secure.

Logging on to a VPN normally means a user will sign into a portal. **Portals** serve as entry points to a variety of resources, such as e-mail, financial records, schedules, and employment and benefits files. They can even include streaming video of the company's day care center. Portals are more than simply Web pages with links. They identify users and allow them access to areas of the intranet according to their roles: customers, suppliers, employees, and so on. For example, when a supervisor logs on, she may be able to see performance reviews on the employees she manages. She might also be able to see her personal work schedule and other information necessary for her job, such as her job description.

Software

Computer **software** provides the instructions that enable you to tell the computer what to do. Although many people looking to buy a computer think first of the equipment, it is important to find the right software before finding the right hardware. Some programs are easier to use than others. Some are more sophisticated and can perform more functions than others. A businessperson or a person buying a computer for personal use at home must decide what functions he or she wants the computer system to perform, and then choose the appropriate software. That

hackers

People who unlawfully break into computer systems.

virtual private network (VPN)

A private data network that creates secure connections, or "tunnels," over regular Internet lines.

portal

An entry point into a Web site.

software

The product that tells your computer what to do.

Allowing employees to access the company's network remotely increases productivity and efficiency, especially when an employee is frequently traveling for the job.

Make Good Career Planning Habits a Life Skill

In order to find that very first job after graduation, you find sooner rather than later that a positive outcome will come from your own work and hard efforts. While there are courses and professionals who can help you along the way, ultimately your successful career will happen because of your commitment to the skills and habits that will be required to move you from an average achiever to a high achiever.

Separate your career "planning functions" into career preparation and career execution. *Career preparation* involves all the activities that can help you in career/job research, improving reading and writing skills, assessing your strengths and weaknesses, learning job/industry terminology, and establishing career goals and objectives. *Career execution* involves establishing high levels of skills in filling out job applications, interviewing, career etiquette, resume writing, personal planning, and effective communication.

choice will help determine what brand of computer to buy, how much power it should have, and what peripherals it needs.

Businesspeople most frequently need and use software for:

1. Writing (word processors)
2. Manipulating numbers (spreadsheets)
3. Filing and retrieving data (databases)
4. Presenting information visually (graphics)
5. Communicating (e-mail and instant messaging)
6. Accounting
7. Internet or intranet use

Software today is often bundled together so that it can perform many functions in one kind of program known as *integrated software* or a *software suite.*

One of the newer types of software still in development is called *expert systems.* According to the Association for the Advancement of Artificial Intelligence, an expert system is a type of software that is meant to solve problems in a variety of industries. For example, a health care provider might use an expert system to diagnose a skin problem someone in her early 20s is experiencing. The doctor would input the symptoms and the possible issues would then be viewable. As you can imagine, the implications of expert systems may affect every industry and at the very least save workers time.

Although most software is distributed commercially through suppliers such as Best Buy or other electronic retailers, there is some software called **shareware** that is copyrighted but distributed to potential customers free of charge. The users are asked to send a specified fee to the

shareware

Software that is copyrighted but distributed to potential customers free of charge.

Word Processing Programs	With word processors, standardized letters can be personalized quickly, documents can be updated by changing only the outdated text and leaving the rest intact, and contract forms can be revised to meet the stipulations of specific customers. The most popular word-processing programs include Corel WordPerfect, Microsoft Word, and Lotus WordPro.
Desktop Publishing (DTP) Software	DTP combines word processing with graphics capabilities that can produce designs that once could be done only by powerful page-layout design programs. Popular DTP programs include Microsoft Publisher, Adobe PageMaker Plus, and Corel Print Office.
Spreadsheet Programs	A spreadsheet program is simply the electronic equivalent of an accountant's worksheet plus such features as mathematical function libraries, statistical data analysis, and charts. Using the computer's speedy calculations, managers have their questions answered almost as fast as they can ask them. Some of the most popular spreadsheet programs are Lotus 1-2-3, Quattro Pro, and Excel.
Database Programs	A database program allows users to work with information that is normally kept in lists: names and addresses, schedules, inventories, and so forth. Using database programs, you can create reports that contain exactly the information you want in the form you want it to appear in. Leading database programs include Q&A, Access, Approach, Paradox, PFS: Professional File, PC-File, R base, and FileMaker Pro for Apple computers.
Personal Information Managers (PIMs)	PIMs or contact managers are specialized database programs that allow users to track communication with their business contacts. Such programs keep track of everything—every person, every phone call, every e-mail message, every appointment. Popular PIMs include Goldmine, Lotus Organizer, ACT, and ECCO Pro.
Graphics and Presentation Programs	Computer graphics programs can use data from spreadsheets to visually summarize information by drawing bar graphs, pie charts, line charts, and more. Inserting sound clips, video clips, clip art, and animation can turn a dull presentation into an enlightening one. Some popular graphics programs are Illustrator and Freehand for Macintosh computers, Microsoft PowerPoint, Harvard Graphics, Lotus Freelance Graphics, Active Presenter, and Corel Draw.
Communications Programs	Communications software enables a computer to exchange files with other computers, retrieve information from databases, and send and receive electronic mail. Such programs include Microsoft Outlook, ProComm Plus, Eudora, and Telik.
Message Center Software	Message center software is more powerful than traditional communications packages. This new generation of programs has teamed up with fax/voice modems to provide an efficient way of making certain that phone calls, e-mail, and faxes are received, sorted, and delivered on time, no matter where you are. Such programs include Communicate, Message Center, and WinFax Pro.
Accounting and Finance Programs	Accounting software helps users record financial transactions and generate financial reports. Some programs include online banking features that allow users to pay bills through the computer. Others include "financial advisers" that offer users advice on a variety of financial issues. Popular accounting and finance programs include Peachtree Complete Accounting, Simply Accounting, Quicken, and QuickBooks Pro.
Integrated Programs	Integrated software packages (also called suites) offer two or more applications in one package. This allows you to share information across applications easily. Such packages include word processing, database management, spreadsheet, graphics, and communications. Suites include Microsoft Office, Lotus SmartSuite, and Corel WordPerfect Suite.
Groupware	Groupware is software that allows people to work collaboratively and share ideas. It runs on a network and allows people in different areas to work on the same project at the same time. Groupware programs include Lotus Notes, Frontier's Intranet Genie, MetaInfo Sendmail, and Radnet Web Share.

figure 11.4

TYPES OF POPULAR COMPUTER SOFTWARE

program Limewire. Limewire is a peer-to-peer file sharing client for Java platform.[10] The shareware concept has become very popular and has dramatically reduced the price of software. **Public domain software (freeware)** is software that is free for the taking. The quality of shareware and freeware varies greatly. To give you an idea of the quality of such programs, find a Web site that rates shareware and freeware programs. For example, tucows.com and topshareware.com list such things as the programs downloaded most often, editors' picks, and links to downloadable programs.

SELF-CHECK QUESTIONS

1. Differentiate between hardware and software.
2. What is a VPN? What is the difference between an intranet and an extranet?
3. What do businesspeople use software for? Provide an example of each.
4. What is the difference between freeware and shareware?

INFORMATION TECHNOLOGY CHALLENGES

With all of the advantages we have with technology, there are some challenges as well. According to the FTC, more than 9 million people experienced identity theft in 2006,[11] much of this due to hackers and their ability to break into computers, allowing them access to credit card numbers and social security numbers. In 2005, computer crime, such as identity theft and viruses in general cost $67 billion, according to the FBI[12], and this number is expected to be higher every year. At costs this high, people are continually working on new ways to prevent this from happening. The type of content available on the Internet is also cause for concern. Adult content, harassment, and spam messages are all areas that, as users of the Internet, we are all vulnerable to. Privacy is a hot topic in technology as well. People are concerned that the government and business will be able to track the Web sites they are viewing, creating lack of personal privacy. Stability of the Internet continues to be an issue. Things such as glitches are a concern to all of us, but glitches in business can cost millions of dollars, as we will discuss in the upcoming section.

Hackers and Viruses

One ongoing problem with computer technology, which is likely to persist in the future, is that computers are susceptible to hackers. For example, according to *Information Week*, hackers broke into computers of TJX, the owners of TJMaxx, and allegedly stole customer credit card numbers. This kind of security breach can cause millions of dollars worth of damage both directly to the bottom line and indirectly to a company's reputation.[13]

Computer security is more complicated today than ever before. When information was processed on mainframes (a single computer that ran all of the computers in a company), the single data center was easier to control because there was limited access to it. Today computers and their information are accessible not only in all areas within the company, but through extranets, affecting all areas of other companies with which the firm does business.

An ongoing security issue involves the spread of computer viruses over the Internet. A **virus** is a piece of programming code inserted into other programming to cause some unexpected, and for the victim, usually undesirable, event. Viruses are spread by downloading infected programming over the Internet or by sharing an infected file. The user is usually unaware of the source of the culprit download file containing the virus. The virus lies dormant until circumstances cause its code to be executed by the computer. Some viruses are playful, but some can be quite harmful, erasing data or causing your hard drive to crash. There are programs, such as Norton's AntiVirus, that "inoculate" your computer so that it does not "catch" a known virus. New viruses are being developed constantly and consequently, antivirus programs have only limited success. Therefore, computer users should keep their antivirus protection program up-to-date and, more important, practice "safe computing" by not downloading files from unknown sources, and by scanning file storage devices, such as CDs and USB flash drives, before accessing any of the files on them. Even businesses protected by firewalls can unwittingly be affected by computer viruses that have been accidentally downloaded by employees. Figure 11.5 offers steps you should take to minimize the threat of virus infection to your computer. Following these steps, however, does not guarantee that you will not get a virus.

virus

Programming codes inserted into other programming to cause unexpected events.

MyDoom is a mass-mailing worm that flooded e-mail servers worldwide. The worm stole e-mail addresses from the infected machine and generated e-mails with a fake "From:" field, so incoming messages appeared to be from users they already knew. Similar new viruses are found constantly. How can you protect your computer from such attacks?

Governmental Security

Until September 11, 2001, corporate and government security officials worried mostly about online theft, credit card fraud, and

figure 11.5

PROTECT YOUR
COMPUTER FROM
VIRUSES

There are several actions that you should take to protect your computer from virus infections:

- **Use a high-quality anti virus program.** Scan your computer and all files using the virus check program regularly and install the updates.
- **If you get public domain software,** (1) ensure the source is reliable and (2) scan the software using the anti virus program.
- **Before using a disk that has been in another computer,** scan it for viruses.
- **Practice "safe computing":** (1) Do not download files from unknown sources, and (2) if and when you do have to download, always scan all Internet downloads and e-mail attachments with an anti virus program.

hackers. Today, however, they are most concerned about cyberterrorism.[14] According to Mike McConnell, former director of the National Security Agency, if 30 terrorists with hacker skills and $10 million attacked the United States today, they could shut down entire communications, money supply, electricity, and transportation systems.

In order to prevent this disaster from happening, government agencies need the cooperation of businesses across the country, because 85 percent of the systems the government needs to protect are in the private sector.

Technology workers are reluctant to give information to the government in exchange for increased protection for fear that the public will fnd out about security breaches and lose faith in the company's ability to protect its assets and reputation. In addition, there are a number of people who believe providing this kind of information is a breach of privacy. They feel the government should not be privy to this kind of information. In addition, some feel that allowing the government this kind of information will result in the government wanting even more information, thereby further affecting right to privacy. The Critical Infrastructure Information Act passed in 2002 gives businesses assurance that any information they provide to the government regarding critical infrastructure (information might be water supply data, electrical systems data, and telecommunications data) is exempt from disclosure by the Freedom of Information Act.

Privacy

The increasing use of technology creates major concerns about privacy. E-mail is no more private than a postcard. You do not need to be the target of a criminal investigation to have your e-mail reviewed by someone in your company or in your personal life. More than one-fourth of U.S. companies scan employee e-mail regularly and legally. Just as employers can listen to employees' telephone conversations, they can track e-mail in a search for trade secrets being passed, non-work-related traffic, harassing messages, and conflicts of interest. According to an AMA research study,

Cyber Ethics

According to a survey taken in 2007 by salary.com, employees waste an average of 1.7 hours per day (not including lunch) surfing the Internet and replying to personal e-mails.[15] The extra unproductive time equals $759 billion in salary cost per year.

1. As an employee, do you think it should be okay to surf the Internet for personal use while at work?

Under what circumstances would it be okay, or not okay?

2. As a manager, you have the ability to access e-mails written by employees. You suspect one of your employees is spending way too much time writing personal e-mails. Should you check his or her account? Why or why not?

25 percent of the companies surveyed have fired workers for misusing the Internet and 5 percent have terminated employees for e-mail misuse.[16] Most e-mail travels over the Internet in **unencrypted** plain text, meaning that the information being sent is not in a secret code, and therefore anyone can view it. Some e-mail systems, such as Lotus Notes, can encrypt messages to ensure corporate messages are kept private. People who use browser-based e-mail (such as Google mail) can obtain a certificate that has an encryption key from a company such as VeriSign, which costs about $10 a year.[17] Of course, legitimate users who want to decrypt your mail need to get a key.

> **unencrypted**
> An encryption is a secret code given to information when it is passing through the Internet. An unencrypted piece of data means anyone can see it and it is less secure.

The Internet presents increasing threats to your privacy, as more personal information is stored in computers and more people are able to access that data both legally *and* illegally. The Internet allows Web surfers to access all sorts of information about both businesses, and individual, Web sites. Myspace.com allows individuals to post personal information about themselves—sometimes too personal. Keep in mind that anything you send through cyberspace could potentially come back to haunt you! Some employers even check the Internet to see if their employees or prospective employees are portraying themselves unprofessionally. Need more proof? Just ask any number of beauty pageant contestants who have had their titles challenged due to bad conduct— the images on the Internet provide compelling evidence.

Average computer users are concerned that Web sites have gotten downright nosy. In fact, many Web servers track users' movements online. Web surfers seem willing to swap personal details for free access to online information. This personal information can then be shared with others without your permission. Web sites often send **cookies** to your computer that stay on your hard drive. These are pieces of information, such as registration data or user preferences, sent by a Web site over the Internet to a Web browser. The browser is expected to save and send back the information to the server whenever the user

> **cookies**
> Pieces of information, such as registration data or user preferences, sent by a Web site over the Internet to your Web browser that the browser is expected to save and send back to the server whenever the user returns to that Web site.

So, You Want to Be in . . . Computer Information Systems

According to the U.S. Department of Labor, careers in information systems are expected to grow faster than average through 2014.[19] Due to this growth, job opportunities in this area should remain plentiful. Examples of entry-level jobs in computer information systems include junior database administrators and technical support specialists. Once experience is gained, a person could become an information systems manager. These management positions sometimes earn more than $100,000 per year. Information systems managers often oversee security for intranets and extranets, and they also might administer and manage complex database systems for a company. The manager might also work in systems integration, which means he or she combines two or more existing systems into one more efficient system. Computer systems analysts, computer programmers, and customer support representatives are also positions in this field.

There are many companies that employ specialists in computer information systems. Manufacturing, government, insurance, retail, and financial firms are all examples of possible employers of CIS employees.

Although many programming jobs are outsourced, companies are still going to have a need for local individuals to run and manage their information systems. Opportunities are endless!

returns to that site. These little tidbits often simply contain your name and a password that the Web site recognizes the next time you visit the site so that you don't have to reenter the same information every time you visit. Other cookies track your movements around the Web and then blend that information with a database so that a company can tailor the ads you receive accordingly. The next time you visit a Web site that welcomes you by your first name, you will know that cookies have been placed on your hard drive.

You need to decide how much information about yourself you are willing to give away. Remember, we are living in an information economy, and information is a commodity—that is, an economic good with a measurable value.

Stability

Although technology can provide significant increases in productivity and efficiency, instability in technology also has a significant impact on business. For example, candy maker Hershey discovered it couldn't get its treats to the stores on time during the busy Halloween season. Failure of its new $115 million computer system disrupted shipments, and retailers were forced to order Halloween treats from other companies. Consequently, Hershey suffered a 12 percent decrease in sales that quarter.[18]

We have all experienced computer glitches that caused delays or garbled data. What's to blame? Sometimes problems are caused by human error, such as not thoroughly testing a new computer application before sending it live. Other problems that cause instability are computer viruses, problems with servers, and incompatible hardware and software. An example of how you could be affected by such problems would be if you had a computer older than all of your co-workers' computers when new software applications are introduced, your computer might not be capable of running that software, thus keeping you from being able to do your job. This combination of computer error, human error, malfunctioning software, and an overly complex marriage of software, hardware, and networking equipment is a never-ending challenge for IT administrators and individual users alike.

Reliability of Data

The last challenge we will discuss is the fact that all information we find online may not be reliable. There are many people who take information found on the Internet to be the absolute truth. This, of course, is not always the case. When evaluating data on the Internet, consider the following:

- *Accuracy.* How reliable and free from error is the information? Are there editors and fact checkers?

- *Authority.* What is the authority or expertise of the individual or group that created this site? How knowledgeable is the individual or group on the subject matter of the site? Is the site sponsored or co-sponsored by an individual or group that has created other Web sites? Is contact information for the author or producer included in the document?

- *Objectivity.* Is the information presented with a minimum of bias? To what extent is the information trying to sway the opinion of the audience?

- *Current.* Is the content of the work up-to-date? When was the Web item produced? When was the Web site last revised? How up-to-date are the links? How reliable are the links? That is, are there blind links or references to sites that have moved?

- *Coverage.* Are the topics explored in depth? What is the overall value of the content? What does it contribute to the literature in its field? Given the ease of self-publishing on the Web, this is perhaps even more important in reviewing Web resources than in reviewing print resources.

Understanding that all data might not be reliable, we can make better decisions when determining data to use in our research, eliminating data that may be biased or is not up-to-date.

SELF-CHECK QUESTIONS

1. What are some of the challenges facing information technology today and in the future?

2. What kinds of risks might one face when using the Internet?

After some extensive research, Jose realized his fear of technology was keeping him from making his business as successful as it could be. First Jose hired an IT specialist who interviewed Jose and his employees in order to access the company's technology needs. The IT specialist helped Jose select hardware and software that could support both the creative and financial needs of the company.

Next, Jose and the IT specialist set up an intranet for his five employees. The intranet has information about vacation time, schedules, and health care. When his company grows, he plans on using the intranet for employee-related forms as well. The specialist also set up an extranet to enable Jose to conduct business transactions with suppliers and his large accounts, such as the local grocery store. The system helps Jose manage his inventory of supplies, such as ink and other materials.

Jose felt so comfortable with the new technology at his company that he also purchased a new iPhone—he is now able to check his e-mail and phone messages whenever he wants.

Although Jose was reluctant to confront his fear of technology at first, he now feels comfortable with his decision to implement technology in his workplace. Using the software, he can print the signs directly from the computer to the banner. He is more efficient and can accept more new orders than ever before. Overall, Jose has found his productivity and profits are increasing because of technology!

summary

This chapter discussed the role of technology in helping businesses be more productive in both their internal systems and interfacing with customers. The data processing of the "darkened back room" emerged to be the information systems of the 80s and the information technology of the 90s.

Information technology has liberated business from dependence on time and place. Customers can make purchases online any time they feel like it without going to stores, and employees have real-time collaboration with colleagues even while traveling or doing other things via instant messaging.

A major problem in managing the new technology is to help managers avoid being overloaded with information to the point the problem disappears in a mountain of conflicting data. This phenomenon is called infoglut.

A data warehouse stores huge amounts of information useful for business. Data mining allows businesspeople to find relevant and meaningful patterns in the data that they can use productively.

The chapter provided an introduction to computer hardware and software. Hardware includes the physical devices such as PDAs, computers, cellular phones, printers, multifunction devices, and all the new products coming online today that make businesspeople more productive. Software is the programs and instructions that we use to tell the hardware what to do for us—from producing spreadsheets to executing complex data management tasks.

The chapter concluded with an overview of the challenges businesses face today in the management of information. Security issues, privacy issues, and stability issues are all contemporary challenges that IT people and businesspeople must understand. In addition, understanding how to evaluate the reliability of data we find on the Internet was discussed in this chapter.

key terms

data processing
  (DP) 359
data 359
information 359
information systems
  (IS) 359
information technology
  (IT) 361
virtualization 362
instant messaging
  (IM) 362
e-business 363

e-commerce 363
infoglut 364
data warehouse 365
data mining 365
wireless
  networking 368
wireless fidelity
  (Wi-Fi) 368
intranet 369
firewall 369
extranet 370

hackers 370
virtual private network
  (VPN) 371
portal 371
software 371
shareware 372
public domain software
  (freeware) 374
virus 375
unencrypted 377
cookies 377

applying your skills

1. Imagine that you have $1,000 with which to buy a computer system or to upgrade a computer system you already have. Research the latest in hardware and software in computer magazines and on Web sites such as www.zdnet.com. Then, go to a computer store or to online computer sites, such as Dell, Gateway, and Micron, to find the best value. Make a list of what you would buy, and then write a summary explaining the reasons for your choices.

2. Interview someone who bought a computer system to use in his or her business. Ask that person why he or she bought that specific computer, and how it is used. Ask about any problems that occurred during the purchase process, or in installing and using the system. What would the buyer do differently next time? What software does he or she find especially useful?

3. If you have worked with computers, you've probably experienced times when the hard drive crashed or the software didn't perform as it should have. Describe one computer glitch you've experienced and what you did to resolve it. Analyze and discuss the consequences of the interruption (e.g., decreased productivity, increased stress).

381

4. Discuss how technology has changed your relationship with specific businesses or organizations, such as your bank, your school, and your favorite places to shop. Has it strengthened or weakened your relationship? On a personal level, how has technology affected your relationship with your family, friends, and community? Take a sheet of paper and on one side write down how technology has helped build your business and personal relationships. On the other side of the paper, list how technology has weakened the relationships. What can you and others do to use technology more effectively, and to reduce any negative impact?

5. Discuss the difference between e-commerce and e-business. Give an example of how a business might use both.

the internet in action

1. *Purpose:* To experience the functions and benefits of an enterprise portal.

   Exercise: Log on to www.dynamicintranet.com and take the Portal Tour to see what an enterprise portal can do and how it can help businesses and their employees. (Click through the tour to get a general idea of the benefits of enterprise portals; don't try to understand the technical descriptions—you can save that for another course.) B2E (business to employee) portals are not accessible to outsiders, but you can see what one looks like and use some of its tools by logging on to the demo portal of Toasters, Inc. at http://demo.dynamicintra.net/toaster_en.asp.

   - Using the calendar feature in the demo portal, schedule a meeting with three other employees. (Hint: Click "calendar" and then "search public calendar" to get started.) What are the benefits of using this tool, rather than calling a meeting personally?

   - Suppose you want to work from home one day a week, but you aren't sure what Toasters' policy is on telecommuting. Find the policy in the human resources directory.

   - You're a team leader for Project 996. What's your reward if your team meets its goal?

   - Some of the folks in marketing have a sick sense of humor. See if you can find why office humor isn't reserved for the water cooler anymore. Obviously, Toasters, Inc. allows individual employees to post information to the portal without supervisory approval. What are the advantages and disadvantages of nonmoderated postings?

   Exercise: Unlike most print resources, such as magazines and journals, which go through a filtering process (e.g., editing, peer review), information on the Web is mostly unfiltered. The Web has a lot to offer, but not all sources are equally valuable or reliable. Because almost anyone can publish online, accepting information from the Web can be like accepting advice from strangers. It's best to look at all Web sites with a critical eye. Find two Web sites that discuss possible causes of lung cancer (you can do a search on www.google.com). Then, write a one-paragraph evaluation of each site using the criteria discussed in this chapter.

UNDERSTANDING FINANCIAL INFORMATION AND ACCOUNTING

R. J. Julia Booksellers

Roxanne Coady knew about accounting, but she realized she wasn't applying that knowledge to the business that she loved. Coady had left a job in accounting to open a business in an area for which she had a passion—books. But if she was going to keep what she loved she was going to have to use her accounting skills to bear on some business problems that were cropping up in her new store.

Coady left her 20-year career as a tax director for BDO Seidman, a New York–based international accounting firm, and the secu-

Roxanne Coady

rity of a regular paycheck to open R. J. Julia Booksellers in a small Connecticut town. Coady's new company was successful in its first five years, with growth of 30–75 percent. However, after that point the company began experiencing financial problems.

Coady's employees knew that inventory management was unacceptable, and Coady knew that her costs of doing business were too high. The company was no longer making much of a profit. Of course, the irony in this situation was the fact that the owner was once a high-level New York accountant.

objectives

After reading this chapter, you should be able to:

1. Describe the importance of financial information and accounting.

2. Define and explain different areas of accounting.

3. List the steps in the accounting cycle.

4. Explain how the major financial statements differ.

5. Explain the importance of ratio analysis in reporting financial information.

CHAPTER

12

After some serious introspection, Coady realized that it was the very motivation that had driven her to become a bookseller—her love of books—that was the source of the problem. She was letting her passion for books take over her decision making. She had ignored budgets and gone on a literary fling, misspending about $250,000 of the money she and her husband had saved. The financial standards of the company were lax to nonexistent and the resulting cash flow was poor.

If her business was to recover from these challenges, Coady knew that her accounting procedures needed to improve. Fortunately, as a former accountant, she was just the woman to take charge!

Coady gathered her staff and told them about the changes that would be made. Those changes included reviewing monthly income statements and cash flow analyses. No longer would book-buying decisions be made intuitively and solely from the heart. She made it a goal to focus on costs, since profit margins in book selling are slim. On the selling as well as the buying side, other employee changes would include the provision of a training manual.

Now, Coady is one of the most successful independent book store owners in the country. In fact, she has recently expanded to a second bookstore.

Sources: Cara Baruzzi, "Madison, Conn., Bookseller Gains Ownership of Second Store," *New Haven Register,* July 7, 2005; Julie Fishman-Lapin, "New Canaan, Conn., Gets an Independent Partner," *Stamford Advocate,* June 23, 2005; Cara Baruzzi, "Old Saybrook, Conn., Retailer Given Business Award," *New Haven Register,* August 26, 2005.

INTRODUCTION TO ACCOUNTING

Although you may not have plans to be an accountant, learning about accounting is extremely important because as a businessperson, you will constantly be dealing in numbers. If you are thinking about buying a business, the numbers will be the key to determining if that business is worth the money. Once you own that business, you will constantly look at numbers to see how well your company is doing.[1] This chapter will discuss some basic information on how businesspeople can use accounting to better understand and control their businesses, even if they do not aspire to become accountants.

THE IMPORTANCE OF FINANCIAL INFORMATION

The goal of this chapter is not to show you everything there is to know about accounting; rather, its purpose is to expose you to some basics of accounting as well as to some career opportunities in the accounting field. All individuals can benefit personally and professionally by having a basic working knowledge of accounting.

As you read this chapter, keep in mind that there are many terms used that a person who has never been exposed to accounting may

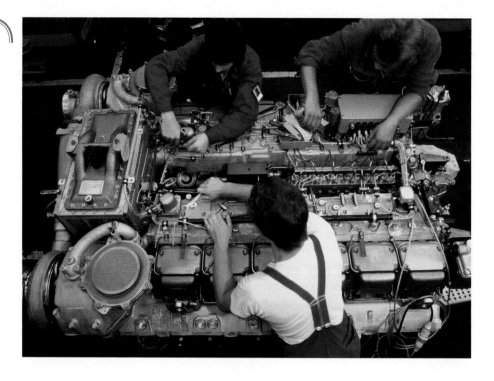

Assembling a marine diesel engine involves many tools, parts, and raw materials. Keeping down costs is the combined effort of managers and accountants.

John Miller recently opened a candle store in downtown Dallas, Texas. Since opening, John has continued to expand the variety of candles offered in his store. John has a two-year degree in business and he took two accounting classes. He had planned to do his own books; however, increasingly he does not feel comfortable doing the accounting for his business. After some thought, he decides he does not have the time even to research the accounting needs of his business and instead sets up a meeting with an accountant who he hopes will help his business manage its finances thoroughly and accurately.

understand to have a different meaning. Consider accounting an entirely new language and it will make the terms in this chapter much easier to comprehend.

In addition, it is important to note that many people use accounting information, not just managers. Suppliers, your competition, and employees are also interested in this kind of information.

Let's start by defining accounting, and then discuss the types of accounting in which you may be involved.

What Is Accounting?

Financial information is primarily based on information generated from accounting. **Accounting** is the recording, classifying, summarizing, and interpreting of financial events and transactions, in order to provide management and other stakeholders the information they need to make good decisions. Financial transactions can include such specifics as buying and selling goods and services, acquiring insurance, paying employees, and using supplies. Once business transactions have been recorded, they are usually classified into groups that have common characteristics. For example, all purchases are grouped together, as are all sales transactions. The method used to record and summarize accounting data into reports is called an *accounting system,* which illustrates the operating performance of the firm and from which management can make informed decisions.

Another major purpose of accounting is to report financial information to people outside the firm, such as owners, creditors, suppliers, investors, and the government (for tax purposes). In sum, accounting is the measurement and reporting of financial information to various users (inside and outside the organization) regarding the economic activities of the firm.

Accounting work is divided into several major areas, which we will discuss next.

accounting
Recording, classifying, summarizing, and interpreting financial events and transactions to provide management and other interested parties the information they need to make good decisions.

AREAS OF ACCOUNTING

The accounting profession is divided into five key areas: managerial and financial, auditing, tax, governmental, and not-for-profit. All five areas are important, and all create career opportunities for students who are interested in accounting.[2]

Managerial and Financial Accounting

Managerial accounting is used to provide information and analysis to managers *within* the organization to assist them in decision making. **Financial accounting,** on the other hand, generates information for use *outside* the organization.

Managerial accounting is concerned with measuring and reporting costs of production, marketing, and other functions; preparing budgets (planning); checking whether or not units are staying within their budgets (controlling); and designing strategies to minimize taxes (i.e., information and analysis for decision makers within the organization). The information and analysis prepared by financial accounting goes not only to the company owners, managers, and employees, but also to creditors and lenders, employee unions, customers, suppliers, government agencies, and the general public. External users are interested in important financial questions such as: Is the organization profitable? Is it able to pay its bills? How much debt does the organization hold? Financial accountants have the important responsibility of preparing **annual reports** which are yearly statements of the financial condition, progress, and expectations of an organization.

Individuals who desire to work in the accounting field are required to take courses in managerial and financial accounting, and then may elect to pursue a career as a certified management accountant or a certified public accountant. A **certified management accountant (CMA)** is a

managerial accounting

Provides information and analysis to managers within the organization to assist them in decision making.

financial accounting

Generates information for use outside the organization.

All public companies publish annual reports on a yearly basis. Many, such as Target, now use the Internet to post their reports.

professional accountant who has met certain educational and experience requirements, passed a qualifying exam in the field, and been certified by the Institute of Certified Management Accountants. An accountant who passes a series of examinations established by the American Institute of Certified Public Accountants (AICPA) and meets the state's requirement for education and experience earns recognition as a **certified public accountant (CPA).** CPAs find careers as private accountants or public accountants, and are often sought out to fill other financial positions within organizations.[3]

Private accountants work for a single firm, government agency, or nonprofit organization, and are on the payroll of the company or organization. However, not all firms or nonprofit organizations want or need a full-time accountant. Accountants who do not work for a specific company are called **public accountants.** Public accountants can be hired to help businesses with payroll, taxes, and other projects but do not need to be employees of the company, which is useful to know, in case you choose to start your own business.

It is vital for the accounting profession to ensure users of financial information that the information provided to them is accurate, especially in light of the scandals that have spanned this decade. The independent **Financial Accounting Standards Board (FASB)** defines the set of **generally accepted accounting principles (GAAP)** that accountants must follow. If financial reports are prepared in accordance with GAAP, users can expect that the information is reported according to standards agreed on by accounting professionals.[4]

> **annual report**
> Yearly statement of the financial condition, progress, and expectations of an organization.

> **certified management accountant (CMA)**
> A professional accountant who has met certain educational and experience requirements, passed a qualifying exam in the field, and been certified by the Institute of Certified Management Accountants.

> **certified public accountant (CPA)**
> An accountant who passes a series of examinations established by the American Institute of Certified Public Accountants (AICPA) and does accounting work for no one particular firm.

Auditing

The job of reviewing and evaluating the records used to prepare a company's financial statements is referred to as **auditing.** Accountants within the organization often perform internal audits to ensure that proper accounting procedures and financial reporting are being followed.

Public accountants also conduct independent audits of accounting and related records. An **independent audit** is an evaluation, an unbiased opinion, regarding the accuracy of a company's financial statements. An accountant who meets educational requirements can be considered for a professional accreditation. The individual receiving this accreditation or certification is called a *certified internal auditor (CIA).*

Edmund L. Jenkins, chair of the Financial Accounting Standards Board, at the FASB meeting. According to its Web site, the mission of the FASB is to establish and improve standards of financial accounting and reporting for the guidance and education for the public, including issuers, auditors, and users of financial information. (See www.fasb.org/facts.)

private accountant

Accountant who works for a single firm, government agency, or nonprofit organization, on the payroll of the company or organization.

public accountant

Accountant who does not work for a specific company.

Financial Accounting Standards Board (FASB)

The group that oversees accounting practices.

generally accepted accounting principles (GAAP)

A set of principles followed by accountants in preparing reports.

Tax Accounting

Taxes are the price we pay for roads, parks, schools, police protection, the military, and other functions provided by government. Federal, state, and local governments require submission of taxes and forms filed at specific times and in a precise format. Of course, for personal taxes, the deadline to file is once per year, on April 15. Businesses, however, generally have to file and pay taxes on a quarterly basis, and the tax accountants ensure that company taxes are filed correctly.

A tax accountant is trained in tax law and is responsible for preparing tax returns or developing tax strategies to save the company money. Because governments often change tax policies according to specific needs or objectives, the job of the tax accountant is certainly challenging. Also, as the burden of taxes grows in the economy, the role of the tax accountant becomes increasingly important to the organization or entrepreneur.[5]

Government and Not-for-Profit Accounting

Government accounting and not-for-profit accounting meet the needs of organizations whose purpose is not generating a profit, but serving ratepayers, taxpayers, or others according to a duly approved budget. Governments (federal, state, and local) require an accounting system that satisfies the needs of their information users. The primary users of government accounting information are citizens, special interest groups, legislative bodies, and creditors. These users want to ensure that government is fulfilling its obligations and making the proper use of taxpayers' money. Governmental accounting standards are set by the **Governmental Accounting Standards Board (GASB).** There are various national, state, and local agencies that provide opportunities for accounting professionals. Some examples of government agencies are the Federal Bureau of Investigation, the Internal Revenue Service, state departments of natural resources, or county departments of revenue.

Not-for-profit organizations also require accounting professionals. In fact, not-for-profit organizations have a growing need for trained accountants because contributors to nonprofits want to see exactly how and where the funds they contribute are being spent. Charities, such as the United Way or the Red Cross, for example, state universities and colleges, hospitals,

Even charitable organizations such as the Red Cross need accounting employees. Robert P. McDonald serves as the CFO for the Red Cross. He ensures that bookkeeping and financial accounts for the organization are accurate and that funds are spent appropriately.

and labor unions all hire accountants to learn and account for how the funds they raise are being spent.

It is important to note that accounting is different from bookkeeping. **Bookkeeping** is simply the recording of business transactions; accounting goes much further. Accountants, rather than simply recording transactions, classify and summarize financial data according to formal standards and principles.

Accounting Tools

Just as construction workers require tools, accountants also have tools to make their job easier. One such tool is called a **journal,** which is basically a record book. The journal is almost always in electronic format. The journal is where the transactions are kept for each day, week, or month. For example, in a retail store the journal would include the data regarding all of the sales, as well as any new inventory that was received on a specific day. The main purpose of a journal is to have a chronological listing of the business transactions that take place.

Most accountants record financial transactions in two places to ensure the accuracy of the information being recorded. They can then check one list of transactions against the other to make sure the numbers add up in both places. The concept of recording every transaction in two places is called **double-entry bookkeeping.** In double-entry bookkeeping, two separate entries, one each in the journal and the *ledger,* are required for each company transaction. A **ledger** is a specialized accounting book or computer program in which information from accounting journals is recorded into specific categories.

The journal, in other words, does not provide information about the different accounts, but is a log of transactions as they happen. Then, the accountant transfers the information from the journal into the ledger.

For example, a manager might want to know how much money has been spent on supplies for the year. She would not likely go to the journal, because that consists of daily transactions, that are not sorted into categories. Instead, she would look at the ledger under the account "supplies." This type of system allows managers to easily find the data they need to make decisions. Today, computerized accounting programs post information from journals into ledgers daily, or instantaneously, which also makes the manager's job easier.

In the next section, we will discuss the *accounting cycle.* Keep in mind as you read that the goal of this chapter is to give you a basic understanding of accounting, and to remind you that understanding accounting will make you a better manager, employee, or entrepreneur! But first, we will briefly look at an important recent piece of federal legislation pertaining to accounting practices.

---

auditing

The job of reviewing and evaluating the records used to prepare a company's financial statements.

independent audit

An evaluation and unbiased opinion about the accuracy of a company's financial statements.

Governmental Accounting Standards Board (GASB)

This group sets standards for governmental agencies' accounting practices.

bookkeeping

The recording of business transactions.

journal

Record book in accounting (can also be a computer program).

double-entry bookkeeping

The concept of writing (or typing) every transaction in two places.

ledger

A specialized accounting book or computer program in which information from accounting journals is recorded into specific categories.

The Enron Fallout Fell Out Years Ago

Forget the fraud and conspiracy trial in federal court in Houston. The most important fallout from the collapse of Enron "fell out" many years ago.

It fell out with the 2002 passage of the Sarbanes-Oxley Act, a sweeping piece of federal legislation that changed the way companies must account for their business. It fell out into the trash, along with all those pensions and 401ks that Enron employees had been urged to buy into, and then hold, even when it should have been reasonably clear that the company was in trouble. It fell out with massive layoffs, the civil lawsuits that are still wending their way through the legal system, and the criminal appeals that surely will follow.

The convictions of former Enron chiefs Kenneth Lay (whose conviction was no longer necessary upon his death in 2006) and Jeffrey Skilling may be the final notable act in the grand drama of the company's rocket-rise and startling fall. But its results will not make a meaningful difference in the lives of anyone outside the relatively small circle of participants. The verdict alone will not put significant money back in anyone's pocket, or give the approximately 5,600 former Enron employees their jobs back, or force lawyers and accountants to honestly assess both the law and their clients' books. In Thomas Jefferson's words, it will neither pick your pocket nor break your leg. Lay and Skilling were convicted using federal laws that were around long before anyone knew who or what Enron was.

The great columnist Michael Kinsley once said that sometimes the true scandal is not what was done illegally, but what instead was permitted as a matter of law. Before the collapse of Enron, we now know, accounting rules were so malleable, and corporate oversight by regulators so lax, that any thoughtful and organized gang of corporate thieves could have accomplished what too many of Enron's officers and directors accomplished, before good journalism and market reality did them all in. Before the collapse of Enron, the rest of us had no idea how poorly our lawmakers were watching our captains of industry.

The disgrace wasn't that a bunch of crooks acted like crooks, but that our government, and our professional class of accountants and lawyers, permitted the crimes to take place, and in many ways implemented (or at least excused) the illegal activities. Government will never be able to legislate away greed, arrogance, and opportunism. But that doesn't mean it has to tolerate them, either. And before Enron, under both Republican and Democrat administrations, as the market soared and our portfolios expanded seemingly without end, too many blind eyes were cast from Washington toward Wall Street.

Enter Sarbanes-Oxley (not-so-affectionately known by those who live with it as "SOX"). By far the most important legacy of the corporate scandals of the 1990s, SOX passed as a direct result of the Enron implosion. It requires companies, large and small, to better track and then account for their financial condition. Executives must implement stringent internal protocols to help promote and ensure accounting accuracy and ethical conduct, and then, in many cases, open up the books to independent auditors who cannot have the conflicts-of-interest that marked the shamefully co-dependent relationship between Enron and the now-defunct Arthur Andersen accounting firm. The idea is to make it, if not impossible, then simply a lot harder for a group of executives to hijack a company and use dense "account-ese" to hide their crimes.

Questions

1. How has SOX affected the business environment? Explain.

2. Should the requirements from SOX be relaxed to "ease the pain" of the organizations and accountants? Why or why not?

Source: Andrew Cohen, *Washington Post*, May 26, 2006.

Sarbanes-Oxley Act
Signed into law in 2002 after many accounting scandals, the act requires higher standards of accounting practices and auditing firms.

Sarbanes-Oxley Act

We mentioned the **Sarbanes-Oxley Act** in the chapter on ethics, but it is extremely important to mention it again here in our discussion of accounting. As you probably remember, the Sarbanes-Oxley Act was signed into law in 2002 after many accounting scandals had rocked the United States. The act requires higher standards of accounting practices and auditing firms.

This act has critics on both sides. Some businesses feel that the standards are too stringent and hinder their ability to make business decisions.[6] Other businesses feel that this act has bogged down their company accountants to the point that they are unable to make effective financial decisions for the company. However, supporters of the act feel that it protects the American public from financial disasters—such as at Enron, World-Com, and the many others that occurred as a result of unethical and illegal accounting practices—and if anything, it does not go far enough.[7] See the nearby Thinking Critically box for more information on the Sarbanes-Oxley Act.

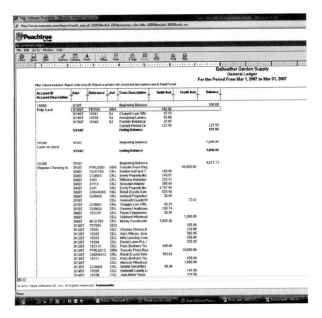

Peachtree is accounting software for small- to medium-size businesses. This is an example of what a general ledger looks like using this software program.

SELF-CHECK QUESTIONS

1. Define *accounting*.
2. What is the difference between managerial accounting and financial accounting?
3. Name and describe the five working areas of accounting.

THE SIX-STEP ACCOUNTING CYCLE

The accounting cycle is a six-step procedure that results in the preparation and analysis of the major financial statements. The accounting cycle generally involves the work of both the bookkeeper and the accountant.

The first three steps are the continual operations we discussed previously: (1) analyzing and categorizing documents, (2) putting the information into journals, and (3) posting that information into ledgers, and (4) preparing a *trial balance*. A **trial balance** is a summary of all the financial data in the account ledgers. It is used to check whether the figures are correct and balanced, much the same way that you balance your checkbook and compare it to your bank statement.

trial balance

A summary of all the financial data in the account ledgers to check whether the figures are correct and balanced.

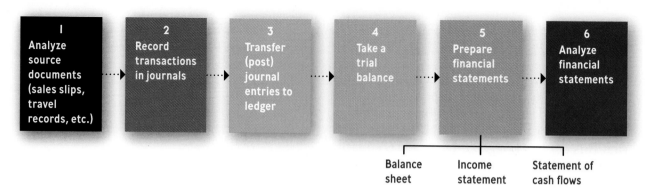

| Balance sheet | Income statement | Statement of cash flows |

figure 12.1

THE STEPS IN THE ACCOUNTING CYCLE

If the information in the account ledgers is not accurate, it must be corrected before the firm's financial statements are prepared and analyzed in the final two steps: (5) preparing the financial statements, including a *balance sheet, income statement,* and *statement of cash flows,* and (6) analyzing the financial statements and evaluating the overall financial condition of the firm. As you can imagine, computers and accounting software have simplified this process considerably.

Keep in mind that the financial statements are a result of the ongoing work of bookkeepers and managerial accountants, and their recording of daily transactions. In the following section of the chapter we discuss preparation of the financial statements.

FINANCIAL STATEMENTS

A **financial statement** is a summary of all the transactions (for example, all expenses and revenues) that have occurred over a particular period. Financial statements indicate a firm's financial health and stability, which is why stockholders (the owners of the firm); bondholders and banks (people and institutions that lend money to the firm); labor unions; employees; and the Internal Revenue Service are all interested in a firm's financial statements.[8] The following are the key financial statements of a business:

financial statement
A summary of all the transactions that have occurred over a particular period.

1. The *balance sheet,* which reports the firm's financial condition on a specific date.

2. The *income statement (sometimes called a profit and loss statement, or "P & L" for short),* which summarizes revenues, cost of goods, and expenses (including taxes), for a specific period of time and highlights the total profit or loss the firm experienced during that period.

3. The *statement of cash flows,* which provides a summary of money coming into, and going out of, the firm and tracks a company's cash receipts and cash payments.

The differences among the financial statements can be summarized this way:

- The *balance sheet* details what the company owns and owes on a certain day.
- The *income statement* shows what a firm sells its products for and what its selling costs are over a specific period.
- The *statement of cash flows* highlights the difference between cash coming into, and cash going out of, a business.

To fully understand important financial information, you must be able to understand the purpose of an organization's financial statements. Let's now explore each statement in more detail.

q: Do you think there might be value in using a company's

»» financial statements to determine if you want to work for that company? Why or why not?

The Accounting Equation

Suppose your company does not owe money to any financial institution (banks, credit card companies, etc). If the company does not owe money, you could say that it has no debt (also called *liabilities*). In this scenario, the company also has assets, which include equipment, cash, and property, and these assets are items for which your company does not owe money. The sum of the value of the assets is your equity. In other words, your assets include anything that your company owns. If your company was to borrow money, it would incur a liability. Your assets are now equal to what you *owe* plus what you own.

Translated into accounting terms:

Assets = Liabilities + Owner's equity

In other words, owner's equity is a way of stating the difference between what is owned versus what is owed. Let's use a specific example to illustrate this point. Assume a person owns a car worth $10,000, but still owes $4,000 on it. The accounting equation would look like this:

Car (assets) = What is owed on the car
+ Owner's equity

or

$10,000 = $4,000 + $6,000

As you can see, owner's equity and liabilities will always be the same number as assets. This formula is called the *fundamental accounting equation*.

Let us assume that the $10,000 car is completely paid off; in other words, you do not owe any more money on it. The equation in this situation would be:

$$\$10,000 = 0 + \$10,000$$

This fundamental equation is the crucial part of the *balance sheet*, which we will cover next.

The Balance Sheet

balance sheet
The financial statement that reports a firm's financial condition at a specific time.

A **balance sheet** is the financial statement that reports a firm's financial condition at a specific time. It is comprised of three major accounts: *assets, liabilities,* and *owner's equity*.[9] The balance sheet gets its name because it shows a balance between two figures: the company's assets on the one hand, and its liabilities plus owner's equity on the other, as we just discussed.

Suppose that you want to know what your financial condition is at a given time. Maybe you want to buy a new house or car; therefore, you need to calculate your available resources. One of the best measuring sticks is your balance sheet. First, add up everything you own—cash, property, money owed you, and so forth (assets). Then subtract from that the money you owe others—credit card debt, IOUs, current car loan, student loans, and so forth (liabilities). The sum equals your net worth, which is the basic principle used for balance sheets.

A balance sheet can help in your personal life, and it can also help you as a manager. For example, as an entrepreneur, you can calculate how much money you owe, how much money you expect to come in, and the value of the business, or owner's equity. This valuable information can help you if you are trying to get a loan, considering growing your business, or considering how much to spend on new inventory or marketing. Again, understanding the balance sheet provides you with an overall picture of your company's financial health, which allows you to make better management decisions.

assets
Economic resources (things of value) owned by a firm.

liquidity
Refers to how fast an asset can be converted into cash.

account receivable
An amount of money owed to the firm that it expects to be paid within one year.

Assets

Assets are economic resources (things of value) owned by a firm. Assets include productive, tangible items (e.g., equipment, buildings, land, furniture, fixtures, and motor vehicles) that help generate income, as well as intangibles with value (e.g., patents, trademarks, copyrights, goodwill, brand names). Think, for example, of the value of brand names, such as Coca-Cola, McDonald's, and Intel. If you were to open an independent fast-food restaurant selling burgers and fries, it may cost you between $40,000 and $50,000 depending on the size of the store, location, and so forth. However, can you imagine what it would cost to open a McDonald's franchise? It is well over $500,000.[10] Why would anyone pay more than 10 times for a McDonald's than what it may cost to open an independent fast-food restaurant? It is the McDonald's goodwill and brand name that brings customers and generates sales. Brand names can be among the firm's most valuable assets.[11]

Liquidity refers to how fast an asset can be converted into cash. For example, an **accounts receivable** is the amount of money owed to the firm that it expects to receive within one year. Accounts receivable are considered liquid assets. Land, however, is not very liquid because it takes time to sell, fill out paperwork, complete legal proceedings, and so on. Thus, assets are divided into three categories according to how quickly they can be turned into cash (see Figure 12.2):

1. *Current assets* are items that can or will be converted into cash within one year. Current assets include cash, accounts receivable, and inventory.
2. *Fixed assets* are long-term assets that are relatively permanent, such as land, buildings, and equipment. These assets are also referred to on the balance sheet as *property, plant, and equipment.*

A company can have many types of assets, including land/buildings (fixed assets), inventory and accounts receivable (current assets), and copyrights and trademarks (intangible assets).

Current assets

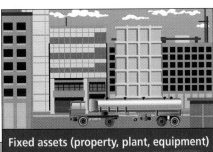

Fixed assets (property, plant, equipment)

Copyright

Intangible assets

figure 12.2

CLASSIFICATIONS OF ASSETS

Assets are classified by how quickly they can be turned into cash (liquidity). The most liquid are called *current assets.* Those that are hard to sell quickly are called *fixed assets* or *property, plant,* and *equipment. Intangible assets* include patents and copyrights.

3. *Intangible assets* are long-term assets that have no real physical form, but do have value. Patents, trademarks, copyrights, and goodwill are examples of intangible assets.

Liabilities

liabilities

What the business owes to others (debts).

Another important accounting term is *liabilities*. **Liabilities** are what the business owes to others (debts). *Current liabilities* are debts due in one year or less; *long-term liabilities* are debts not due for one year or longer. The following are common *liability accounts* recorded on a balance sheet:

1. *Accounts payable* are current liabilities involving money owed to others for merchandise or services purchased on credit, but not yet paid. If you have a bill you haven't paid, you have an account payable.

2. *Notes payable* are short-term or long-term liabilities (e.g., loans from banks) that a business promises to repay by a certain date.

3. *Bonds payable* are long-term liabilities that represent money lent to the firm that must be paid back. If a firm sells someone a bond, it agrees to repay that person the money he or she lent the company, plus interest.

owners' equity

The amount of the business that belongs to the owners minus any liabilities owed by the business.

Your assets minus the amount of money you owe others (liabilities) is called *equity*. The value of what stockholders own in a firm (minus liabilities) is called *stockholders' equity* (or *shareholders' equity*).[12] Because stockholders are the owners of a firm, stockholders' equity can also be called owners' equity. As we discussed earlier, **owners' equity** is the amount of the business that belongs to the owners, minus any liabilities owed by the business. The formula for owners' equity, then, is assets minus liabilities.

Assume you are considering the purchase of a business. The balance sheet is useful because it tells the potential buyer all of the assets the company has, and also what it owes. If a business, for example, had more debt than assets, a person might want to reconsider purchasing that business. For an investor, this financial information is not only useful information, but also extremely important.

The Income Statement

income statement

The income statement summarizes all of the resources (called *revenue*) that have come into the firm from operating activities, the money resources that were used up, the expenses incurred in doing business, and what resources were left after all costs and expenses, including taxes, were paid out.

The financial statement that shows a firm's bottom line—that is, its profit after costs, expenses, and taxes—is the **income statement** (also called the *profit and loss statement*). The income statement summarizes all of the resources (called *revenue*) that have come into the firm from operating activities, the money resources that were used up, the expenses incurred in doing business, and what resources were left after all

VERY VEGETARIAN
Balance Sheet
December 31, 2007

Assets

① Current assets

Cash	$ 15,000	
Accounts receivable	200,000	
Notes receivable	50,000	
Inventory	335,000	
Total current assets		$600,000

② Fixed assets

Land		$ 40,000	
Building and improvements	$200,000		
Less: Accumulated depreciation	−90,000		
		110,000	
Equipment and vehicles	$120,000		
Less: Accumulated depreciation	−80,000		
		40,000	
Furniture and fixtures	$ 26,000		
Less: Accumulated depreciation	−10,000		
		16,000	
Total fixed assets			206,000

③ Intangible assets

Goodwill	$ 20,000	
Total intangible assets		20,000
Total assets		**$826,000**

Liabilities and Owners' Equity

④ Current liabilities

Accounts payable	$ 40,000	
Notes payable (due June 2008)	8,000	
Accrued taxes	150,000	
Accrued salaries	90,000	
Total current liabilities		$288,000

⑤ Long-term liabilities

Notes payable (due Mar. 2012)	$ 35,000	
Bonds payable (due Dec. 2017)	290,000	
Total long-term liabilities		325,000
Total liabilities		$613,000

⑥ Owners' equity

Common stock (1,000,000 shares)	$100,000	
Retained earnings	113,000	
Total owners' equity		213,000
Total liabilities & owners' equity		**$826,000**

figure 12.3

SAMPLE VERY VEGETARIAN BALANCE SHEET

① Current assets are those items that can be converted into cash within one year.

② Fixed assets are those things such as land or buildings that are permanent.

③ Intangible assets are items of value, like copyrights that don't have a physical form.

④ Current liabilities are payments that are due within one year.

⑤ Long-term liabilities are payments not due for one year or longer.

⑥ Owners' equity is the value of what stockholders own in a firm (also called stockholders' equity).

figure 12.4

SAMPLE VERY VEGETARIAN INCOME STATEMENT

① Revenue is the value of what is received from goods sold, services rendered, and other financial sources.

② Cost of goods sold is the cost of merchandise sold (in retail) or the cost of raw materials or parts used in manufacturing an item.

③ Gross profit is how much the firm earned by selling or buying merchandise.

④ Operating expenses are those expenses incurred while running the business.

⑤ Net income after taxes is the profit or loss over a specific period of time, after subtracting all costs and expenses, including taxes.

VERY VEGETARIAN
Income Statement
For the Year Ended December 31, 2007

① **Revenues**			
Gross sales		$720,000	
Less: Sales returns and allowances	$ 12,000		
Sales discounts	8,000	−20,000	
Net sales			$700,000
② **Cost of goods sold**			
Beginning inventory, Jan. 1		$200,000	
Merchandise purchases	$400,000		
Freight	40,000		
Net purchases		440,000	
Cost of goods available for sale	$640,000		
Less ending inventory, Dec. 31		−230,000	
Cost of goods sold			−410,000
③ **Gross profit**			$290,000
④ **Operating expenses**			
Selling expenses			
Salaries for salespeople	$ 90,000		
Advertising	18,000		
Supplies	2,000		
Total selling expenses		$110,000	
General expenses			
Office salaries	$ 67,000		
Depreciation	1,500		
Insurance	1,500		
Rent	28,000		
Light, heat, and power	12,000		
Miscellaneous	2,000		
		112,000	
Total operating expenses			222,000
Net income before taxes			$ 68,000
Less: Income tax expense			19,000
⑤ **Net income after taxes**			$ 49,000

costs and expenses, including taxes, were paid out (see Figure 12.4). The resources (revenue) left over are referred to as *net income* or *net loss*.

The income statement reports the firm's financial operations over a particular period of time, usually a year, a quarter of a year, or a month.[13]

It is the financial statement that reveals whether the business is actually earning a profit or losing money. The formulas used to prepare an income statement are as follows:

Revenue − Cost of goods sold = Gross profit (also called gross margin)

Gross profit − Operating expenses = Net income before taxes

Net income before taxes − Taxes = Net income (or loss)

The income statement includes valuable financial information for stockholders, lenders, investors (or potential investors), suppliers, competitors, and employees. Because this report is so important to businesses, we will define each of the components included in a profit and loss (income) statement. For the remainder of this chapter, all financial information will be based on a company called Very Vegetarian, our fictional retail store.

Revenue

Revenue is the value of what is received from goods sold, services rendered, and other financial sources. Note that there is a difference between revenue and sales. Most revenue (money coming into the firm) comes from sales, but there could be other sources of revenue. For example, a company could earn money by renting a portion of its building to a tenant.

Gross sales are the total of all sales the firm completed. **Net sales** are gross sales minus returns, discounts, and allowances. Returns are merchandise customers send back, discounts are price reductions given to customers, and allowances are any additional costs associated with a specific sale.

Cost of Goods Sold (Cost of Goods Manufactured)

The **cost of goods sold (cost of goods manufactured)** is a measure of the cost of merchandise sold, or the cost of the raw materials and supplies used for producing items for sale. So, cost of merchandise sold (for manufacturing) is calculated by determining how much a business earned by selling merchandise over the period being evaluated compared to how much it spent to buy the merchandise. The cost of goods sold includes the raw materials, plus any freight charges paid to transport goods, plus any costs associated with storing the goods. In other words, all the costs of buying and keeping merchandise for sale are included in the cost of goods sold.

Retail is a bit different than manufacturing when calculating cost of goods sold. Remember, most retailers do not buy directly from the manufacturers; they use wholesalers. As a result, retailers do not have to worry about the cost of raw materials, since this cost is already included in the purchase price. As a result, their main concern is purchase price and the storage cost. See the example in Figure 12.5.

revenue
The value of what is received from goods sold, services rendered, and other financial sources.

gross sales
Total of all sales the firm completed.

net sales
Gross sales minus returns, discounts, and allowances.

cost of goods sold (cost of goods manufactured)
A measure of the cost of merchandise sold, or the cost of the raw materials and supplies used for producing items for sale.

figure 12.5

EXAMPLE OF COST OF GOODS SOLD FOR A RETAIL STORE

These are some of the possible costs for a gallon of milk to a retail store:

Purchase price from wholesaler: $2.10

Freight/Cold storage: $0.10

Total cost to supermarket: $2.20

Total selling price: $2.99

Subtract the two: $0.79 would be the gross margin

Milk

gross profit (gross margin)

How much a firm earned by buying (or making) and selling merchandise, without expenses.

When you subtract the cost of goods sold from net sales, the result is called gross profit or gross margin. **Gross profit (gross margin)** is how much a firm earned by buying (or making) and selling merchandise. Understanding this concept is important because as a manager or employee, you can evaluate how much your firm is spending to make the goods, and you can also evaluate how much you earned on the goods, not including the expenses to sell them. However, the gross profit does not tell you everything you need to know about the financial performance of the firm. The income statement also needs to determine the *net* profit or loss a firm experienced. To find out the net profit or loss, you must subtract the business's expenses.

Operating Expenses and Net Profit or Loss

operating expenses

The costs involved in operating a business.

In the process of selling goods or services, a business experiences certain expenses. **Operating expenses** are the costs involved in operating a business, such as rent, salaries, supplies, utilities, insurance, and even depreciation of equipment (we will look at depreciation a little later). Expenses can generally be classified into two categories: selling and general expenses. *Selling expenses* are expenses related to the marketing and distribution of the firm's goods or services, such as salaries for salespeople, advertising, and supplies. *General expenses* are the administrative expenses of the firm, such as office salaries, depreciation, insurance, and rent. Accountants are trained to help businesses record all applicable expenses and find other relevant expenses they need to deduct. There are also nonoperating expenses, such as interest. If a company purchases land and pays 6 percent a year interest on the loan, this interest would be considered a nonoperating expense.

After all expenses are deducted, the firm's *net income before taxes* is determined. Net income is also referred to as *net earnings* or *net profit*. Although you may not realize it, you use income statements all the time in your personal life. For example, if you are preparing a household budget, you must know what your expenses are, such as rent, telephone, and cable TV. You obviously do not want your expenses to be greater than your income—it would mean you are spending too much.

The same is true for companies. A net income statement reveals if the company is spending too much for certain expenses. If so, stockholders may not want to invest in the company, or the business owners may want to consider changing spending habits.[14] On the other hand, if a company is not spending enough in selling expenses, such as marketing, it could mean that it is missing out on selling to potential customers.

Sometimes lack of sales, or too many expenses, can result in cash flow problems. *Cash flow* is the amount of money coming in and going out. Have you ever run out of money a few days before you were to receive your paycheck? *Cash flow statements* help companies prevent this situation from happening.

The Statement of Cash Flows

The **statement of cash flows** reports cash receipts and disbursements (or money going out of the firm) related to the three major activities of a firm:

- *Operations:* cash transactions associated with running the business.
- *Investments:* cash used in, or provided by, the firm's investment activities.
- *Financing:* cash raised from the issuance of debt, such as taking out a loan

Accountants analyze all of the cash changes and financial transactions that have occurred from operating, investing, and financing the firm's activities and that appear in the statement of cash flows to determine the firm's net cash position. Among other things, the statement of cash flows gives the firm some insight into how to handle cash better, so that no cash flow problems (e.g., having no cash on hand) occur.

The statement of cash flows (see Figure 12.6) may simply seem like a repeat of the income statement, but it is actually quite different because the statement of cash flows shows a cash position—that is, how much money is on hand at any given time. Companies do not want to have too much money on hand, yet they need to have enough to pay their expenses, which is where the statement comes in handy. Although yearly cash flow statements are most common, a cash flow statement can be done on a weekly or monthly basis as well.

> **statement of cash flows**
>
> Reports cash receipts and disbursements related to the three major activities of a firm.

Cash flow is the difference between money coming in and money going out of a business. Careful cash flow management is a must for all businesses, such as a ski resort, for instance. Can you think of a key reason why cash flow is important for a ski resort?

figure 12.6

SAMPLE VERY VEGETARIAN STATEMENT OF CASH FLOWS

① Cash receipts from sales, commissions, fees, interest, and dividends. Cash payments for salaries, inventories, operating expenses, interest, and taxes.

② Includes cash flows that are generated through a company's purchase or sale of long-term operational assets, investments in other companies, and lending activities.

③ Cash outflows and inflows associated with the company's equity transactions or borrowing activities.

VERY VEGETARIAN
Statement of Cash Flows
For the Year Ended December 31, 2007

① Cash flows from operating activities		
Cash received from customers	$150,000	
Cash paid to suppliers and employees	(90,000)	
Interest paid	(5,000)	
Income tax paid	(4,500)	
Interest and dividends received	1,500	
Net cash provided by operating activities		$52,000
② Cash flows from investing activities		
Proceeds from sale of plant assets	$ 4,000	
Payments for purchase of equipment	(10,000)	
Net cash provided by investing activities		(6,000)
③ Cash flows from financing activities		
Proceeds from issuance of short-term debt	$ 3,000	
Payment of long-term debt	(7,000)	
Payment of dividends	(15,000)	
Net cash inflow from financing activities		(19,000)
Net change in cash and equivalents		$27,000
Cash balance (beginning of year)		(2,000)
Cash balance (end of year)		$25,000

Regular review of the cash flow statements allows the business owner to be assured he or she will have enough cash on hand to pay employees, and for other immediate needs.[15]

q : In what way might you use a statement of cash flows
» » for your personal finances?

To discuss cash flow on a personal level, let's say you borrow $100 from a friend to buy a used bike and agree to pay back your friend at the end of the week. You then sell the bike to someone else for $150, who also agrees to pay you in a week. Unfortunately, at the end of the week

Create a Career Plan

By now, all the improved work habits you have practiced and skill development you have achieved have you ready for successfully establishing your career objectives. However, to ensure all this work will pay off in the short and long term, you need to carefully and consciously create a career plan.

The process of "setting the bar for success" can be powerful for your career. Career plans can be lengthy or brief, but to begin the career plan process, ask yourself three basic questions:

- What are the career goals you would like to set for yourself?

- When would you like to achieve these goals?
- What obstacles exist that might keep you from reaching these goals?

These are powerful questions. They deserve careful thought. If you can answer these three questions with sincere, well-thought-out answers, you are well on your way to establishing a career plan that can enhance your career goals and objectives early on in your career!

---

the person who bought the bike from you does not have the money, as promised. This person says that he will have to pay you next month. Meanwhile, your friend wants the $100 you agreed to pay her by the end of the week! What seemed like a great opportunity to make an easy $50 profit is not so easy because you owe $100 and have no cash.

What do you do when your friend shows up at the end of the week and demands to be paid? If you were a business, this might cause you to default on the loan and possibly go bankrupt, even though you had the potential for profits. As you can see, it is very possible that a business can increase sales and increase profit, and still suffer greatly from cash flow problems.

A Word about Depreciation

Before we move on, there is one last accounting term we should define—*depreciation*. **Depreciation** is the systematic write-off of the cost of a tangible asset over its estimated useful life. Have you ever heard the comment that a new car depreciates in market value as soon as you drive it off the dealer's lot? The same principle holds true for equipment and other specific assets of the firm that are considered depreciable, such as machinery and computers. Companies are permitted to recapture the cost of these assets over time, using depreciation as an operating expense of the business. There are several ways depreciation can be calculated, but we won't go into that in this book—we will save that for an accounting class.

> **depreciation**
> The systematic write-off of the cost of a tangible asset over its estimated useful life.

ETHICAL challenge

The Accounting Hot Seat

Suppose you are the accountant for a small cabinet building shop, and it is the end of January. Your manager, who is also the owner of the business, is in the process of trying to get a loan from the bank. The owner must show financial statements from the previous year. The company had several thousand dollars in sales in January, and the owner wants you to include those sales in the previous year's accounting records. You are worried, because you don't want to upset your boss, but you also want to do what is right.

Questions

1. Is this an ethical dilemma or a basic legal dilemma? Why?
2. Explain how you would handle this situation.

Now that we have gone over the basic accounting statements, in the next section we will talk about how to analyze the financial position of a company.

SELF-CHECK QUESTIONS

1. What does an income statement show? What about a statement of cash flow? What does the balance sheet show?
2. How are these statements useful for small businesses?
3. What is the accounting equation?
4. What is depreciation?

Section Outline

Analyzing Financial Statements: Ratio Analysis

- Liquidity Ratios
- Leverage (Debt) Ratios
- Profitability (Performance) Ratios
- Activity Ratios

ANALYZING FINANCIAL STATEMENTS: RATIO ANALYSIS

Accurate information from the firm's financial statements is the basis of the financial analysis performed by accountants, both inside and outside the firm. Accountants and financial people perform calculations as part of their analysis. These calculations are called ratios. Keep in mind that accountants are not the only individuals who use these ratios. People considering investing in a company can view a company's annual report, perform the calculations, and then decide if they think the company is a good investment. Likewise, people who are considering buying a business would also find financial ratios valuable in order to evaluate whether the purchase is a sound investment or not.

Ratio analysis is the assessment of a firm's financial condition and performance through calculations and interpretation of financial ratios developed from the firm's financial statements. We will perform ratios for the company Very Vegetarian, since we saw its financial statements earlier in this chapter in Figures 12.3, 12.4, and 12.6.

At first glance, ratio analysis may seem complicated. The fact is most of us already use ratios, and often. For example, in basketball, the number of shots made from the foul line is expressed by a ratio: shots made to shots attempted. A player who shoots 85 percent from the foul line is considered an outstanding foul shooter, and the idea is not to foul him or her in a close game.

Whether ratios measure an athlete's performance or the financial health of a business, they provide a good deal of valuable information. Financial ratios provide key insights into how a firm compares to other firms in its industry in the important areas of liquidity (speed of changing assets into cash), debt (leverage), profitability, and business activity.[16] Let's look briefly at four key types of ratios businesses use to measure financial performance.

> **ratio analysis**
> The assessment of a firm's financial condition and performance through calculations and interpretation of financial ratios developed from the firm's financial statements.

Liquidity Ratios

As explained earlier, the word *liquidity* refers to how fast an asset can be converted to cash in order to pay a company's short-term debts (liabilities that must be repaid within one year).[17] These short-term debts are of particular importance to creditors of the firm, who expect to be paid on time. Two key liquidity ratios are the current ratio and the acid-test ratio.

The *current ratio* is the ratio of a firm's current assets to its current liabilities. This information can be found on the firm's balance sheet. Look back at Figure 12.3, the sample balance sheet for Very Vegetarian. Very Vegetarian lists current assets of $600,000 and current liabilities of $288,000. The firm therefore has a current ratio of 2.08, which means Very Vegetarian has $2.08 of current assets for every $1.00 of current liabilities. The current ratio was calculated by:

$$\text{Current ratio} = \frac{\text{Current assets}}{\text{Current liabilities}}$$

$$= \frac{\$600,000}{\$288,000} = \$2.08$$

Generally, a number higher than two means a company is a safe risk for granting a short-term loan because of the quantity of assets. If the number is lower than two, it is likely the business has few assets and a significant amount of debt. Another way to determine what the current ratio means is by comparing the current ratio of a firm with industry norms.

Another key liquidity ratio, called the *acid-test* or *quick ratio*, measures the cash, marketable securities (such as stocks and bonds), and receivables of a firm, compared to its current liabilities. This ratio is particularly important to firms having difficulty converting inventory into quick cash. It helps answer such questions as: What if sales drop off and we can't sell our inventory? Can we still pay our short-term debt? To answer these questions, the calculation would consist of the following:

$$\text{Acid-test ratio} = \frac{\text{Cash} + \text{Accounts receivable} + \text{Marketable securities}}{\text{Current liabilities}}$$

Looking at our balance sheet for Very Vegetarian once again, the numbers would look like this:

$$\frac{\$265,000}{\$288,000} = \$0.92$$

A number between 0.50 and 1.0 is usually considered satisfactory, but a ratio under 1.0 could also be a hint of cash flow problems. Because the calculation is based on all of the money coming in versus what is owed, a higher number would indicate the company owes uncomfortably more than the cash it has flowing into the company. Therefore, Very Vegetarian's acid-test ratio of 0.92 could raise concerns that perhaps the firm may not meet its short-term debt and may therefore have to go to a high-cost lender for financial assistance.

Leverage (Debt) Ratios

Leverage (debt) ratios measure the degree to which a firm relies on borrowed funds in its operations. A firm that takes on too much debt could experience problems repaying lenders or meeting promises made to stockholders. The *debt to owners' equity ratio* measures the degree to which the company is financed by borrowed funds that must be repaid. Again, we can use Figure 12.3 to measure Very Vegetarian's level of debt:

The calculation here would be:

$$\text{Debt to owners' equity ratio} = \frac{\text{Total liabilities}}{\text{Owners' equity}} = \frac{\$613,000}{\$213,000} = 287\%$$

Anything above 100 percent shows that a firm has more debt than equity. With a ratio of 287 percent, Very Vegetarian has a rather high level of debt compared to its equity, which implies that the firm may be quite risky to lenders and investors. However, it is always important to compare a firm's debt ratios to those of other firms in its industry (see Figure 12.7), because financing operations with debt is more acceptable in some industries than it is in others. Comparisons with past debt ratios can also identify trends that may be occurring within the firm or industry.

One way to determine how to use ratios is to determine the standard for the industry. The Web site www.bizstats.com compiles industry data from annual reports, trade associations, and the Internal Revenue Service and averages the information based on the type of ownership. It even provides information such as average executive compensation for that industry and operating expenses, such as salaries and supplies. The data listed here are for corporations for the first half of 2007:

figure 12.7

INDUSTRY RATIO AVERAGES

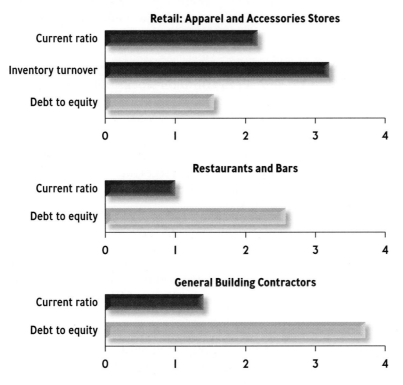

So, as a business owner, what does this mean to you? Researching and comparing ratio averages of companies in the same industry can help you set benchmarks and compare how well you are doing with other firms.

Profitability (Performance) Ratios

Profitability (performance) ratios measure how effectively a firm is using its various resources to achieve profits. Management's performance is often measured by these ratios. Three of the more important ratios are earnings per share, return on sales, and return on equity.

The *basic earnings per share (basic EPS) ratio* helps determine the amount of profit earned by a company for each share of outstanding common stock (stock sold on the stock market; we will discuss this concept further in the next chapter).

Earnings per Share

The *diluted earnings per share (diluted EPS) ratio* measures the amount of profit earned by a company for each share of outstanding common stock, but this ratio also takes into consideration stock options, warrants, preferred stock, and convertible debt securities, which can be converted into common stock. For simplicity's sake, we will compute only the basic earnings per share (EPS).[18]

EPS is a very important ratio for a company, because earnings help stimulate growth in the firm and pay for such things as stockholders' dividends. Continued earnings growth is well received by both investors and lenders. The basic EPS ratio calculated for Very Vegetarian is as follows:

$$\text{EPS} = \frac{\text{Net income after taxes}}{\text{Number of common stocks outstanding}}$$
$$= \frac{\$49,000}{\$1,000,000} = \$0.049 \text{ per share}$$

This number is useful for investors, as well as anyone who is considering the purchase of a business. A larger number would mean the company either has high net income after taxes, which is good, or it does not have much outstanding stock.

Return on Sales (Net Profit Margin)

Another reliable indicator of performance is obtained by using a ratio that measures the return on sales based on how much profit a company earns for every dollar it generates in revenue.[19] The formula for return on sales is:

$$\text{Return on sales} = \frac{\text{Net income}}{\text{Net sales}} = \frac{\$49,000}{\$700,000} = 0.07 \text{ or } 7\%$$

This figure is an indicator of the company's ability to generate income from sales. It is important to compare the net profit margin number to the industry average, as margins for grocery stores can be very low, while profits for other types of retail goods can be high.

Return on Equity

Risk is a market variable that concerns investors. The higher the risk involved in an industry, the higher the return investors expect on their investment. Therefore, the level of risk involved in an industry and the return on investment of competing firms is important in comparing the firm's performance.

Return on equity measures how much was earned for each dollar invested by owners. It shows how well a company manages the money invested in the company. The calculation is:

$$\text{Return on equity} = \frac{\text{Net income after tax}}{\text{Total owners' equity}} = \frac{\$49,000}{\$213,000} = 23\%$$

A figure of 23 percent means the company gets 23 percent back on each dollar it invests into the business. Similar to the return on sales ratio, it is best to compare this ratio with other firms in the same industry.

Activity Ratios

The last type of ratio we will discuss explores how well a company converts its resources to profits. The *inventory turnover ratio*[20] measures the speed of inventory moving through the firm and its conversion into sales. Inventory sitting by idly in a business costs money. Think of the cost to store inventory in a warehouse, as opposed to the revenue that can be earned when the merchandise is sold.

The more efficiently a firm manages its inventory, the higher the return. The inventory turnover ratio for Very Vegetarian is measured as follows:

$$\text{Inventory turnover} = \frac{\text{Cost of goods sold}}{\text{Average inventory}}$$

$$\frac{\$410,000}{\$215,000} = 1.9 \text{ times}$$

An acceptable turnover ratio is usually determined industry by industry. In most retail firms, a turnover of 4 would be acceptable, which means that the entire inventory in a company is sold four times per year. A lower number could mean the company is trying to sell obsolete merchandise, or poor buying practices on the part of the organization.

Home Depot stocks over 40,000 items. Imagine managing that entire inventory. Poor inventory turnover results in old merchandise and implies poor buying decisions. What tools are necessary to keep track of incoming and outgoing inventory?

spotlight

So, You Want to Be . . . an Accounting Professional

As you have learned from this chapter, there are several types of accounting in which you can be involved. What is important is that you choose the area that holds the most interest for you.

A relatively new accounting field, called *forensic accounting,* entails investigating possible securities fraud, contract disputes, and other complex and possibly criminal financial transactions, such as money laundering, or the kinds of problematic accounting involved in the Enron debacle. Forensic accountants have an accounting background, but also have experience in law.

Similar to jobs in information systems, accounting is expected to grow faster than most industries, through the year 2014. This is great news for those of you who may choose accounting as a future career!

A 2005 salary survey conducted by Robert Half International[21] (a staffing services firm specializing in accounting and finance) concluded that accountants and auditors with less than a year of experience earned between $28,250 and $45,000 a year. Those with 1 to 3 years of experience earned between $33,000 and $52,000. Senior accountants and auditors earned between $40,750 and $69,750, managers between $48,000 and $90,000, and directors of accounting and auditing between $64,750 and $200,750. As with our discussions of salary in all the Career Spotlight boxes in previous chapters in the book, the variation in salaries reflects differences in size of firm, location, level of education, and professional credentials.

If you want to succeed in business, you need to know about accounting. It is almost impossible to run any size business or understand business operations without being able to read, understand, and analyze accounting reports and financial statements. Accounting reports and financial statements reveal as much about a business's health as pulse rate and blood pressure readings tell us about a person's health.

---

figure 12.8

PUTTING TOGETHER RATIO ANALYSES

In groups, analyze the following ratios, keeping in mind industry averages might be useful information to have if you were in a situation where you had to make these decisions.

John Miller asked his accountant candidate to sit down with him and explain some basic accounting concepts, so he could better understand his financial information for his new store. The accountant, Ashley, explained that she was a certified public accountant, which is different from a private accountant or an auditor. The difference is that she works on several different companies' books at any given time and does not work for any one company. In order to do her job, Ashley had to take exams and pass a test to become a CPA.

Ashley then explained the process she would go through if John hired her to keep his books. First, she would look at all of the transactions for the month. Then, she would record every transaction in a journal. Next, she would use an accounting software program to post those transactions to the ledger (usually in a Microsoft Excel file which records both in the ledger and the journal at the same time), making sure the journal and ledger match. Assuming they did match, she would then prepare a balance sheet, income statement, and statement of cash flows for John's candle business to see how healthy it was. John asked Ashley if she could go over the basics of financial statements, because it had been awhile since he had taken accounting.

She explained that the balance sheet looks at the owner's equity, assets, and debts. The income statement looks at sales and expenses, and then provides a net income figure. Finally, the cash flow statement shows John's cash position during the month.

John asked her, "So what does all this mean to my business?" Ashley replied that John could use those statements to calculate some meaningful information using financial ratios. He could use the information derived from these calculations to see how liquid his business happens to be, and determine how much debt the store has, compared with its assets. He could also see the business profitability and compare it to other stores similar to his. Finally, he could use the activity ratios to determine how quickly turnover occurs at his store. John was especially interested in this number, since his store was a retail store.

John decides to hire Ashley because of her ability, but also because of the customer service she has provided him by explaining her processes to him. John feels confident that with this sort of review, he will be able to analyze his financial statements and even learn to perform some of the ratio calculations himself.

Accountants and other finance professionals use several other specific ratios, in addition to the ones we have briefly discussed here, to learn more about a firm's financial condition. As you continue in your studies and career, you will become familiar with more of them. These ratios can be very useful to business owners, business buyers, and investors. Review Figure 12.8 to try your hand at ratio analysis for two companies.

SELF-CHECK QUESTIONS

1. What is the current ratio used for?
2. What does debt to owners' equity tell us?
3. What is the major benefit of performing a ratio analysis using the financial statements?

summary

This chapter introduced you to the basics of accounting, including basic types of accountants: managerial, financial, auditors, tax accountants, government and not-for-profit, private, and public. Several tools of the accountant were described: journal, double-entry bookkeeping, and ledger. The Financial Accounting Standards Board (FASB) oversees the accounting industry and prescribes the basic principles of the accounting profession, known as generally accepted accounting principles or GAAP.

The Enron scandal and other financial scandals at the turn of the new century resulted in Congress's passing of the Sarbanes-Oxley Act, which prescribes stricter new regulations for the accounting profession and internal accounting procedures in businesses.

The steps of the accounting process were described. First, documents such as sales slips are analyzed. Then, any transaction that occurs within the business is recorded in a journal and in a ledger, called double-entry accounting. Next, a trial balance makes sure the journal and the ledger match up. At that point, financial statements are prepared and analyzed.

The chapter presented a basic discussion of the major financial statements: the balance sheet, the income statement, and the statement of cash flows. The financial statements of a company give a picture of its financial health that is of interest to all stakeholders in the business. The balance sheet reports a firm's financial condition at a specific time and is composed of three major accounts: assets, liabilities, and owner's equity. The income statement shows a firm's bottom line. It is also called a profit and loss statement. The statement of cash flows reports cash receipts and cash disbursements related to operations, investments, and financing.

Finally, the various ratios that can be used to analyze the financial statements were discussed and illustrated. Four major categories of ratios were addressed: liquidity, leverage, profitability, and activity ratios. Again, use of these ratios gives a quick insight into a company's financial condition.

key terms

accounting 387
managerial
  accounting 388
financial
  accounting 388
annual report 389
certified management
  accountant (CMA) 389

certified public
  accountant (CPA) 389
private
  accountant 389
public accountant 390
Financial Accounting
  Standards Board
  (FASB) 390

generally accepted
  accounting principles
  (GAAP) 390
auditing 391
independent audit 391
Governmental
  Accounting Standards
  Board (GASB) 391

applying your skills

1. Visit, telephone, or e-mail a CPA from a local company in your area, or talk with a CPA in your college's business department. Ask what challenges, changes, and opportunities he or she foresees in the accounting profession in the next five years. List the forecasts on a sheet of paper and share with your classmates.

2. Obtain the most recent annual report for a company of your choice. (Hint: Choose a company, type it in a search engine, and go to the company Web site and click on where it says "investor relations" or something similar.) Discuss at least two important conclusions auditors reached after reading the financial statements.

3. Place yourself in the role of a small-business consultant. One of your clients, Pretty Fashions, is considering opening two new stores. The problem is that the business often experiences cash flow problems, due to the continuous style changes that occur in the fashion industry. Prepare an e-mail memo to Pretty Fashions explaining the difficulties a firm experiences when it encounters the cash flow problems that typically occur with such change or growth. Think of a business option Pretty Fashions could try in order to avoid cash flow problems.

4. Using the same company you researched earlier to find an annual report, find its financial statements and answer these questions:

   • What is the return on equity figure? What is the return on sales? If this were your business, would you feel comfortable with these results?

   • What is the debt to owners' equity? If you were the owner of this business, would you feel comfortable with this percentage?

   • What is the current ratio for this firm? Acid-test ratio?

5. Find the financial statements of a retail store. Compare the turn-over to the industry average, presented under the discussion on activity ratio in this chapter. How does the store compare?

6. Name four ways that accounting information can be used by managers, suppliers, employees, or investors.

the internet in action

1. *Purpose:* To calculate and analyze current ratios and quick (acid-test) ratios.

   Exercise: Thingamajigs and Things, a small gift shop, has total assets of $45,000 (including inventory valued at $30,000) and $9,000 in liabilities. WannaBees, a specialty clothing store, has total assets of $150,000 (including inventory valued at $125,000) and $85,000 in liabilities. Both businesses have applied for loans. Use the calculators on the www.Bankrate.com Web site to answer the following questions:

   • Calculate the current ratio for each company. Comparing the ratios, which company is more likely to get the loan? Why?

   • The quick (acid-test) ratio is considered an even more reliable measure of a business's ability to repay loans than the current ratio. Because inventory is often difficult to liquidate, the value of the inventory is subtracted from the total current assets. Calculate the quick ratio for each business. Do you think either business will get the loan? Why?

2. *Purpose:* To become familiar with annual reports.

   Exercise: Visit www.microsoft.com. Find its annual report and review it.

   • According to its report, what success did Microsoft have over the last year? What challenges does the company have in the future?

   • What was its gross income? Net income?

MONEY, FINANCIAL INSTITUTIONS, AND SECURITIES MARKETS

The Motley Fool

According to David and Tom Gardner, their interest in stocks and other investments began with chocolate pudding. Sound unusual? It's really quite simple. When the two brothers were young, they would often go to the supermarket with their father, who was both a lawyer and an economist. As the three of them traveled down the various aisles, their dad would tell them, "See that pudding? We own the company that makes it! Every time someone buys that pudding, it's good for our company. Boys, go get some more pudding!"

Those supermarket lessons about investing stuck with David and Tom. After graduating from the Univer-

David Gardner and Tom Gardner, the Motley Fool

sity of North Carolina, David became a writer for respected investment guru Louis Rukeyser's *Wall Street* newsletter. His brother Tom graduated from Brown University and went on to teach business at the University of Montana. In 1993, the two brothers, along with their friend Erik Rydholm, founded the Motley Fool, with the self-imposed mission "to educate, amuse and enlighten everyday people about the power of investing." Based in Alexandria, Virginia, the company has become one of the most successful multimedia financial-education firms in the nation.

Today, the Motley Fool includes a popular financial Web site (www.fool.com); five books—*The Motley Fool*

objectives

After reading this chapter, you should be able to:

1 Understand the importance of money and its basic characteristics.

2 Describe how the Federal Reserve controls the money supply.

3 Explain the functions of the Federal Reserve.

4 Understand how securities markets work.

5 Explain the differences among stocks, bonds, and mutual funds.

CHAPTER

13

Investment Guide, You Have More Than You Think, The Motley Fool Investment Workbook, Rule Breakers, Rule Makers, and *What To Do With Your Money Now*—that have all become bestsellers; a syndicated newspaper column that appears in over 200 papers; and a weekly program carried on National Public Radio. David and Tom chose the name Motley Fool from Shakespeare to reflect the spirit of truthful fun that the company brings to the world of investments.

Though they often sport jester hats and are humorous in their analyses, both David and Tom are intense in their passion to spread the message that securities markets can offer financial opportunity to all. The mission of the Motley Fool (to provide quality financial information to the masses—regardless of education or income) remains the primary focus of the two founders.

In 2000, the company took advantage of the interactivity of the Internet and began offering online seminars to help interested or would-be investors get specific knowledge about particular investment topics. The Fool also offers in-depth, company-specific research reports on companies that are most widely owned by the members of the Fool community. Because foolishness has no boundaries, the Motley Fool has expanded its business globally. The company even has a "Foolanthropy" program that invites readers to nominate charities they feel are worthy of the Fool's efforts. Since 1997, the Motley Fool has raised close to $2 million for such charities.

Sources: Based on www.fool.com; "David Gardner," NPR Biographies, www.npr.org/templates/story/story.php?storyId=2100501, accessed November 29, 2007; and "The Motley Fool Selects Charities for Foolanthropy 2005 Campaign," www.heifer.org/site/c.edJRKQNiFiG/b.1267917, accessed November 8, 2007.

THE IMPORTANCE OF MONEY

The U.S. economy depends heavily on money, its availability, and its value relative to other currencies. Economic growth and the creation of jobs depend on money. Money is so important to the economy that many institutions have evolved to manage money and to make it available to you when you need it. Today, you can easily get cash from an automated teller machine (ATM) almost anywhere in the world, but in many places cash is not the only means of payment you can use. Most organizations will accept a credit card, debit card, smart card, and sometimes checks for purchases. Behind the scenes of this free flow of money is a complex system of banking that makes the transactions possible.

money

Anything that people generally accept as payment for goods and services.

Money is anything that people generally accept as payment for goods and services. Long ago, objects such as salt, feathers, stones, rare shells, tea, and horses were used as money. In fact, until the 1880s, cowries (shells of marine animals) were one of the world's most abundant currencies.[1]

barter

The trading of goods and services for other goods and services directly.

Barter is the direct trading of goods and services for other goods and services. Although barter may sound like something from the past, this is far from so; many people have discovered the benefits of bartering online. Others still barter goods and services the old-fashioned way—face-to-face. Some of the trade in Russia over recent years has been done in barter. For example, in Siberia two eggs have been used to buy one admission to a movie, and customers of Ukraine's Chernobyl nuclear plant have paid in sausages and milk.

The problem is that eggs and milk are difficult to carry around. People need some object that is portable, divisible, durable, and stable, so they can trade goods and services without carrying the actual goods around with them. One answer to that problem over the years was to create coins made of silver or gold. Coins met all the standards of a useful form of money:

- *Portability.* Coins are a lot easier to take to market than are pigs or other heavy products.
- *Divisibility.* Different-size coins could be made to represent different values. For example, prior to 1963, a U.S. quarter had half as much silver content as a half dollar, and a dollar had four times the silver of a quarter. Because silver is now too expensive, today's coins are made of other metals, but the accepted values remain.
- *Stability.* When everybody agrees on the value of coins, the value of money is relatively stable. In fact, U.S. money has become so stable that much of the world uses the U.S. dollar as the measure of value.

Alan Wong just inherited $25,000 from his grandmother. Although he has considered taking several months off work and using the money to relax and to purchase new furniture for his entire apartment, he also knows it might be a good idea to invest some of the money. Somehow, he feels un- easy about that plan, but he is also unsure of how he might invest the money. Besides, he is only 25 and knows that he has a long time to save for retirement. After meeting one of his friends, Lydia, for coffee and discussing the money he just inherited, Alan changes his mind.

Can you tell if the bills are real or fake? Governments are making it more difficult to create counterfeit money. Paper money and coin money are portable, divisible, durable, unique, and stable but paper money is easier to counterfeit. The bills in this photo are counterfeit.

- *Durability.* Coins last for thousands of years, even when they have sunk to the bottom of the ocean, as evidenced when divers find old Roman coins in sunken ships.
- *Uniqueness.* It is difficult to counterfeit, or copy, elaborately designed and minted coins and printed dollars.

As a result of the advances in technology that make possible such duplicating of printed money, the government has had to go to extra lengths to make sure real dollars are readily identifiable, which is why we have new paper money with the picture slightly off center and with new, invisible lines that quickly show up when reviewed by banks and stores. Note the blue, peach, and green colors in the new $20 bill. Other denominations of bills also have new colors.[2]

When coins and paper money become units of value, they simplify exchanges. Most countries have their own coins and paper money, and they are all nearly equally portable, divisible, and durable. However, they are not always equally stable. For example, in the past, the value of money in Russia, Brazil, and Turkey was so uncertain and so unstable that other countries did not want to accept these countries' money in international trade.

Electronic cash (e-cash) is the latest form of money. In addition to being able to make online bill payments using software programs such as Quicken or Microsoft Money, you can e-mail e-cash to anyone using Web sites such as Pay-Pal.com (now owned by eBay). Recipients will receive an e-mail message telling them they have several choices for how they can receive the money: automatic deposit (the money will be sent to their bank), e-dollars for spending online, or a traditional check in the mail.

q: Do you bank online? Why or why not?

Bank customers can now access accounts online to check balances and make payments. NetBank is a fully online financial institution.

Because of the importance of money in our society and economy, the Federal Reserve plays a key role in managing our money supply in the United States. We will explore that topic next.

money supply

The amount of money the Federal Reserve Bank makes available for people to buy goods and services with.

M-1

Coins and paper bills, money that's available by writing checks, and money that's held in traveler's checks.

SELF-CHECK QUESTIONS

1. What is money and why is it important?
2. What are the five characteristics of useful money?

MONEY SUPPLY

Because of the importance of currency, the government takes some control in managing the money supply. Additionally, the Federal Reserve is a quasi-government/quasi-private agency. The **money supply** is the amount of money the Federal Reserve Bank makes available for people to purchase goods and services. There are several classifications of money in the money supply: M-1, M-2, and M-3. The *M* stands for money, and the *1* and *2* and so on stand for different definitions of the money supply.[3]

M-1 includes coins and paper bills, money available by writing checks (demand deposits and share drafts), and money held in traveler's checks—that is, money that can be accessed quickly and easily. This class of money is the one most commonly used. **M-2** includes everything in M-1 plus money in savings accounts, money market accounts, mutual funds, certificates of deposit, and the like. The M-2 class of money may take a bit more time to convert to use than coins and paper bills. **M-3** is M-2 plus big deposits (e.g., institutional money-market funds and agreements among banks).

M-2

Everything in M-1 plus money in savings accounts, money market accounts, mutual funds, and certificates of deposit.

To get an idea of the significance of maintaining control over the money supply, imagine what would happen if governments (or in the case of the United States, the Federal Reserve) were to generate twice as much money as exists now. There would be double the money available, but there would be the same amount of goods and services. What would happen to prices in that case? Think about the answer for a moment.

The answer is that prices would go up because more people would try to buy goods and services with their money and would bid up the price to get what they want. This effect is called *inflation,* and it is why some people define inflation as "too much money chasing too few goods."[4] If you need a review of inflation and deflation, refer back to Chapter 2.

M-3

M-2 plus big deposits, which would include agreements among banks.

Now think about the opposite: What would happen if the Fed took some of the money out of the economy? What would happen to prices? Prices would go down because there would be an oversupply of goods and services compared to the money available to buy them; this is called *deflation.* If too much money is taken out of the economy, a recession might occur. That is, people would lose jobs and the economy would stop growing.

Federal Reserve

The organization that oversees the money supply of the United States.

As you can see, the Federal Reserve does not want inflation or deflation to occur, beyond some manageable limits, which is why the money supply must be managed.

Basics about the Federal Reserve

The **Federal Reserve** system ("the Fed") consists of five major parts: (1) the board of governors (the current chair is Ben Bernanke); (2) the Federal Open Market Committee (FOMC); (3) 12 Federal Reserve banks; (4) three advisory councils; and (5) the member banks of the system. Figure 13.1 shows where the 12 Federal Reserve banks are located. Member banks may be chartered by the federal government or by the state in which they're located.

The Board of Governors administers and supervises the 12 Federal Reserve banks. The seven members of the board are appointed by the president and confirmed by the Senate. The board's primary function is to set *monetary policy*

figure 13.1

THE 12 FEDERAL RESERVE DISTRICT BANKS

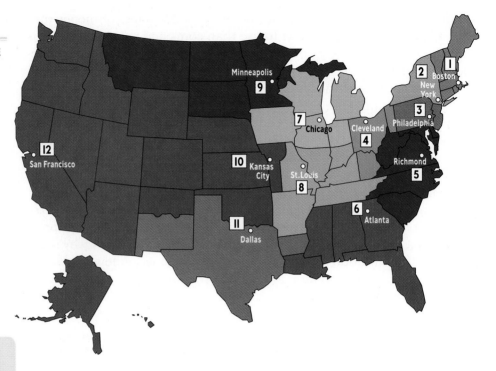

monetary policy

Policies used by the Federal Reserve to control factors such as inflation, deflation, exchange rates, and economic growth.

Federal Open Market Committee (FOMC)

The group that oversees the entire Federal Reserve process.

figure 13.2

THE FOUR FUNCTIONS OF THE FEDERAL RESERVE

Source: Federal Reserve Banks of Atlanta.

(see Figure 13.2). **Monetary policies** are the policies used by the Federal Reserve to control factors such as inflation, deflation, exchange rates, and economic growth.

The **Federal Open Market Committee (FOMC)** has 12 voting members and is the policymaking body of the Federal Reserve. The committee is made up of the seven-member board of governors plus the president of the New York reserve bank. Four others rotate in from the other reserve banks. The advisory councils offer suggestions to the

Services to depository institutions
- Similar to what our banks do for us, the Fed does for banks: tasks such as transferring funds, providing cash, and accepting and safeguarding deposits

Monetary policy
- Controlling of inflation, deflation, exchange rates, and economic growth

Supervision of banks
- Insurance that banks are in compliance of reserve requirements, and consumer protection laws

Services to U.S. Treasury
- Management of incoming revenues for the federal government, and lending of funds to the federal government

board and to the FOMC. The councils represent the various banking districts, consumers, and member institutions, including banks, savings and loan institutions, and credit unions.

The Fed buys and sells foreign currencies, regulates various types of credit, supervises banks, and collects data on the money supply and other economic activity. As part of monetary policy, the Fed determines the *reserve requirement;* that is, the level of reserves that must be kept at the 12 Federal Reserve banks by all financial institutions. It also lends money to member banks and sets the rate for such loans (called the *discount rate*). Finally, it buys and sells government securities in what are known as *open-market operations.*

It is important to understand how the Fed controls the money supply (see Figure 13.3), so we will explore that in some depth next. As just noted, the three basic tools the Fed uses to manage the money supply are reserve requirements, open-market operations, and the discount rate.

Ben S. Bernanke is the current chair of the Federal Reserve; because of that, he is one of the most powerful men in the United States. His challenges include the national trade deficit, the cooling of the housing market, rising inflation, potential economic downturn, and the possible continuation of high energy prices.

Reserve Requirement

First, a **reserve** is an amount of money that must be kept on hand and not lent to individuals or institutions. Therefore, the **reserve requirement** is a percentage of commercial banks' checking and savings accounts that must be physically kept in the banks (e.g., as cash in the vault) or in a non-interest-bearing deposit at the local Federal Reserve district bank. The current requirement in the United States is between 3 to 10 percent (as of 2007, according to the Federal Reserve Web site) depending on the account totals of the banks.

The reserve requirement is one of the Fed's most powerful tools. When the Federal Reserve increases the reserve requirement, banks have less money for loans (because they must keep more stored away) and thus make fewer loans. Money becomes scarcer, which in the long run tends to reduce inflation. For instance, if Omaha Security Bank holds deposits of $100 million and the reserve requirement is 10 percent, then the bank must keep $10 million on reserve either in the bank or at the local Federal Reserve district bank. If the Fed were to increase the reserve requirement to 11 percent, then the bank would have to put an additional $1 million on reserve, thus reducing the amount it could lend out. Because this increase in the reserve requirement would affect all banks, the money supply would be reduced and prices would likely fall.

A decrease of the reserve requirement, in contrast, increases the funds available to banks for loans, so banks make more loans and money

reserve
An amount of money that must be kept on hand and not lent to individuals or institutions.

reserve requirement
Percentage of commercial banks' checking and savings accounts that must be physically kept in the banks.

The Federal Reserve system was designed to prevent the run on the banks that occurred in 1907, then again in 1929.

becomes more readily available. An increase in the money supply stimulates the economy.

Open-Market Operations

open-market operations

Another tool commonly used by the Fed consisting of buying and selling government bonds.

Open-market operations are another common tool used by the Fed consisting of buying and selling government bonds. To decrease the money supply, the federal government sells U.S. government bonds to the public. The money it gets as payment is no longer in circulation, decreasing the money supply. If the Fed wants to increase the money supply, it buys government bonds from individuals, corporations, or organizations that are willing to sell. The money paid by the Fed in return for these securities enters circulation, resulting in an increase in the money supply.

The Discount Rate

discount rate

The interest rate that the Fed charges for loans to member banks.

The Fed has often been called the banker's bank. One reason for this is that member banks can borrow money from the Fed and then pass it on to their customers in the form of loans. The **discount rate** is the interest rate that the Fed charges for loans to member banks. When you see in the paper that the Fed is raising or lowering interest rates, it is usually the discount rate that is being discussed, which is an important point to remember should you ever wish to obtain a loan. An increase in the

To Return the Money or Not

You have been banking at the same bank for about three years. One aspect you really like about the bank is that it has ATMs at every corner and does not charge any fees for their use. One Friday evening, getting ready to go out with your friends, you decided to stop at the corner ATM and withdraw $100 for the weekend. The machine gave you $200 but the receipt indicated that the machine gave you $100.

Questions

1. What would you do? Why?
2. What *should* you do? Why?

discount rate by the Fed discourages banks from borrowing, and consequently reduces the number of available loans, resulting in a decrease in the money supply. In contrast, lowering the discount rate encourages member banks to borrow money and increases the funds available for loans, which increases the money supply. The Fed also sets the rate that banks charge each other (the federal funds rate). During wars and other hard economic times, the Fed is ready to slash both the discount rate and federal funds rate to prevent a monetary crisis.

figure 13.3

HOW THE FEDERAL RESERVE CONTROLS THE MONEY SUPPLY

CONTROL METHOD	IMMEDIATE RESULT	LONG-TERM EFFECT
Reserve Requirements		
A. Increase.	Banks put more money into the Fed, *reducing* money supply; thus, there is less money available to lend to customers.	Economy slows.
B. Decrease.	Banks put less money into the Fed, *increasing* the money supply; thus, there is more money available to lend to customers.	Economy speeds up.
Open-Market Operations		
A. Fed sells bonds.	Money flows from the economy to the Fed.	Economy slows.
B. Fed buys bonds.	Money flows into the economy from the Fed.	Economy speeds up.
Managing the Discount Rate		
A. Rate increases.	Banks borrow less from the Fed; thus, there is less money to lend.	Economy slows.
B. Rate decreases.	Banks borrow more from the Fed; thus, there is more money to lend.	Economy speeds up.

The exchange rate for international money is constantly fluctuating, which impacts both travelers and international business.

Global Exchange of Money

One other key point that must be discussed in this section is the value of the dollar compared to other currencies. A *falling dollar value* means that the amount of goods and services you can buy with a dollar decreases compared to other currencies. However, it also means that other currencies that are rising against the dollar can buy U.S. products at a cheaper price which increases U.S. exports. A *rising dollar value* means that the amount of goods and services you can buy with a dollar goes up. Thus, in real terms, the price you paid for a weekend get-away in Canada was lower in 1999, for example, than it is today because the American dollar was stronger when compared with the Canadian dollar.[5] However, the Canadian dollar is growing and gaining strength compared to the American dollar today; therefore, the cost of that same weekend has gone up in price. Of course, part of this situation can be due to inflation, but part is also due to the weakening American dollar, which can be a good sign for some American businesses because it means that with the currencies more equivalent in value, it is worthwhile for Canadian companies to do business with American companies.

What makes the dollar weak (falling dollar value) or strong (rising dollar value) is the position of the U.S. economy relative to other economies, such as the strength of our economy and the amount of debt we have. When the U.S. economy is strong, the demand for dollars is high, and the value of the dollar rises. When the U.S. economy is perceived as weakening, however, the demand for dollars declines and the value of the dollar falls.[6] The value of the dollar thus depends on the strength of the U.S. economy.

q: How does a strong or weak dollar affect you personally?

Major issues arise when the dollar is weak compared to other currencies. Let's assume you are a manufacturing firm in the United States and you want to purchase specialized equipment from France. If the value of the dollar is lower compared to the value of the euro, it will take more dollars to buy that same equipment, making it much more expensive. So, when the dollar is weak, companies are not able to trade as much, or are unwilling to trade as often with firms in other countries. Because this is a global market, the weaker dollar is a huge concern to American business, and foreign competitors can use this situation to their advantage.

THE FUNCTION OF SECURITIES MARKETS

Because we have been discussing money, it is appropriate to discuss money in terms of securities markets at this point in our chapter. First, **securities** are stocks and bonds that are traded, and the **securities market** is a financial marketplace where stocks and bonds are traded. The **New York Stock Exchange (NYSE)** and the **NASDAQ** (a completely electronic exchange) are examples of securities markets. Figure 13.4 shows the companies represented in the DOW, the most widely used indicator of the stock market.

These institutions serve two major functions: First, they assist businesses in finding long-term funding to finance capital needs, such as beginning operations, expanding their businesses, or buying major goods and services. Second, they provide private investors a place to buy and sell securities (investments), such as stocks, bonds, and mutual funds that can help them build their financial future.

Securities markets are divided into primary and secondary markets. *Primary markets* handle the sale of new securities. Corporations make money on the sale of their securities only once—when they are first sold on the primary market. The first public offering of a corporation's stock is called an **initial public offering (IPO).** After that, the *secondary market* handles the trading of securities between investors, with the proceeds of a sale going to the investor selling the stock, not to the corporation whose stock is sold. For example, if Very Vegetarian offers 2 million shares of stock in the company at $15 a share, the company would raise $30 million at the initial offering. However, if Shareholder Jones sells 100 shares of the company stock to Investor Smith, Very Vegetarian collects nothing from this transaction. Smith bought the stock from Jones, not from Very Vegetarian. However, it is possible for companies like Very Vegetarian to offer additional shares of stock in order to raise additional capital. Also, many people within the company, executives and workers alike, may own shares in a company. When the demand is high for the shares, the executives or workers can

Section Outline

The Function of Securities Markets

- Bonds
- Stocks
- Mutual Funds
- Stock Exchanges
- Investing in Securities
- Reading Stock, Bond, and Mutual Fund Quotes

securities
Stocks and bonds that are traded.

securities market
A place where stocks and bonds are traded.

New York Stock Exchange (NYSE)
A securities market.

NASDAQ
Completely electronic securities market.

initial public offering (IPO)
The first public offering of a corporation's stock.

figure 13.4

WHAT IS THE DOW?

The DOW is the most widely used indicator of the overall stock market. The DOW consists of 30 stocks chosen by the *Wall Street Journal* editors (which is published by DOW Jones and Company). The picks are generally called "blue chip stocks" which are large national companies with a record of stable earnings. As of July 2007, according to Dow Jones Indexes, the following companies were part of the DOW:

Altria Group Inc.	McDonald's Corp.
Pfizer Inc.	Intel Corp.
Citigroup Inc.	Wal-Mart Stores Inc.
Verizon Communications, Inc.	Alcoa Inc.
AT&T Inc.	Honeywell International Inc.
JPMorgan Chase & Co.	Caterpillar Inc.
E.I. DuPont de Nemours & Co.	Exxon Mobil Corp.
General Motors Corp.	United Technologies Corp.
Merck & Co. Inc.	Microsoft Corp.
General Electric Co.	Boeing Co.
Johnson & Johnson	International Business Machines Corp.
Coca-Cola Co.	American International Group Inc.
Home Depot Inc.	American Express Co.
Procter & Gamble Co.	Walt Disney Co.
3M Co.	Hewlett-Packard Co.

sell their shares and make money from the transaction. For example, in May 2006, the world's second largest credit card issuer and one of the best known brands, MasterCard, floated 61.5 million shares at an IPO price of $39 per share.[7] In November 2007, the shares of MasterCard were trading on the NYSE at $195 per share.[8] In October 2007, three officers of the company collectively sold 35,500 shares at prices ranging from $162 to $178 per share.[9] Following MasterCard's lead, the world's largest credit card company, Visa, filed plans in November 2007 for a $10 billion IPO.[10]

Issuing stock or "going public" (IPO) is one way companies can gain new funding. Unfortunately, new companies often start without sufficient capital, and many established firms fail to do adequate long-term financial planning. If given a choice, businesses normally prefer to meet long-term financial needs by using retained earnings (past profit) or by borrowing from a lending institution (bank, pension fund, insurance company). However, if such types of long-term funding are not available, a company may be able to raise funds by issuing corporate bonds (debt) or selling stock (ownership). Issuing corporate bonds is a form of *debt financing* and selling stock in the corporation is a form of *equity financing.* These forms of debt or equity financing are not available to all companies, especially small businesses. However, many firms use such financing options to meet long-term financial needs.

Investment bankers can help companies meet these financial needs. These individuals are specialists who assist in the issue and sale of new securities, understanding as they do the surrounding regulations and the necessity of gaining the **Securities and Exchange Commission's (SEC's)** permission for stock or bond issuances. The investment bank also underwrites new issues of stocks or bonds.[11] In other words, the investment bank buys all of the stocks or bonds (or signs a good faith effort to do so), and then sells all (or most) of the stocks and bonds.

Bonds

A **bond** is a corporate certificate indicating that a person has lent money to a firm. A company that issues bonds has a legal obligation to make regular interest payments to investors and to repay the entire bond principal amount at a prescribed time, called the **maturity date.**

The interest rate paid on a bond varies according to factors such as the state of the economy, the reputation of the company issuing the bond, and the going interest rate for government bonds or bonds of similar companies. Once an interest rate is set for a corporate bond issue, except in the case of floating-rate bonds, it cannot be changed. The interest rate being paid by U.S. government bonds clearly affects the interest rate a firm must agree to pay, because government bonds are considered safe investments. Bonds offer several long-term financing advantages to an organization. The decision to issue bonds is often based on advantages such as the following:

- Bondholders are creditors, not owners, of the firm and seldom have a vote on corporate matters. Thus, management maintains control over the firm's operations.
- Interest paid on bonds is tax deductible to the firm issuing the bond.
- Bonds are a temporary source of funding for a firm. They are eventually repaid and the debt obligation eliminated.
- Bonds can be repaid before the maturity date if they contain a call provision, and can also be convertible to common stock.

However, bonds also have several drawbacks:

- Bonds increase debt (long-term liabilities) and may adversely affect the market's perception of the firm.
- Paying interest on bonds is a legal obligation. If interest is not paid, bondholders can take legal action to force payment.

Securities and Exchange Commission (SEC)

A governmental organization that has responsibility at the federal level for regulating activities in the various exchanges.

bond

A corporate certificate indicating that a person has lent money to a firm.

maturity date

The date that a bond can be cashed in.

figure 13.5

TYPES OF GOVERNMENT BONDS

BOND	DESCRIPTION
U.S. government bond	Issued by the federal government; considered the safest type of bond investment
Treasury bill (T-bill)	Matures in less than a year; issued with a minimum denomination of $1,000
Treasury note	Matures in 10 years or less; sold in denominations of $1,000 and $5,000
Treasury bond	Matures in 25 years or more; sold in denominations of $1,000 and $5,000
Municipal bond	Issued by states, cities, counties, and other state and local government agencies; usually exempt from federal taxes
Yankee bond	Issued by a foreign government; payable in U.S. dollars

- The face value (denomination) of bonds must be repaid on the maturity date. Without careful planning, this repayment can cause cash flow problems when the bonds come due.

The government can issue bonds as well. Figure 13.5 shows some different types of bonds that can be issued by governments. Both corporate and government bonds are given ratings by Moody's and by Standard & Poor's. These ratings can help investors determine the likelihood that they will be repaid. Both Moody's and Standard & Poor's provide independent credit ratings, risk analysis, and research to assist investors in their investment decision making. Figure 13.6 shows the types of ratings.

figure 13.6

BOND RATINGS AND THEIR MEANINGS

Rating		DESCRIPTIONS
MOODY'S	**STANDARD & POOR'S**	
Aaa	AAA	Highest quality (lowest default risk)
Aa	AA	High quality
A	A	Upper medium grade
Baa	BBB	Medium grade
Ba	BB	Lower medium grade
B	B	Speculative
Caa	CCC, CC	Poor (high default risk)
Ca	C	Highly speculative
C	D	Lowest grade

Stocks

Stocks can be another way for companies to gain financing. **Stocks** are shares of ownership in a company. A *stock certificate* is evidence of stock ownership that specifies the name of the company, the number of shares it represents, and the type of stock being issued (see Figure 13.7). Today stock certificates are generally held electronically for the owners of the stock. Certificates sometimes indicate a stock's **par value,** which is a dollar amount assigned to each share of stock by the corporation's charter. Some states use par value as a basis for calculating the state's incorporation charges and fees. Because par values do not reflect the market value of the stock, most companies issue "no-par" stock.

Dividends are part of a firm's profits that may be distributed to stockholders as either cash payments or additional shares of stock. Dividends are declared by a corporation's board of directors and are generally paid quarterly.[12] Although it is a legal obligation for companies that issue bonds to pay interest, companies that issue stock are not required to pay dividends.[13] Many companies that are growing instead opt to reinvest those funds that would have gone to dividends to continue growing, which satisfies shareholders. Take, for instance, two technology companies, Microsoft and Apple. Microsoft does pay a dividend to its shareholders. In 2007, it paid $0.44 per share. In other words, if you owned 100 shares of Microsoft, you received $44 in dividends from the company in 2007. On the other hand, Apple does not pay dividends to its shareholders but chooses to reinvest the money in the company's growth.[14]

stock
Share of ownership in a company.

par value
The dollar amount assigned to each stock certificate on the corporation's charter.

dividend
Part of a firm's profits that may be distributed to stockholders as either cash payments or additional shares of stock.

figure 13.7

STOCK CERTIFICATE FOR PET INC.

The following are some advantages to the firm that is issuing stock:

- As owners of the business, stockholders never have to be repaid.
- There is no legal obligation to pay dividends to stockholders. Therefore, income (retained earnings) can be reinvested in the firm for future financing needs.
- Selling stock can improve the condition of a firm's balance sheet, because issuing stock creates no debt.

A corporation can buy back its stock to improve its balance sheet and make the company appear stronger financially. When the stock price of the company is low, the board of the company can authorize a stock repurchase program. When fewer shares are available for purchase to outsiders, the price of the shares goes up. Remember demand and supply from Chapter 2.

Disadvantages of issuing stock include the following:

- As owners, stockholders (usually only common stockholders) have the right to vote for the company's board of directors. Typically, one vote is granted for each share of stock. Hence, the direction and control of the firm can be altered by the sale of additional shares of stock.
- Dividends are paid out of profit after taxes, and thus are not tax deductible.
- Management's decisions can be affected by the need to keep stockholders happy.

Companies can issue two classes of stock: preferred and common. Let's see how these two forms of equity financing differ.

preferred stock

A preference (hence the term *preferred*) in the payment of dividends.

Preferred Stock

Owners of **preferred stock** enjoy a preference (hence the term *preferred*) in the payment of dividends; they also have a priority claim on company assets if the firm is forced out of business and its assets sold. Normally, however, preferred stock does not include voting rights in the firm. Preferred stock is frequently referred to as a hybrid investment because it has characteristics of both bonds and stocks. To illustrate this, consider the treatment of preferred stock dividends.

Preferred stock dividends differ from common stock dividends in several ways. Preferred stock is generally issued with a par value that becomes the base for the dividend the firm is willing to pay. For example, if the par value of a preferred stock is $25 a share and its dividend rate is 4 percent, the firm is committing to a $1 dividend for each share of preferred stock the investor owns (4 percent of $25 = $1). An owner of 100 shares of this preferred stock is promised a fixed yearly dividend of $100. In addition, the preferred stockholder is also assured that this dividend must be paid in full before any common stock dividends can be distributed.

Preferred stock is, therefore, quite similar to bonds: both have a face (or par) value and both have a fixed rate of return.[15] Preferred stock is rated by Standard & Poor's and Moody's Investors Service according to risk, similar to the manner in which bonds are rated.

So how do bonds and preferred stock differ? Remember that companies are legally bound to pay bond interest and to repay the face value (denomination) of the bond on its maturity date. In contrast, even though preferred stock dividends are generally fixed, they do not legally have to be paid. Also, stock (preferred or common) never has to be repurchased. Although both bonds and stocks can increase in market value, the price of stocks generally increases at a higher percentage than does the price of bonds. Of course, the market value of both could also go down.

Preferred stock can have special features that do not apply to common stock. For example, like bonds, preferred stock can be callable, which means that preferred stockholders could be required to sell back their shares to the corporation. Preferred stock can also be convertible to shares of common stock (in some situations, but not all). Another important feature of preferred stock is that it can often be cumulative. That is, if one or more dividends are not paid when promised, the missed dividends will be accumulated and paid later. All dividends, including any back dividends, must be paid in full before any common stock dividends can be distributed.

Common Stock

Common stock is the most basic form of ownership in a firm. In fact, if a company issues only one type of stock, it must be common. Holders of common stock have the right (1) to vote for company board directors and on important issues affecting the company and (2) to share in the firm's profits through dividends, if approved by the firm's board of directors. Having voting rights in a corporation allows common stockholders to influence corporate policy, because the elected board chooses the firm's top management and makes major policy decisions. Common stockholders used this influence in the early 2000s against major companies such as Tyco, Hewlett-Packard, and smaller firms, such as Luby's Cafeterias.[16] Common stockholders also have a *preemptive right*, which is the first right to purchase any new shares of common stock the firm decides to issue. This right allows common stockholders to maintain a proportional share of ownership in the company.

It is important to mention the two types of financing a company can use to get money. Suppose a company wants to expand its manufacturing units by 50 percent, but does not have the cash to do so. It can *debt finance*, which would be borrowing money from a bank or investor, putting the company into debt. *Equity financing*, on the other hand, is selling stock in a company. Because the company does not have to pay that money back, it is not considered a debt.

> **common stock**
> The most basic form of ownership in a firm.

mutual fund

Like an investment company, it pools investors' money and then buys stocks or bonds in many companies.

figure 13.8

TYPES OF MUTUAL FUNDS

Source: InvestorGuide.com, accessed November 29, 2007.

Mutual Funds

A **mutual fund** is like an investment company, in that it pools investors' money and then buys stocks or bonds in many companies, in accordance with the specific purpose of the fund. Mutual fund managers are experts who pick what they consider to be the best stocks and bonds available. Investors can buy shares of the mutual funds and thus take part in the ownership of the many different companies that they could not afford to invest in individually. Thus, for a normally small fee, mutual funds provide professional investment management and help investors diversify.

Buying shares in a mutual fund is probably the best way for a small or beginning investor to get started. Funds range in purpose from very conservative, investing only in government securities or secure corporate bonds, to risky (see Figure 13.8). Mutual funds that

Growth Funds
- Mutual fund that invests in stocks with the potential for long-term growth
- Focus on companies experiencing significant earnings growth
- Do not generally pay dividends
- More volatile (can change quickly) than other types of mutual funds

Value Funds
- Invest in companies that are thought to be bargains
- Stocks that have fallen out of favor with mainstream investors due to changing investor preference, poor quarterly earnings, or hard times in an industry
- Often are stocks of mature companies that may not be growing
- Usually pay dividends

Aggressive Growth Funds
- Similar to growth funds but even more extreme
- Target companies with very rapid growth and/or earnings or in risky industries

Blend Funds
- Combine both growth and value funds
- Can result in a balanced portfolio
- Less risky than growth funds but more risky than value funds

Sector Funds
- Mutual funds that invest in only one sector of the market, such as energy or biotechnology companies
- To be considered, it must invest at least 25% of its portfolio in one sector, although many invest all funds within the one sector

Large Cap, Mid Cap, Small Cap, and Micro Cap Funds
- Can be classified as the total value of the company on the stock market; in other words, the number of outstanding shares
- Large cap funds might invest only in companies whose holdings are more than $10 billion, while a small cap might invest in companies with market caps below $1 billion

Charles Schwab & Co. offices at One Madison Avenue. The Charles Schwab Corporation provides securities brokerage and financial services to individual investors and independent investment advisors. As one of the nation's largest financial services firms, Schwab serves more than 6.8 million client brokerage accounts, 535,000 corporate retirement plan participants, and 181,000 banking accounts, all representing more than $1.3 trillion in client assets.

specialize in emerging high-tech firms, Internet companies, foreign companies, precious metals, and other investments often have greater risk. Some mutual funds even invest exclusively in "socially responsible" companies.[17]

An **index fund** is a fund that invests in stocks that follow the Standard & Poor's 500 (S&P 500) or other similar index. The S&P 500 is a basket of 500 stocks that are thought to represent the overall market.[18] It is used as an indicator as to how the marketing is doing overall. The main difference between a mutual fund and an index fund is the fact that the index fund is managed passively—that is, it follows an index rather than having someone actively selecting stocks in which to invest. As a result, the fees for an index fund are usually lower than for mutual funds.

To *diversify* means to invest in a number of different types of investments to safeguard against a loss by one part of your portfolio not doing well. For example, you could put your money into an index fund that focuses on large companies, one that focuses on small companies, one that invests in emerging countries, and one that invests mainly in real estate (real estate investment trusts, or REITs), among others. This example represents a *diversified portfolio*.

Bonds, stocks, and mutual funds are generally traded on a *stock exchange*. The types of stock exchanges will be discussed next.

Stock Exchanges

As its name implies, a **stock exchange** is an organization whose members can buy and sell (exchange) securities for companies and investors.

index fund
A fund that invests in stocks that follow the Standard & Poor's 500 (S&P 500) or other similar index.

stock exchange
An organization whose members can buy and sell (exchange) securities for companies and investors.

Brokerage firms, such as A. G. Edwards and Merrill Lynch, purchase memberships—or seats—on the exchanges, but the number of seats available is limited. The New York Stock Exchange, for example, has only 1,366 members, a number that had not changed from 1953 to 2006, when NYSE merged with Archipelago. Archipelago is a securities trading company that specializes in electronic trading. In April 2007, NYSE merged with Euronext to create NYSE Euronext, a milestone in global financial markets.[19] The price of a seat on the NYSE varies with the strength of the market. In August 1999, the price was $2.65 million. With the declining market, the price had dropped to around $2 million in 2002.[20] However, the highest price of $4 million for a seat was recorded in 2005. In December 2005, sale of the seats was ended in anticipation of NYSE's transformation into a publicly traded company.[21]

The largest stock exchange in the United States, the NYSE was founded in 1792. The NYSE is a floor-based exchange (trades take place on the floor of the stock exchange) but it also exchanges electronically. The NYSE lists about 2,800 companies, most of which are large. For example, in 2002 the 2,800 companies listed on the NYSE had a total market value of about $13.5 trillion. Because of such a large market value, the NYSE is often referred to as the *Big Board*. The second largest floor-based U.S. exchange is the American Stock Exchange (AMEX).[22] These two exchanges are considered national exchanges because they handle stocks of companies from all over the United States. In addition to the national exchanges, there are several regional exchanges in cities such as Chicago, San Francisco, Philadelphia, Cincinnati, Spokane, and Salt Lake City. The regional exchanges deal mostly with firms in their own areas but also handle the stock of many large corporations listed on the Big Board. Regional exchanges are often used by big institutional investors to trade stock because their transaction costs are less than those of large exchanges such as the NYSE.

over-the-counter (OTC) market

Provides companies and investors with a means to trade stocks not listed on the national securities exchanges.

Not all securities are traded on registered stock exchanges. The **over-the-counter (OTC) market** provides companies and investors with a means to trade stocks not listed on the national securities exchanges. The OTC market is a network of several thousand brokers who maintain contact with one another and buy and sell securities through a nationwide electronic system.

The NASDAQ stock market (originally known as the National Association of Securities Dealers Automated Quotations) evolved from the OTC market, but is no longer part of it. As of this writing, the SEC is considering NASDAQ's application for exchange registration.[23] Unlike a floor-based exchange like the NYSE, the NASDAQ is a telecommunications network. It links dealers across the nation so that they can buy and sell securities electronically, rather than in person. Originally, the NASDAQ dealt mostly with small firms. Today, however, well-known companies such as Microsoft, Intel, Starbucks, Cisco, and Dell trade their stock on the NASDAQ. The NASDAQ handles federal, state, and city government

The NYSE and the NASDAQ are securities markets. Stock owners use traders on the floor of the New York Stock Exchange to buy and sell stocks, hopefully at a profit.

bonds as well. Today, the **NASDAQ** lists approximately 3,800 companies and its average is reported every business day.[24]

Figure 13.9 lists the requirements for registering (listing) stocks on the various exchanges. It is important to note that stocks can be delisted from an exchange if a company fails to hold to the exchange's minimum requirements.[25]

Securities Exchange Regulation

The Securities Act of 1933 protects investors by requiring full disclosure of financial information by firms selling bonds or stock.[26] The U.S. Congress passed this legislation to deal with the free-for-all atmosphere

EXCHANGE	REQUIREMENTS	TYPE OF COMPANY
New York Stock Exchange (NYSE)	Pretax income of $2.5 million; 2,000 shareholders holding at least 100 shares; market value of $50 million	Oldest, largest, and best-known companies
American Stock Exchange (AMEX)	Pretax income of $750,000; 500,000 shares publicly held at a minimum market value of $3 million; minimum of 400 public shareholders	Midsize growth companies
NASDAQ	Total market value of all shares of $8 million; 400 shareholders holding at least 100 shares	Large, midsize, and small growth companies

figure 13.9

REQUIREMENTS FOR LISTING STOCK ON THE TWO MAJOR SECURITIES EXCHANGES

Job Interviewing—Make It Count!

The job interview—what an opportunity to impress! And what an opportunity to *learn*. Mistakes will happen but can become knowledge for your future interviews that might mean better opportunities and bigger implications for your career later. So don't get down on yourself if things don't go right—but learn to be better prepared for your interview in the future.

What is a job interview? A particular company has opened its doors for the right person to walk through and if you understand the interviewing process, that "right" person can be you.

Come to the interview prepared to be hired. Ask good questions, take notes, research the prospective company, use good posture, and make good eye contact. These behaviors might seem basic but more often than not, they are not carried out by prospective new hires. As a result, if you are poised, focused, and confident about the hiring opportunity and carry out these basic interview practices, your odds of being hired increase significantly!

Securities and Exchange Commission (SEC)

The group that oversees the stock markets.

prospectus

A document that provides information about a company to investors. Required to be sent out at least once per year.

insider trading

The use of knowledge or information that individuals gain through their position that allows them to benefit unfairly from fluctuations in security prices.

that existed in the securities markets during the Roaring 20s and the early 1930s.

The Securities and Exchange Act of 1934 created the **Securities and Exchange Commission (SEC),** which has responsibility at the federal level for regulating activities in the various exchanges. Companies trading on the national exchanges must register with the SEC and provide it annual updates. The 1934 act also established specific guidelines that companies must follow when issuing financial securities, such as bonds or stock. For example, before issuing either bonds or stock for sale to the public, a company must file a detailed registration statement with the SEC that includes extensive economic and financial information relevant to the firm. The condensed version of that registration document—called a **prospectus**—must be sent to prospective investors.

The 1934 act also established guidelines to prevent company insiders from taking advantage of privileged information they may have. **Insider trading** involves the use of knowledge or information that individuals gain through their position that allows them to benefit unfairly from fluctuations in security prices. The key words here are *benefit unfairly*. Insiders within a firm are permitted to buy and sell stock in the company they work for, so long as they do not take unfair advantage of information. Originally, the SEC defined the term *insider* rather narrowly as consisting of a company's directors, employees, and relatives. Today, the term has been broadened to include just about anyone with securities information that is not available to the general public. For example, say the chief financial officer of Very Vegetarian tells her next-door neighbor that she is finalizing paperwork to sell the company to a major grocer. The neighbor buys the stock based on this information. A court may well consider the purchase an insider trade. Penalties for insider trading can include fines and/or imprisonment.

Investing in Securities

Investing in bonds, stocks, or other securities is not very difficult. First, you decide what bond or stock you want to buy. After that, it is necessary to find a registered representative, authorized to trade stocks and bonds, who can call a member of the stock exchange to execute your order. Another option is to use an online trading service, such as E*Trade or TD Ameritrade. A *stockbroker* is a registered representative who works as a market intermediary to buy and sell securities for clients. Stockbrokers place an order with a stock exchange member, who goes to the place at the exchange where the bond or stock is traded and negotiates a price. After the transaction is completed, the trade is reported to your broker, who notifies you and confirms your purchase. Large brokerage firms, such as Merrill Lynch or A. G. Edwards, maintain automated order systems that allow their brokers to enter your order the instant you make it. Seconds later, the order can be confirmed. Online brokers, such as E*Trade, can also confirm investor trades in a matter of seconds.[27] The same procedure is followed if you wish to sell stocks or bonds. Brokers historically held on to stock or bond certificates for investors to ensure safekeeping and to allow investors to sell their securities easily and quickly. Today, brokers keep most records of bond or stock ownership electronically, and transactions are almost instantaneous. A broker can be a valuable source of information about what stocks or bonds would best meet your financial objectives.

q: Do you invest in and own stocks? If not, would you be
»» interested in stock investment? Why or why not?

It is important, however, that you learn about and follow stocks and bonds on your own, because investment analysts' advice may not always meet your specific expectations and needs. In fact, several years back, a Stockholm newspaper gave five Swedish stock analysts and a chimpanzee each the equivalent of $1,250 to make as much money as they could in the stock market. The chimp made his selections by throwing darts—and won the competition.[28]

The Wall Street Journal also periodically compares the predictions of a panel of experts to those of "dart throwers." Make sure to look for these

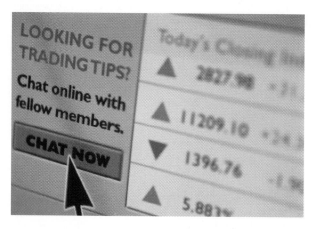

Do you have a feeling about a stock you believe is the next Microsoft, but don't have a stockbroker? Well, relief is just a click away. Investors can use online trading services such as E*Trade for their investment needs for a fraction of the cost charged by traditional brokers. Investors, however, must do their own research and make their own decisions. Check out www.etrade.com for more information.

contests in the *Journal*. You might want to compete against the experts to test your knowledge. If you choose to invest on your own, Web sites discussed earlier, such as E*Trade, provide investors not only the ability to make trades, but also to conduct research on potential purchases.

There are several considerations people should be aware of before investing:

1. *Investment risk.* The chance that an investment will be worth less, at some future time, than it is worth now.

2. *Yield.* The expected rate of return on an investment, such as interest or dividends, usually over a period of one year.

3. *Duration.* The length of time money is committed to an investment.

4. *Liquidity.* How quickly invested funds can be recovered if an investor wants or needs them.

5. *Tax consequences.* How the investment will affect an investor's tax situation.

Because new investors are not generally well versed in the world of investing or in choosing proper investment strategies, an investment planner, such as a chartered financial analyst (CFA) or a certified financial planner (CFP), can be very helpful. A short course in investments can also be very useful. Setting investment objectives, such as growth or income, should clearly set the tone for a person's investment strategy.

See Figure 13.10 to compare the types of investments we have discussed in this chapter.

figure 13.10

A COMPARISON OF DIFFERENT SECURITIES INVESTMENTS

Investment	Degree of risk	Expected income	Possible growth (capital gain)
Bonds	Low	Secure	Little
Preferred stock	Medium	Steady	Little
Common stock	High	Variable	Good
Mutual funds	Medium	Variable	Good
Commodities	Very high	Very volatile	Very volatile

Reading Stock, Bond, and Mutual Fund Quotes

Do you ever wonder what all of those numbers mean in the stock section of the newspaper? This section will explore how to read stock, bond, and mutual fund quotes.

Look at Figure 13.11. Moving from left to right, the stock quote tells us the following:

- The percentage of change in the stock's price for the year to date (YTD).
- The highest and lowest price the stock has sold for over the past 52 weeks.
- The company name and the company's stock symbol.
- The last dividend paid per share.
- The stock's dividend yield (annual dividend as a percentage of the price per share).
- The price/earnings ratio (P/E), which is the price of the stock divided by the firm's per-share earnings. For example, if the price of Very Vegetarian stock was $50, and the company earnings were $5 per share, Very Vegetarian's price/earnings ratio would be 10.

figure 13.11

SAMPLE STOCK QUOTES

YTD % CHG	52-WEEK HI	52-WEEK LO	STOCK (SYM)	DIV	YLD %	PE	VOL 100s	CLOSE	NET CHG	
16.7	22.36	15.05	Mattel MAT	.05	.2	21	9838	20.08	0.13	Price of Mattel stock is 21 times its earnings
4.4	19.15	8.21↓	MayrckTube MVK		...	cc	2300	13.52	0.60	
−6.2	7.90	1.77	Maxtor MXO		...	dd	28648	5.95	0.05	
−36.5	38.86	20.10	MayDeptStrs' MAY	.95	4.0	13	10482	23.47	0.17	Closing price of May Department Stores stock
−10.9	47.94	18.84	Maytag MYG	.72	2.6	13	5707	27.66	0.56	
19.9	65.55	45.10	McClatchy A MNI x	.40	.7	23	1561	56.35	0.52	
13.7	27.25	20.67	McCrmkCo MKC s	.44f	1.8	21	3053	23.85	0.05	Stock yields a 1.8% dividend
−70.3	17.29	2.34	McDermint MDR		...	dd	15706	3.65	0.64	
−34.3	30.72	15.75	McDonalds MCD	.24f	1.4	14	57791	17.40	0.20	
−2.5	69.70	50.71	McGrawH MHP	1.02	1.7	26	6296	59.48	−0.69	
−27.8	42.09	24.99	McKesson MCK	.24	.9	17	15741	27.01	0.16	McKesson went up 16¢ since the previous close
−15.2	6.35	2.54	McMoRanExpl MMR	.35p	...	dd	196	4.91	0.16	
21.6	4.14	1.55↓	MdwbrkinsGp MIG		...	20	416	2.42	−0.02	
−25.1	36.50	15.57	MeadWVaco MWV	.92	4.0	dd	4169	23.15	−0.43	
30.8	4.50	1.57	MediaArts MDA		...	dd	45	3.44	0.14	
16.0	69.49	46.55	MediaGen A MEG	.72	1.2	dd	644	57.80	−0.03	Stock pays a dividend of 72¢
−34.7	29.75	9.25	MedStaffNtwk MRN n		...	...	454	14.04	−0.05	
−25.0	64.60	33.85	MediclsPhrm MRX		...	31	5997	48.45	−0.42	

High and low price for last 52 weeks

Change in stock price for year to date

Symbol for company

599,700 shares of this stock traded today

Socially Responsible Investing Movement Grows Up

Whether it's getting pharmaceutical giants, such as Bristol Myers, to waive patent rights in Africa so AIDS medicines can be produced cheaply, or negotiating with Occidental Petroleum to establish a corporatewide human rights policy, Doris Gormley knows it is not just the value of the financial assets of the 10 Jesuit regions she represents that gets her a seat in the corporate suite.

"When we're engaging a company for the first time, they always ask us to keep it confidential," said Gormley, socially responsible investment consultant to the National Jesuit Conference and a member of the Sisters for Christian Community, a non-canonical religious order. "They don't want us to go to the press because they don't want the world to know that all these religious denominations have problems with what they are doing," said Gormley, who also co-chairs the human rights working group of the New York–based Interfaith Center on Corporate Responsibility. "This is our real leverage."

It is leverage the socially responsible investment movement has learned to exploit. Once perceived as nettlesome do-gooders, gadflies whose stock certificates provided access to annual shareholder meetings but not much more, the movement has matured.

Socially responsible investing—the idea that institutional and retail investors should look beyond the financial bottom line and include an approach that, according to the Social Investment Forum, "integrates social and environmental concerns into investment decisions"—is a growth industry. More than 10 percent of all professionally managed money in the U.S. economy, $2.2 trillion, is invested according to socially responsible guidelines. That's up 40 percent between 1985 and 2005.

Questions

1. Should you consider the level of social responsibility of the company before making an investment commitment? Why or why not?

2. What are the five things to consider before investing in a particular stock?

3. What aspects of social responsibility are important to you that you certainly would want to consider in a company before investing?

Source: Joe Feuerherd, "Socially Responsible Investing Movement Grows Up," *National Catholic Reporter,* March 11, 2005.

- The number of shares of stock in the company traded that day, in 100s.
- The stock's closing price for the day.
- The net change in the stock's price from the previous day.

Look down the columns and find the stock that has the biggest price change over the past 52 weeks, the stock that pays the highest dividend, and the stock that has the highest and lowest price/earnings ratio. The more you look through the figures, the more sense they begin to make.

When reading mutual fund quotations (see Figure 13.12), the fund's name is in the first column, followed by the fund's net asset value (NAV), which is the market value of the mutual fund's portfolio divided by the number of shares it has outstanding. The NAV is the price per share of the mutual fund. The next column lists the net change in the NAV from the previous day's trading. The fund's year-to-date (YTD) return is in the next column. Finally, in this example, the fund's three-year return is listed. Publications such as *The Wall Street Journal* list a fund's 13-week return, one-year return, and five-year return on different days of the week, in order to provide investors with detailed information about the

So, You Want to Be . . . in the Stock Market

Stockbrokers manage their corporate or private client investment portfolios. To be successful in this field, math skills are required, but equally important are interpersonal skills and the ability to work with clients. The first few years in this business can be tough, as a client base is built, but the financial rewards can be large! Of course, the job of the stockbroker is to generate maximum return for clients' money, resulting in the possibility for large commissions and bonuses.

Some stockbrokers may make independent decisions on their client's behalf, or work closely with the client to determine where investment money should be placed. Even if you do not have an interest in being a stockbroker, understanding the mechanics of a stock market has profound impact on your personal investments in stock,

bonds, and mutual funds, and your retirement accounts such as 401(k). It is your money and you should work closely with your broker to understand and impact the investment decisions. You can also invest on your own using online trading companies. However, in any investment decisions, knowledge and understanding of the markets and companies or investment tools are a must. There are several financial newspapers and Web sites that can be of help: *Wall Street Journal, Investor's Business Daily, Money, BusinessWeek,* www.finance.yahoo.com, The Street.com, MSN Money, and so on.

The investment field is fast paced and allows a person to use his or her analytical skills, while utilizing human relations skills as well.

funds that are listed. It is simple to change investment objectives with mutual funds. Switching money, for example, from a bond fund to a stock fund, and then back, is generally no more difficult than calling an 800 number or clicking a mouse.

Finally, let's look at reading bond quotations, as shown in Figure 13.13. First, the ZR in the first column means it is a zero-coupon bond,

	FUND	NAV	NET CHG	YTD %RET	3-YR %RET
	American Century Ist				
Name of the fund family	DivBnd	10.33	−0.01	7.1	8.3
	EqIndex	3.62	−0.01	−20.3	−12.9
The price at which a fund's shares can be purchased or sold; called net asset value (NAV)	EqGro	15.58	−0.01	−18.4	−12.0
	EqInc	6.58	−0.03	−4.7	9.3
	IncGro	22.29	−0.03	−17.6	−10.8
	IntlDisc r	9.01	0.04	−12.4	−13.7
Name of the specific fund	IntlGr	6.51	0.02	−18.4	−16.8
	Select	29.49	−0.05	−20.7	−15.1
	StrMod	5.32	...	−8.6	NS
	Ultra	22.05	−0.03	−20.7	−15.8
	Value	6.03	−0.02	−11.8	6.6

The rate of percentage return of the fund year to date

Change from the previous day's NAV

Rate of percentage return of the fund for the past 3 years

figure 13.12

SAMPLE MUTUAL FUND QUOTES

Alan Wong was facing a dilemma. He had just inherited $25,000 and was considering taking several months off from work and purchasing new furniture. After meeting with his friend, Lydia, for coffee, however, he realized he might be much better off investing the money. First, Lydia explained to him that furniture does not "appreciate" (that is, gain value); rather, it depreciates (loses value). Therefore, she reminded him (perhaps reading her friend's mind), an expensive car would not be a good investment either.

Lydia pointed out to him that with his Associate's degree in business, now was the best time to work and maximize his earning power and to build his resume, rather than taking time off from work. She also explained some of the basics of the stock market to him: stocks, bonds, and mutual funds. Stocks represent ownership of a company, while a mutual fund is ownership of many different companies. Bonds are really like a loan to a company, where the purchaser of the bond gets interest from the money "lent" to the company. The advantage of a mutual fund is being able to diversify risk. In other words, rather than putting all of his money in one stock, he could put it into several stocks, which would spread the risk.

Lydia explained to Alan that he could use a stock-broker to manage his investments, rather than having to do it all himself. Hundreds, if not thousands of companies handle investments for clients.

Although Alan really wanted the new furniture, he decided to buy only a bedroom set rather than a houseful and to invest the rest of the money and continue working. In fact, he decided to automatically deduct 5 percent of his salary every month to go into his investment account. After meeting with a stockbroker and seeing how much his money will grow in a mere five years, he knows he has made the right decision.

which means the bond does not pay any interest to the buyer until maturity date, although interest is being earned throughout the duration of the bond. After the name of the bond is the interest rate and the year interest will be paid. Next is the current yield of the bond. Next to the current yield is the volume, which indicates the number of bonds traded within that day. The last two columns contain the price of the bond and the change from the previous trading day.

figure 13.13

SAMPLE BOND QUOTES

This is a zero-coupon bond

CV means this is a convertible bond

These IBM bonds pay 8.375% interest and mature in 2019

Bonds	Yld	Vol	Bond Close	Chg
GMA zr 5	...	27	368.88	...
Hilton 5.06	cv	30	96.13	–0.13
Honywhl zr09	...	5	68.13	...
HousF 6.750,11	6.8	10	99.00	+2.00
IBM 7.500,13	6.5	4	115.00	...
IBM 8.375,19	6.8	94	123.00	...
IBM 6.500,28	6.2	10	104.38	...
JCPL 7.125,04	7.1	10	101.00	...

Number of bonds traded this day

The price of this bond increased $20 from the previous day

This bond is currently selling at a premium ($101.00)

This bond is currently yielding 6.2%

SELF-CHECK QUESTIONS

1. Why does a company issue stocks or bonds?
2. What is the difference between a mutual fund and a stock?
3. Find a stock quotation and explain the meaning of each of the columns.

summary

This chapter has been all about money! Money has the basic characteristics of portability, divisibility, stability, durability, and uniqueness. The three categories of money are M-1 (cash); M-2 (cash plus liquid assets like savings and CDs); and M-3 (large institutional deposits and transactions between banks).

The Federal Reserve is the institution that controls the money supply in the United States. The chapter discussed the basic operations of the Fed in exercising this responsibility. What the Federal Reserve does dramatically affects our day-to-day lives. For example, the choices the Federal Reserve makes can change how much, or how little, we pay for a house or a car. In this chapter, we discussed how the Fed tries to control the money supply in order to control inflation or deflation. The basic tools with which the Fed controls the money supply are reserve requirements, open-market operations, and the discount rate.

The second half of the chapter explained the securities markets. We defined and discussed the stock market, stocks, bonds, mutual funds, index funds, the SEC, and insider trading. A stock represents ownership of one company, while investing in a mutual fund is having ownership of several companies. Bonds, on the other hand, are basically a loan to a company, for which you receive interest.

We discussed the different securities exchange areas, pointing out that there are many smaller, regional securities exchanges, besides the larger ones we generally think about. Finally, we discussed how to read the stock market pages of the newspaper.

key terms

money 420
barter 420
money supply 422
M-1 422
M-2 422
M-3 423

Federal Reserve 423
monetary policy 424
Federal Open Market
  Committee (FOMC) 424
reserve 425
reserve requirement 425

open-market
  operations 426
discount rate 426
securities 429
securities market 429

applying your skills

1. In small groups, take out some bills ($1 and $5) and look at them closely. Note that it says "Federal Reserve Note" on the top. Look at your $1 notes. You will find a jagged circle in the middle of the left side. What states are they from? Note also the words "This note is legal tender for all debts, public and private." What role does the Fed play in making such money?

2. In small groups, discuss the role of the Federal Reserve and its current chair, Ben Bernanke. Do you think it has too much power? Too little power? Explain.

3. Go to your campus library and ask the reference librarian for information from Standard & Poor's and Moody's Investors Service concerning bond ratings. Analyze the process used by these two firms in evaluating and rating corporate bonds, and then report what you find to the class.

4. Go to the Web sites of Charles Schwab (www.schwab.com), E*Trade (www.etrade.com), and Ameritrade (www.ameritrade.com). Investigate each of the brokerage companies and compare what they offer to investors in terms of research and advice, and how their price structures work. Evaluate each of the brokers according to specific services they offer, and then decide which service you consider most appropriate to your investment objectives. Be prepared to defend your choice to the class.

5. Read *The Wall Street Journal, Investor's Business Daily,* or the business section of your local newspaper each day for two weeks and then select three stocks for your portfolio from the New York Stock Exchange and three from the NASDAQ. Track your stocks for three days and discuss the daily changes that occurred in each of the stocks.

6. Compare the benefits a bank offers versus a credit union. Make a chart comparing advantages and disadvantages of each.

7. If you had to make investing decisions, would you prefer to invest in bonds, mutual funds, or stocks? Why? What are the advantages and disadvantages of investing in each?

8. Research two IPOs that have been offered in the past six months. Discuss their performance from the first day of trading compared to today.

the internet in action

1. *Purpose:* To experience the excitement of the New York Stock Exchange (NYSE) trading floor and to explain the anatomy of a stock trade.

   Exercise: Go to the NYSE's Web site at www.nyse.com.

   - Click on the Trading Floor button to find panoramic views of the NYSE trading floor from a variety of perspectives. How many people work on the trading floor? What roles do the specialists play in stock exchanges?

   - Describe the anatomy of a trade from the moment an investor places an order until the investor receives confirmation that the trade has been made.

   - If you have a high-speed connection (higher than 56k), you can experience the fast pace of the trading floor for yourself by clicking About NYSE, then Education. There you will find a series of videos prepared in conjunction with Cornell University. Click on the segment "Broker Technology." How has technology helped brokers keep up with the pace of the trading floor?

2. *Purpose:* To learn a few fun facts about U.S. currency.

   Exercise: Your parents always told you that money doesn't grow on trees. Other than that, what else do you know about money? Go to the Web site of the Bureau of Engraving and Printing (BEP) at www.moneyfactory.com and answer the following questions:

   - What is "paper" currency made of?

   - How much ink does the BEP use to print money each day?

   - How much does it cost to produce a paper currency note?

   - Approximately how many times could you fold a piece of currency before it would tear?

   - How long is the life span of a $1 bill?

   - What is the origin of the dollar sign ($)?

   - Why did the BEP print paper notes in 3-, 5-, 10-, 25-, and 50-cent denominations during the Civil War?

   - If you had 10 billion $1 notes and spent one every second of every day, how long would it take you to go broke?

   - Who was the only woman whose portrait appeared on a U.S. paper currency note?

   - When did "In God We Trust" become part of the U.S. currency design?

   - Whose picture is on a $100 bill? (If you're still a kid at heart, you might enjoy playing the money trivia games at the Treasury Dome at www.bep.treas.gov/kids_site/tdome.html.)

PERSONAL FINANCE

The Forbes 400

One billion dollars is no longer enough. The price of admission to the 2007 Forbes 400 list, the 25th anniversary edition of the Forbes 400, is $1.3 billion, up $300 million from 2006. The collective net worth of the nation's mightiest plutocrats rose $290 billion to $1.54 trillion.

Bill Gates, founder and CEO of Microsoft.

Let's face it—the chances of becoming a billionaire are not really very good; chances of becoming a millionaire are much better, though. There are about 7 million people in the world with more than $1 million in financial assets. More than 2 million of these millionaires live in the United States. One of the best ways to learn how to become a millionaire is to do what compa-nies do: benchmark those who are successful. That is, find out what all those millionaires did to make their money. For over 20 years, Thomas Stanley has been doing just that—studying wealthy people. His research is available in a book called *The Millionaire Next Door: The Surprising Secrets of America's Wealthy,* which he co-authored with William Danko. Stanley and Danko found that the majority of millionaires are entrepreneurs who own one or more small businesses. Self-employed people are four times as likely to be millionaires as people who earn a paycheck working for others. The average income of American millionaires is $131,000 a year.

CHAPTER 14

After reading this chapter, you should be able to:

1. Describe the six steps to successful financial management.

2. Explain strategies for building a financial base.

3. Define the different types of insurance and how they can protect your financial base.

4. Describe strategies for effective retirement planning.

So how did they get to be millionaires? They saved their money. To become a millionaire by the time you are 50 or so, you have to save about 15 percent of your income every year—starting when you are in your 20s. If you start later, you have to save an even larger percentage. The secret is to put your money in a place where it will grow without you having to pay taxes on it. You'll learn how to do that in this chapter. To save that 15 percent a year, you have to spend less than you earn. Discipline in spending must begin with your first job and stay with you all your life. To save money, the millionaires Stanley studied tended to own modest homes and to buy used cars. In short, becoming a millionaire has more to do with thrift than with how much you earn.

Sources: The Forbes 400, edited by Matthew Miller, *Forbes Magazine,* September 20, 2007; and Thomas Stanley and William Danko, *The Millionaire Next Door: The Surprising Secrets of America's Wealthy* (Thorndike Press, 1999).

This chapter provides information on becoming a financial success.

INTRODUCTION TO PERSONAL FINANCE

Do you want to be a billionaire or, more plausibly, a millionaire? If so, then you need to do what other rich people have done. You need to get an education, work hard, save your money, and make purchases carefully. This chapter will give you more insight into how to manage your finances. Are you ready to do the hard work it takes to become a millionaire? To reach your goal, your final answer must be "Yes!"

WHY PLAN PERSONAL FINANCES?

America is a capitalist country. It follows, then, that the secret to success in such a country is to have capital. With capital, you can take nice vacations, raise a family, invest in stocks and bonds, buy the goods and services you want, give generously to others, and retire with enough money to live out your years in comfort. Money management, however, is not easy. You have to earn the money in the first place. Then you have to learn how to save money, spend money wisely, and insure yourself against the risks of serious accidents, illness, or death. We will discuss each of these issues in this chapter, so that you can begin making financial plans for the rest of your life. With a bit of luck, and a lot of discipline, you could be one of the millionaires Stanley and Danko interview for their next book (see the chapter's opening profile).

After you complete your education, the chances are good that you will find a well-paying job. Throughout history, an investment in education has paid off, regardless of the state of the economy. Education has become even more important since we entered the information age. The lifetime income of families headed by individuals with varied levels of education include the following: no high school degree, $630,000; high school degree, $994,080; Associate's degree, $1,269,850; and bachelor's degree, $1,667,700.[1] One way to begin to be a millionaire, therefore, is to get further education.

Many people use their education to find successful careers and to improve their earning potential, but at retirement they have little to show for their efforts. Making money is one thing; saving, investing, and spending it wisely is something else. Less than 10 percent of the U.S. population has accumulated enough money by retirement age to

Margie Keen is working on earning her Associate's degree in business. She enrolled in college because she was injured at her manufacturing job last year. She knew she needed to retrain in order to start a new career. Margie has two small children and her life partner earns slightly above minimum wage. Margie is worried that after she finishes school, she still won't have enough to save money for her kids' education and her own retirement. Margie decides to do some research to see how she can work through this challenge.

live comfortably.[2] Despite the messages we receive from many get-rich schemes, getting rich means saving and investing properly. Only slightly more than half of all households have a retirement account. Following the six steps listed in the next section will help you become one of those with enough to live comfortably after retirement. Keep in mind that these steps are useful whether you have $500 in your savings account or $500,000.

Steps to Controlling Your Assets

The only way to save enough money to achieve your financial goals is to make more than you spend! We all know that saving money can be difficult, but saving money is not only possible, it is imperative in order to accumulate enough to be financially secure. People can save money and still live comfortably, purchase the goods and services they need, and still save for their futures.

Step 1: Take an Inventory of Your Financial Assets

To take inventory, you need to develop a balance sheet for yourself. Remember from Chapter 12 that a balance sheet starts with the fundamental accounting equation:

$$\text{Assets} - \text{Liabilities} = \text{Owner's Equity}$$

You can develop your own balance sheet, similar to the one presented, by listing your assets (e.g., savings, checking account, investments, TV, DVD, computer, bicycle, car, jewelry, and clothes) on one side and liabilities (e.g., mortgage, school loans, credit card debt, and auto loans) on the other. Assets include anything you own. For our purpose, evaluate your assets on the basis of their current value, not the purchase price, as is required in formal accounting statements. If you have no debts (liabilities), then your assets equal your net worth (in a corporation it's called owner's equity). If you do have debts, you must subtract them from your assets to get your net worth. If the value of your liabilities exceeds the value of your assets, you are not on the path to financial security. You may need more financial discipline in your life. However, many students find that their liabilities *do* exceed their assets. If this is the case, you will likely be able to change this once you are finished with college and get a well-paying job.

Now is an excellent time to think about how much money you will need to accomplish all your goals. The more you visualize your goals, the easier it is to begin saving for them.

Step 2: Keep Track of All Your Expenses

You may often find yourself running out of cash (cash flow). In such circumstances, the only way to trace where the money is going is to keep track of every cent you spend. Keeping records of your expenses can be a rather tedious but necessary chore if you want to learn discipline. Actually, tracking your expenses could turn out to be an enjoyable task because you will be completely in control of your own finances. Here is what to do: Carry a notepad with you wherever you go and record what you spend as you go through the day. That notepad is your journal. At the end of the week, record your journal entries into a record book or computerized accounting program. Develop certain categories (accounts) to make the task easier and more informative. For example, you can have a category called "food" for all food you bought from the grocery or the convenience store during the week. You might want to have a separate account for meals eaten away from home, because you can dramatically cut such costs if you bring lunches that you made at home. Other categories could include automobile (including car payments, insurance, gas, and maintenance), clothing, utilities, entertainment, donations to charity, and gifts. Most people like to have a category called "miscellaneous" for spontaneous purchases that do not fit into any of your other categories. People are often surprised by how much they spend on miscellaneous items after monitoring their expenses over time. You can develop your accounts on the basis of what is most important to you, or where you spend the most money. Once you have recorded all of your expenses, it is relatively easy to see where you are spending too much money and what you have to do to save more money.

Keeping accurate records of all your income and expenses can help you control your finances.

Step 3: Prepare a Budget

Once you understand your current financial situation and your sources of revenue and expenses, prepare a personal budget.[3] Remember, budgets are financial

FIRST CHOICE COST PER MONTH	ALTERNATE CHOICE COST PER MONTH	SAVINGS PER MONTH
Starbucks caffe latté $3.00 for 20 days = $60.00	Quick Trip's Cappuccino $0.60 for 20 days = $12.00	$48.00
Fast-food lunch of burger, fries, and soft drink $4.00 for 20 days = $80.00	Lunch brought from home $2.00 for 20 days = $40.00	40.00
Evian bottled water $1.50 for 20 days = $30.00	Generic bottled water $0.50 for 20 days = $10.00	20.00
CD = $15.00	Listen to your old CDs = $0.00	15.00
Banana Republic T-shirt = $34.00	Old Navy T-shirt = $10.00	24.00
	Total savings per month	$147.00
		$\times$ 48 months
	Total savings through 4 years of college	$7,056.00

plans. Items that are important in a household budget include mortgage or rent, utilities, food, clothing, vehicles, furniture, life insurance, car insurance, and medical care. It is also important to make choices regarding how much to allow for such expenses as dining out, entertainment, and so on. Keep in mind that what you spend now reduces what you can save later. For example, spending $3.50 a day for cigarettes adds up to about $25 a week, $100 a month, $1,200 a year. If you can save $4 or $5 a day, you'll have almost $1,800 saved by the end of the year. Keep up this savings during all four years of college and you will have saved more than $7,000 by graduation. And that's before adding any interest earned. Cost-saving choices you might consider to reach this goal are listed in Figure 14.1.

Running a household is similar to running a small business. It takes the same careful record keeping, the same budget processes and forecasting, the same control procedures, and often the same need to periodically borrow funds. Suddenly, concepts such as credit and interest rates become only too real, which is where some knowledge of finance, investments, and budgeting pays off. Thus, the time spent learning budgeting techniques will benefit you throughout your life.

figure 14.1

POSSIBLE COST-SAVING CHOICES

Saving money can be challenging, but it does not mean you have to give up things that are important to you forever; it just means that by changing spending habits, you can save lots of money!

q: Why do you think some people choose
» » not to live by a budget?

Step 4: Pay Off Your Debts

After paying off your monthly bills, the first thing to do with the remaining money is to pay off your debts. Start with the debts that carry the highest interest rates. Credit card debt, for example, may be costing you 14 percent or more a year. Merely paying off such debts will set you on a path toward financial freedom. It is better to pay off a debt that costs 14 percent than to put the money in a bank account that earns, say, 2 percent or less. Another recommendation is to call your credit card companies and ask for lower interest rates.

On another note, savings in the United States is at an all-time low. In 2007, the United States consumer had a personal savings rate of less than 1 percent.[4] This problem is deeply concerning because it means more and more Americans are not only avoiding saving any money, but are also getting into debt.

Step 5: Start a Savings Plan

Saving money every month in a separate account for large purchases will help you in the future, such as when you need to purchase a car or a house. When it comes time to make those purchases, you will have more cash to use for your down payment. Saving for significant down payments will enable you to reduce finance charges and can even help you obtain a lower interest rate. The best way to save money is to *pay yourself first*. If you have created a budget that realistically identifies your expenses, every time you receive a paycheck you will be able to first put money in savings and then plan what to do with the rest.[5] You can arrange with your bank or mutual fund to deduct a certain amount every month. You will be pleasantly surprised when the money starts accumulating and earning interest over time. With some discipline, you can eventually reach your goal of becoming financially secure. Figure 14.2 shows how $5,000 invested over 25 years can grow to nearly $70,000! Look at Figure 14.3 to see how money grows with monthly deposits.

figure 14.2

HOW MONEY GROWS

This chart illustrates how $5,000 would grow at various rates of return over a 25-year period.

TIME	ANNUAL RATE OF RETURN			
	2%	**5%**	**8%**	**11%**
5 years	$5,520	$ 6,381	$ 7,347	$ 8,425
10 years	6,095	8,144	10,795	14,197
15 years	6,729	10,395	15,861	23,923
20 years	7,430	13,266	23,305	40,312
25 years	8,203	16,932	34,242	67,927

TIME	2%	5%	8%	11%
5 years	$ 9,308	$10,487	$11,857	$ 13,414
10 years	14,069	17,551	22,075	27,965
15 years	19,330	26,605	37,296	53,121
20 years	25,144	38,225	59,975	96,613
25 years	31,569	53,137	93,762	171,807

figure 14.3

HOW MONEY GROWS WITH MONTHLY DEPOSITS

Source: Math.com, 2007.

This calculation is based on an initial deposit of $5,000 with monthly deposits of $60. How can you save $60 in a month?

Step 6: Borrow Money Only to Buy Assets That Have the Potential to Increase in Value or Generate Income

Never borrow money for ordinary expenses, such as food, because you will only get into more debt. If you have budgeted for emergencies, such as car repairs and health care costs, you should be able to stay financially secure. Most financial experts will tell you to save about six months of earnings for contingency purposes, which means keeping the money in highly liquid accounts (money that is easily accessible), such as the bank or a money market fund. Only the most unexpected of expenses should cause you to borrow. It is hard to wait until you have enough money to buy what you want, but learning to wait is a critical part of self-discipline. Of course, you can always try to produce more income by working overtime, or by working on the side, for extra revenue.

Keep in mind that borrowing money for education expenses or to purchase a home is a *good* type of borrowing. In other words, these are investments that will likely grow in value over time. Review Figure 14.4 to see how much more you can earn with an education.

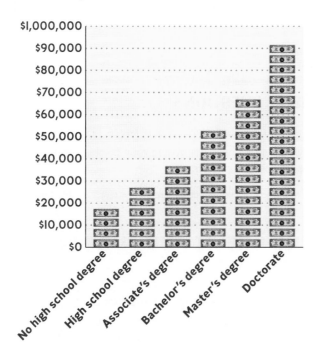

figure 14.4

WHO SAYS COLLEGE DOESN'T PAY?

Source: U.S. Census Bureau, table 8, "Income in 2005 by Educational Attainment."

This figure shows the average income of Americans with various levels of education. A reduction in your standard of living now can have great benefits in the future!

Borrowing money to buy a car, while sometimes necessary, is the sort of debt that does not pay you back in the long run because cars depreciate in value. In almost all cases, cars you purchase will never be worth more than the day you make the purchase. Likewise, charging items on a credit card is the same as borrowing money. A good rule of thumb is to never charge more on a credit card than you are able to pay off at the end of the month. The credit card company is giving you the money now, and you will have to pay it back later, with fees and interest. For example, suppose you paid $4.00 for a fast-food value meal with your credit card. Every month you do not pay off your credit card, the interest you must pay on your balance is 14 percent. After one month of not paying the credit card balance in full, that value meal's cost to you is $4.56; after two months it is $5.20; after six months that $4.00 value meal now has cost you $8.79—over double what you would have paid if you had simply used cash!

People can prevent themselves from overspending by resisting the urge to spend. Consumers are constantly bombarded by advertisements and salespeople wanting them to buy. It is sometimes difficult to discern the purchases we make in order to survive (fresh fruits and vegetables) versus the purchases we make because we want that good or service (a French manicure or a bag of Cheetos). Attempting to cut down on wants and focusing only on needs is a huge step toward becoming a millionaire.

By following these six steps, individuals will not only have money for investment but also will have developed most of the financial techniques needed to become financially secure. At first, people may find it hard to live within a budget. Nonetheless, the payoff is well worth the pain.

SELF-CHECK QUESTIONS

1. What is the role education plays in your lifetime income?
2. Write down the six steps to controlling your assets. Which ones are you good at? Which may need improvement?

Section Outline

Managing Credit and Building a Financial Base

- Real Estate: A Relatively Secure Investment
- Where to Put Savings
- Learning to Manage Credit

MANAGING CREDIT AND BUILDING A FINANCIAL BASE

Living *frugally* (not participating in unnecessary spending) is extremely difficult for the average person.[6] Most people are eager to spend their money on a new car, furniture, CDs, and clothes.[7] They tend to look for a fancy apartment with all the amenities. A capital-generating strategy may require forgoing most, though not all, of these purchases to accumulate investment money. The living style required is similar to the one adopted by most college students: a relatively inexpensive apartment furnished in hand-me-downs from parents, friends, and resale shops. It means not buying the expensive new car but instead purchasing a used car and saving the difference or at least not going into debt. These suggestions do not imply that people can never make purchases based on wants, but they do mean that people must balance the purchase of "wants" while making sure they are saving at the same time. Many students feel that immediately after graduating college they should have the same standard of living as their parents. It is imperative to keep in mind that it took years for parents to get to the standard of living that allowed them to buy a house or new cars.

People are wise to plan their financial futures with the same excitement and dedication they bring to other aspects of their lives. When individuals marry or commit to a lifetime partner, it is important to discuss financial issues. Conflicts over money are a major cause of separations and divorce, so agreeing on a financial strategy before making commitments is very important. A great strategy is to try to live on one income and to save the other. The longer people wait before marriage or assuming joint financial responsibilities, the more likely it will be that one or the other of you can be earning enough to make that savings plan work—as college graduates. If one person nets $36,000 per year after taxes, saving that income for five years quickly adds up to $198,000 (plus interest).

What do you do with the money you accumulate? The first investment might be a low-priced home.[8] You should make this investment as early as possible. The purpose of this investment is to lock in payments for your shelter at a fixed amount, which is possible by owning a home, but not by renting. Through the years, home ownership has been a wise investment. We will discuss home buying next.

Real Estate: A Relatively Secure Investment

Owning a home can be a great investment—one that you live in! The tax savings from owning a home are also very beneficial.

Homes provide several investment benefits. First, a home is the one investment that you can live in. Second, once people buy a home, the payments are relatively fixed (though taxes and utilities go up). As incomes rise, the house payments get easier and easier to make, but renters often find that rent tends to go up at least as fast as income. Paying for a home is a good way of forcing yourself to save because every month you must make the payments. Those payments are an investment that proves very rewarding over time for most people. As capital accumulates and

figure 14.5

TYPES OF HOME MORTGAGES

Fixed rate	The interest rate is fixed and payment is the same throughout the life of the loan.
Adjustable rate mortgage (ARM)	The interest rate changes, therefore the payment throughout the life of the loan will change.
Interest only mortgage	The interest is not charged for a certain period of time. After the period of time, the payment will change once interest is added.
80/20 loan	If a buyer does not have a down payment, he or she takes out two loans, one for 80% of the value of the home and one for 20% for the down payment.

values rise, people can sell the first homes and then buy different homes (in better locations or which offer more living space), or they may even be able to purchase investment properties. Furthermore, a home is a good asset to use when applying for a loan. There are several types of home loans, which are shown in Figure 14.5. When choosing a loan, it is important not to get sold on the "product of the day," but rather look at what type of mortgage best suits your needs.

After understanding the benefits of home ownership versus renting, decide whether those same principles apply should you decide to start your own business (can you purchase the work space or do you need to rent it?)—or owning versus renting equipment, vehicles, and the like. Figure 14.6 will give you some idea of how expensive a house you can afford, given your income. You can find current mortgage interest rates and mortgage calculators at www.interest.com.

Another advantage to buying a home is that the interest paid on the mortgage is tax deductible, and so are the property taxes. During the first few years, virtually all the mortgage payments go toward the interest on the loan, so almost all the early payments are tax deductible—a tremendous benefit for home owners and investors. For example, if your payments are $1,000 a month, most of that $1,000 will go toward interest. At the end of the year, a large percentage of the $12,000 you

figure 14.6

HOW MUCH HOUSE CAN YOU AFFORD?

Mortgage payments shouldn't amount to more than 28% of your net income.

Source: Federal Housing Finance Board.

		INTEREST RATES			
INCOME	MONTHLY PAYMENT	5%	6%	7%	15%
$ 30,000	$ 700	$106,263	$ 98,303	$ 91,252	$ 56,870
50,000	1,167	180,291	167,081	155,376	98,606
80,000	1,867	287,213	266,056	247,308	155,916
100,000	2,333	361,240	334,832	311,433	198,013

| | | Loan amount: $10,000 | | Monthly loan payments: $212.47 |
Term of loan: 5 years — Total interest paid over life of loan: $2,478.23
Interest rate: 10%

YEAR	LOAN BALANCE	YEARLY INTEREST PAID	YEARLY PRINCIPAL PAID	TOTOAL INTEREST
2006	$8377.32	$926.96	$1622.68	$ 926,96
2007	6584.72	757.05	1792.6	1684.01
2008	4604.42	569.34	1980.31	2253.35
2009	2416.75	361.98	2187.67	2515.33
2010	0	132.9	2416.75	2748.23

paid throughout the year can be deducted from your income, thereby reducing your taxes. Property taxes reduce your taxable income in this way as well. **Amortization** is the gradual elimination of a liability, such as a mortgage.

Where to Put Savings

You have learned that one place to invest the money you have saved is in a home. Where are some other good places to save your money? For a young person, one of the worst places to keep long-term investments is in a bank or savings and loan. As noted earlier, it is important to have about six months' savings in the bank for emergencies, but the bank is not the best place to invest. One of the best places to invest over time has been the stock market. The stock market does tend to go up and down, but over a longer period of time it has proved to be one of the best investments. That's important, because about half of U.S. households own stock and roughly the same percentage own mutual funds. Stocks and mutual funds should not be viewed as daily trading commodities. There must be a long-term investment perspective. You can start small and build your investments for long-term.

Remember, the greater the risk, the greater the return. The time to purchase stocks is when the prices are low. Actually, when stocks collapse—as they have in recent years—it is an opportunity to get into the stock market, not avoid it. The average investor buys when the market is high and sells when it is low. Clearly, that approach is not a good idea. It takes courage to buy when everyone else is selling, and this is called a **contrarian approach** to investing. In the long run, however, the contrarian approach is the way the rich get richer. Chapter 12 gave you a foundation for starting an investment program. That chapter also talked about bonds, but bonds have traditionally lagged behind stocks as a long-term investment.

figure 14.7

SAMPLE AMORTIZATION SCHEDULE

As you can see, the bulk of the interest is paid in the first two years of the loan.

Source: Freddie Mac, accessed November 29, 2007.

amortization
The gradual elimination of a liability.

contrarian approach
Purchasing stock when others are selling.

Whatever you decide to do, putting your money somewhere it can grow is important to long-term financial health. Spending below your means, taking tax advantages where you can, and saving as much as you can are very important to remember—and put into practice.

Learning to Manage Credit

You are no doubt familiar with credit cards. Companies like Visa, MasterCard, American Express, and Discover are well known to most people, not always to their benefit, even though the availability of credit can be helpful at times. However, credit card purchases have finance charges that usually amount to anywhere from 12 to 20 percent annually, which means that if you finance a TV, home appliances, and other purchases with a credit card, you may end up spending much more than if you had paid with cash (think back to the fast-food example earlier in the chapter). A good manager of personal finances, like a good businessperson, pays off debt on time and takes advantage of the savings made possible by paying early. People who have established a capital fund can tap that fund to make large purchases and then pay back the fund (with interest if so desired), rather than paying finance charges.

Credit cards are an important element in a personal financial system, even if the wise person rarely uses them. First, some merchants request credit cards as a form of identification. It may be difficult to buy certain goods or services, such as renting a car, without having a credit card because businesses use them for identification and assured payment. Second, credit cards can be used to keep track of purchases. A gasoline credit card, for example, provides records of purchases over time for income tax and financial planning purposes. It is sometimes easier to write one check at the end of the month for several purchases than to carry around cash. Besides, when cash is stolen or lost, it is simply gone; a stolen credit card can be canceled to protect your account.

Finally, a credit card is simply more convenient than cash or checks. If you come upon a special sale and need more money than you usually carry, paying by credit is quick and easy (but remember—it *is* borrowing money!). You can carry less cash and do not have to worry about keeping your checkbook balanced as often. As mentioned before, if you do use a credit card, pay the balance in full during the period when no interest is charged. Also, you may want to choose a card that pays you back in cash, like the Discover card, or others that offer paybacks, such as credit toward the purchase of a car, free

Credit companies like First USA are quite willing to give students credit cards. Credit card offers can be enticing, including free gifts for applying and low interest rates in the first year. Why are the companies so eager to give you a card?

long-distance minutes, or frequent-flier miles. The value of these givebacks can be from 1 to 5 percent.[9] Rather than paying 14 percent interest, you actually earn a certain percentage—quite a difference. Some cards have no annual fees; others have lower interest rates.[10]

The danger of a credit card is the flip side of its convenience. Too often, consumers buy goods and services that they would not normally buy if they had to pay cash or write a check on funds in the bank. Using credit cards, consumers often pile up debts to the point where they are unable to pay. If you are not the type of person who can stick to a financial plan or household budget, *it may be better not to have a credit card at all.*

Reducing debt now can help you save for the future.

q : What are some ways to reduce the amount of debt you
» » have, or some ways to ensure you don't have debt in the future?

Credit cards are a helpful tool for the financially careful buyer. They're a financial disaster to people with little financial restraint and tastes beyond their income.[11] College students take note: Of the debtors seeking help at the National Consumer Counseling Service, more than half were between 18 and 32 years of age.

Credit Reports

Every person should get a credit report at least once a year. It can be obtained by contacting one, or all, of the three main credit reporting agencies: Equifax, Experian, and Trans Union. A recent amendment to the Fair Credit Reporting Act requires these companies to provide credit reports at no cost, once per year.[12]

The advantage to seeing your credit report, first and foremost, is so you may monitor activity. If someone got your social security number and managed to open an account in your name, the credit report would provide you with this information.

The information on a credit report includes the names of companies that have checked your credit score, as well as the names of companies to whom you owe money. The report also includes a FICO score, which is based on several factors, such as on-time payments to creditors and amounts owed. **FICO** is an acronym for Fair Isaac Corporation, the company that provides the most well-known and widely used credit score model in the United States.

FICO
This is a credit score assigned by the three major credit reporting bureaus.

ETHICAL challenge

Credit Card Offers

The offers come in the mail and over the Internet. Get a credit card now! People eager to give away free gifts, such as T-shirts and pennants in exchange for you purchasing items on credit, seem to be everywhere. All you have to do is fill out an application for a credit card. Do you want an extra 10 percent off a store purchase? Just fill out the application for a store credit card. Even students in high school are targeted for such free offers. More than 70 percent of students in college now have at least one credit card. The average balance is $3,066. For many students, the balance is a lot higher.[13]

Suppose you have a chance to work part-time for a credit card company passing out free gifts and urging students to sign up. You have noticed that many students abuse such cards and build up debt way beyond what they can afford. The pay for this job is pretty good, however, and it is not your fault that students don't always handle credit cards well.

Questions

1. Would you accept the job?
2. What are the ethical issues involved? Why?

The FICO score is the information that is used to determine the interest rate you should pay, and whether or not you should get a loan. In other words, it predicts how likely you are to default on a loan. Obviously, your credit report can affect your ability to buy a car, a home, or obtain school loans, which is why it is so important to track.

Knowing what is in your credit report can help you plan for future purchases and investments. Consumers are allowed access to their credit reports from all three major agencies once per year. You can now access them online through sites like www.freecreditreport.com.

BUYING INSURANCE

One of the last things young people think about is the idea that they may get sick or have an accident and die. It is not a pleasant thought. Even more unpleasant, though, is the reality of young people dying every day in accidents and other unexpected ways. You have to know only one of these families to see the emotional and financial havoc such a loss causes. Purchasing insurance is one of those tasks we all must do. **Insurance** is a written contract between the party being insured and the insurer where the financial responsibility for losses transfers to the insurer up to a specified limit. Figure 14.8 shows the reasons for buying insurance.

insurance
A written contract between the party being insured and the insurer where the financial responsibility for losses transfers to the insurer up to a specified limit.

Auto Insurance

The first type of insurance we will discuss is auto insurance. Most states require auto insurance, and if you owe money on your car, the lender will require insurance as well. *Liability insurance* means that if you hit someone else with your car, your insurance would pay to repair the damage on the other vehicle, but not your vehicle. *Full coverage* means that the insurance would pay for both your car and the other person's car. *Uninsured motorist coverage* pays for damages to your car if you are hit by someone who does not have insurance.

Life Insurance

Today, with so many husbands and wives both working, the loss of a spouse can also mean a sudden severe drop in income. To provide protection from

INSURANCE NEEDS IN EARLY YEARS ARE HIGH	INSURANCE NEEDS DECLINE AS YOU GROW OLDER
1. Children are young and need money for education.	1. Children are grown.
2. Mortgage is high relative to income.	2. Mortgage is low or completely paid off.
3. Often there are auto payments and other bills to pay.	3. Debts are paid off.
4. Loss of income would be disastrous.	4. Insurance needs are few.
	5. Retirement income is needed.

figure 14.8

REASONS FOR BUYING INSURANCE

Finding the right insurance is important. Be sure to research all your needs to make the best decision. Web sites such as www. insweb.com can help.

term insurance

Pure insurance protection with no savings feature for a given number of years that typically costs less the younger you buy it.

such risks, a couple or business should buy life insurance. Today, the least expensive and simplest form of life insurance is **term insurance.**[14] It is pure insurance protection, with no savings features, for a given number of years, that typically costs less the younger you are when you buy it. Typically, life insurance costs increase as your age does. With term life insurance, the price is fixed for the term of the policy (for example, with a 10-year-term policy, the price will not change for 10 years). When you renew the policy, however, your premium will be based on your attained age and the premiums are likely to be higher. It is helpful to check out prices for term insurance through a Web-based service.

How much insurance do you need? *Newsweek* magazine posed this question: We just had our first baby; how much life insurance should we have? Answer: Seven times your family income plus $100,000 for college. To be fair, apportion it so that a spouse earning 60 percent of the income carries 60 percent of the insurance. It is a good idea before buying life insurance to check out the insurance company through a rating service, such as A. M. Best (www.ambest.com) or Moody's Investors Service (www.moodys.com).

whole life insurance

Life insurance where some part of the money you pay goes toward pure insurance and another part goes toward savings, so you are buying both insurance and a savings plan.

Whole life insurance is another type of life insurance that is also called permanent life insurance—you pay the same premium for your entire life. However, some part of the money you pay for whole life insurance goes toward pure insurance and another part goes toward savings, so you are buying both insurance and a savings plan. This option may be a good idea for those people who have trouble saving money. A **universal life** policy is also permanent insurance plan that allows flexibility in your insurance and

universal life

A permanent insurance plan that allows flexibility in your insurance and savings amounts.

savings amounts. The investments traditionally are very conservative, but pay a steady interest rate.

Variable life insurance is similar to universal life insurance except that your excess premium is invested in stocks, mutual funds, or other high-yielding securities. Death benefits may thus vary, reflecting the performance of the investments. Some people, seeing the stock market go up for so many years, switched out of whole life policies to get the higher potential returns of variable life insurance. When the stock market plunged, they were not so certain of the wisdom of their choice. In the long run, however, stocks should rise again.

Life insurance companies recognized the desire that people had for higher returns on their insurance, and for protecting themselves against running out of money before they died, and began selling annuities. An **annuity** is a contract to make regular payments to a person for life or for a fixed period. With an annuity, you are guaranteed an income until you die. There are two kinds of annuities: fixed and variable. *Fixed annuities* are investments that pay the policyholder a specified interest rate. They are not as popular as *variable annuities,* which provide investment choices identical to mutual funds. Such annuities are gaining in popularity relative to term or whole life insurance.

Clearly, people have been choosing more risk to get greater returns when they retire. This means, however, that people must be more careful in selecting an insurance company and what investments are made with their money. Because life insurance is getting much more complex, it may be wise to consult a financial adviser who is not an insurance agent, before buying an insurance policy. He or she can help you make the wisest decision about insurance.

Health Insurance

Individuals need to consider protecting themselves from losses due to health problems.[15] You may have health insurance coverage through your employer. If not, you can buy insurance from a health insurance provider (e.g., Blue Cross/Blue Shield), a health maintenance organization (HMO), or a preferred provider organization (PPO). For quick online help in picking a health insurance provider, try www.EHealthInsurance.com or www.healthaxis.com (not available in all areas). You may be able to buy health insurance for less by buying it through a professional organization. When buying insurance, keep in mind that deductibles sometimes have to be met. A **deductible** is the amount that must be spent on health care before insurance companies will cover the remaining expenses. A co-payment some-

variable life insurance
A form of whole life insurance that invests the cash value of the policy in stocks or other high-yielding securities.

annuity
A contract to make regular payments to a person for life or for a fixed period.

deductible
The amount that must be spent on health care before insurance companies will cover the remaining expenses.

co-payment

An amount paid by the insured party when medical services are rendered.

disability insurance

A type of insurance that pays part of the cost of a long-term sickness or an accident.

rider

Supplemental insurance; also means an amendment to a contract.

times is required as well. A **co-payment** is an amount paid when medical services are rendered. A co-payment can be as little as $10, but could be quite a bit more. Another important consideration is whether or not doctors will accept your health care plan. Since there are so many varieties, be sure to do a careful search to find the best program for you and your family.

It is financially dangerous not to have health insurance. Hospital costs are simply too high to risk financial ruin by going uninsured. In fact, it is often a good idea to supplement health insurance policies with **disability insurance,** which pays part of the cost of a long-term sickness or an accident. Your chances of becoming disabled at an early age are much higher than are your chances of dying from an accident. Therefore, individuals must have the proper amount of disability insurance. Call an insurance agent or check the Internet for possible costs of such insurance. The cost is relatively low to protect yourself from losing your income for an extended period of time.

Homeowner's or Renter's Insurance

As you begin to accumulate possessions, consider getting insurance to protect against their loss. You might be surprised to total up how much it would cost to replace all your clothes, furniture, pots and pans, appliances, sporting goods, electronic equipment (e.g., computers), and other belongings. Apartment or homeowner's insurance covers losses of your possessions, but you must be careful to specify that you want *guaranteed replacement cost,* which means that the insurance company will give you whatever it costs to buy all of those things *new.* Such insurance costs a little more than a policy without guaranteed replacement, but you will get a lot more if you have a loss.

The other option is to buy insurance that covers the depreciated cost of the items. For example, a sofa you bought five years ago for $600 may be worth only $150 now. The current value is what you would get from insurance, not the $700 or more you may need to buy a brand-new sofa. The same is true for a computer that you paid $950 for a few years ago. If it were to be stolen, you would get only a few hundred dollars for it, rather than the replacement cost. Most policies do not cover expensive items, such as engagement and wedding rings and silver pieces of all kinds. You can buy a **rider** *(sometimes called supplemental insurance)* to your insurance policy that will cover such items at a very reasonable cost. Ask your agent about such coverage.

Cherie Froeba photographs the inside of her home in St. Bernard's Parish, Louisiana, for insurance purposes when she visits it for the first time after the floods following Hurricane Katrina. Froeba with her husband returned to salvage any personal effects, including her grandmother's heirloom Bible. St. Bernard's Parish was one of the worst-hit areas in Louisiana. What things do you think about when making insurance decisions?

Homeowner's insurance will be required by your mortgage company, and is sometimes paid with your mortgage payment. Often, flood and earthquake insurance are sold as separate policies.

SELF-CHECK QUESTIONS

1. What types of insurance should you consider purchasing now? What insurance might you need in the future?
2. What is the difference between a variable life insurance policy and a term policy?

PLANNING FOR RETIREMENT

No matter how young or old you are, not planning for retirement is a big mistake. Successful financial planning means long-range planning, and retirement is a critical phase of life. Even if you have begun planning late, it is still better than not planning at all! What you do now could make a world of difference in your quality of life after age 65, or whenever you retire. According to a study published in the *Journal of Financial Planning,* researchers recommended savings rates for various ages. To be able to have 80 percent of your income after retirement, the researchers suggest saving 12 percent of the income, if you are at age 25. If you wait until age 45, you will have to save twice as much from each paycheck.[16] The cost of procrastination can be quite high. For example, if at age 30 Laura saves $2,000 every year in a retirement account until age 65, she will have accumulated $222,870 (assuming a modest earning of 6 percent tax deferred on her money). If Kelly, on the other hand, at age 40 saves $2,000 in a similar account at 6 percent interest until age 65, she will have saved $109,729 by the age 65.[17] Clearly, starting to save early is a lesson we all need to take seriously.

Social Security

Social Security is the common term used for the Old-Age, Survivors, and Disability Insurance Program established by the Social Security Act of 1935. There is little question that by the time the youth of our society retire, there will have been significant changes in the Social Security system. There is even talk today of making part of the system private.[18] Although the media talk about it all the time, there really is no Social Security trust fund. The money individuals receive when they retire comes directly from the Social Security taxes being paid by others. The problem is that the number of people retiring and living longer is increasing dramatically, and the number of workers paying into Social

Section Outline

Planning for Retirement

- Social Security
- Individual Retirement Accounts (IRAs)
- 401(k) Plans
- Keogh Plans
- Financial Planners
- Estate Planning

Social Security

The common name for the Old-Age, Survivors, and Disability Insurance Program established by the Social Security Act of 1935.

Social Security benefits are important to today's retirees as well as those just entering the workforce. Knowing what changes are being made is important to your financial future. Senators Pete Domenici (R-New Mexico) and Diane Feinstein (D-California) announce a plan to reform Social Security and Medicare during a press conference on Capitol Hill.

individual retirement account (IRA)

Allows a person to save a percentage of income tax free.

Security per retiree is declining. The results are likely to include serious cuts in benefits, a much later average retirement age, reduced cost-of-living adjustments (COLAs), and possibly much higher Social Security taxes. The moral of the story is this: Do not count on Social Security to provide ample funds for retirement. Rather, plan now to save funds for nonworking years. Recognizing Social Security's potential limitations, the government has established incentives for people to save money now for retirement, which we describe next.

Individual Retirement Accounts (IRAs)

Traditionally, an **individual retirement account (IRA)** has been a tax-deferred investment plan that enables a person (and the person's spouse, if he or she is married) to save part of his or her income for retirement. A traditional IRA allows people who qualify to deduct from their reported income the money they put into the IRA account. Such tax-deferred contributions are those for which no current taxes are paid, but the earnings gained in the IRA are taxed as income when they are withdrawn. Let's see why a traditional IRA is a good deal for an investor. The tremendous benefit is that the invested money is not taxed, which means fast, and good, returns for individuals. For example, suppose you put $3,000 into an IRA each year. (The maximum will be $5,000 by 2008. If you're 50 or older, you can make an additional $500–$1,000 "catch-up" contribution.) Normally, you would pay taxes on that $3,000 when you receive it as income. But because you put the money into an IRA, you will not have to pay those taxes. If you're in the 25 percent tax bracket, that means you save $750 in taxes! Put another way, the $3,000 you save costs you only $2,250—a huge bargain.

The earlier you start saving the better, because your money has a chance to double, and then double again. Saving $3,000 a year for 35 years in an IRA and earning 11 percent interest per year will accumulate savings of more than $1 million. Individuals who start saving at age 22 can be millionaires by the time they are 55. By increasing the contribution to the maximum allowable each time it is raised, a person can reach his or her million-dollar goal even earlier. The actual rate of return depends on the type of investments chosen. It is important to remember that future rates of return cannot be predicted with certainty, and that investments that pay higher rates of return also have higher risk and volatility. For example, the stock market was booming in the mid- to late 1990s and then plummeted for several years starting in 1999. The actual rate of return on investments can vary widely over time, but the average for the S&P 500, between 1970 and 2003, was 11 percent a year.

Consider this: If you were to start contributing $3,000 to an IRA earning 11 percent when you were 22 years old, and do so for only five years, you'd have nearly $21,000 by the time you turned 27. Even if you *never added another penny* to the IRA, by the time you were 65 you would have a little more than $1 million. If you wait until you are 30 to start saving, you must save $3,000 every year for 35 years to have the same nest egg. And what would you have if you started saving at 22 *and* continued nonstop every year until 65? More than $2.6 million! This $2.6 million is called **future value.** It is the value of a sum of money at some point in the future. **Present value,** on the other hand, is the worth of an investment right now. Can you see why investment advisers often say that an IRA is the best way to invest in your retirement?

A more recent kind of IRA is called a **Roth IRA.**[19] People who invest in a Roth IRA do not get up-front deductions on their taxes as they would with a traditional IRA, but the earnings grow tax free and are also tax free when they are withdrawn.

So, traditional IRAs offer tax savings when they are deposited and Roth IRAs offer tax savings when they are withdrawn. Financial planners highly recommend IRAs, but they differ as to which kind is best. Both have advantages and disadvantages, so check with a financial adviser to determine which option is best. You may even decide to have both kinds of accounts.

For more information on IRAs, check out the Money Chimp Web site (www.moneychimp.com), run by a group of self-proclaimed amateur investors. See Figure 14.9 for a brief comparison of Roth versus traditional IRAs.

A key point to remember is the money in either type of IRA may not be withdrawn until an individual is 59 1/2 years old without having to pay 10 percent penalty and paying taxes on the income. Such a requirement can be a benefit because people cannot tap into IRAs when emergencies happen or if they are tempted to make a large impulse purchase. On the other hand, the money is there if a real need or emergency arises. All IRAs are different and the government often changes the rules on them. Be sure to fully understand your IRA before purchasing.

There are many types of IRAs that offer a wide range of investment choices. Banks, savings and loans, and credit unions all have different types of IRAs. Insurance companies offer

future value

The value of an investment at some future point in time.

present value

The worth of an investment right now.

Roth IRA

An investment that does not get up-front deductions on taxes, but the earnings grow tax-free and are tax-free when they are withdrawn.

Online financial calculators like this one from Harris Bank can help you determine how much money you will need for things like retirement.

	TRADITIONAL IRA	ROTH IRA
Maximum Contributions	$3,000 per person for the 2002–2004 tax years; $3,500 if age 50 or over. Contributions must be from earned income.	$3,000 per person for the 2002–2004 tax years; $2,500 if age 50 or over. Contributions must be from earned income.
Eligibility	No income-based limits for nondeductible contributions, but you must be under age 70½.	Anyone with an AGI subject to the following income limits. **Single filers:** Up to $95,000 for a full contribution; $95,000 to $110,000 for a partial contribution. **Joint filers:** Up to $150,000 for a full contribution; $150,000 to $160,000 for a partial contribution. (If you're married and filing separately, the eligibility phase-out range is between $0 and $10,000.)
Contribution Deductibility	For the 2002 tax year, contributions are fully tax deductible for single filers with an adjusted gross income (AGI) of up to $34,000 and joint filers with an AGI of up to $54,000. Deductibility phases out for single filers with an AGI over $44,000 and for joint filers with an AGI over $64,000. Contributions are also tax deductible for anyone not covered by an employer-sponsored retirement plan, regardless of their AGI.	Contributions are not tax deductible.
Taxation on Earnings	Earnings are tax deferred until withdrawn. You can take withdrawals prior to age 59½ without facing the IRS's 10 percent penalty tax on early withdrawals (although you'll owe income taxes) for certain qualified reasons, which include: a first-time home purchase (up to $10,000); qualified higher education expenses; deductible medical expenses that exceed 7.5 percent of your AGI; death; or disability. Other withdrawals prior to age 59½ are generally subject to the 10 percent IRS penalty tax in addition to regular income tax.	Earnings are tax deferred until withdrawn. You can withdraw earnings *completely tax-free* provided the IRA has been in place for at least five years and the withdrawal meets at least one of the additional requirements: It's made after age 59½; the taxpayer becomes disabled; the distribution goes to a beneficiary of the taxpayer's estate after the taxpayer's death; the withdrawal is used to pay for first-time homebuyer expenses (up to $10,000). Otherwise, earnings are subject to ordinary income taxes and, if applicable, the IRS's 10 percent early withdrawal penalty. To avoid this penalty tax, the taxpayer must meet one of the IRS's qualifying events, which include: reaching age 59½; using the funds for qualified higher education expenses or a first-time home purchase; deductible medical expenses that exceed 7.5 percent of AGI; disability; or death.
Advantages	• Tax-deferred earnings. • Tax-deductible contributions, if you qualify. • You can take early withdrawals penalty-tax free (but not income-tax free) if your withdrawals qualify (see above).	• Tax-deferred earnings. • You can withdraw contributions penalty-tax and income-tax free whenever you wish. • Earnings can be withdrawn completely tax free if your withdrawals qualify (see above). • No required minimum distribution rules at age 70½. You can also contribute past age 70½.
Disadvantages	• The ability to deduct contributions is not available to everyone. • You must take required minimum distributions at age 70½, and you cannot contribute past age 70½.	• Contributions are never tax deductible.

figure 14.9

TRADITIONAL VERSUS
ROTH IRAS

such plans as well. People may prefer to be a bit aggressive with this money in order to earn a higher return. In that case, they can put IRA funds into stocks, bonds, mutual funds, or precious metals. Some mutual funds have multiple options (gold stocks, government securities, high-tech stocks, and more). Investors can switch from fund to fund, or from investment to investment, with IRA funds and can even open several different IRAs, as long as the total amount invested does not exceed the government's limit. Consider contributing to an IRA through payroll deductions to ensure that the money is invested before you are tempted to spend it. Opening an IRA may be one of the wisest investments you make.

401(k) Plans

A **401(k) plan** is a savings plan that allows people to deposit pretax dollars and whose earnings compound tax free until withdrawal, when the money is taxed at ordinary income tax rates. 401(k) plans now account for 49 percent of America's private pension savings. More than 220,000 companies now offer 401(k) retirement plans, covering some 55 million workers. For 28 percent of these employees, a 401(k) or similar defined-contribution plan is their only pension. One problem is that only 72 percent of eligible employees make any contributions.[20] That is a huge mistake, as you will see.

These plans have three benefits: (1) the money put in reduces present taxable income, (2) tax is deferred on the earnings, and (3) employers often match part of the deposits made. More than 80 percent of 401(k) plans offer a match, sometimes 50 cents on a dollar. No investment will give you a better deal than an instant 50 percent return on your money. You should deposit at least as much as your employer matches, often up to 15 percent of your salary. Funds may not normally be withdrawn from a 401(k) account until individuals reach 59 1/2, but they may be able to borrow from the account. Usually people may select how the money in a 401(k) plan is invested: stocks, bonds, and in some cases real estate.

Be careful not to invest all your money in the company where you work. Although the company may be doing quite well, there is always the possibility that it could collapse and leave you with almost nothing. During the scandals of the early 2000s, many employees, such as those at Enron, lost their 401(k) money. It is always best to diversify funds among different companies and among stocks, bonds, and real estate investment trusts.

401(k) plan

Savings plan that allows you to deposit pretax dollars and whose earnings compound tax free until withdrawal, when the money is taxed at ordinary income tax rates.

q: Why do you think some people would choose not to
»» participate in their company's 401(k)?

Winning Resumes . . . It's All about You!

Writing a resume for the first time can seem to be a strange exercise because often we are not used to describing ourselves, our own job experiences, our education, and our accomplishments. However, writing a resume is indeed all about you and the more there is to write about, the more a potential company can learn about you and the unique reasons they might hire you over other potential job candidates.

When writing your resume, remember that companies that are hiring new employees are looking for goal-oriented, ambitious individuals who have leadership qualities, who have good potential for further training and development, who are responsible and ethical, and who will be good representatives of their company. Does this sound like you?

Begin now to see where you have made accomplishments that will help you in your career. Companies will be interested in you because of what you bring to the table in terms of your abilities, experience, and willingness to learn. Take time to visit your placement office, talk to an instructor, or review some books about how you can create a winning resume!

Keogh Plans

Keogh

Similar to an IRA but designed for entrepreneurs with higher maximum contributions.

Millions of small-business owners do not have the benefit of a corporate retirement system.[21] Such people can contribute to an IRA, but the amount they can invest is limited. The alternative for all those doctors, lawyers, real estate agents, artists, writers, and other self-employed people is to establish their own Keogh plan. **Keogh** plans are like IRAs for entrepreneurs. (Also check into simplified employee pension (SEP) plans, which are the best types of IRAs for sole proprietors.) The advantage of Keogh plans is that the maximum that can be invested is $40,000 per year. The original amount was much lower, but the government wanted to encourage self-employed people to build retirement funds. Like traditional IRAs, Keogh funds are not taxed until the funds are withdrawn, nor are the returns the funds earn. Thus, a person in the 25 percent tax bracket who invests $10,000 yearly in a Keogh saves $2,500 in taxes. That means, in essence, that the government is financing 25 percent of the person's retirement fund. As with an IRA, Keogh plans are excellent deals. However, there is a 10 percent penalty for early withdrawal. Also like an IRA, funds may be withdrawn in a lump sum or spread out over the years.

The key decision is the one you make now—to begin early to put funds into an IRA, a Keogh plan, or both, so that the "magic" of compounding can turn that money into a sizable retirement fund.

Financial Planners

If the idea of developing a comprehensive financial plan for yourself or your business seems overwhelming, relax; help is available. The people who assist in developing a comprehensive program that covers

Credit Card Debt

Students today use cash for only 42 percent of their purchases. The rest of their purchases are conducted with credit, debit, or ATM cards, or even their school IDs. Over 35 percent of first-year students and 60 percent of seniors have their own credit cards. The change from paying cash to buying goods and services on credit is often a traumatic one for students. Often, they simply do not have the experience, or sometimes the self-control, to manage such freedom. Some students are taking on "substantial debt loads that will clearly affect them for the rest of their lives," says a law professor at the University of Houston.

A student with a balance of $3,000 on a credit card, with an 18 to 20 annual percentage rate, who pays the minimum 3 percent monthly payment, would need about 15 years to pay off the debt (and that is without using the card again to purchase so much as a candy bar). In addition, the student would end up paying *double* the initial amount of the purchases. Students are nearly three times as likely to be at least 90 days delinquent on their credit card payments as are older adults. Yet, credit card issuers do not experience large losses, because parents often bail out their children.

Many adults have similar problems handling the freedom of having credit cards available, often resulting in staggering debt from their purchases of expensive new cars and over-the-top items they do not really need. Changing from a lifestyle of spending freely to one of carefully watching every dime is a major undertaking, but a crucial one for such people.

Critical Thinking Questions

1. Do you know people who suffer from credit card debt? How hard does it seem for them to get rid of that debt?

2. If you are one of these people, do you have a plan for getting out of debt?

3. Why do you think so many college students are in debt?

Sources: Ruth Simon and Christine Whelan, "The New Credo on Campus: Just Charge It," *The Wall Street Journal*, September 3, 2002, pp. D1, D4; "College Students Rake in Too Much Credit Card Debt," *U-Wire*, Chicago, IL, May 13, 2002 (northernlight.com); and "By the Numbers," *Washington Times*, February 12, 2003, p. A3.

investments, taxes, insurance, and other financial matters are called financial planners. Be careful, though—anybody can claim to be a financial planner today. Often it is best to find a person who has earned the distinction of being a **certified financial planner (CFP).** A CFP must have completed a curriculum on 106 financial topics and passed a 10-hour examination. In the United States today, there are about 36,000 certified financial planners. Businesspeople often turn to their accountants or finance department for legitimate financial planning help.

In the past few years, there has been an explosion in the number of companies offering financial services. Such companies are sometimes called one-stop financial centers, or financial supermarkets, because they provide a variety of financial services, ranging from banking service to mutual funds, insurance, tax assistance, stocks, bonds, and real estate. It pays to shop around for financial advice. Ask friends and family for referrals. Good financial planners take time to understand their clients' needs before making suggestions. Most financial planners begin with life insurance. They feel that most people should have basic term insurance coverage. They also explore your health insurance plans. They look for both medical expense and disability coverage. They may also recommend major medical protection to cover catastrophic illnesses. Financial planning covers all aspects of investing, all the way to retirement and

certified financial planner (CFP)
A licensed person who manages investments.

So, You Want to Be . . . Financially Secure for Your Future

The concepts discussed in this chapter, but also throughout the text, have identified ways for you to become financially successful. The first step is finding a job you like and one that pays enough to meet and exceed your expected expenses. As you consider job offers, it will be important for you to consider benefits beyond salary. Does the prospective employer have a 401(k) that matches part of your contributions? Does the company provide or subsidize health insurance for its employees? Can you purchase disability insurance through the company? The second step, however, is careful financial planning. By saving and investing your money and not spending beyond your means, you can substantially increase your ability to become financially secure through your retirement and beyond. Make sure you also protect yourself from unexpected losses by ensuring that you have the appropriate auto, life, and health insurance. We hope this chapter has given you some basic ideas and tools with which you can begin thinking about financial planning. Whether you use a financial advisor or do your own planning, now is the time to begin doing such planning for a successful financial future.

death. Financial planners can advise you on the proper mix of IRAs, stocks, bonds, real estate, and so on.

Estate Planning

It is never too early to begin thinking about estate planning and retirement. No matter how close a person is to retirement it is importance to understand the basics. An important first step is to select a guardian for minor children, which is a difficult decision to make. Guardians should have genuine concern for the children and should match a parent's parental style and moral beliefs. As part of the process, parents must ensure that sufficient resources are provided to rear your children, not only for living expenses, but also for medical expenses, college, and other major expenses. Life insurance is often a good way to ensure such a fund. Be sure to discuss all these issues with the guardian, and choose a contingent guardian in case the first choice is unable to perform the functions.

A second step is to prepare a will. A **will** is a document that names the guardian for children, states how assets are to be distributed, and names the executor of the estate. An **executor** assembles and values the estate, files income and other taxes, and assists with the distribution of assets. Often the executor will work closely with the deceased person's attorney to ensure that the terms of the will are properly administered.

A third step is to prepare a durable **power of attorney.** This document gives an individual the power to take over finances if a person becomes incapacitated. A durable power of attorney for health care

will

Document that names the guardian for your children, states how you want your assets distributed, and names the executor for your estate.

executor

A person who assembles and values your estate, files income and other taxes, and distributes assets.

power of attorney

A contract that gives signing power from one person to another to make decisions.

Margie Keen studied this chapter and did a lot of reading on the Internet to find solutions to her financial situation. Margie and her partner have decided to cut down on expenses. First, after studying the six steps for controlling finances outlined in this chapter, they realized they spend too much on dining out. Both of them purchase lattés and go out for lunch every day. They calculated that by bringing a lunch from home three days a week, and limiting lattés to three days per week, they could save $12 per week on lattés and $18 a week on lunches, which results in a savings of over $1,500 per year!

Margie decided that this $1,500 savings can be invested in a traditional IRA, which will allow them to start saving for retirement. Margie is very comfortable with this plan because she will still be able to enjoy the things she likes, but she will also save money.

Margie also decided they must put together a will. Currently, they do not have a will, but having one is a necessity, especially for guardianship of their children.

Although Margie and her partner do not have a lot of extra money now, she is planning for the day when she gets out of school and gets a good job. She has planned budgets and scenarios of different income levels to see what they would be able to afford. With a mid-level paying job, Margie figures they can save several hundred dollars per month at their current lifestyle, which means if their money is invested properly they could have enough money for a down payment on a house within just a few years of graduating!

Margie feels a lot more positive about her financial situation. She has realized that being financially secure is not about making hundreds of thousands of dollars, but instead, planning properly with what she has!

delegates power to a person named to make health decisions for individuals who are unable to make such decisions for themselves.

There are other steps to follow that are beyond the scope of this text. You may need to contact a financial planner or attorney to help you prepare the paperwork and do the planning necessary to preserve and protect your investments for your children, spouse, and others. Estate planning is very complex, but good planning begins with a strong financial base.

As you have read thus far, accumulating enough funds to be financially secure is a complex and difficult matter. Investing that money and protecting it from loss makes the process even more involved. It is never too early to start a saving and investment program. As you have learned, there are many, many millionaires in the United States and around the world. They have taken various paths to their wealth, but the most common ones are entrepreneurship and wise money management.[22] We hope this chapter helps you join their ranks.

SELF-CHECK QUESTIONS

1. What is the difference between a Roth and a traditional IRA?
2. What is a 401(k) plan and why is it a good idea to participate in one?
3. What tasks do financial planners perform?

summary

This chapter presented the six basic steps for managing personal assets:

1. Take an inventory of your financial assets. That means you need to develop a balance sheet for yourself: Assets – Liabilities = Net worth.
2. Keep track of all your expenses.
3. Prepare a budget.
4. Pay off your debts.
5. Start a savings plan (the best way to save money is to pay yourself first).
6. If you have to borrow money, borrow only when it is to buy assets that have the potential to increase in value or generate income, such as a house or business.

The second part of the chapter discussed building a financial base and managing credit. First, purchasing real estate is a great investment. A home is a great investment because you can live in it, and the payments are relatively stable compared to renting. Also, a house appreciates in value. Second, you can also invest money in mutual funds or the stock market. A good adviser can help you do this. The chapter discussed the problem of credit card debt. Pay off all credit cards every month. That is, never carry a balance.

Term insurance is pure insurance with no savings feature. Whole life insurance is part insurance and part savings plan. Variable life insurance is a form of whole life, except the money is invested, which also makes this a good option for part insurance and part retirement planning. In addition to life insurance, we discussed the importance of disability insurance, in case something happens that would not allow you to work. Homeowner's and renter's insurance are also important to protect your property. Having enough life, health, disability, and property protection is important to insure your financial security if a disaster occurs.

The chapter concluded with a discussion of planning for your retirement. You might think you are too young to think about this, but it is never too early to get started. Saving for retirement might include participating in your company's 401(k) plan or purchasing long-term retirement options such as IRAs and Keoghs, since these options have tax advantages.

Finally, in order to make sure your family is financially secure after you are gone, it is imperative to have a will in place. It is also important to choose someone you trust to grant power of attorney, who can make decisions on your behalf in case you are unable to. All of the things discussed in this chapter will help make your financial life a success!

key terms

amortization 461	**annuity** 467	**present value** 471
contrarian approach 461	**deductible** 467	**Roth IRA** 471
FICO 463	**co-payment** 468	**401(k) plan** 473
insurance 465	**disability insurance** 468	**Keogh** 474
term insurance 466	**rider** 468	**certified financial**
whole life insurance 466	**Social Security** 469	**planner (CFP)** 475
universal life 466	**individual retirement**	**will** 476
variable life	**account (IRA)** 470	**executor** 476
insurance 467	**future value** 471	**power of attorney** 476

applying your skills

1. Check your local paper or use an online realtor to gather information regarding the cost to rent a two-bedroom apartment and compare that to purchasing a two-bedroom condominium in your area. Go to www.dinkytown.net and use the site's "rent-versus-buy calculator" to compare the costs. How do the costs compare? Discuss your findings in small groups.

2. Compose a list of the benefits and the drawbacks of owning a home, and real estate in general, as an investment. Be prepared to give a one-minute presentation on what you learn.

3. Check with your family or others in your area to determine the cost of major medical/hospital treatments, such as the cost for minor surgery, an ambulance ride to the hospital, or a daily rate for a hospital room. Ask them about medical insurance and the dangers of not having any. What insurance program would they recommend? Discuss your results with the class.

4. The best time to start saving for the future is *now*. Find a retirement calculator online and prove this point to yourself. Calculate how much you will have at age 65 if you begin saving $100 a month now, versus $100 a month 10 years from now. You can go onto the Internet to find such calculations. Just type in "compound interest" in Google and find an appropriate site.

5. Check out the benefits and drawbacks of both traditional and Roth IRAs. Be prepared to make a two-minute presentation on the benefits of each and to discuss your findings in class.

6. What are your financial goals 5 years from now, 20 years from now, and 35 years from now? What kinds of things can you be doing to make those goals happen?

the internet in action

1. *Purpose:* To use online resources to make smart personal finance decisions.

   Exercise: Use the calculators on the FinanCenter Web site (www. financenter.com) to answer the following questions:

   - You need $5,000 for a trip to Europe in two years. How much would you have to deposit monthly into a savings account that pays 3 percent in order to meet your goal?

   - Assume that you are investing $1,000 at 6 percent for five years. What is the difference in purchasing power of your savings if inflation increases by 2 percent annually during that time? By 4 percent?

   - Starting today, how much would you need to save each month in order to become a millionaire before you retire?

   - You need a new car. What car can you afford if you have $1,500 for a down payment, can make monthly payments of $300, and get $1,000 for trading in your old clunker?

   - How much house can you afford if you earn $36,000 a year and have $10,000 in savings for a down payment, a $6,000 car loan balance, and no credit card debts?

endnotes

CHAPTER 1

1. Based on an interview with Curt Greenberg, Central Bark, Seattle, Washington, July 2006.
2. "The World's Billionaires," *Forbes,* March 8, 2007, www.forbes.com/lists/2007/10/07billionaires_William-Gates-III_BH69.html, accessed October 7, 2007.
3. Steve Forbes, "Ignorance Is Not Bliss," *Forbes*, December 23, 2002, p. 45.
4. www.boxofficemojo.com/movies/?id=gigli.htm, accessed October 16, 2007.
5. www.boxofficemojo.com/movies/?id=mybigfatgreekwedding.htm, accessed October 16, 2007.
6. "Levi Strauss Closes Last Two U.S. Plants," CNN.com, January 8, 2004.
7. Pete Engardio, "The Future of Outsourcing," *BusinessWeek,* February 6, 2006, pp. 50–58.
8. www.nass.usda.gov/quickstats/PullData_US.jsp, accessed September 28, 2007.
9. David C. Korten, *When Corporations Rule the World* (San Francisco: Berrett-Koehler Publishers, 2001).
10. "Service Economy Growth Below Forecast," *New York Times,* October 3, 2007.
11. "Small Business Makes a Big Impact," NFIB.com, February 23, 2007.
12. Christian Zappone, "Which States Love Small Businesses?" CNNMoney.com, October 31, 2006.
13. Sarel Reza, "Privatization and Private Sector Growth in China and Russia: A Comparison from the Institutional Perspective," *China: An International Journal* 5, no. 2 (September 2007).
14. Transparency International, 2006, www.transparency.org, accessed October 8, 2007.
15. "CEO Justice," *The Wall Street Journal,* March 16, 2005, p. A24.
16. Chuck Carlson, "Liar Liar," *Bloomberg Personal Finance,* July 28, 2002.
17. Matt Richtel, "Charges Dismissed in Hewlett-Packard Spying Case," *New York Times,* March 15, 2007.
18. Brad Stone, "High Tech's New Day," *Newsweek,* April 11, 2005, pp. 60–64.
19. Paul Sloan, "Retail without the Risk," *Business 2.0,* March 2006, p. 118.
20. Michael V. Copeland, "Everyone's Investing in B to B," *Business 2.0,* April 2006, p. 30.
21. Fred Reichheld, "The Microeconomics of Customer Relationships," *MIT Sloan Management Review,* Winter 2006, pp. 73–78.
22. Tom Lester, "The Cost of Not Caring for Your Customer," *Financial Times,* January 30, 2006, p. 10.
23. Mike Richman, "The Quest for Zero Defects," *Quality Digest,* April 2005, pp. 40–43.
24. www.buildabear.com/aboutUs/OurCompany/FactSheet.pdf, accessed October 8, 2007.
25. http://factfinder.census.gov, *2006 American Community Survey,* published September 27, 2007, accessed October 16, 2007.
26. Ibid.
27. Ibid.
28. "Chevron Establishes Multi-Million Dollar Strategic Alliance in Australia: Global Scope to Benefit Chevron's Worldwide Operations," *PR Newswire,* April 7, 2005.

CHAPTER 2

1. Personal interview with Jim Williams, WTRG Consulting, June 2006.
2. Moon Ihlwan, "Hands across the DMZ," *BusinessWeek,* March 20, 2006, p. 48.
3. Kathleen Holder, "China Road," *UC Davis Magazine Online,* Fall 2006.
4. "Taiwan Sees Expanding Gaps between Rich and Poor," *Taiwan Headlines,* September 14, 2007.
5. Kristine Ohlson, "Burst of Energy," *Entrepreneur,* February 2006, pp. 46–47.
6. Deborah Whitman, "Genetically Modified Foods: Harmful or Helpful," April 2000, www.csa.com/discoveryguides/gmfood/overview.php, accessed October 15, 2007.
7. "Comrade Capitalists," *The Wall Street Journal,* January 31, 2006, p. A14.
8. "Overview of Financial Statements," *2006 Annual Report,* Bill and Melinda Gates Foundation.
9. "The Forbes 400," *Forbes,* September 20, 2007.
10. Matt Richtel, "Demand Outpaced Supply for New Game Consoles," *New York Times,* January 12, 2007.
11. "China Car Sales Rev Up Nearly 26%," *Asia Times Online,* July 10, 2007, www.atimes.com/atimes/China_Business/IG10Cb02.html, accessed October 17, 2007.
12. www.worldwide-tax.com/, accessed October 16, 2007.
13. State Sales Tax Rates, January 1, 2007, www.taxadmin.org/FTA/rate/sales.html, accessed October 16, 2007.
14. www.worldwide-tax.com/, accessed October 16, 2007.
15. Mary Anastasia O'Grady, "Overcoming Castro's 'Culture of Fear,'" *The Wall Street Journal,* May 6, 2005, p. A15.

16. Mark Henricks, "New China?" *Entrepreneur,* February 2006, pp. 17–18.

17. Dexter Roberts, "How Rising Wages Are Changing the Game in China," *BusinessWeek,* March 27, 2006, pp. 32–35.

18. Laura D'Andrea Tyson, "How Europe Is Revving Its Engine," *BusinessWeek,* February 21, 2005, p. 24.

19. *The World Fact Book,* "The CIA," www.cia.gov, accessed October 16, 2007.

20. Ibid.

21. James C. Cooper and Kathleen Madigan, "The GDP Report: No Reason to Sweat," *BusinessWeek,* May 16, 2005, p. 21.

22. Economic and Labor Market Information Bureau, www.nhes. state.nh.us/elmi/unempnr.htm, accessed October 17, 2007.

23. Nell Henderson, "Inflation Hit Five-Year High of 3.4% Last Year," *Washington Post,* January 19, 2006, p. D1.

24. Carmen M. Reinhart and Miguel A. Savastano, "The Realities of Modern Hyperinflation," *Finance & Development,* June 2003, pp. 20–23.

25. David Pilling, "Japan Still in Grip of Deflation as Prices Fall," *Financial Times,* April 27, 2005, p. 7.

26. Consumer Price Index, U.S. Department of Labor, www.bls. gov/cpi/cpifaq.htm, accessed October 17, 2007.

27. Bureau of Labor Statistics, U.S. Department of Labor, www. bls.gov/ppi/ppifaq.htm, accessed October 17, 2007.

28. U.S. National Debt Clock, http://brilling.com/debt_clock/, accessed October 16, 2007.

CHAPTER 3

1. Personal interview, Joe Sample, Brett Bats, June 2006.

2. Erin White, "Executives with Global Experience Are among the Most In-Demand," *The Wall Street Journal*, January 25, 2005, p. B6.

3. "World Population Clock," U.S. Census Bureau, www.census. gov/ipc/www/popclockworld.html, accessed October 17, 2007.

4. Anup Shah, "Poverty Factors and Stats," *Global Issues,* http://72.14.253.104/search?q=cache:cOmKQMCeu-wJ: www.globalissues.org/TradeRelated/Facts.asp+how+many+ people+live+in+developing+countries&hl=en&ct=clnk&cd= 1&gl=us, accessed October 17, 2007.

5. Erin Kelly, "Sanders Going to China to Battle Trade Imbalance," *Gannett News Service,* January 8, 2003.

6. Thomas Friedman, *The World Is Flat* (New York: Picador Publishing, 2007).

7. Thuy-Doan Le, "U.S. Wine Exports Jump 28 Percent," *Sacramento Bee,* February 19, 2005.

8. Peter Coy, Adrienne Carter, and Michael Arndt, "The Export Engine Needs a Turbocharge," *BusinessWeek,* February 14, 2005, p. 32; and Martin Ladner, "Trade-Offs: Understanding Legal Basics of Importing and Exporting," *Houston Business Journal,* January 13, 2006.

9. "Small Businesses Big in Exports," *The Small Business Advocate* 22, no. 5 (May 2003); Katherine Kobe, "The Small Business Share of GDP: 1998–2004, April 2007, www.sba.gov/advo;

and Matt Quinn, "U.S. Agency Working to Promote Small Business Exports," Inc.com, July 4, 2004, www.inc.com/news/ articles/200407/exports.html, accessed October 17, 2007.

10. Frank Vargo, "U.S. Trade Policy: Free Trade Agreements Level the Playing Fields for Everyone," *Rubber and Plastics News,* May 2, 2005; and "Free Trade Winds in the Mideast," *The Wall Street Journal,* January 11, 2006.

11. Greg Hitt, "Congress Set to Debate Free Trade," *The Wall Street Journal,* April 13, 2005, p. A17.

12. Stacie Driebusch, "Washington U–St Louis Professor Aims for Understandable Economics," *University Wire,* January 14, 2003.

13. Chris Smith, "Globalization Provides Mixed Blessings," *University Wire,* April 19, 2005; and Robert Batterson, "Resolutions for 2006 Start with Embracing Free Trade," *St. Louis Post-Dispatch,* January 1, 2006.

14. Marcel Kohler, "Comparative Advantage and Trade Performance in South African Manufactures," *Journal of African Economics,* www.essa.org.za/download/2003Conference/ KohlerMRAR&%20Bruce-BrandJanetO_Comparative %20Cost%20Advantage%20And%20Trade%20Performance %20In%20South%20African%20Manufactures%201970- 2000.pdf, accessed October 17, 2007.

15. Ralph Byrns, "Comparative and Absolute Advantage," *Economics Interactive,* www.unc.edu/depts/econ/byrns_web/ Economicae/Essays/ABS_Comp_Adv.htm, accessed October 17, 2007.

16. www.census.gov/foreign-trade/statistics/historical/gands. txt, accessed October 21, 2007.

17. "U.S.-China Trade Statistics and China's World Trade Statistics," U.S.-China Business Council, www.uschina.org/statistics/ tradetable.html, accessed October 17, 2007.

18. International Monetary Fund Statistics, www.imf.org/external/ np/res/mmod/mark3/html/us.htm, accessed October 17, 2007.

19. Dermot McGrath, "The High Price of Setting Up or Not Setting Up a Global Net Presence," *International Herald Tribune,* June 24, 2002.

20. Naomi Koppel, "Fifteen Countries Call for Tightening of Anti-Dumping Rules in WTO," *AP World Stream,* February 5, 2003; John Zarocostas, "EU Prepared to Impose Sanctions on the U.S.," *WWD,* April 1, 2005; and "Mandleson Warns China It Must Crack Down on Illegal Dumping," *AP Worldstream,* January 10, 2006.

21. Rick Barrett, "Tariffs on Foreign Steel Spark Debate," *Milwaukee Journal Sentinel,* April 19, 2005; and "Prime Minister Must Take Action in the Softwood Lumber Dispute," *PR Newswire,* February 9, 2005.

22. Peter Passel, "Tough U.S. Enforcement on Trade, Is It Fair?" *New York Times*, July 20, 2003, http://query.nytimes.com/gst/ fullpage.html?res=9F0CE3DD173BF933A15754C0A9659582 60&sec=&spon=&pagewanted=print, accessed October 17, 2007.

23. Jagdish Bhagwati, "Free Trade or Protectionism?" *Financial Times,* October 11, 2007, www.ft.com/cms/s/2/cb0b204a-7683- 11dc-ad83-0000779fd2ac.html, accessed October 17, 2007.

24. Jeffery Birnbaum, "Business to Bush, Let Us into Cuba," *Fortune,* May 27, 2002, p. 36.

25. Chester Dawson, "Japan: Mitsubishi Moves into High Gear," *BusinessWeek International,* February 10, 2004, p. 16.

26. General Agreement on Tariffs and Trade, http://en.wikipedia. org/wiki/General_Agreement_on_Tariffs_and Trade, accessed October 17, 2007.

27. www.wto.org/english/thewto_e/whatis_e/tif_e/org6_e.htm, accessed October 21, 2007.

28. Ernesto Xedillo, "Will the Doha Round Implode?" *Forbes,* February 3, 2003, p. 29.

29. History of the European Union, http://europa.eu/abc/treaties/ index_en.htm, accessed October 17, 2007.

30. Member Information, The European Union, http://europa.eu/ abc/european_countries/index_en.htm, accessed October 17, 2007.

31. Peggy Crawford, "The Dollar v. the Euro," *Graziadio Business Report,* Pepperdine University, http://gbr.pepperdine. edu/041/devaluation.html, accessed October 17, 2007.

32. Organization of the Petroleum Exporting Countries, www. opec.org/home/, accessed October 17, 2007.

33. John Cavanagh and Sarah Anderson, "Happily Ever NAFTA," *Foreign Policy,* September 1, 2002, p. 58.

34. *NAFTA: A Preliminary Report,* www.dfait-maeci.gc.ca/eet/ research/nafta/nafta-en.asp#lec, accessed October 17, 2007.

35. Randy L. Gahn, "Trade Agreements Would Harm Workers," *Fresno Bee,* May 12, 2005.

36. Data & Statistics, World Bank, http://web.worldbank.org/ WBSITE/EXTERNAL/DATASTATISTICS/0,,contentMDK: 20394802~menuPK:1192714~pagePK:64133150~piPK: 64133175~theSitePK:239419,00.html, accessed October 22, 2007.

37. Raymond Lopez, "Disney in Asia, Again," *Lubin School of Business Case Studies,* http://digitalcommons.pace.edu/cgi/ viewcontent.cgi?article=1002&context=business_cases, accessed October 17, 2007.

38. http://trade.gov/media/publications/pdf/epg_2006-ch1.pdf, accessed October 21, 2007.

39. International Trade Administration, http://trade.gov/cs/, accessed October 17, 2007.

40. Alan Hughes, "Time to Venture Abroad: Exporting Is a Multibillion Dollar Industry That Can Be Extremely Lucrative—If You Are Properly Prepared," *Black Enterprise,* June 1, 2004.

41. "Rocky Mountain Chocolate Factory," *Reuters,* http://stocks. us.reuters.com/stocks/fullDescription.asp?rpc=66&symbol= RMCF.O, accessed October 17, 2007.

42. www.rmcf.com, accessed October 21, 2007.

43. "Success and Failure in the Chinese Fast Food Industry: It's All about Standardization," Wharton School of Business, May 10, 2006, http://knowledge.wharton.upenn.edu/article. cfm?articleid=1470, accessed October 17, 2007.

44. *McDonald's Netherlands: Facts and Figures,* www.alpha-group. biz/content/News/press2000_archiv.asp?Suchen=Nein& Index1=9, accessed October 22, 2007.

45. *Pizza Industry Facts,* www.pizzacam.tv/faqs/index.asp, accessed October 22, 2007.

46. Gil Bassak, "Homegrown Outsourcing," *Product Design & Development,* March 1, 2005; and S. Srinivasan, "U.S. Senator Supports Outsourcing to India," *AP Online,* January 13, 2006.

47. "Global Markets-U.S. Stocks Surge on Cisco, Bonds Drop," *Reuters,* May 18, 2002.

48. Carolyn Brown, "Partnering for a Profit," *Black Enterprise,* June 2006.

49. Lee Hawkins Jr. and Joann S. Lublin, "Emergency Repairman: GM's Wagoner Aims to Make Auto Company More Global," *The Wall Street Journal,* April 6, 2005, p. B1; "Shanghai Automotive Industry Corporation Guide to China's Auto Market," *Automotive News,* March 9, 2005; and Martin Strathnairn, "SAIC Car Sales to Get Boost from GM," *Birmingham Post,* January 9, 2006.

50. Haig Simonian, "A Case of Two Heads Being Better than One," *Financial Times,* March 4, 2005, p. 9.

51. Oracle Corporation, www.oracle.com/partnerships/index. html, accessed October 17, 2007.

52. Matthew Fordahl, "Haagen Dazs Scoops Up Dreyers in Cool Deal for Shareholders," *Associated Press,* June 18, 2002.

53. Mark Srite, "Levels of Culture and Individual Behavior: An Integrative Perspective," *Journal of Global Information Management,* April 1, 2005.

54. Geert Hofstede, ITIM International, www.geert-hofstede.com/, accessed October 17, 2007.

55. Greg Bensinger, "GM Probably Led Drop in Sales," Bloomberg, www.bloomberg.com/apps/news?pid=20601087&sid= aSdqZKQfQGMo&refer=home, accessed October 17, 2007.

56. www.chachich.com/blog/b.2006-04-30-Global-Marketing-Mistakes.html, accessed December 3, 2007.

57. Eric Bellman and Kris Hudson, The High Price of Setting Up or Not Setting Up a Global Net Presence "Wal-Mart Trains Sights on India's Retail Market," *The Wall Street Journal,* January 18, 2006, p. A9.

58. Manjeet Kripalani and Mark Clifford, "India: Coke Finally Gets It Right," *BusinessWeek,* February 10, 2003, p. 18.

59. Timothy Aeppel, "Weak Dollar, Strong Sales," *The Wall Street Journal,* January 20, 2005, pp. B1–B2; and Rick Carew, "China Takes Further Step towards Freeing Up Yuan," *The Wall Street Journal,* January 4, 2006.

60. Christopher Swan, "U.S. Exporters Fail to Reap the Full Benefits of a Weaker Greenback," *Financial Times,* March 22, 2005, p. 3.

61. Ed Zwirn, "Dollar Doldrums," *CFO,* May 2005, pp. 35–38.

62. www.hbfuller.com, accessed October 17, 2007.

63. Angie C. Marek and Nisha Ramachandran, "Wanna Swap?" *U.S. News & World Report,* September 6, 2004; Rob Kaiser, "Bartering Makes a Comeback through Evolving Business Networks," *Chicago Tribune,* October 4, 2004; and Steve Gutterman, "Russia, Ukraine Companies Reach Deal," *AP Online,* January 4, 2006.

64. http://en.wikipedia.org/wiki/Counter_trade, accessed October 17, 2007.

65. "The Jails Where Time Is Money," *Financial Times,* February 17, 2005, p. 8.

66. Glenn R. Simpson, "Multinational Companies Unite to Fight Bribery," *The Wall Street Journal,* January 27, 2005, p. A2.

67. Peter Fritsch and Timothy Mapes, "In Indonesia, a Tangle of Bribes Creates Trouble for Monsanto," *The Wall Street Journal,* April 5, 2005, pp. A1–A6.

68. Matt Rosenburg, "The Population Growth of the World's Largest Country," http://geography.about.com/od/populationgeography/a/chinapopulation.htm, accessed October 17, 2007.

CHAPTER 4

1. "Corporate Fraud—Enron: An Investigation into Corporate Fraud, Further Readings," www.law.jrank.org/pages/5759/corporate-fraud.html, accessed October 18, 2007.

2. "A Framework for Ethical Decision Making," Santa Clara University, Markkula Center for Applied Ethics, www.scu.edu/ethics/practicing/decision/framework.html, accessed October 17, 2007.

3. Booz Allen Hamilton, "New Study Finds Link between Financial Success and Focus on Corporate Values," *Business Wire,* February 3, 2005.

4. Richard Coughlan, "Demystifying Business Ethics," *Successful Meetings* 52, no. 5 (May 2003), p. 33.

5. Kathryn Tyler, "Do the Right Thing: Ethics Training Programs Help Employees Deal with Ethical Dilemmas," *HRMagazine,* February 1, 2005.

6. "Whistleblower," http://en.wikipedia.org/wiki/whistleblower, accessed October 23, 2007.

7. "Sarbanes-Oxley 101, Info Guide to the Sarbanes-Oxley Act of 2002," www.sarbanes-oxley-101.com/sarbanes-oxley-compliance.htm, accessed October 23, 2007.

8. www.americanshredding.com/index.php?section=sarbanes, accessed October 23, 2007.

9. Matt Olberding, "For Some Companies, Cost Outweighs Good of Corporate Fraud Law," *Lincoln Journal Star,* January 8, 2006.

10. National Park Service, www.nps.gov/partnerships/fundraising_individual_statistics, accessed October 23, 2007.

11. Ronald McDonald House, www.mcdonalds.com/rmhc/index/programs/ronald_mcdonald_house.html, accessed November 6, 2007.

12. David Raths, "Business Ethics Announces Its 2006 Best Corporate Citizens," *Business Ethics,* November 6, 2006.

13. Coleman Murphy, "Xerox Social Service Leave Press Release," January 22, 2007.

14. Jessi Hempel, "A Corporate Peace Corps Catches On," *BusinessWeek,* January 31, 2005.

15. Raths, "Business Ethics Announces Its 2006 Best Corporate Citizens."

16. S. J. Suzuki, www.answers.com/topic/suzuki-sj?cat=biz-fin, accessed October 24, 2007.

17. Andrew English, "Bouncing Baby Benz to get £100M Redesign," *Electronic Telegraph,* June 28, 1997.

18. Wanda Gluckert-Menke, "Baby Benz Faces the Moose," *Europe,* February 2, 1998, pp. 40–44.

19. John Porretto, "WorldCom Files Suit against Former Controller, Wants Him to Repay $800,000," *CRN,* July 17, 2002.

20. John Reh, "What Good People Really Cost," http://management.about.com/cs/people/a/WhatPeopleCost.htm, accessed November 6, 2007.

21. RhinoAbout Us, www.rhino.com/about/support.html, accessed October 17, 2007.

22. www.cibasc.com/index/cmp-index/cmp-ehs.htm, accessed October 17, 2007.

23. Starkist Tuna, www.starkist.com/template.asp?section=faqs.html, accessed October 17, 2007.

24. "Japan Needs to Tackle Bribery," BBC News, June 29, 2006.

25. Scott Allen, "The Greening of McDonalds," www.uoregon.edu/~recycle/events_topics_McDonalds_text.htm, accessed October 24, 2007.

26. Mark Pieth, "Taking Stock: Making the OECD Initiative against Corruption Work," www.oas.org/juridico/english/pieth2000.htm, accessed October 24, 2007.

CHAPTER 5

1. DuPont.com, "DuPont Overview: 200 Years of History," www.apoloinformatica.com.br/imagens/parceiros/DuPont_com%A0DuPont%20Overview%20200%20Years%20of%20History.htm, accessed October 18, 2007.

2. "Avon, History and Timeline," www.avoncompany.com/about/history.html, accessed November 9, 2007.

3. "History of Kodak," www.kodak.com/global/en/corp/historyOfKodak/eastmanTheMan.jhtml?pq-path=2/8/2217/2687/2689, accessed November 7, 2007.

4. Procter and Gamble, www.pg.com/canada, accessed October 18, 2007.

5. Wikipedia, http://en.wikipedia.org/wiki/Henry_Ford, accessed October 18, 2007.

6. Answers.com, www.answers.com/topic/jeff-bezos?cat=biz-fin, accessed October 18, 2007.

7. Wikipedia, http://en.wikipedia.org/wiki/History_of_Google, accessed October 18, 2007.

8. Sarah Swak, "Students' Success as Entrepreneurs," *University Wire,* June 3, 2005; Karen Klein, "Rekindling an Entrepreneur's Passion," *BusinessWeek,* December 15, 2005; and Pallavi Gogoi, "Start-up Secrets of the Successful," *BusinessWeek Online,* January 18, 2006.

9. Amy Joyce, "After the Pink Slip, a Rosier Outlook; Laid Off Workers Take Chances as Entrepreneurs," *Washington Post,* July 4, 2002, p. T5.

10. John Challenger, "As Entrepreneurs, Seniors Lead U.S. Start-ups," *Franchising World,* August 1, 2005; DeTienne, "Prior Knowledge, Potential Financial Reward," *Entrepreneurship: Theory and Practice,* January 1, 2005; "List of Richest People Was Topped by Microsoft Corp. Founder Bill Gates for 11th Year in a Row," *Capper's,* March 29, 2005; and John Fried, "How I Did It," *Inc.,* March 2005, pp. 88–90.

11. Nancy Flexman and Thomas Scanian, *Running Your Own Business* (New York: Argus Publications, October 1982).

12. FAQs, U.S. Small Business Administration, http://app1.sba.gov/faqs/faqindex.cfm?areaID=24, accessed November 8, 2007.

13. Zoe Galland, "A Stew of Small Business Stats," *BusinessWeek*, May 2, 2006, www.businessweek.com/smallbiz/content/may2006/sb20060502_489185.htm?chan=search, accessed November 11, 2007.

14. Internal Revenue Service, Department of the Treasury, www.irs.gov/businesses/small/article/0,,id=98202,00.html, accessed October 19, 2007.

15. *Forbes Financial Glossary,* www.forbes.com/tools/glossary/search.jhtml?term=unlimited_liability, accessed October 19, 2007.

16. Jill Elswick, "Loaded Statements: Web Based Total Compensation Statements Keep Employees in the Know," *Employee Benefit News*, May 1, 2005.

17. "Types of Partnerships," Find Law, http://smallbusiness.findlaw.com/business-structures/partnership/partnerships-types.html, accessed October 19, 2007.

18. "Revised Uniform Partnership Act," West Law, http://lawschool.westlaw.com/shared/marketinfodisplay.asp?code=RE&id=216&rtcode=re&rtid=203&subpage=2, accessed October 19, 2007.

19. Jeff Opdyke, "When Business and Friendship Don't Mix," *The Wall Street Journal*, March 17, 2005; and Paulette Thomas, "One Sweet Solution to a Sour Partnership,"*The Wall Street Journal,* March 23, 2005.

20. "Types of Corporations: S Corp versus C Corp," Learn About Law, www.learnaboutlaw.com/Corporations/types_of_corps.htm, accessed October 19, 2007.

21. Wikipedia, http://en.wikipedia.org/wiki/S-corporation, accessed October 18, 2007.

22. Megan E. Mowrey, "Choice of Business Entity after JGTRRA and AJCA," *Strategic Finance,* March 1, 2005.

23. Investopedia: A Forbes Media Company, www.investopedia.com/terms/d/double_taxation.asp, accessed October 19, 2007.

24. "Franchise Ownership," Transition Assistance Program, www.transitionassistanceprogram.com/portal/transition/lifestyles/Entrepreneurship/Franchise_Ownership, accessed October 19, 2007.

25. McDonald's Career Website, www.mcdonalds.com/corp/career/hamburger_university.html, accessed October 19, 2007.

26. Nina Wu, "Couple Takes Road to Fiscal Fitness," *Pacific Business Journal,* December 2, 2006; and Rebecca Reiser, "Finding a Whole New Grind," *BusinessWeek Online*, January 20, 2006.

27. "CSPI Withdraws from Lawsuit after KFC Cuts Trans Fat," CSPI NEWSROOM, www.cspinet.org/new/200610301.htm, October 30, 2006, accessed October 18, 2007.

28. Peter Klarfeld, "Covenants against Competition in Franchise Agreements," American Bar Association, 2004www.chachich.com/blog/b.2006-04-30-Global-Marketing-Mistakes.html.

29. "NRECA Programs Benefit 825 Co-Ops, 37 Million Consumers," *Rural Cooperative Magazine,* May/June 2005; and Jack Cassazza and Frank Dela, "Understanding Electric Power Systems," March 19, 2004, www.usabizmart.com/blog/posts/536-selling-a-business.php, accessed October 19, 2007.

30. "National Cooperatives Bank Acknowledges the 'Cooperative Spirit' of Our Nation's Businesses; Cooperatives Are Stable Business Model; Form 'www.chachich.com/blog/b.2006-04-30-Global-Marketing-Mistakes.htmlFourth Sector' of the Economy," http://findarticles.com/p/articles/mi_m0EIN/is_2001_Nov_2/ai_79650482/print, November 2, 2001, accessed October 18, 2007.

31. "Vertical Mergers," www.learnmergers.com/mergers-vertical.shtml, accessed October 18, 2007; and Steve Case, "It's Time to Take It Apart," *Washington Post,* December 11, 2006.

32. Olga Kharif, "For Singular, Now Comes the Hard Part," *BusinessWeek,* October 1, 2004.

33. Jack Craven, "Sale of Snapple and a Comeback for Wendy's," www.bevnet.com/news/1997/04-17-1997-snapple.asp, accessed October 18, 2007; and John Deighton, "How a Juicy Brand Came Back to Life," Harvard Business School, http://hbswk.hbs.edu/item/2752.html, accessed October 19, 2007.

34. Thomas Scholtes, "Board Guidance for Going Private," *Directors and Boards,* March 22, 2005.

35. Matthew Benjamin, "Deal Mania," *U.S. News & World Report,* April 18, 2005.

36. Patricia Schaefer, "The Seven Pitfalls of Business Failures and How to Avoid Them," *Business Know-how,* www.businessknowhow.com/startup/business-failure.htm, accessed November 11, 2007; and "Why Do Many Small Businesses Fail?" www.allbusiness.com/business-planning-structures/business-plans/1440-1.html, accessed November 11, 2007.

37. "U.S. Department of Labor and Small Business Administration Launch Project GATE, a One-Stop Service for Entrepreneurs," www.dol.gov/opa/media/press/eta/ETA2002503.htm, August 8, 2002, accessed October 18, 2007.

38. Carrie Mason-Draffen, "SBA's Micro Loan Program Helps Tint Businesses Get off the Ground," *NewsDay,* February 15, 2005; Kathy Mayer, "Small Business Bucks," *Indiana Business Magazine,* January 1, 2005; Tinana Velez, "Senate Amendment Would Bolster SBA Funding," *Arizona Daily Star,* March 28, 2005; Jim Wyss, "Micro Loans Provide Massive Assistance," *Miami Herald,* April 18, 2005; and Rachel Stone, "Small Business Administration Approves More than $2.5 Billion in Disaster Loans," *Beaumont (Texas) Enterprise,* January 16, 2006.

39. Jane Applegate, "Family Business Challenges Need Novel Solutions," Entrepreneur.com, March 22, 2001.

40. Heida Thurlow, "A Spirit That Never Gives Up—Entrepreneur's Notebook-Column," *Nation's Business,* May 1993.

41. John Canter, "How and Why I Hired My Tax Accountant," *The Wall Street Journal,* February 25, 2005.

CHAPTER 6

1. John E. West, "Listening to the Customer," *Quality Digest*, February 2006, p. 16.

2. Jack Welch, "It's All in the Sauce," *Fortune*, April 18, 2005, pp. 78–83.

3. "Brief Company History," www.dogwise.com/HelpCont/AboutUs.cfm, accessed September 4, 2007

4. Bill Green, "The Clear Leader," *Fast Company*, March 2005, pp. 65–67.

5. Peter Drucker, *Management: Tasks, Responsibilities, and Practices* (New York: Harper & Row, 1974), p. 61.

6. http://home.earthlink.net/~lindberg_b/GECGrwth.htm, accessed September 8, 2007.

7. Moira Herbst, "Why Oil Could Be Headed Even Higher," *BusinessWeek*, August 3, 2007.

8. John Tozzi, "Minimum Wage Hike Means Tax Breaks," *BusinessWeek*, July 25, 2007.

9. David Bogoslaw, "Stocks Slammed on Dismal Jobs Report," *BusinessWeek*, September 7, 2007.

10. www.cdc.gov/nchs/fastats/lifexpec.htm, accessed September 7, 2007.

11. Lucy Kellaway, "Beware the Senseless Dumbing Up of Management Thinking," *Financial Times*, May 23, 2005, p. 8.

12. Thaddeus Herrick, "Leadership as Layup? Lessons from Basketball," *The Wall Street Journal Online*, March 21, 2005.

13. Amy Joyce, "Big Bad Boss Tales," *Washington Post*, May 29, 2005, pp. F1 and F4.

14. www.patriots.com/team/index.cfm?ac=coachbio&bio=506, accessed September 5, 2007.

15. Douglas McGregor, *The Human Side of Enterprise* (New York: McGraw-Hill, 1960), pp. 33–48.

16. Lisa Miller, "Ethics: It Isn't Just the Big Guys," *BusinessWeek Online*, July 25, 2003.

17. http://investor.thq.com/phoenix.zhtml?c=96376&p=irol-homeProfile&t=&id=&, accessed September 9, 2007.

18. Steve Hamm, "Guess Who's Hiring in America," *BusinessWeek*, June 14, 2007.

CHAPTER 7

1. *BusinessWeek*, "Special Report: The Art of Motivation," May 1, 2006.

2. www.nucor.com, accessed October 8, 2007.

3. David Rooke and William R. Torbert, "Transformations of Leadership," *Harvard Business Review*, April 2005, pp. 67–76.

4. Compiled and adapted from R. M. Stogdill, *Handbook of Leadership* (New York: Free Press, 1974); William Cohen, *The Stuff of Heroes: The Eight Universal Laws of Leadership* (Longstreet Press, 1998); Lisa Dewey, "Five Qualities Good Leaders Express," Girl Scouts, www.girlscouts.org/for_adults/leader_magazine/2004_fall/five_qualities.asp, accessed September 17, 2007; and Sarah Lourie, "Six Qualities Every Great Leader Needs," *CIO News*, September 20, 2004.

5. Susan Casey, "Patagonia: Blueprint for Green Business," *Fortune*, May 29, 2007, http://money.cnn.com/magazines/fortune/fortune_archive/2007/04/02/8403423/index.htm, accessed September 17, 2007.

6. www.abcsupply.com/About.aspx?id=532&ekmensel=56_submenu_0_link_4, accessed September 17, 2007.

7. Alison Stein Wellner, "Everyone's a Critic," *Inc.*, July 2004, www.inc.com/magazine/20040701/managing.html, accessed September 17, 2007.

8. Lindsey Gerdes, "The Best Places to Launch a Career," *BusinessWeek*, September 24, 2007, pp. 49–60.

9. Lucas Conley, "25 Top Business Leaders, #11 Julie Rodriguez," *Fast Company*, May 2005, p. 72; Chuck Salter, "It's Never Been This Hard," *Fast Company*, November 2005, pp. 72–79; and Jon Berger, "Man on a Mission," *Fortune*, April 3, 2006, pp. 86–92.

10. Sarah Goldstein, "How I Did It: Amy Rees Lewis, CEO, MediConnect Global," *Inc.*, September 2007.

11. Swahilya, "Hard Work Gets 98 Percent but Attitude Gets 100 Percent," *The Hindu*, July 5, 2005.

12. "100 Best Companies to Work for 2007," *Fortune*, January 22, 2007.

13. Elain Pofeldt, "Best Bosses," *Fortune Small Business*, July 1, 2007, http://money.cnn.com/2006/09/25/magazines/fsb/betterbosses.fsb/index.htm, accessed September 17, 2007.

14. Shannon Kalvar, "Understand and Use Your Informal Leadership Role," *Tech Republic Online*, July 7, 2003, http://articles.techrepublic.com.com/5100-10878_11-5035204.html, accessed July 10, 2007.

15. B. M. Bass, "From Transactional to Transformational Leadership: Learning to Share the Vision," *Organizational Dynamics* 18 (1990), pp. 19–36.

16. Casey, "Patagonia: Blueprint for Green Business."

17. Michael Wilson, "The Psychology of Motivation and Employee Retention," *Maintenance Supplies*, July 1, 2005; Jeff Kirby, "Light Their Fires: Find Out How to Improve Employee Motivation and Increase Overall Company Productivity," *Security Management*, June 1, 2005; and Michael Arndt, "Nice Work If You Can Get It," *BusinessWeek*, January 9, 2006.

18. Richard DiPaolo, "Ergonomically Inclined," *Maintenance Supplies*, June 1, 2005.

19. Jay Velury, "Empowerment to the People," *Industrial Engineer*, May 1, 2005.

20. Sean Priestley, "Scientific Management in 21st Century," www.articlecity.com, November 7, 2005, www.articlecity.com/articles/business_and_finance/article_4161.shtml, accessed September 19, 2007.

21. Robert Frank, "Efficient UPS Tries to Increase Efficiency," *The Wall Street Journal*, May 24, 1995, p. B1.

22. "America's Most Admired Companies," *Fortune*, March 19, 2007.

23. www.accel-team.com/motivation/hawthorne_03.html, accessed September 19, 2007.

24. Steven Bratman, "The Double-Blind Gaze," *Altadena (California) Skeptic*, January 1, 2005.

25. A. Maslow, *Motivation and Personality* (New York: Harper & Row, 1954).

26. F. Herzberg, B. Mausner, and B. Snyderman, *The Motivation to Work* (New York: Wiley, 1959); and F. Herzberg, "One More

Time: How Do You Motivate Employees?" *Harvard Business Review,* January–February 1968, pp. 54–63.

27. J. R. Hackman and G. R. Oldham, "Motivation through the Design of Work: Test of a Theory," *Organizational Behavior and Human Performance,* August 1976, pp. 250–279.

28. "100 Best Companies to Work for 2007," *Fortune,* January 22, 2007.

29. For a complete discussion on MBO, please see P. F. Drucker, *The Practice of Management* (New York: Harper, 1954); and P. F. Drucker, "What Results Should You Expect? A User's Guide to MBO," *Public Administration Review,* January–February 1976, pp. 12–19.

30. K. Davis and J. Newstom, *Human Behavior at Work: Organizational Behavior* (New York: McGraw-Hill, 1989); and J. L. Mendelson, "Goal Setting: An Important Management Tool," in *Executive Skills: A Management by Objectives Approach* (Dubuque, IA: Brown, 1980).

31. Rebecca M. Chory-Assad, "Motivating Factors: Perceptions of Justice and Their Relationship with Managerial and Organizational Trust," *Communication Studies,* March 1, 2005; and Christine A. Henle, "Predicting Workplace Deviance from the Interaction between Organizational Justice and Personality," *Journal of Managerial Issues,* June 22, 2005.

CHAPTER 8

1. Dick Youngblood, "Making Workers Happy Helps Business Thrive," *Certes Financial Pros,* http://certesfinancialpros.com/news/article_apr_00.cfm, accessed October 9, 2007.

2. Anthony Wheeler, "Post-Hire Human Resource Practices and Person-Organization Fit: A Study of Blue Collar Employees," *Journal of Managerial Issues,* March 22, 2005.

3. Tom Shehan, "How to Retain Employees: A High Turnover Rate Is Costly in Both Direct and Indirect Costs," *Detroiter,* January 1, 2005; and "Hiring Is Stymied by the Search for the Perfect Candidate," *Business Wire,* January 6, 2005.

4. Alison Overholt, "True or False: You Are Hiring the Right People," *Fast Company,* February, 2002, p. 110.

5. Liz Kislik, "A Hire Authority," *Catalog Age,* April 1, 2005; and "HR by Numbers: How to Hire the Right People and Then Lead Them to Success," *Prosales,* January 1, 2006.

6. Marcela Creps, "What Not to Ask Applicants at a Job Interview," *Bloomington (Indiana) Herald Times,* May 31, 2005.

7. Tara Pepper, "Inside the Head of an Applicant," *Newsweek,* February 21, 2005; and "Personality Assessment Tests," *PR Newswire,* April 12, 2005.

8. David Hench, "Maine Overwhelmed as Background Checks Balloon," *Portland (Maine) Press Herald,* April 18, 2005; Carol Hymowitz, "Add Candidate's Character to Boards' Lists of Concerns," *The Wall Street Journal,* March 17, 2005; James Swann, "Guarding the Gates with Employee Background Checks," *Community Banker,* August 1, 2005; Carol Patton, "To Tell the Truth: It's an Institution's Duty to Ensure That New Hires Are Who They Say They Are," *University Business,* January 1, 2006; and Mary Jane Maytum, "Look a Little Closer: Investigators Say Employers Can Thwart Value of Background Checks; Some Should Dig Deeper," *Business First,* January 27, 2006.

9. Deborah J. Myers, "You're Fired! Letting an Employee Go Isn't Easy for Any Manager," *Alaska Business Monthly,* May 1, 2005.

10. Robert Green, "Effective Training Programs: How to Design In-House Training on a Limited Budget," *CADalyst,* March 1, 2005; and Lynne M. Connelly, "Welcoming New Employees," *Journal of Nursing Scholarship,* June 22, 2005.

11. Patrick Sauer, "The Problem: Magnetech Wants to Triple Its Workforce," *Inc.,* January 2005, pp. 38–39.

12. Tara Weiss, "Lifetime of Learning," *Forbes,* September 19, 2007, www.forbes.com/leadership/2007/09/19/training-flowers-hamburger-lead-careers-cx_tw_0919universities.html, accessed November 19, 2007.

13. www.webex.com, accessed October 9, 2008.

14. Weiss, "Lifetime of Learning."

15. Steve Cooper, http://findarticles.com/p/articles/mi_m0DTI/is_12_33/ai_n15896773/print, accessed November 14, 2007.

16. Wendy Tanaka, "Googlaires," *Forbes,* November 6, 2007, www.forbes.com/technology/2007/11/05/billionaires-google-options-tech-cx_wt_1106googlaires.html, accessed November 19, 2007.

17. "Telework Facts," The Telework Coalition, www.telcoa.org/id33.htm, accessed October 28, 2007.

18. Leslie Turex, "Top Ten Telecommuting Questions Answered," *Jobsnake,* www.jobsnake.com/seek/articles/index.cgi?openarticle&8599&Top_10_Telecommuting_Questions_Answered, accessed October 9, 2007.

19. www.incomesdata.co.uk/studies/job-sharing.htm, accessed November 15, 2007.

20. Betsy Morris, "How Corporate America Is Betraying Women," *Fortune,* January 10, 2005, pp. 64–74; and Mitchell Pacelle, "Citigroup Faces Gender Bias Suit over Broker Account Assignments," *The Wall Street Journal,* April 1, 2005, p. C4.

21. Law Center, "Narrow Use of Affirmative Action Preserved in College Admissions," CNN, December 25, 2003, www.cnn.com/2003/LAW/06/23/scotus.affirmative.action/, accessed October 9, 2007.

22. http://caselaw.lp.findlaw.com/scripts/getcase.pl?court=US&vol=000&invol=02-516, accessed November 15, 2007.

23. "Compliance Assistance—Family Medical Leave Act (FMLA)," www.dol.gov/esa/whd/fmla/, accessed October 25, 2007.

24. Daniel E. Bender, *Sweated Work, Weak Bodies: Anti-Sweatshop Campaign and Languages of Labor* (New Brunswick: Rutgers University Press, 2004).

25. Shelia Burt, "Festival Gears to Honor Legendary Labor Leader Mother Jones," *St. Louis Post-Dispatch,* June 13, 2005.

26. Stephan Franklin, "Sunday Not Just Another Working Day," *Chicago Tribune,* May 2, 2005.

27. www.aflcio.org, accessed December 3, 2007; and William Glanz, "Sweeney Smooths Over Split in Labor; AFL-CIO Still a Player with Clout," *Washington Times,* January 7, 2006.

28. "A Crack in Big Labor's Armor," *Washington Times,* June 23, 2005.

29. William Glanz, "Unions to Quit AFL-CIO; Four Dissatisfied Groups Walk Out on Convention," *Washington Times*, July 25, 2005.

30. Terence Chea, "Service Workers Board OKs AFL-CIO Split," *AP Online*, June 11, 2005; Stephen Franklin, "Child-Care Coup Only a Baby Step for Labor," *Chicago Tribune*, January 7, 2006; and Will Lester, "United Farm Workers Leave AFL-CIO," *AP Online*, January 13, 2006.

31. www.aflcio.org, accessed December 3, 2007; and William Glanz, "Farm Union Leaves AFL-CIO," *Washington Times*, January 13, 2006.

32. Jennifer C. Kerr, "Dissident Unions Press AFL-CIO," *Capital Times*, June 16, 2005; and John B. Schnapp, "Auto Workers of the World Unite," *The Wall Street Journal*, January 25, 2006.

33. John Hoerr, "Lucky Strike," *Harper's*, June 1, 2005; and Kris Maher, "Share of the U.S. Work Force in Unions Held Steady in 2005," *The Wall Street Journal*, January 21, 2006.

34. Dayna Sason, "Talks Restart in Writers' Strike," *Washington Square News*, November 19, 2007; and Michael Cieply, "Screenwriters on Strike over Stake in New Media," *New York Times*, November 6, 2007.

35. Rebecca Winters Keegan, "What a Writers' Strike Means for Us," *Time*, October 20, 2007, www.time.com/time/arts/article/ 0,8599,1674063,00.html, accessed November 20, 2007.

36. Rachel Osterman, "UFW Ready to Boycott Gallo—Again," *Sacramento Bee*, June 14, 2005.

37. Samuel Estreicher, Michael Heise, and David Sherwyn, "Assessing the Case of Employment Arbitration: A New Path for Empirical Research," *Stanford Law Review*, April 1, 2005.

38. Scott DeCarlo, "Big Paychecks," *Forbes*, May 3, 2007.

39. Paul La Monica, "Google CEO, Co-founders Stick with $1," *CNN Money*, March 5, 2007, http://money.cnn.com/2007/03/05/news/companies/google_salaries/index.htm, accessed October 9, 2007.

40. Jeffery Pfeffer, "The Pay-for-Performance Fallacy," *Business 2.0*, July 2005, p. 64.

41. DeCarlo, "Big Paychecks."

42. David Nicklaus, "CEO Pay and Performance," *St. Louis Post-Dispatch*, April 18, 2005, p. B1.

43. Louis Lavelle, "Consulting Even beyond the Grave," *Business-Week*, February 28, 2005, p. 14.

44. D. C. Denison, "The Increasingly Short-Term CEO: Last Month, 80 CEOs with an Average Tenure of 4.2 Years Left Their Jobs," *News and Information*, Kellogg School of Management, http://kellogg.northwestern.edu/news/hits/011106np.htm, accessed October 29, 2007.

45. U.S. Department of Labor, www.dol.gov/wb/stats/main.htm, accessed November 15, 2007.

46. "The Sexual Harassment Charges," U.S. Equal Employment Opportunity Commission, www.eeoc.gov/stats/harass.html, accessed October 29, 2007.

CHAPTER 9

1. Tom Englehoff, "How to Use the Eight Functions of Marketing," *Small Business Marketing*, www.smalltownmarketing.com/eightbasic.html, accessed October 10, 2007.

2. Terry Dodson, "Minority Groups of 10 Trillion Dollar Consumer Market," Terry College Selig Center for Economic Growth, July 31, 2007.

3. Daniel Yankelovich and David Meer, "Rediscovering Market Segmentation," *Harvard Business Review*, February 2006, pp. 122–131.

4. "Hard Rock Café Increases Sales with E.Piphany Software," www.crm2day.com/news/crm/EppAAyVEyFOFZebtfq.php, accessed November 23, 2007.

5. Michael V. Copeland, "Everyone Is Investing in B-to-C B," *Business 2.0*, April 2006, p. 30.

6. E. Jerome McCarthy, "The Concept of the Marketing Mix," *Journal of Advertising Research*, June 1964, pp. 2–7.

7. Louise Lee, "Too Many Surveys, Too Little Passion," *Business-Week*, August 1, 2005, p. 38.

8. Thomas H. Davenport, "Competing on Analytics," *Harvard Business Review*, January 2006, pp. 99–107.

9. Alison Stein Wellner, "Boost Your Bottomline by Taking the Guesswork Out of Pricing," *Inc.*, June 2005, pp. 72–82.

10. Parija Kavilanz, "Coke Expects More Weakness at Home in 2007," *CNN Money*, April 17, 2007, http://money.cnn.com/2007/04/17/news/companies/coke/index.htm, accessed October 10, 2007.

CHAPTER 10

1. B. H. Boom and M. J. Bitner, "Marketing Strategies for Service Firms," *Journal of Marketing*, 1981, pp. 83–105.

2. Rob Carter, "The FedEx Edge," *Fortune*, April 3, 2006, pp. 77–84.

3. Food Marketing Institute, "Facts and Figures," www.fmi.org/facts_figs/superfact.htm, accessed October 10, 2007.

4. Offshore Outsourcing Staff, "Globalization Drives Offshore Outsourcing," March 24, 2004, www.enterblog.com/200403240849.html, accessed October 10, 2007.

5. Melody Vargas, "Retail Industry Profile," About.com, http://retailindustry.about.com/od/abouttheretailindustry/p/retail_industry.htm, accessed November 25, 2007.

6. www5.toysrus.com/about, accessed November 1, 2007.

7. http://beta.bordersstores.com/online/store/BGIView_bgiaboutstores, accessed November 25, 2007.

8. www.fundinguniverse.com/company-histories/Petco-Animal-Supplies-Inc-Company-History.html, accessed November 1, 2007.

9. Jim Collins, "Bigger, Better, Faster," *Fast Company*, June 3, 2003.

10. www.roadsideamerica.com/sights/sightstory.php?tip_AttrId=%3D11761, accessed November 25, 2007.

11. www.basspro.com/webapp/wcs/stores/servlet/CFPage?appID=94&storeId=10151&catalogId=10001&langId=-1&CMID=MH_IN_EVENTS, accessed November 25, 2007.

12. www.mustseesanfrancisco.com/attractions/sony-metreon. html, accessed November 25, 2007.

13. www.vans.com/vans/skateparks/, accessed October 10, 2007.

14. www.rei.com, accessed October 10, 2007.

15. Alan Farnham, "The Party That Crashed Retailing," *Forbes*, November 1, 2005, pp. 80–81.

16. Randall Rothenburg, "Despite All the Talk, Ad and Media Shops Aren't Truly Integrated," *Advertising Age*, March 27, 2006, p. 24.

17. www.tvb.org/nav/build_frameset.asp?url=/rcentral/index. asp, accessed November 25, 2007.

18. Paul R. La Monica, "Super Prices for Super Bowl Ads," CNN Money.com, January 3, 2007, http://money.cnn. com/2007/01/03/news/funny/superbowl_ads/index.htm, accessed November 25, 2007.

19. Paul R. La Monica, "CBS Scores with Super Bowl Ratings," CNN Money.com, February 5, 2007, http://money.cnn. com/2007/02/05/news/companies/superbowl_ratings/index. htm, accessed November 25, 2007.

20. "The 78th Annual Academy Awards," Internet Movie Database, www.imdb.com/title/tt0497318/news, accessed October 10, 2007.

21. U.S. Department of Labor, "Occupational Outlook," www.bls. gov/oco/home.htm, accessed October 10, 2007.

22. Lora Kolodny, "The Art of the Press Release," *Inc.*, March 2005, p. 36.

23. http://07.the3day.org/site/pp.asp?c=pmL6JnO8KzE&b=218 3617, accessed November 25, 2007.

24. Matthew Creamer, "Word of Mouth Gaining Respect of Marketers," *Advertising Age*, January 23, 2006, pp. 3 and 28.

CHAPTER 11

1. Steve Hamm, "A Virtual Revolution," *BusinessWeek*, June 20, 2005, pp. 98–102; and Robert L. Mitchell, "Virtualization's Real Impact," *Computerworld*, March 13, 2006.

2. www.ecommerceprogram.com/ecommerce/Ebusiness-Info. asp, accessed October 10, 2007.

3. John Foley, "Managing Information: Infoglut," www. informationweek.com/551/51,mtif.htm, accessed October 10, 2007.

4. Charles Fishman, "How to SMASH Your Strategy," *Fast Company*, July 2002.

5. Janice Schroer, "Wireless Internet Turns Hotels into High-Tech Havens," www.hotel-online.com/Trends/Wayport/ WirelessTakesOff.html, accessed November 5, 2007.

6. Fox Pimm, "Plugging into Portal Returns," *Computerworld* April 8, 2002, p. 38.

7. Stephen S. Standifird and J. Christopher Sandvig, "Control of B2B Commerce and the Impact on Industry Structure," *First Monday*, www.firstmonday.org/issues/issue7_11/standifird/ index.html, accessed November 5, 2007.

8. Olga Kharif, "Brad Boston: No Paper," *BusinessWeek Online*, October 1, 2002.

9. Tom Nolle, "IP VPNs," Telecommunications Americas, June 1, 2005; and "Network Based IP VPN Equipment Enabling Key Services for Service Providers Reports In-Stat," *Business Wire*, January 4, 2006.

10. www.limewire.com/about/, and http://en.wikipedia.org/wiki/ LimeWire, accessed November 25, 2007.

11. Beth Ryan, "Unsecure Identity," *The State Journal*, November 1, 2007, www.statejournal.com/story.cfm?func=viewstory& storyid=30903, accessed November 7, 2007.

12. Joris Evers, "Computer Crime Cost 67 Billion, FBI says," *Cnet News*, January 19, 2006, www.news.com/2100-7349_3- 6028946.html, accessed November 7, 2007.

13. Martin Bosworth, "Hackers Hit TJ Maxx, Marshalls," *Consumer Affairs*, www.consumeraffairs.com/news04/2007/01/ tj_maxx_data.html, accessed October 10, 2007.

14. Douglas Schweitzer, "Be Prepared for Cyberterrorism," *Computerworld*, March 28, 2005; John Mallery, "Cyberterrorism: Real Threat or Media Hype?" *Security Technology and & Design*, May 1, 2005; "Are We Prepared for the Latest Type of Terrorism—Cyberterrorism?" *Business Wire*, September 20, 2005; and Ted Bridis, "U.S. Concludes 'Cyber Storm' Mock Attacks," *AP Online*, February 10, 2006.

15. "Wasting Time at Work? You Are Not Alone: Survey," Salary.com, www.reuters.com/article/lifestyleMolt/ idUSN2541395620070726, accessed November 25, 2007.

16. "2005 Electronic Monitoring & Surveillance Survey," American Management Association, 2005, AMA/ePolicy Institute Research.

17. Jane Black, "Faceless Snoopers Have Upper Hand," *BusinessWeek*, June 5, 2002.

18. Marc Songini, "Halloween Less Haunting for Hershey This Year," *Computerworld*, November 2, 2000.

19. *Computer and Information Systems Managers Occupational Outlook Handbook*, Bureau of Labor Statistics, U.S. Department of Labor, www.bls.gov/oco/ocos258.htm, accessed November 25, 2007.

CHAPTER 12

1. Maureen Costello, "Why Is a Good Understanding of Accounting Important for Running Your Business?" www. myownbusiness.org/videos/html/m_costello_t4.html, accessed October 15, 1007.

2. Ellen Heffes, "Accounting Trends Affecting the Next Generation of Accountants," *Financial Executive*, September 1, 2005.

3. Scott Leibs, "Who's Counting?" *CFO*, May 2005, p. 15; and Maureen Nevin Duffy, "Oh, the Places You Will Go! CPAs Today Have Career Options Even They Never Envisioned 100 Years Ago," *Journal of Accountancy*, October 1, 2005.

4. Robert Tie, "The Case for Private Company GAAP," *Journal of Accountancy*, May 1, 2005; Ian P. N. Hauge, "Convergence: In Search for the Best: CPAs Should Understand How U.S. and Foreign Accounting Standards Influence Each Other," *Journal of Accountancy*, January 1, 2006; and C. J. Prince, "Closing the GAAP," *Entrepreneur,* January 1, 2006.

5. Floyd Norris, "How KPMG Was Given a Lesson in Humility," *International Herald Tribune,* August 30, 2005; and Celia Whitaker, "Bridging the Book-Tax Accounting Gap," *Yale Law Journal,* December 1, 2005.

6. Paul Barr, "New Guidance Helps Boards Navigate Sarbanes-Oxley," *Modern Healthcare,* August 8, 2005.

7. Steve Hamm, "Death, Taxes and Sarbanes-Oxley," *Business-Week,* January 17, 2005, pp. 28–32.

8. Richard W. Rahn, "Where Is the Balance Sheet?" *Washington Times,* April 21, 2005; and Lisa Kianoff, "Financial Statements: An Often Unused Tool for the Masses," *CPA Technology Advisor,* January 1, 2006.

9. Mike Vorster, "Balance Sheet Basics," *Construction Equipment,* February 1, 2005; and Joseph S. Eastern, "How to Read a Balance Sheet," *Family Practice News,* January 1, 2006.

10. The Franchise Mall, www.thefranchisemall.com/franchises/details/10357-0-McDonalds.htm, accessed November 27, 2007.

11. David Whelan, "Beyond the Balance Sheet: Hot Brand Values," *Forbes,* June 20, 2005, pp. 113–115.

12. "Shareholders Equity," www.investorwords.com/4529/shareholders_equity.html, accessed October 15, 2007.

13. Jennifer Heebner, "Snapshot of an Income Statement," *Jewelers Circular Keystone,* May 1, 2005; "Minority Groups of 10 Trillion Dollar Consumer Market" and "Here's a Sweet Lesson on Income Statements," *The Bergen County (New Jersey) Record,* April 14, 2005.

14. Nicole Torres, "Count Me In," *Entrepreneur,* April 2005, http://findarticles.com/p/articles/mi_m0DTI/is_4_33/ai_n13659356, accessed October 15, 2007.

15. Phil Campbell, "How Do You Define Cash Flow?" *Inc.,* www.inc.com/welcome.html?aw=600&ah=600, accessed October 15, 2007.

16. "Financial Ratios," www.netmba.com/finance/financial/ratios/, accessed October 15, 2007.

17. Tom Judge, "Liquidity Ratio Can Help Spot Cash Gap," *Powersports Business,* March 14, 2005.

18. Ken Little, "Understanding Earnings Per Share," http://stocks.about.com/od/evaluatingstocks/a/eps1.htm, accessed October 15, 2007.

19. "Calculating Return on Sales," www.effectiveinventory.com/article2.html, accessed October 15, 2007.

20. Jon Schribefeder, "The Concept of Inventory Turnover," *Effective Inventory Management,* www.effectiveinventory.com/article2.html, accessed October 15, 2007.

21. "Accounting," www.educationforadults.com/career/accounting. html, accessed November 6, 2007.

CHAPTER 13

1. Chris Gregory, *Savage Money* (New York: Routledge Publishing, 1997), pp. 233–234.

2. "Anybody Got a Ten-Spot?" *Money,* November 2005, pp. 166–170; and "Government Debuts Colorful $10 Currency," *Washington Times,* March 3, 2006, p. C11.

3. FED101, www.federalreserveeducation.org/FED101_HTML/glossary/glossary.cfm, accessed November 29, 2007.

4. Federal Reserve Bank of Dallas, www.dallasfed.org/educate/everyday/ev9.html, accessed October 15, 2007.

5. Financial Forecast Center, www.neatideas.com/cdollar.htm, accessed October 15, 2007.

6. "Strong Dollar, Weak Dollar," Federal Reserve Bank of Chicago, www.chicagofed.org/consumer_information/strong_dollar_weak_dollar.cfm, accessed October 15, 2007.

7. "Buy or Sell MasterCard," *The Motley Fool,* www.fool.com/personal-finance/general/2006/05/26/buy-or-sell-mastercard.aspx, accessed November 28, 2007.

8. http://finance.yahoo.com/q?s=ma, accessed November 28, 2007.

9. http://finance.yahoo.com/q/it?s=MA, accessed November 28, 2007.

10. Alistair Barr and Matt Andrejczak, "Visa Plans $10 bln IPO, Following Rival MasterCard," *MarketWatch,* November 9, 2007, www.marketwatch.com/news/story/visa-plans-10-bln-ipo/story.aspx?guid=%7B4FB14AF9-B97A-44D6-891A-6D6E0C72E83B%7D, accessed November 28, 2007.

11. John J. Oslund, "JARGON; Investment Bankers," *Minneapolis Star Tribune,* March 24, 2006.

12. David Landis, "Dividends with Room to Grow," *Kiplinger's Personal Finance,* February 10, 2006.

13. Jim Mueller, "Dividend Myths Foolishly Debunked, Part 2," *The Motley Fool,* March 9, 2006.

14. www.finance.yahoo.com, accessed November 28, 2007.

15. "Preferred Stock, Explained," *The Motley Fool,* January 26, 2006.

16. "Voices in Corporate Wilderness," The Street.com, October 15, 2002; and Gary Weiss, "Revenge of the Investor," *BusinessWeek,* December 16, 2002.

17. Meg Richards, "Socially Responsible Funds a Challenge," *AP Online,* October 12, 2005; and Julie Tripp, "Social(k) Funds Aim for Greener Portfolios," *Oregonian,* February 26, 2006.

18. "Stock Market Terms & Definitions," www.stockrhythms.com/stock-market-terms.htm, accessed November 8, 2007.

19. "Timeline," NYSE Euronext, www.nyse.com/about/history/timeline_2000_Today_index.html, accessed November 29, 2007.

20. "NYSE: The World Puts Its Stock in Us," http://everything2.com/index.pl?node_id=136130, accessed November 8, 2007.

21. "Timeline," NYSE Euronext.

22. www.amex.com, accessed December 3, 2007.

23. Peter Chapman, "In the Footsteps of NASDAQ at Chicago Stock Exchange, *Traders,* March 1, 2005; and Gregory Bresiger, "Traders, Lawmakers Back NASDAQ Exchange Plan," *Traders,* January 1, 2006.

24. www.nasdaq.com, accessed December 3, 2007.

25. Andrew McIntosh, "Taser Stock Faces Delisting," *Sacramento Bee,* November 26, 2005; and Tom Murphy, "Standard Stock Sinks Close to Crucial Mark," *Indianapolis Business Journal,* February 20, 2006.

26. Robert Kuttner, "Cox's SEC: Investors Beware," *Business-Week*, June 27, 2005, p. 134; and Amy Borrus, "The Unlikely Hardnose at the SEC," *BusinessWeek*, January 23, 2006.

27. www.etrade.com, accessed December 3, 2007.

28. "Animal Antics," www.eco-action.org/dod/no10/animal_antics.htm, accessed November 29, 2007.

CHAPTER 14

1. "Education and Income," Education-Online-Search.com, accessed November 29, 2007.

2. Cox News Service, "Americans Unprepared for Retirement," *Washington Times*, April 5, 2006, p. C7.

3. Jane Bennett Clark, "Budgets That Work (Honest)," *Kiplinger's*, January 2005, pp. El and E9.

4. "Personal Savings Rate," Bureau of Economic Analysis, www.bea.gov/briefrm/saving.htm, accessed November 29, 2007.

5. Sakina Spruell, "Here's to 50 Years of DOFT," *Black Enterprise*, January 2005, pp. 61–64.

6. Kelly Greene, "Workers Lag on Retirement Savings," *The Wall Street Journal*, April 5, 2005, p. D2.

7. Robert J. Samuelson, "Our Vanishing Savings Rate," *Newsweek*, August 22, 2005, p. 38.

8. Matthew S. Scott, "5 Trends That Will Make You Rich," *Black Enterprise*, August 2005, p. 46.

9. Maggie Dunphy, "The Best Credit Card for You," *SmartMoney*, August 2005, pp. 94–99; and Brooke Kosofysky Glassberg, "Go Ahead, Pick a Card, but Not Just Any Card," *Budget Travel*, April 2006, pp. 55–56.

10. Amanda Gengler, "Nab a Lower Credit-Card Rate," *Money*, May 2006, p. 45.

11. Frank Norton, "Buried Alive," *Washington Times*, January 31, 2006, pp. C7 and C8.

12. Justin Prichard, "Government Mandates Free Credit Reports to All Consumers," http://banking.about.com/od/loans/a/freecreditrpt.htm, accessed October 15, 2007.

13. George Mannes, "I Owe U," *Money*, September 2005, pp. 106–110.

14. Jane Bryant Quinn, "Planning for Trouble," *Newsweek*, January 9, 2006, pp. 57–59.

15. Elizabeth Warren, "Sick and Broke," *Washington Post*, February 9, 2005, p. A23.

16. Mary Dalrymple, "Want to Retire? Start Saving Now," *The Motley Fool*, May 1, 2007.

17. "The High Cost of Procrastination," Retirement Planning, TransAmerica.com, accessed November 29, 2007.

18. Barbara Basler, "Risky Business," *AARP Bulletin*, February 2005, pp. 10 and 13.

19. Mary Beth Franklin, "Family-Friendly Relief," *Kiplinger's*, July 2006, p. 88.

20. Laura D'Andrea Tyson, "Retirement Savings: A Boost for the Needy," *BusinessWeek*, June 6, 2005, p. 30.

21. Ibid.

22. Justin Steele, "How to Make a Million," *Kiplinger's*, May 2006, pp. 77–85.

glossary

401(k) plan Savings plan that allows you to deposit pretax dollars and whose earnings compound tax free until withdrawal, when the money is taxed at ordinary income tax rates.

4Ps The ingredients that go into a marketing program: product, price, place, and promotion.

absolute advantage Occurs when a country has a monopoly on producing a specific product or is able to produce it more efficiently than all other countries.

accounting Recording, classifying, summarizing, and interpreting financial events and transactions to provide management and other interested parties the information they need to make good decisions.

account receivable An amount of money owed to the firm that it expects to be paid within one year.

acquisition One company's purchase of the property and obligations of another company.

affirmative action Activities designed to "right past wrongs" by increasing opportunities for minorities and women.

agents/brokers Marketing intermediaries who bring buyers and sellers together and assist in negotiating an exchange, but don't take title to the goods (don't own the goods at any point in the process).

American Federation of Labor (AFL) An organization of craft unions that championed fundamental labor issues; founded in 1886.

amortization The gradual elimination of a liability.

angel investors Individuals, usually wealthy, who invest their own money in a business for a share of the company.

annual report Yearly statement of the financial condition, progress, and expectations of an organization.

annuity A contract to make regular payments to a person for life or for a fixed period.

apprentice programs Involve a period during which a learner works alongside an experienced employee to master the skills and procedures of a craft.

arbitration Occurs when both parties agree on an unbiased third party to make a decision about the disagreement.

assets Economic resources (things of value) owned by a firm.

auditing The job of reviewing and evaluating the records used to prepare a company's financial statements.

autocratic leadership Making managerial decisions without consulting others.

balance of payments The difference between money coming into a country (from exports) and money leaving the country (for imports) plus money flows coming into or leaving a country from other factors such as tourism, foreign aid, military expenditures, and foreign investment.

balance of trade Ratio of a country's exports to imports.

balance sheet The financial statement that reports a firm's financial condition at a specific time.

barter The trading of goods and services for other goods and services directly.

bartering The exchange of merchandise for merchandise or service for service with no money involved.

benefit segmentation   Determining which benefits are preferred and using those benefits to promote a product.

board of directors   A group that oversees the activities of a corporation. Generally represents a mix—a small number of company executives and a greater number of outsiders. The group ultimately responsible for the decisions of a business.

bond   A corporate certificate indicating that a person has lent money to a firm.

bookkeeping   The recording of business transactions.

boycott   Occurs when organized labor encourages both its members and the general public not to buy the products of a firm involved in a labor dispute.

brain drain   The loss of the best and brightest people to other countries.

brand   The name and symbol that identify the product of one seller over another.

brand equity   Refers to the combination of factors that people associate with a given brand name, such as image and perceived quality.

brand loyalty   The extent to which a customer will choose one product over another on a continual basis.

bundling   Grouping two or more products together and pricing them as a unit.

business   An individual or organization that seeks to provide goods and services to others while operating at a profit.

business cycle   The periodic rises and falls that occur in all economies over time.

business plan   Detailed written statement that describes the nature of the business, the target market, the advantages the business will have in relation to competition, and the resources and qualifications of the owner(s).

business-to-business (B2B)   A business that produces products to sell to another business.

business-to-consumer (B2C)   A business that produces products to sell directly to the consumer.

capitalist system   Companies and businesses are owned by citizens instead of government.

cash-and-carry wholesalers   Serve mostly smaller retailers with a limited assortment of products. Office Depot would be an example.

category killer   Stores that offer a wide selection of goods in a specific category (such as Toys "R" Us), at competitive prices.

certified financial planner (CFP)   A licensed person who manages investments.

certified management accountant (CMA)   A professional accountant who has met certain educational and experience requirements, passed a qualifying exam in the field, and been certified by the Institute of Certified Management Accountants.

certified public accountant (CPA)   An accountant who passes a series of examinations established by the American Institute of Certified Public Accountants (AICPA) and does accounting work for no one particular firm.

channel of distribution   The whole set of marketing intermediaries, such as agents, brokers, wholesalers, and retailers, that join together to transport and store goods in their path (or channel) from producers to consumers.

command economies   The government largely decides what goods and services get produced, who gets them, and how the economy grows.

common market   Regional group of countries that have a common external tariff, no internal tariffs, and the coordination of laws to facilitate exchange among member countries (also called a trading bloc).

common stock   The most basic form of ownership in a firm.

communism   An economic and political system in which the state (the government) makes almost all economic decisions and owns almost all the major factors of production.

company stores   A store owned by a chain that owns and franchises stores.

comparable worth   The concept that people in jobs that require similar levels of education, training, or skills should receive equal pay.

comparative advantage theory The theory that a country should sell to other countries those products that it produces most effectively and efficiently and buy from other countries those products it cannot produce as effectively or efficiently.

compensation The combination of salary, vacation time, paid health care, and other benefits.

compliance-based ethics codes Prevent unlawful behavior by increasing control and penalizing violations.

compressed workweek When an employee works a full number of hours in less than the standard number of days.

conceptual skills Ability to see the "big" picture.

conglomerate merger Unites firms in completely unrelated industries.

Congress of Industrial Organizations (CIO) Union organization of unskilled workers; broke away from AFL in 1935 and rejoined it in 1955.

consumer price index (CPI) Consists of monthly statistics that measure the pace of inflation or deflation. It tracks the price of 400 goods.

contingency planning Planning for "what if" scenarios and secondary plans in case the original ones do not work.

contingent workers Workers who do not have the expectation of regular, full-time employment.

contract manufacturing When one country produces goods with another country's company label on it.

contrarian approach Purchasing stock when others are selling.

controlling Establishing clear standards to determine whether an organization is progressing toward its goals and objectives, rewarding people for doing a good job, and taking corrective action if they are not.

conventional (C) corporation A form of business ownership that provides limited liability.

cookies Pieces of information, such as registration data or user preferences, sent by a Web site over the Internet to your Web browser that the browser is expected to save and send back to the server whenever the user returns to that Web site.

cooperative A business owned and controlled by the people who use it—producers, consumers, or workers with similar needs who pool their resources for mutual gain.

co-payment An amount paid by the insured party when medical services are rendered.

core time Refers to the period when all employees are expected to be at their job stations, when referring to a flextime plan.

corporate governance The processes, customs, policies, laws, and institutions affecting the way in which a corporation is directed, administered, or controlled.

corporate philanthropy An indicator of social responsibility that includes charitable donations.

corporate policy The position a firm takes on social and political issues.

corporate responsibility An indicator of social responsibility that includes the actions the company takes that could affect others.

corporate social responsibility The level of concern a business has for the welfare of society.

cost of goods sold (cost of goods manufactured) A measure of the cost of merchandise sold, or the cost of the raw materials and supplies used for producing items for sale.

countertrading A complex form of bartering in which several countries may be involved, each trading goods for goods or services for services with the others.

cross-functional teams A group of people with different expertise working together to achieve a common goal.

culture The set of values, beliefs, rules, and institutions held to by a specific group of people.

data Raw, unanalyzed, and unorganized facts and figures.

data mining Looking for hidden patterns in the data in a data warehouse and discovering relationships among the data.

data processing (DP) The name for business technology in the 1970s. Its primary purpose was to improve the flow of financial information.

data warehouse An electronic storage place for data on a specific subject (such as sales) over a period of time.

database An electronic storage file where information is kept.

deductible The amount that must be spent on health care before insurance companies will cover the remaining expenses.

deflation Prices are actually declining. It occurs when countries produce so many goods that people cannot afford to buy them all.

demand The quantity of goods that buyers will purchase at a particular price.

demographic segmentation Segmentation by age, income, and education level, race, profession, or religion.

depreciation The systematic write-off of the cost of a tangible asset over its estimated useful life.

depression A severe recession, when the GDP falls for several quarters, and recovery is a long time off.

direct selling Selling to consumers in their homes or where they work.

disability insurance A type of insurance that pays part of the cost of a long-term sickness or an accident.

discount rate The interest rate that the Fed charges for loans to member banks.

diversity Broad differences among people (ethnicity, gender, color, sexual orientation, body size, age).

dividend Part of a firm's profits that may be distributed to stockholders as either cash payments or additional shares of stock.

double-entry bookkeeping The concept of writing (or typing) every transaction in two places.

double taxation Occurs when the owners of the corporation are taxed twice—once when the corporation itself gets taxed and a second time when the dividends are taxed.

downsizing (rightsizing) Elimination of many management jobs, and other types of jobs, by using cost-cutting methods and technology, such as computers.

drop shippers Solicit orders from retailers and other wholesalers and have the merchandise shipped directly from a producer to a buyer.

dumping The practice of selling products in a foreign country at lower prices than those charged in the producing country.

e-business Any electronic business data exchange using any electronic device.

e-commerce Business conducted electronically over the Internet selling products or services online through e-business.

economics The study of how society chooses to employ resources to produce goods and services and distribute them for consumption among various competing groups and individuals.

effectiveness Producing the desired results.

efficiency The ability to produce using the least amount of resources.

embargo Complete ban on goods to or from a country.

employee orientation The activity that initiates new employees to the organization; to fellow employees; to their immediate supervisors; and to the policies, practices, and objectives of the firm.

empower Giving employees as much freedom as possible to become self-directed and self-motivated.

empowerment To give power or authority; allowing employees the ability and trust to make decisions.

entrepreneur A person who owns and operates his or her own business.

equity theory The idea that employees try to maintain equity between inputs and outputs compared to others in similar positions.

ethics The standards of moral behavior; that is, behavior that is accepted by society as right versus wrong.

ethnocentricity Attitude that one's own culture is superior to all others.

European Union (EU) An agreement among European member countries to eventually reduce all barriers to trade and become unified both economically and politically.

event marketing Sponsoring events such as rock concerts or being at various events to promote your products.

everyday low pricing (EDLP) A pricing strategy where a store sets prices lower than other stores and does not have many special sales.

exchange rate The value of one nation's currency relative to the currencies of other countries.

exclusive distribution Distribution that sends products to only one retail outlet in a given geographic area.

executor A person who assembles and values your estate, files income and other taxes, and distributes assets.

exporting Selling products to another country.

expropriation When a host government takes over a foreign subsidiary in a country.

external candidates People who are not currently working within the company.

extranet A semiprivate network that uses Internet technology and allows more than one company to access the same information or allows people on different servers to collaborate.

extrinsic reward A reward given to an employee, such as a promotion or pay raise.

factors of production The resources used to create wealth: land, labor, capital, entrepreneurship, and knowledge.

Family and Medical Leave Act (FMLA) Passed in 1993, stipulates that companies with more than 50 employees must provide up to 12 weeks of unpaid leave to an employee upon birth or adoption of a child or upon serious illness of a parent, spouse, or child.

Federal Open Market Committee (FOMC) The group that oversees the entire Federal Reserve process.

Federal Reserve The organization that oversees the money supply of the United States.

FICO This is a credit score assigned by the three major credit reporting bureaus.

financial accounting Generates information for use outside the organization.

Financial Accounting Standards Board (FASB) The group that oversees accounting practices.

financial statement A summary of all the transactions that have occurred over a particular period.

firewall Can consist of hardware or software; prevents outsiders from accessing information the user does not want others to see.

fiscal policy The federal government's efforts to keep the economy stable by increasing or decreasing taxes or government spending.

flextime plan A type of scheduling that gives employees some freedom to choose when to work, as long as they work the required number of hours.

focus group A small group of people who meet under the direction of a discussion leader who tries to discover their opinions about a product.

foreign direct investment (FDI) The buying of permanent property and businesses in foreign nations.

foreign subsidiary A company that is owned in a foreign country by another company (called the parent company).

formal leadership   Someone has been given authority to make decisions or lead a group.

franchise agreement   An arrangement whereby someone with a good idea for a business sells the rights to use the business name and sell a product or a service to others in a given territory.

franchisee   A person who buys a franchise.

franchisor   A company that develops a product concept and sells others the rights to make and sell the product.

free market   A system in which decisions about what to produce and in what quantities are made by the market.

free market economies   The market largely determines what goods and services get produced, who gets them, and how the economy grows.

free-rein (laissez-faire) leadership   Managers setting objectives and then employees being relatively free to do whatever it takes to accomplish those objectives.

free trade   The reduction of barriers to trade, such as elimination of tariffs (or taxes) on goods brought into another country; the movement of goods and services among nations without political or economic trade barriers.

future value   The value of an investment at some future point in time.

General Agreement on Tariffs and Trade (GATT)   An agreement signed by many countries to reduce the restrictions on trade with one another. It is overseen by the WTO.

generally accepted accounting principles (GAAP)   A set of principles followed by accountants in preparing reports.

general partner   An owner (partner) who has unlimited liability and is active in managing the firm.

general partnership   A partnership in which all owners share in operating the business and in assuming liability for the business's debts.

geographic segmentation   Dividing the market by geographic area (cities, counties, states, regions, etc.).

global business   Any activity that seeks to provide goods and services to others across national borders while operating at a profit.

global marketing   The term used to describe selling the same product in essentially the same way everywhere in the world.

global trade   The exchange of goods and services across national borders.

goals   The broad, long-term accomplishments an organization wishes to attain.

goal setting theory   The idea that setting ambitious but attainable goals can motivate workers and improve performance.

golden parachute   Aptly refers to the massive amount of bonuses received by upper-level executives upon leaving a company.

Governmental Accounting Standards Board (GASB)   This group sets standards for governmental agencies accounting practices.

gray market   The flow of goods in a distribution channel other than those intended by the manufacturer.

Greenfield investment   When a company decides to enter a country and build offices and production facilities.

gross domestic product (GDP)   The total value of final goods and services produced in a country in a given year.

gross national product (GNP)   Similar to GDP, but only counts Americans producing products in the country, not other foreign nationals.

gross profit (gross margin)   How much a firm earned by buying (or making) and selling merchandise, without expenses.

gross sales   Total of all sales the firm completed.

hackers   People who unlawfully break into computer systems.

Harmonized Tariff Schedule A publication by the U.S. government that lists the tariffs and quotas for every imported good.

Hawthorne effect The tendency for people to behave differently when they know they are being studied.

high–low pricing strategy With this strategy, a store's regular prices are higher than those at stores using EDLP, but it has many special sales in which the prices are lower.

horizontal merger Joins two firms in the same industry and allows them to diversify or expand their products.

hostile takeover Attempts by the bidder to acquire a firm against the interest of the latter's management.

hostile work environment An environment created as a result of sexual harassment.

human relations skills The ability to communicate and work with others.

human resource management The process of determining human resource needs and then recruiting, selecting, training and developing, compensating, appraising, and scheduling employees to achieve organizational goals.

hygiene factors Job factors that can cause dissatisfaction if missing but do not necessarily motivate employees if increased.

hyperinflation When inflation increases beyond 50 percent in a given time period.

illegal An action for which you could be fined or imprisoned.

importing Buying products from another country.

import quota Limits the number of products in certain categories that a nation can import.

income statement The income statement summarizes all of the resources (called *revenue*) that have come into the firm from operating activities, the money resources that were used up, the expenses incurred in doing business, and what resources were left after all costs and expenses, including taxes, were paid out.

independent audit An evaluation and unbiased opinion about the accuracy of a company's financial statements.

index fund A fund that invests in stocks that follow the Standard & Poor's 500 (S&P 500) or other similar index.

individual retirement account (IRA) Allows a person to save a percentage of income tax free.

industrial good A product that is used to produce or as a component of other products.

industrial unions Labor organizations of unskilled and semiskilled workers in mass-production industries such as automobiles and mining.

inflation A general rise in the prices of goods and services over time.

infoglut The phenomenon of information overload in business.

informal leadership Someone does not have "official" authority but is recognized as a leader by the group.

information The processed and organized data that can be used for managerial decision making.

information systems The name for business technology in the 1980s. Its role changed from supporting the business to doing business. Technology such as ATMs and voice mail are examples.

information technology (IT) The name given to business technology in the 1990s. Its role became the way of doing business, rather than just using technology to help with business functions.

initial public offering (IPO) The first public offering of a corporation's stock.

injunction A court order directing someone to do, or to refrain from doing, certain acts.

insider trading Insiders of a company (such as employees) using private company information to further their own financial situation. The use of knowledge or information that individuals gain through their position that allows them to benefit unfairly from fluctuations in security prices.

instant messaging (IM)   Allows businesses to communicate in real time, for free, via computer.

insurance   A written contract between the party being insured and the insurer where the financial responsibility for losses transfers to the insurer up to a specified limit.

integrated marketing communication (IMC)   Combines all the promotional tools into one comprehensive and unified promotional strategy.

integrity-based ethics codes   Define the organization's guiding values and create an environment that supports ethically sound behavior.

intensive distribution   Distribution that puts products into as many retail outlets as possible.

internal candidates   Employees who are already within the firm.

intranet   A companywide network, closed to public access, that uses Internet-type technology.

intrapreneuring   The process of continuing to innovate a small business.

intrinsic reward   The personal satisfaction you feel when you perform well and achieve goals.

invisible hand   A theory developed by Adam Smith that says that self-directed gain turns into social and economic benefits for all.

job analysis   A study of what is done by employees who hold various job titles.

job description   Specifies the objectives of the job, the type of work to be done, the responsibilities and duties, the working conditions, and the relationship of the job to other functions.

job enlargement   A motivation technique that involves combining a series of tasks into one challenging assignment.

job enrichment   A motivational strategy that involves making the job more interesting in order to motivate employees.

job rotation   A motivation technique that involves moving employees from one job to another.

job sharing   An arrangement whereby two part-time employees share one full-time job.

job simulation   The use of equipment that duplicates job conditions and tasks so that trainees can learn skills before attempting them on the job.

job specifications   A written summary of the minimum qualifications (education, skills, etc.) required of workers to do a particular job.

joint venture   A partnership in which two or more companies (often from different countries) join to undertake a major project for a specified time period.

journal   Record book in accounting (can also be a computer program).

Keogh   Similar to an IRA but designed for entrepreneurs with higher maximum contributions.

Knights of Labor   The first national labor union; formed in 1869.

labor intensive   A type of business where the primary cost of operations is the cost of labor.

leadership   The process of offering guidance or direction.

leading   Creating a vision for the organization and communicating, guiding, training, coaching, and motivating others to work effectively to achieve the organization's goals and objectives.

ledger   A specialized accounting book or computer program in which information from accounting journals is recorded into specific categories.

leveraged buyout (LBO)   An attempt by employees, management, or a group of investors to purchase an organization primarily through borrowing.

liabilities   What the business owes to others (debts).

licensing   Selling the right to manufacture a product or use a trademark to a foreign company (the licensee) for a fee (a royalty).

limited liability   Means limited partners are not responsible for the debts of the business beyond the amount of their investment—their liability is *limited* to the amount they put into the company; their personal assets are not at risk.

limited liability partnership (LLP)   LLPs limit partners' risk of losing their personal assets to only their own acts and omissions and to the acts and omissions of people under their supervision.

limited partner   An owner who invests money in the business but does not have any management responsibility or liability for losses beyond the investment.

limited partnership   A partnership with one or more general partners and one or more limited partners.

liquidity   Refers to how fast an asset can be converted into cash.

lockout   An attempt by managers to put pressure on union workers by temporarily closing the business.

logistics   Planning, implementing, and controlling the physical flow of materials, goods, and related information from points of origin to points of consumption.

loss   This occurs when a business's expenses are more than its revenues.

loss leader   When a store advertises certain products at or below cost to attract people to the store.

M-1   Coins and paper bills, money that's available by writing checks, and money that's held in traveler's checks.

M-2   Everything in M-1 plus money in savings accounts, money market accounts, mutual funds, and certificates of deposit.

M-3   M-2 plus big deposits, which would include agreements among banks.

macroeconomics   The study of the operation of a nation's economy as a whole.

management   The process of planning, organizing, leading, and controlling people and other available resources to accomplish organizational goals and objectives.

management buyout   When employees of the company get together to purchase the business.

management by objectives (MBO)   A system of goal setting and implementation that involves a cycle of discussion, review, and evaluation of objectives among top and mid-level managers, supervisors, and employees.

management development   The process of training and educating employees to become good managers and then monitoring the progress of their managerial skills over time.

managerial accounting   Provides information and analysis to managers within the organization to assist them in decision making.

market   Consists of people with unsatisfied wants and needs who have both the resources and the willingness to buy.

market segmentation   The process of dividing the total market into several groups whose members have similar characteristics.

marketing   The process of planning and executing the conception, pricing, promotion, and distribution of goods and services to facilitate exchanges that satisfy individual and organizational objectives.

marketing intermediaries   Organizations that assist in moving goods and services from producers to business and consumer users.

marketing management   The process of overseeing all of the aspects of marketing a particular product or service for the purpose of attracting and retaining customers.

marketing research The analysis of markets to determine opportunities and challenges, and to find the information needed to make good marketing decisions.

Maslow's hierarchy of needs Theory of motivation based on unmet human needs from basic physiological needs to safety, social, esteem, and self-actualization needs.

master limited partnership (MLP) Structured much like a corporation in that it acts like a corporation and is traded on the stock exchanges like a corporation, but taxed like a partnership and thus avoids the corporate income tax.

maturity date The date that a bond can be cashed in.

mediation The use of a third party who encourages both sides in a dispute to come to an agreement.

merchant wholesalers Independently owned firms that take title to the goods they handle.

merger The result of two firms forming one company.

microeconomics The study of the behavior of people and organizations in particular markets.

middle management General managers, division managers, district managers, and plant managers or supervisors.

mission statement An outline of the fundamental purposes of an organization.

mixed economies Economies where some allocation of resources is made by the market and some by the government.

monetary policy Policies used by the Federal Reserve to control factors such as inflation, deflation, exchange rates, and economic growth. The management of the money supply and interest rates.

money Anything that people generally accept as payment for goods and services.

money supply The amount of money the Federal Reserve Bank makes available for people to buy goods and services with.

monopolistic competition Exists when a large number of sellers produce products that are very similar but are perceived by buyers as different.

monopoly Occurs when there is only one seller for a product or service.

motivation The drive to satisfy a need.

motivators Job factors that cause employees to be productive and give them satisfaction.

multinational corporation An organization that manufactures and markets products in many different countries; it has multinational stock ownership and multinational management.

mutual fund Like an investment company, it pools investors' money and then buys stocks or bonds in many companies.

NASDAQ Completely electronic securities market.

national debt The sum of government deficits over time.

negotiated labor–management agreement An agreement signed between unions and management for agreed-upon working conditions, benefits, and pay.

net sales Gross sales minus returns, discounts, and allowances.

New York Stock Exchange (NYSE) A securities market.

niche marketing The process of finding small but profitable market segments and designing or finding products for them.

nonprofit organization An organization whose goals do not include making a personal profit for its owners and organizers but rather the alleviation of some social problem.

nontariff barriers Restrictive standards that detail exactly how a product must be sold in a country.

North American Free Trade Agreement (NAFTA) An agreement signed by the United States, Mexico, and Canada to reduce or eliminate tariffs on goods and to encourage trade between the countries.

objectives Specific, short-term statements detailing how to achieve the organization's goals.

off-the-job training It occurs away from the workplace and consists of internal or external programs to develop any of a variety of skills or to foster personal development, such as health or stress management classes.

oligopoly A form of competition in which just a few sellers dominate a market.

online training Employees "attend" classes via the Internet to get the necessary training.

on-the-job training This type of training immediately begins with the new employee learning by doing, or watching others for a while and then imitating them.

OPEC An organization, consisting of 12 oil-producing countries, to work collectively for oil interests.

open-market operations Another tool commonly used by the Fed consisting of buying and selling government bonds.

operating expenses The costs involved in operating a business.

operational planning Scheduling, budgeting, and any other necessary plans used to meet the tactical objectives.

organization chart Visual diagram that shows relationships among people and divides the organization's work.

organizing Designing the structure of the organization and creating conditions and systems in which everyone and everything work together to achieve the organization's goals and objectives.

over-the-counter (OTC) market Provides companies and investors with a means to trade stocks not listed on the national securities exchanges.

owners' equity The amount of the business that belongs to the owners minus any liabilities owed by the business.

participative (democratic) leadership Managers and employees work together to make decisions.

partnership Legal form of business with two or more owners.

par value The dollar amount assigned to each stock certificate on the corporation's charter.

penetration strategy A pricing strategy in which a product is priced low to attract more customers and discourage competitors.

pension A promise made by a company to pay a monthly dollar amount to employees who have worked a minimum number of years.

perfect competition Exists when there are many sellers in a market, no seller is large enough to dictate the price of a product, and the products are similar.

performance appraisal An evaluation in which the performance level of employees is measured against established standards to make decisions about promotions, compensation, additional training, or firing.

performance improvement plan (PIP) A detailed document explaining what the employee needs to change and detailed steps on how to accomplish the change.

personal selling Face-to-face presentation and promotion of goods and services.

PEST analysis An analysis of outside factors that could affect a business: political, economic, social, and technological.

place The process of getting products to the places where they will be sold, or *distribution*, and to how the actual locations where the products are sold is determined.

planning Anticipating trends and determining the best strategies and tactics to achieve organizational goals and objectives.

portal An entry point into a Web site.

power of attorney A contract that gives signing power from one person to another to make decisions.

preferred stock A preference (hence the term *preferred*) in the payment of dividends.

present value The worth of an investment right now.

price indexes Indexes of the changes in goods and prices of goods and services based on the prices of the same goods and services from a previous period.

price leadership The procedure by which one or more dominant firms set the pricing practices that all competitors in an industry follow.

primary research Research that a marketer creates and implements.

principle of motion economy Theory developed by Frank and Lillian Gilbreth that every job can be broken down into a series of elementary motions.

private accountant Accountant who works for a single firm, government agency, or nonprofit organization, on the payroll of the company or organization.

producer price index (PPI) Similar to the consumer price index, but measures prices at the wholesale level.

product differentiation The creation of real or perceived product differences.

product life cycle A theoretical model of what happens to sales and profits for a product class over time.

product line A group of products that are physically similar or intended for a similar market.

product placement Paying to put products into TV shows and movies where they will be seen.

productivity The amount of output you generate given the amount of input (e.g., hours worked).

profit The amount of money a business earns above and beyond what it pays out for salaries and other expenses.

promotion mix The combination of tools a marketer uses: advertising, personal selling, public relations, and sales promotion.

prospecting Researching potential buyers and choosing those most likely to buy.

prospectus A document that provides information about a company to investors. Required to be sent out at least once per year.

psychographic segmentation Segmentation by lifestyle, values, attitudes, and interests.

psychological pricing (odd pricing) Pricing goods and services at price points that make them appear less expensive than they are.

public accountant Accountant who does not work for a specific company.

public domain software (freeware) Software that is free for the taking.

publicity Any information about an individual, product, or organization that's distributed to the public through the media and that's not paid for, or controlled by, the seller.

public relations (PR) The management function that evaluates public attitudes, changes policies and procedures accordingly, and executes a program of action and information to earn public understanding and acceptance.

quid pro quo An employee's submission to sexual harassment is made either explicitly or implicitly a term or condition of employment, or an employee's submission to or rejection of such conduct is used as the basis for employment decisions affecting the worker's status.

rack jobbers Furnish racks or shelves full of merchandise to retailers, display products, and sell on consignment.

ratio analysis The assessment of a firm's financial condition and performance through calculations and interpretation of financial ratios developed from the firm's financial statements.

reasonable accommodation An adjustment to the work environment that does not have high costs.

recession When the GDP falls for two consecutive quarters.

recovery An improvement in the economy, marking the end of a recession or decline.

recruitment The set of activities used to obtain a sufficient number of the right people at the right time; its purpose is to select those who best meet the needs of the organization.

reinforcement theory The idea that positive and negative reinforcement motivate a person to behave in certain ways.

relationship marketing A marketing strategy with a goal to keep individual customers over time by offering them new products that exactly meet their requirements.

reserve An amount of money that must be kept on hand and not lent to individuals or institutions.

reserve requirement Percentage of commercial banks' checking and savings accounts that must be physically kept in the banks.

resource Something used in the production of goods.

resource development The study of how to increase resources and to create the conditions that will make better use of those resources.

retailer Organization that sells ultimately to consumers.

return on investment (ROI) The money gained from taking a business venture risk. In addition to money, investment of time is also an important consideration for businesspeople.

revenue The total amount of money a business takes in during a given period by selling goods and services.

revenue The value of what is received from goods sold, services rendered, and other financial sources.

reward The gratification as a result of some action.

rider Supplemental insurance; also means an amendment to a contract.

risk Exposure to the chance of a financial or time loss due to something that is not successful.

Roth IRA An investment that does not get upfront deductions on taxes, but the earnings grow tax free and are tax free when they are withdrawn.

sales promotion Promotional tool that stimulates consumer purchasing and dealer interest by means of short-term activities.

sampling Letting consumers have a small sample of the product for no charge.

Sarbanes-Oxley Act Signed into law in 2002 after many accounting scandals, the act requires higher standards of accounting practices and auditing firms; set new standards for ethical codes of conduct within organizations.

scientific management Studying workers to find the most efficient processes and then teaching people those techniques.

S-corporation A type of legal entity in which the biggest advantage is that it is taxed like a sole proprietorship.

secondary research Data already available to the marketer, such as in government publications and journal articles.

securities Stocks and bonds that are traded.

Securities and Exchange Commission (SEC) A governmental organization that has responsibility at the federal level for regulating activities in the various exchanges.

securities market A place where stocks and bonds are traded.

selection The process of gathering information and deciding who should be hired, under legal guidelines, for the best interests of the individual and the organization.

selective distribution Distribution that sends products to only a preferred group of retailers in an area.

services Intangible products (i.e., products that can't be held in your hand) such as education, health care, insurance, recreation, and travel and tourism.

sexual harassment Unwelcome sexual advances, requests for sexual favors, and other conduct (verbal or physical) of a sexual nature.

shareholder A person who actually owns stock in a company.

shareware Software that is copyrighted but distributed to potential customers free of charge.

skimming price strategy   A pricing strategy in which a new product is priced high to make optimum profit while there's little competition.

Small Business Administration (SBA)   U.S. government agency that advises and assists small businesses by providing management training and financial advice and loans.

social audit   A systematic evaluation of a company's progress toward implementing programs that are socially responsible.

socialism   An economic system based on the premise that some, if not most, basic businesses—such as steel mills, coal mines, and utilities—should be owned by the government so that profits can be evenly distributed among the people.

social leader   A leader who ensures everyone in the group is getting along and agrees with the direction the group is going.

Social Security   The common name for the Old-Age, Survivors, and Disability Insurance Program established by the Social Security Act of 1935.

software   The product that tells your computer what to do.

sole proprietor   The name given to a person who owns a sole proprietorship.

sole proprietorship   A form of ownership that involves one individual.

span of control   The optimal number of subordinates (employees) a manager supervises.

staffing   Recruiting, hiring, motivating, and retaining the best people available to accomplish the company's objectives.

stagflation   When unemployment rates and inflation rates are high.

stakeholders   All the people who stand to gain or lose from the policies and activities of a business.

standard of living   A grade or level of subsistence (basic needs) and comfort in everyday life enjoyed by a community, class, or individual.

statement of cash flows   Reports cash receipts and disbursements related to the three major activities of a firm.

stock   Share of ownership in a company.

stock exchange   An organization whose members can buy and sell (exchange) securities for companies and investors.

strategic alliance   An agreement between two or more companies to work together to achieve competitive market advantages.

strategic planning   Setting of long-term goals for the company.

strike   A tactic by unions to negotiate a labor contract. It occurs when workers collectively refuse to go to work.

supervisory (first-line) management   Those who are directly responsible for supervising workers and evaluating their daily performance.

supply   The quantity of products that manufacturers or owners are willing to sell at different prices at a specific time.

supply chain management   The process of moving goods and materials from one place to another.

SWOT analysis   An analysis of the organization's strengths, weaknesses, opportunities, and threats.

tactical planning   The development of several objectives for each goal. These are the short-term goals that must be achieved to attain long-term goals.

target costing   Means to price based upon demand. A product is designed so it satisfies needs and meets the profit margins desired by the company.

target marketing   Choosing the market segment for a marketer to focus its efforts on.

tariff   A tax on imported goods.

task leader   A leader who plans activities and helps keep the group on task.

technical skills The skills required to do a specific job.

telecommuting Scheduling workers and work arrangements from home.

telemarketing The sale of goods and services by telephone.

term insurance Pure insurance protection with no savings feature for a given number of years that typically costs less the younger you buy it.

Theory X Managers believe the average person dislikes work, has relatively little ambition, and wishes to avoid responsibility, so workers must be forcefully directed or threatened with punishment. Primary motivators are fear and money.

Theory Y Managers believe most people like work and naturally work toward goals to which they are committed. People are capable of using imagination and creativity to solve problems. Each worker is stimulated by rewards unique to that worker.

Theory Z Management theory that focuses on trust and intimacy within the work group.

time and motion studies Studies of the tasks performed to complete a job and the time needed to do each task.

Title VII Prohibits discrimination in hiring, firing, compensation, apprenticeships, training, terms, conditions, or privileges of employment based on race, religion, creed, sex, or national origin.

top management It is the highest level of management and consists of the president and other key company executives.

total product offer Consists of everything that consumers evaluate when deciding whether to buy something.

total quality management (TQM) A management strategy where quality is reviewed at every phase of the production process, even in service organizations.

tradable currency Money that is allowed to be exchanged for another country's money.

trade deficit Occurs when a country imports more than it exports.

trade protectionism The use of government regulations to limit the import of goods and services.

trade surplus When a country exports more than it imports.

training and development Include all attempts to improve productivity by increasing an employee's ability to perform. Training focuses on short-term skills, whereas development focuses on long-term abilities.

transactional leader A leader who gets people to do things by providing structure and guidelines based on the exchange process.

transformational leader A leader who can transform the ideas of employees through inspiration, charisma, and a shared vision.

trial balance A summary of all the financial data in the account ledgers to check whether the figures are correct and balanced.

unemployment rate The number of civilians at least 16 years old who are unemployed and who have tried to find a job within the prior four weeks.

unencrypted An encryption is a secret code given to information when it is passing through the Internet. An unencrypted piece of data means anyone can see it and it is less secure.

Uniform Commercial Code (UCC) A comprehensive set of commercial laws, adopted by every state in the United States, that covers sales laws and other commercial laws.

Uniform Product Code (UPC) A series of lines and numbers that you see on most consumer packaged goods. The UPC identifies the type of product.

union An employee organization that has the main goal of representing members in employee– management bargaining over job-related issues.

universal life   A permanent insurance plan that allows flexibility in your insurance and savings amounts.

unlimited liability   The responsibility of business owners for all of the debts of the business.

value   The relative worth, merit, or importance.

variable life insurance   A form of whole life insurance that invests the cash value of the policy in stocks or other high-yielding securities.

variable pay   Pay based on employees earning some percentage of sales.

venture capitalists   A company that has money to invest in small and large businesses, and in return for its investment will generally take a stake in the business.

vertical merger   The joining of two firms involved in different stages of related businesses.

vestibule training   Also called near-the-job training, is done in classrooms where employees are taught on equipment similar to that used on the job.

viral marketing   The term now used to describe everything from paying people to say positive things on the Internet to setting up multilevel selling schemes whereby consumers get commissions for directing friends to specific Web sites.

virtualization   Accessibility through technology that allows business to be conducted independent of location.

virtual private network (VPN)   A private data network that creates secure connections, or "tunnels," over regular Internet lines.

virus   Programming codes inserted into other programming to cause unexpected events.

vision   A forward-looking statement that provides an encompassing explanation of why the organization exists and where it is headed in the future.

volume (usage) segmentation   Separating the market by usage (volume of product use) or how often a product is used.

whistleblowers   People who report illegal or unethical behavior.

whole life insurance   Life insurance where some part of the money you pay goes toward pure insurance and another part goes toward savings, so you are buying both insurance and a savings plan.

wholesaler   Marketing intermediary that sells to other organizations.

will   Document that names the guardian for your children, states how you want your assets distributed, and names the executor for your estate.

wireless fidelity (Wi-Fi)   The technology used to obtain an Internet connection without having to connect to a phone line or cable line.

wireless networking   Refers to the ability of a computer or device to transport signals through the air.

word-of-mouth promotion   A promotional tool that involves people telling other people about products that they've purchased.

work–life balance   The idea that an individual should have control over interactions between work and home.

World Trade Organization (WTO)   An organization that mediates trade disputes between countries and also sets policies in place to encourage trade.

photo credits

CHAPTER 1

2: Courtesy Curt Greenberg; 4: © The McGraw-Hill Companies, Inc./John Flournoy, photographer; 5: © Corbis; 6: © PictureNet/Corbis; 10: © Ben Fink/Brand X/Corbis; 11: © The McGraw-Hill Companies, Inc./Andrew Resek, photographer; 16: © Sven Hagolani/zefa/Corbis; 17: © The McGraw-Hill Companies, Inc./Jill Braaten, photographer; 18 (*left*): © The McGraw-Hill Companies, Inc./Ken Cavanagh, photographer; 18 (*right*): © The Mc-Graw-Hill Companies, Inc./John Flournoy, photographer; 19: © Comstock/PunchStock; 22: © Ramin Talaie/Corbis; 25 (*top*): © Comstock/Corbis; 25 (*bottom*): © Digital Vision; 26: © BananaStock/PunchStock; 28 (*top*): United Nations; 28 (*bottom*): © Don Tremain/Getty Images; 33: © Corbis

CHAPTER 2

38: Courtesy James Williams; 40 (left): © TongRo Image Stock/Brand X/Corbis; 40 (right): © AP Photo/World Food Program, HO; 41: © Digital Vision/PunchStock; 43: © Naashon Zalk/Corbis; 44: © Ryan McVay/Getty Images; 48: © The McGraw-Hill Companies, Inc./John Flournoy, photographer; 52: © Dr. Parvinder Sethi; 64: © Royalty-Free/Corbis; 65: © Digital Vision/PunchStock

CHAPTER 3

70: Courtesy Joe Sample; 72: © AP Photo/Kathy Willens; 73: © Janis Christie/Getty Images; 76: © Layne Kennedy/Corbis; 80: © AP Photo/Christopher Rolinson; 81: © AP Photo/Bullit Marquez; 88 (*top*): © Dr. Parvinder Sethi; 88 (*bottom*): © Peter Wilson; Cordaiy Photo Library Ltd./Corbis; 94: © Andersen Ross/Blend Images/Corbis; 98: © Getty Images; 99: Courtesy of The Persuaders, LLC; 101: © Antoine Gyori/AGP/Corbis; 103: © Steve Cole/Getty Images

CHAPTER 4

108: Courtesy of WomenVenture; 110: © Coby Burns/ZUMA/Corbis; 111: © Digital Vision; 112: © Getty Images; 117: © Martin H. Simon/Corbis; 119: © John Gillooly, Professional Event Images, Inc.; 123: © Reuters/Corbis; 126: © Ed Quinn/Corbis; 130: © Image Source/Corbis; 131: © Digital Vision

CHAPTER 5

136: Courtesy of Chuck Loomis; 138: © Matthew Gilson; 139: © Amos Morgan/Getty Images; 140: © AP Photo/Paul Sakuma; 145: © Max Hirshfeld; 148: © Craig Sands; 153: © InterContinental Hotels Group; 159: © Ted Rice Photography; 162: © Laura Mueller/Charlotte Observer; 164: © Chris Fanning; 168: © Amos Morgan/Getty Images

CHAPTER 6

174: Courtesy of Jim Beebe; 176: © Stockbyte/Getty Images; 177: © The McGraw-Hill Companies, Inc./John Flournoy, photographer; 195: © Brent Smith/Reuters/Corbis; 196: © The McGraw-Hill Companies, Inc./John Flournoy, photographer; 202: © Digital Vision; 204: © The McGraw-Hill Companies, Inc./John Flournoy, photographer

CHAPTER 7

208: © Lee Jae-Won/Reuters/Corbis; 210: © AP Photo/Elaine Thompson; 211: © Royalty-Free/Corbis; 213: © Galen Rowell/Corbis; 214: Courtesy of ABC Supply; 216: Courtesy of MediConnect Global; 217: Courtesy of Rackspace Managed Hosting; 223: © Underwood & Underwood/Corbis; 224(*top*): © The McGraw-Hill Companies/Andrew Resek, photographer;224 (*bottom*): Courtesy of AT&T Archives and History Center; 227: © Jim Sugar/Corbis; 233: Courtesy of Mini Maid; 234: © Royalty-Free/Corbis

CHAPTER 8

240: Courtesy of Karen Oman/Certes Financial Pros; 242: Courtesy of Wegman's Food Markets; 243:© Stockbyte/Getty Images; 246: Courtesy of Microsoft Corporation; 247: Courtesy of CareerBuilder.com; 249: Courtesy of Kronos Incorporated; 250: © Jay LaPrete/Landov; 253: Courtesy of Worldchefs; 255: Courtesy of RSM McGladrey, Inc.; 265: © The McGraw-Hill Companies/John Flournoy, photographer; 268: © Richard H. Cohen/Corbis; 270: © Peter DaSilva/Corbis; 276: © Stockbyte/Getty Images

CHAPTER 9

282: © Andrea Sorani; 284: © Daniel Hennessy Photography; 285: © Stockbyte/PunchStock; 287: © Envision/Corbis; 289: © Najlah Feanny/Corbis SABA; 292: © Annie Engel/zefa/Corbis; 293: James Leynse/Corbis; 296: © Mark Peterson/Corbis; 297: © BananaStock/PictureQuest; 298: © Bill Aaron/PhotoEdit; 300: © David Young-Wolff/PhotoEdit; 301: © James Sparshatt/Corbis; 306: Courtesy of Ben & Jerry's Homemade, Inc.; 308: Courtesy of Shopping.com; 312: © Stockbyte/PunchStock

CHAPTER 10

316: Courtesy of Nancy Engel; 318: Photo provided by Grey Worldwide, © Grey Worldwide, www.covergirl.com; 319: © Christian Kober/Robert Harding World Imagery/Corbis; 322: © Erik Freeland/Corbis; 325: © Copyright 1997 IMS Communications Ltd/Capstone Design. All Rgihts Reserved; 327: © David Butow/Corbis SABA; 328: © Jeff Zelevansky/Reuters/Corbis; 329: © Mark E. Gibson/Corbis; 330: © Charles Jean Marc/Corbis SYGMA; 332 (*left*): Used with the permission of Inter IKEA Systems; 332 (*right*): Used with the permission of Inter IKEA Systems; 333: © Mel Nathanson/The News and Observer; 338 (*top*): © Horst Ossinger/DPA/Landov; 338 (*bottom*): © Thinkstock/Jupiter Images; 345: International Manufacturing Technology Show; 347: Courtesy of Mind Storm Labs, www.mindstormlabs.com; 351: © James Leynse/Corbis

CHAPTER 11

356: Courtesy of Karen Clark; 358: © Helen King/Corbis; 359: © Pablo Corral V/Corbis; 360 (*top*): © Maranello/Corbis; 360 (*bottom*): © C. Borland/PhotoLink/Getty Images; 363 (*top*): © Ken Cedeno/Corbis; 363(*bottom*): © Getty Images; 364: © Beathan/Corbis; 366: Microsoft product screen shot reprinted with permission from Microsoft Corporation; 368: © James Leynse/Corbis; 369: © Heide Benser/zefa/Corbis; 370: © Rick Friedman/Corbis; 371: © Artiga Photo/Corbis; 375: © Lucas Schifres/Landov; 380: © Pablo Corral V/Corbis

CHAPTER 12

384: Courtesy of Roxanne Coady; photo by Tricia Bohan Photography; 386: © Michael Rosenfeld/Getty Images; 387: © Comstock/PunchStock; 389: © Najlah Feanny/Corbis; 390: © Andrew Holbrooke/Corbis; 397: © Steve Allen/Getty Images; 403: © AP Photo; 411: © James Leynse/Corbis; 413: © Image Source/PunchStock

CHAPTER 13

418: Courtesy of The Motley Fool; 425: © Ken Cedeno/Corbis; 421 (*top*): © Ryan McVay/Getty Images; 421 (*bottom*): © Stephan Jansen/epa/Corbis; 422: Courtesy of First Internet Bank of Indiana; 426: © Bettmann/Corbis; 428: © Tetra Images/Corbis; 437: © Najlah Feanny/Corbis; 439: © Royalty-Free/Corbis; 442: © Brand X/SuperStock; 446: © Brand X Pictures

CHAPTER 14

450: © AP Photo/William Fernando Martinez; 452: © Don Farrall/PhotoDisc/Getty Images; 453: © Keith Brofsky/Getty Images; 454: © Brand X/JupiterImages/Getty Images; 455: © Serge Kozak/zefa/Corbis; 459: © Ryan McVay/Getty Images; 462: © Keith Meyers/*The New York Times*; 463: © Don Farrall/Getty Images; 464: © Digital Vision; 466: Courtesy of InsWeb Corporation; 468: © Lynsey Addario/Corbis; 470: © Shawn Thew/epa/Corbis; 471: Courtesy of Harris N.A.; 477: © Keith Brofsky/Getty Images